Lecture Notes in Computer Science 15932

Founding Editors

Gerhard Goos
Juris Hartmanis

The series Lecture Notes in Computer Science (LNCS), including its subseries Lecture Notes in Artificial Intelligence (LNAI) and Lecture Notes in Bioinformatics (LNBI), has established itself as a medium for the publication of new developments in computer science and information technology research, teaching, and education.

LNCS enjoys close cooperation with the computer science R & D community, the series counts many renowned academics among its volume editors and paper authors, and collaborates with prestigious societies. Its mission is to serve this international community by providing an invaluable service, mainly focused on the publication of conference and workshop proceedings and postproceedings. LNCS commenced publication in 1973.

Ruzica Piskac · Zvonimir Rakamarić
Editors

Computer Aided Verification

37th International Conference, CAV 2025
Zagreb, Croatia, July 23–25, 2025
Proceedings, Part II

 Springer

Editors
Ruzica Piskac
Yale University
New Haven, CT, USA

Zvonimir Rakamarić
Amazon (United States)
Seattle, WA, USA

ISSN 0302-9743   ISSN 1611-3349 (electronic)
Lecture Notes in Computer Science
ISBN 978-3-031-98678-9   ISBN 978-3-031-98679-6 (eBook)
https://doi.org/10.1007/978-3-031-98679-6

This Springer imprint is published by the registered company Springer Nature Switzerland AG
The registered company address is: Gewerbestrasse 11, 6330 Cham, Switzerland

If disposing of this product, please recycle the paper.

Preface

It was our privilege to serve as the program chairs for CAV 2025, the 37th International Conference on Computer-Aided Verification. CAV 2025 was held in Zagreb, Croatia, on July 23–25, 2025, and the pre-conference workshops were held on July 21–22, 2025.

CAV is an annual conference dedicated to the advancement of the theory and practice of computer-aided formal analysis methods for hardware and software systems. The primary focus of CAV is to extend the frontiers of verification techniques by expanding to new domains such as security, quantum computing, and machine learning. This puts CAV at the cutting edge of formal methods research. This year's program is a reflection of this commitment.

CAV 2025 received 305 submissions. We accepted 24 tool papers, 4 case-study papers, and 51 regular papers, which amounts to an acceptance rate of roughly 25.9% overall. The accepted papers cover a wide spectrum of topics, from theoretical results to applications of formal methods. These papers apply or extend formal methods to a wide range of domains such as concurrency, machine learning and neural networks, quantum systems, as well as hybrid and stochastic systems. The program featured keynote talks by Corina Păsăreanu (Carnegie Mellon University, USA), Emina Torlak (Amazon Web Services and University of Washington, USA), and Roderick Bloem (Graz University of Technology, Austria). In addition to the contributed talks, CAV 2025 also hosted the CAV Award ceremony, and a report from the Synthesis Competition (SYNTCOMP) chairs. Furthermore, we continued the tradition of Logic Lounge, a series of discussions on computer science topics targeting a general audience. This year's Logic Lounge speakers were Moshe Y. Vardi (Rice University) and Henry Shevlin (University of Cambridge) who invited us to examine the nature of mind itself and whether artificial intelligence met its defining criteria.

In addition to the main conference, CAV 2025 hosted the following workshops: Verification Mentoring Workshop (VMW), Workshop on Synthesis (SYNT), Workshop on Verification of Quantum Computing (VQC), Workshop on Automated Reasoning for Tensor Compilers (AR4TC), International Workshop on Trustworthy Cyber-Physical Systems (TACPS), Workshop on Hyperproperties: Advances in Theory and Applications (HYPER), Symposium on AI Verification (SAIV), Meeting on String Constraints and Applications (MOSCA), Workshop on Horn Clauses for Verification and Synthesis (HCVS), and Workshop on Verification of Probabilistic Programs (VeriProP). Furthermore, CAV 2025 also included the following events dedicated to two prominent members of the CAV community: Ken McMillan Celebration and Allen Emerson Memorial.

Organizing a flagship conference like CAV requires a great deal of effort from the community. The Program Committee for CAV 2025 consisted of 122 members and two co-chairs—a committee of this size ensures that each member has to review only a reasonable number of papers in the allotted time. In all, the committee members wrote 958 reviews while investing significant effort to maintain and ensure the high quality of the conference program. We are grateful to the CAV 2025 Program Committee for their outstanding efforts in evaluating the submissions and making sure that each paper got a fair chance.

Like recent years in CAV, we made artifact evaluation mandatory for tool paper submissions, but optional for the rest of the accepted papers. This year we received 68 artifact submissions, all of which received at least one badge. We rejected 5 tool papers because the associated artifacts did not meet the functional badge criteria. The Artifact Evaluation Committee consisted of 83 members and two co-chairs, who put in significant effort to evaluate each artifact. The goal of this process was to provide constructive feedback to tool developers and help make the research published in CAV more reproducible. We are also very grateful to the Artifact Evaluation Committee for their hard work and dedication in evaluating the submitted artifacts.

CAV 2025 would not have been possible without the tremendous help we received from a number of individuals, and we would like to thank everyone who helped make CAV 2025 a success. First, we would like to thank our area chairs Anthony Widjaja Lin, Azadeh Farzan, Erika Ábrahám, Eva Darulova, Guy Katz, Peter Müller, Philipp Rümmer, and Roderick Bloem. Moreover, we would like to thank Matthias Heizmann and Tanja Schindler for chairing the Artifact Evaluation Committee. We also thank Grigory Fedyukovich for chairing the workshop organization. Ferhat Erata and Hadar Frenkel for leading publicity efforts, Ning Luo as the fellowship chair, Borzoo Bonakdarpour and Jana Hofmann as sponsorship chairs, and Jordan Schmerge as the website chair. Steve Siegel helped prepare the proceedings, while Alan Jović spearheaded the local organization. We also thank Grigory Fedyukovich, Mukund Raghothaman, Elizabeth Polgreen, Kaushik Mallik, and Thom Badings for organizing the Verification Mentoring Workshop. Last but not least, we would like to thank the members of the CAV Steering Committee (Kenneth McMillan, Aarti Gupta, Orna Grumberg, and Daniel Kroening) for helping us with several important aspects of organizing CAV 2025.

We hope that you will find the proceedings of CAV 2025 scientifically interesting and thought-provoking!

June 2025   Ruzica Piskac
Zvonimir Rakamarić

Organization

Steering Committee

Orna Grumberg	Technion, Israel
Aarti Gupta	Princeton University, USA
Daniel Kroening	Amazon, USA
Kenneth McMillan	University of Texas at Austin, USA

Conference Co-chairs

Ruzica Piskac	Yale University, USA
Zvonimir Rakamarić	Amazon Web Services, USA

Artifact Evaluation Co-chairs

Matthias Heizmann	University of Stuttgart, Germany
Tanja Schindler	University of Basel, Switzerland

Local Chair

Alan Jović	University of Zagreb, Croatia

Area Chairs

Anthony Widjaja Lin	Technical University of Kaiserslautern, Germany
Azadeh Farzan	University of Toronto, Canada
Erika Ábrahám	RWTH Aachen University, Germany
Eva Darulova	Uppsala University, Sweden
Guy Katz	Hebrew University of Jerusalem, Israel
Peter Müller	ETH Zurich, Switzerland
Philipp Rümmer	University of Regensburg, Germany
Roderick Bloem	Graz University of Technology, Austria

Workshop Chair

Grigory Fedyukovich   Florida State University, USA

Fellowship Chair

Ning Luo   University of Illinois Urbana-Champaign, USA

Publicity Chairs

Ferhat Erata   Yale University, USA
Hadar Frenkel   Bar Ilan University, Israel

Publication Chair

Stephen Siegel   University of Delaware, USA

Website Chair

Jordan Schmerge   Yale University, USA

Program Committee

Aarti Gupta	Princeton University, USA
Ahmed Bouajjani	Université Paris Cité, France
Aina Niemetz	Stanford University, USA
Alan J. Hu	University of British Columbia, Canada
Alberto Griggio	Fondazione Bruno Kessler, Italy
Alessandro Cimatti	Fondazione Bruno Kessler, Italy
Alexander J. Summers	University of British Columbia, Canada
Alexander Nadel	Technion & Intel, Israel
Alfons Laarman	Leiden University, Netherlands
Aman Goel	Amazon Web Services, USA
Anastasia Isychev	TU Wien, Austria
Anastasia Mavridou	KBR/NASA Ames Research Center, USA
Anca Muscholl	LaBRI, Université Bordeaux, France

Andreas Pavlogiannis	Aarhus University, Denmark
Andreas Podelski	University of Freiburg, Germany
Anna Lukina	TU Delft, Netherlands
Anne-Kathrin Schmuck	Max Planck Institute for Software Systems, Germany
Anthony Widjaja Lin	TU Kaiserslautern, Germany
Anton Wijs	Eindhoven University of Technology, Netherlands
Arie Gurfinkel	University of Waterloo, Canada
Armin Biere	University of Freiburg, Germany
Azadeh Farzan	University of Toronto, Canada
Barbara Jobstmann	Cadence Design Systems, Switzerland
Benjamin Kaminski	Saarland University, Germany
Bernd Finkbeiner	CISPA Helmholtz Center for Information Security, Germany
Bettina Könighofer	Graz University of Technology, Austria
Borzoo Bonakdarpour	Michigan State University, USA
Burcu Kulahcioglu Ozkan	Delft University of Technology, Netherlands
Cesar Sanchez	IMDEA Software Institute, Spain
Christoph M. Wintersteiger	Imandra, UK
Christoph Matheja	University of Oldenburg, Germany
Clark Barrett	Stanford University, USA
Claudia Cauli	Huawei Ireland Research Center, Ireland
Corina Pasareanu	NASA Ames Research Center, USA
Cristina David	University of Bristol, UK
Damien Zufferey	NVIDIA, Switzerland
Daniel Kröning	Amazon, USA
Daniel Stan	LRE EPITA Research Laboratory, France
Dirk Beyer	LMU Munich, Germany
Dominik Winterer	ETH Zurich, Switzerland
Đorđe Žikelić	Singapore Management University, Singapore
Dorra Ben Khalifa	ENAC – University of Toulouse, France
Duc-Hiep Chu	Google Research, USA
Elizabeth Polgreen	University of Edinburgh, UK
Elvira Albert	Complutense University of Madrid, Spain
Enrico Magnago	Amazon Web Services, Germany
Erika Ábrahám	RWTH Aachen University, Germany
Eva Darulova	Uppsala University, Sweden
Gidon Ernst	LMU Munich, Germany
Guowen Xu	University of Electronic Science and Technology of China, China
Guy Amir	Cornell University, USA
Guy Katz	Hebrew University of Jerusalem, Israel

Hadar Frenkel	Bar Ilan University, Israel
Haoze (Andrew) Wu	Amherst College, USA
Harald Ruess	SRI International, USA
Hari Govind Vediramana Krishnan	University of Waterloo, Canada
Hazem Torfah	Chalmers University of Technology, Sweden
He Zhu	Rutgers University, USA
Hossein Hojjat	Tehran Institute of Advanced Studies, Iran
Ichiro Hasuo	National Institute of Informatics, Japan
Jana Hofmann	Max Planck Institute for Security and Privacy, Germany
Ji Guan	Institute of Software, Chinese Academy of Sciences, China
Jianan Yao	Amazon Web Services, USA
Jingbo Wang	Purdue University, USA
Jocelyn (Qiaochu) Chen	New York University, USA
Joey Dodds	Amazon Web Services, USA
Joost-Pieter Katoen	RWTH-Aachen University, Germany
Jorge A. Pérez	University of Groningen, Netherlands
Junkil Park	Aptos Labs, USA
Kaushik Mallik	IMDEA Software Institute, Spain
Kedar Namjoshi	Bell Labs, Nokia, USA
Kshitij Bansal	Google, USA
Kyungmin Bae	POSTECH, South Korea
Laura Kovacs	TU Wien, Austria
Magnus Myreen	Chalmers University of Technology, Sweden
Marco Faella	University of Naples Federico II, Italy
Marieke Huisman	University of Twente, Netherlands
Mark Santolucito	Barnard College, Columbia University, USA
Michael Emmi	Amazon Web Services, USA
Mihaela Sighireanu	University Paris-Saclay, France
Mirco Giacobbe	University of Birmingham, UK
Natasha Sharygina	University of Lugano, Switzerland
Nian-Ze Lee	National Taiwan University, Taiwan
Ning Luo	University of Illinois Urbana-Champaign, USA
Ondřej Lengál	Brno University of Technology, Czech Republic
Pablo Castro	Universidad Nacional de Río Cuarto - CONICET, Argentina
Pavithra Prabhakar	Kansas State University, USA
Peter Müller	ETH Zurich, Switzerland
Philipp Ruemmer	University of Regensburg, Germany
Qinxiang Cao	Shanghai Jiao Tong University, China
Ravi Mangal	Colorado State University, USA

Rayna Dimitrova	CISPA Helmholtz Center for Information Security, Germany
Roderick Bloem	Graz University of Technology, Austria
S. Akshay	Indian Institute of Technology Bombay, India
S. Krishna	Indian Institute of Technology Bombay, India
Shaobo He	Amazon Web Services, USA
Shibashis Guha	Tata Institute of Fundamental Research, India
Soham Chakraborty	TU Delft, Netherlands
Stefan Leue	University of Konstanz, Germany
Stefan Zetzsche	Amazon Web Services, UK
Stephen F. Siegel	University of Delaware, USA
Subhajit Roy	Indian Institute of Technology Kanpur, India
Sylvie Putot	Ecole Polytechnique, France
Sébastien Bardin	CEA List, Université Paris Saclay, France
Tachio Terauchi	Waseda University, Japan
Tatjana Petrov	University of Trieste, Italy
Thomas Wahl	Trusted Science and Technology, Inc., USA
Tim King	Amazon Web Services, USA
Timos Antonopoulos	Yale University, USA
Tom van Dijk	University of Twente, Netherlands
Tomas Vojnar	Masaryk University, Czech Republic
Vijay Ganesh	Georgia Tech, USA
Viktor Kunčak	EPFL, Switzerland
Wenxi Wang	University of Virginia, USA
William Hallahan	Binghamton University, USA
Xi (James) Zheng	Macquarie University, Australia
Yakir Vizel	Technion, Israel
Yedi Zhang	National University of Singapore, Singapore
Yu-Fang Chen	Academia Sinica, Taiwan
Yuting Wang	Shanghai Jiao Tong University, China
Yuxin Deng	East China Normal University, China
Yuyang Sang	Alibaba Cloud, USA

Artifact Evaluation Committee

Abdalrhman Mohamed	Stanford University, USA
Abhishek Kr Singh	National University of Singapore, Singapore
Adwait Godbole	UC Berkeley, USA
Akshatha Shenoy	Università della Svizzera italiana, Switzerland
Alejandro Hernández-Cerezo	Complutense University of Madrid, Spain
Ameer Hamza	Florida State University, USA

Amit Samanta	University of Utah, USA
Anna Becchi	Fondazione Bruno Kessler, Italy
Annelot Bosman	Universiteit Leiden, Netherlands
Avaljot Singh	University of Illinois Urbana-Champaign, USA
Avraham Raviv	Bar Ilan University, Israel
Benjamin F. Jones	Amazon Web Services, USA
Bruno Andreotti	Federal University of Minas Gerais, Brazil
Calvin Chau	Technische Universität Dresden, Germany
Cayden Codel	Carnegie Mellon University, USA
Chenyu Zhou	University of Southern California, USA
Christoph Weinhuber	University of Oxford, UK
Clara Rodríguez-Núñez	Universidad Complutense de Madrid, Spain
Daniel Ajeleye	University of Colorado, Boulder, USA
Diptarko Roy	University of Birmingham, UK
Ehsan Kafshdar Goharshady	Institute of Science and Technology, Austria
Enrico Magnago	Amazon Web Services, Germany
Filip Cano	Graz University of Technology, Austria
Filip Macák	Brno University of Technology, Czech Republic
Filipe de Arruda	Universidade Federal de Pernambuco, Brazil
Florian Sextl	TU Wien, Austria
Frédéric Recoules	CEA LIST, France
Geunyeol Yu	Pohang University of Science and Technology, South Korea
Guangyu Hu	Hong Kong University of Science and Technology, China
Hichem Rami Ait-El-Hara	Université Paris-Saclay, France
Idan Refaeli	Hebrew University of Jerusalem, Israel
Jacqueline Mitchell	University of Southern California, USA
Jaime Arias	CNRS, LIPN, Université Sorbonne Paris Nord, France
Jiong Yang	Georgia Institute of Technology, USA
Joseph Tafese	University of Waterloo, Canada
Kadiray Karakaya	Paderborn University, Germany
Konstantin Britikov	University of Lugano, Switzerland
Konstantin Kueffner	Institute of Science and Technology, Austria
Leni Aniva	Stanford University, USA
Lutz Klinkenberg	RWTH Aachen University, Germany
Mahboubeh Samadi	Tehran Institute for Advanced Studies, Iran
Mahyar Karimi	Institute of Science and Technology, Austria
Marek Chalupa	Institute of Science and Technology, Austria
Mário Pereira	NOVA School of Science and Technology, Portugal

Mathias Fleury	University of Freiburg, Germany
Mehrdad Karrabi	Institute of Science and Technology, Austria
Miguel Isabel	Complutense University of Madrid, Spain
Mihai Nicola	Stevens Institute of Technology, USA
Mihály Dobos-Kovács	Budapest University of Technology and Economics, Hungary
Mikael Mayer	Amazon Web Services, USA
Muqsit Azeem	Technical University of Munich, Germany
N. Ege Saraç	Institute of Science and Technology, Austria
Neea Rusch	Augusta University, USA
Nicolas Koh	Princeton University, USA
Omar Inverso	Gran Sasso Science Institute, Italy
Omkar Tuppe	IIT Bombay, India
Omri Isac	Hebrew University of Jerusalem, Israel
Oyendrila Dobe	Amazon Web Services, USA
Pablo Gordillo	Complutense University of Madrid, Spain
Patrick Trentin	Amazon Web Services, USA
Pei-Wei Chen	UC Berkeley, USA
Peixin Wang	Nanyang Technological University, Singapore
Philipp Kern	Karlsruhe Institute of Technology, Germany
Pinhan Zhao	University of Michigan, USA
Po-Chun Chien	LMU Munich, Germany
Rajarshi Roy	University of Oxford, UK
Sankalp Gambhir	EPFL, Switzerland
Sascha Klüppelholz	Technische Universität Dresden, Germany
Shantanu Kulkarni	IIT Bombay, India
Simon Guilloud	EPFL, Switzerland
Stefan Zetzsche	Amazon Web Services, UK
Timo Lang	Huawei Ireland Research Center, Ireland
Xuan Xie	University of Alberta, Canada
Yanju Chen	University of California, Santa Barbara, USA
Yannik Schnitzer	University of Oxford, UK
Yibo Dong	East China Normal University, China
Yizhak Elboher	Hebrew University of Jerusalem, Israel
Yogev Shalmon	Technion, Israel
Yuning Wang	Rutgers University, USA
Yusen Su	University of Waterloo, Canada
Zhengyang John Lu	University of Waterloo, Canada
Zhiyang Chen	University of Toronto, Canada
Zunchen Huang	CWI, Netherlands

Additional Reviewers

Abha Chaudhary
Adam Husted Kjelstrøm
Adam Rogalewicz
Alejandro Luque-Cerpa
Alejandro Villoria Gonzalez
Alex Ozdemir
Alexander Bork
Alexander C. Wilton
Alexander Stekelenburg
Andoni Rodriguez
Andrew Reynolds
Anja Petkovic Komel
Anton Varonka
Antonina Skurka
Antonio Casares
Arend-Jan Quist
Áron Ricardo Perez-Lopez
Arshia Rafieioskouei
Ashwani Anand
Benedikt Maderbacher
Benjamin Monmege
Che Cheng
Chia-Hsuan Su
Christian Lidström
Christina Gehnen
Christophe Chareton
Christopher Brix
Christopher Watson
Corto Mascle
Cruise Song
Daniela Kaufman
David Boetius
Dimitrios Thanos
Fabio Mogavero
Faezeh Labbaf
Felix Stutz
Filip Cano
Gianluca Redondi
Grigory Fedyukovich
Grégoire Menguy
Hangcheng Cao
Henrik Wachowitz
Igor Walukiewicz

Irmak Saglam
Iwo Kurzidem
Jan Martens
Jannick Strobel
Jasper Nalbach
Jia Hu
Jingyi Mei
Jinhua Wu
Johannes Haring
Joonhwan Yoo
Konstantin Britikov
Ling Zhang
Lutz Klinkenberg
Marc Farreras I Bartra
Marek Jankola
Marian Lingsch-Rosenfeld
Marvin Brieger
Massimo Benerecetti
Mathias Preiner
Matthew Davis
Matthias Kettl
Matthieu Bovel
Matthieu Lemerre
Michal Hečko
Milad Rabizadeh
Min Wu
Mingyu Huang
Muhammad Mahmoud
Pengzhi Xing
Pierre Ganty
Piyush Jha
Po-Chun Chien
Pranshu Gaba
Prithwish Jana
Rachel Cleaveland
Rafael Dewes
Raffael Senn
Ritam Raha
Robert Mensing
Roy Hermanns
Satya Prakash Nayak
Simon Guilloud
Steef Hegeman

Stefan Pranger
Subhajit Bandopadhyay
Thomas Hader
Thomas Lemberger
Tian-Fu Chen
Timm Spork
Tobias Winkler
Tomas Kolarik
Tomáš Dacík
Tzu-Han Hsu

Valentin Promies
Xieting Chu
Xin Hong
Xinyuan Qian
Yanis Sellami
Yicheng Ni
Yizhou Mao
Zhengyang Lu
Zhengyu Li
Zihao Li

Keynote Talks

Through the Looking Glass: Semantic Analysis of Neural Networks

Corina Păsăreanu

Carnegie Mellon University, USA

Abstract. Neural networks are known for their lack of transparency, making them difficult to understand and analyze. In this talk, we explore methods designed to interpret, formally analyze, and even shape the internal representations of neural networks using human-understandable abstractions. We review recent techniques including the use of vision-language models to investigate perception modules, the application of probing and steering vectors to identify vulnerabilities in code models, and an axiomatic approach for validating mechanistic interpretation of transformer models.

Bio. Corina Păsăreanu is an ACM Fellow working at NASA Ames. She is affiliated with KBR and Carnegie Mellon University's CyLab. Her research interests include model checking, symbolic execution, compositional verification, AI safety, autonomy, and security. She is the recipient of several awards, including an ETAPS Test of Time Award and an ACM Impact Paper Award. She has served as Program/General Chair for several conferences, including CAV in 2015, and more recently ICSE in 2025. More information can be found on her website: https://www.andrew.cmu.edu/user/pcorina/.

Cedar: A New Language for Expressive, Fast, Safe, and Analyzable Authorization

Emina Torlak

Amazon Web Services and University of Washington, USA

Abstract. Authorization is the problem of deciding who has access to what in a multi-user system. Every cloud-based application has to solve this problem, from photo sharing to online banking to health care. This talk presents Cedar, a new language for authorization that is designed to be ergonomic, fast, safe, and analyzable by reduction to SMT. Cedar's simple and intuitive syntax supports common authorization use-cases with readable policies, naturally expressing concepts from role-based, attribute-based, and relation-based access control models. Cedar's policy structure enables authorization requests to be decided quickly. Its policy validator uses optional typing to help policy writers avoid mistakes, but not get in their way. Cedar's design has been finely balanced to allow for a sound, complete, and decidable logical encoding, which enables precise policy analysis, e.g., to ensure that policy refactoring preserves existing permissions. We have implemented Cedar in Rust and used Lean to formally verify important properties of its design. Cedar is used at scale in Amazon Verified Permissions and Amazon Verified Access, and it is freely available at https://github.com/cedar-policy.

Bio. Emina Torlak is a Senior Principal Scientist at Amazon Web Services and an Affiliate Professor at the University of Washington. Emina works on new languages and tools for program verification and synthesis. She received her Bachelors (2003), Masters (2004), and Ph.D. (2009) degrees from MIT. Emina is the creator of Rosette and Kodkod, and leads the development of Cedar. Rosette is a solver-aided language that powers verification and synthesis tools for all kinds of systems, from radiation therapy control to Linux JIT compilers. Kodkod is a solver for relational logic, used widely in tools for software analysis and design. Cedar is an expressive, fast, and analysable language for authorization, used at scale at Amazon Web Services and beyond. Emina is a recipient of the Robin Milner Young Researcher Award (2021), NSF Career Award (2017), Sloan Research Fellowship (2016), and the AITO Dahl-Nygaard Junior Prize (2016).

Side Channel Secure Software: A Hardware Question

Roderick Bloem

Graz University of Technology, Austria

Abstract. We will present a method to prove the absence of power side channels in systems that are protected using masking. Power side channels may allow attackers to discover secret information by measuring electromagnetic emanations from a chip. Masking is a countermeasure to hide secrets by duplication and addition of randomness. We will discuss how to formally prove security against power side channel techniques for circuits. We will then move on to software running on a CPU, where hardware details can have surprising effects. We will present some vulnerabilities on a small CPU and how to fix them, and we will talk about contracts that take side channels into account.

Bio. Roderick Bloem is a professor at Graz University of Technology. He received his M.Sc. degree in Computer Science from Leiden University, the Netherlands, in 1996, and his Ph.D. degree in Computer Science from the University of Colorado at Boulder in 2001. From 2002 until 2008, he was an Assistant at Graz University of Technology, Graz, Austria. From 2008, he has been a full professor of Computer Science at the same university. He is a co-editor of the *Handbook of Model Checking* and has published over 140 peer reviewed papers in formal verification, reactive synthesis, Safe AI, and security.

References

1. Bloem, R., Gigerl, B., Gourjon, M., Hadzic, V., Mangard, S., Primas, R.: Power contracts: provably complete power leakage models for processors. In: Yin, H., Stavrou, A., Cremers, C., Shi, E. (eds.) Proceedings of the 2022 ACM SIGSAC Conference on Computer and Communications Security, CCS 2022, Los Angeles, CA, USA, 7–11 November 2022. pp. 381–395. ACM (2022). https://doi.org/10.1145/3548606.3560600
2. Bloem, R., Gross, H., Iusupov, R., Könighofer, B., Mangard, S., Winter, J.: Formal verification of masked hardware implementations in the presence of glitches. In: Nielsen, J., Rijmen, V. (eds.) EUROCRYPT 2018. LNCS, vol. 10821, pp. 321–353. Springer, Cham (2018). https://doi.org/10.1007/978-3-319-78375-8_11

3. Hadzic, V., Bloem, R.: COCOALMA: a versatile masking verifier. In: Formal Methods in Computer Aided Design, FMCAD 2021, New Haven, CT, USA, 19–22 October 2021, pp. 1–10. IEEE (2021). https://doi.org/10.34727/2021/ISBN.978-3-85448-046-4_9

4. Haring, J., Hadzic, V., Bloem, R.: Closing the gap: Leakage contracts for processors with transitions and glitches. IACR Trans. Cryptogr. Hardw. Embed. Syst. 2024(4), 110–132 (2024). https://doi.org/10.46586/TCHES.V2024.I4.110-132

Contents – Part II

Neural Networks

Markov Decision Process
and Probabilistic Reasoning

Quantitative Supermartingale Certificates

Alessandro Abate[1], Mirco Giacobbe[2], and Diptarko Roy[2(✉)]

[1] University of Oxford, Oxford, UK
alessandro.abate@cs.ox.ac.uk
[2] University of Birmingham, Birmingham, UK
{m.giacobbe,d.s.roy}@bham.ac.uk

Abstract. We introduce a general methodology for quantitative model checking and control synthesis with supermartingale certificates. We show that every specification that is invariant to time shifts admits a stochastic invariant that bounds its probability from below; for systems with general state space, the stochastic invariant bounds this probability as closely as desired; for systems with finite state space, it quantifies it exactly. Our result enables the extension of every certificate for the almost-sure satisfaction of shift-invariant specifications to its quantitative counterpart, ensuring completeness up to an approximation in the general case and exactness in the finite state case. This generalises and unifies existing supermartingale certificates for quantitative verification and control under reachability, safety, reach-avoidance, and stability specifications, as well as asymptotic bounds on accrued costs and rewards. Furthermore, our result provides the first supermartingale certificate for computing upper and lower bounds on the probability of satisfying ω-regular and linear temporal logic specifications. We present an algorithm for quantitative ω-regular verification and control synthesis based on our method and demonstrate its practical efficacy on several infinite-state examples.

Keywords: Probabilistic model checking · Stochastic control synthesis · Probability bounds · LTL · Martingale theory · Converse theorems

1 Introduction

Quantitative model checking for probabilistic systems is the problem of computing the probability that a given stochastic dynamical system or probabilistic program satisfies a specification of intended behaviour. Quantitative control synthesis extends this to the construction of a control policy that maximises or meets a threshold for the probability of satisfying a desired objective within a given stochastic environment. Computing provable bounds on the probability that a system satisfies its specification is crucial for model checking and control synthesis when neither worst-case nor almost-sure satisfaction can be achieved and failure to comply must be tolerated within acceptable margins. Notable examples

© The Author(s) 2025
R. Piskac and Z. Rakamarić (Eds.): CAV 2025, LNCS 15932, pp. 3–28, 2025.
https://doi.org/10.1007/978-3-031-98679-6_1

include many randomized distributed algorithms and cryptographic protocols, cyber-physical systems and biochemical processes under random parameter and input uncertainty, and machine learning algorithms facing aleatoric uncertainty in their data and epistemic uncertainty in their models.

Algorithmic technologies for quantitative model checking and control synthesis have been developed extensively for probabilistic systems. The standard techniques rely on computing the absorbing components, reduction to linear programming, tabular value and policy iteration as well as symbolic algorithms based on multi-terminal binary decision diagrams [45,46,56,68,86]. This represents the state of the art for systems with a finite state space but, falls short for systems with a countably infinite or continuous state space, which is common in probabilistic programs, control systems, and machine learning models. The automated verification and control of infinite-state probabilistic systems builds upon either the construction of finite abstractions—grounded in concurrency theory—or the construction of proof certificates—grounded in martingale theory [5,15–17,69].

Proof certificates for the analysis of dynamical systems and computer programs are typically expressed as functions or regions of the state space that evidence invariant properties of the system [44,52]. Certificates for the quantitative and qualitative analysis of stochastic processes—known as supermartingale certificates—have been widely studied, especially in stochastic control with a focus on asymptotic stability, reachability, and avoidance objectives [37,67,78]. While traditionally these proof certificates are characterised analytically, hence requiring significant manual effort for their actual derivation, their automated construction has recently gained momentum due to advances in numerical methods [85,87,90,91], as well as machine learning techniques for this purpose [1]. Automation in the construction of supermartingale certificates has stimulated their adoption in termination analysis [3,16,20,22,28,79], reachability, safety and reach-avoidance analysis [13,57,59,71,105], cost bound analysis [23,81,97,106], stochastic control synthesis and learning [4,60,72,76,102,103].

We present a general methodology for the formalisation of quantitative proof certificates for probabilistic systems and demonstrate its practical application in developing model checking and control synthesis algorithms. We show that every specification that falls within the class of *shift-invariant* events admits a stochastic invariant that bounds its probability from below. A stochastic invariant is a region of the state space associated with a supermartingale that is sufficient to bound from above the probability of leaving the invariant. We provide two converse theorems for their necessary existence: for systems with general state space, we establish the existence of a stochastic invariant that is sufficiently strong to bound the probability of the shift-invariant specification up to arbitrary approximation; for systems with finite state space, we establish the existence of a stochastic invariant that quantifies its probability exactly.

Our result reduces the problem of computing a lower bound on the probability of a shift-invariant specification to the problem of computing a stochastic invariant alongside a proof certificate for the almost-sure satisfaction of the specification. Our reduction is complete up to arbitrary approximation for systems with general state space, complete for systems with finite state space, and applies to a rich class of specifications. Shift-invariant specifications encompass Büchi and co-Büchi acceptance conditions, which have existing quantitative certificates [8], as well as Muller, parity, Rabin, and Streett conditions, for which no quantitative certificates have previously been presented. As such, our method not only unifies existing results but also lays the foundations for developing new quantitative supermartingale certificates.

We instantiate our theory to the design and implementation of the first supermartingale certificate for the quantitative verification and control of ω-regular and linear temporal logic (LTL) specifications. We leverage our theory alongside two existing results. Firstly, ω-regular and LTL specifications enjoy reduction to Streett acceptance conditions through composition with deterministic Streett automata [92]. Secondly, Streett acceptance conditions have supermartingale certificates for their almost-sure satisfaction with supporting invariants [4]. Since Streett acceptance conditions are shift-invariant, our theory extends the existing supermartingale certificates for almost-sure Streett acceptance to additionally quantify lower and upper bounds on the acceptance probability. This enables the algorithmic ω-regular quantitative verification and control of probabilistic systems with general state space, encompassing and generalising safety, reachability, reach-avoidance, recurrence, persistence properties and LTL.

We demonstrate the practical efficacy of our method with a prototype for the simultaneous construction of parametrised supermartingale certificates alongside parametrised control policies expressed as polynomials of known degree. We leverage polynomial Positivstellensatz results to reduce it to a decision problem over the existential theory of the reals, amenable to satisfiability solving modulo quantifier-free non-linear real arithmetic [14,61]. Our algorithm is sound and complete relatively to the existence of the almost-sure component of our certificates and up to a desired approximation error. We compute upper and lower probability bounds using polynomials of varying degree on several examples with infinite state space, which are beyond the reach of the existing tools.

Our contribution is threefold. First, we present a general theory of quantitative supermartingale certificates, which extends every certificate for almost-sure acceptance of shift-invariant specifications to their quantitative counterpart. Second, we introduce a special theory of quantitative Streett supermartingale certificates based on our methodology, which results in the first quantitative supermartingale certificate for ω-regular specifications and LTL. Third, we implement our theory in an algorithm for quantitative ω-regular verification and control, and demonstrate its practical efficacy on examples.

2   Stochastic Invariants

We consider stochastic systems over general state space (S, Σ), where S denotes the set of states and Σ denotes the associated σ-algebra. We treat quantitative model checking and control synthesis problems for specifications over an infinite time horizon measured over $(\Omega, \mathcal{F})$, where the set of outcomes $\Omega = S^\omega$ are the infinite trajectories and the set of events $\mathcal{F} = \bigotimes_{i \in \omega} \Sigma_i$ (with $\Sigma_i = \Sigma$) are the measurable specifications. As is standard in stochastic analysis [78], we rely on the result that every initial probability measure and transition probability kernel gives rise to a well-defined probability measure over specifications.

Theorem 1. *Let $\mu : \Sigma \to [0,1]$ be an initial probability measure and $P : S \times \Sigma \to [0,1]$ be a transition probability kernel. Then, there exists a stochastic process $\Phi = (\Phi_0, \Phi_1, \ldots)$ on the trajectory space $(\Omega, \mathcal{F})$ and a probability measure $\mathsf{P}_\mu : \mathcal{F} \to [0,1]$ where $\mathsf{P}_\mu(\Phi \in L)$ is the probability that Φ satisfies the specification $L \in \mathcal{F}$ and, for every $n \in \mathbb{N}$ and $A_0 \in \Sigma, \ldots, A_n \in \Sigma$, the following holds:*

$$\mathsf{P}_\mu(\Phi_0 \in A_0 \wedge \cdots \wedge \Phi_n \in A_n) =$$
$$\int_{s_0 \in A_0} \cdots \int_{s_{n-1} \in A_{n-1}} \mu(\mathrm{d}s_0) P(s_0, \mathrm{d}s_1) \cdots P(s_{n-1}, A_n). \quad (1)$$

We frame our work around the operation of *time shift*, which encapsulates the forgetfulness of the process with respect to its past—i.e., the Markov property. We define the (time) shift operator θ as the measurable mapping on Ω

$$\theta(s_0, s_1, \ldots, s_n, \ldots) = (s_1, s_2, \ldots, s_{n+1}, \ldots). \quad (2)$$

This characterises time-homogeneous Markov chains over general state spaces, our reference model throughout the paper unless stated otherwise. Also, henceforth we use $\delta_s : \Sigma \to [0,1]$ to denote the Dirac measure at $s \in S$.

Definition 1 (Time-Homogeneous Markov Chains). *A time-homogeneous Markov chain is a stochastic process Φ defined in terms of an initial probability measure $\mu : \Sigma \to [0,1]$ and probability transition kernel $P : S \times \Sigma \to [0,1]$, having a natural filtration $\mathcal{F}_n^\Phi = \sigma(\Phi_0, \ldots, \Phi_n) \subseteq \mathcal{F}$ satisfying the Markov property, i.e.,*

$$\mathsf{E}_\mu[H \circ \theta^n \mid \mathcal{F}_n^\Phi] = \mathsf{E}_{\delta_{\Phi_n}}[H] \qquad a.s. \ [\mathsf{P}_\mu] \quad (3)$$

for every random variable H on $(\Omega, \mathcal{F}, \mathsf{P}_\mu)$ and every $n \in \mathbb{N}$ [78, p. 70].

Time-homogeneity allows us to derive global properties of the stochastic process by locally reasoning about the transition probability kernel P and the initial probability measure μ. For this purpose, we define the post-expectation $(Ph) : S \to \mathbb{R}$ and the init-expectation $(\mu h) \in \mathbb{R}$ operations of any real-valued measurable function $h : S \to \mathbb{R}$, with respect to the process, as follows:

$$Ph(s) = \int_{u \in S} h(u) \, P(s, \mathrm{d}u), \qquad \mu h = \int_{s \in S} h(s) \, \mu(\mathrm{d}s). \quad (4)$$

These two operators are the essential elements in the formalisation and the construction of supermartingale certificates. Specifically, the post-expectation $Ph(s)$ of the function h at state $s \in S$ gives the expected value of h at the next state conditional on s being the current state; similarly, the init-expectation μh gives the expected value of h at the initial time. The algorithmic synthesis of certificates relies on expressing the post- and init-expectation of value functions in a closed form, for which appropriate procedures are available [47].

Our methodology leverages the proof rule for stochastic invariants, which is the most basic form of a quantitative supermartingale certificate [66, Theorem 1]. A stochastic invariant is a region of the state space I associated with a value function V_0 that bounds from above the probability that the process escapes I.

Theorem 2 (Stochastic Invariants). *Suppose that there exists a measurable set $I \in \Sigma$ and a measurable function $V_0 : S \to \mathbb{R}_{\geq 0}$ such that*

$$\forall s \in I : PV_0(s) \leq V_0(s), \tag{5}$$
$$\forall s \notin I : V_0(s) \geq 1. \tag{6}$$

Then, $\mathsf{P}_\mu(\mathbf{\Phi} \notin I^\omega) \leq \mu V_0$.

We show that stochastic invariants are sufficient to characterise the probability of the rich class of specifications that are invariant to time shift, i.e., the specifications that are invariant to addition or deletion of finite prefixes.

Definition 2 (Shift-Invariant Specifications). *A specification $L \in \mathcal{F}$ is invariant to time shift if it satisfies the following property:*

$$\theta^{-1}L = L. \tag{7}$$

Remark 1 (Connection to Tail Objectives). Specifications satisfying Eq. (7) are sometimes referred to as *tail objectives* [18, 26, 64]. In fact, every shift-invariant event is also a tail event, i.e., a member of the tail σ-algebra $\cap_{i \in \omega} \sigma(\Phi_i, \Phi_{i+1}, \dots)$. The converse is not true, and not every tail event is shift-invariant [37, p. 260]. □

Remark 2 (Connection to Liveness Properties [9]). Shift invariance is strictly stronger than liveness. For example, consider the liveness property $L = \{\exists n \in \mathbb{N} : \Phi_n \in A\}$, specifying that $A \in \Sigma$ eventually happens. Under a shift we obtain $\theta^{-1}L = \{\exists n \in \mathbb{N} : \Phi_{n+1} \in A\} \neq L$, excluding the option to hit A at time 0. □

We address the question of determining the probability for which a time-homogeneous Markov chain $\mathbf{\Phi}$ satisfies a shift-invariant specification L using supermartingale certificates. Our methodology is underpinned by the relation between a shift-invariant specification and the random variable characterising its satisfaction probability, which we show in the following technical result.

Theorem 3. *Suppose that $L \in \mathcal{F}$ is shift-invariant. Then*

$$\mathsf{P}_\mu(\mathbf{\Phi} \in L) = \mathsf{P}_\mu(\ \inf_n \mathsf{P}_{\delta_{\Phi_n}}(\mathbf{\Phi} \in L) > 0\ ). \tag{8}$$

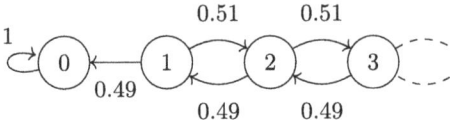

Fig. 1. Gambler's Ruin.

Example 1 (Intuition for Theorem 3). Consider a Markov chain on the countable state space $S = \mathbb{N}$ as illustrated in Fig. 1, defining a biased random walk that, at each time, increments the state with probability 0.51, and otherwise decrements the state with probability 0.49, unless it reaches the state 0, at which it remains thereafter. Consider the event $L = \{\sum_{n=0}^{\infty} \mathbf{1}_A(\Phi_n) = \infty\}$, which specifies that $A \in \Sigma$ is visited infinitely often ($\mathbf{1}_A$ denotes the indicator function of A). Notably, this specification is shift-invariant because $\theta^{-1}L = \{\sum_{n=0}^{\infty} \mathbf{1}_A(\Phi_{n+1}) = \infty\} = L$.

Suppose that $A = \{0\}$. Then, for a state $x \in \mathbb{N}$, the probability that the Markov chain above satisfies L corresponds to

$$\mathsf{P}_{\delta_x}(\mathbf{\Phi} \in L) = \begin{cases} (49/51)^x & \text{if } x > 0, \\ 1 & \text{if } x = 0. \end{cases} \tag{9}$$

Our main observation is that the expression $\mathsf{P}_{\delta_{\Phi_n}}(\mathbf{\Phi} \in L)$ defines a random variable on the probability space $(\Omega, \mathcal{F}, \mathsf{P}_\mu)$, which for shift-invariant properties is equal to the probability $\mathsf{P}_\mu(\mathbf{\Phi} \in L \mid \mathcal{F}_n^\Phi)$ of the system satisfying the specification, conditional on the information contained in the stochastic process up to time n. In fact, this random variable can be simulated in a computer program as we illustrate in Fig. 2, which shows 10 random simulations of the associated stochastic process under initial distribution $\mu = \delta_{10}$.

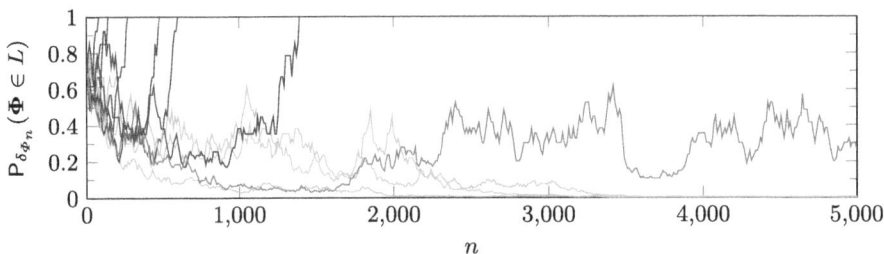

Fig. 2. Random simulations of the satisfaction probability process of Example 1.

There are two central reasons why Eq. (8) holds. Firstly, the stochastic process $\mathsf{P}_{\delta_{\Phi_n}}(\mathbf{\Phi} \in L)$ is a non-negative martingale. This implies that, if the value of the stochastic process ever hits 0, it must remain at 0 at all times thereafter. Secondly, the process $\mathsf{P}_{\delta_{\Phi_n}}(\mathbf{\Phi} \in L)$ almost-surely converges to 1 when $\mathbf{\Phi} \in L$

and to 0 otherwise, as a consequence of Lévy's 0-1 Law. Since $\mathsf{P}_{\delta_{\phi_n}}(\mathbf{\Phi} \in L)$ converges to either 0 or 1 almost surely, the probability of the variable $\mathsf{P}_{\delta_{\phi_n}}(\mathbf{\Phi} \in L)$ converging to 1 corresponds to the probability of not converging to 0, and since 0 is an absorbing value for a non-negative martingale, this corresponds to the probability that its infimum is positive.   □

A consequence of the relation between shift-invariant specifications and the random variables associated with their satisfaction probability is that, for every desired approximation error $\epsilon > 0$, we can always choose an appropriate level set of this random variable to define a sufficiently tight stochastic invariant.

Theorem 4. *Suppose that $L \in \mathcal{F}$ is shift-invariant. Then, for every $\epsilon > 0$ there exists a measurable set $I \in \Sigma$ such that $\mathsf{P}_\mu(\mathbf{\Phi} \in I^\omega \wedge \mathbf{\Phi} \notin L) = 0$ and*

$$\mathsf{P}_\mu(\mathbf{\Phi} \in L) - \epsilon \leq \mathsf{P}_\mu(\mathbf{\Phi} \in I^\omega) \leq \mathsf{P}_\mu(\mathbf{\Phi} \in L). \tag{10}$$

Example 2 (The Gambler's Ruin). The Markov chain in Example 1 corresponds to the Gambler's Ruin problem [41, p. 345]. It is a classic result that if the process starts from $x > 0$, the probability of hitting any other value $y > x$—equivalent to the probability of exiting the set $I = \{0, \dots, y - 1\}$—is given by

$$\mathsf{P}_{\delta_x}(\mathbf{\Phi} \notin I^\omega) = \frac{1 - (49/51)^x}{1 - (49/51)^y}. \tag{11}$$

It follows that the probability of avoiding y converges asymptotically, for increasing y, to the probability of hitting 0:

$$\lim_{y \to \infty} \underbrace{1 - \frac{1 - (49/51)^x}{1 - (49/51)^y}}_{\mathsf{P}_{\delta_x}(\mathbf{\Phi} \in I^\omega)} = \underbrace{(49/51)^x}_{\mathsf{P}_{\delta_x}(\mathbf{\Phi} \in L)}. \tag{12}$$

This shows that, for every $\epsilon > 0$, there exists a sufficiently large y such that I satisfies Eq. (10) with $\mu = \delta_x$. Moreover, for every y the event of eventually hitting either 0 or y has probability 1; in other words $\mathsf{P}_{\delta_x}(\mathbf{\Phi} \in I^\omega \wedge \mathbf{\Phi} \notin L) = 0$.   □

We further demonstrate that, for finite systems, a stochastic invariant that exactly quantifies the probability of the specification always exists.

Theorem 5. *Suppose that $L \in \mathcal{F}$ is shift-invariant and S is finite. Then, there exists a measurable set $I \in \Sigma$ such that $\mathsf{P}_\mu(\mathbf{\Phi} \in I^\omega \wedge \mathbf{\Phi} \notin L) = 0$ and*

$$\mathsf{P}_\mu(\mathbf{\Phi} \in I^\omega) = \mathsf{P}_\mu(\mathbf{\Phi} \in L). \tag{13}$$

Example 3. Assume that the Markov chain in Example 1 has an upper bound $N > 0$ that is a sink state, making its state space finite. Then, the event of hitting 0—which is the event L—corresponds exactly to the event of avoiding N—which is the event I^ω with $I = \{0, \dots, N - 1\}$. Since the two events are equivalent, their probabilities are as well, satisfying Eq. (13).   □

Remark 3 (Existence of Value Functions). Our converse theorems establish the existence of invariant regions $I \in \Sigma$. This implies the existence of appropriate value functions, which can be defined as $V_0(s) = \mathsf{P}_{\delta_s}(\Phi \notin I^\omega)$. These are necessarily measurable and are guaranteed to satisfy Eqs. (5) and (6).   □

3   Quantitative Supermartingale Certificates

We propose a general methodology for the formalisation of proof rules to establish probability bounds for a broad variety of specifications. We show that the problem of computing lower bounds for the probability of satisfaction of shift-invariant specifications can be decomposed into two problems: computing a stochastic invariant alongside a lower bound for its probability, and deciding the almost-sure satisfaction of the specification conditional to the stochastic invariant.

Theorem 6. *Suppose that $L \in \mathcal{F}$ is shift-invariant and, for some probability bound $p \in (0, 1]$ and measurable set $I \in \Sigma$, the following two conditions hold:*

$$\mathsf{P}_\mu(\Phi \in I^\omega) \geq p, \tag{14}$$

$$\mathsf{P}_\mu(\Phi \in L \mid \Phi \in I^\omega) = 1. \tag{15}$$

Then, $\mathsf{P}_\mu(\Phi \in L) \geq p$.

This result enables the extension of every supermartingale certificate proof rule for almost-sure satisfaction, conditional to a deterministic invariant, towards a quantitative proof rule for the same specification. Specifically, our proof rule for stochastic invariants presented in Theorem 2 provides the appropriate constraints for the formalisation of quantitative supermartingale certificates.

Example 4 (A Proof Rule for Quantitative Termination [22, Theorem 4]). Using our methodology, we formalise a supermartingale certificate proof rule for the quantitative finite-time termination of probabilistic programs. For the set of terminal states $A \in \Sigma$, which are assumed to be sink states, this corresponds to determining the probability of $L = \{\sum_{n=0}^{\infty} \mathbf{1}_A(\Phi_n) = \infty\}$, which is shift-invariant. We combine the proof rule for ranking supermartingales [16, Definition 9] (cf. Eq. (18))—which proves almost-sure termination in expected finite time—with Theorem 2, and obtain the following (known) proof rule:

$$\forall s \in I : PV_0(s) \leq V_0(s), \tag{16}$$

$$\forall s \notin I : V_0(s) \geq 1, \tag{17}$$

$$\forall s \in I \setminus A : PV_1(s) \leq V_1(s) - \varepsilon. \tag{18}$$

Here, any region $I \in \Sigma$, non-negative value functions $V_0, V_1 : S \to \mathbb{R}_{\geq 0}$, and positive constant $\varepsilon > 0$ constitute a quantitative supermartingale certificate where $1 - \mu V_0$ is a lower bound upon the probability of hitting target A.

Consider the quantitative verification problem developed in Examples 1 and 2, which corresponds to the termination question with terminal state $A = \{0\}$. A valid supermartingale certificate is given by the following components:

$$V_0(x) = \frac{1 - (49/51)^x}{1 - (49/51)^y}, \quad V_1(x) = y - x, \quad I = \{0, \ldots, y - 1\}, \quad \varepsilon = 0.02, \quad (19)$$

where $y \in \mathbb{N}$ is any value larger than the initial state. For initial state 10, the true probability is approximately $0.6703 \approx (49/51)^{10}$. With $y = 50$, we obtain bound $1 - V_0(10) \approx 0.62$; with $y = 100$, we obtain the tighter bound $1 - V_0(10) \approx 0.66$; with $y = 200$, we obtain the much tighter bound $1 - V_0(10) \approx 0.6702$. Notably, the true probability $(49/51)^x$ would violate Eq. (17), and in this example a bounded invariant is essential to construct a ranking supermartingale V_1. □

Our converse results presented in Theorems 4 and 5 guarantee that our methodology yields complete certificates up to arbitrary approximation for systems with general state space, and complete certificates for finite systems.

Theorem 7 (ϵ-Completeness for General Markov Chains). *Suppose that $L \in \mathcal{F}$ is shift-invariant. Then, for every arbitrary $\epsilon > 0$, there exists a measurable set $I \in \Sigma$ such that Eqs. (14) and (15) hold with $p = \mathsf{P}_\mu(\Phi \in L) - \epsilon$.*

Theorem 8 (Completeness for Finite Markov Chains). *Suppose that $L \in \mathcal{F}$ is shift-invariant and S is finite. Then, there exists a measurable set $I \in \Sigma$ such that Eqs. (14) and (15) hold with $p = \mathsf{P}_\mu(\Phi \in L)$.*

Remark 4. Composing stochastic invariants and almost-sure certificates, as described in Theorem 6, results in complete proof rules for probabilistic lower bounds under the assumption that the proof rule for conditional almost-sure satisfaction is complete. In other words, all completeness guarantees of the proof rule for almost-sure satisfaction carry over to their quantitative extension, up to approximation or exactly, as described in Theorems 7 and 8 respectively. □

Our methodology generalises and unifies existing proof rules for quantitative model checking and control synthesis, while providing the foundation for formalising quantitative supermartingale certificates for new specifications and objectives. It applies to the rich class of shift-invariant specifications, which includes and extends beyond a broad variety of special cases. This includes specifications defined as limits [37, Lemma 5.1.6], such as the limit objectives on cost and reward considered in reinforcement learning, and asymptotic stability considered in control theory, all of which are also tail events (cf. Remark 1). Moreover, it also includes Büchi, co-Büchi, Rabin, Streett, Muller, and parity acceptance conditions of automata over infinite words [18]. As we demonstrate, this enables in particular the development of quantitative supermartingale certificates for ω-regular specifications.

4 Quantitative ω-Regular Verification and Control

We present the first quantitative supermartingale certificate for ω-regular specifications, which we obtain as a result of Theorems 2 and 6 and the supermartingale certificate for the almost-sure acceptance of Streett conditions [4].

An ω-regular specification (or language) over a finite set of atomic propositions Π, which we define as predicates over the state space of the system under analysis, corresponds to the language of an ω-regular expression whose alphabet is the Boolean truth valuations of Π. An important class of ω-regular specifications is the temporal behaviour described using linear temporal logic (LTL). An LTL formula φ extends propositional logic (over the atomic propositions Π) with the temporal *next* operator $\mathsf{X}\varphi$, indicating that φ holds after one step in the future, the *eventually* operator $\mathsf{F}\varphi$, indicating that φ holds at some point in the future, the *always* operator $\mathsf{G}\varphi$, indicating that φ holds at all times in the future, and the *until* operator $\varphi\mathsf{U}\psi$, indicating that φ holds at all times in the future before ψ, which in turn holds at some point in the future [88].

We treat the problem of determining the probability of satisfying an ω-regular specification over Π for a system under analysis corresponding to a time-homogeneous Markov chain $\hat{\mathbf{\Phi}} = (\hat{\Phi}_0, \hat{\Phi}_1, \dots)$ with general state space $(\hat{S}, \hat{\Sigma})$, initial probability measure $\hat{\mu}$ and transition probability kernel $\hat{P}$. The problem is defined in terms of a measurable labelling function $\langle\!\langle \cdot \rangle\!\rangle : \hat{S} \to \mathcal{P}(\Pi)$ where $\langle\!\langle \hat{s} \rangle\!\rangle \subseteq \Pi$ indicates the set of atomic propositions that hold true in state $\hat{s} \in \hat{S}$, which we call the labelling of $\hat{s}$, and interpret the ω-regular specification according to its usual semantics over the set of traces $\mathcal{P}(\Pi)^\omega$. Notably, ω-regular specifications lack shift invariance. For example, the LTL formula $\varphi = \mathsf{F}a$, defining the event $L_\varphi = \{\exists n \in \mathbb{N} : a \in \langle\!\langle \hat{\Phi}_n \rangle\!\rangle\}$, is not shift-invariant (cf. Remark 2).

Automata over infinite words reduce ω-regular specifications to equivalent acceptance conditions that are shift-invariant, by extending the state space with additional memory which is given by the states of an ω-automaton. Büchi automata are the canonical example, but they require the presence of non-determinism, with which standard probability theory is limited. Conversely, automata with Muller, Rabin, parity, and Streett acceptance conditions recognise ω-regular languages in their deterministic form [50], which preserves the probabilistic nature of the system. We consider the case of Streett automata, and generalise the existing supermartingale certificates for their almost-sure acceptance (from the literature [4]) to additionally produce lower and upper probability bounds for ω-regular specifications.

Definition 3 (Deterministic Streett Automata). *A deterministic Streett automaton (DSA) over the finite set of propositions Π consists of a finite set of states Q, an initial state $q_0 \in Q$, a transition function $T : Q \times \mathcal{P}(\Pi) \to Q$, and an acceptance condition $(F_1, G_1), \dots, (F_k, G_k)$ where $F_i, G_i \subseteq Q$ for $i = 1, \dots k$. An infinite input trace $(p_0, p_1, p_2, \dots) \in \mathcal{P}(\Pi)^\omega$ is accepted if there exists an infinite run $(q_0, q_1, q_2, \dots) \in Q^\omega$ such that $q_{n+1} = T(q_n, p_n)$ for every $n \in \mathbb{N}$ and, for every $i = 1, \dots, k$, either $\sum_{n=0}^\infty \mathbf{1}_{F_i}(q_n) < \infty$ or $\sum_{n=0}^\infty \mathbf{1}_{G_i}(q_n) = \infty$.*

There are multiple algorithms for the automatic construction of DSA, in particular from LTL formulae [38,65]. Given a DSA, the original ω-regular verification question reduces to a question of Streett acceptance over the synchronous composition between the Markov chain under analysis $\hat{\Phi}$ and the automaton. Their synchronous composition results in another Markov chain $\Phi = (\Phi_0, \Phi_1, \dots)$ over state space $S = \hat{S} \times Q$ with the σ-algebra $\Sigma = \hat{\Sigma} \otimes \mathcal{P}(Q)$, whose transition probability kernel $P : S \times \Sigma \to [0,1]$ and initial probability measure $\mu : \Sigma \to [0,1]$ are defined as follows:

$$P((\hat{s}, q), A) = \int_{(u,r) \in A} \hat{P}(\hat{s}, du) \cdot \mathbf{1}_{\{r\}}(T(q, \langle\!\langle \hat{s} \rangle\!\rangle)), \tag{20}$$

$$\mu(A) = \int_{(u,r) \in A} \hat{\mu}(du) \cdot \mathbf{1}_{\{r\}}(q_0). \tag{21}$$

This is associated with the Streett acceptance condition $(A_1, B_1) \in \Sigma^2, \dots, (A_k, B_k) \in \Sigma^2$ defined as $A_i = \hat{S} \times F_i, B_i = \hat{S} \times G_i$ for $i = 1, \dots k$.

Remark 5 (Streett Acceptance is Shift-Invariant). As we establish in Example 1, the Büchi acceptance condition $\{\sum_{n=0}^{\infty} \mathbf{1}_A(\Phi_n) = \infty\}$ is shift-invariant. We note that shift-invariant events are closed under countable Boolean operations [37, Proposition 5.1.5], and that Streett acceptance corresponds to the event $\cap_{i=1}^{k}(\{\sum_{n=0}^{\infty} \mathbf{1}_{A_i}(\Phi_n) = \infty\}^c \cup \{\sum_{n=0}^{\infty} \mathbf{1}_{B_i}(\Phi_n) = \infty\})$. □

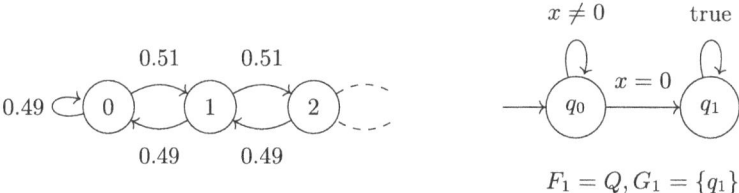

Fig. 3. A biased random walk over $\mathbb{N}$ and a DSA for the LTL specification $\mathsf{F}(x = 0)$.

Example 5 (Reachability as Recurrence). Consider the biased random walk over state space $\hat{S} = \mathbb{N}$ illustrated in Fig. 3, which on all states increments with probability 0.51 and decrements with probability 0.49. Consider the LTL formula $\varphi = \mathsf{F}(x = 0)$, requiring that the process hits 0 at least once. This is not shift-invariant (cf. Remark 2). A DSA for this ω-regular specification has two states $Q = \{q_0, q_1\}$ as depicted in Fig. 3, where q_1 is a sink state that is entered exactly when the random walk hits value 0. The acceptance condition of this automaton requires that q_1 is visited infinitely often—recurrence—which is shift invariant. Notably, their synchronous composition results in a Markov chain where every state $\{q_1\} \times \mathbb{N}$ essentially indicates that value 0 has been hit at least once in the past. As a result, visiting q_1 infinitely often is equivalent to visiting 0 at least once, and has reduced our reachability question to an equivalent recurrence question. This is analogous to the termination problem developed in Example 4, which in fact requires the terminal state 0 to be a recurrent sink state.   □

Our new (and the first) quantitative supermartingale certificate for ω-regular specifications combines the proof rule for stochastic invariants in Theorem 2 with the following (known) proof rule for the almost-sure acceptance of Streett conditions over general state space.

Theorem 9 (Streett Supermartingales [4]). *Let* $(A_1, B_1) \in \Sigma^2, \ldots, (A_k, B_k) \in \Sigma^2$ *be a Streett acceptance condition. Suppose that* $\mathsf{P}_\mu(\boldsymbol{\Phi} \in I^\omega) > 0$ *and there exist* k *measurable functions* $V_1, \ldots, V_k : S \to \mathbb{R}_{\geq 0}$ *such that*

$$\forall s \in I \cap (A_i \setminus B_i) : PV_i(s) \leq V_i(s) - \varepsilon, \tag{22}$$

$$\forall s \in I \cap B_i : PV_i(s) \leq V_i(s) + M, \tag{23}$$

$$\forall s \in I \setminus (A_i \cup B_i) : PV_i(s) \leq V_i(s), \tag{24}$$

for some constants $\varepsilon, M > 0$. *Then,*

$$\mathsf{P}_\mu \left(\bigwedge_{i=1}^{k} \sum_{n=0}^{\infty} \mathbf{1}_{A_i}(\boldsymbol{\Phi}_n) < \infty \vee \sum_{n=0}^{\infty} \mathbf{1}_{B_i}(\boldsymbol{\Phi}_n) = \infty \mid \boldsymbol{\Phi} \in I^\omega \right) = 1. \tag{25}$$

Our quantitative ω-regular supermartingale certificate requires synchronous composition between the system and a DSA recognising the same specification. Suppose that k is the number of pairs in the acceptance condition. Then, we require the simultaneous construction of a measurable set $I \in \Sigma$ and a sequence of measurable functions $V_0, \ldots, V_k : S \to \mathbb{R}_{\geq 0}$ such that V_0 satisfies Eqs. (6) and (5) and V_i satisfies Eqs. (22) to (24) for every $i = 1, \ldots, k$. As a consequence of Theorems 2, 6 and 9, we have that $1 - \mu V_0$ is a lower bound on the probability that the system under analysis satisfies the ω-regular specification.

Theorem 10 (Quantitative Streett Supermartingales). *Let* $(A_1, B_1) \in \Sigma^2, \ldots, (A_k, B_k) \in \Sigma^2$ *be a Streett acceptance condition. Suppose that there exists a measurable set* $I \in \Sigma$ *and* $k + 1$ *measurable functions* $V_0, \ldots, V_k : S \to \mathbb{R}_{\geq 0}$ *such that the following conditions hold:*

$$\forall s \in I : PV_0(s) \leq V_0(s), \tag{26}$$

$$\forall s \notin I : V_0(s) \geq 1, \tag{27}$$

$$\forall s \in I \cap (A_i \setminus B_i) : PV_i(s) \leq V_i(s) - \varepsilon \qquad \textit{for } i = 1, \ldots, k, \tag{28}$$

$$\forall s \in I \cap B_i : PV_i(s) \leq V_i(s) + M \qquad \textit{for } i = 1, \ldots, k, \tag{29}$$

$$\forall s \in I \setminus (A_i \cup B_i) : PV_i(s) \leq V_i(s) \qquad \textit{for } i = 1, \ldots, k, \tag{30}$$

for some constants $\varepsilon, M > 0$. *Then,*

$$\mathsf{P}_\mu \left(\bigwedge_{i=1}^{k} \sum_{n=0}^{\infty} \mathbf{1}_{A_i}(\boldsymbol{\Phi}_n) < \infty \vee \sum_{n=0}^{\infty} \mathbf{1}_{B_i}(\boldsymbol{\Phi}_n) = \infty \right) \geq 1 - \mu V_0. \tag{31}$$

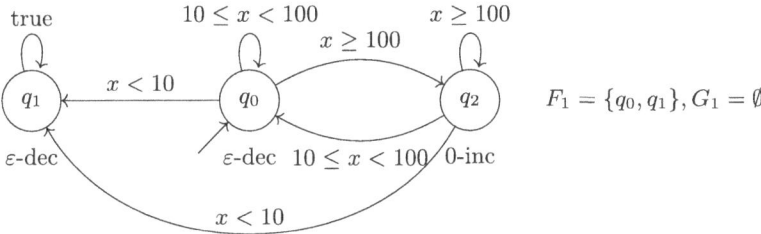

Fig. 4. A DSA for the LTL specification $(x \geq 10)\mathsf{U}\mathsf{G}(x \geq 100)$.

Example 6 (Becoming Rich Without Getting Too Thin). Consider the Gambler's Ruin model of Fig. 1, or similarly the random walk of Fig. 3. Consider the specification for which the amount x eventually persists above 100 without ever going below 10. This is a stabilise-while-avoid requirement specified as the LTL formula $\varphi = (x \geq 10)\mathsf{U}\mathsf{G}(x \geq 100)$, and corresponds to the language accepted by the DSA in Fig. 4. Our proof rule requires a region I and two value functions V_0 and V_1 that simultaneously satisfy Eqs. (5), (6), (22) and (24) on the synchronous composition. Firstly, we observe that it is impossible for any non-negative function V_1 to indefinitely decrease in the sink state q_1. Therefore, we must present a region I that excludes q_1 and characterises every other reachable state, which we associate with a function V_0 that bounds from above the probability of leaving I:

$$V_0(x,q) = \begin{cases} \left(\frac{49}{51}\right)^{x-9} & \text{if } (x,q) \in I \\ 1 & \text{otherwise,} \end{cases} \quad I = \left\{ (x,q) : \begin{matrix} (q = q_0 \wedge 9 \leq x \leq 100) \\ \vee \ (q = q_2 \wedge 99 \leq x) \end{matrix} \right\}. \tag{32}$$

Secondly, we observe that the expected value of V_1 must decrease by ε in q_0 while never increasing in q_2. We present a function with negative drift $PV_1(x,\cdot) - V_1(x,\cdot) < 0$ and choose an $\varepsilon > 0$ that upper-bounds the drift on q_0, which essentially indicates almost-sure finite permanence within q_0 conditional to I^ω:

$$V_1(x,q) = 1 - e^{-x}, \quad \varepsilon = PV_1(100,\cdot) - V_1(100,\cdot). \tag{33}$$

As a result, we obtain the lower bound $1 - V_0(x,q_0) \leq \mathsf{P}_{\delta_x}(\mathbf{\Phi} \in L_\varphi)$ on the probability of satisfying φ from any initial state $x \in \mathbb{N}$. □

Remark 6 (Upper Probability Bounds). Our quantitative ω-regular supermartingale certificates also produce upper probability bounds. As ω-regular languages are closed under complementation, it suffices to compute a lower bound for the complementary specification. According to the original representation of the specification, this requires the use of an appropriate complementation procedure [92]. In the special case of LTL, it is sufficient to negate the formula. □

Example 7. Consider the LTL verification problem of Example 6. A DSA for the complementary property $\neg\varphi$ has the same structure of the automaton in Fig. 4, but has the alternative acceptance condition $F_1 = Q$ and $G_1 = \{q_0, q_1\}$. This requires presenting a region $\bar{I}$ and value function $\bar{V}_0$ satisfying Eqs. (5) and (6) and, as a consequence of Eqs. (22) and (23), a value function $\bar{V}_1$ whose expected value must decrease by at least $\bar{\varepsilon} > 0$ on q_2 and can increase by at most $M > 0$ on q_0 and q_1. Given any chosen bound $y \geq 9$ on the invariant, we present

$$\bar{V}_0(x, q) = \begin{cases} \frac{1-(49/51)^{x-9}}{1-(49/51)^{y-9}} & \text{if } x \geq 10 \wedge q \neq q_1 \\ 0 & \text{otherwise,} \end{cases} \quad \bar{I} = \{(x,q) : 0 \leq x \leq y-1\}, \quad (34)$$

$\bar{V}_1(x, q) = y - x$, and $\bar{\varepsilon} = 0.02$. As a result, for every $x \in \mathbb{N}$ we have the probability upper bound $\mathsf{P}_{\delta_x}(\boldsymbol{\Phi} \in L_\varphi) \leq \bar{V}_0(x, q_0)$. Similarly to Eq. (19), the tightness of $\bar{V}_0$ improves as y increases. For example, suppose the initial state is 50. Under conservative numerical approximation, we obtain $0.80 \leq \mathsf{P}_{\delta_{50}}(\boldsymbol{\Phi} \in L_\varphi) \leq 0.83$ with $y = 100$ and $0.80 \leq \mathsf{P}_{\delta_{50}}(\boldsymbol{\Phi} \in L_\varphi) \leq 0.81$ with $y = 200$. □

Our proof rule reduces the quantitative ω-regular model checking question to the problem of computing an appropriate region I and appropriate value functions $V_0, \ldots V_k$ satisfying the conditions of Eqs. (5), (6) and (22) to (24). Our methodology similarly applies to alternative acceptance conditions (see Remark 4), such as Rabin, parity and Muller automata, but requires proof rules for the almost-sure acceptance of these conditions. Our approach also extends to quantitative synthesis of parametrised control policies for stochastic processes whose transition probability kernel is conditional on control inputs, i.e., Markov decision processes (MDPs), as we show in Sect. 5. This involves finding the parameters of a parameterised control policy that ensure the system satisfies an ω-regular objective with sufficiently high probability. We reduce this problem to simultaneously synthesising the control parameters and the corresponding parameters for a parameterised quantitative supermartingale certificate.

5   Algorithmic Synthesis of Supermartingale Certificates

The construction of certificates is a central objective in verification and control, supported by numerous algorithms for the automated synthesis of invariants and Lyapunov functions. One standard approach for this purpose is to restrict the search within a specific class of parametrised function templates, which reduces their synthesis to the problem of computing appropriate parameters.

We consider the problem of computing appropriate parameters $\zeta_0 \in Z_0, \ldots,$ $\zeta_k \in Z_k$ for the parametrised value functions $V_i : Z_i \times S \to \mathbb{R}_{\geq 0}$ for $i = 0, \ldots, k$, parameter $\eta \in H$ for the parametrised constraint $I : H \times S \to \{\text{true}, \text{false}\}$, as well as control parameter $\kappa \in K$ for the parametrised transition probability kernel $P : K \times S \times \Sigma \to [0, 1]$. In other words, we introduce functional templates for our stochastic invariant and Streett supermartingales, and assume a parametrised controller that governs the system behaviour according to its control parameter; the control parameter is constant throughout the system execution, whereas the control input varies over time as determined by the control policy.

This results in a parametric model checking problem that encompasses the quantitative ω-regular control synthesis of memory-less parametrised control policies $\pi : K \times S \rightarrow U$ over MDPs with general state space S and general control inputs U. Given an MDP with kernel $\hat{P} : S \times U \times \Sigma \rightarrow [0,1]$ conditional on input, it suffices to express our parametrised transition kernel as $P(\kappa; s, A) = \hat{P}(s, \pi(\kappa; s), A)$. This also includes finite-memory parametrised policies, where it is required to augment S with sufficient memory. The quantitative model checking of closed systems is the special case where $|K| = 1$.

Given a desired lower probability bound $p \in (0,1]$, our objective is to compute values for the parameters $\zeta_0 \in Z_0, \ldots, \zeta_k \in Z_k, \eta \in H, \kappa \in K$ and $\varepsilon, M > 0$ such that $p \leq 1 - \mu V_0(\zeta_0)$ and the following universally quantified first-order logic formulae hold true:

$$\forall s \in S : I(\eta; s) \implies PV_0(\zeta_0, \kappa; s) \leq V_0(\zeta_0; s), \tag{35}$$

$$\forall s \in S : \neg I(\eta; s) \implies V_0(\zeta_0; s) \geq 1, \tag{36}$$

$$\forall s \in (A_i \setminus B_i) : I(\eta; s) \implies PV_i(\zeta_i, \kappa; s) \leq V_i(\zeta_i; s) - \varepsilon \quad \text{for } i = 1, \ldots, k, \tag{37}$$

$$\forall s \in B_i : I(\eta; s) \Rightarrow PV_i(\zeta_i, \kappa; s) \leq V_i(\zeta_i; s) + M \quad \text{for } i = 1, \ldots, k, \tag{38}$$

$$\forall s \notin A_i \cup B_i : I(\eta; s) \implies PV_i(\zeta_i, \kappa; s) \leq V_i(\zeta_i; s) \quad \text{for } i = 1, \ldots, k. \tag{39}$$

We require that post-expectations $(PV_i) : Z_i \times K \times S \rightarrow \mathbb{R}_{\geq 0}$ and init-expectation $(\mu V_0) : Z_0 \rightarrow \mathbb{R}_{\leq 0}$ are expressed in closed form, for which appropriate procedures exist [47]. Then, any algorithm that finds a satisfying assignment for the free parameters $\zeta_0, \ldots, \zeta_k, \eta, \kappa, \epsilon$ and M for the first-order formulae Eqs. (35) to (39) would suffice. According to the resulting form of the formulae above, one may select an appropriate decision procedure for this purpose.

There are multiple approaches to solving the parameter synthesis problem expressed above. Firstly, we observe that the problem is decidable when the value functions and their expected values are expressed as polynomials of known degree and the constraints are expressed as semi-algebraic sets [100]. As a consequence, we have a relatively complete algorithm under these assumptions, in the sense that if polynomial certificates with sufficient precision on the probability bound exist and their degree is known then we have an algorithm to compute their coefficients. Under the additional assumption that S is compact, then polynomials with sufficiently high degree necessarily exist and we obtain complete algorithms for (relative to the existence of the almost-sure component $V_1, \ldots, V_k$, see Remark 4) that refine lower and upper bounds incrementally until a desired approximation gap is attained, leveraging the guarantees of Theorems 7 and 8.

Decision procedures for quantified polynomial formulae are computationally intensive and, while theoretically feasible, pursuing arbitrary bounds is often impractical. A more practical approach (not reliant on compactness) is to select a polynomial template of desired degree while minimising the gap between upper and lower bounds on the probability of satisfaction, and possibly increase the degree until an allocated time budget is exhausted. Although this practical strategy is incomplete in general, in the sense that it may stop with trivial bounds, it is sound and produces useful results with sufficient time budget.

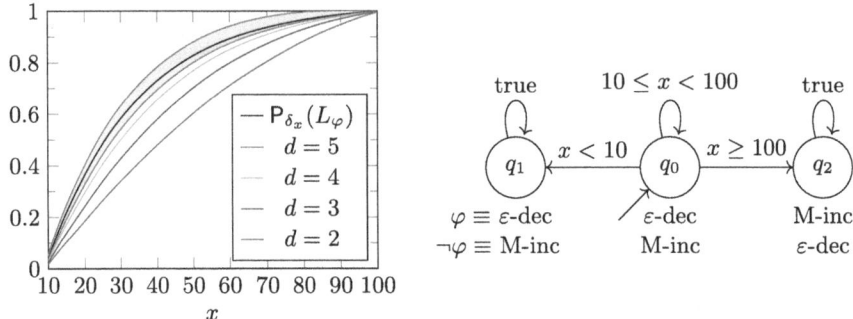

Fig. 5. Polynomial approximations (and DSA) for the probability that the Gambler's Ruin in Fig. 1 satisfies $\varphi = (x \geq 10)\mathsf{U}(x \geq 100)$; d indicates the degree of the polynomial.

Example 8 (Becoming Rich Once). Consider the Gambler's Ruin example of Fig. 1 and the specification for which the process exceeds 100 before possibly falling below 10, i.e., $\varphi = (x \geq 10)\mathsf{U}(x \geq 100)$. This is recognised by the DSA in Fig. 5, with the acceptance condition $F_1 = Q, G_1 = \{q_2\}$. This acceptance condition requires avoidance of q_1 and finite permanence in q_0, while imposing no restrictions on q_2. We assume $\mu = \delta_{50}$ and optimise the bounds accordingly. For the invariant region, we associate each automaton state with a parametrised semi-algebraic set, and for this example we obtain the rectangular region associating q_0 with the interval $[9, 100]$, q_1 with the empty set, and q_2 with $[0, \infty)$. For each value function V_i, we adopt a polynomial template of degree d, whose coefficients are piecewise-defined according to the automaton state q_j:

$$V_i(c_{i,j,0}, \ldots, c_{i,j,d}; x, q_j) = c_{i,j,0} + c_{i,j,1} \cdot x + c_{i,j,2} \cdot x^2 + \cdots + c_{i,j,d} \cdot x^d. \quad (40)$$

We obtain a piecewise-defined linear Streett supermartingale function given by $V_1(x, q_0) = 101 - x$, $V_1(x, q_1) = 101$, $V_1(x, q_2) = 0$, along with a piecewise-defined polynomial value function $V_0(x, q_1) = 1$, $V_0(x, q_2) = 0$, and higher-degree polynomials for $V_0(x, q_0)$, yielding the lower probability bounds depicted in Fig. 5 for the degrees $d = 2, 3, 4, 5$. As shown, the lower probability bound becomes increasingly tighter with higher polynomial degrees.

We further compute a polynomial upper approximation on the probability of satisfying φ by computing a dual lower approximation on the probability of satisfying $\neg\varphi$. This specification corresponds to the DSA of Fig. 5 with the acceptance condition $\bar{F}_1 = Q, \bar{G}_1 = \{q_0, q_1\}$, requiring avoidance of q_2. We obtain the invariant region $\bar{I}$ where q_0 is associated with $[9, 100]$, q_1 with $[0, 10]$, and q_2 with the empty set, along with a constant function $\bar{V}_1$. We then obtain the value function $\bar{V}_0(x, q_0)$ yielding the upper bound shown in Fig. 5 for $d = 5$ (and more conservative bounds for lower degrees, not shown), with the remaining components defined as the constant functions $\bar{V}_0(x, q_1) = 0$ and $\bar{V}_0(x, q_2) = 1$. □

We apply our algorithm to a number of infinite-state Markov chains and ω-regular specifications. We consider polynomial templates for which we use

Table 1. Output of our quantitative verification experiments.

Benchmark	ω-Regular Specification	Attained Bounds	Time [s]
Gambler's Ruin $(d = 2, a^x)$	$\mathsf{GF}(x = 0)$	[0.380, 0.671]	8.64
Gambler's Ruin $(d = 3, a^x)$	$\mathsf{GF}(x = 0)$	[0.545, 0.671]	9.87
Gambler's Ruin $(d = 4, a^x)$	$\mathsf{GF}(x = 0)$	[0.601, 0.671]	24.02
Gambler's Ruin $(d = 5, a^x)$	$\mathsf{GF}(x = 0)$	[0.621, 0.671]	88.17
BecomingRichOnce $(d = 2)$	$(x \geq 10) \cup (x \geq 100)$	[0.610, 1.000]	4.68
BecomingRichOnce $(d = 3)$	$(x \geq 10) \cup (x \geq 100)$	[0.709, 0.974]	7.39
BecomingRichOnce $(d = 4)$	$(x \geq 10) \cup (x \geq 100)$	[0.776, 0.908]	12.15
BecomingRichOnce $(d = 5)$	$(x \geq 10) \cup (x \geq 100)$	[0.807, 0.880]	59.04
Reactivity1 $(d = 2)$	$\mathsf{GF}(x \leq 6) \rightarrow \mathsf{GF}(x \leq 0)$	[0.166, 0.166]	8.18
Reactivity2 $(d = 2)$	$\mathsf{GF}(x \leq 10) \rightarrow \mathsf{GF}(x \geq 100)$	[0.250, 0.250]	8.26

Table 2. Output of our quantitative control synthesis experiments.

Benchmark	ω-Regular Specification	Target Bounds	Time [s]
Gambler's Ruin $(d = 2)$	$\mathsf{GF}(x = 0)$	[0.999, 1.000]	0.69
Becoming Rich Once $(d = 5)$	$(x > 10) \cup (x \geq 100)$	[0.950, 1.000]	12.93
Reactivity1 $(d = 2)$	$\mathsf{GF}(x \leq 6) \rightarrow \mathsf{GF}(x \leq 0)$	[0.187, 1.000]	4.22
Reactivity2 $(d = 2)$	$\mathsf{GF}(x \leq 10) \rightarrow \mathsf{GF}(x \geq 100)$	[0.542, 1.000]	4.26
RepeatedCoin $(d = 3)$	$\mathsf{GF}(x \geq 20)$	[0.499, 0.501]	0.87

Handelman's Theorem [53, Proposition I.1] to reduce the synthesis problem of Streett supermartingales and a stochastic invariant (Eqs. (35) to (39)) to a decision problem in the existential theory of the reals; for deriving upper bounds upon Gambler's Ruin, we use an exponential template for the stochastic invariant [105]. We solve our decision problems using Z3 [61].

Our quantitative verification experiments in Table 1 seek to compute tight bounds upon the satisfaction probability of a specification. Notably, in verification the problem of lower bounding is independent of that of upper bounding the satisfaction probability, and both are solved as separate SMT queries. Our control synthesis experiments in Table 2 seek to compute a control parameter for which the probability of satisfaction lies within given target upper and lower bounds. Notably, in control synthesis the first-order logic formulae corresponding to the upper and lower bound are combined in a conjunction and solved as part of the same SMT query.

Our encoding exploits the structure of the DSA and the Streett supermartingale drift conditions. We heuristically constrain the stochastic invariant to take value 0 (i.e., satisfaction probability of 1) in sink states identified as surely accepting, and value 1 (i.e., satisfaction probability of 0) and sink states identified as surely rejecting, whereas we synthesise the parameters in every other case.

6 Related Work

The problem of quantitative model checking and control under ω-regular specifications for finite state Markov chains (and MDPs) is a classic topic for which scalable and automated tools exist [33,51,63,68,79,80]. As a consequence of the limit behaviour of Markov chains (cf. [12, Theorem 10.27] and [39, Theorem 6.4.5]), the quantitative model-checking question reduces to the computation of probabilities to reach accepting bottom strongly connected components. However, this approach does not apply to infinite state Markov chains, where instead finite abstractions [2,6,34,96,101,108] and proof certificates [16,22,27,28,36,70,82,89,98] constitute two major approaches.

Considering *almost-sure* satisfaction, proof certificates based on martingale theory have been introduced for the specifications of reachability (cf. [37, Corollary 4.4.8] and [16,58,77,99]), persistence [17, Section 3.1], recurrence [17, Section 3.2], and for reactivity specifications [4,35]. For quantitative specifications, supermartingale proof rules for stochastic invariance (cf. [66, Theorem 1], [37, Corollary 4.4.7], and [22,28,62,98,109]), reach-avoidance [27], and persistence [8] have been developed, establishing *lower bounds* on the satisfaction probability. Almost-sure proof certificates and stochastic invariants have been combined (cf. Theorem 6) to yield proof rules for *upper bounding* the probability of termination (cf. [29, Proposition 4], [73, Lemma 4.6], and [28, Section 6.1]), and in the context of cost analysis [97,104,106] to prove tail bounds on costs accrued prior to termination (cf. [23, Section 6.3] and [23, Theorem 6.8]). In the context of assertion-violation analysis for almost-surely terminating probabilistic programs, a supermartingale certificate (repulsing supermartingales) for stochastic invariance [28,98] is combined with a ranking supermartingale [105, Section 5.1] to yield upper and lower bounds on the probability of assertion violation. This need to combine supermartingale certificates has been interpreted and explained using order theory [54,55], also yielding new order-theoretic justifications for classic results in martingale theory [98, Corollary 4.3(2)].

Our results are reminiscent of prior observations in proof rules for quantitative termination analysis, and more generally weakest pre-expectation bounds, in the analysis of probabilistic programs. The notion of *guard-strengthening* [42] may be applied to derive arbitrarily tight lower bounds on the probability of termination by, in effect, restricting attention to a stochastic invariant (and yielding a new program that enjoys stronger termination probabilities). This same approximation property is established in countable-state MDPs [73, Lemma 4.6] with bounded discrete probabilistic choices. Our Theorem 4 shows that this applies not just to reachability, but to the richer class of shift-invariant specifications over general state-space Markov chains, by applying Lévy's 0-1 Law to the satisfaction probability process. Prior work has exploited the connection between infinite-horizon specifications and Lévy's 0-1 Law (cf. [64, Section 3.3], [35, Proposition 4], [18, Lemma 2]), but we are the first to connect it with the existence of stochastic invariants. Furthermore, in the context of termination analysis, prior work has observed that in finite state spaces there exists a stochastic invariant that characterises the quantities of interest without approximation error (cf. [42,

Theorem 23] and [73, Lemma 4.5]). Both results may be interpreted by apply-ing Theorem 5 to the case where the specification under study is reachability (Example 5).

Converse results for the existence of proof certificates have been established under further topological assumptions [78, Chapter 6 and Theorem 9.4.2] about the transition kernel (e.g. the weak Feller property [74, Theorem 3.2]). Under the assumption of a countable state space and bounded discrete probabilistic choices, recent work has introduced a sound and complete supermartingale proof rule for almost-sure termination [73, Lemma 3.4], that is applicable to programs that are almost-surely terminating but not with finite expected time [43].

The algorithmic synthesis of supermartingale certificates and stochastic invariants draws upon techniques originally developed for the synthesis of invari-ants and ranking functions for deterministic systems [30,40,75,84,94]. These exploit Farkas' Lemma [7,16,20,28,31,32] and Positivstellensatz [11,19,19,21,24, 85,93,95] results, including Handelman's theorem [25,53,107,110] which yields a linear decision problem in certain cases. These reduce the problem of construct-ing a proof certificate to that of solving a problem in quantifier-free nonlinear real arithmetic, and under further assumptions (including the provision of invariants a priori and for autonomous systems) to a linear program. Beyond one-shot syn-thesis procedures, methods based on counterexample-guided inductive synthesis [13] and certificate learning have been proposed [10,27,48,49,72,83,102,103].

7   Conclusion

Our result shows that, to bound the probability of a shift-invariant specifica-tion from below, it suffices to present a stochastic invariant together with an almost-sure certificate conditional to this invariant. It additionally shows the necessary existence of appropriate invariants, bounding the probability with arbi-trary approximation gap in the general case, and with no error in the finite case.

Leveraging our result, we have introduced the first quantitative supermartin-gale certificates for ω-regular specifications, encompassing safety, reachability, reach-avoidance and LTL properties. Our new quantitative ω-regular certificates are amenable to algorithmic synthesis using symbolic procedures (e.g., polynomi-als Positivstellensatz), and are additionally prone to future extensions towards machine learning techniques [1]. Our approach provides lower and upper bounds on the probability of satisfaction of these properties and readily extends to auto-mated control synthesis with parametrised control policies.

Our decomposition into stochastic invariants and almost-sure certificates pro-vides the basis for the future development of further quantitative certificates, restricting the focus on (1) proving shift invariance of the specification under study and (2) defining a proof rule for its almost-sure satisfaction. Our converse results guarantee completeness relative to the adopted proof rule for almost-sure acceptance and the adopted algorithm for their automated construction. Our work lays the foundations for developing new model checking, control synthesis and policy learning algorithms with quantitative formal guarantees.

Acknowledgment. This work was funded in part by the Advanced Research + Invention Agency (ARIA) under the Safeguarded AI programme.

Disclosure of Interests. The authors have no competing interests to declare that are relevant to the content of this article.

References

1. Abate, A., Edwards, A., Giacobbe, M., Punchihewa, H., Roy, D.: Quantitative verification with neural networks. In: CONCUR. LIPIcs, vol. 279, pp. 22:1–22:18. Schloss Dagstuhl - Leibniz-Zentrum für Informatik (2023)
2. Abate, A., Giacobbe, M., Micheletti, C., Schnitzer, Y.: Branching bisimulation learning. In: CAV (2025)
3. Abate, A., Giacobbe, M., Roy, D.: Learning probabilistic termination proofs. In: Silva, A., Leino, K. (eds.) CAV 2021. LNCS, vol. 12760, pp. 3–26. Springer, Cham (2021). https://doi.org/10.1007/978-3-030-81688-9_1
4. Abate, A., Giacobbe, M., Roy, D.: Stochastic omega-regular verification and control with supermartingales. In: CAV (3). Lecture Notes in Computer Science, vol. 14683, pp. 395–419. Springer, Heidelberg (2024). https://doi.org/10.1007/978-3-031-65633-0_18
5. Abate, A., Giacobbe, M., Roy, D., Schnitzer, Y.: Model checking and strategy synthesis with abstractions and certificates. In: Principles of Verification: Cycling the Probabilistic Landscape: Essays Dedicated to Joost-Pieter Katoen on the Occasion of His 60th Birthday, Part II. Lecture Notes in Computer Science, vol. 12261, pp. 360–391. Springer, Heidelberg (2024). https://doi.org/10.1007/978-3-031-75775-4_16
6. Abate, A., Giacobbe, M., Schnitzer, Y.: Bisimulation learning. In: CAV (3). Lecture Notes in Computer Science, vol. 14683, pp. 161–183. Springer, Heidelberg (2024). https://doi.org/10.1007/978-3-031-65633-0_8
7. Agrawal, S., Chatterjee, K., Novotný, P.: Lexicographic ranking supermartingales: an efficient approach to termination of probabilistic programs. Proc. ACM Program. Lang. 2(POPL), 34:1–34:32 (2018)
8. Ajeleye, D., Zamani, M.: Co-büchi control barrier certificates for stochastic control systems. IEEE Control. Syst. Lett. 8, 2529–2534 (2024)
9. Alpern, B., Schneider, F.B.: Recognizing safety and liveness. Distrib. Comput. 2(3), 117–126 (1987)
10. Ansaripour, M., Chatterjee, K., Henzinger, T.A., Lechner, M., Zikelic, D.: Learning provably stabilizing neural controllers for discrete-time stochastic systems. In: ATVA (1). Lecture Notes in Computer Science, vol. 14215, pp. 357–379. Springer, Heidelberg (2023). https://doi.org/10.1007/978-3-031-45329-8_17
11. Asadi, A., Chatterjee, K., Fu, H., Goharshady, A.K., Mahdavi, M.: Polynomial reachability witnesses via stellensätze. In: PLDI, pp. 772–787. ACM (2021)
12. Baier, C., Katoen, J.: Principles of Model Checking. MIT Press, Cambridge (2008)
13. Batz, K., Chen, M., Junges, S., Kaminski, B.L., Katoen, J., Matheja, C.: Probabilistic program verification via inductive synthesis of inductive invariants. In: TACAS (2). Lecture Notes in Computer Science, vol. 13994, pp. 410–429. Springer, Heidelberg (2023). https://doi.org/10.1007/978-3-031-30820-8_25
14. Bjørner, N.S., Nachmanson, L.: Arithmetic solving in Z3. In: CAV (1). Lecture Notes in Computer Science, vol. 14681, pp. 26–41. Springer, Heidelberg (2024). https://doi.org/10.1007/978-3-031-65627-9_2

15. Blute, R., Desharnais, J., Edalat, A., Panangaden, P.: Bisimulation for labelled markov processes. In: LICS, pp. 149–158. IEEE Computer Society (1997)
16. Chakarov, A., Sankaranarayanan, S.: Probabilistic program analysis with martingales. In: Sharygina, N., Veith, H. (eds.) CAV 2013. LNCS, vol. 8044, pp. 511–526. Springer, Heidelberg (2013). https://doi.org/10.1007/978-3-642-39799-8_34
17. Chakarov, A., Voronin, Y.-L., Sankaranarayanan, S.: Deductive proofs of almost sure persistence and recurrence properties. In: Chechik, M., Raskin, J.-F. (eds.) TACAS 2016. LNCS, vol. 9636, pp. 260–279. Springer, Heidelberg (2016). https://doi.org/10.1007/978-3-662-49674-9_15
18. Chatterjee, K.: Concurrent games with tail objectives. Theor. Comput. Sci. **388**(1–3), 181–198 (2007)
19. Chatterjee, K., Fu, H., Goharshady, A.K.: Termination analysis of probabilistic programs through Positivstellensatz. In: CAV (1). Lecture Notes in Computer Science, vol. 9779, pp. 3–22. Springer, Heidelberg (2016). https://doi.org/10.1007/978-3-319-41528-4_1
20. Chatterjee, K., Fu, H., Novotný, P., Hasheminezhad, R.: Algorithmic analysis of qualitative and quantitative termination problems for affine probabilistic programs. ACM Trans. Program. Lang. Syst. **40**(2), 7:1–7:45 (2018)
21. Chatterjee, K., Goharshady, A.K., Goharshady, E.K., Karrabi, M., Zikelic, D.: Sound and complete witnesses for template-based verification of LTL properties on polynomial programs. In: FM (1). Lecture Notes in Computer Science, vol. 14933, pp. 600–619. Springer, Heidelberg (2024). https://doi.org/10.1007/978-3-031-71162-6_31
22. Chatterjee, K., Goharshady, A.K., Meggendorfer, T., Žikelić, Ð.: Sound and complete certificates for quantitative termination analysis of probabilistic programs. In: CAV (1). Lecture Notes in Computer Science, vol. 13371, pp. 55–78. Springer, Heidelberg (2022). https://doi.org/10.1007/978-3-031-13185-1_4
23. Chatterjee, K., Goharshady, A.K., Meggendorfer, T., Žikelić, Ð: Quantitative bounds on resource usage of probabilistic programs. Proc. ACM Program. Lang. **8**(OOPSLA1), 362–391 (2024)
24. Chatterjee, K., Goharshady, E.K., Karrabi, M., Motwani, H.J., Seeliger, M., Zikelic, D.: Quantified linear and polynomial arithmetic satisfiability via template-based skolemization. In: AAAI, pp. 7326–7336. AAAI Press (2025)
25. Chatterjee, K., Goharshady, E.K., Novotný, P., Zikelic, D.: Equivalence and similarity refutation for probabilistic programs. Proc. ACM Program. Lang. **8**(PLDI), 2098–2122 (2024)
26. Chatterjee, K., Henzinger, T.A., Horn, F.: Stochastic games with finitary objectives. In: Královič, R., Niwiński, D. (eds.) MFCS 2009. LNCS, vol. 5734, pp. 34–54. Springer, Heidelberg (2009). https://doi.org/10.1007/978-3-642-03816-7_4
27. Chatterjee, K., Henzinger, T.A., Lechner, M., Zikelic, D.: A learner-verifier framework for neural network controllers and certificates of stochastic systems. In: TACAS (1). Lecture Notes in Computer Science, vol. 13993, pp. 3–25. Springer, Heidelberg (2023). https://doi.org/10.1007/978-3-031-30823-9_1
28. Chatterjee, K., Novotný, P., Žikelić, Ð.: Stochastic invariants for probabilistic termination. In: POPL, pp. 145–160. ACM (2017)
29. Chatterjee, K., Quatmann, T., Schäffeler, M., Weininger, M., Winkler, T., Zilken, D.: Fixed point certificates for reachability and expected rewards in mdps. In: TACAS. Lecture Notes in Computer Science (2025)
30. Colón, M.A., Sankaranarayanan, S., Sipma, H.B.: Linear invariant generation using non-linear constraint solving. In: Hunt, W.A., Somenzi, F. (eds.) CAV 2003.

LNCS, vol. 2725, pp. 420–432. Springer, Heidelberg (2003). https://doi.org/10.1007/978-3-540-45069-6_39

31. Colóon, M.A., Sipma, H.B.: Synthesis of linear ranking functions. In: Margaria, T., Yi, W. (eds.) TACAS 2001. LNCS, vol. 2031, pp. 67–81. Springer, Heidelberg (2001). https://doi.org/10.1007/3-540-45319-9_6

32. Colón, M.A., Sipma, H.B.: Practical methods for proving program termination. In: Brinksma, E., Larsen, K.G. (eds.) CAV 2002. LNCS, vol. 2404, pp. 442–454. Springer, Heidelberg (2002). https://doi.org/10.1007/3-540-45657-0_36

33. Dehnert, C., Junges, S., Katoen, J.-P., Volk, M.: A storm is coming: a modern probabilistic model checker. In: Majumdar, R., Kunčak, V. (eds.) CAV 2017. LNCS, vol. 10427, pp. 592–600. Springer, Cham (2017). https://doi.org/10.1007/978-3-319-63390-9_31

34. Desharnais, J., Laviolette, F., Tracol, M.: Approximate analysis of probabilistic processes: logic, simulation and games. In: QEST, pp. 264–273. IEEE Computer Society (2008)

35. Dimitrova, R., Fioriti, L.M.F., Hermanns, H., Majumdar, R.: Probabilistic ctl*: the deductive way. In: TACAS. Lecture Notes in Computer Science, vol. 9636, pp. 280–296. Springer, Heidelberg (2016). https://doi.org/10.1007/978-3-662-49674-9_16

36. Dimitrova, R., Majumdar, R.: Deductive control synthesis for alternating-time logics. In: EMSOFT, pp. 14:1–14:10. ACM (2014)

37. Douc, R., Moulines, E., Priouret, P., Soulier, P.: Markov Chains. Springer Series in Operations Research and Financial Engineering. Springer, Heidelberg (2018)

38. Duret-Lutz, A., et al.: From spot 2.0 to spot 2.10: what's new? In: CAV (2). Lecture Notes in Computer Science, vol. 13372, pp. 174–187. Springer, Heidelberg (2022). https://doi.org/10.1007/978-3-031-13188-2_9

39. Durrett, R.: Probability: Theory and Examples. Cambridge Series in Statistical and Probabilistic Mathematics, 5th edn. Cambridge University Press, Cambridge (2019)

40. Ernst, M.D., Perkins, J.H., Guo, P.J., McCamant, S., Pacheco, C., Tschantz, M.S., Xiao, C.: The daikon system for dynamic detection of likely invariants. Sci. Comput. Program. **69**(1–3), 35–45 (2007)

41. Feller, W.: An Introduction to Probability Theory and its Applications, vol. 1. Wiley, Hoboken (1968)

42. Feng, S., Chen, M., Su, H., Kaminski, B.L., Katoen, J., Zhan, N.: Lower bounds for possibly divergent probabilistic programs. CoRR arxiv:2302.06082 (2023)

43. Fioriti, L.M.F., Hermanns, H.: Probabilistic termination: soundness, completeness, and compositionality. In: POPL, pp. 489–501. ACM (2015)

44. Floyd, R.W.: Assigning meanings to programs. In: Program Verification: Fundamental Issues in Computer Science, pp. 65–81. Springer, Heidelberg (1993). https://doi.org/10.1007/978-94-011-1793-7_4

45. Forejt, V., Kwiatkowska, M., Norman, G., Parker, D.: Automated verification techniques for probabilistic systems. In: Bernardo, M., Issarny, V. (eds.) SFM 2011. LNCS, vol. 6659, pp. 53–113. Springer, Heidelberg (2011). https://doi.org/10.1007/978-3-642-21455-4_3

46. Forejt, V., Kwiatkowska, M., Norman, G., Parker, D., Qu, H.: Quantitative multiobjective verification for probabilistic systems. In: Abdulla, P.A., Leino, K. (eds.) TACAS 2011. LNCS, vol. 6605, pp. 112–127. Springer, Heidelberg (2011). https://doi.org/10.1007/978-3-642-19835-9_11

47. Gehr, T., Misailovic, S., Vechev, M.T.: PSI: exact symbolic inference for probabilistic programs. In: CAV (1). Lecture Notes in Computer Science, vol. 9779, pp. 62–83. Springer, Heidelberg (2016). https://doi.org/10.1007/978-3-319-41528-4_4
48. Giacobbe, M., Kroening, D., Pal, A., Tautschnig, M.: Neural model checking. In: NeurIPS (2024)
49. Giacobbe, M., Kroening, D., Parsert, J.: Neural termination analysis. In: ESEC/SIGSOFT FSE, pp. 633–645. ACM (2022)
50. Grädel, E., Thomas, W., Wilke, T. (eds.): Automata, Logics, and Infinite Games: A Guide to Current Research [outcome of a Dagstuhl seminar, February 2001], Lecture Notes in Computer Science, vol. 2500. Springer, Heidelberg (2002)
51. Hahn, E.M., Li, Y., Schewe, S., Turrini, A., Zhang, L.: ISCASMC: a web-based probabilistic model checker. In: Jones, C., Pihlajasaari, P., Sun, J. (eds.) FM 2014. LNCS, vol. 8442, pp. 312–317. Springer, Cham (2014). https://doi.org/10.1007/978-3-319-06410-9_22
52. Hahn, W.: Theory and Application of Liapunov's Direct Method. Dover Books on Mathematics, Dover Publications, New York (2019)
53. Handelman, D.: Representing polynomials by positive linear functions on compact convex polyhedra. Pacific J. Math. **132** (1988)
54. Hark, M., Kaminski, B.L., Giesl, J., Katoen, J.: Aiming low is harder: induction for lower bounds in probabilistic program verification. Proc. ACM Program. Lang. **4**(POPL), 37:1–37:28 (2020)
55. Hasuo, I., Shimizu, S., Cîrstea, C.: Lattice-theoretic progress measures and coalgebraic model checking. In: POPL, pp. 718–732. ACM (2016)
56. Hensel, C., Junges, S., Katoen, J., Quatmann, T., Volk, M.: The probabilistic model checker storm. Int. J. Softw. Tools Technol. Transf. **24**(4), 589–610 (2022)
57. Huang, C., Chen, X., Lin, W., Yang, Z., Li, X.: Probabilistic safety verification of stochastic hybrid systems using barrier certificates. ACM Trans. Embed. Comput. Syst. **16**(5s), 186:1–186:19 (2017)
58. Huang, M., Fu, H., Chatterjee, K., Goharshady, A.K.: Modular verification for almost-sure termination of probabilistic programs. Proc. ACM Program. Lang. **3**(OOPSLA), 129:1–129:29 (2019)
59. Jagtap, P., Soudjani, S., Zamani, M.: Temporal logic verification of stochastic systems using barrier certificates. In: Lahiri, S.K., Wang, C. (eds.) ATVA 2018. LNCS, vol. 11138, pp. 177–193. Springer, Cham (2018). https://doi.org/10.1007/978-3-030-01090-4_11
60. Jagtap, P., Soudjani, S., Zamani, M.: Formal synthesis of stochastic systems via control barrier certificates. IEEE Trans. Autom. Control **66**(7), 3097–3110 (2021)
61. Jovanovic, D., de Moura, L.: Solving non-linear arithmetic. ACM Commun. Comput. Algebra **46**(3/4), 104–105 (2012)
62. Katoen, J.-P., McIver, A.K., Meinicke, L.A., Morgan, C.C.: Linear-invariant generation for probabilistic programs. In: Cousot, R., Martel, M. (eds.) SAS 2010. LNCS, vol. 6337, pp. 390–406. Springer, Heidelberg (2010). https://doi.org/10.1007/978-3-642-15769-1_24
63. Katoen, J., Zapreev, I.S., Hahn, E.M., Hermanns, H., Jansen, D.N.: The ins and outs of the probabilistic model checker MRMC. In: QEST, pp. 167–176. IEEE Computer Society (2009)
64. Kiefer, S., Mayr, R., Shirmohammadi, M., Totzke, P., Wojtczak, D.: How to play in infinite mdps (invited talk). In: ICALP. LIPIcs, vol. 168, pp. 3:1–3:18. Schloss Dagstuhl - Leibniz-Zentrum für Informatik (2020)

65. Křetínský, J., Meggendorfer, T., Sickert, S., Ziegler, C.: Rabinizer 4: From LTL to your favourite deterministic automaton. In: Chockler, H., Weissenbacher, G. (eds.) CAV 2018. LNCS, vol. 10981, pp. 567–577. Springer, Cham (2018). https://doi.org/10.1007/978-3-319-96145-3_30
66. Kushner, H.J.: On the stability of stochastic dynamical systems. Proc. Natl. Acad. Sci. **53**(1), 8–12 (1965)
67. Kushner, H.: Stochastic Stability and Control. Mathematics in science and engineering. Academic Press (1967)
68. Kwiatkowska, M., Norman, G., Parker, D.: PRISM 4.0: verification of probabilistic real-time systems. In: Gopalakrishnan, G., Qadeer, S. (eds.) CAV 2011. LNCS, vol. 6806, pp. 585–591. Springer, Heidelberg (2011). https://doi.org/10.1007/978-3-642-22110-1_47
69. Larsen, K.G., Skou, A.: Bisimulation through probabilistic testing. Inf. Comput. **94**(1), 1–28 (1991)
70. Lavaei, A., Soudjani, S., Abate, A., Zamani, M.: Automated verification and synthesis of stochastic hybrid systems: a survey. In: Automatica, vol. 146 (2022)
71. Lavaei, A., Soudjani, S., Frazzoli, E.: Safety barrier certificates for stochastic hybrid systems. In: ACC, pp. 880–885. IEEE (2022)
72. Lechner, M., Žikelić, Đ., Chatterjee, K., Henzinger, T.A.: Stability verification in stochastic control systems via neural network supermartingales. In: AAAI, pp. 7326–7336. AAAI Press (2022)
73. Majumdar, R., Sathiyanarayana, V.R.: Sound and complete proof rules for probabilistic termination. Proc. ACM Program. Lang. **9**(POPL), 1871–1902 (2025)
74. Majumdar, R., Sathiyanarayana, V.R., Soudjani, S.: Necessary and sufficient certificates for almost sure reachability. IEEE Control. Syst. Lett. **8**, 2703–2708 (2024)
75. Manna, Z., Pnueli, A.: Temporal Verification of Reactive Systems - Safety. Springer, Heidelberg (1995)
76. Mathiesen, F.B., Calvert, S.C., Laurenti, L.: Safety certification for stochastic systems via neural barrier functions. IEEE Control. Syst. Lett. **7**, 973–978 (2023)
77. McIver, A., Morgan, C., Kaminski, B.L., Katoen, J.: A new proof rule for almost-sure termination. Proc. ACM Program. Lang. **2**(POPL), 33:1–33:28 (2018)
78. Meyn, S., Tweedie, R.L.: Markov Chains and Stochastic Stability. Cambridge Mathematical Library, 2nd edn. Cambridge University Press, Cambridge (2009)
79. Moosbrugger, M., Bartocci, E., Katoen, J., Kovács, L.: Automated termination analysis of polynomial probabilistic programs. In: ESOP. Lecture Notes in Computer Science, vol. 12648, pp. 491–518. Springer, Heidelberg (2021)
80. Moosbrugger, M., Bartocci, E., Katoen, J.-P., Kovács, L.: The probabilistic termination tool amber. In: Huisman, M., Păsăreanu, C., Zhan, N. (eds.) FM 2021. LNCS, vol. 13047, pp. 667–675. Springer, Cham (2021). https://doi.org/10.1007/978-3-030-90870-6_36
81. Moosbrugger, M., Stankovic, M., Bartocci, E., Kovács, L.: This is the moment for probabilistic loops. Proc. ACM Program. Lang. **6**(OOPSLA2), 1497–1525 (2022)
82. Morgan, C.: Proof rules for probabilistic loops. In: Proceedings of the BCS-FACS 7th Conference on Refinement. p. 10. FAC-RW'96, BCS Learning & Development Ltd., Swindon, GBR (1996)
83. Neustroev, G., Giacobbe, M., Lukina, A.: Neural continuous-time supermartingale certificates. In: AAAI. AAAI Press (2025)
84. Nguyen, T., Kapur, D., Weimer, W., Forrest, S.: DIG: a dynamic invariant generator for polynomial and array invariants. ACM Trans. Softw. Eng. Methodol. **23**(4), 30:1–30:30 (2014)

85. Papachristodoulou, A., Prajna, S.: On the construction of Lyapunov functions using the sum of squares decomposition. In: CDC, pp. 3482–3487. IEEE (2002)
86. Parker, D.A.: Implementation of symbolic model checking for probabilistic systems. Ph.D. thesis, University of Birmingham, UK (2003)
87. Parrilo, P.A.: Structured semidefinite programs and semialgebraic geometry methods in robustness and optimization. California Institute of Technology (2000)
88. Pnueli, A.: The temporal logic of programs. In: FOCS, pp. 46–57. IEEE Computer Society (1977)
89. Prajna, S.: Barrier certificates for nonlinear model validation. Automatica (J. IFAC) 42(1), 117–126 (2006)
90. Prajna, S., Jadbabaie, A., Pappas, G.J.: Stochastic safety verification using barrier certificates. In: CDC, pp. 929–934. IEEE (2004)
91. Prajna, S., Jadbabaie, A., Pappas, G.J.: A framework for worst-case and stochastic safety verification using barrier certificates. IEEE Trans. Autom. Control 52(8), 1415–1428 (2007)
92. Safra, S.: On the complexity of omega-automata. In: FOCS, pp. 319–327. IEEE Computer Society (1988)
93. Sankaranarayanan, S., Chen, X., Ábrahám, E.: Lyapunov function synthesis using handelman representations. IFAC Proc. Vol. 46(23), 576–581 (2013)
94. Sankaranarayanan, S., Sipma, H.B., Manna, Z.: Constraint-based linear-relations analysis. In: Giacobazzi, R. (ed.) SAS 2004. LNCS, vol. 3148, pp. 53–68. Springer, Heidelberg (2004). https://doi.org/10.1007/978-3-540-27864-1_7
95. She, Z., Li, H., Xue, B., Zheng, Z., Xia, B.: Discovering polynomial lyapunov functions for continuous dynamical systems. J. Symb. Comput. 58, 41–63 (2013)
96. Soudjani, S., Abate, A.: Adaptive and sequential gridding for abstraction and verification of stochastic processes. SIAM J. Appl. Dyn. Syst. 12(2), 921–956 (2012)
97. Sun, Y., Fu, H., Chatterjee, K., Goharshady, A.K.: Automated tail bound analysis for probabilistic recurrence relations. In: CAV (3). Lecture Notes in Computer Science, vol. 13966, pp. 16–39. Springer, Heidelberg (2023). https://doi.org/10.1007/978-3-031-37709-9_2
98. Takisaka, T., Oyabu, Y., Urabe, N., Hasuo, I.: Ranking and repulsing supermartingales for reachability in randomized programs. ACM Trans. Program. Lang. Syst. 43(2), 5:1–5:46 (2021)
99. Takisaka, T., Zhang, L., Wang, C., Liu, J.: Lexicographic ranking supermartingales with lazy lower bounds. In: CAV (3). Lecture Notes in Computer Science, vol. 14683, pp. 420–442. Springer, Heidelberg (2024). https://doi.org/10.1007/978-3-031-65633-0_19
100. Tarski, A.: A decision method for elementary algebra and geometry. In: Quantifier Elimination and Cylindrical Algebraic Decomposition, pp. 24–84. Springer, Heidelberg (1998). https://doi.org/10.1007/978-3-7091-9459-1_3
101. Tkachev, I., Abate, A.: Formula-free finite abstractions for linear temporal verification of stochastic hybrid systems. In: HSCC, pp. 283–292. ACM (2013)
102. Žikelić, Đ., Lechner, M., Henzinger, T.A., Chatterjee, K.: Learning control policies for stochastic systems with reach-avoid guarantees. In: AAAI, pp. 11926–11935. AAAI Press (2023)
103. Žikelić, Đ., Lechner, M., Verma, A., Chatterjee, K., Henzinger, T.A.: Compositional policy learning in stochastic control systems with formal guarantees. In: NeurIPS (2023)
104. Wang, D., Hoffmann, J., Reps, T.W.: Central moment analysis for cost accumulators in probabilistic programs. In: PLDI, pp. 559–573. ACM (2021)

105. Wang, J., Sun, Y., Fu, H., Chatterjee, K., Goharshady, A.K.: Quantitative analysis of assertion violations in probabilistic programs. In: PLDI, pp. 1171–1186. ACM (2021)
106. Wang, P., Fu, H., Goharshady, A.K., Chatterjee, K., Qin, X., Shi, W.: Cost analysis of nondeterministic probabilistic programs. In: PLDI, pp. 204–220. ACM (2019)
107. Wang, P., Yang, T., Fu, H., Li, G., Ong, C.L.: Static posterior inference of bayesian probabilistic programming via polynomial solving. Proc. ACM Program. Lang. 8(PLDI), 1361–1386 (2024)
108. Zhang, L., She, Z., Ratschan, S., Hermanns, H., Hahn, E.M.: Safety verification for probabilistic hybrid systems. Eur. J. Control. 18(6), 572–587 (2012)
109. Zhi, D., Wang, P., Liu, S., Ong, C.L., Zhang, M.: Unifying qualitative and quantitative safety verification of dnn-controlled systems. In: CAV (2). Lecture Notes in Computer Science, vol. 14682, pp. 401–426. Springer, Heidelberg (2024). https://doi.org/10.1007/978-3-031-65630-9_20
110. Zikelic, D., Chang, B.E., Bolignano, P., Raimondi, F.: Differential cost analysis with simultaneous potentials and anti-potentials. In: PLDI, pp. 442–457. ACM (2022)

Supermartingale Certificates for Quantitative Omega-Regular Verification and Control

Thomas A. Henzinger[1] , Kaushik Mallik[2(✉)] , Pouya Sadeghi[3] ,
and Đorđe Žikelić[3]

[1] Institute of Science and Technology Austria (ISTA),
Klosterneuburg, Austria
tah@ist.ac.at
[2] IMDEA Software Institute, Madrid, Spain
kaushik.mallik@imdea.org
[3] Singapore Management University, Singapore, Singapore
{pouyas,dzikelic}@smu.edu.sg

Abstract. We present the first supermartingale certificate for quantitative ω-regular properties of discrete-time infinite-state stochastic systems. Our certificate is defined on the product of the stochastic system and a limit-deterministic Büchi automaton that specifies the property of interest; hence we call it a limit-deterministic Büchi supermartingale (LDBSM). Previously known supermartingale certificates applied only to quantitative reachability, safety, or reach-avoid properties, and to qualitative (i.e., probability 1) ω-regular properties.We also present fully automated algorithms for the template-based synthesis of LDBSMs, for the case when the stochastic system dynamics and the controller can be represented in terms of polynomial inequalities. Our experiments demonstrate the ability of our method to solve verification and control tasks for stochastic systems that were beyond the reach of previous supermartingale-based approaches.

Keywords: Supermartingales · Probabilistic verification · Stochastic control

1 Introduction

Stochastic (or probabilistic) systems provide a framework for modeling and quantifying uncertainties in computational models. They are ubiquitous in many areas of computer science, including randomized algorithms [55], security and privacy protocols [8], stochastic networks [30], control theory [6], and artificial intelligence [33]. Many of these systems are safety critical in nature; hence formal methods for guaranteeing their correctness have become an important topic of research.

While the correctness of stochastic systems can be accomplished using a variety of complementary approaches, such as abstraction-based [26,27,38,64],

© The Author(s) 2025
R. Piskac and Z. Rakamarić (Eds.): CAV 2025, LNCS 15932, pp. 29–55, 2025.
https://doi.org/10.1007/978-3-031-98679-6_2

symbolic integration-based [9,32,54], or logical calculi-based methods [35,42,48], there is a growing interest in martingale-based approaches, which do not only guarantee correctness but also provide *supermartingale certificates* as locally checkable correctness proofs for improving the trustworthiness of stochastic system design. A *supermartingale certificate* is a mathematical witness that the desired specification is satisfied. Their name is due to their usage of super-martingale processes from probability theory [62] towards proving properties of stochastic systems.

Recent years have seen significant theoretical and algorithmic advances in utilizing supermartingale certificates for reasoning about stochastic systems with a wide range of specifications, such as termination and reachability [2,11,14,15,20,39,43], safety [1,12,16,21,58,59,61], Büchi and co-Büchi (aka, stability) [13], and cost analysis [17,47,60]. These certificates have also been used for the synthesis and verification of controllers with respect to reachability [29,37], safety [41,51,57,65], reach-avoid [63,66], and stability [4] objectives, and extensions to continuous-time stochastic systems were also considered [46]. However, existing supermartingale certificates are limited to atomic specifications or to small fragments of logical specification languages. Designing a new, bespoke supermartingale certificate for each complex automaton-based or composite logical specification is not a feasible approach. Ideally, we would like to have a systematic method for designing supermartingale certificates for an entire, rich *class of specifications*, which captures all different properties that one might care about. The recent work of Abate et al. [3] has considered this problem and proposed a supermartingale certificate for the general class of ω-regular specifications. However, their certificate is restricted to properties that hold with probability 1, so-called *qualitative* specifications. To the best of our knowledge, no supermartingale certificates for *quantitative ω-regular properties* have been proposed. That is, existing supermartingale certificates are insufficient for reasoning about whether an ω-regular specification is satisfied with a probability $p \in [0, 1]$, which would allow the fine-grained probabilistic analysis that is often needed in practice.

In this work, we present the first supermartingale certificate for reasoning about the full class of *quantitative ω-regular specifications* for discrete-time infinite-state stochastic systems. In order to design our certificate, we use the fact that each ω-regular language can be represented by a limit-deterministic Büchi automaton (LDBA) [24]. This allows us to reduce the problem of proving that an ω-regular specification is satisfied with probability at least $p \in [0, 1]$ to the problem of proving that some set of states in the product of the stochastic system and the LDBA is reached infinitely many times with probability at least p. Hence, we call our certificiate a *limit-deterministic Büchi supermartingale (LDBSM)*. The design of LDBSMs builds upon and significantly generalizes several existing supermartingale certificates for both quantitative and qualitative reasoning about stochastic systems.

We supplement our theoretical developments with *fully automated algorithms for the verification and control* of infinite-state stochastic systems using LDB-

SMs. Our algorithms apply to the setting in which the system dynamics and the controller can be represented in terms of a system of polynomial inequalities over real-valued variables. We show how the verification problem (i.e., the synthesis of a supermartingale certificate) and the control problem (i.e., the synthesis of a controller together with a supermartingale certificate) can be reduced to solving a system of polynomial inequalities, for which an off-the-shelf SMT solver may be used. Not only does this give rise to the first *certificate-based* algorithm, but also the *first* algorithm for the verification and control of general *quantitative ω-regular specifications* for polynomial dynamical systems with a general form of stochastic uncertainties. We implemented a prototype of our method and experimentally evaluated it on a number of random walk examples with quantitative ω-regular specifications. Our results show that our method can reason about a range of quantitative ω-regular properties, including those that were beyond the reach of prior works.

Finally, while our focus is on the verification and control of infinite-state stochastic systems, our LDBSM certificates are applicable to general Borel-measurable stochastic dynamic systems, and hence they naturally extend to probabilistic programs with real- and integer-valued variables. Moreover, our automated synthesis algorithm also extends to polynomial probabilistic programs, similarly to existing works on supermartingale-based verification of probabilistic programs [14,16,21].

In short, our contributions are as follows:

1. **Theory: Supermartingale certificates.** We present limit-deterministic Büchi supermartingales (LDBSMs), the first supermartingale certificate for arbitrary quantitative ω-regular specifications of discrete-time infinite-state stochastic systems.
2. **Automation: Template-based certificate synthesis.** We present the first fully automated algorithms for the verification and control of polynomial stochastic dynamical systems with respect to arbitrary quantitaitve ω-regular specifications.

2   Preliminaries

We assume that the reader is familiar with basic notions of probability theory such as probability space, expected value, etc., which can also be found in standard textbooks on probability theory [62]. For a set S, we use $\mathcal{D}(S)$ to denote the set of all probability distributions over S, and use 2^S to denote the set of all subsets of S.

2.1   Stochastic Dynamical Systems and the Problem Statement

Stochastic Dynamical Systems. A discrete-time *stochastic dynamical system* (SDS) is a tuple $\mathcal{S} = (\mathcal{X}, \mathcal{U}, \mathcal{W}, d, f, \mathrm{Init})$, where $\mathcal{X} \subseteq \mathbb{R}^n$ is the state space, $\mathcal{U} \subseteq \mathbb{R}^m$ is the control input space, $\mathcal{W} \subseteq \mathbb{R}^p$ is the stochastic disturbance space,

$d \in \mathcal{D}(\mathcal{W})$ is the stochastic disturbance distribution, $f \colon \mathcal{X} \times \mathcal{U} \times \mathcal{W} \to \mathcal{X}$ is the *system dynamics* function, and Init $\subseteq \mathcal{X}$ is the set of initial system states. We refer to the elements of $\mathcal{X}$ as *states*, the elements of $\mathcal{U}$ as *control inputs*, and the elements of $\mathcal{W}$ as *stochastic disturbances*. A *path* in $\mathcal{S}$ is an infinite sequence of states $x_0, x_1, \ldots$ in $\mathcal{X}$ where $x_0 \in$ Init and for every $t \geq 0$, there exist a control input $u_t \in \mathcal{U}$ and a stochastic disturbance $w_t \in \mathcal{W}$ such that $x_{t+1} = f(x_t, u_t, w_t)$.

A *controller* in $\mathcal{S}$ is a function $\pi \colon \mathcal{X} \to \mathcal{U}$, mapping every state to a control input. To avoid clutter, we define controllers as being memoryless, i.e., only depending on the current state and without using any information about the past. Our setting organically extends to *finite memory* controllers, which are able to remember bounded amount of information from the past. We will use one such finite memory controller in Sect. 2.2, which will use its memory to track the current state of the specification automaton.

Our model of SDS subsumes the cases of SDS without control inputs (using $|\mathcal{U}| = 1$, making the control input ineffective) and without disturbances (using $|\mathcal{W}| = 1$, making the disturbance ineffective and giving rise to deterministic dynamical systems).

Semantics of SDS. We assume that the sets $\mathcal{X}$, Init $\subseteq \mathbb{R}^n$, $\mathcal{U} \subseteq \mathbb{R}^m$ and $\mathcal{W} \subseteq \mathbb{R}^p$ as well as the functions $f \colon \mathcal{X} \times \mathcal{U} \times \mathcal{W} \to \mathcal{X}$ and $\pi \colon \mathcal{X} \to \mathcal{U}$ are all Borel-measurable. These assumptions are necessary for the semantics of SDS to be mathematically well defined.

Under these assumptions, for every initial state $x_0 \in$ Init, the SDS $\mathcal{S}$ and the controller π together define a continuous-state, discrete-time Markov decision process that takes values in the set of states $\mathcal{X}$ and whose trajectories correspond to paths in $\mathcal{S}$ [52]. Initially, the process starts in x_0. Then, at every time step $t \in \mathbb{N}_0$, the next state of the process is defined by the equation $x_{t+1} = f(x_t, \pi(x)_t, w_t)$, where $w_t \sim d$ is a stochastic disturbance sampled from the stochastic disturbance distribution d, independently from the previous samples.

This process gives rise to a probability space over the set of all paths in $\mathcal{S}$ [52]. We use $\mathbb{P}_{x_0}^{\mathcal{S},\pi}$ and $\mathbb{E}_{x_0}^{\mathcal{S},\pi}$ to denote the probability measure and the expectation operators in this probability space, respectively.

Specifications. A *specification* φ in an SDS $\mathcal{S}$ is a set of paths in $\mathcal{S}$. We write $\mathbb{P}_{x_0}^{\mathcal{S},\pi}[\varphi]$ to denote the probability that a path in $\mathcal{S}$ randomly sampled from the underlying probability space (over all paths) satisfies the specification φ. We will consider ω-regular specifications, which constitute a broad class of properties subsuming linear temporal logic (LTL) and computation tree logics [7]. Every ω-regular specification can be represented using limit deterministic Büchi automata, which will be defined in Sect. 2.2. We will occasionally use the standard LTL notation [7] for convenience; in particular, G a will stand for "always a," F a will stand for "eventually a," and $a \cup b$ will stand for "a until b."

Problem Statement. We now formally define the formal verification and control problems that we consider in this work. Consider an SDS $\mathcal{S}$, an ω-regular specification φ in $\mathcal{S}$, and a probability threshold $p \in [0, 1]$:

1. *Verification problem.* Given a controller π, prove that $\mathbb{P}^{\mathcal{S},\pi}_{x_0}[\varphi] \geq p$ for all $x_0 \in \text{Init}$.
2. *Control problem.* Synthesize a controller π such that $\mathbb{P}^{\mathcal{S},\pi}_{x_0}[\varphi] \geq p$ for all $x_0 \in \text{Init}$.

Example 1 (Running example: 1D random walk). For our running example, we will use a simple 1D random walk denoted as $\mathcal{S}^{\text{rw}}$, whose state space is the real line $\mathbb{R}$, input space is a singleton set $\{\perp\}$ with a dummy input $\perp$, i.e., the system is uncontrolled, stochastic disturbance space is $\mathcal{W} = [-2, 1]$ with a continuous uniform distribution over $\mathcal{W}$, system dynamics is given as

$$f(x, \perp, w) = \begin{cases} x & \text{if } x > 100, \\ x + w & \text{otherwise,} \end{cases} \tag{1}$$

and the set of initial states is [2,3]. Although this simple SDS does not contain control inputs in its dynamics, it will be sufficient for us to illustrate our technical contributions; a variation of $\mathcal{S}^{\text{rw}}$ with control inputs will be considered in Sect. 5. Essentially, at every step, the random walk $\mathcal{S}^{\text{rw}}$ has a higher probability of moving towards the left than towards the right. If however, it ever crosses 100, it becomes stationary. Consider the specification that is the set of all paths that visit the negative half of the real line infinitely many times, formalized as $\{x_0 x_1 \ldots \mid \forall i \geq 0 \ . \ \exists j > i \ . \ x_j \leq 0\}$. Using the standard notation of linear temporal logic, we will write this specification as $\text{GF}\,(x \leq 0)$. For this example, we will refer to the set $\{x \mid x \leq 0\}$ as the *target*.

2.2   Limit-Deterministic Büchi Automata

To specify properties of a given SDS, we label its state space with a finite set of *atomic propositions* P. A *labeling function* $L : \mathcal{X} \to 2^P$ maps each state $x \in \mathcal{X}$ to the set of atomic propositions that are true in x, and we assume that each atomic proposition $p \in P$ has an associated Borel-measurable arithmetic expression $\exp_p : \mathcal{X} \to \mathbb{R}$ such that for every $x \in \mathcal{X}$, $p \in L(x)$ iff $\exp_p(x) \geq 0$. Hence, a path $(x_i)_{i=0}^{\infty}$ in the SDS gives rise to an *infinite word* $(L(x_i))_{i=0}^{\infty}$ over the alphabet 2^P.

We use the classical result that for every ω-regular specification φ defined over a finite set of atomic predicates P, there exists a limit-deterministic Büchi automaton with alphabet $\Sigma = 2^P$ which accepts the same set of infinite words over 2^P as φ [24].

Nondeterministic Büchi Automata. A *nondeterministic Büchi automaton (NBA)* is a tuple $\mathcal{A} = (Q, q_{\text{init}}, \Sigma, \Delta, \mathcal{F})$ where Q is a finite set of states, $q_{\text{init}} \in Q$ is an initial state, Σ is a finite alphabet that includes the empty word symbol ϵ, $\Delta : Q \times \Sigma \to 2^Q$ is a nondeterministic transition function, and $\mathcal{F} \subseteq 2^Q$ is a set of accepting states. An infinite word $\sigma_0, \sigma_1, \ldots$ of letters in the alphabet Σ is *accepted* by $\mathcal{A}$, if it gives rise to at least one Büchi accepting run in $\mathcal{A}$, i.e., if there exists a run $q_0, q_1, \ldots$ of states in Q such that $q_0 = q_{\text{init}}$, for each $i \in \mathbb{N}_0$,

$q_{i+1} \in \Delta(q_i, \sigma_i)$, and for every $i \in \mathbb{N}_0$ there exists a $j > i$ such that $q_j \in \mathcal{F}$ (infinitely many visits to $\mathcal{F}$).

Limit-Deterministic Büchi Automata. *Limit-deterministic Büchi automata (LDBA)* are particular types of NBAs with a restricted form of nondeterminism. In particular, an NBA $\mathcal{A} = (Q, q_{\mathsf{init}}, \Sigma, \Delta, \mathcal{F})$ is said to be an LDBA, if there exists a partition $\{Q_n, Q_d\}$ of the set of states Q (i.e., $Q = Q_n \cup Q_d$ and $Q_n \cap Q_d = \emptyset$) such that for every $q \in Q_d$ and for every $\sigma \in \Sigma$, (i) the transitions from q are deterministic, i.e., $|\Delta(q, \sigma)| = 1$, and (ii) there is no transition from q going outside of Q_d, i.e., $\Delta(q, \sigma) \subseteq Q_d$. We call Q_n the *nondeterministic part* of the LDBA and Q_d the *deterministic part* of the LDBA.

As mentioned above, for every ω-regular specification φ defined over a finite set of atomic predicates P, there exists a canonical LDBA $\mathcal{A}$ with the alphabet $\Sigma = 2^P$ accepting the same set of infinite words as φ. Hence, a path $(x_i)_{i=0}^{\infty}$ in $\mathcal{S}$ satisfies ω-regular specification φ if and only if the infinite word $(L(x_i))_{i=0}^{\infty}$ is accepted by the LDBA $\mathcal{A}$. Our verification and control problems thus reduce to ensuring that a random run in $\mathcal{S}$ induces an infinite word over 2^P accepted by the LDBA $\mathcal{A}$ with probability at least p.

Product SDS. In order to reason about paths and infinite words that they induce in the LDBA, we consider a (synchronous) product of the SDS and the LDBA. A *product SDS* of the SDS $\mathcal{S} = (\mathcal{X}, \mathcal{U}, \mathcal{W}, d, f, \mathrm{Init})$ and the LDBA $\mathcal{A} = (Q, q_{\mathsf{init}}, 2^P, \Delta, \mathcal{F})$ is a tuple $\mathcal{S}^{\times} = (\mathcal{X}^{\times}, \mathcal{U}^{\times}, \mathcal{W}, d, f^{\times}, \mathrm{Init}^{\times})$, where

- $\mathcal{X}^{\times} = \mathcal{X} \times Q$ is the state space of the product SDS,
- $\mathcal{U}^{\times} = \mathcal{U} \times Q$ is the control input space of the product SDS,
- $\mathcal{W} \subseteq \mathbb{R}^p$ is the stochastic disturbance space of the product SDS,
- $d \in \mathcal{D}(\mathcal{W})$ is the stochastic disturbance distribution of the product SDS,
- $f^{\times} \colon \mathcal{X}^{\times} \times \mathcal{U}^{\times} \times \mathcal{W} \to \mathcal{X}^{\times}$ is the system dynamics function, and
- $\mathrm{Init}^{\times} = \mathrm{Init} \times \{q_{\mathsf{init}}\}$ is the set of initial states of the product SDS.

Similarly as before, a *controller* in $\mathcal{S}^{\times}$ is a function $\pi^{\times} \colon \mathcal{X}^{\times} \to \mathcal{U}^{\times}$ mapping every state to a control input. However, we require that for every $(x, q) \in \mathcal{X}^{\times}$, the corresponding control input $\pi^{\times}(x, q) = (u, q') \in \mathcal{U} \times Q$ satisfies $q' \in \Delta(q, L(x))$. Hence, the product SDS indeed models a synchronous product of the SDS and the LDBA, where the controller $\pi^{\times}$ resolves nondeterminism both in the SDS and in the LDBA. To distinghuish between the two controller components, we write $\pi^{\times}(x, q) = (\pi^{\mathcal{S}}(x, q), \pi^{\mathcal{A}}(x, q))$. The semantics of the product SDS are defined analogously to Sect. 2.1, with

$$(x_{t+1}, q_{t+1}) = \left(f(x_t, \pi^{\mathcal{S}}(x_t, q_t), w_t), \pi^{\mathcal{A}}(x_t, q_t) \right)$$

for every time step $t \in \mathbb{N}_0$ and w_t sampled according to d and independent from w_i for every $i \leq t - 1$. For each initial state $(x_0, q_{\mathsf{init}}) \in \mathrm{Init}^{\times}$, we denote by $\mathbb{P}^{\mathcal{S}^{\times}, \pi^{\times}}_{(x_0, q_{\mathsf{init}})}$ and $\mathbb{E}^{\mathcal{S}^{\times}, \pi^{\times}}_{(x_0, q_{\mathsf{init}})}$ the probability measure and the expectation operator in the probability space of all paths in $\mathcal{S}^{\times}$ with controller $\pi^{\times}$, respectively.

Finally, the following proposition will allow us to reduce our verification and control problems to the problems of synthesizing a controller for the product

SDS. Denote by Büchi(B) the set of all runs in $\mathcal{S}^\times$ that visit states in $B \subseteq \mathcal{X}^\times$ infinitely many times.

Proposition 1. *Consider an SDS $\mathcal{S}$ and a controller π in $\mathcal{S}$. Let φ be an ω-regular specification over a finite set of atomic propositions P, $\mathcal{A} = (Q, q_{\text{init}}, 2^P, \Delta, \mathcal{F})$ be an LDBA for the specification φ, and $\mathcal{S}^\times$ be the product MDP of $\mathcal{S}$ and $\mathcal{A}$. Then, for every controller $\pi^\times = (\pi^\mathcal{S}, \pi^\mathcal{A})$ in $\mathcal{S}^\times$ with $\pi^\mathcal{S} = \pi$ and for every initial state $(x_0, q_{\text{init}}) \in \text{Init}^\times$, we have*

$$\mathbb{P}_{x_0}^{\mathcal{S}, \pi}\left[\varphi\right] \geq \mathbb{P}_{(x_0, q_{\text{init}})}^{\mathcal{S}^\times, \pi^\times}\left[\text{Büchi}(\mathbb{R}^n \times \mathcal{F})\right].$$

Proof. Consider a controller $\pi^\times = (\pi^\mathcal{S}, \pi^\mathcal{A})$ in $\mathcal{S}^\times$ with $\pi^\mathcal{S} = \pi$. Let Π be the set of all paths in $\mathcal{S}$, and $\Pi^\times$ be the set of all paths in $\mathcal{S}^\times$. Define the map $g : \Pi \to \Pi^\times$ via

$$g(x_0, x_1, x_2, \dots) = ((x_0, q_0), (x_1, \pi^\mathcal{A}(x_0, q_0)), (x_2, \pi^\mathcal{A}(x_1, q_1)), \dots).$$

Now, observe that

$$
\begin{aligned}
\mathbb{P}_{x_0}^{\mathcal{S}, \pi}\left[\varphi\right] &= \mathbb{P}_{x_0}^{\mathcal{S}, \pi}\left[(x_i)_{i=0}^\infty \in \Pi \mid (x_i)_{i=0}^\infty \models \varphi\right] \\
&= \mathbb{P}_{x_0}^{\mathcal{S}, \pi}\left[(x_i)_{i=0}^\infty \in \Pi \mid (L(x_i))_{i=0}^\infty \text{ infinite word accepted by } \mathcal{A}\right] \\
&\geq \mathbb{P}_{x_0}^{\mathcal{S}, \pi}\left[(x_i)_{i=0}^\infty \in \Pi \mid (g(x_i))_{i=0}^\infty \text{ visits infinitely many times } \mathbb{R}^n \times \mathcal{F}\right] \\
&= \mathbb{P}_{(x_0, q_{\text{init}})}^{\mathcal{S}^\times, \pi^\times}\left[\text{Büchi}(\mathbb{R}^n \times \mathcal{F})\right],
\end{aligned}
$$

where the inequality holds due to the first set of paths in Π containing the second set of paths in Π. This proves the proposition claim. □

The inequality in Proposition 1 is strict whenever $\pi^\mathcal{A}$ chooses a sub-optimal resolution of non-determinisms in the LDBA $\mathcal{A}$. Consider, e.g., the property FG a (eventually always a), whose LDBA representation has three states q_0, q_1, q_2. The initial state is q_0, and upon seeing an a the controller $\pi^\mathcal{A}$ needs to non-deterministically decide whether to wait at q_0 or to proceed to the accepting state q_1. The system can stay in q_1 as long as only a is seen, and seeing a !a forces the automaton (deterministically) to the rejecting sink q_2. For $\pi^\mathcal{S} = \pi$, satisfying the specification FG a on the SDS with probability $p > 0$, if $\pi^\mathcal{A}$ always chooses to stay at q_0 after seeing every a, then the left side of the inequality will be p but the right side will be 0.

Rejecting States. An LDBA $\mathcal{A} = (Q, q_{\text{init}}, \Sigma, \Delta, \mathcal{F})$ induces a graph over its states with edges defined by all possible nondeterministic transitions in the automaton, i.e., it induces a graph $G = (Q, E)$ with $E = \{(q, q') \in Q \times Q \mid \exists \sigma \in \Sigma. \, q' \in \Delta(q, \sigma)\}$.

We denote by $Q_{\text{reject}} \subseteq Q$ the set of all states in the LDBA from which no state in the set of accepting states $\mathcal{F}$ can be reached in the graph G. Thus, if an infinite run $q_0, q_1, \ldots$ in the LDBA contains a state in Q_{reject}, then it cannot be an accepting run as it will contain no states in $\mathcal{F}$ after the first occurence of a state in Q_{reject}. To that end, we call Q_{reject} the set of *rejecting states* in the LDBA.

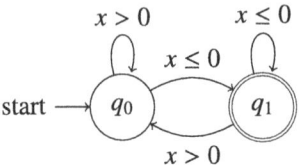

Fig. 1. The specifications GF $(x \leq 0)$ from Example 1 represented using LDBA, which in this case is a deterministic Büchi automaton, where q_1 is the Büchi accepting state.

Example 2. The specification GF $(x \leq 0)$ from the 1D random walk is shown in the LDBA form in Fig. 1. The atomic predicates are given by $(x \leq 0)$ and $(x > 0)$. The product state remains in the automaton state q_0 until $x > 0$ is true, and each time the target $x \leq 0$ is true, the automaton visits the state q_1, which is the accepting state.

3 Supermartingale Certificate for ω-Regular Specifications

We now present the theory behind our novel supermartingale certificates for quantitative ω-regular specifications, which is the main technical contribution of our work. Definition 1 formally defines the certificates and Theorem 1 establishes their soundness. The computational aspects of the certificate will be discussed in Sect. 4. We also assume that a controller is provided as input, and in Sect. 4 we will show how to compute it when it is not provided.

In what follows, suppose the following are given: an SDS $\mathcal{S} = (\mathcal{X}, \mathcal{U}, \mathcal{W}, d, f, \text{Init})$, a controller π in $\mathcal{S}$, an ω-regular specification φ over a set of atomic propositions P, and a minimum probability $p \in [0, 1]$ with which the specification should be satisfied.

3.1 Intuitive Overview

Let $\mathcal{A} = (Q, q_{\text{init}}, 2^P, \Delta, \mathcal{F})$ be an LDBA that accepts the same set of infinite words over 2^P as the specification φ. Our certificate is defined over the product SDS $\mathcal{S}^\times$ of the SDS $\mathcal{S}$ and the LDBA $\mathcal{A}$. By Proposition 1, this reduces the problem of certifying

$$\text{the specification } \varphi \text{ is satisfied with probability} \geq p$$

to the problem of certifying that

$$\text{there exists a controller } \pi^\times = (\pi^{\mathcal{S}}, \pi^{\mathcal{A}}) \text{ in } \mathcal{S}^\times \text{ with } \pi^{\mathcal{S}} = \pi, \text{ such that}$$
$$\text{the set of states } \mathbb{R}^n \times \mathcal{F} \text{ in } \mathcal{S}^\times \text{ is reached infinitely many times with probability} \geq p.$$

To prove this, it suffices to show that there exists a controller $\pi^\times = (\pi^{\mathcal{S}}, \pi^{\mathcal{A}})$ in $\mathcal{S}^\times$ with $\pi^{\mathcal{S}} = \pi$, such that the following two properties are satisfied:

1. *Safety property.* There exists a set of states *SI* in the product SDS $\mathcal{S}^\times$ that contains all initial states $\mathrm{Init} \times \{q_0\}$, no rejecting states $\mathbb{R}^n \times Q_{\mathrm{reject}}$, and such that *SI* is left with probability at most $1 - p$. In other words, the pair (SI, p) is a *stochastic invariant* [21].
2. *Liveness property.* A random run in the product SDS $\mathcal{S}^\times$ either visits $\mathbb{R}^n \times \mathcal{F}$ infinitely many times or eventually leaves the set *SI* with probability 1.

The conjunction of the safety and the liveness properties guarantees that the set of states $\mathbb{R}^n \times \mathcal{F}$ is visited infinitely many times with probability at least p.

The safety-liveness decomposition of the problem is reflected in the design of our supermartingale certificate. In particular, our certificate V consists of two components V^{safe} and V^{live}, called the *safety certificate* and the *liveness certificate*, which are connected in a hierarchical fashion: the certificate V^{safe} is independent of V^{live} and generates the stochastic invariant *SI*, whereas the certificate V^{live} depends on V^{safe} to use the set *SI* as a "safety net" and make sure that the liveness condition is fulfilled. A crucial aspect of this hierarchical composition is that the two certificates agree on their choices of control inputs and resolutions of the nondeterminisms in the LDBA at all time. From this, we obtain a single joint controller $\pi^\times = (\pi^{\mathcal{S}}, \pi^{\mathcal{A}})$ in $\mathcal{S}^\times$ with $\pi^{\mathcal{S}} = \pi$, and formally certify that both the safety and the liveness property specified above are satisfied.

Invariants. Supermartingale certificates need to satisfy a set of conditions in the reachable parts of the state space, starting from the initial states. Since computing the exact set of reachable states is in general infeasible, we define our supermartingale certificates with respect to an over-approximation, called a *(supporting) invariant*. In this section, we assume that the invariant is given, and in Sect. 4, we will describe how to automatically compute it along with the certificate and the controller.

Formally, a state x in the SDS $\mathcal{S}$ is *reachable*, if there exists a path $x_0, x_1, \ldots$ in $\mathcal{S}$ with $x_t = x$ for some $t \in \mathbb{N}_0$. An *invariant* in $\mathcal{S}$ is a set of states $I \subseteq \mathcal{X}$ which contains all reachable states in $\mathcal{S}$. The definition of an invariant in a product SDS $\mathcal{S}^\times$ is analogous.

Invariants are integral components of supermartingale certificates, because they determine within which part of the state space the certificate conditions are required to be fulfilled; outside of the invariant, the certificates may behave arbitrarily. Therefore, our formal definition of LDBSM certificates will include their supporting invariants as their "domains" of operation.

3.2   Supermartingale Certificates for LDBA Specifications

To formalize the certificate components V^{safe}, V^{live}, and I, as described above, we build upon and generalize the existing supermartingale certificates for reasoning about quantitative safety and qualitative recurrence (i.e., Büchi) properties.

Safety Certificates. Our safety certificate V^{safe} draws insight from *repulsing supermartingales* [21], which were introduced for reasoning about quantitative safety. Intuitively, given some set of unsafe states $U \subseteq \mathcal{X}$ in an SDS $\mathcal{S}$ under a controller π, a repulsing supermartingale for U is a function $V^{\mathrm{safe}} : \mathcal{X} \to \mathbb{R}$, along with an invariant I, which to every system state assigns a real value that is required to satisfy the following conditions at the states in I: **(S1)** at initial states, the value of V^{safe} is below some negative threshold $\eta \leq 0$, **(S2)** at unsafe states in $U \cap I$, the value of V^{safe} is above the threshold 0, and **(S3)** at states in I in which $V^{\mathrm{safe}} \leq 0$, the value of V^{safe} must strictly decrease in expectation by $\epsilon > 0$ upon every one-step execution of the SDS under the controller π, while also ensuring that the absolute change in its value lies within some interval of length $M > 0$, and ensuring that the next state remains within I. It was shown that, if a repulsing supermartingale for the unsafe set exists, then the SDS stays within the set of states $SI = \{x \in \mathcal{X} \mid V^{\mathrm{safe}}(x) < 0\}$—the *stochastic invariant*—and thus does not reach the unsafe set U with probability at least $p \geq 1 - \exp(\frac{8 \cdot \epsilon \cdot \eta}{M^2})$ [59] (the bound of [59] is an improved version of the bound in [21]).

For us, the set of unsafe states of the product SDS $\mathcal{S}^{\times}$ is given by $U = \mathbb{R}^n \times Q_{\mathrm{reject}}$, where recall that Q_{reject} is the set of rejecting states in the LDBA, and our goal is to ensure that there exists a controller $\pi^{\times}_{\mathrm{safe}} = (\pi^{\mathcal{S}}, \pi^{\mathcal{A}})$ in $\mathcal{S}^{\times}$ with $\pi^{\mathcal{S}} = \pi$, under which the product SDS is safe with probability at least p. To this end, we extend repulsing supermartingales by requiring condition (S3) to be satisfied only for *some* outgoing LDBA transition at a state in $\mathcal{S}^{\times}$—call it condition **(S3+)**. The stochastic invariant also gets generalized to the state space of the product SDS in the obvious way: $SI^{\times} = \{(x, q) \in \mathcal{X} \times Q \mid V^{\mathrm{safe}}(x, q) < 0\}$. The controller $\pi^{\mathcal{A}}$ then picks that LDBA transition towards satisfying the quantitative safety property.

Liveness Certificates. Our liveness certificate V^{live} draws insight from the supermartingale certificate of Chakarov et al. [13] for proving that a given set of target states $T \subseteq \mathcal{X}$ in $\mathcal{S}$ under a given controller π is visited infinitely many times with probability 1. Intuitively, a supermartingale certificate for T is a function $V^{\mathrm{live}} : \mathcal{X} \to \mathbb{R}$, along with an invariant I, which to every system state assigns a real value that is required to satisfy the following conditions at the states in I: **(L1)** the value of V^{live} is non-negative, **(L2)** at non-target states outside T, the value of V^{live} must strictly decrease in expected value by $\epsilon > 0$ upon every one-step execution of the system under the controller π, and **(L3)** at target states in $T \cap I$, the value of V^{live} is allowed to increase in expectation by at most $M > 0$ in every one-step execution of the system under the controller π, while making sure that the next state does not go outside of I. If such a certificate for the target set T exists, then T is reached infinitely many times with probability 1 [13].

For us, the set of target states of the product SDS $\mathcal{S}^{\times}$ is given by $T = \mathbb{R}^n \times \mathcal{F}$, where recall that $\mathcal{F}$ is the set of Büchi accepting set in the LDBA. In our LDBSM certificate, we extend the certificate of Chakarov et al. [13] in two ways. First, we present a supermartingale certificate for proving that, with probability 1, *either* the Büchi accepting set $\mathcal{X} \times \mathcal{F}$ of the product SDS is reached infinitely many times *or* the stochastic invariant set $SI^{\times}$ is eventually left—call it condition **(L3+)**. This is in line with the overview in Sect. 3.1 and our requirements for a liveness certificate. Second, in the product MDP $\mathcal{S}^{\times}$, our goal is again to ensure that there exists a controller $\pi_{\text{live}}^{\times} = (\pi^{\mathcal{S}}, \pi^{\mathcal{A}})$ in $\mathcal{S}^{\times}$ with $\pi^{\mathcal{S}} = \pi$, under which this property is satisfied. This is accounted for by requiring conditions (L2) and (L3) of the certificate of Chakarov et al. [13] to be satisfied only for *some* outgoing LDBA transition at a state in $\mathcal{S}^{\times}$.

The Hierarchical Composition of Safety and Liveness Certificates. The challenge in combining the safety and liveness components lies in ensuring that the properties implied by the two components are satisfied with respect to the *same controller* $\pi^{\times} = (\pi^{\mathcal{S}}, \pi^{\mathcal{A}})$ in $\mathcal{S}^{\times}$ with $\pi^{\mathcal{S}} = \pi$; in other words, we need to ensure that the controllers $\pi_{\text{safe}}^{\times}$ and $\pi_{\text{live}}^{\times}$ are the same. Otherwise, we cannot conclude that the set of states $\mathbb{R}^n \times \mathcal{F}$ is reached infinitely many times with probability at least p. In particular, we need to ensure that condition (S3+) on one hand, and conditions (L2) and (L3+) on the other hand, are always satisfied with respect to the same resolution of non-determinism, i.e., with respect to the same transition $q' \in \Delta(q, a)$ in the LDBA. We will pinpoint how this is achieved after presenting our novel LDBSM certificate in the following.

Definition 1 (LDBMS certificates). *Consider an SDS $\mathcal{S}$ and a controller π in it. Let $\mathcal{A} = (Q, q_{\text{init}}, 2^P, \Delta, \mathcal{F})$ be an LDBA, $\mathcal{S}^{\times}$ be the product SDS of $\mathcal{S}$ and $\mathcal{A}$, and $I \subseteq \mathcal{X} \times Q$ be an invariant in $\mathcal{S}^{\times}$.*

An LDBSM certificate is a triple $V = (V^{\text{safe}}, V^{\text{live}}, I)$, where $V^{\text{safe}} : \mathcal{X} \times Q \to \mathbb{R}$ and $V^{\text{live}} : \mathcal{X} \times Q \to \mathbb{R}$ assign real values to each state in $\mathcal{S}^{\times}$, and $I \subseteq \mathcal{X} \times Q$ is an invariant in $\mathcal{S}^{\times}$. We require that there exist $\eta^{S} \leq 0$, $\epsilon^{S} > 0$, $M^{S} > 0$, and $\beta^{S} \in \mathbb{R}$, as well as $\epsilon^{L} > 0$, $M^{L} > 0$, such that the following conditions are satisfied:

(a) Initial condition of the invariant: *the initial state is inside the invariant, i.e.,*

$$\forall (x, q) \in Init^{\times}. (x, q) \in I.$$

(b) Initial condition of the safety certificate: *the value of V^{safe} at initial states is at most η^{S}, i.e.,*

$$\forall x \in Init. V^{\text{safe}}(x, q_{\text{init}}) \leq \eta^{S}. \tag{Cond. S1}$$

(c) Safety condition of the safety certificate: *the value of V^{safe} at reachable rejecting states is non-negative, i.e.,*

$$\forall (x, q) \in (\mathcal{X} \times Q_{reject}) \cap I. V^{\text{safe}}(x, q) \geq 0. \tag{Cond. S2}$$

(d) Non-negativity condition of the liveness certificate: *the value of V^{live} is non-negative at states in the invariant I, which over-approximates the set of reachable states, i.e.,*

$$\forall (x, q) \in I. V^{\text{live}}(x, q) \geq 0. \tag{Cond. L1}$$

(e) Strict expected decrease of the liveness certificate until $\mathcal{X} \times \mathcal{F}$ or $SI = \{(x, q) \in \mathcal{S}^\times \mid V^{\text{safe}}(x, q) < 0\}$ is reached with the safety condition: *we have*

$$\forall (x, q) \in \mathcal{X} \times (Q \setminus (\mathcal{F} \cup Q_{reject})) \cap I. \, V^{\text{safe}}(x, q) \leq 0 \Longrightarrow$$

$$\bigvee_{a \in \Sigma} \bigvee_{q' \in \Delta(q,a)} \left[\left(\overbrace{\begin{bmatrix} x \models a \wedge \forall w \in \mathcal{W}. \, (f(x, \pi(x), w), q') \in I \wedge \\ V^{\text{safe}}(x, q) \geq \mathbb{E}_w^\pi[V^{\text{safe}}(f(x, \pi(x), w), q')] + \epsilon^S \wedge \\ \forall w \in \mathcal{W}. \, \beta^S \leq V^{\text{safe}}(x, q) - V^{\text{safe}}(f(x, \pi(x), w), q') \leq \beta^S + M^S \end{bmatrix}}^{SafetyCond(x,q,a,q') \quad \text{Cond. S3+}} \right) \\ \wedge \\ \underbrace{V^{\text{live}}(x, q) \geq \mathbb{E}_w^\pi[V^{\text{live}}(f(x, \pi(x), w), q')] + \epsilon^L}_{\text{Cond. L2}} \right]$$

(f) Bounded expected increase of the liveness certificate in $(\mathcal{X} \times \mathcal{F}) \setminus SI$ with the safety condition: *we have*

$$\forall (x, q) \in (\mathcal{X} \times \mathcal{F}) \cap I. \, V^{\text{safe}}(x, q) \leq 0 \Longrightarrow$$

$$\bigvee_{a \in \Sigma, \Delta(q,a)=q'} \left[\overbrace{SafetyCond(x, q, a, q')}^{\text{Cond. S3+}} \cdot \\ \wedge \\ \underbrace{\mathbb{E}_w^\pi[V^{\text{live}}(f(x, \pi(x), w), q')] \leq V^{\text{live}}(x, q) + M^L}_{\text{Cond. L3+}} \right] .$$

Conditions (b), (c), and (d) in Def. 1 formalize the (S1), (S2), and (L1) conditions that were informally introduced beforehand. Conditions (e) and (f) combine (S3+) with (L2) and (L3+), respectively, which are concerned about states that are, respectively, outside of $\mathcal{F} \cup Q_{reject}$ and inside of $\mathcal{F}$. Additionally, in both (e) and (f), the left hand sides of the implications require that the state (x, q) is in the stochastic invariant SI, which is formalized by the inequality $V^{\text{safe}}(x, q) \leq 0$, and the right hand sides require the satisfaction of (S3+) which is captured using the formula $SafetyCond(x, q, a, q')$. The formula $SafetyCond(x, q, a, q')$ encodes that the strict expected decrease and the bounded differences conditions are satisfied at a state (x, q) of $\mathcal{S}^\times$, upon taking the LDBA transition to q' by using a. The assertion $x \models a$ guarantees the satisfaction of a at x, ensuring the availability of the LDBA transition to $q' \in \Delta(q, a)$. The clause $V^{\text{safe}}(x, q) \geq \mathbb{E}_w^\pi[V^{\text{safe}}(f(x, \pi(x), w), q')] + \epsilon^S$ encodes strict expected decrease, i.e., that the value of V^{safe} decreases in expected value by at least ϵ^S upon one-step execution of the SDS under the controller π. The clause $\forall w \in \mathcal{W}. \, \beta^S \leq V^{\text{safe}}(x, q) - V^{\text{safe}}(f(x, \pi(x), w), q') \leq \beta^S + M^S$ encodes the bounded differences condition, i.e., that for every stochastic disturbance $w \in \mathcal{W}$, the change in the value of V^{safe} is contained in the interval $[\beta^S, \beta^S + M^S]$. Finally, the clause $\forall w \in \mathcal{W}. \, (f(x, \pi(x), w), q') \in I$ guarantees that after the one-step execution of the SDS under the controller π, the new state is within the invariant I. Moreover, the right hand sides of the implications of (d) and (e) also respectively implement (L2) and (L3+), which are straightforward.

The following theorem establishes the soundness of our certificate for proving satisfaction of quantitative ω-regular specifications in SDSs.

Theorem 1 (Soundness of LDBSM certificates). *Consider an SDS S and a controller π. Let φ be an ω-regular specification in S, $p \in [0,1]$ be a probability threshold, and $\mathcal{A} = (Q, q_{\text{init}}, 2^P, \Delta, \mathcal{F})$ be an LDBA that accepts the same language as φ. Let $S^\times$ be the product SDS of S and $\mathcal{A}$.*

Suppose that there exists an LDBSM certificate $V = (V^{\text{safe}}, V^{\text{live}}, I)$ with the associated constants η^S, ϵ^S, and M^S, such that $p \leq 1 - \exp \frac{8 \cdot \eta^S \cdot \epsilon^S}{(M^S)^2}$. Then, there exists a controller $\pi^\times = (\pi^S, \pi^{\mathcal{A}})$ in $S^\times$ with $\pi^S = \pi$, such that for every initial state $(x_0, q_{\text{init}}) \in \text{Init}^\times$, we have

$$\mathbb{P}_{x_0}^{S,\pi}\left[\varphi\right] \geq \mathbb{P}_{(x_0,q_{\text{init}})}^{S^\times,\pi^\times}\left[\text{Büchi}(\mathbb{R}^n \times \mathcal{F})\right] \geq p. \qquad (2)$$

Proof. We first define $\pi^{\mathcal{A}} : S^\times \to Q$ in order to specify the controller $\pi^\times = (\pi^S, \pi^{\mathcal{A}})$ in $S^\times$ with $\pi^S = \pi$. In what follows, we fix an ordering of the states in Q. For each $(x, q) \in S^\times$, we define $\pi^{\mathcal{A}}(x, q)$ as follows:

- If $(x, q) \in I$, $V^{\text{safe}}(x, q) \leq 0$ and $q \in Q \backslash (\mathcal{F} \cup Q_{\text{reject}})$, we define $\pi^{\mathcal{A}}(x, q)$ to be $q' \in Q$ of the smallest order for which the predicate on the right-hand-side of condition ((e)) in Def. 1 is satisfied.
- If $(x, q) \in I$, $V^{\text{safe}}(x, q) \leq 0$ and $q \in \mathcal{F}$, we define $\pi^{\mathcal{A}}(x, q)$ to be $q' \in Q$ of the smallest order for which the predicate on the right-hand-side of condition ((f)) in Def. 1 is satisfied.
- If $(x, q) \in I$, $V^{\text{safe}}(x, q) \leq 0$ and $q \in Q_{\text{reject}}$, by condition (c) in Def. 1, if $(x, q) \in I$ then $V^{\text{safe}}(x, q) \geq 0$. Hence, $V^{\text{safe}}(x, q)$ must be 0. We define $\pi^{\mathcal{A}}(x, q)$ to be $q' \in Q$ of the smallest order for which there exists a letter $a \in \Sigma$ with $x \models a$ and $q' \in \Delta(q, a)$. Such $q' \in Q$ is guaranteed to exist, as it is always possible to take at least one transition in the LDBA.
- If $(x, q) \notin I$ or $V^{\text{safe}}(x, q) > 0$, we define $\pi^{\mathcal{A}}(x, q)$ exactly as in the previous case above, i.e., $\pi^{\mathcal{A}}(x, q)$ is $q' \in Q$ of the smallest order for which there exists a letter $a \in \Sigma$ with $x \models a$ and $q' \in \Delta(q, a)$.

We note that fixing an order of states in Q and picking a state q' of the smallest order is done in order to ensure that $\pi^{\mathcal{A}} : S^\times \to Q$ is a measurable function, for the semantics of the controller to be mathematically well defined.

We now show that the controller $\pi^\times = (\pi^S, \pi^{\mathcal{A}})$ with $\pi^S = \pi$ and $\pi^{\mathcal{A}}$ defined as above satisfies the theorem's claim. The first inequality follows from Proposition 1, hence we only need to prove the second inequality. We show that the certificate component V^{safe} defines a repulsing supermartingale for the unsafe set $\mathbb{R}^n \times Q_{\text{reject}}$ [21] in the product SDS $S^\times$ controlled by our controller $\pi^\times = (\pi^S, \pi^{\mathcal{A}})$. To prove this, we need to show that V^{safe} and I satisfy conditions **(S1)-(S3)** defined earlier in this section. Condition **(S1)** is implied by condition ((b)) in Definition 1. Condition **(S2)** is implied by condition ((c)) in Definition 1. Finally, condition **(S3)** is implied by conditions ((e)) and ((f)) in Definition 1. Hence, V^{safe} indeed defines a repulsing supermartingale for the unsafe set $\mathbb{R}^n \times Q_{\text{reject}}$, and I is the respective invariant. Thus, by [59, Theorem 5.1], it follows that for every initial state $(x, q_{\text{init}}) \in \mathcal{X}^\times$, we have

$$\mathbb{P}^{\mathcal{S}^\times, \pi^\times}_{(x_0, q_{\text{init}})} \left[\mathit{Safe}\Big(\{(x,q) \in \mathcal{X}^\times \mid V^{\text{safe}}(x,q) \geq 0\} \Big) \right] \geq 1 - \exp \frac{8 \cdot \eta^S \cdot \epsilon^S}{(M^S)^2} \geq p, \quad (3)$$

where the inequality indeed holds with respect to our controller $\pi^\times = (\pi^S, \pi^A)$ and $\mathit{Safe}(U)$ denotes the set of all paths in $\mathcal{S}^\times$ that do not contain states from some set U.

Next, we show that, under our controller $\pi^\times = (\pi^S, \pi^A)$, either the set of states $\mathbb{R}^n \times \mathcal{F}$ is visited infinitely many times or the set of states $SI = \{(x,q) \in \mathcal{X}^\times \mid V^{\text{safe}}(x,q) \leq 0\}$ is eventually left with probability 1. To prove this, we first define a new product SDS $\mathcal{S}^\times_{\text{new}}$ by modifying its dynamics function $f^\times : \mathcal{X}^\times \times \mathcal{U}^\times \times W \to \mathcal{X}^\times$ to

$$f^\times_{\text{new}}((x,q),(u,q),w) = \begin{cases} f^\times((x,q),(u,q),w), & \text{if } V^{\text{safe}}(x,q) < 0 \\ (x,q), & \text{if } V^{\text{safe}}(x,q) \geq 0. \end{cases}$$

Intuitively, we are redefining the product SDS to make the complement of SI, i.e., the set of all states at which $V^{\text{safe}}(x,q) \geq 0$, into a sink where the system remains stuck forever once entered. Then, in order to prove that either the set of states $\mathbb{R}^n \times \mathcal{F}$ is visited infinitely many times or the set of states $SI = \{(x,q) \in \mathcal{X}^\times \mid V^{\text{safe}}(x,q) \leq 0\}$ is eventually left with probability 1, it suffices to prove that the set of states $(\mathbb{R}^n \times \mathcal{F}) \cup \neg SI$ in the *new product SDS* $\mathcal{S}^\times_{\text{new}}$ is visited infinitely many times with probability 1. To show this, we prove that the certificate component V^{live} defines an instance of the supermartingale certificate of [13] for proving that the target set $(\mathbb{R}^n \times \mathcal{F}) \cup \neg SI$ is reached infinitely many times with probability 1 in the *new product SDS* $\mathcal{S}^\times_{\text{new}}$ controlled by our controller $\pi^\times = (\pi^S, \pi^A)$. To prove this, we need to show that V^{live} and I satisfy conditions **(L1)**-**(L3)** defined earlier in this section. Condition **(L1)** is implied by condition ((d)) in Definition 1. Condition **(L2)** is implied by condition ((e)) in Definition 1. Finally, condition **(L3)** is implied by conditions ((f)) in Definition 1 and by our construction of the new product SDS $\mathcal{S}^\times_{\text{new}}$, since it ensures that the value of V^{live} remains constant once a state in $\neg SI$ is reached. Hence, V^{live} indeed defines an instance of the supermartingale certificate of [13] for proving that the target set $(\mathbb{R}^n \times \mathcal{F}) \cup \neg SI$ is reached infinitely many times with probability 1 in $\mathcal{S}^\times_{\text{new}}$, and it follows that in the product SDS $\mathcal{S}^\times$ we have

$$\mathbb{P}^{\mathcal{S}^\times, \pi^\times}_{(x_0, q_{\text{init}})} \left[\mathit{Büchi}(\mathbb{R}^n \times \mathcal{F}) \cup \mathit{Reach}(\neg SI) \right] = 1, \quad (4)$$

where the equality indeed holds with respect to our controller $\pi^\times = (\pi^S, \pi^A)$, $\mathit{Büchi}(T)$ denotes the set of all paths in $\mathcal{S}^\times$ that visit states in T infinitely many times, and $\mathit{Reach}(T)$ denotes the set of all paths in $\mathcal{S}^\times$ that eventually visit a state in T.

Combining eq. (3) and eq. (4) above, we conclude that for every initial state $(x, q_{\text{init}}) \in \mathcal{X}^\times$ we have

$$\mathbb{P}^{S^{\times},\pi^{\times}}_{(x_0,q_{\text{init}})}\Big[B\ddot{u}chi(\mathbb{R}^n \times \mathcal{F})\Big] \geq \mathbb{P}^{S^{\times},\pi^{\times}}_{(x_0,q_{\text{init}})}\Big[B\ddot{u}chi(\mathbb{R}^n \times \mathcal{F}) \cup Reach(\neg SI)\Big] - \mathbb{P}^{S^{\times},\pi^{\times}}_{(x_0,q_{\text{init}})}\Big[Reach(\neg SI)\Big]$$

$$\geq \mathbb{P}^{S^{\times},\pi^{\times}}_{(x_0,q_{\text{init}})}\Big[B\ddot{u}chi(\mathbb{R}^n \times \mathcal{F}) \cup Reach(\neg SI)\Big] - \Big(1 - \mathbb{P}^{S^{\times},\pi^{\times}}_{(x_0,q_{\text{init}})}\Big[Safe(\neg SI)\Big]\Big)$$

$$\geq 1 - (1 - p) = p.$$

This concludes the proof of the theorem claim. □

Example 3 (LDBSM certificates). Consider the 1D random walk from Example 1 and 2 with specification GF $(x \leq 0)$. The following constitute an LDBSM certificate: The invariant I in q_0 is $73 + (1/2)x$ and in q_1 is the constant 0, $V^{\text{safe}}(\cdot, q_0) = V^{\text{safe}}(\cdot, q_1) = -9 + (5/16)x$, $V^{\text{live}}(\cdot, q_0) = (367/2) + (3/4)x$, $V^{\text{live}}(\cdot, q_1) = (4747/128) - (1/256)x$, with the variables $\eta^S = -8$, $\epsilon^S = 5/32$, $M^S = 1$, $\beta^S = -11/32$, $\epsilon^L = 3/8$, and $M^L = 260$. It can be checked that $\{V^{\text{safe}}, V^{\text{live}}, I\}$ is a valid LDBSM that satisfies all the constraints in Definition 1.

Remark 1 (On the incompleteness of LDBSM certificates). Our LDBSM certificates are incomplete: it is possible that a certificate does not exist even though there exists a controller that fulfills the given ω-regular specification. The incompleteness of LDBSM certificates follows from the incompleteness of our safety (based on repulsing supermartingales [21]) and liveness certificates (based on almost-sure recurrence certificates of Chakarov et al. [13]). The incompleteness of repulsing supermartingales was discussed in Chatterjee et al. [16], and we omit the details. An example of incompleteness of the liveness certificate is when the target set is closed under system dynamics and cannot be left once entered. In this case, infinitely many visits to the target is equivalent to reaching it once. For almost-sure reachability, the liveness certificate satisfying conditions (L1) and (L2) (see Sect. 3.1) becomes a ranking supermartingale of Chakarov and Sankaranarayanan [11]. Ranking supermartingales are sound and complete for finite expected time reachability [31], but are incomplete for almost-sure reachability.

4   Polynomial Template-Based Synthesis Algorithms

We now present our algorithms for automated verification and control of stochastic dynamical systems via our LDBSM certificates. While our theory on LDBSM certificates in Sect. 3 is applicable to general SDS and controllers, the algorithms in this section are restricted to systems that can be specified via polynomial arithmetic.

Assumption: Polynomial Systems. We assume that the system dynamics function f, the controller π, and arithmetic expressions for all atomic propositions appearing in the ω-regular specification φ are *polynomial functions* over the state, control input, and stochastic disturbance variables. More generally, we allow the system dynamics function f to be piecewise-polynomial. That is, it can be of the form

$$f(x, u, w) = \begin{cases} f_1(x, u, w), & \text{if } \wedge_{i=1}^{N_1} g_i^1(x) \leq 0, \\ \dots & \\ f_k(x, u, w), & \text{if } \wedge_{i=1}^{N_k} g_i^k(x) \leq 0, \end{cases} \tag{5}$$

where all f_i's and g_i^j's are polynomial functions over their input variables. Later, we will fix d as the specified maximum degree of our polynomial templates, and we assume that the first d moments of $f(x, u, W)$—with W being the random variable representing the distribution over noise—be representible and given as polynomials over x and u. For example, the system dynamics function in Example 1 is piecewise linear with $k = 2$.

Input. Our verification and control algorithms take as input an SDS S whose system dynamics function is piecewise polynomial, an LDBA $\mathcal{A}$ for an ω-regular specification φ defined over a set of polynomial atomic prepositions P, and a minimum probability threshold $p \in [0, 1]$ with which the ω-regular specification φ should be satisfied. The verification algorithm also takes as input the polynomial controller π.

In addition, the algorithms take as input two parameters: (1) the polynomial degree d of polynomial templates used in the synthesis of the LDBSM certificate and the controller, and (2) the number of polynomial inequalities n_I used to define the supporting invariant. These two parameters are formally defined in Step 1 below.

The verification algorithm may accept polynomial supporting invariants as inputs, and if an invariant I is provided, then the algorithm only computes V^{safe} and V^{live} for the fixed I. For the control algorithm, the invariant depends on the controller, and is therefore always synthesized as a part of the certificate. For the uniformity of presentation, we will assume that the verification algorithm is not provided an input invariant.

Output. Both the verification and the control algorithms return as output the LDBSM certificate $V = (V^{\text{safe}}, V^{\text{live}}, I)$, as defined in Definition 1. The control algorithm also returns the SDS controller π computed by the algorithm. If the algorithms fail due to, e.g., the SMT solver timing out or returning "UNSAT," they return "Unknown."

Algorithm Outline. Our algorithms employ the classical *template-based synthesis* approach to synthesize an LDBSM certificate $V = (V^{\text{safe}}, V^{\text{live}}, I)$ (and also the controller π for the control problem). This automation approach is similar to those employed in prior works on algorithmic synthesis of supermartingales for analyzing stochastic systems and programs with respect to reachability or safety properties [14, 16, 21, 58].

In Step 1, both the verification and the control algorithms fix symbolic polynomial templates with *unknown coefficients* for all objects that they need to compute. Namely, the verification algorithm fixes templates for the LDBSM certificate $V = (V^{\text{safe}}, V^{\text{live}}, I)$, while the control algorithm also fixes a template for the controller π. The templates for V^{safe}, V^{live}, and π are polynomial *expressions*, whereas the template for I is a conjunction of n_I polynomial inequalities of the form "$P_I^j(x, q) \geq 0$," with each P_I^j being a polynomial expression. In Step 2, the algorithms encode all certificate conditions in Definition 1 as a system of quantified polynomial entailments over the unknown template coefficients. In Step 3, the resulting system of quantified polynomial entailments is solved by employing existing algorithms and efficient tooling support provided by the POLYQENT tool [19], which reduces the problem to solving a purely existentially quantified system of polynomial constraints for which an off-the-shelf SMT solver is used. In the rest of this section, we provide a more detailed description of these steps.

Step 1: Setting Up Templates. The algorithms fix symbolic polynomial templates for all objects that they need to compute:

- *LDBSM certificate.* Suppose $x_1, \ldots, x_n$ represent the state variables for the n dimensions. For each LDBA state $q \in Q$, we set up the polynomial templates for $V^{\text{safe}}(\cdot, q)$ and $V^{\text{live}}(\cdot, q)$, as well as for polynomial expressions $P_I^1(\cdot, q), \ldots, P_I^{n_I}(\cdot, q)$ over the state variables, each of polynomial degree d and with unknown coefficients whose values are to be found out in the subsequent steps of the algorithm. Here, the polynomial degree d and the number n_I of polynomial inequalities that define the invariant I are algorithm parameters. For example, if $n = 2$, $d = 2$, and $n_I = 1$, then
$V^{\text{safe}}(x_1, x_2, q) = \theta_{11}^{q,\text{safe}} x_1^2 + \theta_{22}^{q,\text{safe}} x_2^2 + \theta_{12}^{q,\text{safe}} x_1 x_2 + \theta_1^{q,\text{safe}} x_1 + \theta_2^{q,\text{safe}} x_2 + \theta_0^{q,\text{safe}}$,
$V^{\text{live}}(x_1, x_2, q) = \theta_{11}^{q,\text{live}} x_1^2 + \theta_{22}^{q,\text{live}} x_2^2 + \theta_{12}^{q,\text{live}} x_1 x_2 + \theta_1^{q,\text{live}} x_1 + \theta_2^{q,\text{live}} x_2 + \theta_0^{q,\text{live}}$,
and $(x_1, x_2, q) \in I$ is expressed as $P_I^1(x, q) \geq 0$ where $P_I^1(x, q) = \theta_{11}^{q,I} x_1^2 + \theta_{22}^{q,I} x_2^2 + \theta_{12}^{q,I} x_1 x_2 + \theta_1^{q,I} x_1 + \theta_2^{q,I} x_2 + \theta_0^{q,I} \geq 0$.
- *Certificate parameters.* The algorithm introduces variables $\underline{\eta}^S$, $\underline{\epsilon}^S$, $\underline{M}^S$, β^S, $\underline{\epsilon}^L$, $\underline{M}^L$, whose values will represent the constant parameters $\eta^S \leq 0$, $\epsilon^S, M^S, \epsilon^L, M^L > 0$, and $\beta^S \in \mathbb{R}$ from Definition 1.
- *Controller (for the control algorithm).* For every LDBA state $q \in Q$, we set up a polynomial controller $\pi(\cdot, q)$ over the state variables with degree d and with unknown coefficients. For example, if $n = 2$ and $d = 2$, then $\pi(x_1, x_2, q) = \lambda_{11}^q x_1^2 + \lambda_{22}^q x_2^2 + \lambda_{12}^q x_1 x_2 + \lambda_1^q x_1 + \lambda_2^q x_2 + \lambda_0^q$, where $\lambda.$-s are the unknown coefficients.

We will use Ω to denote the set of all unknown coefficients (i.e., $\theta_{11}^{q,\text{safe}}, \theta_{11}^{q,\text{live}}, \theta_{11}^{q,I}, \ldots$) in the polynomial templates for V^{safe}, V^{live}, I, and π, and the variables (i.e., $\underline{\epsilon}^S$, β^S, $\ldots$). For a given set of unknowns such as Ω, we will write $[\![\Omega]\!]$ to denote the set of all possible valuations of the unknowns in Ω.

Step 2: Constraint Collection. The goal of this step is to symbolically evaluate the conditions in Definition 1, and rearrange them in a way that we finally obtain a system of polynomial inequality predicates in the prenex normal form

$$\exists \omega \in [\![\Omega]\!] \ . \ \underbrace{\bigwedge_i (\forall q \in Q \ . \ \forall x \in \mathbb{R}^n \ . \forall w \in \mathbb{R}^p \ . \ \Phi_i^\omega(q,x,w) \implies \Psi_i^\omega(q,x,w))}_{R_i}, \quad (6)$$

where Φ_i^ω and Ψ_i^ω are boolean combinations of polynomial inequalities over the variables q, x, and w and unknown coefficients whose values conform with ω. First, observe that the constraints (a)-(d) of Definition 1 generate constraints that are trivially of the form R_i. We explain the derivation for constraint ((e)), the procedure for ((f)) is analogous:

(A) **Prenex normal form:** First, we need to take out the two quantifications "$\forall w \in \mathcal{W}$" from within "$SafetyCond(x,q,q')$." We show the process for the clause "$\forall w \in \mathcal{W}. \beta^S \leq V^{\text{safe}}(x,q) - V^{\text{safe}}(f(x,\pi(x),w),q') \leq \beta^S + M^S$," call it γ_1, and for "$\forall w \in \mathcal{W}. (f(x,\pi(x),w),q') \in I$," call it γ_2, the procedure is identical. There are two possibilities:

  (i) Suppose the safety component of the LDBSM certificate V^{safe} and q''s invariant polynomials $\{P_I^i(\cdot,q')\}_{i \in [1;n_I]}$ are linear, i.e., $d = 1$, the disturbance in the system is additive, i.e., $\forall x, u, w \ . \ f(x,u,w) = g(x,u) + w$ for some function g, and the domain $\mathcal{W}$ of the disturbance is bounded within a given range $[w_{\min}, w_{\max}]$. Then, for γ_1, we can altogether suppress "$\forall w \in \mathcal{W}$" and replace $SafetyCond(x,q,a,q')$ with

$$\begin{pmatrix} x \models a \wedge \forall w \in \mathcal{W}. (f(x,\pi(x),w),q') \in I \\ \wedge V^{\text{safe}}(x,q) \geq \mathbb{E}_w^\pi[V^{\text{safe}}(f(x,\pi(x),w),q')] + \epsilon^S \\ \wedge \left(\beta^S \leq V^{\text{safe}}(x,q) - V^{\text{safe}}(g(x,\pi(x)),q') - V^{\text{safe}}(w_{\min},q') \leq \beta^S + M^S\right) \\ \wedge \left(\beta^S \leq V^{\text{safe}}(x,q) - V^{\text{safe}}(g(x,\pi(x)),q') - V^{\text{safe}}(w_{\max},q') \leq \beta^S + M^S\right) \end{pmatrix}.$$

  This transformation is sound since for every $w \in \mathcal{W}$, by the additivity of the noise and by the linearity of V^{safe}, we have $V^{\text{safe}}(f(x,u,w)) = V^{\text{safe}}(g(x,u)+w) = V^{\text{safe}}(g(x,u)) + V^{\text{safe}}(w)$, which is bounded between $V^{\text{safe}}(g(x,u)) + V^{\text{safe}}(w_{\min})$ and $V^{\text{safe}}(g(x,u)) + V^{\text{safe}}(w_{\max})$ from the boundedness of the noise and the linearity of V^{safe}. We can use the same idea for the clause γ_2.

  (ii) In general, the above restrictions could be insufficient, in which case we resort to the following stricter requirement at the expense of added incompleteness of the solution. The idea is that, instead of allowing w to depend on the choice of $a \in \Sigma$ and $q' \in \Delta(q,a)$, for γ_1, we require the following the hold true:

$$\forall a \in \Sigma \ . \ \forall q' \in \Delta(q,a) \ . \ \forall w \in \mathcal{W} \ .$$
$$\left(\beta^S \leq V^{\text{safe}}(x,q) - V^{\text{safe}}(f(x,\pi(x),w),q') \leq \beta^S + M^S\right).$$

  Let the expression above be written as $D(x,q)$ in short, and it is easy to see that $D(x,q)$ can be expressed in the desired form (6). We can now write the constraint ((e)) of Definition 1 as:

$$D(x, q) \wedge$$

$$\forall x \in \mathbb{R}^n. V^{\text{safe}}(x, q) \leq 0 \implies \bigvee_{a \in \Sigma} \bigvee_{q' \in \Delta(q, a)}$$

$$\left(\begin{array}{c} x \models a \wedge \forall w \in \mathcal{W}. (f(x, \pi(x), w), q') \in I \\ \wedge V^{\text{safe}}(x, q) \geq \mathbb{E}_w^\pi [V^{\text{safe}}(f(x, \pi(x), w), q')] + \epsilon^S \\ \wedge V^{\text{live}}(x, q) \geq \mathbb{E}_w^\pi [V^{\text{live}}(f(x, \pi(x), w), q')] + \epsilon^L \end{array} \right)$$

The same idea will work for γ_2.

(B) **Simplifications.** After moving the quantification "$\forall w \in \mathcal{W}$" from the inside of "$SafetyCond(x, q, a, q')$" to the outermost part of 2(b) and 2(c), we substitute all the variables and functions with the templates that we set up in Step 1. For the expected value $\mathbb{E}_w^\pi [V^{\text{safe}}(f(x, \pi(x), w), q')]$, we use the linearity of the expectation operator to break it down into a polynomial over x whose coefficients are functions of the moments of the distribution over w (assumed to be given as input). For instance, since $V^{\text{safe}}(x, q)$ is a polynomial over x, and $f(x, \pi(x), w) = C_2(x)w^2 + C_1(x)w + C_0(x)$ where C_2, C_1, C_0 are polynomials over x, it follows that $V^{\text{safe}}(f(x, \pi(x), w), q) = \hat{C}_2(x)w^2 + \hat{C}_1(x)w + \hat{C}_0(x)$ where $\hat{C}_2, \hat{C}_1, \hat{C}_0$ are polynomials over x. This gives us: $\mathbb{E}_w^\pi [V^{\text{safe}}(f(x, \pi(x), w), q)] = \hat{C}_2(x) \cdot \mathbb{E}_w^\pi [w^2] + \hat{C}_1(x) \cdot \mathbb{E}_w^\pi [w] + \hat{C}_0(x)$, where $\mathbb{E}_w^\pi [w^i]$ is the i-th moment of the distribution (therefore, a constant) of the noise.

Step 3: Constraint Solving. Finally, the system of quantified polynomial entailments collected in Step 2 is solved. This is achieved by first employing Putinar's theorem [53] (or Farkas' lemma [28], if all involved polynomials have degree 1) to translate each quantified polynomial entailment into a system of purely existentially quantified polynomial constraints over the unknown template variables, as well as fresh variables introduced by the Putinar's theorem translation. Since this step is standard in the template-based synthesis literature, including that on the synthesis of supermartingale ceritificates [14,16,21,58], we omit the details. The resulting system of purely existentially quantified polynomial constraints over real-valued variables is then solved by using an SMT solver. In our implementation, the application of Putinar's theorem and reduction to SMT solving are achieved via the PolyQEnt tool [19]. See [19] for details, including on how boolean combinations of polynomial inequalities are handled prior to applying Putinar's theorem. It is straightforward to note that if the encoding (6) is satisfiable, then we obtain an LDBSM certificate, and in case of control problem, we also get a controller. Then from the soundness of the PolyQEnt tool [19] that we use to solve (6), Theorem 2 follows.

Theorem 2 (Algorithm soundness). *Suppose that the verification algorithm returns an LDBSM certificate $V = (V^{\text{safe}}, V^{\text{live}}, I)$. Then, V is an LDBSM certificate with respect to the invariant I as in Definition 1, and the SDS $\mathcal{S}$ under controller π satisfies specification φ with probability at least p.*

Suppose that the control algorithm returns an LDBSM certificate $V = (V^{\text{safe}}, V^{\text{live}}, I)$ and an SDS controller π. Then, V is an LDBSM certificate with respect to the invariant I as in Definition 1, and the SDS S under controller π satisfies specification φ with probability at least p. Similar to existing template-based synthesis methods for polynomial program verification and controller synthesis [5, 14], the runtime complexity of our vertification and control algorithms is in PSPACE when the polynomial degree d is treated as a constant parameter. This is because the size of the final SMT query produced by our method is $\mathcal{O}(n_I * |Q| * n^d)$. As the final SMT query is a sentence in the existential theory of the reals, the parameterized PSPACE runtime complexity follows.

5   Experiments

We implemented our algorithm as a proof-of-concept tool in Python, where our tool automatically translates the given inputs to quantified polynomial entailments by using the procedure outlined in Sect. 4, and then uses the tool POLYQENT [19] as its back end to compute solutions. POLYQENT uses Putinar's theorem [53] (or Farkas' lemma [28] for linear systems and certificate and controller templates) and translates the provided entailments into existentially quantified polynomial constraints over unknown template variables, and uses off-the-shelf SMT solvers Z3 [25] and MathSAT [10] to find satisfying assignments of the variables. Our prototype tool is availabe at https://github.com/Ipouyall/Omega-Regular-Stoch-Cert.

We used our tool to automatically compute LDBSM certificates for the verification of the random walk SDS S^{rw} from Example 1, and for the control of a modified version of S^{rw} defined as follows. The system S^{rw}_c has the state space $\mathbb{R}$, input space $\mathcal{U} = [-2, 2]$, disturbance space $\mathcal{W} = [0, 1]$ with a continuous uniform distribution over $\mathcal{W}$, system dynamics given as

$$f_c(x, u, w) = \begin{cases} x & \text{if } x > 100, \\ x + u + w & \text{otherwise,} \end{cases} \tag{7}$$

and the set of initial states $[2, 3]$. Both the verification and the control example were solved with a number of different specifications as listed in Table 1. For each specification, the general requirement is to push the state towards the origin (eventually for $F\,a$, always eventually for $GF\,a$, etc.). For the verification problems, the disturbances in $W = [-2, 1]$ create an automatic bias towards the origin, which ultimately helps satisfying the specifications. For the control problems, the disturbances in $W = [0, 1]$ create a challenge by introducing bias *away* from the origin, so the controller needs to counteract with negative control inputs at each step.

All the experiments were performed on an Apple Macbook Air with M2 chip and 16 GB RAM, and we report the results in Table 1. In both the verification and control problems, the SDS's have small probabilities of violating the objectives, by reaching the region $x > 100$ and not being able to come out afterwards.

Therefore, existing approaches supporting only qualitative (almost sure satisfaction) ω-regular specifications would not work, and no single supermartingale-based approach for quantitative specifications would support all the specifications at once. In contrast, our tool achieved 99% probability for satisfying the specifications, and computed LDBSM certificates (and controllersfor the control problem) within minutes.

Table 1. Experimental results for verification and control of the random walk examples. The predicates are: $a := x \leq 0$ and $b := x \leq 100$. Each experiment was run with polynomial degree $d = 1$.

	Specification	Probability	Time (s)
Verification (SDS $\mathcal{S}^{\mathrm{rw}}$)	F a	0.9999	0.35
	GF a	0.9999	27.28
	bU a	0.9999	6.13
	G$b \wedge$ Fa	0.9999	27.78
	Gb	0.9999	28.60
	F$a \wedge$ Fb	0.9999	172.28
Control (SDS $\mathcal{S}_c^{\mathrm{rw}}$)	F a	0.9999	0.39
	GF a	0.9999	4.90
	bU a	0.9999	18.90
	G$b \wedge$ Fa	0.9999	46.68
	Gb	0.9999	4.04

6 Related Work

Earliest known types of certificates in control theory date back to mid-twentieth century, and were developed for certifying stability [34,36] and invariance [44] of dynamical systems. However, back then, obtaining suitable certificates for general nonlinear systems was largely a manual process. It was in early 2000s, when the seminal work of Parrilo [50] first proposed the use of Positivstellensätze to automate the process of certificate computation, which were later strengthened and refined [49,56].

In parallel to control theory, from early 2000s, program analysis also experienced an emergence of certificate-based approaches for proving termination of deterministic programs [22,23]. In the landmark paper by Chakarov and Sankarnarayanan [11], ranking functions for deterministic programs were generalized to ranking supermartinagles for probabilistic programs. This has sparked interest in using supermartingale certificates for the analysis of probabilistic programs, with signifiant advances in supermartingale certificates and automated algorithms for termination [2,14,15,20,39,43], safety [12,16,21,58,59], Büchi and co-Büchi (stability) [13], and cost analysis [17,47,60]. These results were also exported to control theory to solve the verification and control problem for stochastic dynamical systems with logical specifications [51,63,66].

A majority of existing supermartingale certificates for stochastic systems only support fragments of ω-regular specifications. Only recently, Abate et al. [3] proposed a new class of supermartingale certificates for ω-regular specifications represented using Streett automata. However, their certificate is restricted to the probability 1 satisfaction of the specification, contrary to our quantitative certificate that allows arbitrary probability thresholds to be imposed as a requirement for satisfying the specification. It is important to note that our certificate is incomplete, like most other existing supermartingale certificates that are available in the literature, see Remark 1.

It is important to mention that there are also other non-certificate-based approaches to verification and control of stochastic systems. For example, there is a long line of research that falls under the abstraction-based control paradigm, where a given system model is abstracted to a simpler graph, so that graph theoretic techniques can be applied to approximately solve the original verification and control problem [26,27,38,40,64]. Among these works, only one is known to be able to support quantitative ω-regular specifications [26], though their functionalities are complementary to ours: They support general nonlinear systems but only having additive control input and additive stochastic noise with unimodal, symmetric distribution. We support polynomial systems and controllers and stochastic noise that can have arbitrary distributions.

7   Discussions

We present LDBSM certificates, the first supermartingale-based certificates for quantiative ω-regular verification and control of infinite-state stochastic systems. LDBSM certificates are defined on the product of the system and the equivalent LDBA representation of the given ω-regular specification, and they generalize and combine existing safety and liveness supermartingale certificates in a hierarchical manner to achieve soundness. We supplement the theoretical development with a standard template-based synthesis algorithm for solving the verification and control problems in polynomial stochastic systems.

There are several interesting future directions. First, we will explore alternate methods for computing LDBSM certificates, including learning-assisted approaches [18,66], alongside optimizing our template-based approach that relies on off-the-shelf constraint solvers. Even the state-of-the-art constraint solvers struggled to compute LDBSM certificates, and eliminating this tooling bottleneck will be a priority in future works. Second, in the same vein as the previous one, we will explore compositional approaches for LDBSM certificates for better scalability; such approaches are well-studied for existing classes of certificates [45,67]. Finally, we will explore completeness questions. Right now, LDBSM certificates provide sound but incomplete solutions: if they exist, then it follows that the specification holds, but not the other way round.

Acknowledgments. This work was supported in part by the Singapore Ministry of Education (MOE) Academic Research Fund (AcRF) Tier 1 grant (Project ID:22-SIS-SMU-100) and the ERC project ERC-2020-AdG 101020093.

Disclosure of Interests. The authors have no competing interests to declare that are relevant to the content of this article.

References

1. Abate, A., Edwards, A., Giacobbe, M., Punchihewa, H., Roy, D.: Quantitative verification with neural networks. In: CONCUR. LIPIcs, vol. 279, pp. 22:1–22:18. Schloss Dagstuhl - Leibniz-Zentrum für Informatik (2023)
2. Abate, A., Giacobbe, M., Roy, D.: Learning probabilistic termination proofs. In: Silva, A., Leino, K. (eds.) CAV 2021. LNCS, vol. 12760, pp. 3–26. Springer, Cham (2021). https://doi.org/10.1007/978-3-030-81688-9_1
3. Abate, A., Giacobbe, M., Roy, D.: Stochastic omega-regular verification and control with supermartingales. In: International Conference on Computer Aided Verification, pp. 395–419. Springer, Heidelberg (2024). https://doi.org/10.1007/978-3-031-65633-0_18
4. Ansaripour, M., Chatterjee, K., Henzinger, T.A., Lechner, M., Žikelić, Ð.: Learning provably stabilizing neural controllers for discrete-time stochastic systems. In: International Symposium on Automated Technology for Verification and Analysis, pp. 357–379. Springer, Heidelberg (2023). https://doi.org/10.1007/978-3-031-45329-8_17
5. Asadi, A., Chatterjee, K., Fu, H., Goharshady, A.K., Mahdavi, M.: Polynomial reachability witnesses via stellensätze. In: PLDI, pp. 772–787. ACM (2021)
6. Åström, K.J.: Introduction to Stochastic Control Theory. Courier Corporation, Chelmsford (2012)
7. Baier, C., Katoen, J.P.: Principles of Model Checking. MIT press, Cambridge (2008)
8. Barthe, G., Gaboardi, M., Grégoire, B., Hsu, J., Strub, P.: Proving differential privacy via probabilistic couplings. In: Grohe, M., Koskinen, E., Shankar, N. (eds.) Proceedings of the 31st Annual ACM/IEEE Symposium on Logic in Computer Science, LICS '16, New York, NY, USA, 5–8 July 2016, pp. 749–758. ACM (2016). https://doi.org/10.1145/2933575.2934554
9. Beutner, R., Ong, C.L., Zaiser, F.: Guaranteed bounds for posterior inference in universal probabilistic programming. In: PLDI, pp. 536–551. ACM (2022)
10. Bruttomesso, R., Cimatti, A., Franzén, A., Griggio, A., Sebastiani, R.: The mathsat 4 smt solver: Tool paper. In: Computer Aided Verification: 20th International Conference, CAV 2008 Princeton, NJ, USA, 7–14 July 2008 Proceedings 20, pp. 299–303. Springer, Heidelberg (2008). https://doi.org/10.1007/978-3-540-70545-1_28
11. Chakarov, A., Sankaranarayanan, S.: Probabilistic program analysis with martingales. In: Sharygina, N., Veith, H. (eds.) CAV 2013. LNCS, vol. 8044, pp. 511–526. Springer, Heidelberg (2013). https://doi.org/10.1007/978-3-642-39799-8_34
12. Chakarov, A., Sankaranarayanan, S.: Expectation Invariants for Probabilistic Program Loops as Fixed Points, pp. 85–100. Springer, Heidelberg (2014). https://doi.org/10.1007/978-3-319-10936-7_6

13. Chakarov, A., Voronin, Y.-L., Sankaranarayanan, S.: Deductive proofs of almost sure persistence and recurrence properties. In: Chechik, M., Raskin, J.-F. (eds.) TACAS 2016. LNCS, vol. 9636, pp. 260–279. Springer, Heidelberg (2016). https://doi.org/10.1007/978-3-662-49674-9_15

14. Chatterjee, K., Fu, H., Goharshady, A.K.: Termination analysis of probabilistic programs through positivstellensatz's. In: Chaudhuri, S., Farzan, A. (eds.) CAV 2016. LNCS, vol. 9779, pp. 3–22. Springer, Cham (2016). https://doi.org/10.1007/978-3-319-41528-4_1

15. Chatterjee, K., Fu, H., Novotný, P., Hasheminezhad, R.: Algorithmic analysis of qualitative and quantitative termination problems for affine probabilistic programs. TOPLAS **40**(2), 7:1–7:45 (2018). https://doi.org/10.1145/3174800

16. Chatterjee, K., Goharshady, A.K., Meggendorfer, T., Žikelić, Ð.: Sound and complete certificates for quantitative termination analysis of probabilistic programs. In: International Conference on Computer Aided Verification, pp. 55–78. Springer, Heidelberg (2022). https://doi.org/10.1007/978-3-031-13185-1_4

17. Chatterjee, K., Goharshady, A.K., Meggendorfer, T., Žikelić, Ð: Quantitative bounds on resource usage of probabilistic programs. Proc. ACM Program. Lang. **8**(OOPSLA1), 362–391 (2024)

18. Chatterjee, K., Henzinger, T.A., Lechner, M., Žikelić, Ð.: A learner-verifier framework for neural network controllers and certificates of stochastic systems. In: International Conference on Tools and Algorithms for the Construction and Analysis of Systems, pp. 3–25. Springer, Heidelberg (2023). https://doi.org/10.1007/978-3-031-30823-9_1

19. Chatterjee, K., et al.: Polyqent: a polynomial quantified entailment solver. arXiv e-prints pp. arXiv–2408 (2024)

20. Chatterjee, K., Kafshdar Goharshady, E., Novotnỳ, P., Zárevúcky, J., Žikelić, Ð: On lexicographic proof rules for probabilistic termination. Formal Aspects Comput. **35**(2), 1–25 (2023)

21. Chatterjee, K., Novotný, P., Zikelic, D.: Stochastic invariants for probabilistic termination. In: Castagna, G., Gordon, A.D. (eds.) Proceedings of the 44th ACM SIGPLAN Symposium on Principles of Programming Languages, POPL 2017, Paris, France, 18–20 January 2017, pp. 145–160. ACM (2017). https://doi.org/10.1145/3009837.3009873

22. Colón, M.A., Sipma, H.B.: Practical methods for proving program termination. In: Brinksma, E., Larsen, K.G. (eds.) CAV 2002. LNCS, vol. 2404, pp. 442–454. Springer, Heidelberg (2002). https://doi.org/10.1007/3-540-45657-0_36

23. Colóon, M.A., Sipma, H.B.: Synthesis of linear ranking functions. In: Margaria, T., Yi, W. (eds.) TACAS 2001. LNCS, vol. 2031, pp. 67–81. Springer, Heidelberg (2001). https://doi.org/10.1007/3-540-45319-9_6

24. Courcoubetis, C., Yannakakis, M.: The complexity of probabilistic verification. J. ACM **42**(4), 857–907 (1995)

25. de Moura, L., Bjørner, N.: Z3: an efficient SMT solver. In: Ramakrishnan, C.R., Rehof, J. (eds.) TACAS 2008. LNCS, vol. 4963, pp. 337–340. Springer, Heidelberg (2008). https://doi.org/10.1007/978-3-540-78800-3_24

26. Dutreix, M., Huh, J., Coogan, S.: Abstraction-based synthesis for stochastic systems with omega-regular objectives. Nonlinear Anal. Hybrid Syst **45**, 101204 (2022)

27. Esmaeil Zadeh Soudjani, S., Abate, A.: Adaptive and sequential gridding procedures for the abstraction and verification of stochastic processes. SIAM J. Appl. Dyn. Syst. **12**(2), 921–956 (2013)

28. Farkas, J.: Theorie der einfachen ungleichungen. Journal für die reine und angewandte Mathematik (Crelles J.) **1902**(124), 1–27 (1902)
29. Florchinger, P.: Lyapunov-like techniques for stochastic stability. SIAM J. Control. Optim. **33**(4), 1151–1169 (1995)
30. Foster, N., Kozen, D., Mamouras, K., Reitblatt, M., Silva, A.: Probabilistic NetKAT. In: Thiemann, P. (ed.) ESOP 2016. LNCS, vol. 9632, pp. 282–309. Springer, Heidelberg (2016). https://doi.org/10.1007/978-3-662-49498-1_12
31. Fu, H., Chatterjee, K.: Termination of nondeterministic probabilistic programs. In: Enea, C., Piskac, R. (eds.) VMCAI 2019. LNCS, vol. 11388, pp. 468–490. Springer, Cham (2019). https://doi.org/10.1007/978-3-030-11245-5_22
32. Gehr, T., Misailovic, S., Vechev, M.T.: PSI: exact symbolic inference for probabilistic programs. In: CAV (2016)
33. Ghahramani, Z.: Probabilistic machine learning and artificial intelligence. Nature **521**(7553), 452–459 (2015). https://doi.org/10.1038/nature14541
34. Kalman, R.E., Bertram, J.E.: Control system analysis and design via the "second method" of lyapunov: I—continuous-time systems (1960)
35. Kaminski, B.L., Katoen, J., Matheja, C., Olmedo, F.: Weakest precondition reasoning for expected runtimes of randomized algorithms. J. ACM **65**(5), 30:1–30:68 (2018). https://doi.org/10.1145/3208102
36. LaSalle, J., Lefschetz, S.: Stability by Lyapunov's Second Method with Applications. Academic Press, New York (1961)
37. Lechner, M., Žikelić, Đ., Chatterjee, K., Henzinger, T.A.: Stability verification in stochastic control systems via neural network supermartingales. In: Proceedings of the AAAI Conference on Artificial Intelligence, vol. 36, pp. 7326–7336 (2022)
38. Majumdar, R., Mallik, K., Schmuck, A.K., Soudjani, S.: Symbolic control for stochastic systems via finite parity games. Nonlinear Anal. Hybrid Syst **51**, 101430 (2024)
39. Majumdar, R., Sathiyanarayana, V.: Sound and complete proof rules for probabilistic termination. Proc. ACM Program. Lang. **9**(POPL), 1871–1902 (2025)
40. Mallik, K., Soudjani, S.E.Z., Schmuck, A.K., Majumdar, R.: Compositional construction of finite state abstractions for stochastic control systems. In: 2017 IEEE 56th Annual Conference on Decision and Control (CDC), pp. 550–557. IEEE (2017)
41. Mathiesen, F.B., Calvert, S.C., Laurenti, L.: Safety certification for stochastic systems via neural barrier functions. IEEE Control Syst. Lett. **7**, 973–978 (2022)
42. McIver, A., Morgan, C.: Abstraction, Refinement and Proof for Probabilistic Systems. Monographs in Computer Science. Springer, Heidelberg (2005)
43. McIver, A., Morgan, C., Kaminski, B.L., Katoen, J.P.: A new proof rule for almost-sure termination. Proc. ACM Program. Lang. **2**(POPL), 1–28 (2017)
44. Nagumo, M.: Über die lage der integralkurven gewöhnlicher differentialgleichungen. Proc. Physico-Math. Soc. Jpn. 3rd Series **24**, 551–559 (1942)
45. Nejati, A., Soudjani, S., Zamani, M.: Compositional construction of control barrier functions for continuous-time stochastic hybrid systems. Automatica **145**, 110513 (2022)
46. Neustroev, G., Giacobbe, M., Lukina, A.: Neural continuous-time supermartingale certificates. In: AAAI, pp. 27538–27546. AAAI Press (2025)
47. Ngo, V.C., Carbonneaux, Q., Hoffmann, J.: Bounded expectations: resource analysis for probabilistic programs. ACM SIGPLAN Not. **53**(4), 496–512 (2018)
48. Olmedo, F., Kaminski, B.L., Katoen, J.P., Matheja, C.: Reasoning about recursive probabilistic programs. In: LICS, pp. 672–681 (2016). https://doi.org/10.1145/2933575.2935317

49. Papachristodoulou, A., Prajna, S.: A tutorial on sum of squares techniques for systems analysis. In: Proceedings of the 2005, American Control Conference, 2005, pp. 2686–2700. IEEE (2005)
50. Parrilo, P.A.: Structured semidefinite programs and semialgebraic geometry methods in robustness and optimization. California Institute of Technology (2000)
51. Prajna, S., Jadbabaie, A., Pappas, G.J.: Stochastic safety verification using barrier certificates. In: 2004 43rd IEEE Conference on Decision and Control (CDC)(IEEE Cat. No. 04CH37601), vol. 1, pp. 929–934. IEEE (2004)
52. Puterman, M.L.: Markov Decision Processes: Discrete Stochastic Dynamic Programming. Wiley Series in Probability and Statistics. Wiley, Hoboken (1994). https://doi.org/10.1002/9780470316887
53. Putinar, M.: Positive polynomials on compact semi-algebraic sets. Indiana Univ. Math. J. **42**(3), 969–984 (1993)
54. Sankaranarayanan, S., Chakarov, A., Gulwani, S.: Static analysis for probabilistic programs: inferring whole program properties from finitely many paths. In: Boehm, H., Flanagan, C. (eds.) ACM SIGPLAN Conference on Programming Language Design and Implementation, PLDI '13, Seattle, WA, USA, 16–19 June 2013, pp. 447–458. ACM (2013). https://doi.org/10.1145/2491956.2462179
55. Segala, R.: Verification of randomized distributed algorithms. In: Brinksma, E., Hermanns, H., Katoen, J.-P. (eds.) EEF School 2000. LNCS, vol. 2090, pp. 232–260. Springer, Heidelberg (2001). https://doi.org/10.1007/3-540-44667-2_6
56. Sloth, C.: On the computation of lyapunov functions for interconnected systems. In: 2016 IEEE Conference on Computer Aided Control System Design (CACSD), pp. 850–855. IEEE (2016)
57. Steinhardt, J., Tedrake, R.: Finite-time regional verification of stochastic non-linear systems. Int. J. Rob. Res. **31**(7), 901–923 (2012)
58. Takisaka, T., Oyabu, Y., Urabe, N., Hasuo, I.: Ranking and repulsing supermartingales for reachability in randomized programs. ACM Trans. Program. Lang. Syst. (TOPLAS) **43**(2), 1–46 (2021)
59. Wang, J., Sun, Y., Fu, H., Chatterjee, K., Goharshady, A.K.: Quantitative analysis of assertion violations in probabilistic programs. In: Freund, S.N., Yahav, E. (eds.) PLDI '21: 42nd ACM SIGPLAN International Conference on Programming Language Design and Implementation, Virtual Event, Canada, 20–25 June 2021, pp. 1171–1186. ACM (2021). https://doi.org/10.1145/3453483.3454102
60. Wang, P., Fu, H., Goharshady, A.K., Chatterjee, K., Qin, X., Shi, W.: Cost analysis of nondeterministic probabilistic programs. In: McKinley, K.S., Fisher, K. (eds.) Proceedings of the 40th ACM SIGPLAN Conference on Programming Language Design and Implementation, PLDI 2019, Phoenix, AZ, USA, 22–26 June 2019, pp. 204–220. ACM (2019). https://doi.org/10.1145/3314221.3314581
61. Wang, P., Yang, T., Fu, H., Li, G., Ong, C.L.: Static posterior inference of bayesian probabilistic programming via polynomial solving. Proc. ACM Program. Lang. **8**(PLDI), 1361–1386 (2024)
62. Williams, D.: Probability with Martingales. Cambridge mathematical textbooks, Cambridge University Press, Cambridge (1991)
63. Xue, B., Zhan, N., Fränzle, M.: Reach-avoid analysis for polynomial stochastic differential equations. IEEE Trans. Autom. Control (2023)
64. Zamani, M., Esfahani, P.M., Majumdar, R., Abate, A., Lygeros, J.: Symbolic control of stochastic systems via approximately bisimilar finite abstractions. IEEE Trans. Autom. Control **59**(12), 3135–3150 (2014)

65. Zhi, D., Wang, P., Liu, S., Ong, C.L., Zhang, M.: Unifying qualitative and quantitative safety verification of dnn-controlled systems. In: CAV (2). Lecture Notes in Computer Science, vol. 14682, pp. 401–426. Springer, Heidelberg (2024). https://doi.org/10.1007/978-3-031-65630-9_20
66. Žikelić, Đ., Lechner, M., Henzinger, T.A., Chatterjee, K.: Learning control policies for stochastic systems with reach-avoid guarantees. In: Proceedings of the AAAI Conference on Artificial Intelligence, vol. 37, pp. 11926–11935 (2023)
67. Žikelić, Đ., Lechner, M., Verma, A., Chatterjee, K., Henzinger, T.: Compositional policy learning in stochastic control systems with formal guarantees. Adv. Neural Inf. Process. Syst. **36** (2024)

Approximate Probabilistic Bisimulation for Continuous-Time Markov Chains

Timm Spork[1]([✉]) [iD], Christel Baier[1] [iD], Joost-Pieter Katoen[2] [iD],
Sascha Klüppelholz[1] [iD], and Jakob Piribauer[1,3] [iD]

[1] Technische Universität Dresden, Dresden, Germany
{timm.spork,christel.baier,sascha.klueppelholz,
jakob.piribauer}@tu-dresden.de
[2] RWTH Aachen University, Aachen, Germany
katoen@cs.rwth-aachen.de
[3] Universität Leipzig, Leipzig, Germany

Abstract. We introduce (ε, δ)-bisimulation, a novel type of approximate probabilistic bisimulation for continuous-time Markov chains. In contrast to related notions, (ε, δ)-bisimulation allows the use of different tolerances for the transition probabilities (ε, additive) and total exit rates (δ, multiplicative) of states. Fundamental properties of the notion, as well as bounds on the absolute difference of time- and reward-bounded reachability probabilities for (ε, δ)-bisimilar states, are established.

Keywords: Continuous-Time Markov Chains · Approximate
Probabilistic Bisimulation · Quasi-Lumpability · Time-Bounded
Reachability

1 Introduction

Continuous-time Markov chains (CTMCs) are a prominent probabilistic model in various application fields, e.g., reliability engineering, systems biology, modeling of chemical reactions, and performance evaluation. CTMCs are state-based models whose transitions yield a discrete probability distribution over states—as in discrete-time Markov chains (DTMCs)—while the state residence times are governed by exponential distributions. Various model-checking approaches for CTMCs exist [7,11,22,64] and are supported by tools such as PRISM [40] and Storm [34]. CTMC model checking is used to analyze, e.g., stochastic Petri nets [6], fault trees [8,62], biological systems [41,46], and chemical reactions [2,4].

The central issue in CTMC model checking is computing timed reachability probabilities: what is the probability to reach a set of goal states within a given deadline from a given start state? The reliability of a fault tree, or the probability that all molecules have been catalyzed within two days, are instances of this question. Computing timed reachability probabilities reduces to computing transient probabilities in a uniformized CTMC, i.e., a CTMC in which the state

R. Piskac and Z. Rakamarić (Eds.): CAV 2025, LNCS 15932, pp. 56–81, 2025.
https://doi.org/10.1007/978-3-031-98679-6_3

residence times are "normalized" [13]. This method is quite efficient, numerically stable, and scales to CTMCs with millions of states.

In practical applications, however, transition probabilities and state residence time distributions—defined by exit rates—are usually not known exactly. Component failure rates in fault trees are vulnerable to environmental conditions, and reaction rates of molecules are obtained experimentally. This raises the question whether CTMC model-checking results are robust w.r.t. perturbations of their stochastic aspects. The aim of this paper is to investigate to what extent transition probabilities and exit rates in a given CTMC can be altered while ensuring that timed reachability probabilities are preserved up to a small tolerance θ.

To this end we define the novel notion of (ε, δ)-bisimulation on CTMCs, investigate its fundamental properties and derive bounds for timed reachability probabilities. The results yield under which (absolute) ε-tolerance on transition probabilities and (relative) δ-tolerance on exit rates, timed reachability probabilities are close up to θ. This enables, e.g., to determine the maximal tolerances in components' failure rates while ensuring the fault tree's (i.e., overall systems') reliability. Our notion generalizes strong probabilistic bisimulation [19] (also known as lumpability) that preserves timed reachability probabilities exactly.

Let us illustrate the conceptual difference of perturbing exit rates and transition probabilities separately in (ε, δ)-bisimulations compared to existing notions such as τ-quasi-lumpability (also known as near-lumpability) [19,29,30] that consider *transition rates*, i.e., products of exit rates and transition probabilities.

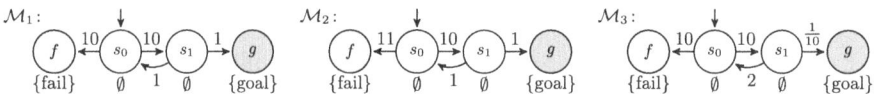

Fig. 1. Three CTMCs where the copies of the states can be related by a τ-quasi-lumpability iff $\tau \geq 1$. The numbers indicate the transition rates between states.

Example 1. Consider the CTMCs in Fig. 1. The value attached to an arrow from state s to state s' describes the *transition rate* $R(s, s')$ between s and s', given as the product of the total exit rate $E(s)$ of s and the probability $P(s, s')$ to move from s to s'. The colors of the states indicate their labels (also written next to the states). Note that the CTMCs $\mathcal{M}_1$ and $\mathcal{M}_2$ behave very similarly— in $\mathcal{M}_2$, the transition to f is only taken with a slightly higher rate, and the probability to reach the goal state g until time t is almost the same in the two models. The CTMCs $\mathcal{M}_1$ and $\mathcal{M}_3$, however, behave very differently—reaching g until t is much less likely in $\mathcal{M}_3$ because of the significantly lower rate $R(s_1, g)$. A τ-quasi-lumpability [19,29,30] is an equivalence relation such that related states have the same label and the total transition rates to move to any other equivalence class from related states differ by at most τ. If we want to relate the states of $\mathcal{M}_1$ with their copies in $\mathcal{M}_2$ with a τ-quasi-lumpability, τ has to be at least 1 due to the change of the transition rate from s_0 to f from 10 to 11. For

$\tau = 1$, however, we can also relate the states of $\mathcal{M}_1$ with their copies in $\mathcal{M}_3$. Hence, τ-quasi-lumpability does not allow us to capture the intuition that $\mathcal{M}_1$ and $\mathcal{M}_2$ behave similarly while $\mathcal{M}_1$ and $\mathcal{M}_3$ behave very differently.

The central idea behind (ϵ, δ)-bisimulations is to decouple the changes of exit rates and transition probabilities of related states. In $\mathcal{M}_1$ and $\mathcal{M}_2$ from Fig. 1, the total exit rate $E(s_0) = \sum_{s'} R(s_0, s')$ of s_0 changes by a factor of 1.05 from 20 to 21, and the probability $P(s_0, f) = \frac{R(s_0, f)}{E(s_0)}$ to transition from s_0 to f is $1/2$ and $11/21$, respectively. The absolute change of transition probabilities and the relative change of exit rates is small, so the chains behave similarly. For $\mathcal{M}_1$ and $\mathcal{M}_3$, however, $P(s_1, g)$ changes from $1/2$ to $1/21$, a huge difference. In this way, (ϵ, δ)-bisimulation can express (dis)similarities of CTMCs in a more fine-grained manner than notions that consider the transition rates between states.

Main Contributions. Our main contributions are the following:

- We introduce (ε, δ)-*bisimulation* for CTMCs, a novel type of approximate probabilistic bisimulation that allows an absolute tolerance of ε for the transition probabilities of related states, and a relative tolerance of δ for their total exit rates. We prove that the union of all (ε, δ)-bisimulations, called (ε, δ)-bisimilarity, is an (ε, δ)-bisimulation itself, that it is additive in ε and δ, and that it coincides with strong bisimilarity [15, 19] iff $\varepsilon = \delta = 0$. Moreover, we discuss how quasi-lumpability [19, 29, 30] and (ε, δ)-bisimilarity relate, and show how to "split" (ε, δ)-bisimilarity into $(\varepsilon, 0)$- and $(0, \delta)$-bisimilarity, allowing an individual treatment of the parameters (Sect. 3).
- We derive bounds on the absolute difference of timed reachability probabilities of (ε, δ)-bisimilar states by uniformizing the CTMC and applying a bound from [18] for the difference in finite horizon reachability probabilities of ε-bisimilar states of DTMCs [25]. The bounds are tight if $\delta = 0$ (Sect. 4).
- We analyze the absolute difference of timed reachability probabilities between $(0, \delta)$-bisimilar states in more detail. Using so-called *Erlang CTMCs* [28] we show how to compute them *exactly* if $\varepsilon = 0$. Subsequently, we derive different bounds on the difference: an easy-to-compute one based on an Erlang CTMC of a specific length, and bounds that utilize a spectral decomposition of the transition probability matrix of the given CTMC (Sect. 5).
- We extend (some of) our results to reward-bounded reachability probabilities in CTMCs with nonnegative rewards, by utilizing a method from [12] that allows us to express them as timed reachability probabilities (Sect. 6).

Missing proofs can be found in the full version of the paper [59].

Related Work. In the discrete-time setting of DTMCs a lot of work has been done on approximate probabilistic bisimulations, mainly focusing on ε-bisimulations as introduced by Desharnais *et al.* [18, 25]. Other notions include approximate probabilistic bisimulations with precision ε [1, 3, 27], up-to-(n, ε)-bisimulations

[16,25], or approximate versions of weak- and branching probabilistic bisimulation [5,60]. See, e.g., [60] for a comparison of several different notions.

For CTMCs, an approximate version of lumpability, called τ-*quasi-* or *near-lumpability*, is known [19,29,30]. It is best suited for the analysis of long-run or stationary properties of a chain, but does not provide good guarantees on its *transient* behavior. A more recent notion is *proportional lumpability* [48,49, 55,56]. Intuitively, states s, s' are proportionally lumpable w.r.t. a function κ that maps states to values in $\mathbb{R}_{>0}$ iff there is an equivalence R such that the transition rates of s and s' to any equivalence class of R differ by the constant factors $\kappa(s)$ resp. $\kappa(s')$. Proportional lumpability preserves the *exact* stationary distributions.

Uncertain continuous-time Markov chains (*UCTMC*) [20,21] are CTMCs with time-varying transition rates. At each time $t \geq 0$ and for all states s, s', the transition rate to move from s to s' must be contained in a fixed interval $[m(s, s'), M(s, s')] \subseteq \mathbb{R}_{\geq 0}$. Lumpabilities for UCTMCs are equivalences that require related states to have the same "extremal realizations", defined as the (time-invariant) CTMCs in which all transition rates $R(s, s')$ coincide with $m(s, s')$ resp. $M(s, s')$. These lumpabilities can be computed efficiently and are characterized both via value functions and satisfaction equivalence of formulas in a variant of the continuous stochastic logic CSL [9,13]. However, there does not seem to be a direct connection to our notion of (ε, δ)-bisimulation.

Another related line of research is *perturbation theory* for Markov chains. Given a CTMC $\mathcal{M}$ and a (slightly) perturbed $\mathcal{M}'$, the goal is to bound the difference of (some) performance measures of the models. See, e.g., [43–45,51,58] or the overview article [52]. The bounds presented in the literature are usually on the *total* error between the *stationary* distributions of $\mathcal{M}$ and $\mathcal{M}'$. Furthermore, they are oftentimes obtained under the assumption of *drift conditions* or rely on the *ergodicity* of the chain. This is in contrast to our work, which focuses on the *componentwise* difference in *transient* reachability probabilities up to time t.

2 Preliminaries

Distributions and Vectors. Let $S \neq \emptyset$ be finite. The set of *distributions* on S is $\mathrm{Distr}(S) = \{\mu\colon S \to [0,1] \mid \sum_{s \in S} \mu(s) = 1\}$. The *support* of $\mu \in \mathrm{Distr}(S)$ is $\mathrm{supp}(\mu) = \{s \in S \mid \mu(s) > 0\}$. Given $A \subseteq S$, we set $\mu(A) = \sum_{a \in A} \mu(a)$. The *Dirac-distribution* 1_s satisfies $1_s(s') = 1$ if $s = s'$ and $1_s(s') = 0$ otherwise. We may associate $\mu \in \mathrm{Distr}(S)$ with a row vector $\boldsymbol{\mu} \in [0,1]^{1 \times |S|}$ such that $\boldsymbol{\mu}[i] = \mu(i)$ for every $i \in S$. Vectors are written in bold face, and $\boldsymbol{\mu}^\top$ is the transpose of $\boldsymbol{\mu}$.

Relations. Given a relation $R \subseteq S \times S$, the *image* of $A \subseteq S$ under R is $R(A) = \{t \in S \mid \exists s \in A\colon (s,t) \in R\}$. A is called *R-closed* if $R(A) \subseteq A$. If R is an equivalence, we write S/R for the set of R equivalence classes. The R-closed sets of an equivalence R are precisely the (unions of) elements of S/R.

Markov Chains. Fix a countable set AP of *atomic propositions*. A *discrete-time Markov chain* (*DTMC*) is a tuple $\mathcal{D} = (S, P, s_{init}, L)$, with S a finite set of *states*, $P\colon S \to \mathrm{Distr}(S)$ a *transition distribution function*, $s_{init} \in S$ a unique *initial state* and $L\colon S \to 2^{AP}$ a *labeling function*. $P(s, s') = P(s)(s')$ denotes the probability to move from s to s' in one step, and we write $\mathbf{P} \in [0, 1]^{|S| \times |S|}$ for the *transition probability matrix* of $\mathcal{D}$ with entries $\mathbf{P}_{s,s'} = P(s, s')$. $\mathrm{Succ}(s) = \{s' \in S \mid P(s, s') > 0\}$ is the set of *successors* of s. Given $s \in S$, let $\mathcal{D}_s$ be the DTMC that is exactly like $\mathcal{D}$, but with initial state s. The *direct sum* $\mathcal{D} \oplus \mathcal{D}'$ of DTMCs $\mathcal{D}, \mathcal{D}'$ is the DTMC obtained from the disjoint union of $\mathcal{D}$ and $\mathcal{D}'$. The initial state of $\mathcal{D} \oplus \mathcal{D}'$ is not relevant for our purposes.

A *continuous-Time Markov Chain* (*CTMC*) is a tuple $\mathcal{M} = (S, P, E, s_{init}, L)$ such that $\mathcal{D}_{\mathcal{M}} = (S, P, s_{init}, L)$ is a DTMC, called the *embedded* or *underlying* DTMC of $\mathcal{M}$, and $E\colon S \to \mathbb{R}_{>0}$ is an *exit rate function*. We use the same notations for CTMCs as for DTMCs, and we let $\mathcal{M}, \mathcal{N}$ range over CTMCs. Note that we do not exclude the possibility of $P(s, s) > 0$, i.e., we allow self-loops in CTMCs. The residence time in a state s of $\mathcal{M}$ is negative exponentially distributed with rate $E(s)$, so the probability to take *any* outgoing transition of s until time $t \geq 0$ (including self-loops) is $1 - e^{-E(s) \cdot t}$, and the probability to take a transition from s to some specific state s' until t is $P(s, s') \cdot (1 - e^{-E(s) \cdot t})$. $\mathbf{Q} \in \mathbb{R}^{|S| \times |S|}$ denotes the *(infinitesimal) generator* of $\mathcal{M}$. The entries of $\mathbf{Q}$ are given as $\mathbf{Q}_{i,j} = P(i, j) \cdot E(i)$ if $i \neq j$ and $\mathbf{Q}_{i,i} = -\sum_{j \neq i} \mathbf{Q}_{i,j}$. For more information on CTMCs and DTMCs see, e.g., [14, 36, 39].

Paths and Probability Measures. Let $\mathcal{D}$ be a DTMC. A sequence $\sigma = s_0 s_1 \ldots \in S^{\omega}$ is an *(infinite) path* of $\mathcal{D}$ if $s_{i+1} \in \mathrm{Succ}(s_i)$ for all $i \in \mathbb{N}$. $\sigma[i] = s_i$ is the state at position i of σ, and $trace(\sigma) = L(s_0)L(s_1) \ldots \in (2^{AP})^{\omega}$ is the *trace* of σ. The set of infinite paths is $\mathrm{Paths}(\mathcal{D})$. *Finite paths* $\sigma = s_0 s_1 \ldots s_k \in S^{k+1}$ and their traces are defined similarly. $\mathrm{Paths}^*(\mathcal{D})$ is the set of finite paths of $\mathcal{D}$.

Let $s \in S$. We consider the standard probability measure $\mathrm{Pr}_s^{\mathcal{D}}$ on subsets of $\mathrm{Paths}(\mathcal{D})$, defined via *cylinder sets* $Cyl(\rho) = \{\sigma \in \mathrm{Paths}(\mathcal{D}) \mid \rho \text{ is a prefix of } \sigma\}$ for $\rho \in \mathrm{Paths}^*(\mathcal{D})$. See, e.g., [14] for details. We write $\mathrm{Pr}^{\mathcal{D}}$ for $\mathrm{Pr}_{s_{init}}^{\mathcal{D}}$ and drop the superscript if $\mathcal{D}$ is clear from the context.

Now, let $\mathcal{M}$ be a CTMC. $\sigma = s_0 t_0 s_1 t_1 \ldots \in (S \cdot \mathbb{R}_{>0})^{\omega}$, where $\cdot$ denotes concatenation, is an *(infinite) timed path* of $\mathcal{M}$ if $s_{i+1} \in \mathrm{Succ}(s_i)$ for all $i \in \mathbb{N}$. $\sigma[i]$ and $trace(\sigma)$ are defined as for DTMCs. A *finite* timed path is a finite prefix of a timed path that ends in a state. We write $\mathrm{Paths}(\mathcal{M})$ (resp. $\mathrm{Paths}^*(\mathcal{M})$) for the set of infinite (resp. finite) timed paths of $\mathcal{M}$. The value $\sigma_i = t_i$ describes the residence time in state s_i along σ. Given some $t \in \mathbb{R}_{\geq 0}$, $\sigma@t$ is the state of σ at time t, i.e., $\sigma@t = \sigma[k]$ for k the smallest index such that $t \leq \sum_{i=0}^{k} t_i$ [13].

Let $k \in \mathbb{N}$, $s, s_0, \ldots, s_{k+1} \in S$ and $I_0, \ldots, I_k$ nonempty intervals in $\mathbb{R}_{\geq 0}$. We consider the standard probability measure $\mathrm{Pr}_s^{\mathcal{M}}$ on subsets of $\mathrm{Paths}(\mathcal{M})$, defined via *timed cylinder sets* $Cyl(s_0 I_0 \ldots s_k I_k s_{k+1}) = \{\sigma \in \mathrm{Paths}(\mathcal{M}) \mid \sigma[i] = s_i$ for $i \leq k + 1$ and $\sigma_j \in I_j$ for $j \leq k\}$. See, e.g., [13] for details. We use the same abbreviations as for DTMCs regarding $\mathrm{Pr}_s^{\mathcal{M}}$. For a finite untimed path $\pi = s_0 s_1 \ldots s_n$, let $\mathrm{Pr}^{\mathcal{M}}(\pi)$ denote the probability of $\mathcal{M}$ to follow any timed path with a state sequence prefixed by π.

Given $G \subseteq S$ and $t \geq 0$, $\mathrm{Pr}_s^{\mathcal{M}}(\Diamond^{\leq t} G)$ is the probability to reach in $\mathcal{M}$ from $s \in S$ a state in G after time at most t. For a DTMC $\mathcal{D}$, $\mathrm{Pr}_s^{\mathcal{D}}(\Diamond^{\leq k} G)$ is the probability to reach in $\mathcal{D}$ from s a state in G after at most $k \in \mathbb{N}$ steps.

Transient Probabilities. Let $n \in \mathbb{N}$. The probability of a DTMC $\mathcal{D}$ to be in state s' after n steps when starting in state s is $\pi_n^{\mathcal{D}}(s, s') = \mathbf{P}_{s,s'}^n$.

For CTMC $\mathcal{M}$, the values $\pi_t^{\mathcal{M}}(s)$ of the *transient probability distribution* $\pi_t^{\mathcal{M}} \in \mathrm{Distr}(S)$ describe the probabilities of $\mathcal{M}$ to be in s at time t. Let $\boldsymbol{\pi}_t^{\mathcal{M}} \in [0,1]^{1 \times |S|}$ denote the vector representation of $\pi_t^{\mathcal{M}}$, and let $\pi_t^{\mathcal{M}}(s, s') = \boldsymbol{\pi}_t^{\mathcal{M}_s}(s')$ be the probability to be in s' after time t when starting in s. $\boldsymbol{\pi}_t^{\mathcal{M}}$ can be computed by solving the following system of forward Kolmogorov differential equations [38]:

$$\frac{d}{dt} \boldsymbol{\pi}_t^{\mathcal{M}} = \boldsymbol{\pi}_t^{\mathcal{M}} \cdot \mathbf{Q} \qquad \text{given } \boldsymbol{\pi}_0^{\mathcal{M}} = \mathbf{1}_{s_{init}}.$$

Let $q \geq \max_{s \in S} E(s)$. The DTMC $\mathrm{unif}(\mathcal{M}, q) = (S, \overline{P}, s_{init}, L)$ with $\overline{P}(s, s') = \frac{P(s,s') \cdot E(s)}{q}$ if $s \neq s'$, and $\overline{P}(s, s) = 1 + \frac{P(s,s) \cdot E(s)}{q} - \frac{E(s)}{q}$ is the *uniformization* of $\mathcal{M}$ w.r.t. q. $\boldsymbol{\pi}_t^{\mathcal{M}}$ can also be computed by the *uniformization method* via [32,35]

$$\boldsymbol{\pi}_t^{\mathcal{M}} = \sum_{k=0}^{\infty} e^{-q \cdot t} \cdot \frac{(q \cdot t)^k}{k!} \cdot \mathbf{1}_{s_{init}} \cdot \overline{\mathbf{P}}^k.$$

We omit the superscript from $\boldsymbol{\pi}_t^{\mathcal{M}}$ (resp. $\pi_n^{\mathcal{D}}$) if no confusion can arise.

Bisimulation. A *(probabilistic) bisimulation* $R \subseteq S \times S$ for DTMC $\mathcal{D}$ is an equivalence such that for all $(s, s') \in R$ it holds that $L(s) = L(s')$ and $P(s, C) = P(s', C)$ for every $C \in S/R$ [42]. For CTMC $\mathcal{M}$, an equivalence R is a *strong (probabilistic) bisimulation* if it is a bisimulation on $\mathcal{D}_{\mathcal{M}}$, and additionally satisfies $E(s) = E(s')$ for all $(s, s') \in R$ [15,19]. States s and s' of $\mathcal{M}$ are *strongly (probabilistic) bisimilar*, written $s \sim s'$, if there is a strong bisimulation R on $\mathcal{M}$ with $(s, s') \in R$. CTMCs $\mathcal{M}$ and $\mathcal{N}$ are strongly (probabilistic) bisimilar, written $\mathcal{M} \sim \mathcal{N}$, if $s_{init}^{\mathcal{M}} \sim s_{init}^{\mathcal{N}}$ in $\mathcal{M} \oplus \mathcal{N}$.

3 (ε, δ)-Bisimulation on CTMCs

If not specified otherwise, we always assume that $\varepsilon, \delta \geq 0$. In this section, after a short recap on ε-bisimulation for DTMCs (Sect. 3.1), we formally define (ε, δ)-bisimulation for CTMCs (Sect. 3.2) and establish fundamental properties of this notion (Sect. 3.3).

3.1 ε-Bisimulation in the Discrete-Time Setting

In the discrete-time setting of DTMCs, the most well-known and well-studied [18,25,37] notion of approximate probabilistic bisimulation are ε-*bisimulations*. They were introduced by Desharnais *et al.* [25] for *labeled Markov processes* [23,24] and have since been adjusted to other models like DTMC [18,37].

Definition 2 ([18,25]). *Let $\mathcal{D}$ be a DTMC. A reflexive[1] and symmetric relation $R \subseteq S \times S$ is an ε-bisimulation if for all $(s,t) \in R$ and any $A \subseteq S$*

$$\text{(i) } L(s) = L(t) \quad and \quad \text{(ii) } P(s,A) \leq P(t, R(A)) + \varepsilon.$$

States s and t are ε-bisimilar, denoted $s \sim_\varepsilon t$, if there is an ε-bisimulation R with $(s,t) \in R$. DTMCs $\mathcal{D}_1$ and $\mathcal{D}_2$ are ε-bisimilar, denoted $\mathcal{D}_1 \sim_\varepsilon \mathcal{D}_2$, if $s_{init}^{\mathcal{D}_1} \sim_\varepsilon s_{init}^{\mathcal{D}_2}$ in $\mathcal{D}_1 \oplus \mathcal{D}_2$.

The tolerance ε describes by how much the transition probabilities of related states may differ. If $\varepsilon \approx 1$, many states can be related, but their behavior might be significantly different, whereas an ε close to 0 allows us to only relate states with almost the same behavior, decreasing the number of relatable states.

The satisfaction of condition (ii) of Definition 2 can be characterized by the existence of suitable *weight functions* that describe how to split the successor probabilities of related states such that the condition holds. This approach is used in, e.g., [33,37,61]. We will later use the following characterization (where we slightly abuse notation and write $\Delta_{s,t}(s',t')$ instead of $\Delta_{s,t}(s')(t')$).

Lemma 3 ([60]). *A reflexive and symmetric relation $R \subseteq S \times S$ that only relates states with the same label is an ε-bisimulation iff for all $(s,t) \in R$ there is a map $\Delta_{s,t}: \text{Succ}(s) \to \text{Distr}(\text{Succ}(t))$ such that*

1. *for all $t' \in \text{Succ}(t)$ we have $P(t,t') = \sum_{s' \in \text{Succ}(s)} P(s,s') \cdot \Delta_{s,t}(s',t')$, and*
2. *$\sum_{s' \in \text{Succ}(s)} P(s,s') \cdot \Delta_{s,t}(s', R(s') \cap \text{Succ}(t)) \geq 1 - \varepsilon$.*

Furthermore, step-bounded reachability probabilities $\text{Pr}_*(\lozenge^{\leq n} g)$ of a goal state g for ε-bisimilar states s, s' are related as follows.

Theorem 4 ([18]). *Let $\mathcal{D}$ be a DTMC, $k \in \mathbb{N}$ and $s \sim_\varepsilon s'$. Then*

$$|\text{Pr}_s(\lozenge^{\leq k} g) - \text{Pr}_{s'}(\lozenge^{\leq k} g)| \leq 1 - (1-\varepsilon)^k.$$

3.2   Definition of (ε, δ)-Bisimulation

In contrast to the discrete-time case, the behavior of a CTMC $\mathcal{M}$ is not only influenced by the transition probabilities, but also by the exit rates of the states. Thus, it is natural to consider two different tolerance values ε and δ for the probabilities resp. the exit rates. As the values of $P(s, \cdot)$ are in $[0,1]$ for any $s \in S$, similar to the discrete-time case an additive tolerance ε is suitable.

The rates $E(s)$, however, can take on any (finite) positive value. This makes the use of *additive* tolerances δ for the rates difficult. Consider, for example, a CTMC with states s, s' such that $E(s) = 1$ and $E(s') = 100$, and assume that the exit rates of related states are allowed to differ by at most 10%. For s, an additive δ would need a value of 0.1 (i.e., all states with a rate in $[0.9, 1.1]$ are

---

[1] In contrast to [18,25] we require reflexivity of ε-bisimulations. This assumption is rather natural (a state should always simulate itself) and does not affect $\sim_\varepsilon$.

considered to behave almost the same as s), while $\delta = 10$ would be necessary for s'. The former allows virtually no tolerance for $E(s')$ (only 0.001% instead of the desired 10%), while the latter allows a tolerance of up to 1000% for $E(s)$.

To circumvent this issue we propose the use of a *multiplicative* tolerance δ for the exit rates of related states, so that the tolerable difference is relative to the actual rates. For the rest of the paper, let $\ln(\cdot)$ denote the natural logarithm.

Definition 5 *Let $\mathcal{M}$ be a CTMC and let $R \subseteq S \times S$ be a reflexive and symmetric relation. R is an (ε, δ)-bisimulation if for all $(s, s') \in R$ it holds that*

1. $L(s) = L(s')$ (labeling condition)
2. $|\ln(E(s)) - \ln(E(s'))| \leq \delta$ (δ-condition)
3. *for all $A \subseteq S$:* $P(s, A) \leq P(s', R(A)) + \varepsilon$.   ($\varepsilon$-condition)

States $s, s' \in S$ are (ε, δ)-bisimilar, written $s \sim_{\varepsilon, \delta} s'$, if $(s, s') \in R$ for an (ε, δ)-bisimulation R. CTMCs $\mathcal{M}_1$ and $\mathcal{M}_2$ are (ε, δ)-bisimilar, written $\mathcal{M}_1 \sim_{\varepsilon, \delta} \mathcal{M}_2$, if $s_{init}^{\mathcal{M}_1} \sim_{\varepsilon, \delta} s_{init}^{\mathcal{M}_2}$ in $\mathcal{M}_1 \oplus \mathcal{M}_2$.

Any (ε, δ)-bisimulation on $\mathcal{M}$ induces an ε-bisimulation on the embedded DTMC $\mathcal{D}_{\mathcal{M}}$, i.e., $s \sim_{\varepsilon, \delta}^{\mathcal{M}} t$ implies $s \sim_{\varepsilon}^{\mathcal{D}_{\mathcal{M}}} t$. Hence, there are weight functions $\Delta_{s,t}$ as in Lemma 3 (w.r.t. the probabilities of $\mathcal{M}$) for (ε, δ)-bisimilar states s, t.

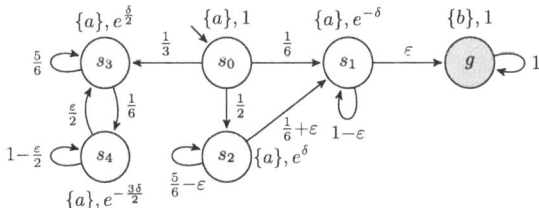

Fig. 2. The CTMC used in Example 6.

Example 6. Let $\varepsilon < \frac{1}{2}$ and $\delta > 0$. In Fig. 2, $\sim_{\varepsilon, \delta}$ is the reflexive and symmetric closure of $\{(s_0, s_2), (s_0, s_3), (s_1, s_4), (s_2, s_3)\}$. States s_1 and s_2 are not (ε, δ)-bisimilar as they violate the δ-condition: $|\ln(E(s_1)) - \ln(E(s_2))| = 2\delta$. Moreover, $s_0 \not\sim_{\varepsilon, \delta} s_1$ since, although the pair of states satisfies the δ-condition, the ε-condition is violated: $P(s_0, \{s_2\}) = \frac{1}{2} > \varepsilon = P(s_1, \sim_{\varepsilon, \delta}(\{s_2\})) + \varepsilon$.

Note that the steady state distributions of (ε, δ)-bisimilar states can differ significantly: starting from s_0 the probability to reach g (and stay there forever) is $2/3$, from s_2 it is 1 and from s_3 it is 0, even though s_0, s_2, and s_3 are pairwise (ε, δ)-bisimilar.

3.3 Fundamental Properties of $\sim_{\varepsilon, \delta}$

We now establish some fundamental properties of $\sim_{\varepsilon, \delta}$ that are generally desirable for approximate probabilistic bisimulations [25,60].

Theorem 7. *Let $\mathcal{M}$ be a CTMC and $s, s', s'' \in S$.*

1. *$\sim_{\varepsilon,\delta}$ is the largest (ε, δ)-bisimulation on $\mathcal{M}$.*
2. *If $s \sim_{\varepsilon_1,\delta_1} s'$ and $s' \sim_{\varepsilon_2,\delta_2} s''$ then $s \sim_{\varepsilon_1+\varepsilon_2,\delta_1+\delta_2} s''$.*
3. *$s \sim s'$ iff $s \sim_{0,0} s'$.*

Theorem 7 shows that $\sim_{\varepsilon,\delta}$ is itself an (ε, δ)-bisimulation, and that it is the largest such relation (item 1). Furthermore $\sim_{\varepsilon,\delta}$ is additive in both ε and δ (item 2) and coincides with strong bisimilarity $\sim$ iff $\varepsilon = \delta = 0$ (item 3).

By slightly adjusting a procedure proposed in [25] that constructs $\sim_\varepsilon$ for DTMCs by solving flow networks á la [10,57], $\sim_{\varepsilon,\delta}$ can be computed in time polynomial in the number of states of $\mathcal{M}$.

Corollary 8. *For a given CTMC $\mathcal{M}$, $\sim_{\varepsilon,\delta}$ can be computed in time $\mathcal{O}(|S|^7)$.*

Furthermore, (ε, δ)-bisimilarity in $\mathcal{M}$ implies τ-bisimilarity (for a $\tau \geq 0$ that depends on ε and δ) in the uniformization $\text{unif}(\mathcal{M}, q)$ of $\mathcal{M}$ for $q \geq \max_{s \in S} E(s)$.

Lemma 9. *$s \sim_{\varepsilon,\delta}^{\mathcal{M}} s'$ implies $s \sim_\tau^{\text{unif}(\mathcal{M},q)} s'$, where $\tau = e^\delta \cdot (1 + \varepsilon) - 1$.*

A notion from the literature related to (ε, δ)-bisimulations is that of τ-quasi-lumpability, which is also known as τ- or near-lumpability [19,29,30]. It is defined for partitions $\Omega = \{\Omega_1, \ldots, \Omega_m\}$ of the state space S of $\mathcal{M}$. More precisely, Ω is a τ-quasi-lumpability for some $\tau \geq 0$ if for all $1 \leq i, j \leq m$ and all $s, s' \in \Omega_i$ it holds that $|P(s, \Omega_j) \cdot E(s) - P(s', \Omega_j) \cdot E(s')| \leq \tau$ [48]. The partitions of the state space induced by *transitive* (ε, δ)-bisimulations are quasi-lumpabilities.

Proposition 10. *Let R be a transitive (ε, δ)-bisimulation and $q \geq \max_{s \in S} E(s)$. The partition induced by R, i.e., the set S/R, is a $q \cdot (e^\delta \cdot (1+\varepsilon) - 1)$-lumpability.*

In [59] we construct, for given $\varepsilon \in (0, 1), \delta > 0$ and $\tau > 0$, a CTMC $\mathcal{M}(\varepsilon, \delta, \tau)$ with states s, s' such that $\{s, s'\}$ is a block of a τ-quasi lumpability on $\mathcal{M}(\varepsilon, \delta, \tau)$ but the pair (s, s') does neither satisfy the ε- nor the δ-condition.

We finish the section by showing how to "split" (ε, δ)-bisimilarity into $(\varepsilon, 0)$- and $(0, \delta)$-bisimilarity. More precisely, given $\mathcal{M} \sim_{\varepsilon,\delta} \mathcal{N}$ we construct CTMCs $\mathcal{M}', \mathcal{N}'$ with the same graph structure and such that $\mathcal{M} \sim_{\varepsilon,0} \mathcal{M}' \sim_{0,\delta} \mathcal{N}' \sim \mathcal{N}$. This decomposition makes it possible to treat the two parameters individually and, together with the additivity of $\sim_{\varepsilon,\delta}$, allows us to extend results shown for $(\varepsilon, 0)$- and $(0, \delta)$-bisimilar states or chains to (ε, δ)-bisimilar ones.

Theorem 11. *Let $\mathcal{M} \sim_{\varepsilon,\delta} \mathcal{N}$. Then there are CTMCs $\mathcal{M}'$ and $\mathcal{N}'$ with the same graph structure and such that $\mathcal{M} \sim_{\varepsilon,0} \mathcal{M}' \sim_{0,\delta} \mathcal{N}' \sim \mathcal{N}$.*

Proof sketch. We describe how to construct $\mathcal{M}'$ and $\mathcal{N}'$. The models share the state space $S' = S^{\mathcal{M}} \times S^{\mathcal{N}}$, with initial state $(s_{init}^{\mathcal{M}}, s_{init}^{\mathcal{N}})$. The label function L' of both models is $L'((s, t)) = L^{\mathcal{N}}(t)$, and the exit rate functions are defined via

$$E^{\mathcal{M}'}((s, t)) = \begin{cases} E^{\mathcal{M}}(s), & \text{if } s \sim_{\varepsilon,\delta} t \\ E^{\mathcal{N}}(t), & \text{if } s \not\sim_{\varepsilon,\delta} t \end{cases} \quad \text{and} \quad E^{\mathcal{N}'}((s, t)) = E^{\mathcal{N}}(t).$$

Furthermore, the common transition probability function of $\mathcal{M}'$ and $\mathcal{N}'$ is

$$P'((s,t),(s',t')) = \begin{cases} \Delta_{s,t}(s',t')P^{\mathcal{M}}(s,s'), & \text{if } s \sim_{\varepsilon,\delta} t, s' \in \text{Succ}(s), t' \in \text{Succ}(t) \\ P^{\mathcal{M}}(s,s')P^{\mathcal{N}}(t,t'), & \text{if } s \not\sim_{\varepsilon,\delta} t \\ 0, & \text{otherwise} \end{cases}$$

where, for a given pair of (ε,δ)-bisimilar states $(s,t) \in S^{\mathcal{M}} \times S^{\mathcal{N}}$, the function $\Delta_{s,t}: \text{Succ}(s) \to \text{Distr}(\text{Succ}(t))$ is a weight function as in Lemma 3, which exists for all such (s,t) since $s \sim_{\varepsilon} t$ in the underlying DTMCs of $\mathcal{M}$ and $\mathcal{N}$. The proof proceeds by showing the desired relations between the models. □

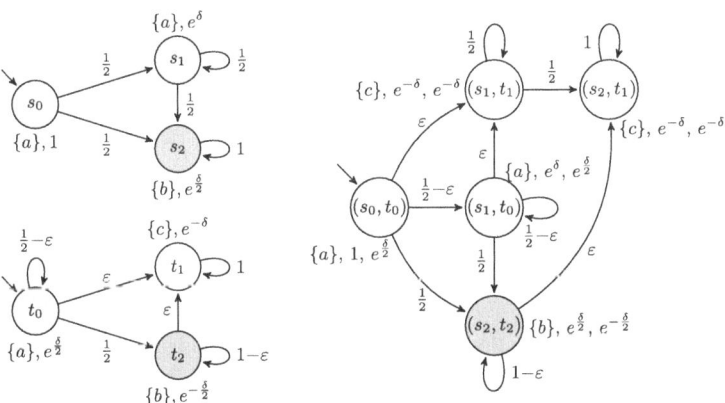

Fig. 3. The CTMCs used in Example 12.

Example 12. We illustrate the construction of Theorem 11 in Fig. 3. The CTMCs $\mathcal{M}$ (top left) and $\mathcal{N}$ (bottom left) are (ε,δ)-bisimilar, as all states with the same label are pairwise (ε,δ)-bisimilar in $\mathcal{M} \oplus \mathcal{N}$. The chains $\mathcal{M}'$ and $\mathcal{N}'$, which only differ in their exit rate functions $E^{\mathcal{M}'}$(first, in blue) and $E^{\mathcal{N}'}$(second, in red) are on the right of the figure. To construct $\mathcal{M}'$ and $\mathcal{N}'$ it is necessary to compute weight functions $\Delta_{s,t}$ for all $s \sim_{\varepsilon,\delta} t$. For example, a suitable choice for (s_0,t_0) is $\Delta_{s_0,t_0}(s_1,t_0) = 1-2\cdot\varepsilon$, $\Delta_{s_0,t_0}(s_1,t_1) = 2\cdot\varepsilon$, $\Delta_{s_0,t_0}(s_2,t_2) = 1$ and $\Delta_{s_0,t_0}(\cdot,\cdot) = 0$ otherwise. It is easy to prove that $\mathcal{M} \sim_{\varepsilon,0} \mathcal{M}' \sim_{0,\delta} \mathcal{N}' \sim \mathcal{N}$.

4 Bounding Timed Reachability Probabilities

Let $\mathcal{M}$ be a CTMC and $t \in \mathbb{R}_{\geq 0}$. We are interested in bounds for the absolute difference of the probabilities of (ε,δ)-bisimilar states s and s' to reach a unique *goal state* g until the deadline t, i.e., in bounds for $|\text{Pr}_s(\Diamond^{\leq t}g) - \text{Pr}_{s'}(\Diamond^{\leq t}g)|$.

For the rest of the paper we therefore assume that $\mathcal{M}$ has such a unique goal state g, which is w.l.o.g. [13] absorbing and uniquely labeled. If there are multiple, potentially non-absorbing goal states, these states can be collapsed to a single absorbing goal state without affecting the time-bounded reachability probabilities. The same pre-processing is also applied in the computation of satisfaction probabilities for time-bounded until-formulas of the *continuous stochastic logic CSL* [9,13]. Similarly, we assume that all states from which g is not reachable are collapsed to a single, uniquely labeled absorbing fail state. Hence, there are at most two absorbing states in $\mathcal{M}$ which are not (ε, δ)-bisimilar to any other state (because of the unique labels) and are eventually reached almost surely. Further, let $q = \max_{s \in S} E(s)$ be the smallest possible uniformization rate of $\mathcal{M}$.

By considering the DTMC unif$(\mathcal{M}, q)$ and applying the bound of Theorem 4 [18], which is possible because of the preservation of approximate bisimilarity in the uniformization (see Lemma 9), we derive an upper bound on the absolute difference of timed reachability probabilities of (ε, δ)-bisimilar states.

Proposition 13. *For $s \sim_{\varepsilon,\delta} s'$: $|\mathrm{Pr}_s(\lozenge^{\leq t}g) - \mathrm{Pr}_{s'}(\lozenge^{\leq t}g)| \leq 1 - e^{-qt(e^{\delta}(1+\varepsilon)-1)}$.*

Considering $\varepsilon = 0$ or $\delta = 0$ in Proposition 13 yields the following corollary.

Corollary 14. *Let $s \sim_{\varepsilon,\delta} s'$.*

1. *If $\delta = 0$ then $|\mathrm{Pr}_s(\lozenge^{\leq t}g) - \mathrm{Pr}_{s'}(\lozenge^{\leq t}g)| \leq 1 - e^{-qt\varepsilon}$.*
2. *If $\varepsilon = 0$ then $|\mathrm{Pr}_s(\lozenge^{\leq t}g) - \mathrm{Pr}_{s'}(\lozenge^{\leq t}g)| \leq 1 - e^{-qt(e^{\delta}-1)}$.*
3. *If $\varepsilon = \delta = 0$ then $\mathrm{Pr}_s(\lozenge^{\leq t}g) = \mathrm{Pr}_{s'}(\lozenge^{\leq t}g)$.*

The third result of Corollary 14 also directly follows from $s \sim_{0,0} s'$ iff $s \sim s'$, which was proved in the third item of Theorem 7, and the fact that $\sim$ exactly preserves transient (reachability) probabilities [13,19].

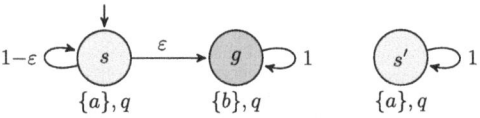

Fig. 4. A CTMC with $s \sim_{\varepsilon,0} s'$ and $|\mathrm{Pr}_s(\lozenge^{\leq t}g) - \mathrm{Pr}_{s'}(\lozenge^{\leq t}g)| = 1 - e^{-qt\varepsilon}$.

We now show that the bound of Proposition 13 is tight if $\delta = 0$.

Example 15. ([18]). In Fig. 4, $s \sim_{\varepsilon,0} s'$, $\mathrm{Pr}_{s'}(\lozenge^{\leq t}g) = 0$ and $\mathrm{Pr}_s(\lozenge^{\leq t}g) = 1 - e^{-qt\varepsilon}$, so $|\mathrm{Pr}_s(\lozenge^{\leq t}g) - \mathrm{Pr}_{s'}(\lozenge^{\leq t}g)| = |1 - e^{-qt\varepsilon} - 0| = 1 - e^{-qt\varepsilon}$ for all t.

A disadvantage of the bounds in Proposition 13 (and Corollary 14) is that they converge to 1 exponentially fast for $t \to \infty$, while the maximal total difference in timed reachability probabilities is usually much smaller for (ε, δ)-bisimilar states. Intuitively, the bounds converge to 1 because the bound of Theorem 4 used in their derivation always assumes the maximal possible error. However it does not consider, e.g., that for growing t some of the probability mass already reached the goal state and can thus not contribute to the total error anymore.

This disadvantage is particularly observable for $(0, \delta)$-bisimilar states, as in this case the actual error converges to 0 for $t \to \infty$ (see also Figs. 6 and 7 in Sect. 5). In Sect. 5, we derive explicit formulas and better bounds for the absolute difference in timed reachability probabilities of $(0, \delta)$-bisimilar states.

For now we consider the problem of computing, for given $\theta \in [0, 1)$ and time $t > 0$, values for ε and δ that guarantee the absolute difference in reachability probabilities of g until t for (ε, δ)-bisimilar states to be $\leq \theta$. By using the bound of Proposition 13 and solving $1 - e^{-qt(e^\delta(1+\varepsilon)-1)} \leq \theta$ w.r.t. ε and δ we obtain:

Theorem 16. *Let* $\theta \in [0, 1)$, $t > 0$, *and* $q = \max_{p \in S} E(p)$. *Then, for all* ε, δ *with* $\varepsilon \in \left[0, \frac{1}{e^\delta} \cdot \left(\frac{q \cdot t - \ln(1 - \theta)}{q \cdot t}\right) - 1\right]$ *and* $\delta \in \left[0, \ln\left(\frac{q \cdot t - \ln(1 - \theta)}{(\varepsilon + 1) \cdot q \cdot t}\right)\right]$, *it holds that*

$$s \sim_{\varepsilon, \delta} s' \ \ implies \ \ |\mathrm{Pr}_s(\lozenge^{\leq t} g) - \mathrm{Pr}_{s'}(\lozenge^{\leq t} g)| \leq \theta.$$

As the bound of Proposition 13 is tight if $\delta = 0$ (see Example 15), the range of admissible values for ε in Corollary 16 is tight in this case as well, in the sense that for a given $\theta \in [0, 1)$ there is a CTMC $\mathcal{M}$ with states $s \sim_{\varepsilon, 0} s'$ such that $|\mathrm{Pr}_s(\lozenge^{\leq t} g) - \mathrm{Pr}_{s'}(\lozenge^{\leq t} g)| \leq \theta$ iff $\varepsilon \leq -\frac{\ln(1 - \theta)}{q \cdot t}$.

5 The Effect of Changing Rates Only

The goal of this section is to obtain more refined bounds for the absolute difference of timed reachability probabilities of $(0, \delta)$-bisimilar CTMCs. This setting is relevant in different scenarios like, e.g., queuing theory. Consider a CTMC $\mathcal{M}$ modeling a single server queue with a buffer of size n, in which tasks arrive with a constant rate τ and are served with a constant rate μ. If the buffer is full and a new task arrives, it has to be dropped and an absorbing fail state f is entered. The timed reachability probability $\mathrm{Pr}^{\mathcal{M}}(\lozenge^{\leq t} f)$ describes the probability of failure until t. Now let $\mathcal{M}'$ be like $\mathcal{M}$, but with an increased service rate $\mu' = \mu \cdot c$ for some $c > 1$. Then $\mathcal{M} \sim_{0, \delta} \mathcal{M}'$ for $\delta \geq \ln(c)$ and $|\mathrm{Pr}^{\mathcal{M}}(\lozenge^{\leq t} f) - \mathrm{Pr}^{\mathcal{M}'}(\lozenge^{\leq t} f)|$ describes how much higher the probability of failure until t is when using the slower server instead of the faster one, making it easy to compare their performance.

We first show how to compute the absolute difference in timed reachability probabilities of $(0, \delta)$-bisimilar CTMCs $\mathcal{M}$ and $\mathcal{M}'$ exactly, without relying on the uniformization method [32, 35] or the Kolmogorov forward equations [38]. We then derive two bounds for the difference: an easy-to-compute constant value (that depends on t and δ), and a bound that yields better results if $t \to \infty$.

Remark 17. Throughout this section we assume that the CTMCs are uniform, i.e., that all states have the same exit rates. For *transitive* $(0, \delta)$-bisimulations R on non-uniformized CTMCs, the following procedure allows us to construct uniformized CTMCs for the analysis of time-bounded reachability probabilities: Let $\mathcal{M}$ and $\mathcal{N}$ be related by such an R. In all equivalence classes C of R, we change the exit rates in $\mathcal{M}$ to the minimal exit rate $E_{\min}^{\mathcal{M}}(C)$ present in C and all rates in $\mathcal{N}$ to $E_{\min}^{\mathcal{M}}(C) \cdot e^{\delta}$. As the transition probabilities of the chains are not affected by this change, and the rates of related states differ by a factor of at most e^{δ}, R is also a $(0, \delta)$-bisimulation on the transformed chains. Afterwards, $\mathcal{M}$ and $\mathcal{N}$ can be uniformized with rates q and $q \cdot e^{\delta}$, respectively, for a suitable q. This again preserves the fact that R is a $(0, \delta)$-bisimulation and results in uniform CTMCs. During the procedure, the difference $|\mathrm{Pr}^{\mathcal{M}}(\lozenge^{\leq t} g) - \mathrm{Pr}^{\mathcal{N}}(\lozenge^{\leq t} g)|$ in the original CTMCs is at most as big as in the resulting uniformized CTMCs. For more details on the transformation, see [59].

Our formula for $|\mathrm{Pr}^{\mathcal{M}}(\lozenge^{\leq t} g) - \mathrm{Pr}^{\mathcal{M}'}(\lozenge^{\leq t} g)|$ depends on the corresponding differences in CTMCs of a specific form, which we call *Erlang CTMCs* [28].

Definition 18. *Let* $n \in \mathbb{N}$. *The* $(n\text{-})$*Erlang CTMC* $\mathcal{E}_n$ *is a CTMC with* n *non-goal states* $s_0, \ldots, s_{n-1}$ *and a unique goal state* $s_n = g$, *such that* $L(s_i) = L(s_j)$ *for* $0 \leq i, j < n$, $L(g) \neq L(s_i)$ *for any* $i < n$, $E(s_i) = 1$ *for* $0 \leq i \leq n$ *and* $P(s_i, s_{i+1}) = 1$ *for* $0 \leq i < n$, *as well as* $P(g, g) = 1$.

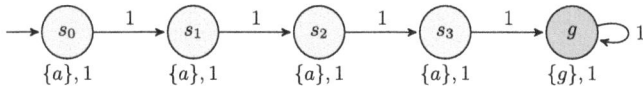

Fig. 5. The Erlang CTMC $\mathcal{E}_4$.

$\mathcal{E}_4$ is illustrated in Fig. 5. Given $\mathcal{M}$ and $c \in \mathbb{R}_{>0}$, let $c \cdot \mathcal{M}$ be the CTMC obtained from $\mathcal{M}$ by multiplying all rates with c. Then $\mathcal{M} \sim_{0, \delta} c \cdot \mathcal{M}$ for $\delta \geq \ln(c)$. For an absorbing, uniform CTMC $\mathcal{M}$ it is clear that an acceleration $c \cdot \mathcal{M}$ with $c = e^{\delta} \geq 1$ or a deceleration $1/c \cdot \mathcal{M}$ induces the maximal possible difference in timed reachability probabilities compared to $\mathcal{M}$ among all $\mathcal{M}'$ with $\mathcal{M} \sim_{0, \delta} \mathcal{M}'$. In the sequel, results are formulated for the comparison of $\mathcal{M}$ with $c \cdot \mathcal{M}$. By switching the roles of $\mathcal{M}$ and $c \cdot \mathcal{M}$, we obtain symmetric results for the deceleration.

Proposition 19. *Let* $n \in \mathbb{N}$, $t \geq 0$, *and* $\mathcal{E}'_n = c \cdot \mathcal{E}_n$ *for some* $c \geq 1$. *Then*

$$\mathrm{Diff}_t(\mathcal{E}_n) := |\mathrm{Pr}^{\mathcal{E}_n}(\lozenge^{\leq t} g) - \mathrm{Pr}^{\mathcal{E}'_n}(\lozenge^{\leq t} g)| = \sum_{k=0}^{n-1} \frac{t^k}{k!} \cdot \left(e^{-t} - c^k e^{-ct}\right).$$

If $c > 1$, $\mathrm{Diff}_t(\mathcal{E}_n)$ *has a local maximum at* $t = \frac{n \cdot \ln(c)}{c-1}$ *that is global on* $[0, \infty)$.

Remark 20. We could have also allowed arbitrary (but uniform) rates for $\mathcal{E}_n$ in Definition 18, i.e., $E(s) = r$ for all $s \in S$ and some $r > 0$. In this case,

$$\mathrm{Diff}_t(\mathcal{E}_n) = \sum_{k=0}^{n-1} \frac{(r \cdot t)^k}{k!} \cdot \left(e^{-r \cdot t} - c^k e^{-c \cdot r \cdot t}\right),$$

with a (local) maximum at $t^* = \frac{n \cdot \ln(c)}{r \cdot (c-1)}$ for $c > 1$. Note that $\mathrm{Diff}_{t^*}(\mathcal{E}_n)$ does not depend on r. Moreover, the assumption that $r = 1$ can be made w.l.o.g., as in the case of $r \neq 1$ the time-bounded reachability probabilities until t are the same as those of the corresponding CTMC with uniform exit rate 1 until $r \cdot t$.

Proposition 19 induces a way to exactly compute the absolute difference in timed reachability probabilities of a CTMC $\mathcal{M}$ and its acceleration $c \cdot \mathcal{M}$.

Theorem 21. *Let $\mathcal{M}$ be a CTMC with $E(s) = 1$ for all $s \in S$, and let g be a unique absorbing goal state. Let $\delta > 0$, $c = e^\delta > 1$, and $\mathcal{M}' = c \cdot \mathcal{M}$. Then*

$$\mathrm{Diff}_t(\mathcal{M}) = |\mathrm{Pr}^{\mathcal{M}'}(\Diamond^{\leq t} g) - \mathrm{Pr}^{\mathcal{M}}(\Diamond^{\leq t} g)| = \sum_{n=1}^{\infty} p_n \cdot \mathrm{Diff}_t(\mathcal{E}_n),$$

where p_n denotes the probability to reach g after exactly n (discrete) steps.

Proof sketch. Let Π_n contain all finite paths entering g after exactly n steps, and let $\mathrm{Traj}^*(\pi)$ contain all timed versions of $\pi \in \Pi_n$ that enter g in $(t, c \cdot t]$. Then $\mathrm{Diff}_t(\mathcal{M}) = \sum_{n=0}^{\infty} \sum_{\pi \in \Pi_n} \mathrm{Pr}^{\mathcal{M}}(\mathrm{Traj}^*(\pi)) = \sum_{n=0}^{\infty} \sum_{\pi \in \Pi_n} \mathrm{Pr}^{\mathcal{M}}(\mathrm{Traj}^*(\pi) \mid \pi) \cdot \mathrm{Pr}^{\mathcal{M}}(\pi)$ by Bayes' rule. As $\mathrm{Pr}^{\mathcal{M}}(\mathrm{Traj}^*(\pi) \mid \pi) = \mathrm{Diff}_t(\mathcal{E}_n)$ for all $\pi \in \Pi_n$, $\mathrm{Diff}_t(\mathcal{E}_0) = 0$ for all t, and $\sum_{\pi \in \Pi_n} \mathrm{Pr}^{\mathcal{M}}(\pi) = p_n$, the claim follows. $\square$

In Theorem 21 (and all other results in this section) we could have also used any (uniform) exit rate $r > 0$ for the states of $\mathcal{M}$ since, as described in Remark 20, we can model different rates by scaling the time bound t.

Next we show how to obtain, for given t and δ, a maximal N (that depends on t, δ) such that $\mathrm{Diff}_t(\mathcal{M}) \leq \mathrm{Diff}_t(\mathcal{E}_N)$. Using the explicit form of $\mathrm{Diff}_t(\mathcal{E}_N)$ from Proposition 19, this yields an easy-to-compute upper bound for $\mathrm{Diff}_t(\mathcal{M})$.

Proposition 22. *Let $N = \left\lceil \frac{(e^\delta - 1) \cdot t}{\delta} \right\rceil$. Under the conditions of Theorem 21,*

$$\mathrm{Diff}_t(\mathcal{M}) \leq \mathrm{Diff}_t(\mathcal{E}_N) = \sum_{k=0}^{N-1} \frac{t^k}{k!} \cdot \left(e^{-t} - c^k e^{-ct} \right).$$

The bound of Proposition 22 is usually tighter than that for $(0, \delta)$-bisimilar states in Corollary 14, since it does not converge to 1 exponentially fast for increasing t. See Figs. 6 and 7 for some examples of the behavior of the bound.

Remark 23. Let $\mathcal{M}$ be as in Theorem 21 and let X be the random variable that describes the probability to reach g for the first time after exactly n steps. Then $p_n \leq \mathrm{Pr}(X \leq n)$, so the Markov inequality implies $p_n \leq \frac{\mathbb{E}(X)}{n}$ for every n, where $\mathbb{E}(X)$ is the expected value of X. Together with Theorem 21 this yields

$$\mathrm{Diff}_t(\mathcal{M}) = \sum_{n=1}^{\infty} p_n \cdot \mathrm{Diff}_t(\mathcal{E}_n) \leq \mathbb{E}(X) \cdot \sum_{n=1}^{\infty} \frac{1}{n} \cdot \mathrm{Diff}_t(\mathcal{E}_n).$$

This bound heavily depends on $\mathbb{E}(X)$, i.e., on the expected number of steps until reaching g. If $\mathbb{E}(X)$ is small the bound can be tighter than those of Propositions 13 and 22, while it can quickly become trivial if $\mathbb{E}(X)$ is large.

Next, we present a way to compute the values of p_n based on a spectral decomposition of the transition probability matrix $\mathbf{P}$ of CTMC $\mathcal{M}$. We start with the case of a diagonalizable $\mathbf{P}$, and afterwards deal with arbitrary $\mathbf{P}$ by using the Jordan canonical form [50]. Moreover, we use the so obtained explicit formulas for p_n to obtain upper bounds for $\mathrm{Diff}_t(\mathcal{M})$. In contrast to the results so far, these bounds converge to 0 for $t \to \infty$, just like the actual difference does.

The transition probability matrix $\mathbf{P}$ of $\mathcal{M}$ is diagonalizable if there is a diagonal matrix $\mathbf{D}$, with diagonal elements corresponding to the eigenvalues of $\mathbf{P}$ (repeated according to their multiplicities), and a regular matrix $\mathbf{S}$ such that $\mathbf{P} = \mathbf{SDS}^{-1}$ [50]. It is well-known that every eigenvalue λ_i of a stochastic matrix satisfies $|\lambda_i| \le 1$, and that $\lambda_1 = 1$ is an eigenvalue of any such matrix. As we assume that an absorbing state is reached almost surely, 1 is the only eigenvalue of modulus 1, and it has a multiplicity $a_{\mathbf{P}}$ of at most 2 (as there are at most two absorbing states in $\mathcal{M}$). Hence, we can w.l.o.g. assume that for the m distinct eigenvalues of $\mathbf{P}$ we have $\lambda_1 = 1 > |\lambda_2| \ge \ldots \ge |\lambda_m|$, and that the diagonal of $\mathbf{D}$ is in descending order w.r.t. the absolute values of these eigenvalues. From now on we denote the second largest (absolute value wise) eigenvalue of $\mathbf{P}$ by λ.

Proposition 24 ([63]). *Let $\mathcal{M}$ be a CTMC such that $\mathbf{P} = \mathbf{SDS}^{-1}$ is diagonalizable. Let $k \in \mathbb{N}$ and $n = |S|$. Then $p_{k+1} = \sum_{j=a_{\mathbf{P}}+1}^{n} \mathbf{S}_{1,j} \cdot \mathbf{S}_{j,n}^{-1} \cdot (\lambda_j - 1) \cdot \lambda_j^k$.*

Combining Theorem 21 and Proposition 24 yields a new bound for $\mathrm{Diff}_t(\mathcal{M})$.

Proposition 25. *Under the conditions of Theorem 21 we have*

$$\mathrm{Diff}_t(\mathcal{M}) \le (n - a_{\mathbf{P}}) \cdot C \cdot \sum_{k=1}^{\infty} |\lambda|^{k-1} \cdot \mathrm{Diff}_t(\mathcal{E}_k),$$

where $n = |S|$ and $C = \max_{i=a_{\mathbf{P}}+1,\ldots,n} |\mathbf{S}_{1,i} \cdot \mathbf{S}_{i,n}^{-1} \cdot (\lambda_i - 1)|$.

Proof sketch. By Proposition 24, $p_{k+1} = \sum_{j=a_{\mathbf{P}}+1}^{n} \mathbf{S}_{1,j} \cdot \mathbf{S}_{j,n}^{-1} \cdot (\lambda_j - 1) \cdot \lambda_j^k$, so by the triangle inequality $p_{k+1} \le \sum_{j=a_{\mathbf{P}}+1}^{n} |\mathbf{S}_{1,j} \cdot \mathbf{S}_{j,n}^{-1} \cdot (\lambda_j - 1)| \cdot |\lambda_j|^k$. Because $|\lambda_j| \le |\lambda|$ for all $j > a_{\mathbf{P}}$ we get $p_{k+1} \le |\lambda|^k \cdot \sum_{j=a_{\mathbf{P}}+1}^{n} C = |\lambda|^k \cdot (n - a_{\mathbf{P}}) \cdot C$ for $C = \max_{i=a_{\mathbf{P}}+1,\ldots,n} |\mathbf{S}_{1,i} \cdot \mathbf{S}_{i,n}^{-1} \cdot (\lambda_i - 1)|$. The claim follows from Theorem 21. □

The bound obtained in Proposition 25 is tight: Consider a CTMC $\mathcal{M}$ with two states s and g, such that $E(s) = E(g) = 1$ and $P(s,s) = p, P(s,g) = 1 - p$ for a $p \in (0,1)$. Let $\mathcal{M}' = e^{\delta} \cdot \mathcal{M}$, so $\mathcal{M} \sim_{0,\delta} \mathcal{M}'$. The probability matrix $\mathbf{P}$ of $\mathcal{M}$ is diagonalizable with eigenvalues $\lambda_1 = 1$ and $\lambda_2 = \lambda = p$. Then $p_k = |\sum_{j=2}^{2} \mathbf{S}_{1,j} \cdot \mathbf{S}_{j,2}^{-1} \cdot (\lambda_j - 1) \cdot \lambda_j^{k-1}| = (1 - p) \cdot p^{k-1} = (n - 1) \cdot C \cdot \lambda^{k-1}$, so here the inequalities in the proof of Proposition 25 are equalities. Furthermore, since always $|\lambda| < 1$, the bounds converge to 0 for $t \to \infty$, just like $\mathrm{Diff}_t(\mathcal{M})$.

Example 26. Consider the CTMC $\mathcal{M}$ on the left of Fig. 6. The probability matrix $\mathbf{P}$ of $\mathcal{M}$ is diagonalizable, with second largest eigenvalue $\lambda = \frac{1}{2}$. The graphic on the right of the figure compares the different error bounds for $\mathrm{Diff}_t(\mathcal{M})$ when $\delta = 0.1$. We can observe that the bound from Proposition 13 based on the uniformization method quickly approaches 1. The bound from Proposition 22

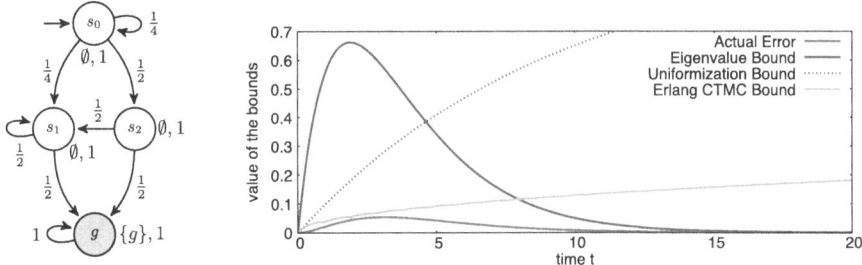

Fig. 6. A CTMC $\mathcal{M}$ with diagonalizable probability matrix (left) and a comparison of the different error bounds for $\mathrm{Diff}_t(\mathcal{M})$.

based on the maximal value of $\mathrm{Diff}_t(\mathcal{E}_n)$ performs well if t is small, but becomes imprecise if t grows. On the other hand, the bound from Proposition 25 that utilizes the diagonalization of $\mathbf{P}$ shows the opposite behavior. It performs bad for small values of t (as here the values of $\mathrm{Diff}(\mathcal{E}_k)$ are big for small k, for which $|\lambda|^k$ is not yet close to 0), while it converges to the actual error with increasing t.

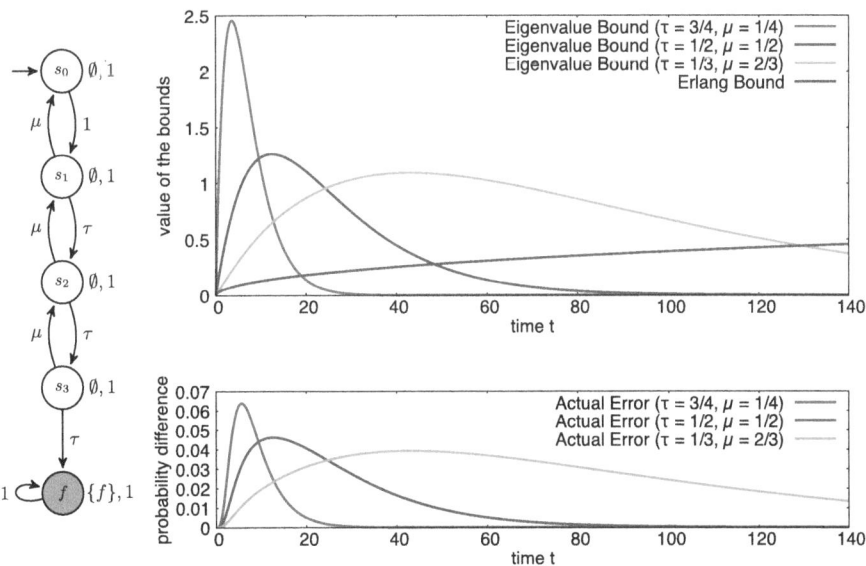

Fig. 7. The queue from Example 27 (left) and the bounds and errors for specific instances (right). The upper graphic depicts the bounds from Propositions 22 and 25 for the considered scenarios, the lower one the actual errors.

Example 27. Consider a single-server queue with capacity 4, modeled by the CTMC $\mathcal{M}$ on the left of Fig. 7. Tasks are completed with rate μ. If the queue is empty, the next task arrives with rate 1, and otherwise tasks arrive with rate τ. We assume that $\tau + \mu = 1$. If the queue is full, i.e., if it already contains four tasks, and a fifth one arrives it has to be dropped, leading to a fail-state f. This setting is close to the example discussed in the beginning of this section.

Let $\mathcal{M}' = e^{0.1} \cdot \mathcal{M}$. In particular, $\mathcal{M} \sim_{0,0.1} \mathcal{M}'$. We analyze the bounds from Propositions 22 and 25 w.r.t. $\mathcal{M}, \mathcal{M}'$ and f by considering three scenarios that are parameterized in τ and μ.[2] In the first scenario, $\tau_1 = \frac{3}{4}$ and $\mu_1 = \frac{1}{4}$, i.e., the arrival rate of tasks is three times higher than their service rate. In the second scenario, arrival and service rates coincide ($\tau_2 = \frac{1}{2} = \mu_2$), while in the third scenario the service rate is twice the arrival rate, i.e., $\tau_3 = \frac{1}{3}$ and $\mu_3 = \frac{2}{3}$. We denote the CTMC corresponding to scenario $i \in \{1, 2, 3\}$ by $\mathcal{M}_i$. Note that for each i the transition probability matrix $\mathbf{P}_i$ of $\mathcal{M}_i$ is diagonalizable.

The resulting bounds, as well as the actual errors, are depicted on the right-hand side of Fig. 7, where the same-colored (and similarly dashed) lines correspond to the same scenario (red and solid for the first, blue and dashed for the second and magenta and dash-dotted for the third). The dotted line in the upper graphic represents the bound from Proposition 22.

We observe that in each scenario the actual error and the bounds of Proposition 25 converge to 0 for $t \to \infty$, while the bound of Proposition 22 converges to 1 for increasing t. The convergence rate to 0 of the former bound can, however, be quite slow. In, e.g., the third scenario, the second largest eigenvalue of $\mathbf{P}_3$ has modulus 0.9778, causing a slow convergence of $|\lambda|^k$ to 0. On the other hand, in the first scenario $\mathcal{M}_1$ enters f quickly, which is reflected in a second largest eigenvalue of 0.7334 whose powers converge to 0 fast.

While the values of the bounds from Proposition 25 are, in particular for small t, significantly larger than the actual error, it is promising that their shape as a function of t closely resembles the actual difference. This scaling of the bounds by a large factor is caused by the constant C, which is obtained by using the triangle inequality and a maximum. Refining this constant in future work might lead to bounds following the actual error much more closely.

As the presented bounds work differently well for small and large t, the following formulation is useful.

Corollary 28. *Let C be as in Proposition 25, and N as in Proposition 22. Then*

$$\mathrm{Diff}_t(\mathcal{M}) \leq \min \left\{ \mathrm{Diff}_t(\mathcal{E}_N), (n - a_\mathbf{P}) \cdot C \cdot \sum_{k=1}^{\infty} |\lambda|^{k-1} \cdot \mathrm{Diff}_t(\mathcal{E}_k) \right\}.$$

Proposition 25 requires the transition probability matrix $\mathbf{P}$ of $\mathcal{M}$ to be diagonalizable. If this is not the case, we can use the *Jordan canonical form (JCF)* [50] instead, which looks as follows: Given an $n \times n$ matrix M over the field of complex numbers $\mathbb{C}$ with distinct eigenvalues $\lambda_1, \ldots, \lambda_m$, given in descending order w.r.t. their absolutes values, the JCF of M is a decomposition of the form $M = \mathbf{SJS}^{-1}$ for matrices $\mathbf{S}, \mathbf{J} \in \mathbb{C}^{n \times n}$. $\mathbf{J}$ is a block diagonal matrix with so-called *Jordan blocks* $\mathbf{J}_i$, $i = 1, \ldots, k$, $m \leq k \leq n$, on the diagonal. The i-th

---

[2] We omit the bound based on uniformization from Proposition 13 as we have already seen in Example 26 that it does not perform well for $(0, \delta)$-bisimilar models.

Jordan block $\mathbf{J}_i$ corresponds to one of M's eigenvalues τ and is a $r_i \times r_i$ matrix for some r_i that is at most the algebraic multiplicity of τ, and such that the sum over all r_i for the Jordan blocks belonging to the same eigenvalue τ equals its geometric multiplicity. The Jordan blocks for eigenvalue τ have τ everywhere on the diagonal and entry 1 directly above the diagonal. All other entries are 0. We w.l.o.g. assume that the Jordan blocks are in descending order w.r.t. the absolute value of the corresponding eigenvalues, and that multiple Jordan blocks for the same eigenvalue are in descending order w.r.t. their size. We write $q_{\mathbf{J}}$ for the total number of Jordan blocks of $\mathbf{J}$ and r_i for the size of the i-th Jordan block $\mathbf{J}_i$.

It is well-known that every matrix over $\mathbb{C}$ has a JCF [50], so the above decomposition exists for the transition probability matrix of *any* CTMC. We now show how to compute p_n, i.e., the probability to reach the goal state after exactly n discrete steps, in the case that $\mathbf{P}$ is not diagonalizable.

Proposition 29. *Denote by λ_i the eigenvalue corresponding to the i-th Jordan block $\mathbf{J}_i$ of $\mathbf{P} = \mathbf{SJS}^{-1}$. Let $N \in \mathbb{N}$, $z \in \{0, \ldots, q_{\mathbf{J}} - 1\}$ the number of Jordan blocks for eigenvalue 0 and $h_l = \sum_{i=1}^{l-1} r_i$. Then p_{N+1} equals*

$$\sum_{l=a_{\mathbf{P}}+1}^{q_{\mathbf{J}}-z} \sum_{j=1}^{r_l} \sum_{k=1}^{j} \mathbf{S}_{1,k+h_l} \cdot \mathbf{S}_{j+h_l,n}^{-1} \cdot \lambda_l^{N+k-j} \cdot \left(\lambda_l \cdot \binom{N+1}{j-k} - \binom{N}{j-k} \right) + R(N,z)$$

where, for $\mathbf{S}_{1,h_l+j}^* = \mathbf{S}_{1,h_l,+j}$ if $j > 0$ and $\mathbf{S}_{1,h_l+j}^* - 0$ if $j = 0$,

$$R(N,z) = \sum_{l=q_{\mathbf{J}}-z+1}^{q_{\mathbf{J}}} \sum_{j=0}^{r_l-(N+1)} (\mathbf{S}_{1,h_l+j}^* - \mathbf{S}_{1,h_l+j+1}) \cdot \mathbf{S}_{h_l+N+j,n}^{-1}.$$

In particular, the term $R(N,z)$ introduced in Theorem 29 equals 0 if $z = 0$ or if $N \geq \max_{q_{\mathbf{J}}-z+1 \leq i \leq q_{\mathbf{J}}} r_i$. Hence, if N is at least the size of the largest Jordan block corresponding to eigenvalue 0, the term $R(N,z)$ vanishes.

Remark 30. The decompositions of $\mathbf{P}$ proved in Propositions 24 and 29 also hold when the Markov chain contains more than 2 (reachable) absorbing states, i.e., if $a_{\mathbf{P}} > 2$. In an absorbing Markov chain, the multiplicity (both geometric and algebraic) of the eigenvalue 1 is the number of absorbing states, and thus each Jordan block for eigenvalue 1 has a size of 1, causing them to get canceled out in the computations of the explicit forms of p_{N+1}.

Combining Theorem 21 and Theorem 29 yields another upper bound on the absolute difference in timed reachability probabilities of $(0, \delta)$-bisimilar CTMCs.

Theorem 31. *In the setting of Theorem 29 let $|\lambda| > 0$. Let R be the maximal size of any Jordan block of $\mathbf{P}$, $r = \max_{i=a_{\mathbf{P}}+1,\ldots,q_{\mathbf{J}}-z} r_i$ the maximal size of any such block corresponding to an eigenvalue $\neq 0, 1$, $\lambda_l^* = \max\{|\lambda_l|, |1 - \lambda_l|\}$ for $l = a_{\mathbf{P}} + 1, \ldots, q_{\mathbf{J}} - z$ and $C = \sum_{l=a_{\mathbf{P}}+1}^{q_{\mathbf{J}}-z} \sum_{j=1}^{r_l} \sum_{k=1}^{j} |\mathbf{S}_{1,k+h_l} \cdot \mathbf{S}_{j+h_l,n}^{-1}| \cdot |\lambda_l^*|$. Then*

$$\mathrm{Diff}_t(\mathcal{M}) \leq \sum_{k=1}^{R-1} p_k \cdot \mathrm{Diff}_t(\mathcal{E}_k) + C \cdot \sum_{k=R}^{\infty} |\lambda|^{k-r} \cdot k^{r-1} \cdot \mathrm{Diff}_t(\mathcal{E}_k).$$

The bound of Proposition 31 is a conservative extension of the one for diagonalizable $\mathbf{P}$ from Proposition 25, as in this case $R = 1 = r$ and so the bound of Proposition 31 collapses to $\mathrm{Diff}_t(\mathcal{M}) \leq C \cdot \sum_{k=1}^{\infty} |\lambda|^{k-1} \cdot \mathrm{Diff}_t(\mathcal{E}_k)$.

Remark 32. In Proposition 31 we have to exclude the case $|\lambda| = 0$, i.e., the case that $\mathbf{P}$ only has eigenvalues 0 and 1. This happens, e.g., if $\mathbf{P}$ (and hence $\mathcal{M}$) is acyclic. In an acyclic CTMC the goal state g is, however, reached after *at most* as many steps as the length of the longest path in the chain. Therefore, if $\mathcal{M}$ is acyclic, $\mathrm{Diff}_t(\mathcal{M})$ can easily be computed exactly, for example by using the identity in Theorem 21 and computing the relevant values of $p_n = \mathbf{P}^{n+1} - \mathbf{P}^n$, or by applying methods like the ACE algorithm of [47] that allow computing the transient distribution functions of acyclic CTMCs directly.

Corollary 33. *Under the conditions and with the notation of Proposition 31 and Proposition 22, $\mathrm{Diff}_t(\mathcal{M})$ is bounded from above by*

$$\min \left\{ \mathrm{Diff}_t(\mathcal{E}_N), \sum_{k=1}^{R-1} p_k \cdot \mathrm{Diff}_t(\mathcal{E}_k) + C \cdot \sum_{k=R}^{\infty} |\lambda|^{k-r} \cdot k^{r-1} \cdot \mathrm{Diff}_t(\mathcal{E}_k) \right\}.$$

We finish the section by noting that the bounds for $(0, \delta)$-bisimilar CTMCs can also be used to derive bounds for the case that $\varepsilon > 0$. Given $\mathcal{M} \sim_{\varepsilon, \delta} \mathcal{N}$, by Theorem 11 there are CTMCs $\mathcal{M}'$ and $\mathcal{N}'$ with $\mathcal{M} \sim_{\varepsilon, 0} \mathcal{M}' \sim_{0, \delta} \mathcal{N}' \sim \mathcal{N}$. Hence, the triangle inequality together with the fact that strong bisimilarity preserves timed reachability probabilities [13,19] implies $|\mathrm{Pr}^{\mathcal{M}}(\Diamond^{\leq t}g) - \mathrm{Pr}^{\mathcal{N}}(\Diamond^{\leq t}g)| \leq |\mathrm{Pr}^{\mathcal{M}}(\Diamond^{\leq t}g) - \mathrm{Pr}^{\mathcal{M}'}(\Diamond^{\leq t}g)| + |\mathrm{Pr}^{\mathcal{M}'}(\Diamond^{\leq t}g) - \mathrm{Pr}^{\mathcal{N}'}(\Diamond^{\leq t}g)|$. As $\mathcal{M} \sim_{\varepsilon, 0} \mathcal{M}'$, the bound from Proposition 13 for the special case of $\varepsilon = 0$ is applicable to the first term, and one of the bounds for $(0, \delta)$-bisimilar chains can be applied to the second term. This yields another upper bound on the absolute difference in timed reachability probabilities for (ε, δ)-bisimilar CTMCs.

6 Bounds for Reward-Bounded Reachability Probabilities

In practice, CTMCs are often extended with *rewards* that allow to model, e.g., the accumulation of costs, the energy consumption, or different performance measures like the availability of the system [12,31]. We consider state-based reward functions $\rho: S \to \mathbb{R}$ that assign to every $s \in S$ a reward $\rho(s)$. Rewards are accumulated in the states, and the cumulative reward along the timed path $\pi = s_0 t_0 s_1 t_1 \ldots \in \mathrm{Paths}(\mathcal{M})$ of $\mathcal{M}$ until time t is given (for $\sigma @ t = s_m$) as [12]

$$\rho(\sigma, t) = \sum_{j=0}^{m-1} t_j \cdot \rho(s_j) + \left(t - \sum_{j=0}^{m-1} t_j \right) \cdot \rho(s_m).$$

Similar to timed reachability probabilities $\mathrm{Pr}_s(\Diamond^{\leq t}g)$, logics like CSRL [12] allow to specify properties in terms of *reward-bounded* reachability probabilities $\mathrm{Pr}_s(\Diamond_{\leq r}g)$, which denote the probability to reach, from state s, a goal state g while accumulating at most reward $r \in \mathbb{R}$.

We extend the results of Sects. 4 and 5 to reward-bounded reachability probabilities. Here, we consider the special case of *nonnegative* rewards, i.e., we assume that $\rho(s) \geq 0$ for all $s \in S$. To accommodate for the addition of rewards to our model, we adjust the definition of (ε, δ)-bisimulations to require related states to have the same reward, i.e., $s \sim_{\varepsilon,\delta} s'$ is possible only if $\rho(s) = \rho(s')$. An extension to a notion of, say, $(\varepsilon, \delta, \mu)$-bisimulation, where μ describes an allowed error in the rewards in related states, is an interesting direction for future work.

First, assume $\rho(s) > 0$ for all s, a setting also analyzed in, e.g., [12]. There, based on ideas from [17], a transformation is proposed that allows to compute reward-bounded reachability probabilities in $\mathcal{M}$ via *time-bounded* reachability probabilities in a modified model $\widehat{\mathcal{M}}$. This model differs from $\mathcal{M}$ only in the exit rates $\widehat{E}(s) = \frac{E(s)}{\rho(s)}$ and rewards $\widehat{\rho}(s) = \frac{1}{\rho(s)}$ of states $s \in S$. A direct consequence of [12, Lem. 1] is that $\Pr_s^{\mathcal{M}}(\Diamond_{\leq r} g) = \Pr_s^{\widehat{\mathcal{M}}}(\Diamond^{\leq r} g)$.

Thus, given $s \sim_{\varepsilon,\delta} s'$ we can directly apply the bounds obtained in Sects. 4 and 5, provided that s and s' are still (ε, δ)-bisimilar in $\widehat{\mathcal{M}}$. However, this is indeed the case as we require $\rho(s) = \rho(s')$, and so the transformation of [12] simply scales the exit rates (and rewards) of s and s' by a common factor.

Proposition 34. *Let* $s \sim_{\varepsilon,\delta} s'$, $r \geq 0$ *and* $\widehat{q} \geq \max_{p \in S} \widehat{E}(p)$. *Then*

$$|\Pr_s(\Diamond_{\leq r} g) - \Pr_{s'}(\Diamond_{\leq r} g)| \leq 1 - e^{-\widehat{q} \cdot t \cdot (e^{\delta}(\varepsilon+1)-1)}.$$

If $\varepsilon = 0$, a similar result can be formulated for the bounds from Sect. 5.

Next, we allow $\rho(s) = 0$. As the reward of the goal state g does not matter for our purpose, we can w.l.o.g. assume $\rho(g) > 0$. The transformation from [12] is not applicable, as it could require division by 0. To circumvent this issue we first construct from $\mathcal{M}$ a CTMC $\mathcal{M}_{>0}$ without states with $\rho(s) = 0$. Intuitively, this is done by redirecting the incoming transitions of states with reward 0 to their successors, allowing us to remove any such state from the chain.

Proposition 35. *Let* $\mathcal{M}$ *be a CTMC. There is a CTMC* $\mathcal{M}_{>0}$ *with* $S^{\mathcal{M}_{>0}} = S^{\mathcal{M}} \setminus \{x \mid \rho(x) = 0\}$ *such that* $\Pr_s^{\mathcal{M}}(\Diamond_{\leq r} g) = \Pr_s^{\mathcal{M}_{>0}}(\Diamond_{\leq r} g)$ *for all* $s \in S^{\mathcal{M}_{>0}}$.

Hence, by first constructing $\mathcal{M}_{>0}$ from $\mathcal{M}$ and afterwards applying the transformation from [12] to $\mathcal{M}_{>0}$, we obtain the following corollary.

Corollary 36. *Proposition 34 also holds for CTMCs with nonnegative rewards.*

7   Conclusion and Future Work

We introduced (ε, δ)-bisimulations, a novel type of approximate probabilistic bisimulation for CTMCs. In contrast to notions from the literature such as quasi-lumpability [19, 29, 30], the separate bounds on changes in transition probabilities and changes in exit rates used in (ε, δ)-bisimulation result in a more flexible, fine-grained notion of behavioral similarity. We established fundamental properties of the notion, and analyzed the difference in timed reachability probabilities of (ε, δ)-bisimilar chains.

We obtained bounds on this difference by uniformizing the chain and applying known results from [18] for the discrete-time setting. Although tight if $\delta = 0$, the bounds usually do not perform well if $\delta > 0$. Hence, we investigated the special case of $(0, \delta)$-bisimilarity in more detail—also as a stepping stone towards a refined treatment of (ε, δ)-bisimilarity in future work. For $(0, \delta)$-bisimilar chains, we provided bounds based on the error in Erlang CTMCs $\mathcal{E}_n$, as well as based on a spectral analysis of the probability matrix $\mathbf{P}$ of the CTMC in question. Furthermore, we extended our results to reward-bounded reachability probabilities, provided that all rewards in the model are nonnegative.

From a theoretical point of view, the behavior of the bounds obtained from the spectral analysis of $\mathbf{P}$ is promising. They are tight and, as can be observed in Fig. 7, seem to evolve similar to the actual error. The bounds are, however, stretched by a (large) factor, which happens since, to obtain the constants C, the triangle inequality and maxima are used. This causes the constants to become significantly larger than necessary, leading to poor performance of the bounds in particular if t is small. Therefore, searching for smaller constants $C' \ll C$ in future work is in order. From a practical point of view, applicability of the bounds seems questionable. They tend to over-approximate the error and, depending on the second largest eigenvalue of $\mathbf{P}$, can take a long time (i.e., require large values of t) to converge to the actual error, even for small chains. Moreover, computing Jordan canonical forms (and diagonalizations) is computationally expensive and numerically unstable [26,53,54]. Consequently, the search for more practically relevant bounds is an important direction for future work.

Other open questions include an extension of (ε, δ)-bisimulation to a notion of $(\varepsilon, \delta, \mu)$-bisimulation that allows a tolerance of μ in the rewards of related states, an analysis of the achievable state space reduction in quotients w.r.t. (transitive) (ε, δ)-bisimulations, and a closer look at the (approximate) preservation of logical properties expressed by, e.g., CSL-formulas [9,13], between (ε, δ)-bisimilar states.

Acknowledgements. This work was partly funded by the DFG through the DFG grant 389792660 as part of TRR 248 (see https://perspicuous-computing.science) and the Cluster of Excellence EXC 2050/1 (CeTI, project ID 390696704, as part of Germany's Excellence Strategy).

Disclosure of Interests. The authors have no competing interests to declare that are relevant to the content of this article.

References

1. Abate, A.: Approximation metrics based on probabilistic bisimulations for general state-space Markov processes: a survey. In: Proceedings of the First Workshop on Hybrid Autonomous Systems. Electronic Notes in Theoretical Computer Science, vol. 297, pp. 3–25 (2013). https://doi.org/10.1016/j.entcs.2013.12.002

2. Abate, A., Brim, L., Češka, M., Kwiatkowska, M.: Adaptive aggregation of Markov chains: quantitative analysis of chemical reaction networks. In: Kroening, D., Păsăreanu, C.S. (eds.) Computer Aided Verification. Lecture Notes in Computer Science (LNCS), vol. 9206, pp. 195–213. Springer International Publishing, Cham (2015). https://doi.org/10.1007/978-3-319-21690-4_12

3. Abate, A., Kwiatkowska, M., Norman, G., Parker, D.: Probabilistic model checking of labelled Markov processes via finite approximate bisimulations. In: van Breugel, F., Kashefi, E., Palamidessi, C., Rutten, J. (eds.) Horizons of the Mind. A Tribute to Prakash Panangaden: Essays Dedicated to Prakash Panangaden on the Occasion of His 60th Birthday, Lecture Notes in Computer Science (LNCS), vol. 8464, pp. 40–58. Springer International Publishing, Cham (2014). https://doi.org/10.1007/978-3-319-06880-0_2

4. Češka, M., Šafránek, D., Dražan, S., Brim, L.: Robustness analysis of stochastic biochemical systems. PLoS ONE 9(4), e94553 (2014). https://doi.org/10.1371/journal.pone.0094553

5. Aldini, A.: A Note on the Approximation of Weak Probabilistic Bisimulation (2009)

6. Amparore, E.G., Beccuti, M., Donatelli, S.: (Stochastic) model checking in Great-SPN. In: Petri Nets. Lecture Notes in Computer Science (LNCS), vol. 8489, pp. 354–363. Springer (2014). https://doi.org/10.1007/978-3-319-07734-5_19

7. Amparore, E.G., Donatelli, S.: Efficient model checking of the stochastic logic CSL^{TA}. Perform. Eval. $\mathbf{123-124}$, 1–34 (2018). https://doi.org/10.1016/j.peva.2018.03.002

8. Arnold, F., Belinfante, A., van der Berg, F.I., Guck, D., Stoelinga, M.: DFTCalc: a tool for efficient fault tree analysis. In: SAFECOMP. Lecture Notes in Computer Science (LNCS), vol. 8153, pp. 293–301. Springer (2013). https://doi.org/10.1007/978-3-642-40793-2_27

9. Aziz, A., Sanwal, K., Singhal, V., Brayton, R.: Model-checking continuous-time Markov chains. ACM Trans. Comput. Logic $\mathbf{1}$(1), 162–170 (2000). https://doi.org/10.1145/343369.343402

10. Baier, C.: Polynomial time algorithms for testing probabilistic bisimulation and simulation. In: Alur, R., Henzinger, T.A. (eds.) Computer Aided Verification. Lecture Notes in Computer Science (LNCS), vol. 1102, pp. 50–61. Springer, Berlin, Heidelberg (1996). https://doi.org/10.1007/3-540-61474-5_57

11. Baier, C., Cloth, L., Haverkort, B.R., Kuntz, M., Siegle, M.: Model checking Markov chains with actions and state labels. IEEE Trans. Software Eng. $\mathbf{33}$(4), 209–224 (2007). https://doi.org/10.1109/TSE.2007.36

12. Baier, C., Haverkort, B., Hermanns, H., Katoen, J.P.: On the logical characterisation of performability properties. In: Montanari, U., Rolim, J.D.P., Welzl, E. (eds.) Automata, Languages and Programming (ICALP 2000). Lecture Notes in Computer Science (LNCS), vol. 1853, pp. 780–792. Springer Berlin Heidelberg, Berlin, Heidelberg (2000). https://doi.org/10.1007/3-540-45022-X_65

13. Baier, C., Haverkort, B.R., Hermanns, H., Katoen, J.P.: Model-checking algorithms for continuous-time Markov chains. IEEE Trans. Softw. Eng. $\mathbf{29}$(6), 524–541 (2003). https://doi.org/10.1109/TSE.2003.1205180

14. Baier, C., Katoen, J.P.: Principles of Model Checking. The MIT Press (2008)
15. Baier, C., Katoen, J.P., Hermanns, H., Wolf, V.: Comparative branching-time semantics for Markov chains. Inf. Comput. **200**(2), 149–214 (2005). https://doi.org/10.1016/j.ic.2005.03.001
16. Bartoletti, M., Murgia, M., Zunino, R.: Sound approximate and asymptotic probabilistic bisimulations for PCTL. Log. Meth. Comput. Sci. **19**(1) (2023). https://doi.org/10.46298/lmcs-19(1:22)2023
17. Beaudry, M.D.: Performance-related reliability measures for computing systems. IEEE Trans. Comput. **C-27**(6), 540–547 (1978). https://doi.org/10.1109/TC.1978.1675145
18. Bian, G., Abate, A.: On the relationship between bisimulation and trace equivalence in an approximate probabilistic context. In: Esparza, J., Murawski, A.S. (eds.) Foundations of Software Science and Computation Structures (FoSSaCS). Lecture Notes in Computer Science (LNCS), vol. 10203, pp. 321–337. Springer, Berlin, Heidelberg (2017). https://doi.org/10.1007/978-3-662-54458-7_19
19. Buchholz, P.: Exact and ordinary lumpability in finite Markov chains. J. Appl. Probab. **31**(1), 59–75 (1994). https://doi.org/10.2307/3215235
20. Cardelli, L., Grosu, R., Larsen, K.G., Tribastone, M., Tschaikowski, M., Vandin, A.: Lumpability for uncertain continuous-time Markov chains. In: Abate, A., Marin, A. (eds.) Quantitative Evaluation of Systems (QEST 2021), Lecture Notes in Computer Science (LNCS), vol. 12846, pp. 391–409. Springer International Publishing, Cham (2021). https://doi.org/10.1007/978-3-030-85172-9_21
21. Cardelli, L., Grosu, R., Larsen, K.G., Tribastone, M., Tschaikowski, M., Vandin, A.: Algorithmic minimization of uncertain continuous-time markov chains. IEEE Trans. Autom. Control **68**(11), 6557–6572 (2023). https://doi.org/10.1109/TAC.2023.3244093
22. Chen, T., Han, T., Katoen, J.P., Mereacre, A.: Quantitative model checking of continuous-time Markov chains against timed automata specifications. In: 24th IEEE Symposium on Logic In Computer Science (LICS), pp. 309–318. IEEE Computer Society (2009). https://doi.org/10.1109/LICS.2009.21
23. Desharnais, J., Edalat, A., Panangaden, P.: A logical characterization of bisimulation for labeled Markov processes. In: Proceedings of the Thirteenth Annual IEEE Symposium on Logic in Computer Science (LiCS), pp. 478–487 (1998). https://doi.org/10.1109/LICS.1998.705681
24. Desharnais, J., Edalat, A., Panangaden, P.: Bisimulation for labelled Markov processes. Inf. Comput. **179**(2), 163–193 (2002). https://doi.org/10.1006/inco.2001.2962
25. Desharnais, J., Laviolette, F., Tracol, M.: Approximate analysis of probabilistic processes: logic, simulation and games. In: Fifth International Conference on Quantitative Evaluation of Systems (QEST 2008), pp. 264–273 (2008). https://doi.org/10.1109/QEST.2008.42
26. Dey, P., Kannan, R., Ryder, N., Srivastava, N.: Bit complexity of Jordan normal form and polynomial spectral factorization. In: Tauman Kalai, Y. (ed.) 14th Innovations in Theoretical Computer Science Conference (ITCS 2023). Leibniz International Proceedings in Informatics (LIPIcs), vol. 251, pp. 42:1–42:18. Schloss Dagstuhl – Leibniz-Zentrum für Informatik, Dagstuhl, Germany (2023). https://doi.org/10.4230/LIPIcs.ITCS.2023.42
27. D'Innocenzo, A., Abate, A., Katoen, J.P.: Robust PCTL model checking. In: Proceedings of the 15th ACM International Conference on Hybrid Systems: Computation and Control (HSCC 2012), pp. 275–286. Association for Computing Machinery, New York, NY, USA (2012). https://doi.org/10.1145/2185632.2185673

28. Erlang, A.K.: Solution to some problems of the theory of probabilities of significance in automatic telephone exchange. Post Office Electric. Eng. J., 189–197 (1917)
29. Franceschinis, G., Muntz, R.R.: Bounds for quasi-lumpable Markov chains. Perform. Eval. **20**(1), 223–243 (1994). https://doi.org/10.1016/0166-5316(94)90015-9
30. Franceschinis, G., Muntz, R.R.: Computing bounds for the performance indices of quasi-lumpable stochastic well-formed nets. IEEE Trans. Softw. Eng. **20**(7), 516–525 (1994). https://doi.org/10.1109/32.297940
31. Gouberman, A., Siegle, M.: Markov reward models and Markov decision processes in discrete and continuous time: performance evaluation and optimization. In: Remke, A., Stoelinga, M. (eds.) Stochastic Model Checking. Rigorous Dependability Analysis Using Model Checking Techniques for Stochastic Systems: International Autumn School (ROCKS 2012). Lecture Notes in Computer Science (LNCS), vol. 8453, pp. 156–241. Springer Berlin Heidelberg, Berlin, Heidelberg (2014). https://doi.org/10.1007/978-3-662-45489-3_6
32. Grassmann, W.K.: Transient solutions in Markovian queueing systems. Computers & Operations Research **4**(1), 47–53 (1977). https://doi.org/10.1016/0305-0548(77)90007-7
33. Haesaert, S., Nilsson, P., Soudjani, S.: Formal multi-objective synthesis of continuous-state MDPs. In: 2021 American Control Conference (ACC), pp. 3428–3433 (2021). https://doi.org/10.23919/ACC50511.2021.9482873
34. Hensel, C., Junges, S., Katoen, J., Quatmann, T., Volk, M.: The probabilistic model checker STORM. Int. J. Softw. Tools Technol. Trans. (STTT) **24**, 589–610 (2022). https://doi.org/10.1007/s10009-021-00633-z
35. Jensen, A.: Markoff chains as an aid in the study of Markoff processes. Scand. Actuar. J. **1953**(sup1), 87–91 (1953). https://doi.org/10.1080/03461238.1953.10419459
36. Kemeny, J.G., Snell, J.L.: Finite Markov Chains. Undergraduate Texts in Mathematics (UTM), Springer, New York (1976)
37. Kiefer, S., Tang, Q.: Approximate bisimulation minimisation. In: Bojańczy, M., Chekuri, C. (eds.) 41st IARCS Annual Conference on Foundations of Software Technology and Theoretical Computer Science (FSTTCS 2021). Leibniz International Proceedings in Informatics (LIPIcs), vol. 213, pp. 48:1–48:16. Schloss Dagstuhl – Leibniz-Zentrum für Informatik, Dagstuhl, Germany (2021). https://doi.org/10.4230/LIPIcs.FSTTCS.2021.48
38. Kolmogorov, A.N.: Über die analytischen methoden in der wahrscheinlichkeitsrechnung. Math. Ann. **104**, 415–458 (1931). https://doi.org/10.1007/BF01457949
39. Kulkarni, V.G.: Introduction to Modeling and Analysis of Stochastic Systems. Springer Texts in Statistics (STS), Springer New York (2010). https://doi.org/10.1007/978-1-4419-1772-0
40. Kwiatkowska, M., Norman, G., Parker, D.: PRISM 4.0: verification of probabilistic real-time systems. In: Gopalakrishnan, G., Qadeer, S. (eds.) Proc. 23rd International Conference on Computer Aided Verification (CAV'11). Lecture Notes in Computer Science (LNCS), vol. 6806, pp. 585–591. Springer (2011). https://doi.org/10.1007/978-3-642-22110-1_47
41. Kwiatkowska, M.Z., Thachuk, C.: Probabilistic model checking for biology. In: Software Systems Safety, NATO Science for Peace and Security Series, D: Information and Communication Security, vol. 36, pp. 165–189. IOS Press (2014). https://doi.org/10.3233/978-1-61499-385-8-165

42. Larsen, K.G., Skou, A.: Bisimulation through probabilistic testing. Inf. Comput. **94**(1), 1–28 (1991). https://doi.org/10.1016/0890-5401(91)90030-6
43. Lin, N., Liu, Y.: Perturbation analysis for continuous-time Markov chains in a weak sense. J. Appl. Probab. **61**(4), 1278–1300 (2024). https://doi.org/10.1017/jpr.2024.20
44. Liu, Y.Y.: Perturbation analysis for continuous-time Markov chains. Sci. China Math. **58**(12), 2633–2642 (2015). https://doi.org/10.1007/s11425-015-5019-z
45. Liu, Y., Li, W.: Error bounds for augmented truncation approximations of Markov chains via the perturbation method. Adv. Appl. Probab. **50**(2), 645–669 (2018). https://doi.org/10.1017/apr.2018.28
46. Madsen, C., Zhang, Z., Roehner, N., Winstead, C., Myers, C.J.: Stochastic model checking of genetic circuits. ACM J. Emerg. Technol. Comput. Syst. **11**(3), 23:1–23:21 (2014). https://doi.org/10.1145/2644817
47. Maire, R.A., Reibman, A.L., Trivedi, K.S.: Transient analysis of acyclic Markov chains. Perform. Eval. **7**(3), 175–194 (1987). https://doi.org/10.1016/0166-5316(87)90039-3
48. Marin, A., Piazza, C., Rossi, S.: Proportional lumpability. In: André, É., Stoelinga, M. (eds.) Formal Modeling and Analysis of Timed Systems (FORMATS) 2019. Lecture Notes in Computer Science (LNCS), vol. 11750, pp. 265–281. Springer International Publishing, Cham (2019). https://doi.org/10.1007/978-3-030-29662-9_16
49. Marin, A., Piazza, C., Rossi, S.: Proportional lumpability and proportional bisimilarity. Acta Inf. **59**(2–3), 211–244 (2022). https://doi.org/10.1007/s00236-021-00404-y
50. Meyer, C.D.: Matrix Analysis and Applied Linear Algebra. Society for Industrial and Applied Mathematics, Philadelphia, PA (2000)
51. Mitrophanov, A.Y.: Sensitivity and convergence of uniformly ergodic Markov chains. J. Appl. Probab. **42**(4), 1003–1014 (2005). https://doi.org/10.1239/jap/1134587812
52. Mitrophanov, A.Y.: The arsenal of perturbation bounds for finite continuous-time Markov chains: a perspective. Mathematics **12**(11) (2024). https://doi.org/10.3390/math12111608
53. Moler, C., Van Loan, C.: Nineteen dubious ways to compute the exponential of a matrix. twenty-five years later. SIAM Rev. **45**(1), 3–49 (2003). https://doi.org/10.1137/S00361445024180
54. Pan, V.Y., Chen, Z.Q.: The complexity of the matrix eigenproblem. In: Proceedings of the thirty-first Annual ACM Symposium on Theory of Computing, pp. 507–516. ACM, Atlanta Georgia USA (1999). https://doi.org/10.1145/301250.301389
55. Piazza, C., Rossi, S.: Reasoning about proportional lumpability. In: Abate, A., Marin, A. (eds.) Quantitative Evaluation of Systems (QEST 2021). Lecture Notes in Computer Science (LNCS), vol. 12846, pp. 372–390. Springer International Publishing, Cham (2021). https://doi.org/10.1007/978-3-030-85172-9_20
56. Piazza, C., Rossi, S., Smuseva, D.: Efficient algorithm for proportional lumpability and its application to selfish mining in public blockchains. Algorithms **17**(4) (2024). https://doi.org/10.3390/a17040159
57. Segala, R., Lynch, N.: Probabilistic simulations for probabilistic processes. In: Jonsson, B., Parrow, J. (eds.) CONCUR '94: Concurrency Theory. Lecture Notes in Computer Science (LNCS), vol. 836, pp. 481–496. Springer, Berlin, Heidelberg (1994). https://doi.org/10.1007/978-3-540-48654-1_35

58. Shardlow, T., Stuart, A.M.: A perturbation theory for ergodic Markov chains and application to numerical approximations. SIAM J. Numer. Anal. **37**(4), 1120–1137 (2000). https://doi.org/10.1137/S0036142998337235
59. Spork, T., Baier, C., Katoen, J.P., Klüppelholz, S., Piribauer, J.: Approximate Probabilistic Bisimulation for Continuous-Time Markov Chains (2025). https://doi.org/10.48550/arXiv.2505.15587
60. Spork, T., Baier, C., Katoen, J.P., Piribauer, J., Quatmann, T.: A spectrum of approximate probabilistic bisimulations. In: Majumdar, R., Silva, A. (eds.) 35th International Conference on Concurrency Theory (CONCUR 2024). Leibniz International Proceedings in Informatics (LIPIcs), vol. 311, pp. 37:1–37:19. Schloss Dagstuhl – Leibniz-Zentrum für Informatik, Dagstuhl, Germany (2024). https://doi.org/10.4230/LIPIcs.CONCUR.2024.37
61. Tracol, M., Desharnais, J., Zhioua, A.: Computing distances between probabilistic automata. In: Massink, M., Norman, G. (eds.) Proceedings of the Ninth Workshop on Quantitative Aspects of Programming Languages (QAPL 2011), Saarbrücken, Germany, April 1-3, 2011. EPTCS, vol. 57, pp. 148–162 (2011). https://doi.org/10.4204/eptcs.57.11
62. Volk, M., Junges, S., Katoen, J.P.: Fast dynamic fault tree analysis by model checking techniques. IEEE Trans. Ind. Info. **14**(1), 370–379 (2018). https://doi.org/10.1109/TII.2017.2710316
63. Watterson, G.A.: Markov chains with absorbing states: a genetic example. Ann. Math. Stat. **32**(3), 716–729 (1961). https://doi.org/10.1214/aoms/1177704967
64. Zhang, L., Jansen, D.N., Nielson, F., Hermanns, H.: Automata-based CSL model checking. Log. Meth. Comput. Sci. **8**(2) (2011). https://doi.org/10.1007/978-3-642-22012-8_21

On the Almost-Sure Termination of Probabilistic Counter Programs

Sergei Novozhilov[1,2], Mingqi Yang[1], Mingshuai Chen[1(✉)], Zhiyang Li[1],
and Jianwei Yin[1(✉)]

[1] Zhejiang University, Hangzhou, China
{mingqiyang,m.chen,misakalzy,zjuyjw}@zju.edu.cn
[2] Hong Kong University of Science and Technology,
Hong Kong, China
snovozhilov@connect.ust.hk

CAV
Artifact
Evaluation
★
Available

CAV
Artifact
Evaluation
★ ★ ★
Reusable

Abstract. This paper introduces k-d PCPs – the class of *probabilistic counter programs* with $k \in \mathbb{N}$ counter variables inducing possibly infinite-state Markov chains. We show that the universal (positive) almost-sure termination problem is *undecidable* for k-d PCPs in general, yet *decidable* for 1-d PCPs. We present an efficient decision procedure for the latter leveraging the technique of *Markov chain finitization*. Moreover, we identify several classes of k-d PCPs that are reducible to 1-d PCPs – thus their termination properties can be inferred automatically. Experiments demonstrate that our decision procedure can certify (positive) almost-sure termination – without resorting to invariants or supermartingales – of non-trivial probabilistic programs beyond the scope of existing tools.

Keywords: Probabilistic (counter) programs · (Positive) almost-sure termination · Decidability · Infinite-state Markov chains

1 Introduction

Probabilistic programming [3,26,34,38,47] is a widely adopted paradigm where programs can make probabilistic choices. Amongst others, the *almost-sure termination* (AST) problem, i.e., whether a program terminates with probability 1, is a fundamental property of probabilistic programs. Both AST and its refined notion called *positive almost-sure termination* (PAST) – whether an AST program terminates within finite expected runtime – are undecidable in general. In fact, reasoning about the termination behavior of probabilistic programs is known to be harder than that for deterministic programs; see [35]. Known classes of probabilistic programs/models admitting decidable (P)AST problems include finite-state Markov chains [2], probabilistic pushdown automata [20], and probabilistic counter programs [9]. However, these decidable fragments are not expressive enough to model randomized algorithms featuring, e.g., infinite state spaces and/or nonlinear guards; see Example 1 in Sect. 2.

S. Novozhilov and M. Yang—Both authors contributed equally to this work.

© The Author(s) 2025
R. Piskac and Z. Rakamarić (Eds.): CAV 2025, LNCS 15932, pp. 82–104, 2025.
https://doi.org/10.1007/978-3-031-98679-6_4

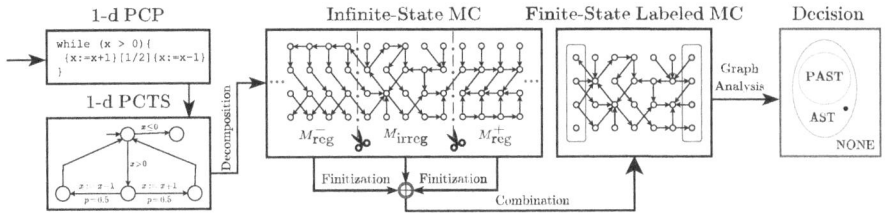

Fig. 1. The general workflow of our procedure for deciding (P)AST of 1-d PCPs.

In this paper, we introduce k-d PCPs – the class of *probabilistic counter programs* with $k \in \mathbb{N}$ counter variables (Sect. 3). This class of programs is a restricted version of the imperative probabilistic programming language pGCL [45] by allowing only assignments of the form $x := x + c$, where x is a counter variable and c is a constant. We show that k-d PCPs induce countable Markov chains with a regular structure and thereby admit an efficient analysis using various techniques established for random walks, queueing processes, finite-state Markov chains, and graph theory. In particular, we show that such Markov chains can be *finitized* while preserving their (positive) almost-sure termination properties, which yields the decidability of both AST and PAST for one-dimensional PCPs (1-d PCPs, Sect. 4) on all inputs (i.e., universal termination). We further identify several classes of k-d PCPs that are reducible to 1-d PCPs (hence called *essentially 1-d PCPs*), and thus their termination properties can be inferred automatically (Sect. 5). These classes include non-trivial practical programs such as the bounded retransmission protocol [30] and the Zeroconf protocol [5]. Moreover, we show that AST and PAST problems are undecidable for k-d PCPs in general, which is established by modeling a two-counter program within the 2-d PCP framework [18] ([54, Appendix F]). Finally, we present PASTRY, a tool implementing the decision procedure for essentially 1-d PCPs. Experimental results on a collection of benchmarks demonstrate that our decision procedure can certify (positive) almost-sure termination of non-trivial probabilistic programs that remain out of reach for existing tools, without resorting to any form of invariants or supermartingales (Sect. 6).

Main Contributions. Our main contributions are summarized as follows.

- We introduce a new class of probabilistic programs called k-d PCPs.
- We establish the decidability of universal (P)AST for 1-d PCPs and present an efficient decision procedure via Markov chain finitization.
- We identify important classes of k-d PCPs that are reducible to 1-d PCPs.
- We implement and conduct an extensive experimental evaluation of the proposed decision procedure against existing termination analysis tools.

2   A Bird's-Eye Perspective

This section outlines our procedure for deciding (P)AST of probabilistic programs with *one* counter. As depicted in Fig. 1, our algorithm takes a 1-d PCP

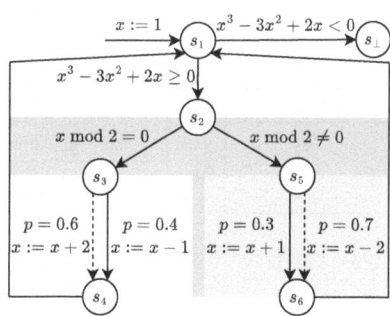

$x := 1$;

$\texttt{while}\left(x^3 - 3x^2 + 2x \geq 0\right)\{$

   $\texttt{if}\ (x \bmod 2 = 0)\ \{$

     $\{x := x+2\}\ [0.6]\ \{x := x-1\}$

   $\}\ \texttt{else}\ \{$

     $\{x := x+1\}\ [0.3]\ \{x := x-2\}$

   $\}$

$\}$

Prog. 1. The parity random walk.   **Fig. 2.** The PCTS of Prog. 1.

as input and converts it to an intermediate representation called probabilistic counter transition systems (PCTSs). Each PCTS induces a countable yet potentially *infinite-state* Markov chain. Our key observation is that such Markov chain is highly *regular*: It can be decomposed into a finite component M_{irreg} and two infinite components $M_{\mathrm{reg}}^-, M_{\mathrm{reg}}^+$ featuring *periodic* behaviors. We then abstract the regular components leveraging the theory of quasi-birth-death processes [56], which yields *finite-state* MCs with *labeled* states. By combining these MCs with M_{irreg}, we obtain a single finite-state labeled MC. Finally, we conclude the termination of the original 1-d PCP by conducting a standard *reachability* analysis (via graph-theoretic techniques) over this MC.

We use the following example to demonstrate our decision procedure.

Example 1 (Parity Random Walk). Consider the 1-d PCP Prog. 1 that models a one-dimensional asymmetric random walk subject to two phases (based on the parity of its current position). This program is adapted from [13] by adding features of nonlinear guards and the modulo operation (mod). These features – together with the unbounded nature of x – render it infeasible to analyze the termination behavior using existing procedures such as AMBER [52] and KoAT [41]. We show below how our decision procedure sketched in Fig. 1 can be employed to certify positive almost-sure termination of Prog. 1 in steps.   ◁

1) Convert 1-d PCP to 1-d PCTS We first adopt a standard procedure to mechanically convert the probabilistic counter program to a probabilistic counter transition system by recursively traversing the underlying syntax tree. The so-obtained 1-d PCTS of Prog. 1 is shown in Fig. 2, where $s_\perp$ denotes the terminal state and a dashed edge denotes a condensed transition of consecutive counting steps, e.g., $s_3 \xrightarrow{p=0.6,\ x:=x+2} s_4$ abbreviates $s_3 \xrightarrow{p=0.6,\ x:=x+1} s' \xrightarrow{x:=x+1} s_4$ for some omitted intermediate state s'. To demonstrate the correspondence between the PCTS and the Markov chain(s) it induces (in later steps), we use colors in Fig. 2 to indicate transitions between different states.

2) Transform 1-d PCTS to Partitioned Infinite-State MC Each 1-d PCTS with state space S induces a countable Markov Chain M over the infinite state space

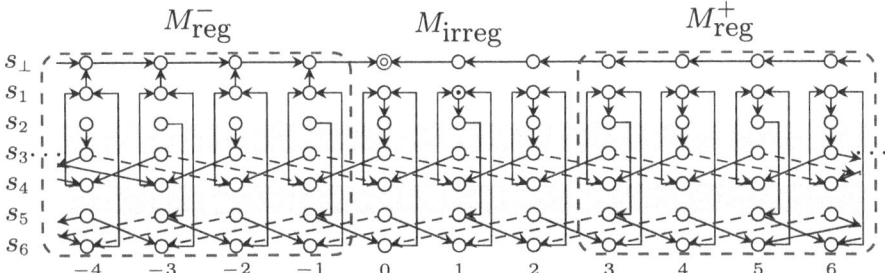

Fig. 3. The partitioned infinite-state MC induced by Prog. 1. Transition probabilities are omitted for clarity. ⊙ and ⊚ mark the initial and terminal state, respectively. We artificially chain the states associated with $s_\perp$ to ensure that the MC has a unique exit state $(s_\perp, 0)$ (see Sect. 3).

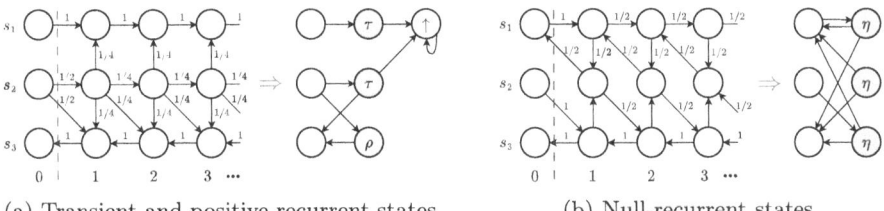

(a) Transient and positive-recurrent states.   (b) Null-recurrent states.

Fig. 4. An illustration of regular MC finitization using *transient* (τ), *positive-recurrent* (ρ), and *null-recurrent* (η) states. A transient state is an abstract state from which a random walk on the MC gets trapped in the regular part (signified by the artificial sink state ↑) with a positive probability. A positive-recurrent state is an abstract state from which the random walk crosses the boundary and enters the irregular part with probability 1 in a finite expected number of steps. In contrast, from a null-recurrent state, a random walk visits the irregular side with probability 1 but in an infinite expected number of steps.

$S \times \mathbb{Z}$; see Fig. 3 for the induced MC of Prog. 1. We then exploit the *regularity* of this Markov chain: Except for finitely many "middle" states around the initial counter value, the behavior of the Markov chain exhibits *periodicity*, i.e., the transitions form specific patterns ad infinitum. We can thus decompose the MC into a finite irregular component and two infinite regular components:[1]

$$M \quad = \quad M_{\mathrm{reg}}^{-} \ \uplus \ M_{\mathrm{irreg}} \ \uplus \ M_{\mathrm{reg}}^{+} \, , \tag{†}$$

where $\uplus$ denotes a disjoint union. We identify the decomposition (†) by means of *guard analysis* over the PCTS. Such an analysis produces (i) the thresholds δ^{-} and δ^{+} where to partition M; and (ii) the periods T^{-} and T^{+} for M_{reg}^{-} and M_{reg}^{+}, respectively. Such information will be used to finitize M in the later step.

---

[1] The components may share states at the intersections for cross-boundary transitions.

3) Finitize the Partitioned MC Next, we finitize the infinite-state Markov chain M by abstracting its regular components M_{reg}^- and M_{reg}^+ respectively into their *finite-state* counterparts $\dot{M}_{reg}^-$ and $\dot{M}_{reg}^+$, where every state is *labeled* with one of the three labels: *transient, positive-recurrent,* and *null-recurrent*; see Fig. 4 for an illustration. These labels are designed to preserve termination-relevant information about M whilst the rest ingredients in the regular components $M_{reg}^{+,-}$, e.g., concrete probabilities and specific states or transitions, are abstracted away from the finitized counterparts $\dot{M}_{reg}^{+,-}$. By integrating these components, we obtain a finite-state labeled Markov chain $\dot{M}$:

$$\dot{M} \quad = \quad \dot{M}_{reg}^- \uplus M_{irreg} \uplus \dot{M}_{reg}^+ . \tag{$\ddagger$}$$

Note that we drop all the explicit transition probabilities in $\dot{M}$ and keep track of only their *positivity*, i.e., zero or non-zero. This is because the (P)AST nature of finite-state MCs does not depend on the concrete probabilities thereof.

Our core labeling algorithm is inspired by the queueing theory [4] since the regular MCs $M_{reg}^{+,-}$ fall into the scope of quasi-birth-death processes (QBDs) [56]. The main technical challenge is that, in queueing theory, it is common to assume that a QBD is strongly connected (i.e., the underlying Markov chain is irreducible, cf. [8]), which is however not always the case for $M_{reg}^{+,-}$. We address this challenge by extending QBD analysis techniques with the

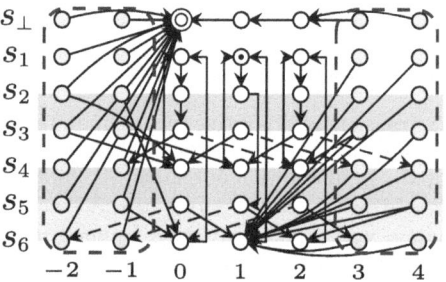

Fig. 5. Finitized labeled MC for Prog. 1.

identification of strongly connected components (SCCs) and reachability analysis between SCCs for infinite regular graphs (see Sect. 4). The resulting finite-state labeled Markov chain for Prog. 1 is depicted in Fig. 5.

4) Decide Termination via Reachability Analysis of the Finite-State Labeled MC. Our finitization technique guarantees that the finite-state labeled Markov chain $\dot{M}$ obtained in the previous step preserves the (positive) almost-sure termination nature of the original 1-d PCP in the following sense: The program is non-AST (and thus non-PAST) if there is a path from the initial state to a bottom SCC (distinct from the terminal state $(s_\perp, 0)$), i.e., an SCC that cannot be escaped once entered; the sink state $\uparrow$ is per se a bottom SCC. Otherwise, if any null-recurrent state is reachable from the initial state, the program is AST but non-PAST. The program is necessarily PAST if none of the above cases holds.

As per the above decision rules, we conclude that the parity random walk modeled by Prog. 1 is PAST (and thus AST), because no bottom SCC (distinct from the terminal state $(s_\perp, 0)$) nor null-recurrent state is reachable from the initial state $(s_1, 1)$; see Fig. 5. We note that, due to the *finiteness* and *non-probabilistic* nature of $\dot{M}$ (as concrete probabilities are abstracted away), the underlying *qualitative* reachability analysis can be done effectively through standard graph-theoretic techniques.

$$C ::= \texttt{skip} \qquad\qquad \varphi ::= e < e \qquad\qquad e ::= c$$

	$\mid\ x := x + c$		$\mid\ \varphi \wedge \varphi$		$\mid\ x$	
	$\mid\ C \,\texttt{;}\, C$		$\mid\ \neg\varphi$		$\mid\ e \bmod c$	$(c \neq 0)$
	$\mid\ \{C\}\,[p]\,\{C\}$				$\mid\ e \div c$	$(c \neq 0)$
	$\mid\ \texttt{if}\,(\varphi)\,\{C\}\,\texttt{else}\,\{C\}$				$\mid\ e \diamond e$	$(\diamond \in \{+, -, \cdot\})$
	$\mid\ \texttt{while}\,(\varphi)\{C\}$					

    (a) k-d PCPs   (b) Guards   (c) Expressions

Fig. 6. Syntax of k-d PCPs and possibly nonlinear guards and expressions. Here, x is an integer *counter* variable taken from the finite set Vars $= \{x_1, x_2, \ldots, x_k\}$ ranging over $\mathbb{Z}^k$, $p \in [0, 1]$ is a probability, and $c \in \mathbb{Z}$ is an integer constant. $x \bmod c$ denotes the unique number in $[0, c)$ congruent to x modulo c and $x \div c$ denotes $(x - x \bmod c)/c$. Moreover, we admit standard predicates in guards that are expressible as syntactic sugar, e.g., true, false, $\varphi \vee \varphi$, $e_1 = e_2$, $e_1 \le e_2$, etc.

3   Problem Formulation

This section formulates our problem of certifying the (positive) almost-sure termination of probabilistic programs with $k \in \mathbb{N}$ counter variables.

Probabilistic Counter Programs. *Probabilistic counter programs* (PCPs) are a subclass of imperative programs described by the *probabilistic guarded command language* (pGCL) [44], where the assignments are restricted to a "counting" form. Specifically, the syntax of a k-d PCP C adheres to the grammar in Fig. 6. The semantics of most program constructs – including skip, sequential composition, conditional, and (possibly nested) loops – is standard. The *probabilistic choice* $\{C_1\}\,[p]\,\{C_2\}$ flips a coin with bias $p \in [0, 1]$ and executes C_1 in case the coin yields heads, and C_2 otherwise; Other forms of discrete random sampling can be mimicked by such coin flips [27]. Notice that PCPs admit *polynomial* and *modulo* operations in guards.[2] Moreover, from the termination point of view, constant assignments of the form $x := c$ are syntactic sugar and can be encoded as certainly terminating loops $\texttt{while}\,(x > c)\,\{x := x - 1\}\,\texttt{;}\,\texttt{while}\,(x < c)\,\{x := x + 1\}$.

We interpret the operational semantics of PCPs as *countably infinite-state Markov chains* [55]. To this end, we define *probabilistic counter transition systems* (PCTSs) as an intermediate representation:

Definition 1 (Probabilistic Counter Transition Systems). *A PCTS is a triple $\langle \boldsymbol{x}, S, \mathcal{T} \rangle$, where $\boldsymbol{x} \in \mathbb{Z}^k$ is a k-dimensional vector of counter variables, S*

---

[2] These operations are essential for reducing k-d PCPs to 1-d PCPs; see Sect. 5.

is a finite set of states including an initial state s_1 (with constant initialization $\boldsymbol{x} := \boldsymbol{c}$) and a terminal state[3] $s_\perp$ (without any outgoing transition), and $\mathcal{T} \subset S \times \mathcal{P}(\boldsymbol{x}) \times [0,1] \times \mathbb{Z}^k \times S$ is a set of transitions. For $(s,g,p,\boldsymbol{u},s') \in \mathcal{T}$,

- $s,s' \in S$ are the source and target states, respectively (s and s' may coincide);
- $g(\boldsymbol{x}) \in \mathcal{P}(\boldsymbol{x})$ is a predicate over $\boldsymbol{x}$, which inherits the guard syntax of PCPs;
- $p \in [0,1]$ is the probability of the transition to be taken;
- $\boldsymbol{u} \in \{-1,0,1\}^k$ is an update vector, i.e., the counters are updated as $\boldsymbol{x} := \boldsymbol{x} + \boldsymbol{u}$ upon taking the transition. Multi-step updates with $\boldsymbol{u} \in \mathbb{Z}^k \setminus \{-1,0,1\}^k$ are broken down to consecutive counting steps (e.g., dashed edges in Fig. 2).

A transition is enabled by its guard $g(\boldsymbol{x})$ if $g(\boldsymbol{x}) = \mathsf{true}$ for the current counter values. If multiple transitions from the same state are enabled by the same guard, then we assume that all the probabilities along these transitions sum up to 1.

Translating PCPs to PCTSs can be done mechanically by recursively traversing the abstract syntax tree; similar procedures are standard in the literature [11].

Next, we convert a PCTS to a countable Markov chain [55] by entangling its state space with the infinitely many counter valuations: Given a PCTS $\langle \boldsymbol{x}, S, \mathcal{T} \rangle$, the induced Markov chain can be constructed as $M = \langle (S \times \mathbb{Z}^k), \mathcal{T}' \rangle$, where

- the initial state $(s_1, \boldsymbol{c}) \in S \times \mathbb{Z}^k$ of M is composed of the initial state s_1 of the PCTS and its initial counter valuations $\boldsymbol{c}$;
- the terminal state $(s_\perp, \boldsymbol{0}) \in S \times \mathbb{Z}^k$ of M is composed of the terminal state $s_\perp$ of the PCTS and special counter valuations $\boldsymbol{0}$;[4]
- for each PCTS transition $(s,g,p,\boldsymbol{u},s') \in \mathcal{T}$, we construct MC transitions $((s,\boldsymbol{x}),p,(s,\boldsymbol{x}+\boldsymbol{u})) \in \mathcal{T}'$ for all $\boldsymbol{x}$ s.t. $g(\boldsymbol{x}) = \mathsf{true}$. Moreover, for $(s_\perp,\boldsymbol{x})$, we add transition $((s_\perp,\boldsymbol{x}),1,(s_\perp,\boldsymbol{x}+1))$ if $\boldsymbol{x} < \boldsymbol{0}$ or $((s_\perp,\boldsymbol{x}),1,(s_\perp,\boldsymbol{x}-1))$ if $\boldsymbol{x} > \boldsymbol{0}$, to ensure that $(s_\perp,\boldsymbol{0})$ is the unique exit of the M (cf. Fig. 3).

Remark that the terminal state $(s_\perp,\boldsymbol{0})$ is also the only *absorbing* state of M, i.e., a state that has no outgoing transitions. The conversion from PCPs to MCs via PCTSs has been illustrated in Sect. 2. Note that the induced MC may contain states unreachable from the initial state.

Given a possibly infinite-state Markov chain M induced by a PCP *prog*, for each path $\pi = \langle (s_1, \boldsymbol{c}), \ldots \rangle$ of M, let T_{prog} be the random variable such that $T_{prog}(\pi)$ represents the number of transitions until π reaching $(s_\perp,\boldsymbol{0})$; If π does not terminate by visiting $(s_\perp,\boldsymbol{0})$, then $T_{prog}(\pi) = \infty$. We call T_{prog} the *runtime* of *prog*. Then, the (P)AST property of a PCP can be defined as follows.

Definition 2 ((Positive) Almost-Sure Termination). *Let prog be a PCP and $\mathbb{P}$ be the probability measure generated by the corresponding Markov chain*

---

[3] For simplicity, we assume a *unique* terminal state for the PCTS (and thus a single exit for the PCP as well). For a program with multiple exits, one can append a ghost statement, e.g., `skip`, to the program end to obtain a unified exit.

[4] The concrete counter valuations do not matter. But, we assume, w.l.o.g., that both $\boldsymbol{0}$ and $\boldsymbol{c}$ will be partitioned into the irregular component of M in the finitization.

with initial state $(s_1, \boldsymbol{c})$ *(cf. [54, Appendix A.1]). Then, prog terminates almost-surely (AST) iff* $\mathbb{P}[T_{prog} < \infty] = 1$. *Moreover, prog positive almost-surely terminates (PAST) iff* $\mathbb{E}[T_{prog}] < \infty$.

Remark 1. Our notion of termination in Definition 2 is *non-universal* as it assumes implicitly a specific input $\boldsymbol{x} = \boldsymbol{c}$ to the program. We will show in Sect. 4.5 how our decidability result can be extended to the *universal* (positive) almost-sure termination (U(P)AST), i.e., (P)AST on *all* inputs. Nonetheless, we note that, in general, deciding AST for *one* input is as hard as ordinary termination for *all* inputs and deciding UPAST is even harder; see [35].   ◁

Example 2 (1-d Random Walk on $\mathbb{Z}$ *[46]).* Consider the following 1-d PCP:

$$x := 1 \, \fatsemi \, \mathtt{while} \, (x > 0) \, \{\{ \, x := x - 1 \, \} \, [p] \, \{ \, x := x + 1 \, \}\}$$

which models a random walk on $\mathbb{Z}$ parameterized by the branching probability $p \in [0, 1]$. The program terminates as soon as the counter x becomes non-positive. It is known from the literature, e.g., [23, 46], that the program is PAST if $p > 1/2$ (i.e., it terminates almost-surely with a finite expected runtime), AST but not PAST if $p = 1/2$ (i.e., it terminates almost-surely yet with an infinite expected runtime), and non-AST if $p < 1/2$ (i.e., it diverges with positive probability). The above termination behavior holds not only for the specific input $x = 1$, but also for all inputs satisfying the loop guard $x > 0$.   ◁

The decision problem concerned in this paper reads as follows:

> **Problem Statement.** Given a k-d probabilistic counter program *prog* with input $\boldsymbol{x} = \boldsymbol{c}$, determine whether *prog* is PAST, AST, or neither.

We show that the problem is undecidable for k-d PCPs in general, yet decidable for 1-d PCPs as well as specific fragments of k-d PCPs. The same conclusion holds for the universal counterpart of the problem (i.e., (P)AST on *all* inputs).

4   Deciding (P)AST for 1-D PCPs

This section stablishes the decidability of (P)AST for 1-d PCPs and presents an efficient decision procedure leveraging the technique of Markov chain finitization.

Decision Procedure. Algorithm 1 outlines our procedure for deciding (P)AST for a 1-d PCP *prog* with input $x = c$. As has been exemplified in Sect. 2, our algorithm works in four main steps: (I) *Preprocessing*: It converts *prog* to the corresponding 1-d PCTS P, which induces a potentially infinite-state Markov chain M (Line 1); (II) *Decomposition*: It decomposes M – based on a guard analysis – into a finite component M_{irreg} and two infinite components $M_{\mathrm{reg}}^-, M_{\mathrm{reg}}^+$ featuring periodic behaviors (Lines 2 and 3); (III) *Finitization*: It abstracts M into a finite-state labeled Markov chain $\dot{M}$ which preserves the termination nature of *prog* (Lines 4 and 5); (IV) *Decision*: It determines the termination of *prog* by conducting a standard reachability analysis over $\dot{M}$ (Lines 6 to 10).

In the rest of this section, we elaborate Steps (II) to (IV) of the above decision procedure and justify its correctness and efficiency afterwards.

Algorithm 1: Deciding AST and PAST for 1-d PCPs

---

    input: 1-d PCP *prog* (with input $x = c$).
    output: PAST, AST (but non-PAST), or non-AST.

    /* convert the program to a 1-d PCTS; see Section 3 */
1 $P \leftarrow$ PCP2PCTS(*prog*) ;

    /* decompose the underlying infinite-state MC; see Section 4.1 */
2 $\langle \delta^-, \delta^+, T^-, T^+ \rangle \leftarrow$ **GuardAnalysis**(P) ;   ▷ generate thresholds and periods
3 $\langle M_{\text{irreg}}, M_{\text{reg}}^-, M_{\text{reg}}^+ \rangle \leftarrow$ **Decompose**($P, \delta^-, \delta^+, T^-, T^+$) ;

    /* obtain the finite-state labeled MC; see Section 4.2 */
4 $\dot{M}_{\text{reg}}^- \leftarrow$ **Abstract**(**Label**(M_{reg}^-)); $\dot{M}_{\text{reg}}^+ \leftarrow$ **Abstract**(**Label**(M_{reg}^+)) ;
5 $\dot{M} \leftarrow \dot{M}_{\text{reg}}^- \uplus M_{\text{irreg}} \uplus \dot{M}_{\text{reg}}^+$;   ▷ combine the finite components

    /* decide termination by reachability analysis of $\dot{M}$ (Section 4.3)
    */
6 **if** $\exists(s', c') \in \dot{M} : (s_1, c) \rightarrow^* (s', c')$ and $(s', c') \not\rightarrow^* (s_\perp, 0)$ **then**
7   ⌊ **return** non-AST ;   ▷ a run may get trapped in a bottom SCC
8 **if** $\exists(s', c') \in \dot{M} :$ NullRec((s', c')) and $(s_1, c) \rightarrow^* (s', c')$ **then**
9   ⌊ **return** AST (but non-PAST) ;   ▷ a null-recurrent state is reachable
10 **return** PAST ;   ▷ *prog* is necessarily PAST otherwise

---

4.1 Infinite-State MC Decomposition

Our decomposition of the countable Markov Chain M exploits its *regularity* over the infinite state space $S \times \mathbb{Z}$. Such regularity roots in the fact that *every (possibly nonlinear) guard of a 1-d probabilistic counter program is eventually periodic*:

Theorem 1 (Periodicity of Guards). *Let $P = \langle x, S, T \rangle$ be the 1-d PCTS of prog and $\mathcal{G} = \{g \mid (s, g, p, u, s') \in T\}$ be the set of guards in P. Then, every guard $g \in \mathcal{G}$ over the counter $x \in \mathbb{Z}$ is eventually periodic, i.e., there exist computable thresholds $\delta^-, \delta^+ \in \mathbb{Z}$ (with $\delta^- < \delta^+$) and periods $T^-, T^+ \in \mathbb{Z}_{>0}$ such that*

$$\forall x < \delta^- : g(x) = g(x - T^-) \quad \text{and} \quad \forall x > \delta^+ : g(x) = g(x + T^+) .$$

Proof (sketch). The proof is done by structural induction on the syntax tree of the guard g: For the base case with a pure polynomial predicate, we construct the thresholds $\delta^{+,-}$ using Cauchy's bound [32] associated with the periods $T^- = T^+ = 1$; For the induction step with nested operators $\div$ or mod, we iteratively replace the innermost $\div$/mod-expression with polynomial expressions while constructing $\delta^{+,-}$ and $T^{+,-}$. See complete proof in [54, Appendix B.1]. □

We refer to the construction in the proof of Theorem 1 as *guard analysis* (cf. Line 2 of Algorithm 1), which ultimately yields two thresholds $\delta^{+,-}$ and periods $T^{+,-}$ such that all guards are periodic with period T^- over $(-\infty, \delta^-)$ and T^+ over (δ^+, ∞), respectively. Recall the parity random walk in Prog. 1, our guard analysis yields $\delta^- = 0, \delta^+ = 2$ and $T^- = T^+ = 2$. Now, to describe the periodic parts beyond $[\delta^-, \delta^+]$, we introduce the model of *regular Markov chains*:

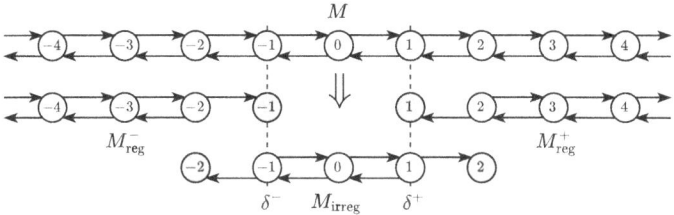

Fig. 7. The decomposition of the infinite-state MC M. Absorbing states (dashed circles) in $M_{\text{reg}}^{+,-}$ correspond to the non-absorbing states in M_{irreg} and vice versa.

Definition 3 (Regular Markov Chains). *Given a Markov chain M_{reg}^{+} over the state space $S \times \mathbb{Z}_{\geq \delta^{+}}$ with a transition probability function $\mu \colon (S \times \mathbb{Z}_{\geq \delta^{+}}) \times (S \times \mathbb{Z}_{\geq \delta^{+}}) \to [0,1]$. For $k \geq \delta^{+}$, we call the sets of the form $S \times \{k\}$ levels and refer to them as level-k. M_{reg}^{+} is called a regular Markov chain with period T^{+} (T^{+}-periodic, for short) if (i) there is no cross-level transition in M_{reg}^{+}, i.e., $\mu((s,k),(s',k')) = 0$ for any $|k'-k| > 1$; ii) all states at level-δ^{+} are absorbing;[5] and (iii) $\mu((s,k),(s',k')) = \mu((s,k+T^{+}),(s',k'+T^{+}))$ for all $k > \delta^{+}, k' \geq \delta^{+}$.[6]*

A T^{+}-periodic regular Markov chain can be represented effectively as a T^{+}-tuple of matrices $\langle (A_i, B_i, C_i) \rangle_{i=1}^{T^{+}}$, where

$$
\begin{aligned}
A_i[s,s'] &= \mu((s,T^{+}+i),(s',T^{+}+i-1)) \,, \\
B_i[s,s'] &= \mu((s,T^{+}+i),(s',T^{+}+i)) \,, \\
C_i[s,s'] &= \mu((s,T^{+}+i),(s',T^{+}+i+1)) \,.
\end{aligned}
\tag{1}
$$

A regular Markov chain M_{reg}^{-} over the state space $S \times \mathbb{Z}_{\leq \delta^{-}}$ with period T^{-} can be defined and represented analogously.

Given the thresholds $\delta^{+,-}$ and periods $T^{+,-}$ from guard analysis, a *decomposition* of infinite-state MC M (Line 3 of Algorithm 1) can be identified as

$$
M = M_{\text{reg}}^{-} \uplus M_{\text{irreg}} \uplus M_{\text{reg}}^{+} \,,
\tag{2}
$$

where M_{irreg} is a finite-state MC over $S \times [\delta^{-}-1, \delta^{+}+1]$ with absorbing states at levels of $\delta^{-}-1$ and $\delta^{+}+1$; M_{reg}^{+} (resp. M_{reg}^{-}) is an infinite-state T^{+}-periodic (resp. T^{-}-periodic) regular MC over $S \times \mathbb{Z}_{\geq \delta^{+}}$ (resp. $\mathbb{Z}_{\leq \delta^{-}}$) with absorbing states at level-δ^{+} (resp. level-δ^{-}). An example of the decomposition is depicted in Fig. 7 and the detailed decomposition algorithm can be found in [54, Appendix C]. We justify in [54, Appendix B.2] that our decomposition as in (2) indeed yields regular Markov chains $M_{\text{reg}}^{+,-}$ in accordance with Definition 3.

---

[5] All outgoing transitions from level-δ^{+} states are allocated to the irregular part of M.

[6] We rule out the case of $k = \delta^{+}$ to ensure that the level-δ^{+} states are absorbing.

4.2 Regular MC Finitization

Next, our goal is to construct a *finite-state* Markov chain $\dot{M}$ via labeling and abstraction (Line 4 of Algorithm 1), which preserves termination nature of M:

$$\dot{M} \quad = \quad \dot{M}_{\mathrm{reg}}^{-} \uplus M_{\mathrm{irreg}} \uplus \dot{M}_{\mathrm{reg}}^{+} , \tag{3}$$

where $\dot{M}_{\mathrm{reg}}^{-}$ and $\dot{M}_{\mathrm{reg}}^{+}$ are finitized MCs abstracting M_{reg}^{-} and M_{reg}^{+}, respectively. Due to the symmetry, we show below how to obtain $\dot{M}_{\mathrm{reg}}^{+}$ by finitizing the T^{+}-periodic regular MC M_{reg}^{+} over $S \times \mathbb{Z}_{\geq \delta^{+}}$, whose transition probability function μ is described by the set of matrices $\langle (A_i, B_i, C_i) \rangle_{i=1}^{T^{+}}$ as per (1).

Without loss of generality, we assume $\delta^{+} = 0$ throughout the rest of this subsection; any other threshold can be aligned to 0 by shifting the MC accordingly. Moreover, we assume $T^{+} = 1$. This is because any T^{+}-periodic regular MC M_{reg}^{+} can be reduced equivalently to a 1-periodic regular MC; see [54, Appendix B.3].

Now, our task is to finitize a 1-periodic regular MC M_{reg}^{+} over $S \times \mathbb{Z}_{\geq 0}$, whose transition probability function μ is described by the matrices (A, B, C). Our approach to solving this task consists of two steps – *labeling* and *abstraction*. The former labels the level-1 states of M_{reg}^{+} whilst the latter replaces the regular part with a labeled Markov chain over the finite state space $S \times \{0, 1\}$.

The Labeling Procedure. Consider a random walk π starting from a level-1 state $(s, 1)$ of M_{reg}^{+}. The *absorbing time* of $(s, 1)$ is a random variable $T(\pi) \triangleq \min\{i \mid \pi(i) \in S \times \{0\}\}$. Let $\mathbb{P}_{(s,1)}$ be the probability measure generated M_{reg}^{+} starting from $(s, 1)$. The state $(s, 1)$ is *recurrent* if $\mathbb{P}_{(s,1)}[T < \infty] = 1$ and *transient* otherwise. In particular, we distinguish *positive-recurrence* with $\mathbb{E}_{(s,1)}[T] < \infty$ from *null-recurrence* with $\mathbb{E}_{(s,1)}[T] = \infty$. The only termination-relevant information from M_{reg}^{+} is which absorbing states at level-0 are reachable from each labeled level-1 state with positive probability. Such information can be obtained by applying [40, Theorem 7.2.3] on *quasi-birth-death processes* (QBDs) established in the queueing theory, which, however, relies on a crucial assumption that M_{reg}^{+} is *irreducible*, i.e., the underneath graph is strongly connected (see [54, Appendix A.2]). This assumption does unfortunately not hold for regular Markov chains induced by 1-d PCPs in general. Our approach drops this assumption by extending QBD analysis techniques with the identification of strongly connected components (SCCs) and reachability analysis between SCCs for infinite regular graphs. The key is to build the so-called *coupled model* – a finite-state Markov chain capturing all asymptotic properties of the infinite walks over M_{reg}^{+}.

To this end, we build a *coupled Markov chain* $\bar{M}$ over the finite state space $S \times \{-1, 0, 1\}$, where the first component represents the current state in M_{reg}^{+} and the second component indicates the *counter change* upon transiting to the current state: -1 for counter decreasing from level-k to level-$(k-1)$, 0 for counter remaining unchanged, and 1 for counter increasing from level-k to level-$(k+1)$. The transition probability function $\bar{\mu}$ of $\bar{M}$, for any $s, s' \in S$, is set as

$$
\begin{aligned}
\bar{\mu}((s,-1),(s',-1)) &= \bar{\mu}((s,0),(s',-1)) = \bar{\mu}((s,1),(s',-1)) = A[s, s'] , \\
\bar{\mu}((s,-1),(s',0)) &= \bar{\mu}((s,0),(s',0)) = \bar{\mu}((s,1),(s',0)) = B[s, s'] , \\
\bar{\mu}((s,-1),(s',1)) &= \bar{\mu}((s,0),(s',1)) = \bar{\mu}((s,1),(s',1)) = C[s, s'] .
\end{aligned}
$$

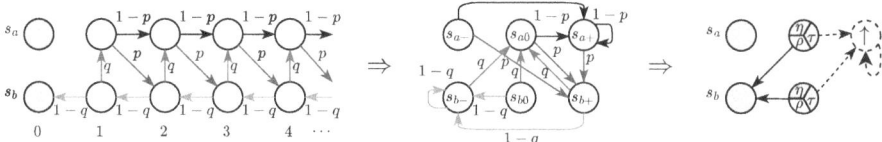

Fig. 8. Distilling from a regular MC M^+_{reg} over $S = \{s_a, s_b\} \times \mathbb{Z}_{\geq 0}$ (left) a coupled MC $\bar{M}$ over $S \times \{-1, 0, 1\} = \{s_{a-}, s_{a0}, s_{a+}, s_{b-}, s_{b0}, s_{b+}\}$ (middle). Based on the labeling of $\bar{M}$ and the abstraction procedure, we obtain the finite-state MC $\dot{M}^+_{\text{reg}}$ with labeled level-1 states (right). The concrete labels depend on the probability values p, q (see Example 3); We introduce an artificial sink state $\uparrow$ succeeding all transient (τ) states (in case of any) to signify that $\dot{M}^+_{\text{reg}}$ can get trapped.

See Fig. 8 for an example of constructing the coupled MC. The intuition behind the coupling is to *measure how much time a random walk over $\bar{M}$ spends in its "decreasing" component $S \times \{-1\}$ compared to that in the "increasing" component $S \times \{1\}$*. For the simple case where $\bar{M}$ is irreducible (assuming the irreducibility of M^+_{reg}), by the ergodic theorem for irreducible Markov chains (see [54, Appendix A.1, Theorem 5]), the ratio of the time spent in any state s converges to the stationary distribution $\bar{\gamma}(s)$. To measure the averaged imbalance between increasing- and decreasing-steps, we define the *imbalance value* $\bar{\nu}$ as

$$\bar{\nu} \quad \triangleq \quad \sum_{s \in S \times \{1\}} \bar{\gamma}(s) \ - \ \sum_{s \in S \times \{-1\}} \bar{\gamma}(s) \, . \tag{4}$$

Then, the sign of $\bar{\nu}$ classifies the coupled Markov chain $\bar{M}$ into three categories: transient ($\bar{\nu} > 0$), null-recurrent ($\bar{\nu} = 0$), and positive-recurrent ($\bar{\nu} < 0$). Note that this is a global property of $\bar{M}$, i.e., all its states are in the same category.

For the more involved case with *reducible* $\bar{M}$, the ergodic theorem does not apply. Nonetheless, every reducible $\bar{M}$ can be partitioned into *bottom SCCs* (BSCCs) and some *dangling states*. Each BSCC $B \subseteq S \times \{-1, 0, 1\}$ forms an irreducible Markov chain with a *local imbalance value* $\bar{\nu}_B$ obtained by restricting in (4) the state space to $B_+ = B \cap S \times 1$ and $B_- = B \cap S \times -1$.

The stationary distribution of B labels all states with $\bar{\nu}_B$. A dangling state s is labeled *transient* if any transient BSCC is reachable, *null-recurrent* if any null-recurrent BSCC is reachable, and *positive-recurrent* otherwise. The detailed labeling algorithm is in [54, Appendix C.3].

Example 3 (Labeling $\bar{M}$). Recall the *reducible* coupled Markov chain $\bar{M}$ in Fig. 8. $\bar{M}$ is composed by one BSCC $B = \{s_{a0}, s_{a+}, s_{b-}, s_{b+}\}$ and two dangling states s_{a-} and s_{b0}. For the MC induced by B, the stationary distribution is given by

$$[\bar{\gamma}(s_{a0}), \bar{\gamma}(s_{a+}), \bar{\gamma}(s_{b-}), \bar{\gamma}(s_{b+})] \ = \ \left[\frac{p \cdot q}{p+q}, \frac{(1-p) \cdot q}{p+q}, \frac{p \cdot (1-q)}{p+q}, \frac{p \cdot q}{p+q} \right] .$$

The local imbalance value $\bar{\nu}_B$ for B is calculated as

$$\bar{\nu}_B \triangleq \sum_{s \in B_+} \bar{\gamma}(s) - \sum_{s \in B_-} \bar{\gamma}(s) = \underbrace{\frac{(1-p)q}{p+q}}_{\bar{\gamma}(s_{a+})} + \underbrace{\frac{pq}{p+q}}_{\bar{\gamma}(s_{b+})} - \underbrace{\frac{p(1-q)}{p+q}}_{\bar{\gamma}(s_{b-})} = \frac{pq-p+q}{p+q} \, .$$

Therefore, the irreducible part B is labeled as transient (if $\bar{\nu}_B > 0$), null-recurrent (if $\bar{\nu}_B = 0$), and positive-recurrent (if $\bar{\nu}_B < 0$). Moreover, since B is the only BSCC that is reachable from the dangling states s_{a-} and s_{b0}, they two will be labeled with the same category as B (depending on the sign of $\bar{\nu}_B$).   ◁

Intuitively, the coupled Markov chain $\bar{M}$ captures the asymptotic, long-term behavior of M_{reg}^+. In principle, we can label level-1 states of M_{reg}^+ in accordance with the labels of $\bar{M}$.[7] However, two corner cases need to be taken into account: (I) A random walk over M_{reg}^+ starting from level-1 can get trapped in a finite set of states, i.e., a finite disconnected region of the infinite graph with no way back to level-0. The coupled Markov chain would capture this behavior as null-recurrent, however, we must label such states as transient; (II) A random walk over M_{reg}^+ starting from level-1 may visit level-0 immediately before exhibiting the asymptotic, long-term behavior as captured by $\bar{M}$.

We address corner case 4.2 by identifying the so-called *trappable states* at level-1 of M_{reg}^+ and corner case 4.2 by allowing a "runway" of length $3 \cdot |S|$ for the random walk to enter the mode of asymptotic, long-term behaviors as captured by $\bar{M}$. Both solutions are implemented, again, via standard qualitative reachability analysis over M_{reg}^+. Due to limited space, we provide the detailed algorithm for labeling the level-1 states of M_{reg}^+ (in the presence of the two corner cases) in Appendices B.4 and C.4 of [54].

The Abstraction Procedure Our abstraction procedure completes the finitization step by truncating M_{reg}^+ – whose level-1 states are labeled – into a labeled finite-state MC $\dot{M}_{\text{reg}}^+$ over $S \times \{0,1\}$ while abstracting away the infinite component beyond level-1. The key in this procedure is to identify *all possible exit states at level-0* for a random walk starting from each state at level-1. Such random walks can be infinite, nevertheless, our "runway" tactic (formulated in [54, Appendix B.4, Lemma 2]) ensures that it suffices to consider only *finite* walks bounded by the first $3 \cdot |S|$ levels (see the detailed abstraction algorithm in [54, Appendix C.2]). An example of the finitized MC $\dot{M}_{\text{reg}}^+$ in depicted in (the right of) Fig. 8.

4.3 Deciding Termination via Reachability Analysis

The finitization step yields two finite-state MCs $\dot{M}_{\text{reg}}^-$ and $\dot{M}_{\text{reg}}^+$ with labels. By combining them with M_{irreg} à la (3), we obtain a finite-state labeled Markov chain $\dot{M}$. The following theorem establishes that the (P)AST nature of the original 1-d PCP can be determined by conducting a reachability analysis over $\dot{M}$ (suppose $s \to^* s'$ means s' is reachable from s in zero or finitely many steps):

Theorem 2 (Decision Rules). *Suppose a 1-d PCP prog induces a finite-state labeled Markov chain $\dot{M}$ over the state space $\dot{S} = S \times [\delta^- - 1, \delta^+ + 1]$ with initial state (s_1, c) and terminal state $(s_\perp, 0)$. Then,*

- *If $\exists (s', c') \in \dot{S} : (s_1, c) \to^* (s', c') \wedge (s', c') \not\to^* (s_\perp, 0)$, then prog is non-AST;*[8]

---

[7] All states in the same row of $\bar{M}$ share the same label due to the construction of $\bar{M}$.

[8] As a special case, if $(s_1, c) \to^* \uparrow$ (through a transient state), then *prog* is non-AST.

– *Otherwise, if there exists a null-recurrent state (s', c') such that $(s_1, c) \rightarrow^*$*
  (s', c'), then prog is AST but non-PAST;
– *Otherwise prog is PAST.*

Remark 2. The reachability analysis over $\dot{M}$ as conducted in Theorem 2 is *qual-itative*: We drop all explicit transition probabilities in $\dot{M}$ and keep track of only their *positivity*, i.e., non-zero (a transition exists) or zero (no transition exists). This is because (positive) almost-sure termination of *finite-state* MCs is a topo-logical property independent of the specific transition probabilities thereof. ◁

4.4   Correctness and Efficiency of Algorithm 1

The decidability of (P)AST problems for 1-d PCPs follows from the correctness (i.e., *soundness* and *completeness*) of our decision algorithm as established below.

Theorem 3 (Correctness). *For any 1-d PCP prog, Algorithm 1 terminates and returns the correct termination category of prog.*

The efficiency of our decision procedure is captured by the following theorem:

Theorem 4 (Time Complexity). *Algorithm 1 runs in time polynomial in the size of the transition system, the thresholds, and the periods, i.e.,*

$$\mathcal{O}\left(\mathrm{poly}(|S|, \delta^+ - \delta^-, T^-, T^+) + StationaryDistribution(\max(T^-, T^+) \cdot |S|)\right) \ ,$$

where StationaryDistribution(n) *denotes the complexity of an oracle for find-ing the stationary distribution of a Markov chain with n states, which can be expressed as a linear programming instance (see [54, Appendix A.1]).*

The proofs of Theorem 3 and Theorem 4 are provided in [54, Appendix B.7].

4.5   Extending the Decidability to U(P)AST

Now, we show how our decidability result can be extended to the U(P)AST problems, i.e., deciding (P)AST on *all* inputs. The key to the extension is that *the termination behavior of a 1-d PCP is eventually periodic w.r.t. the inputs*:

Lemma 1 (Periodicity of (P)AST). *Fix a 1-d PCP prog. Suppose PAST(k) (AST(k), resp.) is a predicate indicating whether prog is PAST (AST, resp.) on input $x = k \in \mathbb{Z}$. Then, there exist thresholds $\delta_t^-, \delta_t^+ \in \mathbb{Z}$ (with $\delta_t^- < \delta_t^+$) and periods $T_t^-, T_t^+ \in \mathbb{Z}_{>0}$ such that*

$$\forall x < \delta_t^-: \ PAST(x) = PAST(x - T_t^-) \quad \text{and} \quad AST(x) = AST(x - T_t^-)$$
$$\forall x > \delta_t^+: \ PAST(x) = PAST(x + T_t^+) \quad \text{and} \quad AST(x) = AST(x + T_t^+) \ .$$

Moreover, the thresholds and periods are computable (cf. Theorem 1) as

$$\delta_t^- = \delta^- - 2^{T^- \cdot |S|}, \quad \delta_t^- = \delta^+ + 2^{T^+ \cdot |S|}, \quad T_t^- \leq 2^{T^- \cdot |S|}, \quad T_t^+ \leq 2^{T^+ \cdot |S|} \ .$$

The decidability of U(P)AST for 1-d PCPs then follows immediately from Lemma 1, since we can enumerate all possible inputs within $[\delta_t^- - T_t^-, \delta_t^+ + T_t^+]$.

5   Decidable Fragments for Multidimensional PCPs

Below, we identify four classes of k-d PCPs that can be reduced to 1-d PCPs:

(i) *All But One Counters are Bounded*: k-d PCPs with counter variables Vars $= \{x_1, x_2, \ldots, x_{k-1}, y\}$, for which there exists constant B such that $|x_i| < B$ for all $i = 1, \ldots, k - 1$ in all reachable program states;

(ii) *Monotone Counters*: k-d PCPs with counter variables Vars $= \{x_1, \ldots, x_m, y_1, \ldots, y_n, z\}$, for which all counters x_i are always non-decreasing while all counters y_i are always non-increasing. An additional requirement is that all atomic propositions in guards must depend on only one variable;

(iii) *Conditionally Bounded Counters*: k-d PCPs with counter variables Vars $= \{x_1, x_2, \ldots, x_{k-1}, y\}$, for which there exist constants $A_i, B_i, C_i, D_i \in \mathbb{Z}$ such that $|A_i \cdot x_i - B_i \cdot y - C_i| \leq D_i$ for all $i = 1, \ldots, k - 1$ in all reachable program states. In other words, all counters lie in a bounded neighborhood of a one-dimensional affine subspace of $\mathbb{Z}^k$;

(iv) *Constant Probability Programs*: The decidable fragment described in [25] can be rewritten as a 1-d PCP via a linear variable substitution.

We call the above classes and their mixtures *essentially 1-d PCPs*. The detailed techniques for reducing essentially 1-d PCPs to 1-d PCPs can be found in [54, Appendix D]. Below, we demonstrate the reduction using a real-world program; additional examples are provided in [54, Appendix E].

Example 4 (Zeroconf Protocol [5,23]). Consider the randomized IPv4 Zeroconf protocol for self-establishing IP connections via bounded retries:

start $:= 1$ ⨾ established $:= 0$ ⨾ probe $:= 0$⨾

while (start $\leq 1 \wedge$ established $\leq 0 \wedge$ probe < 4) {

    if (start $= 1$) {{ start $:= 0$ } [0.5] { start $:= 0$⨾ established $:= 1$ }}

    else { { probe $:=$ probe $+ 1$ } [0.001] { start $:= 1$⨾ probe $:= 0$ }}} .

Observe that all the three variables are bounded and thus – as a special case of Class (i) – the program is an essentially 1-d PCP: By introducing a new variable $z = 16 \cdot$ probe $+ ($start $+ 2) + 4 \cdot ($established $+ 2)$ and applying the substitutions

start $\mapsto (z \bmod 4) - 2$,   established $\mapsto (z \div 4) \bmod 4 - 2$,   probe $\mapsto z \div 16$,

we obtain the reduced 1-d PCP:

$z := 10$⨾

while (($z \bmod 4$) $- 2 \leq 1 \wedge (z \div 4) \bmod 4 - 2 \leq 0 \wedge z \div 16 < 4$) {

    if (($z \bmod 4$) $- 2 = 1$) {{ $z := z - 1$ } [0.5] { $z := z - 1$⨾ $z := z + 4$ }}

    else { { $z := z + 16$ } [0.001] { $z := z + 1$⨾ while ($z \div 16 > 0$) { $z := z - 16$ }}} .

Hence, termination behaviors of the protocol can be inferred automatically.   ◁

6 Implementation and Experimental Results

We have implemented our techniques in Python as a prototypical tool called PASTRY[9] – the Positive Almost-Sure Termination pRototYpe. By interfacing with `Probably` [49] for parsing probabilistic programs, `Sympy` for solving systems of linear equations, `NetworkX` [28] for graph analysis, and `SciPy` [63] for representing and manipulating sparse graphs as COO-encoded matrices, PASTRY decides whether a given essentially 1-d PCP with possibly infinite states is PAST, AST (but non-PAST), or non-AST. All experiments are conducted on a 3.22 GHz Apple M1 Pro processor with 16 GB RAM running macOS Sequoia.

Remark 3. Can one automatically check if a given k-d PCP belongs to one of the four classes of essentially 1-d PCPs as identified in Sect. 5? For Classes (ii) and (iv), the check can be done automatically in a purely *syntactic* way. For Classes (i) and (iii), the check can be automated by leveraging techniques for *synthesizing invariants* of the form $|x_i| < B$ or $|A_i \cdot x_i - B_i \cdot y - C_i| \leq D_i$. For instance, for linear programs, the check can be automated by a reduction to nonlinear constraint solving via Farkas' lemma [15] (though the procedure may not be complete due to integer-valued (counter) variables x_i and y). Our current implementation of PASTRY automates the check for Classes (ii) and (iv).

Baselines and Benchmarks. We compare PASTRY in terms of applicability and efficiency against four state-of-the-art tools for deciding termination of probabilistic programs: AMBER [52] for analyzing *prob-solvable loops*, KOAT1 [25] for analyzing *constant probability programs* (as a subset of essentially 1-d PCPs), and KOAT2 [48] and ABSYNTH [53] – both are for computing *upper bounds on expected costs* and thus are limited to certifying PAST. Our benchmark suite is compiled from seven sources in the literature (see Table 1). To facilitate the comparison, we initialize programs with open inputs (i.e., uninitialized variables and/or parameters) using randomly drawn inputs.

Experimental Results. As reported in Table 1, PASTRY suffices to determine the termination category of *all but 2 benchmarks*, including probabilistic counter programs featuring complex control flows, such as nested loops (e.g., `two_endpoints`) and conditional branches within loops (e.g., `generalized_rw` and `1d_poly_rw`). These program features pose significant challenges for other decision procedures like AMBER and KOAT1. Such benchmarks can be handled by techniques based on stochastic invariants, e.g., [12], which admit, however, only a relatively complete template-based approach for algorithmic synthesis. Moreover, compared to KOAT2 and ABSYNTH which can certify PAST only, PASTRY is capable of deciding both (non-)PAST and (non-)AST within a unified framework. We note that `geometric_gauss` and `polynomial_nast` are out of reach by PASTRY (yet can be handled by AMBER) as they feature continuous sampling and nonlinear updates, respectively (thus beyond PCPs).

---

[9] Available at ⦿ https://github.com/FICTION-ZJU/Pastry.

Table 1. Experimental results (–: inapplicability; TO: timeout in 90 s).

Benchmark	Src	Dim	PAST	AST	Pastry	Amber	KoAT1	KoAT2[2]	Absynth
symmetric_rw1		1	✗	✓	0.171	0.028	0.003	–	–
symmetric_rw2		1	✗	✓	0.137	0.027	0.003	–	–
biased_rw1		1	✗	✗	0.078	0.027	0.003	–	–
biased_rw2		1	✗	✗	0.419	0.073	0.004	–	–
biased_rw3	[52]	1	✗	✗	0.430	0.079	0.004	–	–
biased_rw4		1	✓	✓	0.081	0.023	0.032	0.888	0.011
binomial1		1	✗	✗	0.076	0.028	0.004	–	–
binomial2		1	✓	✓	0.080	0.022	0.031	0.877	0.012
geometric		1	✓	✓	0.074	0.018	0.029	0.661	0.009
2d_bounded_rw		2	✓	✓	3.390	0.031	–	–	–
geometric_gauss		1	✓	✓	–	0.022	–	–	–
polynomial_nast		2	✗	✗	–	1.590	–	–	–
asymmetric_rw1		1	✓	✓	0.075	0.024	0.031	0.980	0.011
complex_roots		1	✓	✓	0.137	0.025	0.056	9.459	0.028
high_multiplicity		1	✓	✓	0.132	0.028	0.052	7.137	0.027
neg_binomial		1	✓	✓	0.073	0.024	0.030	0.924	0.012
nast_prog	[25]	1	✗	✗	0.160	0.046	0.003	–	–
npast_prog		1	✗	✓	0.109	0.040	0.004	–	–
dir_term		1	✓	✓	0.078	–	0.034	–	0.016
irr_runtime		1	✓	✓	0.081	0.024	0.036	0.942	0.012
tortoise_hare_un		1	✓	✓	0.467	0.024	0.130	TO	0.133
tortoise_hare		2	✓	✓	2.450	–	0.159	TO	0.773
tortoise_hare_dt		2	✓	✓	0.185	–	0.032	1.047	–
generalized_rw		1	✗	✗	0.236	–	–	–	–
two_endpoints		1	✗	✗	0.209	–	–	–	–
infinite_loop		1	✗	✗	0.030	–	–	–	–
two_loops		1	✗	✗	0.151	–	–	–	–
ast_loop	[12]	1	✓	✓	0.078	0.022	0.032	1.193	0.013
ast_rw		1	✓	✓	0.174	0.021	0.042	3.114	0.020
biased_rw5		1	✗	✗	0.178	–	–	–	–
skewed_rw		1	✗	✗	0.229	–	–	–	–
asymmetric_rw2		1	✓	✓	0.088	0.031	0.039	0.929	0.011
1d_poly_rw		1	✗	✗	3.720	–	–	–	–
catmouse		1	✓	✓	0.103	–	–	1.079	0.020
speedpldi4		1	✓	✓	0.112	–	–	1.448	0.024
insertsort	[1]	2	✓	✓	0.303	–	–	3.462	0.030
speedpldi2		2	✓	✓	0.135	–	–	2.972	0.020
speedpldi3		2	✓	✓	0.226	–	–	2.235	0.026
counterex1b		2	✓	✓	0.361	–	–	6.758	0.051
Knuth-Yao_dice	[36]	2	✓	✓	0.499	–	–	12.712	53.015
brp_protocol	[30]	3	✓	✓	0.311	–	–	2.135	0.025
zeroconf	[5]	3	✓	✓	0.264	–	–	3.727	0.036

[1] Timings for PASTRY, AMBER, and KOAT1 are the total time for deciding both PAST and AST, whilst timings for KOAT2 and ABSYNTH are for certifying PAST only.
[2] KOAT2 takes inputs in the form of *integer transition systems* (ITS), where semantically equivalent programs may induce ITS with different structures. Thus, for some program that KoAT2 fails to certify PAST, e.g., dir_term, KoAT2 may succeed on its transformed version (by, e.g., eliminating loopy structures).

In terms of efficiency, PASTRY performs on par with its competitors for most 1-d programs yet less efficient for certain multi-dimensional programs. This is primarily due to an unoptimized procedure for constructing potentially large graphs for multi-dimensional programs.

We further note that the efficiency of PASTRY depends on the *size of counter increments* as it affects the size of the underlying Markov chain to be constructed. To investigate the dependency in a quantitative aspect, we examine a simple program with parameters α, β, and p:

$$x := 10 \, \mathring{}\, \texttt{while} \, (x > \alpha) \, \{\{\, x := x + \beta \,\} \, [p] \, \{\, x := x - \beta \,\}\} \,.$$

The expected theoretical time complexity for analyzing this program is $O(\beta^2) + O(|\alpha \cdot \beta|)$. Our empirical results (by varying the parameters α, β, and p) agree with this theoretical estimation; see detailed analysis in [54, Appendix G].

7   Related Work

Program Termination Landscape. As a cornerstone problem in computability, the results concerning termination can be broadly split into four categories: (i) establishing the *undecidability* of the termination problem in a model of computation. Historically the first results were obtained for Turing machines [62] and lambda calculus [14]. Later on, much simpler yet undecidable models were discovered. The most relevant to our work is the counter-machine model. These machines operate on integer registers, and the instructions generally involve incrementing, decrementing, copying, and testing the values in these registers. Different variations of counter machines have been proposed by, e.g., Hermes [31], Ershov [19], Péter [59], Minsky [18,37,50,51], Lambek [39], Shepherdson and Sturgis [60]. Some key differences in these models include: the presence of an accumulator (a special register for arithmetic operations), the use of direct vs. indirect addressing, the availability of instructions for incrementing, decrementing, and comparing the values in the registers, and whether or not the machine allows for unconditional jumps, conditional jumps, or both; (ii) establishing the *hardness* of the termination problem w.r.t. a known hypothesis, such as leveraging the Skolem problem [22,29] to loop termination analysis [57]; (iii) establishing *decidability* results in special cases, such as the decidability of termination for probabilistic pushdown automata (pPDA) [20] or programs in a special restrictive syntax such a single while loop with affine assignments [6,7,24,58,61]; (iv) finding an easily verifiable termination *certificate* (also called a proof). Within this category, we can identify two sub-categories: (a) when the certificate always exists, but the search procedure might be undecidable in general, as for the intersection types [16,17] or recent works on the supermartingale rules [10,42,43,46]; (b) when there is no guarantee of existing certificates, but if exists, it can be found efficiently as for special cases of ranking supermartingales (SMs), e.g., polynomial SMs [11], linear lexicographic ranking SMs [1], repulsing SMs [13]; or for the case of resource-aware programming languages [33].

PCPs in the Landscape. We place our results on k-d PCPs to Categories 7 and 7, especially in the probabilistic setting. For the undecidability category, the most relevant results are on the undecidability of counter machines (with two counters, decrement and jump instructions) [18,37,51] as our proof is based on encoding an arbitrary 2-counter machine inside a 2-d PCP program. For the decidability category, the most relevant works are on probabilistic pushdown automata (pPDA) [20], one-counter automata (pOC) [9], recurrent Markov Chains (RMCs) [21], and one-counter Markov decision procedures (OC-MDPs) [8]. Our work is orthogonal to these models as we allow a wide range of guard expressions that cannot be simulated (or at least we are not aware of the simulation) by pPDA, pOC, RMCs, or OC-MDPs. The non-trivial guards play a crucial role in rewriting the special cases of k-d PCPs into 1-d PCPs. For example, it allows for encoding constant probability programs [25] into 1-d PCPs using a simple transformation. Moreover, we provide the first open-source decision-procedure implementation for PCPs that could be useful for the mentioned models.

8 Conclusion

We have investigated the (positive) almost-sure termination problem of probabilistic counter programs inducing possibly infinite-state Markov chains. Our work establishes the decidability of U(P)AST problems for (essentially) 1-d PCPs – a significant contribution as obtaining stronger decidability results for new classes of programs is inherently challenging. Conversely, we show that these problems are undecidable for k-d PCPs in general. For the decidable class of essentially 1-d PCPs, we developed an efficient decision procedure that relies on decomposing and finitizing the underlying Markov chains. Experimental results demonstrate that our procedure effectively determines (P)AST for non-trivial probabilistic programs, including cases beyond the reach of existing tools.

Future directions include the extension of our results to (i) reasoning about *quantitative aspects* of probabilistic programs beyond almost-sure termination, e.g., termination probabilities and expected runtimes; and (ii) dealing with programs featuring nondeterminism [44] and/or conditioning [55].

Acknowledgments. This work has been partially funded by the ZJNSF Major Program (No. LD24F020013), by the Fundamental Research Funds for the Central Universities of China (No. 226-2024-00140), and by the ZJU Education Foundation's Qizhen Talent program.

Disclosure of Interests. The authors have no competing interests to declare that are relevant to the content of this article.

References

1. Agrawal, S., Chatterjee, K., Novotný, P.: Lexicographic ranking supermartingales: an efficient approach to termination of probabilistic programs. Proc. ACM Program. Lang. **2**(POPL), 34:1–34:32 (2018)
2. Baier, C., de Alfaro, L., Forejt, V., Kwiatkowska, M.: Model checking probabilistic systems. In: Handbook of Model Checking, pp. 963–999. Springer, Cham (2018). https://doi.org/10.1007/978-3-319-10575-8_28
3. Barthe, G., Katoen, J., Silva, A. (eds.): Foundations of Probabilistic Programming. Cambridge University Press (2020)
4. Bhat, U.N.: An Introduction to Queueing Theory: Modeling and Analysis in Applications. Statistics for Industry and Technology, Birkhäuser, Boston, MA (2015)
5. Bohnenkamp, H.C., van der Stok, P., Hermanns, H., Vaandrager, F.W.: Cost-optimization of the IPV4 Zeroconf protocol. In: DSN, pp. 531–540. IEEE Computer Society (2003)
6. Bozga, M., Iosif, R., Konecný, F.: Deciding conditional termination. Log. Methods Comput. Sci. **10**(3), 252–266 (2014)
7. Braverman, M.: Termination of integer linear programs. In: Ball, T., Jones, R.B. (eds.) CAV 2006. LNCS, vol. 4144, pp. 372–385. Springer, Heidelberg (2006). https://doi.org/10.1007/11817963_34
8. Brázdil, T., Brozek, V., Etessami, K., Kucera, A., Wojtczak, D.: One-counter Markov decision processes. In: SODA, pp. 863–874. SIAM (2010)
9. Brázdil, T., Kiefer, S., Kučera, A.: Efficient analysis of probabilistic programs with an unbounded counter. In: Gopalakrishnan, G., Qadeer, S. (eds.) CAV 2011. LNCS, vol. 6806, pp. 208–224. Springer, Heidelberg (2011). https://doi.org/10.1007/978-3-642-22110-1_18
10. Chakarov, A., Sankaranarayanan, S.: Probabilistic program analysis with martingales. In: Sharygina, N., Veith, H. (eds.) CAV 2013. LNCS, vol. 8044, pp. 511–526. Springer, Heidelberg (2013). https://doi.org/10.1007/978-3-642-39799-8_34
11. Chatterjee, K., Fu, H., Goharshady, A.K.: Termination analysis of probabilistic programs through Positivstellensatz's. In: Chaudhuri, S., Farzan, A. (eds.) CAV 2016. LNCS, vol. 9779, pp. 3–22. Springer, Cham (2016). https://doi.org/10.1007/978-3-319-41528-4_1
12. Chatterjee, K., Goharshady, A.K., Meggendorfer, T., Zikelic, D.: Sound and complete certificates for quantitative termination analysis of probabilistic programs. In: CAV (1). LNCS, vol. 13371, pp. 55–78. Springer (2022). https://doi.org/10.1007/978-3-031-13185-1_4
13. Chatterjee, K., Novotný, P., Zikelic, D.: Stochastic invariants for probabilistic termination. In: POPL, pp. 145–160. ACM (2017)
14. Church, A.: An unsolvable problem of elementary number theory. Am. J. Math. **58**(2), 345–363 (1936)
15. Colón, M.A., Sankaranarayanan, S., Sipma, H.B.: Linear invariant generation using non-linear constraint solving. In: Hunt, W.A., Somenzi, F. (eds.) CAV 2003. LNCS, vol. 2725, pp. 420–432. Springer, Heidelberg (2003). https://doi.org/10.1007/978-3-540-45069-6_39
16. Coppo, M., Dezani-Ciancaglini, M.: A new type assignment for λ-terms. Arch. Math. Log. **19**(1), 139–156 (1978)
17. Coppo, M., Dezani-Ciancaglini, M., Venneri, B.: Functional characters of solvable terms. Math. Log. Q. **27**(2–6), 45–58 (1981)

18. Dudenhefner, A.: Certified decision procedures for two-counter machines. In: FSCD. LIPIcs, vol. 228, pp. 16:1–16:18. Schloss Dagstuhl - Leibniz-Zentrum für Informatik (2022)
19. Ershov, A.P.: On operator algorithms. Doklady Akademii Nauk SSSR **122**, 967–970 (1958). English translation in Automat. Express **1**, 20–23 (1959)
20. Esparza, J., Kucera, A., Mayr, R.: Model checking probabilistic pushdown automata. In: LICS, pp. 12–21. IEEE Computer Society (2004)
21. Etessami, K., Yannakakis, M.: Recursive Markov chains, stochastic grammars, and monotone systems of nonlinear equations. J. ACM **56**(1), 1:1–1:66 (2009)
22. Everest, G., van der Poorten, A.J., Shparlinski, I.E., Ward, T.: Recurrence Sequences, Mathematical surveys and monographs, vol. 104. American Mathematical Society (2003)
23. Feng, S., Chen, M., Su, H., Kaminski, B.L., Katoen, J., Zhan, N.: Lower bounds for possibly divergent probabilistic programs. Proc. ACM Program. Lang. **7**(OOPSLA1), 696–726 (2023)
24. Frohn, F., Giesl, J.: Termination of triangular integer loops is decidable. In: Dillig, I., Tasiran, S. (eds.) CAV 2019. LNCS, vol. 11562, pp. 426–444. Springer, Cham (2019). https://doi.org/10.1007/978-3-030-25543-5_24
25. Giesl, J., Giesl, P., Hark, M.: Computing expected runtimes for constant probability programs. In: Fontaine, P. (ed.) CADE 2019. LNCS (LNAI), vol. 11716, pp. 269–286. Springer, Cham (2019). https://doi.org/10.1007/978-3-030-29436-6_16
26. Gordon, A.D., Henzinger, T.A., Nori, A.V., Rajamani, S.K.: Probabilistic programming. In: FOSE, pp. 167–181. ACM (2014)
27. Gryszka, K.: From biased coin to any discrete distribution. Period. Math. Hung. **83**(1), 71–80 (2021)
28. Hagberg, A.A., Schult, D.A., Swart, P.J.: Exploring network structure, dynamics, and function using networkX. Tech. rep, Los Alamos National Laboratory (LANL), Los Alamos, NM, USA (2008)
29. Halava, V., Harju, T., Hirvensalo, M.: Positivity of second order linear recurrent sequences. Discret. Appl. Math. **154**(3), 447–451 (2006)
30. Helmink, L., Sellink, M., Vaandrager, F.W.: Proof-checking a data link protocol. In: Barendregt, H., Nipkow, T. (eds.) TYPES 1993. LNCS, vol. 806, pp. 127–165. Springer, Heidelberg (1994). https://doi.org/10.1007/3-540-58085-9_75
31. Hermes, H.: Die universalität programmgesteuerter rechenmaschinen. Mathematisch-Physikalische Semesterberichte **4**, 42–53 (1954)
32. Hirst, H.P., Macey, W.T.: Bounding the roots of polynomials. Coll. Math. J. **28**(4), 292–295 (1997)
33. Hoffmann, J., Aehlig, K., Hofmann, M.: Resource aware ML. In: Madhusudan, P., Seshia, S.A. (eds.) CAV 2012. LNCS, vol. 7358, pp. 781–786. Springer, Heidelberg (2012). https://doi.org/10.1007/978-3-642-31424-7_64
34. Holtzen, S., den Broeck, G.V., Millstein, T.D.: Scaling exact inference for discrete probabilistic programs. Proc. ACM Program. Lang. **4**(OOPSLA), 140:1–140:31 (2020)
35. Kaminski, B.L., Katoen, J., Matheja, C.: On the hardness of analyzing probabilistic programs. Acta Informatica **56**(3), 255–285 (2019)
36. Knuth, D.E., Yao, A.C.: The complexity of nonuniform random number generation. In: Algorithms and Complexity: New Directions and Recent Results. Academic Press (1976)
37. Korec, I.: Small universal register machines. Theor. Comput. Sci. **168**(2), 267–301 (1996)

38. Kozen, D.: Semantics of probabilistic programs. J. Comput. Syst. Sci. **22**(3), 328–350 (1981)
39. Lambek, J.: How to program an infinite abacus. Math. Bull. **4**(3), 295–302 (1961)
40. Latouche, G., Ramaswami, V.: Introduction to Matrix Analytic Methods in Stochastic Modeling. SIAM, ASA-SIAM Series on Statistics and Applied Mathematics (1999)
41. Lommen, N., Meyer, É., Giesl, J.: Control-flow refinement for complexity analysis of probabilistic programs in Koat (short paper). In: IJCAR (1). LNCS, vol. 14739, pp. 233–243. Springer (2024). https://doi.org/10.1007/978-3-031-63498-7_14
42. Majumdar, R., Sathiyanarayana, V.R.: Positive almost-sure termination: complexity and proof rules. Proc. ACM Program. Lang. **8**(POPL), 1089–1117 (2024)
43. Majumdar, R., Sathiyanarayana, V.R.: Sound and complete proof rules for probabilistic termination. Proc. ACM Program. Lang. **9**(POPL), 1871–1902 (2025)
44. McIver, A., Morgan, C.: Abstraction, refinement and proof for probabilistic systems. Monographs in Computer Science, Springer (2005). https://doi.org/10.1007/b138392
45. McIver, A., Morgan, C.: Introduction to PGCL: its logic and its model. In: Refinement Techniques in Software Engineering. Springer (2005). https://doi.org/10.1007/0-387-27006-X_1
46. McIver, A., Morgan, C., Kaminski, B.L., Katoen, J.: A new proof rule for almost-sure termination. Proc. ACM Program. Lang. **2**(POPL), 33:1–33:28 (2018)
47. van de Meent, J.W., Paige, B., Yang, H., Wood, F.: An introduction to probabilistic programming (2021). https://arxiv.org/abs/1809.10756
48. Meyer, F., Hark, M., Giesl, J.: Inferring expected runtimes of probabilistic integer programs using expected sizes. In: TACAS 2021. LNCS, vol. 12651, pp. 250–269. Springer, Cham (2021). https://doi.org/10.1007/978-3-030-72016-2_14
49. Meyer, P.J.: Probably: probabilistic guarded command language (PGCL) documentation (2023). https://philipp15b.github.io/probably/pgcl.html. Accessed 25 Oct 2023
50. Minsky, M.: Recursive unsolvability of post's problem. Tech. Rep. 54G-0023, Massachusetts Institute of Technology, Lincoln Laboratory (1954)
51. Minsky, M.L.: Computation: Finite and Infinite Machines. Prentice-Hall, Englewood Cliffs, NJ, USA (1967)
52. Moosbrugger, M., Bartocci, E., Katoen, J.-P., Kovács, L.: The probabilistic termination tool amber. In: Huisman, M., Păsăreanu, C., Zhan, N. (eds.) FM 2021. LNCS, vol. 13047, pp. 667–675. Springer, Cham (2021). https://doi.org/10.1007/978-3-030-90870-6_36
53. Ngo, V.C., Carbonneaux, Q., Hoffmann, J.: Bounded expectations: resource analysis for probabilistic programs. In: PLDI, pp. 496–512. ACM (2018)
54. Novozhilov, S., Yang, M., Chen, M., Li, Z., Yin, J.: On the almost-sure termination of probabilistic counter programs (2025). https://hal.science/hal-05082395, hal preprint hal-05082395
55. Olmedo, F., Gretz, F., Jansen, N., Kaminski, B.L., Katoen, J., McIver, A.: Conditioning in probabilistic programming. ACM Trans. Program. Lang. Syst. **40**(1), 4:1–4:50 (2018)
56. Ost, A.: Quasi-birth-and-death processes. In: Performance of Communication Systems: A Model-Based Approach with Matrix-Geometric Methods, pp. 51–102. Springer, Berlin, Heidelberg (2001). https://doi.org/10.1007/978-3-662-04421-6_4
57. Ouaknine, J., Worrell, J.: On linear recurrence sequences and loop termination. ACM SIGLOG News **2**(2), 4–13 (2015)

58. Ouaknine, J., Sousa-Pinto, J., Worrell, J.: On termination of integer linear loops 2015 (2014)
59. Péter, R.: Graphschemata und rekursive funktionen. Dialectica **12**, 373 (1958)
60. Shepherdson, J.C., Sturgis, H.E.: Computability of recursive functions. J. ACM **10**(2), 217–255 (1963)
61. Tiwari, A.: Termination of linear programs. In: Alur, R., Peled, D.A. (eds.) CAV 2004. LNCS, vol. 3114, pp. 70–82. Springer, Heidelberg (2004). https://doi.org/10.1007/978-3-540-27813-9_6
62. Turing, A.M.: On computable numbers, with an application to the entscheidungs problem. Proc. London Math. Soc. **s2-42**(1), 230–265 (1937)
63. Virtanen, P., et al.: SciPy 1.0 Contributors: SciPy 1.0: Fundamental algorithms for scientific computing in Python. Nat. Methods **17**, 261–272 (2020)

POPACheck: A Model Checker for Probabilistic Pushdown Automata

Francesco Pontiggia(✉)🆔, Ezio Bartocci🆔, and Michele Chiari🆔

TU Wien, Vienna, Austria
{francesco.pontiggia,ezio.bartocci,
michele.chiari}@tuwien.ac.at

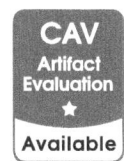
Abstract. We present POPACheck, the first model checking tool for probabilistic Pushdown Automata (pPDA) supporting temporal logic specifications. POPACheck provides a user-friendly probabilistic modeling language with recursion that automatically translates into Probabilistic Operator Precedence Automata (pOPA). pOPA are a class of pPDA that can express all the behaviors of probabilistic programs: sampling, conditioning, recursive procedures, and nested inference queries. On pOPA, POPACheck can solve reachability queries as well as qualitative and quantitative model checking queries for specifications in Linear Temporal Logic (LTL) and a fragment of Precedence Oriented Temporal Logic (POTL), a logic for context-free properties such as pre/post-conditioning.

Keywords: Probabilistic Model Checking · Pushdown Model Checking · Temporal Logic · Operator Precedence Languages

1 Introduction

The last two decades saw great efforts towards the analysis of probabilistic Pushdown Automata (pPDA) [3–6,14,31], and the equivalent model of Recursive Markov Chains (RMCs) [16–20,54] as a succinct formalism to express infinite-state probabilistic systems and to model probabilistic programs with nested and possibly recursive procedures. However, no existing tool implements the presented temporal logic model checking algorithms, due to their computational complexity and many practical obstacles. With

```
# global variables: a[], mid, val
B(u4 left, u4 right) {
  mid = Uniform(left, right);
  if (left < right){
    if (a[mid] < val) {
      left = min(mid +1, right);
      B(left, right);
    } else { if (a[mid] > val) {
      right = max(mid -1, left);
      B(left, right);
    } }
  }
}
```

Fig. 1. Sherwood Binary search.

POPACheck, we leverage various recent results on pPDA analysis to produce an efficient model checking tool that scales beyond toy examples, and forms a baseline for future verification tools for infinite-state probabilistic systems.

Illustrative Example. Consider the Sherwood [34] variant of the binary search (Fig. 1), a well-known recursive algorithm. B() searches for val in the array a[left..right]. Unlike the deterministic version, in each iteration B() selects

© The Author(s) 2025
R. Piskac and Z. Rakamarić (Eds.): CAV 2025, LNCS 15932, pp. 105–121, 2025.
https://doi.org/10.1007/978-3-031-98679-6_5

the pivot mid randomly among the remaining portion of a. Thanks to random-ness, worst-, best- and average runtime align. If a has a finite bound and its elements have a finite domain, B() can be translated into a finite-state pPDA: automaton states model global and local variable values, while stack symbols model procedure parameter values. A relevant property for this program is **par-tial correctness** [37]: when B() is invoked in a state where left ≤ right, a[left..right] is sorted and val occurs in a[left..right], then at return mid stores the index of a where val lies. This property, just like pre/post-conditioning, requires to match each call to B() in the recursion to its correspond-ing return, and skip inner calls to B() in the execution trace. It is a context-free property beyond LTL's expressivity, limited to regular properties. POTL [9] is an expressive logic based on Operator Precedence Languages (OPLs) [22], a subclass of context-free languages, and expresses partial correctness as:

$$\Box(\text{call} \land \text{B} \land \text{sorted} \land \text{valOccurs} \land \text{left} \leq \text{right} \implies \chi_F^u \, \text{a[mid]} == \text{val})$$

Probabilistic Programming. Probabilistic programs have recently gained popular-ity in AI and machine learning [23], where they are employed as succinct models for Bayesian inference [26]. In addition to randomized assignment, a prominent feature of this programming model is *conditioning*, which allows for adding evi-dence of observed events by conditioning the program variables to take certain values. When using rejection sampling, a probabilistic program contains state-ments observe(e), where e is a Boolean condition. If e is not satisfied, the current execution trace is rejected: in such a case, we assume that the program is restarted. The semantics of a probabilistic program is the probability distri-bution in the return statement, also called *posterior*. Probabilistic programs can also be nested: a program samples a value from a distribution represented by another probabilistic program. They are known under the name of *nested queries* [24], and model scenarios beyond the expressivity of flat probabilistic programs: most notably, metareasoning patterns (the so called Theory of Mind) [48,55], linguistics [45], cognitive science [25], multi-agent planning [46] and sequential decision making [21]. To the best of our knowledge, pOPA [40] are the small-est subclass of pPDA that can model effectively these behaviors. OPA traces are OPLs. Unlike general context-free languages, OPLs are closed under most relevant Boolean operations [33]. Let $\mathcal{B}$ be an (deterministic or separated) Oper-ator Precedence Büchi Automaton (ωOPBA), the class of automata recognizing OPLs. When a pOPA $\mathcal{A}$ is defined over the same alphabet as $\mathcal{B}$, we can verify automatically $\mathcal{A}$ against $\mathcal{B}$ via automata-based model checking [40].

Our Approach. The main challenge in pPDA model checking is computing the *termination probabilities*, which involves solving a system of **non-linear** equa-tions. While tools like PReMo [53] approximate them from below, for general model checking we need to know whether these quantities sum up to exactly 1. We could employ off-the-shelf SMT solvers (e.g. Z3 [35]) with decision proce-dures for the Existential first-order Theory of the Reals (ETR) (QF_NRA), but they offer only doubly exponential decision procedures [30], although ETR is in PSPACE [7,43]. We thus devise a semi-algorithm leveraging both certificates for termination probabilities [51] via a numeric method called Optimistic Value

Iteration (OVI), and certificates for expected runtimes [52]. A second challenge is the need for deterministic automata (or weak variants thereof) in probabilistic verification—a common problem already occurring in the far simpler setting of LTL model checking for Markov Chains [1,2,11]. In this regard, we exploit [19,40] which provide resp. single exponential model checking algorithms (i.e., avoiding determinization) for LTL and a fragment of POTL (POTLfχ). These algorithms represent the theoretical ground of POPACheck.

POPACheck is hosted on Github at https://github.com/michiari/POMC/. It is an extension of the POMC tool [8,39,41], and relies on its modules for constructing automata from formulae.

Contributions. We present i) a semi-algorithm overcoming numerical issues regarding computing termination probabilities; ii) POPACheck, a model checker for pPDA based on this semi-algorithm; iii) a user-friendly domain-specific language for recursive probabilistic programs; and iv) an extensive experimental evaluation with a benchmark of programs and LTL/POTLfχ formulae.

2   Background

2.1   Probabilistic Operator Precedence Automata (pOPA)

pOPA are pPDA with state labels from a set Σ. State labels drive the stack behavior of pOPA through three *Precedence Relations (PRs)*: given two labels a and b, we say *a yields precedence* to b iff $a \lessdot b$, a and b are *equal in precedence* iff $a \doteq b$, and a *takes precedence* from b iff $a \gtrdot b$. An Operator Precedence Matrix (OPM) is a total function $M : \Sigma^2 \to \{\lessdot, \doteq, \gtrdot\}$; the special symbol $\#$ is s.t. $\# \lessdot a$ for all $a \in \Sigma$. In the following, let $\mathfrak{D}(S) = \{f : S \to [0,1] \mid \sum_{s \in S} f(s) = 1\}$ denote he set of probability distributions on a finite set S.

Definition 1 ([40]). *A pOPA is a tuple $\mathcal{A} = (\Sigma, M, Q, u_0, \delta, \Lambda)$ where: Σ is a finite set of state labels; M is an OPM; Q is a finite set of states; u_0 is the initial state; $\Lambda : Q \to \Sigma$ is a state labeling function; and δ is a triple of transition functions $\delta_{push} : Q \to \mathfrak{D}(Q)$, $\delta_{shift} : Q \to \mathfrak{D}(Q)$, and $\delta_{pop} : (Q \times Q) \to \mathfrak{D}(Q)$, such that pop moves have the following condition, for all $u, s, v \in Q$:*

$$\delta_{pop}(u,s)(v) > 0 \implies \forall a \in \Sigma : a \gtrdot \Lambda(u) \implies a \gtrdot \Lambda(v).$$

The semantics of $\mathcal{A}$ is an infinite Markov chain [1] $\Delta(\mathcal{A})$ with vertex set $Q \times (\Gamma^*\{\bot\})$ where $\bot$ is the initial stack symbol, which can never be pushed or popped, and $\Gamma = \Sigma \times Q$ is the set of stack symbols. PRs decide whether to push onto the stack, update the topmost symbol, or pop from it. For any stack contents $A \in \Gamma^*\{\bot\}$:

push: $(u, A) \xrightarrow{x} (v, [\Lambda(u), u]A)$ if $smb(A) \lessdot \Lambda(u)$ and $\delta_{push}(u)(v) = x$;
shift: $(u, [a, s]A) \xrightarrow{x} (v, [\Lambda(u), s]A)$ if $a \doteq \Lambda(u)$ and $\delta_{shift}(u)(v) = x$;
pop: $(u, [a, s]A) \xrightarrow{x} (v, A)$ if $a \gtrdot \Lambda(u)$ and $\delta_{pop}(u, s)(v) = x$;

where $smb(\bot) = \#$ and $smb([a, r]) = a$ for $[a, r] \in \Gamma$.

Stack symbols are pairs of a label and a state, and the PR between the label in the topmost stack symbol and that of the current state decides the next move.

If such PR is $<$, a push move puts the current state and its label onto the stack. Since $smb(\bot) = \#$, the first move is always a push. If the PR is $\doteq$, a shift move updates the topmost stack symbol by replacing its label with the current state's. Finally, if the PR is $>$, the topmost stack symbol gets popped.

A run of $\mathcal{A}$ is a path in $\Delta(\mathcal{A})$ starting in $(u_0, \bot)$. The probability space on the set of runs is obtained by the cylinder set construction as for Markov chains [1]. The set of infinite words formed by labels of states in a run is an OPL [40].

PRs guide the stack behavior of pOPA, and PRs between state labels completely determine whether the pOPA pushes, updates, or pops a stack symbol. This dependency of the stack behavior on labels, and hence traces, enables the definition of stack-aware context-free modalities in the specification formalism (POTL), by allowing the definition of a synchronized product between pOPA and a pushdown automaton encoding

	call	ret	qry	obs	stm
call	$<$	$\doteq$	$<$	$>$	$<$
ret	$>$	$>$	$>$	$>$	$>$
qry	$<$	$\doteq$	$<$	$<$	$<$
obs	$>$	$>$	$>$	$>$	$>$
stm	$>$	$>$	$>$	$>$	$>$

Fig. 2. OPM $M_{\mathbf{call}}$.

the specification (cf. [40]). We thus define state labels to describe events that affect the program stack, and we define PRs between state labels so that such events have the same effect on the pOPA stack that they have on the stack of activation frames in a high-level procedural probabilistic programming language with rejection sampling.[1]

State labels in OPM $M_{\mathbf{call}}$ (Fig. 2) represent traces of probabilistic programs. **call** and **ret** are function calls and returns, **stm** statements that do not affect the stack (e.g., randomized assignments). **qry** is the *conditional sampling* operator (roughly corresponding to query in Church [24]): it reifies the posterior distribution of a probabilistic program, allowing for sampling from it. **obs** denotes an unsatisfied observation. The table is to be read by row—e.g., we have **call** $\doteq$ **ret** and **ret** $>$ **call**. PRs are such that a pOPA always pushes from a **call** state (**call** $<$ **call**, etc.), and pops after being in a **ret** state through a shift move (**call** $\doteq$ **ret** and **ret** takes precedence from other symbols). This way, the pOPA stack mimics the program's stack. **stm** causes a push immediately followed by a pop (because **stm** $>$ all labels), thus leaving the stack unchanged. Moreover, **obs** triggers pop moves that unwind the stack until they reach the first **qry** symbol. Thereby, the pOPA excludes (or rejects) the trace at hand from the posterior distribution of the current probabilistic program without affecting outer queries, effectively simulating nested rejection sampling [36].

2.2 Specification Formalism

We express specifications through a temporal logic with the following syntax:

$$\varphi := \mathrm{a} \mid T \mid \neg\varphi \mid \varphi \vee \varphi \mid \bigcirc\varphi \mid \varphi\,\mathcal{U}\,\varphi \mid \bigcirc^t \varphi \mid \chi_F^t\,\varphi \mid \varphi\,\mathcal{U}_\chi^t\,\varphi$$

Formulae are evaluated in the first position of program traces, and subformulae in further positions. a is an *atomic proposition* from a finite set AP containing

---

[1] Note that PRs are not ordering relations, so they need not enjoy standard properties such as reflexivity and transitivity.

labels from Fig. 2 and names of program functions. T is any term of the form $e_1 \bowtie e_2$, where $\bowtie$ is a binary comparison operator ($=$, $>$, etc.) and e_1, e_2 are integer arithmetic expressions involving program variables and constants. $\neg$ and $\vee$ are propositional operators, to which we add the derived operators $\wedge$ and $\implies$ with the usual semantics. $\bigcirc \varphi$ and $\varphi_1 \, \mathcal{U} \, \varphi_2$ are the *next* and *until* operators from LTL [38], resp. meaning that φ will hold in the next time instant, and that φ_1 holds until a time instant in which φ_2 does. We use the derived operators *eventually* $\Diamond \varphi \equiv \top \, \mathcal{U} \, \varphi$, and *globally* $\Box \varphi \equiv \neg \Diamond \neg \varphi$.

The remaining operators form a fragment of POTL called POTLfχ. They move up ($t = u$) and down ($t = d$) among function frames in the program stack. $\bigcirc^d \varphi$ holds if the next time instant belongs to the same or a lower frame and φ holds in it, and *vice versa* for $\bigcirc^u$. χ_F^d moves along a binary relation that links function calls to their returns and inner function calls.

In the program of Fig. 3, the relation links events representing **calls** to f1() to those representing the inner **call** to f2() and f1's return statement. E.g., if evaluated in an instant labeled with a **call** to f1, $\chi_F^d(\textbf{call} \wedge x > 0)$ holds if x > 0 in the instant when f1 calls f2, and $\chi_F^d(\textbf{ret} \wedge y > 0)$ holds if f1 returns in an instant in which y > 0. Moreover, χ_F^u **obs** holds if a

```
f1() {
    ... // other statements
    f2(x);
    ...
    return y;
}
```

Fig. 3. Program stub.

false observe is encountered anytime during the execution of f1. The semantics of $\mathcal{U}_\chi^t$ are the same as the LTL until, except it works on paths obtained by iterating the $\bigcirc^t$ and χ_F^t operators, for $t \in \{u, d\}$. For a complete definition, cf. [10].

3 Model Checking Algorithm

3.1 The Support Chain

Let $\mathcal{A} = (\Sigma, M, Q, u_0, \delta, \Lambda)$ be a pOPA. A *support* is a sequence of pOPA moves $u_0 \to u_1 \dashrightarrow \ldots \dashrightarrow u_\ell \overset{u_0}{\Rightarrow} u_{\ell+1}$, denoted as $u_0 \rightsquigarrow u_{\ell+1}$, that occur from the move pushing a stack symbol $[\Lambda(u_0), u_0]$ to the move popping it. Given $u, v \in Q$ and $\alpha \in \Gamma$, we define $[\![u, \alpha \,|\, v]\!]$ as the probability that $\mathcal{A}$ starting in $(u, \alpha \bot)$ reaches v at the end of the support that put α on top of the stack. Such *termination probabilities* [4,18] are the least non-negative solutions of the equation system $\mathbf{v} = f(\mathbf{v})$, where $\mathbf{v}$ is the vector of triples $[\![u, \alpha \,|\, v]\!]$ for all $u, v \in Q$, $\alpha \in \Gamma$ and $f([\![u, \alpha \,|\, v]\!])$ is given by

$$\begin{cases} \sum_{r,t \in Q} \delta_{push}(u)(r)[\![r, [\Lambda(u), u] \mid t]\!][\![t, \alpha \mid v]\!] & \text{if } \alpha = \bot, \text{ or } \alpha = [a, s] \text{ and } a \lessdot \Lambda(u) \\ \sum_{r \in Q} \delta_{shift}(u)(r)[\![r, [\Lambda(u), s] \mid v]\!] & \text{if } \alpha = [a, s] \text{ and } a \doteq \Lambda(u) \\ \delta_{pop}(u, s)(v) & \text{if } \alpha = [a, s] \text{ and } a \gtrdot \Lambda(u) \end{cases}$$

The probability that $\alpha \in \Gamma$ is never popped after a run visits a configuration $(u, \alpha A)$ for $u \in Q$ and some stack contents A is $[\![u, \alpha \uparrow]\!] = 1 - \sum_{v \in Q} [\![u, \alpha \mid v]\!]$.

The *support chain* is a finite Markov chain that replaces supports with single transitions, and describes the behavior of pOPA runs while preserving their probability distribution.

Definition 2 ([40]). *The* support chain $M_\mathcal{A}$ *of* $\mathcal{A}$ *is a Markov chain with states in* $\mathcal{C} = \{(u, \alpha) \in Q \times \Gamma_\bot \mid [\![u, \alpha \uparrow]\!] > 0\}$, *initial state* $(u_0, \bot)$, *and a transition probability function* $\delta_{M_\mathcal{A}}$ *such that*

- $\delta_{M_\mathcal{A}}(u, [a, s])(v, [\Lambda(u), s]) = \delta_{shift}(u)(v)[\![v, [\Lambda(u), s] \uparrow]\!]/[\![u, [a, s] \uparrow]\!]$
  for all $(u, [a, s]), (v, [\Lambda(u), s]) \in \mathcal{C}$ *such that* $a \doteq \Lambda(u)$;
- *otherwise, for all* $(u, \alpha), (v, \alpha') \in \mathcal{C}$,
  $\delta_{M_\mathcal{A}}(u, \alpha)(v, \alpha') = (P_{push} + P_{supp})[\![v, \alpha' \uparrow]\!]/[\![u, \alpha \uparrow]\!]$ *where*
  - $P_{push} = \delta_{push}(u)(v)$ *if* $smb(\alpha) \lessdot \Lambda(u)$, *and* $P_{push} = 0$ *otherwise;*
  - $P_{supp} = \sum_{v' \in Q} \delta_{push}(u)(v')[\![v', [\Lambda(u), u] \mid v]\!]$, *if* $\alpha = \alpha'$, $smb(\alpha) \lessdot \Lambda(u)$, *and* $\mathcal{A}$ *has a support* $u \rightsquigarrow v$, *and* $P_{supp} = 0$ *otherwise.*

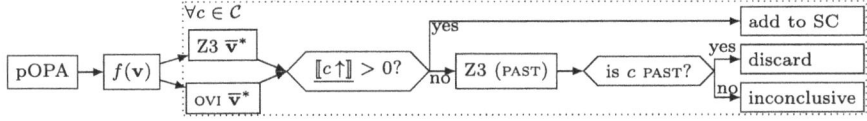

Fig. 4. Overview of the semi-algorithm for building the support chain (SC).

During infinite runs of $\mathcal{A}$, the stack contains symbols that are never popped. States of $M_\mathcal{A}$ consist of such symbols, and the current state of $\mathcal{A}$ when they are put on the stack. $M_\mathcal{A}$ has three types of transitions: push and shift moves that put on the stack (resp. update) a symbol that will never be popped, and *support* edges, which summarize the finite portion of a run from when a stack symbol is pushed to when it is popped—a *support*. Probabilities assigned to edges $c \rightarrow c'$ are conditioned on the fact that the stack symbol in the target node c' is never popped, given that the one in the starting node c is also never popped: hence all probabilities are multiplied by $[\![c' \uparrow]\!]/[\![c \uparrow]\!]$. Probabilities for push and shift edges follow directly from $\mathcal{A}$'s δ distributions, while those for support edges include P_{supp}, the probability that the stack symbol underlying the edge is popped. Thus, $M_\mathcal{A}$ describes the limit behavior of $\mathcal{A}$ by only considering permanent stack symbols and transitions that created them, while summarizing with single edges run portions that involve stack symbols that are eventually popped.

To build the support chain of $\mathcal{A}$, we must check whether $[\![c\!\uparrow]\!] > 0$ for all $c \in Q \times \Gamma_\perp$. We propose the approach sketched in Fig. 4. We further optimize this algorithm by applying all steps bottom-up to Strongly Connected Components (SCCs) of the graph of nodes c.

Let $\mathbf{v}^*$ be the *least* solution of $\mathbf{v} = f(\mathbf{v})$, i.e., the vector of termination probabilities $[\![c \,|\, v]\!]$. Recall that $[\![c\!\uparrow]\!] = 1 - \sum_{v \in Q}[\![c \,|\, v]\!]$. First, we find an upper bound $\overline{\mathbf{v}}^*$ for $\mathbf{v}^*$, which we use to compute a lower bound $[\![c\!\uparrow]\!]$ for $[\![c\!\uparrow]\!]$. If $[\![c\!\uparrow]\!] > 0$, then $[\![c\!\uparrow]\!] > 0$ and we add c to the support chain. Otherwise, we make the hypothesis that $[\![c\!\uparrow]\!] = 0$, i.e., that c is almost-surely terminating (AST), and check the stronger condition that c is positively AST (PAST). A node $c = (u, \alpha)$ is PAST if stack symbol α is popped with probability 1 in *finite expected time*. We check PAST by solving with Z3 a system of linear equations [52] for the expected termination times. If a solution exists, then c is PAST and therefore AST: we do not add c to the support chain. Otherwise, the whole algorithm is inconclusive.

We find the upper bound $\overline{\mathbf{v}}^*$ in two different ways. In both cases, we first find a lower bound $\underline{\mathbf{v}}^*$ to $\mathbf{v}^*$ via a decomposed variant of Newton's method [12,18], after cleaning the system from zero-solution variables via value iteration.

- In the first method, we give $\underline{\mathbf{v}}^*$ as a hint to Z3, and obtain $\overline{\mathbf{v}}^*$ as a model for $\mathbf{v}$ in the query $\underline{\mathbf{v}}^* \leq \mathbf{v} \leq \underline{\mathbf{v}}^* + \varepsilon \wedge \mathbf{v} \geq f(\mathbf{v})$, for a small positive ε.
- The other method employs OVI [51], which computes $\overline{\mathbf{v}}^*$ numerically. We run OVI initialized on $\underline{\mathbf{v}}^*$.

3.2   Avoid Determinization with a Separation-Based Approach

A prominent approach to LTL model checking on probabilistic systems expresses specifications as deterministic automata. Storm [28] and PRISM [32] translate the input formula into a Deterministic Rabin Automaton (DRA) [1], with a worst-case doubly exponential blowup. While singly exponential algorithms that avoid determinization exist [2,11], a common argument for using the conceptually simpler notion of Rabin automata is the existence in practice of effective translations from LTL formulae to relatively small-sized DRA [13]. Unfortunately, the same cannot be said for POTL formulae: the automata construction for POTL is much more involved [8], and easily generates intractable automata.

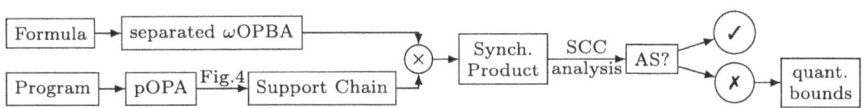

Fig. 5. Overview of model checking probabilistic programs against POTLfχ formulae.

POPACheck takes a different approach, outlined in Fig. 5. LTL formulae can be translated into *separated* Büchi automata, i.e., such that the languages they accept starting from different states are disjoint [11]. Similarly, POTLfχ formulae can be translated into ωOPBA, i.e., pushdown automata that capture the class of infinite-word OPLs, that are *separated*. Thanks to separation, we can build a synchronized product between the support chain of the pOPA modeling the program and the automaton encoding the formula. We then perform qualitative model checking by analyzing the SCCs of the product. Since formulae are translated into automata of exponential size [8,49], the whole procedure requires time exponential in formula size and space polynomial in pOPA size. For quantitative model checking, we compute numerically the probabilities associated with edges in the synchronized product: edges subsuming supports require solving equation systems resembling those for termination probabilities. We compute bounds for them with OVI. Since the product has size exponential in formula length, quantitative model checking is in EXPSPACE. Cf. [40] for details.

4   Input Language

POPACheck analyzes programs written in MiniProb, a simple probabilistic programming language (Fig. 6). MiniProb supports (un)signed integer variables of arbitrary width (u8 is an 8-bit unsigned type) and fixed-size arrays. Functions take parameters by value or value-result (with &). Actual parameters can only be variable identifiers for value-result parameters, and any expression if passed by value. Expressions consist of variables, array indexing, integer constants, and the usual arithmetic and Boolean operators, including comparisons. Boolean operators handle integers (0 means false, everything else true). Programs may sample from $\mathtt{Bernoulli}(e_1, e_2)$, which returns 1 with probability $p = e_1/e_2$, and 0 with probability $1-p$, or from $\mathtt{Uniform}(e_1, e_2)$, which samples uniformly among integers from e_1 to $e_2 - 1$. Random assignments of the form $x = e_1\{e_2/e_3\}e_4$ mean that x is assigned the value of e_1 with probability e_2/e_3, and e_4 with probability $1 - e_2/e_3$. Finally, functions can query the distribution on value-result parameters of another function, and condition on a Boolean expression with observe.

$$prog := [decl; \ldots] \ func \ [func \ldots]$$
$$decl := type \ identifier \ [, identifier \ldots]$$
$$type := \mathtt{bool} \mid uint \mid sint \mid uint[int] \mid sint[int]$$
$$func := f\,(type\;[\&]x_1\;[,\,type\;[\&]x_2\ldots])$$
$$\{[decl; \ldots] \ block\}$$
$$stmt := lval = e$$
$$\mid lval = \mathtt{Distribution}(\ldots)$$
$$\mid lval = e_1\{e_2 : e_3\}[e_4\{e_5 : e_6\}\ldots]e_n$$
$$\mid [\mathtt{query}] \ f\,(e_1 \mid lval_1 \ [, e_2 \mid lval_2 \ldots])$$
$$\mid \mathtt{if} \ (e) \ \{block\} \ \mathtt{else} \ \{block\}$$
$$\mid \mathtt{while} \ (e) \ \{block\}$$
$$\mid \mathtt{observe} \ (e)$$
$$block := stmt; [stmt \ldots;]$$
$$lval := identifier \mid identifier[e]$$

Fig. 6. MiniProb syntax.

Table 1. Benchmark formulae.

#	Formula	#	Formula
Q.1	$\Diamond\square(\neg\text{obs})$	**Q.2**	$\square(\text{qry} \implies \bigcirc^d(\text{call} \wedge \neg\chi_F^u\,\text{obs}) \vee \chi_F^d(\text{call} \wedge \neg\chi_F^u\,\text{obs}))$
Q.3	$\square(\text{call} \wedge \text{Alice} \wedge \text{p} \geq 0.4 \implies \neg\chi_F^u\,\text{obs})$	**Q.4**	$\neg\text{sampleA}\,\mathcal{U}\,(\text{call} \wedge \text{sampleA} \wedge \chi_F^d(\text{qry} \wedge \bigcirc^d(\text{call} \wedge \text{sampleA})))$
Q.5	$\neg\Diamond(\text{qry} \wedge \chi_F^u(\text{sampleA} \wedge \text{opR} == 0 \wedge \text{opC} == 1))$	**Q.6**	$(\neg\text{elder})\,\mathcal{U}_\chi^d\,(\text{young} \wedge f)$
Q.7	$\Diamond(\chi_F^d(\bigcirc^d\,\text{elder}) \wedge \chi_F^u(\text{elder} \wedge \neg f))$	**Q.8**	$\chi_F^u(\text{aliceLoc} == 1)$
Q.9	$\Diamond(\text{ret} \wedge \text{main} \wedge \text{aliceLoc} == 1)$	**Q.10**	$\neg\chi_F^u(\text{R} == 0 \wedge \text{C} == 2)$
Q.11	$\neg\chi_F^u(\text{R} == 0 \wedge \text{C} == 1)$	**Q.12**	$\neg\text{obs}\,\mathcal{U}\,(\text{call} \wedge \text{Bob} \wedge \chi_F^u\,\text{obs})$
Q.13	$\neg\text{Alice}\,\mathcal{U}\,(\text{call} \wedge \text{Alice} \wedge \neg\chi_F^u\,\text{obs})$	**Q.14**	$\Diamond(\text{ret} \wedge \text{main} \wedge \text{R} == 0 \wedge \text{C} == 2)$
Q.15	$\neg\text{obs}\,\mathcal{U}\,(\text{call} \wedge \text{Alice} \wedge \chi_F^u\,\text{obs})$		
Q.16	$\neg\text{sampleA}\,\mathcal{U}\,(\text{call} \wedge \text{sampleA} \wedge \chi_F^d(\text{qry} \wedge \bigcirc^d(\text{call} \wedge \text{sampleA} \wedge \chi_F^d(\text{qry} \wedge \bigcirc^d(\text{call} \wedge \text{sampleA})))))$		
S.1	$\square(\text{call} \wedge \text{B} \wedge \text{sorted} \wedge \text{valOccurs} \wedge \text{left} \leq \text{right} \implies \chi_F^u\,\text{a[mid]} == \text{val})$		
S.2	$\square(\text{call} \wedge \text{B} \wedge \text{sorted} \wedge \neg\text{valOccurs} \wedge \text{left} \leq \text{right} \implies \chi_F^u\,\text{a[mid]} \neq \text{val})$		
S.3	$\square(\text{call} \wedge \text{B} \wedge \text{sorted} \wedge \text{valOccurs} \wedge \text{left} < \text{right} \implies \bigcirc^d\Diamond(\text{call} \wedge \text{B}))$		
S.4	$\square(\text{call} \wedge \text{B} \wedge \text{sorted} \wedge \neg\text{valOccurs} \wedge \text{left} < \text{right} \implies \bigcirc^d\Diamond(\text{call} \wedge \text{B}))$		

5 Evaluation

We devised our experiments around the following questions: can our approach build support chains for probabilistic programs of medium size? How large equations systems arise in quantitative model checking? How scalable is our implementation, i.e., how large programs can our tool solve in a reasonable time?

Setup. Our benchmark consists of three programs (**Schelling**, **Tic-tac-toe** and **Virus**) and 16 mixed LTL/POTLfχ formulae (Table 1, **Q** formulae). All programs consist of a potentially unbounded sequence of nested queries. This places them at the frontier of probabilistic programming: even solving simple questions about their posterior distribution is a hardly tractable problem [42]. Additionally, to inquire scalability, we provide a case study on the **Sherwood** binary search with increasing program state space, against four formulae (Table 1, **S** formulae). We run the experiments on a machine with a 4.5GHz 8-core AMD CPU and 64 GB of RAM running Ubuntu 24.04. We do not offer an experimental comparison with PReMo [53] nor Pray [51], since they only compute termination probabilities on pPDA. This task is not the bottleneck of the overall model checking algorithm—our tool always computes them in less than one second.

We describe in the following the three programs, (some of) the formulae we verify on them, and their results. Afterwards, we present the case study separately. Two formulae inspecting conditioning are of interest for all three (**Q.1** and **Q.2**). If an observe statement conditions on an event with zero probability, all runs of a query are rejected. Such *ill-defined* queries [29] do not represent a valid probability distribution, which is undesired. LTL property **Q.1** means that a run is always sooner or later reinstantiated into a feasible one. However, if queries indefinitely call each other in a nonterminating program, a diverging run indefinitely hits unsatisfied observations in the infinite nesting. POTLfχ formula **Q.2** means that no procedure is indefinitely reinstantiated by an observation: either it terminates, or it diverges.

Schelling (Fig. 7). We consider an instance of a *Schelling coordination game* [44,48]. Two agents wish to meet in town but cannot communicate. However, they know perfectly each other's preferences. Each agent samples both a location according to its preference, and one obtained simulating the behavior of the other agent. Finally, it conditions on the two being equal. The original program [48] bounds the recursion depth by a constant. Conversely, we allow for unbounded recursion, but we introduce a global variable p controlling the recursion probability. We fix p's distribution so that the program is AST. Formula **Q.13** is the event that the first call to Bob is rejected, while **Q.14** that the first call to Alice is *not* rejected. Since Bob is not always fair, his procedure is much less likely to be rejected.

```
u4 p;
main() {
  bool res;
  p = 0{2:6}1{1:6}2{1:6}3{1:6}4;
  query alice(res);
}
Alice(bool &res) {
  aliceLoc = Bernoulli(55,100);
  query Bob(bobLoc);
  observe (aliceLoc == bobLoc);
  res = aliceLoc;
}
Bob(bool &res) {
  bobLoc = Bernoulli(55,100);
  fair = true {p:10} false;
  if (fair) {
    query Alice(aliceLoc);
    observe (bobLoc == aliceLoc);
  }
  res = bobLoc;
}
```

Fig. 7. Schelling.

Tic-tac-toe. Recursive probabilistic programs also model multi-player games involving sequential decision-making, i.e., where the best move in a turn depends on moves in subsequent turns. In these games, players choose actions that maximize future rewards by simulating, through nested queries, other players' turns as the game progresses. We consider tic-tac-toe [48]. A procedure modelling a player's reasoning first marks uniformly at random a cell between those not taken yet; then it recursively queries itself to simulate the other player's behaviour with the updated grid. This way, the whole game is recursively simulated, ending in a draw or in one of the two players winning. Finally, it conditions on a coin flip with weight corresponding to the utility of the outcome, thus performing softmax optimal decision making. We inspect the max/min number of turns until termination of the game, corresponding to the program's max/min recursion depth. **Q.4** means that there are at least two recursive calls (i.e., two turns) —what we would expect from the initial state of Fig. 8, where no move can immediately terminate the game. We also examine the players' meta-reasoning: **Q.5** excludes that a player ever thinks that the other one will pick cell [0, 1] in the next turn, which is indeed already marked at the beginning.

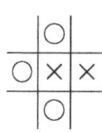

Fig. 8. [48]

Virus (Fig. 9). Recursive probabilistic programs encode epidemiological models and general multi-type Branching Processes [17,27] as models of population dynamics in biology. They consist of an unbounded population of susceptible individuals belonging to distinct species. In the programs, the stack models the individuals currently involved in the system, and different procedures model different species' behaviors. We consider the program from [50, Fig. 1]: a virus outbreak. Our population is composed of either young or elder individuals. We introduce conditioning in the model expressing that young ones are less likely to transmit the virus. **Q.6** encodes the CaRet formula of [50, p. 3]: a chain of infections of young people leads to the death of an elder person.

```
young() {
  bool f;
  ... (other statements)
  ... (sample infecting young)
  if (infect_young) {
    query young();
  }
  ... (sample infecting elders)
  if (infect_elder) {
    query elder(&f);
    query elder(&f);
  }
}
elder(bool &f) {
  ... (same as young())
  ... (sample passing away)
  if (pass_away) {
    f = 1;
  } else { f = 0; }
}
```

Fig. 9. Virus (sketch).

In POTLfχ, $(\neg\texttt{elder})\mathcal{U}_\chi^d(\texttt{young} \wedge f)$, where f is a boolean variable representing an elder person passing away. Young people cannot pass away in our model. Note here the need for the χ variant of the $\mathcal{U}$ operator to capture exactly the property. Consider the case of a young person infecting first an elder person who survives, and then an elder who passes away. There would be only one young person in the chain of infections, however the LTL $(\neg\texttt{elder})\mathcal{U}(\texttt{young} \wedge f)$ would not hold: the first elder's infection happens temporally before the death, although not part of the chain. POTLfχ instead captures this context-free property: $\mathcal{U}_\chi^d$ exploits the χ relation to skip the first call to `elder()`—this example trace would satisfy it. **Q.7** means that eventually an elder person infects at least one elder person, but none of them passes away.

Results. We report the experimental results for building the support chain (Table 3, cf. Fig. 4) and for solving qualitative and quantitative model checking (Table 4, cf. Fig. 5). All times are in seconds and the timeout is 1 h. A key metric is the number of equations arising from each instance. Since we decompose the graph into SCCs and solve it bottom-up, many equations are solved just by propagating already computed values. We thus report how many equations actually require running our semi-algorithm because they introduce circular dependency between variables in the system. We call them **non-trivial** (NT) equations. In Table 3, $|Q_\mathcal{A}|, |f|_{(\mathcal{A})}, |f_{NT}|_{(\mathcal{A})}$ are the number of resp. states, equations and non-trivial equations that arise when analysing pOPA $\mathcal{A}$ modeling the program. To estimate the size of individual SCCs we feed to OVI/Z3, we report also $|f_{NT}(\text{SCC})|_{max(\mathcal{A})}$, the maximum number of non-trivial equations in an SCC of the equation system of $\mathcal{A}$. In Table 4, AS tells whether the formula holds almost surely. If it is not the case, we perform quantitative model checking to get probability P, for which we provide the same metrics as above, but on $\hat{\mathcal{A}}$, the cross-product between $\mathcal{A}$ and the formula automaton (Sect. 3.2).

Sherwood. The pOPA state space is ruled by two parameters: K, the number of bits of each array element, and M, the array's size. We investigate K $\in [1, 4]$ and

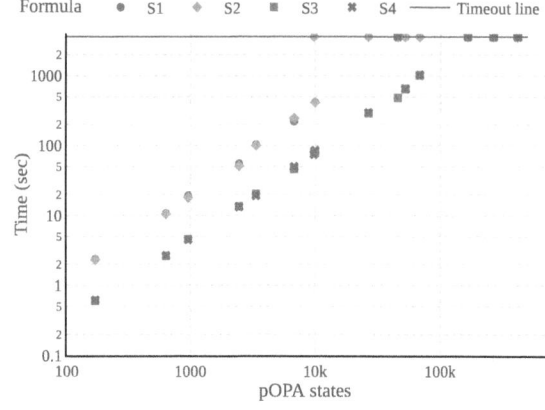

Formula   ● S1   ◆ S2   ■ S3   ✳ S4 ——— Timeout line

Fig. 10. Sherwood binary search: qualitative model checking of all formulae (both axis are on logarithmic scale).

Table 2. Sherwood binary search: quantitative model checking of **S.3** for some values of K and M.

K	M	$|f|_{(\hat{A})}$	t_{tot}	P
		Quantitative MC		
1	1	154k	1.18	1
1	2	2 M	12.12	~ 0.906
1	3	8 M	53.87	~ 0.882
2	1	598k	5.20	1
2	2	15 M	111.36	~ 0.961
3	1	2 M	23.24	1
4	1	9 M	123.63	1

Table 3. Experimental results for the computation of termination probabilities. t_{Z3} (resp. t_{OVI}) is the time required to compute upper bounds with Z3 (OVI).

name	$|Q_A|$	$|f|_{(A)}$	$|f_{NT}|_{(A)}$	$|f_{NT}(SCC)|_{max(A)}$	t_{Z3}	t_{OVI}	t_{PAST}
Schelling	311	1230	266	52	TO	0.03	0.03
Tic-tac-toe	1780	3443	248	36	0.02	0.01	0.08
Virus	427	21211	6490	6488	TO	0.38	0

M ∈ [1, 7]. For each instance, the main procedure randomly initializes the array and a value to search, and calls B(). We assume that calls to uniform() diverge if left > right. Formula **S.1** is partial correctness from Sect. 1. Formula **S.2** is a dual version. Formulae **S.3** and **S.4** are stack-inspection properties: if B() is invoked in a state where left ≤ right, a[left..right] is sorted and val occurs in a[left..right] (does not, in S.4), then there is a recursive call to B(). All formulae hold almost surely except S.3: if the array has multiple elements, the randomized pivot selection may pick the searched value, terminating the program immediately. Figure 10 and Table 2 show results for qualitative model checking on all formulae, and quantitative for some parameters of S.3.

Table 4. Qualitative and quantitative MC. t_G, t_{OVI} are times spent resp. analyzing the synchronized product and computing with OVI upper bounds for non trivial equations.

name	φ	Qualitative MC			Quantitative MC					
		t_G	t_{tot}	AS	$|f|_{(\hat{A})}$	$|f_{NT}|_{(\hat{A})}$	$|f_{NT}(\mathrm{SCC})|_{max(\hat{A})}$	t_{OVI}	t_{tot}	P
Schelling	Q.1	0.02	0.15	✓	-	-		-	-	1
	Q.2	26.28	26.40	✓	-	-		-	-	1
	Q.3	1.25	1.37	✗	893k	68k	7.3k	11.71	20.58	$\sim$ 0.895
	Q.8	0.22	0.34	✗	214k	15k	1.4k	3.80	5.70	$\sim$ 0.610
	Q.9	0.04	0.16	✗	36k	3.2k	252	1.29	1.57	$\sim$ 0.610
	Q.12	1.01	1.14	✗	651k	61k	6.7k	11.56	20.10	$\sim$ 0.096
	Q.13	0.67	0.80	✗	599k	43k	5.7k	6.48	13.28	$\sim$ 0.506
	Q.15	0.95	1.07	✗	762k	63k	7.5k	12.49	23.21	$\sim$ 0.543
Tic-tac-toe	Q.1	0.12	0.2	✓	-	-		-	-	1
	Q.2	122.16	122.33	✓	-	-		-	-	1
	Q.4	9.79	9.98	✓	-	-		-	-	1
	Q.5	8.22	8.41	✓	-	-		-	-	1
	Q.10	2.94	3.10	✗	1.1 M	77k	3k	0.79	10.45	$\sim$ 0.712
	Q.11	2.96	3.13	✓	-	-		-	-	1
	Q.14	0.54	0.71	✗	280k	20k	1.5k	0.17	2.30	$\sim$ 0.288
	Q.16	386.10	386.22	✓	-	-		-	-	1
Virus	Q.1	0.18	2.13	✗	243k	25k	12k	0.50	9.72	$\sim$ 0.239
	Q.2	263.94	265.9	✓	-	-		-	-	1
	Q.6	14.96	16.95	✗	?	?	?	?	?	TO
	Q.7	891.45	893.37	✗	?	?	?	?	?	TO

6   Discussion and Future Work

Experimental results show that OVI scales better than Z3 in solving systems for building the support chain. Z3 already times out when provided with a system of 52 equations. For quantitative model checking, the exponential blow-up on the formula automaton generates in our benchmark hundred of thousands of equations. This suggests that determinization-based approaches, leading to another exponentiation, would not work. Finally, our tool scales up to a few million of equations, supporting checking non-trivial formulae on medium-size pPDA.

Future improvements may come from finding ways of modeling non-trivial probabilistic programs with less expressive pPDA subclasses that have more efficient model checking algorithms. pPDA with one single state (or *stochastic context-free grammars*) admit P-time algorithms for computing the probability of termination [15]; *probabilistic one-counter automata* admit P-time algorithms for model checking ω-regular properties [47].

Acknowledgments. We thank Tobias Winkler and Joost-Pieter Katoen (RWTH Aachen) for the fruitful discussions and advice on implementing OVI. This work was funded by the Vienna Science and Technology Fund (WWTF) grants [10.47379/ICT19018] (ProbInG) and ICT22-023 (TAIGER), and by the Horizon Europe programme grants No. 101034440 (MSCA Doctoral Network LogiCS@TU Wien) and No. 101107303 (MSCA Postdoctoral Fellowship CORPORA) ■.

Disclosure of Interests. The authors declare no competing interests for this article.

References

1. Baier, C., Katoen, J.: Principles of Model Checking. MIT Press (2008)
2. Baier, C., Kiefer, S., Klein, J., Müller, D., Worrell, J.: Markov chains and unambiguous automata. J. Comput. Syst. Sci. **136**, 113–134 (2023). https://doi.org/10.1016/J.JCSS.2023.03.005
3. Brázdil, T., Brozek, V., Holecek, J., Kucera, A.: Discounted properties of probabilistic pushdown automata. In: LPAR 2008. LNCS, vol. 5330, pp. 230–242. Springer (2008). https://doi.org/10.1007/978-3-540-89439-1_17
4. Brázdil, T., Esparza, J., Kiefer, S., Kucera, A.: Analyzing probabilistic pushdown automata. Formal Methods Syst. Des. **43**(2), 124–163 (2013). https://doi.org/10.1007/s10703-012-0166-0
5. Brázdil, T., Esparza, J., Kucera, A.: Analysis and prediction of the long-run behavior of probabilistic sequential programs with recursion (extended abstract). In: FOCS 2005, pp. 521–530. IEEE Computer Society (2005). https://doi.org/10.1109/SFCS.2005.19
6. Brázdil, T., Kiefer, S., Kucera, A., Vareková, I.H.: Runtime analysis of probabilistic programs with unbounded recursion. J. Comput. Syst. Sci. **81**(1), 288–310 (2015). https://doi.org/10.1016/J.JCSS.2014.06.005
7. Canny, J.F.: Some algebraic and geometric computations in PSPACE. In: STOC 1988, pp. 460–467. ACM (1988). https://doi.org/10.1145/62212.62257
8. Chiari, M., Mandrioli, D., Pontiggia, F., Pradella, M.: A model checker for operator precedence languages. ACM Trans. Program. Lang. Syst. **45**(3) (2023). https://doi.org/10.1145/3608443
9. Chiari, M., Mandrioli, D., Pradella, M.: Model-checking structured context-free languages. In: Silva, A., Leino, K. (eds.) CAV 2021. LNCS, vol. 12760, pp. 387–410. Springer, Cham (2021). https://doi.org/10.1007/978-3-030-81688-9_18
10. Chiari, M., Mandrioli, D., Pradella, M.: A first-order complete temporal logic for structured context-free languages. Log. Methods Comput. Sci. **18:3** (2022).https://doi.org/10.46298/LMCS-18(3:11)2022
11. Couvreur, J., Saheb, N., Sutre, G.: An optimal automata approach to LTL model checking of probabilistic systems. In: LPAR 2003. LNCS, vol. 2850, pp. 361–375. Springer (2003). https://doi.org/10.1007/978-3-540-39813-4_26
12. Esparza, J., Kiefer, S., Luttenberger, M.: Computing the least fixed point of positive polynomial systems. SIAM J. Comput. **39**(6), 2282–2335 (2010). https://doi.org/10.1137/090749591
13. Esparza, J., Kretínský, J., Sickert, S.: A unified translation of linear temporal logic to ω-automata. J. ACM **67**(6), 33:1–33:61 (2020). https://doi.org/10.1145/3417995

14. Esparza, J., Kucera, A., Mayr, R.: Model checking probabilistic pushdown automata. In: LICS 2004, pp. 12–21. IEEE Computer Society (2004). https://doi.org/10.1109/LICS.2004.1319596

15. Etessami, K., Stewart, A., Yannakakis, M.: Polynomial time algorithms for multitype branching processes and stochastic context-free grammars. In: STOC 2012, pp. 579–588. ACM (2012). https://doi.org/10.1145/2213977.2214030

16. Etessami, K., Yannakakis, M.: Algorithmic verification of recursive probabilistic state machines. In: TACAS 2005. LNCS, vol. 3440, pp. 253–270. Springer (2005). https://doi.org/10.1007/978-3-540-31980-1_17

17. Etessami, K., Yannakakis, M.: Recursive Markov chains, stochastic grammars, and monotone systems of nonlinear equations. In: STACS 2005. LNCS, vol. 3404, pp. 340–352. Springer (2005). https://doi.org/10.1007/978-3-540-31856-9_28

18. Etessami, K., Yannakakis, M.: Recursive Markov chains, stochastic grammars, and monotone systems of nonlinear equations. J. ACM 56(1), 1:1–1:66 (2009). https://doi.org/10.1145/1462153.1462154

19. Etessami, K., Yannakakis, M.: Model checking of recursive probabilistic systems. ACM Trans. Comput. Log. 13(2), 12:1–12:40 (2012). https://doi.org/10.1145/2159531.2159534

20. Etessami, K., Yannakakis, M.: Recursive Markov decision processes and recursive stochastic games. J. ACM 62(2), 11:1–11:69 (2015). https://doi.org/10.1145/2699431

21. Evans, O., Stuhlmüller, A., Salvatier, J., Filan, D.: Modeling agents with probabilistic programs (2017). http://agentmodels.org

22. Floyd, R.W.: Syntactic analysis and operator precedence. J. ACM 10(3), 316–333 (1963). https://doi.org/10.1145/321172.321179

23. Ghahramani, Z.: Probabilistic machine learning and artificial intelligence. Nat. 521(7553), 452–459 (2015). https://doi.org/10.1038/NATURE14541

24. Goodman, N.D., Mansinghka, V.K., Roy, D.M., Bonawitz, K.A., Tenenbaum, J.B.: Church: a language for generative models. In: UAI 2008, pp. 220–229. AUAI Press (2008)

25. Goodman, N.D., Tenenbaum, J.B., The ProbMods contributors: probabilistic models of cognition. http://probmods.org/v2 (2016). Accessed 22 May 2025

26. Gordon, A.D., Henzinger, T.A., Nori, A.V., Rajamani, S.K.: Probabilistic programming. In: FOSE 2014, pp. 167–181. ACM (2014). https://doi.org/10.1145/2593882.2593900

27. Haccou, P., Jagers, P., Vatutin, V.A.: Branching Processes: Variation, Growth, and Extinction of Populations. Cambridge University Press (2005)

28. Hensel, C., Junges, S., Katoen, J., Quatmann, T., Volk, M.: The probabilistic model checker Storm. Int. J. Softw. Tools Technol. Transf. 24(4), 589–610 (2022). https://doi.org/10.1007/s10009-021-00633-z

29. Jacobs, J.: Paradoxes of probabilistic programming: and how to condition on events of measure zero with infinitesimal probabilities. ACM Program. Lang. 5(POPL), 1–26 (2021). https://doi.org/10.1145/3434339

30. Jovanovic, D., de Moura, L.: Solving non-linear arithmetic. ACM Commun. Comput. Algebra 46(3/4), 104–105 (2012). https://doi.org/10.1145/2429135.2429155

31. Kucera, A., Esparza, J., Mayr, R.: Model checking probabilistic pushdown automata. Log. Methods Comput. Sci. 2(1) (2006). https://doi.org/10.2168/LMCS-2(1:2)2006

32. Kwiatkowska, M.Z., Norman, G., Parker, D.: PRISM 4.0: verification of probabilistic real-time systems. In: CAV 2011. LNCS, vol. 6806, pp. 585–591. Springer (2011). https://doi.org/10.1007/978-3-642-22110-1_47

33. Mandrioli, D., Pradella, M.: Generalizing input-driven languages: theoretical and practical benefits. Comput. Sci. Rev. **27**, 61–87 (2018). https://doi.org/10.1016/j.cosrev.2017.12.001
34. McConnell, J.: Analysis of Algorithms. Jones & Bartlett Publishers (2007)
35. de Moura, L.M., Bjørner, N.S.: Z3: an efficient SMT solver. In: TACAS 2008. LNCS, vol. 4963, pp. 337–340. Springer (2008). https://doi.org/10.1007/978-3-540-78800-3_24
36. Olmedo, F., Gretz, F., Jansen, N., Kaminski, B.L., Katoen, J., McIver, A.: Conditioning in probabilistic programming. ACM Trans. Program. Lang. Syst. **40**(1), 4:1–4:50 (2018). https://doi.org/10.1145/3156018
37. Olmedo, F., Kaminski, B.L., Katoen, J., Matheja, C.: Reasoning about recursive probabilistic programs. In: LICS 2016, pp. 672–681. ACM (2016). https://doi.org/10.1145/2933575.2935317
38. Pnueli, A.: The temporal logic of programs. In: FOCS 1977, pp. 46–57. IEEE Computer Society (1977). https://doi.org/10.1109/SFCS.1977.32
39. Pontiggia, F.: POMC. A model checking tool for operator precedence languages on omega-words. Master's thesis, Politecnico di Milano (2021). http://hdl.handle.net/10589/176028
40. Pontiggia, F., Bartocci, E., Chiari, M.: Model checking probabilistic operator precedence automata. CoRR (2024). https://doi.org/10.48550/arXiv.2404.03515
41. Pontiggia, F., Chiari, M., Pradella, M.: Verification of programs with exceptions through operator precedence automata. In: SEFM 2021. LNCS, vol. 13085, pp. 293–311. Springer, Berlin, Heidelberg (2021). https://doi.org/10.1007/978-3-030-92124-8_17
42. Rainforth, T.: Nesting probabilistic programs. In: Globerson, A., Silva, R. (eds.) UAI 2018, pp. 249–258. AUAI Press (2018). http://auai.org/uai2018/proceedings/papers/92.pdf
43. Renegar, J.: On the computational complexity and geometry of the first-order theory of the reals, parts I-III. J. Symb. Comput. **13**(3), 255–352 (1992). https://doi.org/10.1016/S0747-7171(10)80003-3
44. Schelling, T.C.: The Strategy of Conflict. Harvard University Press (1980)
45. Scontras, G., Tessler, M.H., Franke, M.: Probabilistic language understanding: an introduction to the rational speech act framework. https://www.problang.org/. Accessed 22 May 2025
46. Seaman, I.R., van de Meent, J.W., Wingate, D.: Nested reasoning about autonomous agents using probabilistic programs (2020). https://arxiv.org/abs/1812.01569
47. Stewart, A., Etessami, K., Yannakakis, M.: Upper bounds for Newton's method on monotone polynomial systems, and P-time model checking of probabilistic one-counter automata. J. ACM **62**(4), 30:1–30:33 (2015). https://doi.org/10.1145/2789208
48. Stuhlmüller, A., Goodman, N.D.: Reasoning about reasoning by nested conditioning: modeling theory of mind with probabilistic programs. Cogn. Syst. Res. **28**, 80–99 (2014). https://doi.org/10.1016/J.COGSYS.2013.07.003
49. Vardi, M.Y., Wolper, P.: Reasoning about infinite computations. Inf. Comput. **115**(1), 1–37 (1994). https://doi.org/10.1006/INCO.1994.1092
50. Winkler, T., Gehnen, C., Katoen, J.: Model checking temporal properties of recursive probabilistic programs. In: FOSSACS 2022. LNCS, vol. 13242, pp. 449–469. Springer (2022). https://doi.org/10.1007/978-3-030-99253-8_23

51. Winkler, T., Katoen, J.: Certificates for probabilistic pushdown automata via optimistic value iteration. In: TACAS 2023. LNCS, vol. 13994, pp. 391–409. Springer (2023). https://doi.org/10.1007/978-3-031-30820-8_24
52. Winkler, T., Katoen, J.: On certificates, expected runtimes, and termination in probabilistic pushdown automata. In: LICS 2023, pp. 1–13 (2023). https://doi.org/10.1109/LICS56636.2023.10175714
53. Wojtczak, D., Etessami, K.: PReMo: An analyzer for probabilistic recursive models. In: TACAS 2007. LNCS, vol. 4424, pp. 66–71. Springer (2007). https://doi.org/10.1007/978-3-540-71209-1_7
54. Yannakakis, M., Etessami, K.: Checking LTL properties of recursive Markov chains. In: QEST 2005, pp. 155–165. IEEE (2005). https://doi.org/10.1109/QEST.2005.8
55. Zhang, Y., Amin, N.: Reasoning about "reasoning about reasoning": semantics and contextual equivalence for probabilistic programs with nested queries and recursion. ACM Program. Lang. **6**(POPL), 1–28 (2022). https://doi.org/10.1145/3498677

A Formally Verified IEEE 754 Floating-Point Implementation of Interval Iteration for MDPs

Bram Kohlen[1]([✉])(iD), Maximilian Schäffeler[2](iD), Mohammad Abdulaziz[2,3](iD),
Arnd Hartmanns[1](iD), and Peter Lammich[1](iD)

[1] University of Twente, Enschede, The Netherlands
b.kohlen@utwente.nl
[2] Technical University of Munich, Munich, Germany
maximilian.schaeffeler@tum.de
[3] King's College London, London, UK

Abstract. We present an efficiently executable, formally verified implementation of interval iteration for MDPs. Our correctness proofs span the entire development from the high-level abstract semantics of MDPs to a low-level implementation in LLVM that is based on floating-point arithmetic. We use the Isabelle/HOL proof assistant to verify convergence of our abstract definition of interval iteration and employ step-wise refinement to derive an efficient implementation in LLVM code. To that end, we extend the Isabelle Refinement Framework with support for reasoning about floating-point arithmetic and directed rounding modes. We experimentally demonstrate that the verified implementation is competitive with state-of-the-art tools for MDPs, while providing formal guarantees on the correctness of the results.

1 Introduction

Probabilistic model checking (PMC) [4,5] is a formal verification technique for randomized systems and algorithms like wireless communication protocols [36], network-on-chip (NoC) architectures [51], and reliability and performance models [6]. Typical properties checked by means of PMC relate to *reachability probabilities*: What is the probability that a file will eventually be transmitted successfully [18]? Is the probability that a NoC router's queue will overflow within c clock cycles below 10^{-5}? What is the maintenance strategy that minimizes service outages within a given cost budget [52,53]? The system models that PMC is applied to are specified in higher-level modeling languages such as Modest [12,24] or JANI [15] with a formal semantics in terms of (extensions of) Markov chains and Markov decision processes (MDPs) [11,48].

PMC delivers results with formal guarantees, typically that the computed and (unknown) true probabilities differ by at most a user-specified ε. PMC is thus well-suited for the design and evaluation of safety- and performance-critical systems. Over the past decade, however, we have witnessed several threats to

© The Author(s) 2025
R. Piskac and Z. Rakamarić (Eds.): CAV 2025, LNCS 15932, pp. 122–146, 2025.
https://doi.org/10.1007/978-3-031-98679-6_6

the validity of PMC results. First and foremost, the most-used PMC algorithm, value iteration (VI), was shown to be *unsound* with an absolute- or relative-error stopping criterion, i.e. produce arbitrarily wrong results for certain inputs [22]. Standard VI terminates whenever two successive iterates are sufficiently close in value. However, at this point, the distance to the actual reachability probability may be arbitrarily off, no matter the error threshold [23, Example 1]. Several sound replacements for VI were subsequently developed [23,30,49], yet their soundness proofs have so far been *pen-and-paper* style with room for human error. For example, the pseudocode for the *sound VI* algorithm as stated in [49] contains a subtle omission that only surfaces on 1 of the 78 models of the Quantitative Verification Benchmark Set (QVBS) [31].

This calls for *formal specifications of the algorithms* accompanied by *machine-checked correctness proofs*. Even correct algorithms, however, may be incorrectly implemented in today's manually-coded PMC tools. As a case in point, the implementation of the *interval iteration* algorithm for expected rewards [8] in the mcsta model checker of the MODEST TOOLSET [28] diverges on some inputs. We thus need *correct-by-construction implementations*, too.

VI-based algorithms are iterative numeric approximation schemes that need to be implemented via machine-precision floating-point arithmetic to obtain acceptable performance [16,29]. This introduces approximation and rounding errors that in turn may lead to incorrect Boolean outputs [61]. An efficient solution is to carefully use the directed rounding modes provided by standard IEEE 754 floating-point implementations on modern CPUs [27], which, however, needs careful *reasoning about floating-point errors and rounding* in all formal proofs and correctness-preserving implementation strategies.

Our Contribution. We present a solution to all of the above challenges based on the interval iteration (II) algorithm [23] for sound PMC on MDP models and the interactive theorem prover (ITP) Isabelle/HOL [47] with its Isabelle Refinement Framework (IRF) [42]:

- We formalize (i.e. model) II in Isabelle/HOL's logic and formally prove its correctness using Isabelle/HOL (Sect. 3), making II the first sound PMC algorithm for MDPs with machine-checked correctness.
- We extend the IRF with support for floating-point arithmetic, including directed rounding modes (Sect. 4.2), introducing the first ITP-based algorithm refinement approach suitable for II and similar algorithms.
- Using the IRF, we refine the formalization of II into efficient LLVM bytecode (Sects. 4.3 and 4.4), delivering the first correct-by-construction implementation of a PMC algorithm.
- In Sect. 5, we embed the code into mcsta, a competitive probabilistic model checker. We experimentally evaluate the performance using the QVBS, showing that the verified implementation is efficient. Our formal proofs and the benchmark setup are available online.[1]

---

[1] https://doi.org/10.4121/bf0fef24-4f0f-4de6-a58d-07b9ba601804.

State-of-the-Art: Verification of Algorithms for MDPs. A probabilistic model checker like mcsta performs preprocessing and transformation steps for both correctness and performance. Previously, the strongly connected component [32] and maximal end component decomposition [33] algorithms have been verified down to LLVM, replacing their previous unverified implementations inside mcsta by verified ones of comparable performance. These were fully discrete graph algorithms, however, that neither required reasoning about numerical convergence in their correctness proofs nor floating-point arithmetic in their refinement to an efficient implementation. With this work, we contribute an essential piece for the incremental replacement of unverified by verified algorithms for probabilistic reachability in mcsta's MDP model checking core.

Other work relevant to our setting is the verification of iteration algorithms for MDPs: In Coq by Vajjha et al. [59] and in Isabelle/HOL by Schäffeler and Abdulaziz [54,55]. These works contribute formalizations of the classical version of value iteration and policy iteration that optimize the expected discounted values, and a modified policy iteration algorithm for solving large, factored MDPs. We note that only Schäffeler and Abdulaziz [54,55] also verified practical implementations. However, since their implementations used infinite-precision arithmetic, they could not compete with state-of-the-art floating-point implementations. Thus, the work we present here is the first, to our knowledge, where a full formal mathematical analysis of an algorithm, involving heavy usage of a formal mathematical probabilities library, is performed and a competitive floating-point implementation is also verified. Furthermore, from a formalization-methodology perspective, we note that the correctness argument of II involves a substantial element of graph-theoretic reasoning, in addition to the reasoning about fixed points that is present in II and other verified MDP algorithms. This includes reasoning about connected components, acyclicity, and levels in a directed acyclic graph (DAG), further complicating II's verification compared to other verified iteration algorithms.

State-of-the-Art: Verification of Floating-Point Algorithms. It is widely recognized as a problem that floating-point implementations often deviate from the mathematical models of the underlying algorithms. Bugs with potentially serious consequences were noted in the hardware and aerospace industry [26,46]. Due to the complexity of floating-point algorithms' behavior, and the failure of testing to reliably catch bugs in those algorithms, there is a long tradition of applying formal methods to the verification of floating-point algorithms. This was done in verification systems like Z [10], HOL Light [25,26], PVS [14,45], and Coq [13,20]. Most of that previous work, however, focused on proving correctness of basic algorithms implemented in floating-point arithmetic, such as foundational linear algebra operations [37]. In contrast, we aim to do the correctness proofs on algorithms using real numbers, which we implement as floating-point numbers with directed rounding. This keeps our correctness proofs manageable while preserving interesting properties, even for complex programs.

A related line of work aims to prove correctness by providing error bounds. Tools like PRECiSA [58], VCFloat2 [3], FPTaylor [56], Real2Float [44], and

Fluctuat [21] analyze the floating-point error propagation. They focus on determining the worst-case roundoff error. While more expressive than our approach, these tools have limited to no support for programs with complex control flow like the nested loops in the implementation of II.

The static analysis tool Astrée [17] is used in the aviation and automotive industry to check the absence of runtime errors. While it supports floating-point arithmetic, it cannot verify general correctness properties. Frama-C [38] has similar functionality but also features deductive verification. However, the properties supported are limited to, e.g., proving that outputs lie in a given interval [40]. The situation is similar with other deductive verifiers such as KeY [2], which can verify the absence of exceptional floating-point values like *NaN* and *infinity* [1].

2   Preliminaries

We now present the necessary background for the rest of the paper: we introduce Isabelle and the Isabelle Refinement Framework, followed by IEEE 754 floating-point numbers and Markov decision processes in Isabelle/HOL.

2.1   Isabelle/HOL

An *interactive theorem prover* (ITP) is a program that implements a formal mathematical system in which a user writes definitions and theorem statements, and constructs proofs from a set of axioms. To prove a theorem in an ITP, the user provides high-level steps, and the ITP fills in the details at the axiom-level.

We perform our formalization using the ITP Isabelle/HOL [47], which is a proof assistant for *higher-order logic* (HOL). Roughly speaking, HOL can be seen as a combination of functional programming with logic. Isabelle is designed to be highly trustworthy: a small, trusted kernel implements the inference rules of the logic. Outside the kernel, a large set of tools implement proof automation and high-level concepts like algebraic data types. Bugs in these tools cannot lead to inconsistent theorems being proved, as the kernel refuses flawed proofs.

We aim to represent our formalization as faithfully as possible, but we have optimized the presentation for readability. The notation in Isabelle/HOL is similar to functional programming languages like ML or Haskell mixed with mathematical notation. Function application is written as juxtaposition: we write $f\ x_1\ \dots\ x_n$ instead of the standard notation $f(x_1,\ \dots\ ,x_n)$. Recursive functions are defined using the **fun** keyword and pattern matching. For partial functions, we use the notation $f = (\lambda x \in X.\ g\ x)$, to explicitly restrict the domain of the function to X. Where required, we annotate types as $x :: type$.

Isabelle/HOL provides a keyword **locale** to define a named context with assumptions, e.g. an MDP with well-formedness assumptions [9]. Locales can be interpreted and extended in different contexts, e.g., a locale for MDPs can be instantiated for a specific MDP, which yields all theorems from that locale.

2.2   Isabelle Refinement Framework

Our verification of II spans the mathematical foundations of MDPs, the implementation of optimized algorithms and data structures, and the low-level LLVM intermediate language [43]. To keep the verification effort manageable, we use a stepwise refinement approach: starting with an abstract specification, we incrementally add implementation details, proving that each addition preserves correctness, e.g., computing a fixed point by iteration, or implementing MDPs by a sparse-matrix data structure. The former specifies the control flow of a program, but the data type remains the same. The latter we call *data refinement*.

This approach is supported by the Isabelle Refinement Framework (IRF) [42]. In the IRF, we define algorithms in the *nondeterministic result (nres) monad*, where a program either fails or produces a set of results. The notation $a \leq_R c$ denotes that every (non-deterministic) output of abstract program a is related to an output of concrete program c via the *refinement relation R*. In other words, c is an implementation of a. If a refinement step does not involve data refinement, then we use $\leq := \leq_{R_{id}}$ where R_{id} is the identity relation.

We target LLVM for our code generation, for which the IRF provides semantics, so that we can perform refinements to LLVM in a verified way. LLVM is an intermediate representation, meaning that programming languages like C and Rust can be compiled to LLVM. The LLVM compiler framework can then be used to compile to bytecode and apply optimizations. In our formalization, the refinement chain starts with a high-level specification of the algorithm and ends with an efficient LLVM program. The sepref [41] tool can automatically refine a program to LLVM and prove a refinement theorem, given that we have provided compatible data structures (sepref can automatically refine HOL lists to arrays, nats to 64-bit integers, etc.). Due to transitivity of refinement, the LLVM program satisfies the specification.

2.3   Floating-Point Arithmetic

Our work builds on a formalization of the IEEE 754 floating-point standard in Isabelle/HOL [62]. This library provides a generic type *(e,f) float* resembling scientific notation: e is the number of bits for the *exponent*, and f is the number of bits for the *fraction* (also known as mantissa). We use the type *double = (11,52) float* which is the standard double precision format.

The floating-point format contains positive and negative numbers, as well as designated special values for $\pm\infty$ and *not a number (NaN)*. The function *valof :: (e,f) float $\rightarrow$ ereal* maps non-NaN floating-point numbers to *extended real numbers*, i.e. $\mathbb{R} \,\dot{\cup}\, \{-\infty, +\infty\}$. Finally, the formalization provides standard floating-point instructions like addition, multiplication, and comparisons as well as intuitive predicates to identify special cases (e.g. *is_nan*).

2.4   Markov Decision Processes

Markov decision processes (MDPs) are widely used to model probabilistic systems with nondeterministic choices [48], e.g., in PMC, planning, operations research and reinforcement learning [7,57]. Intuitively, an *agent* interacts with an environment by choosing *actions* that, together with random elements, influence the *state* of the system. The agent has an *objective*, e.g., to reach certain states, and aims to choose actions that optimize the probability to achieve the objective. The important concepts introduced in this section are illustrated in Example 1.

Formally, a finite MDP is a pair $M = (S, K)$ where S is a finite, non-empty set of *states*, and $K : S \to 2^{\mathcal{P}(S)}$ is the transition kernel. It maps every state to a finite, non-empty set of *actions* in the form of transition probabilities. $\mathcal{P}(S)$ denotes the set of probability measures on S, i.e. functions $p : S \to [0,1]$ where $\sum_{s \in S} p(s) = 1$. Furthermore K is closed under S: Actions from S lead to S.

Our formalization of II extends the *Markov Models* [34,35] formalization from *archive of formal proofs* (AFP)—a collection of Isabelle libraries. MDPs are modeled with a generic type *'s mdpc* and a locale *Finite_MDP* that, in combination, contain the states, the transition kernel and well-formedness conditions (Locale 2.1). In the following, we abbreviate the projections *states M* and *actions M* as S and K. The type of the states is *'s*, and the type of probability distributions over *'s* is *'s pmf*. For a distribution $p :: \text{'s pmf}$, $set_{pmf}\ p$ denotes its support, i.e. the set of states with non-zero probability.

locale *Finite_MDP* =   *(Locale 2.1)*
   fixes $M :: \text{'s mdpc}$ **and** S **and** K
   defines $S = states\ M$ **and** $K = actions\ M$
   assumes $S \neq \varnothing$ **and** *finite S* **and** $\forall s.\ K\ s \neq \varnothing$ **and** $\forall s \in S.\ finite\ (K\ s)$
   assumes $\forall s \in S.\ \bigcup a \in K\ s.\ set_{pmf}\ a \subseteq S$

At every state, the agent chooses an action based on the current state and the history of visited states. The agent's choices are captured by a *scheduler* (aka policy, strategy, or adversary), which is a function that maps histories to actions. The MDP formalization works with *configurations*, which are pairs of states and strategies. A configuration is *valid* if the strategy selects only enabled actions and the state of the configuration is in S. $valid_{cfg}$

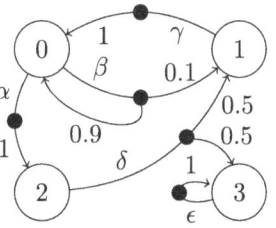

Fig. 1. A simple MDP with four states and five actions.

denotes the set of all valid configurations. Given a configuration and an MDP, the probability space of infinite traces $T\ cfg$ is constructed from the induced Markov chain, where each state is a configuration.

MDP subcomponents play an important role in the analysis of II. A *sub-MDP* $M' = (S', K')$ consists of a subset of states $S' \subseteq S$ and a restricted kernel K' where $\forall s \in S'.\ K'(s) \subseteq K(s)$. A sub-MDP is *strongly connected* if all states are connected via a sequence of actions. A closed, strongly connected sub-MDP is an *end component* (EC). A *maximal end component* (MEC) is an EC that is not a sub-MDP of another EC. Finally, *trivial MECs* are MECs with one state and no actions, and *bottom MECs* are MECs without an exit.

Reachability. In our PMC setting, the objective is to minimize or maximize the long-term reachability probabilities of a set of target states $U \subseteq S$. The value function $P_{cfg} :: {}'s \Rightarrow real$ gives the probability of reaching U in the Markov chain induced by the configuration *cfg*. Minimal and maximal reachability probabilities are denoted by $P_{\inf}$ and $P_{\sup}$ respectively. $P_{\inf}$ is defined as the infimum of P_{cfg} over all valid configurations, $P_{\sup}$ is defined using the supremum. We also introduce the *Bellman optimality operators* $F_{\inf}$ and $F_{\sup}$ (Definition 2.1, $F_{\sup}$ omitted). For a state $s \in S$ and a value vector v, $F_{\inf} \ v \ s$ denotes the minimal expected value of v after taking a single step from s. The symbol $\sqcap$ denotes the infimum.

definition $F_{\inf} \ v = (\lambda s \in S.$ *(Def. 2.1)*
  if $s \in U$ **then** *1*
  else $\sqcap a \in K \ s. \ \sum t \in set_{pmf} \ a. \ v \ t \cdot pmf \ a \ t)$

The *least fixed point* (*lfp*) of $F_{\inf}$ is $P_{\inf}$. In other words, repeatedly applying $F_{\inf}$ to a lower bound of $P_{\inf}$ converges to $P_{\inf}$ in the limit. For II, we preprocess the MDP such that the *greatest fixed point* (*gfp*) of $F_{\inf}$ also equals $P_{\inf}$, and then iterate $F_{\inf}$ on both a lower and an upper bound until they closely approximate $P_{\inf}$. The same holds for $F_{\sup}$ and $P_{\sup}$.

Example 1. Figure 1 shows an MDP with four states, $S = \{0, 1, 2, 3\}$. The outgoing transitions from each state represent the actions in the MDP. Each transition leads to a black dot and branches into the successor states with corresponding probabilities. For example in state 0, $K \ 0 = \{\alpha, \beta\}$. The agent can choose action α to move to state 2, or β to have a 10% chance to move to state 1.

Let the target states $U = \{3\}$. The reachability probabilities are $P_{\inf} \ 2 = 0.5$ and $P_{\sup} \ 2 = 1$. The MDP has a single bottom MEC $\{3\}$ with action $\{\epsilon\}$, and a single trivial MEC $\{2\}$. The states $\{0, 1\}$ form a MEC with actions β and γ.

3   Interval Iteration in Isabelle/HOL

The *interval iteration (II)* algorithm for MDPs is an iterative solution method for reachability problems based on value iteration. In contrast to standard value iteration applied to PMC, II provides a simple and sound stopping criterion.

We present our Isabelle/HOL formalization of definitions and correctness proofs for II and its preprocessing routines. Our formalization is based on the proofs in [23]: We highlight the challenges encountered during formalization and point out differences in our formal proofs to their pen-and-paper equivalents. In particular, we present a more elegant and much more precise proof of [22, Proposition 3]. Moreover, we simplify the definitions of the preprocessing steps significantly. In the following, all statements prefixed with **lemma** or **theorem** are formally verified in Isabelle/HOL. All theorems and definitions for $P_{\sup}$ that are analogous to the ones for $P_{\inf}$ are omitted here for brevity.

3.1   The Interval Iteration Algorithm

The idea of the II algorithm is to start with a lower and an upper bound on the true reachability probabilities and then iterate the Bellman optimality operator F_{inf} (or F_{sup}) on both. Since the optimality operators are monotone, both sequences converge to a fixed point. On arbitrary MDPs, these fixed points are not necessarily the same. However, if the MDP is preprocessed to only contain MECs that are trivial or bottom MECs, both fixed points are equal to the optimal reachability probabilities.

For now, assume an arbitrary MDP with a single target state s_+ and an avoid state s_-, that are both sinks. As the initial lower bound lb_0, we take the function that assigns 1 to s_+ and 0 to all other states. The initial upper bound ub_0 assigns 0 to s_- and 1 to all other states. The II algorithm computes the sequences $lb_{\text{inf}}\ n$ and $ub_{\text{inf}}\ n$, defined as the n-fold application of F_{inf} to either lb_0 or ub_0:

definition $lb_{\text{inf}}\ n = (F_{\text{inf}})^n\ lb_0$ **and** $ub_{\text{inf}}\ n = (F_{\text{inf}})^n\ ub_0$ *(Def. 3.1)*

It is an immediate consequence of the monotonicity of the Bellman optimality operators that the lower (upper) bounds are monotonically increasing (decreasing). Clearly, lb_0 is a lower bound and ub_0 is an upper bound of P_{inf}. Additionally, we formally derive that the Bellman optimality operators preserve upper and lower bounds in Lemma 3.1. These two properties of the abstract II algorithm are required for the refinement proof in Sect. 4.

lemma **assumes** $v \leq P_{\text{inf}}$ **shows** $F_{\text{inf}}\ v \leq P_{\text{inf}}$ *(Lemma 3.1)*
lemma **assumes** $v \geq P_{\text{inf}}$ **shows** $F_{\text{inf}}\ v \geq P_{\text{inf}}$

3.2   Reduced MDPs

II is only guaranteed to converge if the MDP only contains trivial or bottom MECs. We therefore need to preprocess the MDP before applying II. The preprocessing steps differ for P_{inf} and P_{sup}, they are called *min-reduction* and *max-reduction*. In a first step, we extend the existing MDP formalization [34] with *strongly connected components* (SCCs) and bottom MECs (Definition 3.2). The states of an MDP that form trivial or bottom MECs are called *trivials* or *bottoms* respectively. We follow the original presentation of II [23] and call an MDP *reduced* if all of its MECs are either trivial or bottom MECs.

definition $bmec\ M\ b =$ *(Def. 3.2)*
      $mec\ M\ b \wedge (\forall s \in states\ b.\ actions\ b\ s = K\ s)$

Min-Reduction. The min-reduction for MDPs transforms an arbitrary MDP into a reduced MDP whilst P_{inf} remains unchanged. Observe that we may assign a minimal reachability of 0 to all non-trivial MECs (except s_+): There exists a strategy that stays in the MEC forever and therefore never reaches s_+. Hence, all such MECs may be collapsed into a single absorbing state s_-. To formalize this transformation, we first define a function red_{inf} (Definition 3.3) to map single states, and then apply it to the MDP M to obtain the reduced MDP M_{inf} (Definition 3.4). Our formal definition is a substantial simplification compared to the pen-and-paper version [23, Def. 4].

The function map_{mdpc} (defined by Hölzl [35]) applies a function to every state of an MDP. If the function merges states, map_{mdpc} merges the action sets. Finally, $fix\_loop\ s_-$ replaces the actions at s_- with a single self-loop. Figure 2 displays the min-reduced version of the MDP from Fig. 1.

definition $red_{inf}\ s = $ **if** $s \in trivials\ M \cup \{s_+\}$ **then** s **else** s_- *(Def. 3.3)*

definition $M_{inf} = fix\_loop\ s_-\ (map_{mdpc}\ red_{inf}\ M)$ *(Def. 3.4)*

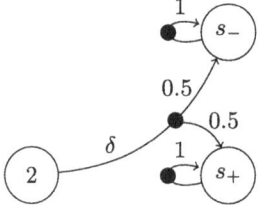

Fig. 2. Min-reduced MDP derived from the MDP in Fig. 1.

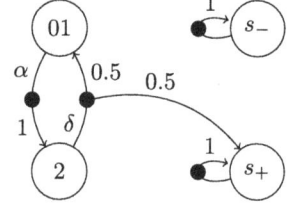

Fig. 3. Max-reduced MDP derived from the MDP in Fig. 1.

Our formal proof of the fact that M_{inf} is in fact a reduced MDP follows the original proof [22]. Next, we also need to show that the transformation preserves P_{inf}. To distinguish the reachability probabilities of the original and the reduced MDP, we use the notation P_{inf} for the original MDP and $M_{inf}.P_{inf}$ for the reduced MDP. Our correctness proof of the transformation is based on the fact that min-reduction preserves the finite-horizon probabilities $P_{inf}^{\leq}\ n$ (Lemma 3.2), i.e., the reachability probability in n steps. Now, the main claim (Theorem 3.1, [23, Proposition 3]) is a direct consequence. Note that our proof is simpler and more precise than the original: Haddad and Monmege [23] only claim without details that for every strategy in the reduced MDP, there exists a strategy in the original MDP with the same P_{inf} and vice versa.

lemma **assumes** $s \in S$ **shows** $P_{inf}^{\leq}\ n\ s = M_{inf}.P_{inf}^{\leq}\ n\ (red_{inf}\ s)$ *(Lemma 3.2)*

theorem **assumes** $s \in S$ **shows** $P_{inf}\ s = M_{inf}.P_{inf}\ (red_{inf}\ s)$ *(Thm. 3.1)*

Max-Reduction. The P_{sup} case can be handled similarly with a max-reduction. Yet the procedure is more involved, as not all non-trivial MECs can be collapsed while preserving P_{sup}—a maximizing strategy might choose to leave a non-trivial MEC. We can, however, first collapse each MEC into a single state to obtain an MDP M_{MEC}. This step keeps the reachability probabilities unchanged. In a second step, we map the bottom MECs to s_-. Finally, we remove self-loops at all states except s_+ and s_-. Our formalization decomposes max-reduction [23, Def. 5] into multiple steps, which in turn simplifies both definitions and proofs.

Collapsing the MECs into a single state is performed by the function *the_mec*, the transformation preserves P_{sup} (Theorem 3.2). Our proof resembles the proof of [19, Theorem 3.8], however we have to work around the fact that the MDP formalization [34] only supports deterministic policies. Note that every state of M_{MEC} now forms its own MEC. The correctness proof of the second phase of the reduction is similar to min-reduction. See Fig. 3 for the max-reduced version of the MDP from Fig. 1.

theorem *(Thm. 3.2)*
    assumes $s \in S$
    shows $P_{\text{sup}}\ s = M_{MEC}.P_{\text{sup}}\ (the\_mec\ M\ s)$

Proof. ($\leq$) As collapsing MECs only shortens paths in the MDP, the proof proceeds similarly to the one for min-reduction via finite-horizon probabilities.

($\geq$) Consider an optimal strategy π_{MEC} in M_{MEC}, we need to show that there exists a strategy in M with the same reachability probability. Every MEC m of M contains a state s_m^π, where the action selected by π_{MEC} is enabled. Moreover, within a MEC, we can obtain a deterministic, memoryless strategy π_m that reaches this state with probability 1. Thus, we can construct a strategy in M that behaves like π_m within each MEC until s_m^π is reached and then follows π_{MEC}. The reachability probability of this strategy in M is the same as the one achieved by π_{MEC} in M_{MEC}.

3.3   Reachability in Reduced MDPs

From now on, we assume that we are working with a reduced, finite MDP M, where each state is either a trivial or a bottom MEC. We show that in such an MDP, over time, any strategy reaches a bottom MEC almost surely. This is the key property that will then allow us to prove the convergence of II.

Level Graph. First, we build a level graph of the MDP, starting at the bottom MECs (Definition 3.5). At level $n+1$, we add all those states where every action has a successor on level n or below. We define I to be the greatest non-empty level of the level graph G, so I is the number of steps that allows us to reach a bottom MEC from every state. We formally show that G has the desired properties, i.e. it is acyclic and contains every state at exactly one level. The proofs in Isabelle/HOL require substantial reasoning about graph-theoretic properties, e.g., we need to show that every MDP contains a bottom MEC.

fun G **where** *(Def. 3.5)*
  $G\ 0 = bottoms\ M$
  $G\ (n+1) = \textbf{let}\ G_{\leq n} = \bigcup i \leq n.\ G\ i\ \textbf{in}$
    $\{s \in S \setminus G_{\leq n}.\ \forall a \in K\ s.\ G_{\leq n} \cap a \neq \varnothing\}$

Reachability of BMECs. We now show that, intuitively, every strategy eventually descends through the levels of G. The rate at which a bottom MEC is encountered is bounded in terms of η, the smallest probability of any transition in the MDP. At every step, the probability of descending a level with respect to G is at least η. Hence, we can show that for any valid configuration, the probability to reach the bottom MECs in I steps is no less than η^I (Lemma 3.3).

lemma assumes $cfg \in valid_{cfg}$ **shows** $\eta^I \leq P_{cfg}^{\leq} I$ *(Lemma 3.3)*

The value $P_{cfg}^{\leq} \ n$ denotes the finite-horizon reachability probability of the bottom MECs in n steps under configuration cfg. Note that the lemma was originally stated for safety instead of reachability problems. We transform it using the well-known equivalence $\mathbb{P}_{cfg}^{\leq n}(\Diamond U) = 1 - \mathbb{P}_{cfg}^{\leq n}(\Box \neg U)$. For n multiples of I, we obtain the stronger lower bound $1 - (1 - \eta^I)^n$ (Theorem 3.3, [23, Proposition 1]). As n increases, $(1 - \eta^I)^n$ converges to 0 and thus $P_{cfg}^{\leq} \ nI$ tends towards 1. Since we chose cfg arbitrarily, we almost surely reach a bottom MEC in the limit.

theorem assumes $cfg \in valid_{cfg}$ **shows** $1 - (1 - \eta^I)^n \leq P_{cfg}^{\leq} \ nI$ *(Thm. 3.3)*

3.4 Convergence of Interval Iteration

We assume a special form of reduced MDPs, where the only bottom MECs are the target state s_+ and avoid state s_-, that are both absorbing (Locale 3.1). The reduced MDPs from Sect. 3.2 are instances of this locale.

locale $MDP\_Reach = Finite\_MDP \ M \ +$ *(Locale 3.1)*
    assumes $s_- \in S$ **and** $s_+ \in S$ **and**
      $\forall s \in S \setminus \{s_+, s_-\}. \ s \in trivials \ M$ **and**
      $K \ s_- = \{return_{pmf} \ s_-\}$ **and** $K \ s_+ = \{return_{pmf} \ s_+\}$

Towards a convergence proof of II, we show that the lower and upper bound sequences are equal to the finite-horizon reachability probabilities towards s_+ and s_- respectively (Lemma 3.4, [23, Lemma 4]). For improved clarity, we indicate target sets explicitly in this section.

lemma *(Lemma 3.4)*
    assumes $s \in S$
    shows $lb_{inf} \ n \ s = P_{inf}^{\leq} \ \{s_+\} \ n \ s$ **and** $ub_{inf} \ n \ s = 1 - P_{sup}^{\leq} \ \{s_-\} \ n \ s$

Combining the above result with Theorem 3.3, we can bound the distance between the sequences (Theorem 3.4). Note that convergence is in general only guaranteed if all computations are carried out with arbitrary precision arithmetic. In a floating-point setting, the convergence to a unique fixed point is not guaranteed. Still, this theoretical result motivates the usage of the II algorithm to optimally solve reachability problems on MDPs. In practice, on most instances the algorithm converges much faster than the theoretical bound suggests (see Sect. 5 for experimental results).

Finally, the theorem does not apply if all probabilities in the MDP are equal to 1, i.e. no branching occurs after action selection [23]. In this case, the MDP is deterministic and is better solved with qualitative solution methods.

theorem *(Thm. 3.4)*
  assumes $s \in S$ **and** $\epsilon > 0$ **and** $\eta \neq 1$ **and** $n \geq \lceil \log_{(1-\eta^I)} \epsilon \rceil * I$
  shows $ub_{\mathrm{inf}} \; n \; s - lb_{\mathrm{inf}} \; n \; s \leq \epsilon$

Proof. As a first step, we show for all i that

$$ub_{\mathrm{inf}} \; iI \; s - lb_{\mathrm{inf}} \; iI \; s = 1 - P^{\leq}_{\mathrm{sup}} \{s_-\} \; iI \; s - P^{\leq}_{\mathrm{inf}} \{s_+\} \; iI \; s \qquad \textit{(Lemma 3.4)}$$
$$\leq 1 - (P^{\leq}_{\mathrm{inf}} \{s_-\} \; iI \; s + P^{\leq}_{\mathrm{inf}} \{s_+\} \; iI \; s) \qquad (P^{\leq}_{\mathrm{inf}} \leq P^{\leq}_{\mathrm{sup}})$$
$$= 1 - P^{\leq}_{\mathrm{inf}} \{s_-, s_+\} \; iI \; s \qquad \textit{(Disjoint events)}$$
$$\leq (1 - \eta^I)^i. \qquad \textit{(Thm. 3.3)}$$

Set $i = \lceil \log_{(1-\eta^I)} \epsilon \rceil$ and the theorem follows from monotonicity.

4   Refinement Using Floating-Point Arithmetic

In the next step, we use the IRF to refine II to an efficient LLVM implementation, refining real numbers to IEEE 754 double precision floating-point numbers (floats). While our framework can be used to refine to floats of any precision, we focus on the widely-adopted double precision variant here for smaller rounding errors than single-precision floats.

To avoid complex reasoning about error bounds, we propose a safe rounding approach that refines reals to *upper bounding* or *lower bounding* floats. As the name suggests, upper bounding floats are always greater than or equal to the real value they refine, while lower bounding floats are always less than or equal.

We first introduce the sepref tool for refinement to LLVM, after which we present our extension of the IRF and sepref for floats. This new reasoning infrastructure for floating-point implementations serves as the framework to obtain correct-by-construction LLVM code for II.

4.1   The Sepref Tool

We use sepref [41] to automatically refine algorithms to LLVM programs. The sepref tool provides a library of verified, reusable data structures. Since LLVM maintains a *heap*, we need to be able to deal with memory allocation and disposal. We use *assertions* from *separation logic* [50] which are refinement relations extended with a heap. Formally $A :: 'a \Rightarrow 'c \Rightarrow 'h \Rightarrow bool$ where $'a$ and $'c$ is the abstract and concrete data and $'h$ is the heap. The assertion holds if $a::'a$ refines $c::'c$ and c is encoded in heap $h::'h$. sepref uses separation logic to ensure memory correctness, e.g., correct disposal and preventing dangling pointers.

Example 2. The following example demonstrates how to employ sepref for automatic refinements to LLVM code.

```
1   definition ls_app x xs = xs @ [x] and half_nat n = n div 2
2   definition app_half n xs = do { let n' = half_nat n; return ls_app n' xs }
3   lemma (rshift1, half_nat) :: A_{size} → A_{size}
4   lemma (arl_app, ls_app) :: [λn xs. length xs < 2^{63}-1] A_{size} → A_{arl}^d → A_{arl}
5   lemma (arl_app_half, app_half) :: [λn xs. length xs < 2^{63}-1] A_{size} → A_{arl}^d → A_{arl}
```

Line 1 defines *ls_app* (insert an element at the end of a list) and *half_nat* (divide a natural number in half). Both are used in the definition of *app_half* in Line 2. The standard library of sepref has LLVM assertions for lists as array lists (A_{arl}), and natural numbers as 64-bit signed words (A_{size}).

Now, *half_nat* can be refined to the LLVM program *rshift1*, which performs an efficient right bit shift. sepref represents refinements using parametric functor notation as in Line 3. The lemma states that *rshift1* and *half_nat* are related as follows: If the inputs of *half_nat* (type *nat*) and *rshift1* (type *size*) are related via A_{size}, then the outputs are related via A_{size}.

Line 4 provides a refinement of the append operation following the same principle, only now with two inputs. Moreover, the precondition *length xs* $< 2^{63} - 1$ limits the length of the input list *xs*. The refinement relation only holds for sufficiently small lists. Finally, the superscript d indicates that the input is destructively updated. With these two rules registered to sepref, we can automatically refine *app_half*. We provide a signature to instruct sepref to use the desired data structures:

$$[\lambda n \ xs. \ length \ xs < 2^{63} - 1] \, A_{size} \to A_{arl}^d \to A_{arl}.$$

sepref can now automatically synthesize the LLVM program *arl_app_half* based on *rshift1* and *arl_app*. Moreover, it proves the refinement relation in Line 5.

4.2   Floating-Point Extension of the Isabelle Refinement Framework

We extend the IRF with data refinements to floats. While we can achieve this with error-bound estimation, the existing frameworks are cumbersome to use. Instead, we propose to refine real numbers to lower bounding (*lb*) or upper bounding (*ub*) floats by employing safe rounding techniques [27]. This allows us to perform a correctness proof on an algorithm that uses real numbers, and in a subsequent refinement replace them with *lb/ub* floats, implemented through AVX512 rounding modes. We eliminate the need to compute error-bounds a-priori while still retaining the information relevant to proving the desired correctness properties.

Since the *ub* case is mostly symmetric to the *lb* case, we focus on *lb* floats. We aim to construct a refinement relation that never produces NaN for the operations we support. The main motivation here is that NaN is incomparable, rendering it incompatible with a framework that reasons about bounds. Furthermore, the operations we support must preserve upper or lower bounds: the float

-2_f (the subscript f denotes floats) is a lower bound of 1, yet $-2_f \times -2_f = 4_f$ is not a lower bound of $1 \times 1 = 1$. To ensure this property, we restrict ourselves to non-negative floats.

We define $R_{lb} = \{(fl,r). \; valof \; fl \leq r \wedge \neg is\_nan \; fl \wedge valof \; fl \geq 0\}$, the refinement relation that relates reals to lb floats, e.g. $(2_f, 3) \in R_{lb}$, but $(-2_f, -1) \notin R_{lb}$, as -2_f is negative. Floats are *pure*, e.g. they do not need to allocate memory on the heap. This means that the assertion A_{lb} is R_{lb} when provided an empty heap.

We now present a non-exhaustive set of operations supported by our framework, where we focus on the operations required for our use-case.

Fused Multiply-Add. The ternary operator $fma \; a \; b \; c = a \times b + c$ (fused multiply-add) yields a smaller floating-point rounding error compared to performing the two operations separately. We name the AVX512 operation for fma that rounds towards negative infinity fma_avx_lb and prove the following refinement:

lemma $(fma\_avx\_lb, fma) :: A_{lb} \rightarrow A_{lb}^{>0} \rightarrow A_{lb} \rightarrow A_{lb}$ *(Lemma 4.1)*

This lemma states that if the inputs are lb, not NaN and non-negative, the output is also lb, not NaN and non-negative. Note that the result of $0_f * \infty_f$ is NaN. We resolve this with the stricter assertion $A_{lb}^{>0}$ that only allows positive finite floats for the second argument. In the case of II, the second argument is the transition probability of the MDP model, which is always positive.

Comparison. Comparing two lb floats does not provide any information about comparing their real counterparts. We can preserve information partially by implementing them as mixed operations, e.g., comparing lb to ub.

definition $leq\_sound \; a \; b = \textbf{spec} \; (\lambda r. \; r \longrightarrow a \leq b)$ *(Lemma 4.2)*
lemma $(leq\_double, leq\_sound) :: A_{lb} \rightarrow A_{lb} \rightarrow A_{bool}$

We use **spec** to introduce non-determinism as follows: the operation must return *False* if the comparison returns *False*, but can return anything otherwise. For illustration of the latter case, consider the following 2 cases when comparing $2 \leq 5$. Case 1: 4_f is a ub of 2, and 3_f is an lb of 5, we have $4_f \not\leq 3_f$; Case 2: 3_f is a ub of 2, and 4_f is an lb of 5, we have $3_f \leq 4_f$. So both outcomes are possible after the refinement.

We use the comparison operation to implement the stopping criterion of II, in which case this partial information is sufficient. For similar reasons, we also implement subtraction as a mixed operator (omitted here).

Min and Max. It is possible to refine the minimum (min) and maximum (max) operations directly using comparisons. We define the following refinement:

definition $min\_double \; fl1 \; fl2 = \textbf{if} \; fl1 \leq fl2 \; \textbf{then} \; fl1 \; \textbf{else} \; fl2$ *(Lemma 4.3)*
lemma $(min\_double, min) :: A_{lb} \rightarrow A_{lb} \rightarrow A_{lb}$

This refinement holds despite the fact that a comparison does not reveal anything about the bounding float number. Consider the following case: 4_f is a lower bound of 5 and 3_f is a lower bound of 6. Also, $min\_double\ 4_f\ 3_f = 3_f$ is a lower bound of $min\ 5\ 6 = 5$, even though the floating-point implementation returns the first argument, while the definition on reals returns the second argument. The refinement works analogously for all combinations of lb/ub and min/max.

Constants. We provide trivial refinements for the real number constants 0 and 1, which can be exactly represented as floating-point numbers.

4.3   Refinement of Interval Iteration

Using our floating-point extension to the IRF, we derive an implementation of II using floats and directed rounding from the abstract specification in Sect. 3. The IRF allows us to reuse the correctness proofs of the abstract specification, and reason about the correctness of the implementation in isolation. Through this separation of concerns we avoid directly proving the floating-point implementation correct.

The plot in Fig. 4 shows a fictive run of II on both reals and their refinement to bounding floats. In the long run, II on reals converges to the dashed red line P_{inf}. The yellow lines denote the valuations of an MDP state using reals, lb starting from lb_0 and ub from ub_0.

Implementing lb with lower-bounding floats (A_{lb}) yields the purple line lb_f (similarly for ub using upper-bounding floats). Note that the deviations are exaggerated on purpose in this example.

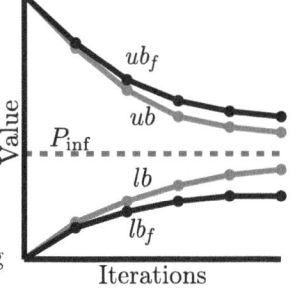

Fig. 4. The valuation of an MDP state over successive iterations: reals (yellow) vs. floats with safe rounding (purple). (Color figure online)

Formally, the following specification states soundness of II, i.e. the outputs are lower and upper bounds of the actual reachability probabilities:

definition $ii\_inf\_spec\ M =$ *(Def. 4.1)*
    spec $(\lambda(x, y).\ \forall s \in states\ M.\ x\ s \leq P_{\mathrm{inf}}\ M\ s \wedge P_{\mathrm{inf}}\ M\ s \leq y\ s)$

Convergence follows from Theorem 3.4, but we do not include this in our correctness proof. With our framework, this statement would be void: The float implementations of x and y are further apart than x and y, which are less than ε apart. As a first step towards the refinement to LLVM, we define II in the nres-monad (the *sup* case is analogous):

```
1   definition  ii_gs_inf M L =                                    (Def. 4.2)
2       x ← lb₀ M;  y ← ub₀ M;  i ← 0;  flag ← True;
3       while (i++ < L ∧ flag) (
4           (x,y) ← F^{gs}_{inf} M x y
5           flag ← spec(λx. True))
6       return (x,y)
```

Line 1: $\textbf{definition}\ ii\_gs\_inf\ M\ L\ =$ *(Def. 4.2)*

Line 2: $x \leftarrow lb_0\ M;\ y \leftarrow ub_0\ M;\ i \leftarrow 0;\ flag \leftarrow True;$

Line 3: $\textbf{while}\ (i{+}{+} < L \wedge flag)\ ($

Line 4: $(x,y) \leftarrow F^{gs}_{inf}\ M\ x\ y$

Line 5: $flag \leftarrow \textbf{spec}(\lambda x.\ True))$

Line 6: $\textbf{return}\ (x,y)$

We define *ii_gs_inf* in Line 1. It takes as inputs an MDP M, and a maximal iteration count L to guarantee termination. Line 2 initializes variables, most importantly the lower bounds *lb* and upper bounds *ub*. The *flag* nondeterministically decides whether to abort the loop. This is sound, because *ii_inf_spec* is satisfied after any number of iterations. In each iteration, we first update the valuations according to a Gauss-Seidel variant of F_{inf} (Line 4): We update *lb* and *ub* in-place, thereby we use the updated values already in the current iteration and converge faster.

The algorithm is now in a format ready for refinement proofs to LLVM. Using the setup from Sect. 3 and Lemma 3.1, it is straightforward to prove that the algorithm refines the specification:

theorem $ii\_gs\_inf\ M\ L \leq ii\_inf\_spec\ M$ *(Thm. 4.1)*

4.4   Refinement of the mcsta Data Structure

The motivation behind refining II to LLVM code is to embed it into the model checker mcsta from the MODEST TOOLSET [28]. mcsta is an explicit-state probabilistic model checker that also supports quantitative model checking of MDPs. To avoid costly conversions of the MDP representation at runtime, we refine the *mdpc* data structure to the MDP data structure of mcsta. This is a two-step process: First, we do a data refinement from *mdpc* to the sparse-matrix representation used by mcsta based on HOL lists. Then, we use sepref to refine this data structure to LLVM. The sparse-matrix representation that we use is a 6-tuple:

$$(St{::}nat\ list,\ Tr{::}nat\ list,\ Br{::}nat\ list,\ Pr{::}real\ list,\ u_a{::}nat,\ u_t{::}nat).$$

For each state, St contains an index to Tr, pointing to the first transition (action) of the state. Similarly, for each transition, Tr contains its first index Br and Pr, pointing to the first branch of the transition and its probability. Finally, Br contains the target of the branch, pointing to St. Additionally, u_a and u_t are the avoid and target states respectively. Example 3 illustrates this data structure.

Example 3. A possible representation of the MDP from Fig. 1 is $St = [0,2,3,4,5]$, $Tr = [0,1,3,4,6,7]$, $Br = [2,0,1,0,1,3,3]$, $Pr = [1.0,0.9,0.1,1,0.5,0.5,1.0]$. The index of the avoid and target state are stored in u_a and u_t. State 0 has two actions: α and β (transitions 0 and 1). Transition 1 (action β) has two branches, 1 and 2, that lead to state 0 and 1 with probability 0.9 and 0.1 respectively.

Refinement Relation. We relate the abstract MDP type *mdpc* to the concrete data structure of mcsta with the refinement relation R_M (definition omitted). For example, R_M contains a tuple of the MDP of Fig. 1 and Example 3 as well as with each other instance of the data structure in Sect. 4.4 along with the MDP it represents. These lists present in the Isabelle/HOL model of the data structure can be directly refined to arrays of 64-bit integers (signed for compatibility with mcsta). Through composition we obtain the assertion A_M from abstract MDP to LLVM.

Refinement of Operations. We use sepref to refine the functions lb_0, ub_0, F_{inf}^{gs} and *flag* that are used by II. Refining lb_0 and ub_0 to the concrete data structure is straightforward: we initialize an array and set entries to constants 0_f or 1_f. The floating-point refinement of F_{inf}^{gs} builds on *fma* and *min* (*max* for F_{sup}^{gs}) from Sect. 4.2. Finally, we implement *flag* as follows: We compare the upper and lower bound, and set the flag if the difference is less than ε, specified by the user. Using the above refinements for all operations in *ii_gs_inf*, we use sepref to obtain an LLVM algorithm *ii_gs_inf_llvm* within Isabelle/HOL.

4.5 Correctness Statement

For the final step in our proof, we combine all of our proofs into one theorem. We use a Hoare triple format, as it allows us to present a concise correctness statement of a program that is not cluttered by intermediary tools such as the parametric functor notation. We show that our LLVM program *ii_gs_inf_llvm* satisfies the specification *ii_inf_spec* (Definition 4.1, unfolded in Theorem 4.2). The resulting triple transitively combines Theorem 4.1 with the refinements from Sect. 4.4:

```
1   theorem llvm_htriple                                          (Thm. 4.2)
2      (A_size n n_i ⋆ A_size L L_i ⋆ A_lb ε ε_f ⋆ A_M M M_i
3         ⋆ ↑(MDP_Reach M ∧ n+1 < max_size ∧ n = card (states M)))
4      (ii_gs_inf_llvm L_i n_i ε_f M_i)
5      (λ(lb_f,ub_f). ∃lb ub. A_lb^out lb lb_f ⋆ A_ub^out ub ub_f
6         ⋆ ↑(∀s ∈ states M. lb s ≤ P_inf M s ∧ P_inf M s ≤ ub s)).
```

Lines 2 and 3 specify the preconditions, where Line 2 concerns the input data: n and L are natural numbers implemented as 64-bit words n_i and L_i; ε is a real number implemented as the float ε_f and M is the MDP implemented as M_i. The separation conjunction $\star$ specifies that these implementations do not overlap on the heap. Line 3 is a boolean predicate lifted to separation logic using $\uparrow$. It states that M satisfies locale *MDP_Reach* (Locale 3.1) and limits the number of states to the largest 64-bit number.

If these preconditions hold, a run of the algorithm (Line 4) yields the arrays lb_f and ub_f that satisfy the postconditions in Lines 5 and 6. These state that lb_f is a lower-bound implementation of lb, which is in turn a lower bound of P_{inf} (similarly for ub). Note that the Hoare triple does not guarantee convergence of lb_f and ub_f to a single fixed point. However, our experiments show that our implementation converges up to the limits of floating-point precision in practice.

5   Experimental Evaluation

The LLVM code generator of the IRF exports the LLVM program $ii\_gs\_inf\_llvm$ for use in the LLVM compiler pipeline. Additionally, it generates a C header that facilitates embedding the program into other software, such as mcsta.

Integration with mcsta. We integrate our verified implementation with mcsta, replacing the existing unverified interval iteration algorithm. This requires a small amount of unverified glue code to convert the MDP's probabilities into a floating-point representation: mcsta stores the probabilities in the MDP as 128-bit rationals (encoded as a pair of 64-bit integers representing the numerator and denominator). Our MDP data structure M_i expects two floats per branch, representing lower and upper bounds of the rational probability. We convert the probabilities to 64-bit doubles by first converting the numerator and denominator to doubles and then performing two separate division operations, once rounding up and once down. We assume that the input MDP as produced by the mcsta pipeline is well-formed. If there were a bug in the parser that produces MDPs that are not well-formed according to the precondition of the Hoare triple, we would lose the formal guarantees. As long as parts of the toolchain remain unverified, we rely on the correctness of the mcsta implementation for the preprocessing.

Evaluation Questions. We have formally verified in Isabelle/HOL that II with precise arithmetic computes lower and upper bounds (lb and ub), and eventually converges to the reachability probability. However, two important questions remain: First, verified implementations tend to be orders of magnitude slower than unverified ones [54]. Since we verified an implementation with efficient numerics down to LLVM, we expect much faster runtimes. So how does our verified implementation compare to state-of-the-art tools in terms of performance? Second, the floating-point outputs (lb_f and ub_f) provably provide conservative bounds. Can we experimentally confirm that the algorithm converges in practice?

Setup. For the first question, we compare the runtime of our verified II implementation to its two unverified counterparts in mcsta: a C# implementation with standard rounding (*Modest* implementation) and a C implementation with safe rounding [27] (*Safe* implementation). The latter is similar to our verified LLVM implementation, also using AVX512 instructions for safe rounding.

We set the maximal iteration count to a high value (10^7) to ensure the computation is never terminated prematurely before convergence. While we anticipate all benchmarks to converge within fewer iterations, this upper limit provides a safeguard. We set the convergence threshold to $\varepsilon = 10^{-6}$. Once the lower and upper bound differ by less than ε, the *Verified, Safe,* and *Modest* implementations terminate. We use all DTMC, MDP and PTA models of the Quantitative Verification Benchmark Set (QVBS) [16] that contain 10^6 to 10^8 states and need at least two iterations to converge to ε. For our benchmarks, we consider both minimal and maximal reachability probabilities. In total, this yields a benchmark set of 49 benchmark instances. We execute all benchmarks on an Intel i9-11900K (3.5–5.3 GHz) system with 128 GB of RAM running Ubuntu Linux 22.04.

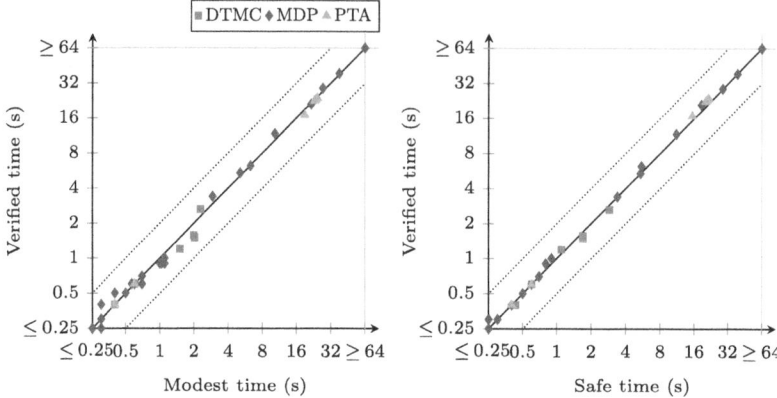

Fig. 5. Comparison of elapsed runtime for completing Interval Iteration

Results. Figure 5 compares the runtimes of the three implementations. Each point $\langle x, y \rangle$ in a plot indicates that, on one benchmark instance, the implementation on the horizontal axis took x seconds while the *Verified* implementation took y seconds. We note that none of our benchmark instances reached the timeout of 10 min. We provide the runtimes for the II algorithm only. Other steps are performed equally by mcsta such as state space exploration or min/max-reduction.

We see that the *Verified* implementation matches the unverified ones in terms of performance. Thus, as far as this benchmark set can show, the answer to the first question is that we have achieved comparable performance to a state-of-the-art unverified tool with a fully verified implementation. We also observed that the *Verified* implementation does not reach the maximal iteration count on any instance, i.e. it always converged up to ε, indicating that the second question can also be answered affirmatively.

Additionally, we did not find any significant discrepancies in the raw data output. The number of iterations to convergence is equal for all instances except for the Haddad-Monmege model [23] between *Verified* and *Modest*. The exception is not surprising, as this model is designed to converge very slowly, increasing the influence of floating-point errors. We also compared the computed results. Due to using different rounding modes, the results of *Verified* and *Modest* show differences well within ε. Despite the fact that *Verified* and *Safe* both implement safe rounding, their outputs still differ by minimal amounts on the order of 10^{-20}. This may be caused by floating-point operations being non-associative, so a different order of operations may yield different outputs.

In terms of memory consumption, *Verified* and *Safe* use almost the same amount of RAM, but use on average 20% more RAM than *Modest*. Since the memory consumption is very similar for *Verified* and *Safe*, we suspect that these differences come from garbage collection effects caused by *Verified* and *Safe* being native code called from within a tool otherwise running in the managed C# runtime, as opposed to the purely-C# *Modest* implementation.

6   Discussion

We provide a framework to verify floating-point LLVM programs which exploits the parametricity principle [60] of the IRF by consistently applying directed rounding to floating-point values. Our approach eliminates complex reasoning about error bounds to prove useful correctness properties of the implementation. We are confident that our framework may be applied to other iterative algorithms that compute lower and upper bounds. The latter is strictly necessary, as—with our approach—we do not a-priori know the size of the error. However, if both bounds converge to a single value, the floating-point error is guaranteed to be smaller than the distance between the bounds. Thus we can determine an a-posteriori error-bound.

We applied our extension to the IRF to the formal verification of the interval iteration algorithm in Isabelle/HOL—all the way to a correct implementation. Our developments formally prove that the algorithm computes lower and upper bounds for the reachability probabilities (soundness) and converges to a single fixed point (completeness) when using real numbers. Furthermore, we show that soundness is preserved if we implement the algorithm using floating-point arithmetic with safe rounding. Our proofs culminate in a single statement, presented as a Hoare triple, leaving no gaps in the link between the specification and the implementation in LLVM.

Finally, we extract verified LLVM code from our formalization and embed it in the mcsta model checker of the Modest toolset. We experimentally verify that our implementation converges in practice and is competitive with manually implemented, optimized, and unverified counterparts. This is an important step towards a fully verified probabilistic model checking pipeline.

We also present our approach as an alternative to the bottom-up approach of building a verified model checker from scratch. With our top-down approach, the full functionality of the model checker is available to the user, possibly in cross-usage with verified components. Verified components are integrated with the model checker incrementally as drop-in replacements for unverified components, designed with competitive performance in mind.

In a next step, we plan to complete the verified II backend for mcsta, the missing part being an efficient verified implementation of the transformations to reduced MDPs. For this purpose, we aim to build on recent advancements that provide a verified and efficiently executable MEC decomposition algorithm in Isabelle/HOL [33].

Verification vs. Certification for II. An alternative to verifying II is to verify a *certifier* that, given the result from an unverified implementation of II plus a compact *certificate*, can efficiently check that the result is indeed correct. The advantage of certification is that the unverified implementation of II can be improved in an agile way independent of the certifier. Also, since the certifier is (presumably) simpler than II, it should be easier to verify, including the verification of a high-performance implementation. One possible certification scheme for II is using the Park induction check of the optimistic value iteration algorithm [30], i.e. performing one iteration of II and checking if the lower/upper bound does not decrease/increase for any state. This could confirm that *some* fixed point lies between the bounds computed by II. This certification scheme would require as input (1) the final lower and upper bound for all states, (2) the full MDP, and (3) *a certificate that the MDP is reduced*. Without the latter, one can not be sure that the certified fixed point corresponds to the reachability probability, i.e. that it is the least fixed point. One challenge with this scheme is that, unlike our verified implementation of II, it cannot guarantee that *all* fixed points lie between the bounds. Also, since the entire reduced MDP is input to the certificate checker, the certificate checking performance might be fundamentally limited.

Data Availability Statement. Proofs and benchmarks presented in this paper are archived and available at DOI 10.4121/bf0fef24-4f0f-4de6-a58d-07b9ba601804 [39].

Disclosure of Interests. The authors have no competing interests to declare that are relevant to the content of this article.

References

1. Abbasi, R., Schiffl, J., Darulova, E., Ulbrich, M., Ahrendt, W.: Deductive verification of floating-point java programs in KeY. In: Tools and Algorithms for the Construction and Analysis of Systems - 27th International Conference, TACAS 2021, Held as Part of the European Joint Conferences on Theory and Practice of Software, ETAPS 2021, Luxembourg City, Luxembourg, March 27 - April 1, 2021, Proceedings, Part II. pp. 242–261 (2021). https://doi.org/10.1007/978-3-030-72013-1_13
2. Ahrendt, W., Beckert, B., Bubel, R., Hähnle, R., Schmitt, P.H., Ulbrich, M. (eds.): Deductive Software Verification - the KeY Book - from Theory to Practice (2016)
3. Appel, A.W., Kellison, A.: Vcfloat2: Floating-point error analysis in Coq. In: CPP. pp. 14–29. ACM (2024)
4. Baier, C.: Probabilistic Model Checking. In: Dependable Software Systems Engineering, pp. 1–23. IOS Press (2016). https://doi.org/10.3233/978-1-61499-627-9-1
5. Baier, C., de Alfaro, L., Forejt, V., Kwiatkowska, M.: Model Checking probabilistic systems. In: Handbook of Model Checking, pp. 963–999. Springer (2018). https://doi.org/10.1007/978-3-319-10575-8_28
6. Baier, C., Haverkort, B.R., Hermanns, H., Katoen, J.P.: Performance evaluation and Model Checking join forces. Commun. ACM **9**, 76–85 (2010). https://doi.org/10.1145/1810891.1810912
7. Baier, C., Katoen, J.P.: Principles of Model Checking. MIT Press (2008)
8. Baier, C., Klein, J., Leuschner, L., Parker, D., Wunderlich, S.: Ensuring the reliability of your model checker: Interval iteration for Markov Decision Processes. In: 29th International Conference on Computer Aided Verification (CAV). pp. 160–180 (2017). https://doi.org/10.1007/978-3-319-63387-9_8

9. Ballarin, C.: Locales and locale expressions in Isabelle/Isar. In: TYPES. pp. 34–50 (2003)
10. Barrett, G.: Formal methods applied to a floating-point number system. IEEE Trans. Software Eng. **5**, 611–621 (1989). https://doi.org/10.1109/32.24710
11. Bellman, R.: A Markovian decision process. Journal of Mathematics and Mechanics **5**, 679–684 (1957)
12. Bohnenkamp, H.C., D'Argenio, P.R., Hermanns, H., Katoen, J.P.: MoDeST: A compositional modeling formalism for hard and softly timed systems. IEEE Trans. Software Eng. **10**, 812–830 (2006). https://doi.org/10.1109/TSE.2006.104
13. Boldo, S., Melquiond, G.: Flocq: A unified library for proving floating-point algorithms in Coq. In: 2011 IEEE 20th Symposium on Computer Arithmetic. pp. 243–252 (2011). https://doi.org/10.1109/ARITH.2011.40
14. Boldo, S., Munoz, C.: A high-level formalization of floating-point number in PVS. Tech. rep. (2006)
15. Budde, C.E., Dehnert, C., Hahn, E.M., Hartmanns, A., Junges, S., Turrini, A.: JANI: Quantitative model and tool interaction. In: 23rd International Conference on Tools and Algorithms for the Construction and Analysis of Systems (TACAS). pp. 151–168 (2017). https://doi.org/10.1007/978-3-662-54580-5_9
16. Budde, C.E., Hartmanns, A., Klauck, M., Kretínský, J., Parker, D., Quatmann, T., Turrini, A., Zhang, Z.: On correctness, precision, and performance in quantitative verification (QComp 2020 competition report). In: 9th International Symposium on Leveraging Applications of Formal Methods (ISoLA). pp. 216–241 (2020). https://doi.org/10.1007/978-3-030-83723-5_15
17. Cousot, P., Cousot, R., Feret, J., Mauborgne, L., Miné, A., Monniaux, D., Rival, X.: The ASTREÉ analyzer. In: Programming Languages and Systems, 14th European Symposium on Programming, ESOP 2005, Held as Part of the Joint European Conferences on Theory and Practice of Software, ETAPS 2005, Edinburgh, UK, April 4-8, 2005, Proceedings. pp. 21–30 (2005). https://doi.org/10.1007/978-3-540-31987-0_3
18. D'Argenio, P.R., Jeannet, B., Jensen, H.E., Larsen, K.G.: Reachability analysis of probabilistic systems by successive refinements. In: Joint International Workshop on Process Algebra and Probabilistic Methods, Performance Modeling and Verification (PAPM-PROBMIV). pp. 39–56 (2001). https://doi.org/10.1007/3-540-44804-7_3
19. de Alfaro, L.: Formal verification of probabilistic systems. Ph.D. thesis, Stanford University, USA (1997)
20. De Dinechin, F., Lauter, C., Melquiond, G.: Certifying the floating-point implementation of an elementary function using Gappa. IEEE Trans. Comput. **2**, 242–253 (2010). https://doi.org/10.1109/TC.2010.128
21. Goubault, E., Putot, S.: Static analysis of finite precision computations. In: Verification, Model Checking, and Abstract Interpretation - 12th International Conference, VMCAI 2011, Austin, TX, USA, January 23-25, 2011. Proceedings. pp. 232–247 (2011). https://doi.org/10.1007/978-3-642-18275-4_17
22. Haddad, S., Monmege, B.: Reachability in MDPs: Refining convergence of Value Iteration. In: 8th International Workshop on Reachability Problems (RP). pp. 125–137 (2014). https://doi.org/10.1007/978-3-319-11439-2_10
23. Haddad, S., Monmege, B.: Interval Iteration algorithm for MDPs and IMDPs. Theoretical Computer Science pp. 111–131 (2018). https://doi.org/10.1016/J.TCS.2016.12.003

24. Hahn, E.M., Hartmanns, A., Hermanns, H., Katoen, J.P.: A compositional modelling and analysis framework for stochastic hybrid systems. Formal Methods Syst. Des. **2**, 191–232 (2013). https://doi.org/10.1007/S10703-012-0167-Z
25. Harrison, J.: Formal verification at Intel. In: 18th Annual IEEE Symposium of Logic in Computer Science, 2003. pp. 45–54 (2003). https://doi.org/10.1109/LICS.2003.1210044
26. Harrison, J.: A machine-checked theory of floating point arithmetic. In: Theorem Proving in Higher Order Logics. pp. 113–130 (1999). https://doi.org/10.1007/3-540-48256-3_9
27. Hartmanns, A.: Correct probabilistic Model Checking with floating-point arithmetic. In: TACAS (2). pp. 41–59 (2022). https://doi.org/10.1007/978-3-030-99527-0_3
28. Hartmanns, A., Hermanns, H.: The Modest Toolset: An integrated environment for quantitative modelling and verification. In: 20th International Conference on Tools and Algorithms for the Construction and Analysis of Systems (TACAS). pp. 593–598 (2014). https://doi.org/10.1007/978-3-642-54862-8_51
29. Hartmanns, A., Junges, S., Quatmann, T., Weininger, M.: A practitioner's guide to MDP Model Checking algorithms. In: 29th International Conference on Tools and Algorithms for the Construction and Analysis of Systems (TACAS). pp. 469–488 (2023). https://doi.org/10.1007/978-3-031-30823-9_24
30. Hartmanns, A., Kaminski, B.L.: Optimistic Value Iteration. In: 32nd International Conference on Computer Aided Verification (CAV). pp. 488–511 (2020). https://doi.org/10.1007/978-3-030-53291-8_26
31. Hartmanns, A., Klauck, M., Parker, D., Quatmann, T., Ruijters, E.: The Quantitative Verification Benchmark Set. In: 25th International Conference on Tools and Algorithms for the Construction and Analysis of Systems (TACAS). pp. 344–350 (2019). https://doi.org/10.1007/978-3-030-17462-0_20
32. Hartmanns, A., Kohlen, B., Lammich, P.: Fast verified SCCs for probabilistic Model Checking. In: ATVA (1). pp. 181–202 (2023). https://doi.org/10.1007/978-3-031-45329-8_9
33. Hartmanns, A., Kohlen, B., Lammich, P.: Efficient formally verified Maximal End Component decomposition for MDPs. In: FM (1). pp. 206–225 (2024). https://doi.org/10.1007/978-981-99-8664-4
34. Hölzl, J.: Markov Chains and Markov Decision Processes in Isabelle/HOL. J. Autom. Reason. **3**, 345–387 (2017). https://doi.org/10.1007/S10817-016-9401-5
35. Hölzl, J., Nipkow, T.: Markov models. Arch, Formal Proofs (2012)
36. Kamali, M., Katoen, J.P.: Probabilistic Model Checking of AODV. In: 17th International Conference on the Quantitative Evaluation of Systems (QEST). pp. 54–73 (2020). https://doi.org/10.1007/978-3-030-59854-9_6
37. Kellison, A.E., Appel, A.W., Tekriwal, M., Bindel, D.: LAProof: A library of formal proofs of accuracy and correctness for linear algebra programs. In: ARITH. pp. 36–43. IEEE (2023)
38. Kirchner, F., Kosmatov, N., Prevosto, V., Signoles, J., Yakobowski, B.: Frama-C: A software analysis perspective. Formal Aspects Comput. **3**, 573–609 (2015). https://doi.org/10.1007/S00165-014-0326-7
39. Kohlen, B., Schäffeler, M., Abdulaziz, M., Hartmanns, A., Lammich, P.: Artifact for the paper "A Formally Verified IEEE 754 Floating-Point Implementation of Interval Iteration for MDPs". 4TU.ResearchData (2025). https://doi.org/10.4121/bf0fef24-4f0f-4de6-a58d-07b9ba601804
40. Kosmatov, N., Prevosto, V., Signoles, J.: Guide to software verification with Frama-C. Springer (2024)

41. Lammich, P.: Generating verified LLVM from Isabelle/HOL. In: 10th International Conference on Interactive Theorem Proving (ITP). pp. 22:1–22:19 (2019). https://doi.org/10.4230/LIPICS.ITP.2019.22

42. Lammich, P., Tuerk, T.: Applying data refinement for monadic programs to Hopcroft's algorithm. In: 3rd International Conference on Interactive Theorem Proving (ITP). pp. 166–182 (2012). https://doi.org/10.1007/978-3-642-32347-8_12

43. Lattner, C., Adve, V.: LLVM: A compilation framework for lifelong program analysis and transformation. In: CGO. pp. 75–88 (2004)

44. Magron, V., Constantinides, G.A., Donaldson, A.F.: Certified roundoff error bounds using Semidefinite Programming. ACM Trans. Math. Softw. (4), 34:1–34:31 (2017). https://doi.org/10.1145/3015465

45. Miner, P.S.: Defining the IEEE-854 floating-point standard in PVS. Tech. rep. (1995)

46. Moscato, M., Titolo, L., Dutle, A., Muñoz, C.A.: Automatic estimation of verified floating-point round-off errors via Static Analysis. In: Computer Safety, Reliability, and Security. pp. 213–229 (2017). https://doi.org/10.1007/978-3-319-66266-4_14

47. Nipkow, T., Paulson, L.C., Wenzel, M.: Isabelle/HOL – a proof assistant for Higher-Order Logic. Springer (2002)

48. Puterman, M.L.: Markov Decision Processes: Discrete stochastic Dynamic Programming. Wiley (1994). https://doi.org/10.1002/9780470316887

49. Quatmann, T., Katoen, J.P.: Sound Value Iteration. In: 30th International Conference on Computer Aided Verification (CAV). pp. 643–661 (2018). https://doi.org/10.1007/978-3-319-96145-3_37

50. Reynolds, J.C.: Separation logic: A logic for shared mutable data structures. In: 17th IEEE Symposium on Logic in Computer Science (LICS 2002), 22-25 July 2002, Copenhagen, Denmark, Proceedings. pp. 55–74 (2002). https://doi.org/10.1109/LICS.2002.1029817 <error l="305" c="Invalid <error l="303" c="Invalid command: paragraph not started." /> command: paragraph not started." /> <error l="305" c="Invalid command: paragraph not started." />

51. Roberts, R., Lewis, B., Hartmanns, A., Basu, P., Roy, S., Chakraborty, K., Zhang, Z.: Probabilistic verification for reliability of a two-by-two network-on-chip system. In: 26th International Conference on Formal Methods for Industrial Critical Systems (FMICS). pp. 232–248 (2021). https://doi.org/10.1007/978-3-030-85248-1_16

52. Ruijters, E., Guck, D., Drolenga, P., Peters, M., Stoelinga, M.: Maintenance analysis and optimization via statistical Model Checking – evaluating a train pneumatic compressor. In: 13th International Conference on the Quantitative Evaluation of Systems (QEST). pp. 331–347 (2016). https://doi.org/10.1007/978-3-319-43425-4_22

53. Ruijters, E., Guck, D., van Noort, M., Stoelinga, M.: Reliability-centered maintenance of the electrically insulated railway joint via fault tree analysis: A practical experience report. In: 46th Annual IEEE/IFIP International Conference on Dependable Systems and Networks (DSN). pp. 662–669 (2016). https://doi.org/10.1109/DSN.2016.67

54. Schäffeler, M., Abdulaziz, M.: Formally verified solution methods for infinite-horizon Markov Decision Processes. In: The 37th AAAI Conference on Artificial Intelligence (AAAI) (2023). https://doi.org/10.1609/aaai.v37i12.26759

55. Schäffeler, M., Abdulaziz, M.: Formally verified Approximate Policy Iteration. In: The 38th AAAI Conference on Artificial Intelligence (AAAI) (2025)

56. Solovyev, A., Baranowski, M.S., Briggs, I., Jacobsen, C., Rakamaric, Z., Gopalakrishnan, G.: Rigorous estimation of floating-point round-off errors with symbolic Taylor expansions. ACM Trans. Program. Lang. Syst. (1), 2:1–2:39 (2019). https://doi.org/10.1145/3230733
57. Sutton, R.S., Barto, A.G.: Reinforcement Learning – an introduction. MIT Press (1998)
58. Titolo, L., Moscato, M., Feliu, M.A., Masci, P., Muñoz, C.A.: Rigorous Floating-Point Round-Off Error Analysis in PRECiSA 4.0. In: Formal Methods. pp. 20–38 (2025). https://doi.org/10.1007/978-3-031-71177-0_2
59. Vajjha, K., Shinnar, A., Trager, B.M., Pestun, V., Fulton, N.: CertRL: Formalizing convergence proofs for value and policy iteration in Coq. In: The 10th International Conference on Certified Programs and Proofs (CPP). pp. 18–31 (2021). https://doi.org/10.1145/3437992.3439927
60. Wadler, P.: Theorems for free! In: Proceedings of the Fourth International Conference on Functional Programming Languages and Computer Architecture, FPCA 1989, London, UK, September 11-13, 1989. pp. 347–359 (1989). https://doi.org/10.1145/99370.99404
61. Wimmer, R., Kortus, A., Herbstritt, M., Becker, B.: Probabilistic Model Checking and reliability of results. In: 11th IEEE Workshop on Design & Diagnostics of Electronic Circuits & Systems (DDECS). pp. 207–212 (2008). https://doi.org/10.1109/DDECS.2008.4538787
62. Yu, L.: A formal model of IEEE floating point arithmetic. Arch, Formal Proofs (2013)

INTERLEAVE: A Faster Symbolic Algorithm for Maximal End Component Decomposition

Suguman Bansal[1] and Ramneet Singh[2](✉)

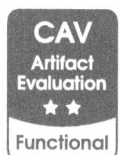

[1] Georgia Institute of Technology, Atlanta, GA 30332, USA
suguman@gatech.edu
[2] Indian Institute of Technology Delhi, Delhi 110016, India
ramneet2001@gmail.com

Abstract. This paper presents a novel symbolic algorithm for the *Maximal End Component (MEC)* decomposition of a *Markov Decision Process (MDP)*. The key idea behind our algorithm INTERLEAVE is to interleave the computation of Strongly Connected Components (SCCs) with eager elimination of redundant state-action pairs, rather than performing these computations sequentially as done by existing state-of-the-art algorithms. Even though our approach has the same complexity as prior works, an empirical evaluation of INTERLEAVE on the standardized Quantitative Verification Benchmark Set demonstrates that it solves **19 more benchmarks** (out of 368) than the closest previous algorithm. On the 149 benchmarks that prior approaches can solve, we demonstrate a **3.81× average speedup** in runtime.

Keywords: Probabilistic model checking · Symbolic algorithms · Maximal end components

1 Introduction

Maximal End Component (MEC) Decomposition is a fundamental problem in *probabilistic model checking*. An *end-component* of an MDP is a set of state-action tuples such that the directed graph induced by the non-zero probability transitions of all state-action tuples in the end-component is (a) *strongly connected* i.e. there is a path from every state to every other state and (b) *self-contained* i.e. no edge in the induced graph enters a state not present in the end-component. An end-component is *maximal* if it is not contained in any other end component. The problem of *MEC decomposition* that obtains all the MECs of an MDP is crucial to computing almost-sure reachability sets [4], interval iteration for maximum reachability probabilities [2,11], verification of ω-regular properties [1], learning approaches for probabilistic verification [14] and so on. Furthermore, its implementations are critical to the performance of state-of-the-art probabilistic model checkers such as STORM [13] and PRISM [15].

R. Piskac and Z. Rakamarić (Eds.): CAV 2025, LNCS 15932, pp. 147–168, 2025.
https://doi.org/10.1007/978-3-031-98679-6_7

In this work, we focus on the design of practically efficient symbolic algorithms for MEC decomposition. A previous evaluation [9] has found that a symbolic version of the naive explicit-state algorithm, hereby referred to as BASIC [7], has the best runtime performance among symbolic MEC decomposition algorithms. BASIC demonstrates better performance than more recent algorithms with better theoretical complexity [5,6].

The BASIC algorithm closely follows the definition of Maximal End Components (MECs). Since an MEC is a strongly connected subgraph with the additional constraint of self-containment, BASIC begins by computing all the Strongly Connected Components (SCCs) in the underlying graph of the MDP. Next, for each SCC, it checks whether there are any outgoing state-action pairs that violate self-containment. If no such pairs exist, the SCC is output as an MEC. Otherwise, all edges corresponding to violating state-action pairs are removed. Since the remaining sub-MDP may no longer be strongly connected, the process is repeated until either no violating state-action pairs remain or the component becomes empty. BASIC employs a symbolic SCC decomposition algorithm, referred to as SKELETON [10]: Given a directed graph (V, E), SKELETON picks a start vertex v, computes its SCC (call it C_v) and the set of vertices forward-reachable from v (call it F_v). It outputs C_v and recursively computes the SCCs of the subgraphs induced by the following two partitions - $(F_v \setminus C_v)$ and $(V \setminus F_v)$.

The need for our algorithm stems from noticing that when SKELETON is called within BASIC, the recursive call on $(V \setminus F_v)$ does some unnecessary work: Consider an edge (s, α, t) such that $s \in V \setminus F_v$ and $t \in F_v$, i.e., an edge that crosses from $V \setminus F_v$ to $F_v \setminus C_v$. We observe that the state-action pair (s, α) cannot be part of any MEC of the MDP. If (s, α) were to be in an MEC, the MEC would be required to intersect the two sets $V \setminus F_v$ and F_v. Since an MEC is also strongly connected, this would require a strongly connected component to intersect the two sets. But this is not possible since there is no path from a state in F_v to a state in $V \setminus F_v$ (as F_v is the forward-reachable set of v). Hence, all such edges and state-action pairs can be immediately removed from the MDP. However, BASIC would process these edges/state-action pairs several times since it will first compute the SCCs in $V \setminus F_v$. This edge would be processed at least twice – at least once during SCC computation within $V \setminus F_v$ and once when it is being removed from the SCC that state s belongs to because it will be violating self-containment.

To eliminate this redundant work, we propose a novel symbolic MEC decomposition algorithm, called INTERLEAVE, that interleaves the SCC decomposition with eager removal of such state-action pairs that will not be present in any MEC. Given an MDP, INTERLEAVE picks a starting vertex v, computes the SCC of v (C_v) and the forward-reachable set of v (F_v), then recursively computes the MECs of the following three partitions - C_v, $(F_v \setminus C_v)$ and $(V \setminus F_v)$. Before INTERLEAVE recurses on these, it identifies outgoing state-action pairs from each and removes their edges. If an SCC C_v has no outgoing state-action pairs, it is output as an MEC. By performing early removal of edges out of $(V \setminus F_v)$, INTERLEAVE avoids the wasted work that BASIC does.

Table 1. Theoretical complexity of symbolic algorithms for MEC Decomposition where $n = |S| \cdot |A|$ and $m = |S|^2 \cdot |A|$ in an MDP with states S and actions A.

Algorithm	Symbolic Operations	Symbolic Space
BASIC	$\mathcal{O}(n^2)$	$\mathcal{O}(\log n)$
LOCKSTEP	$\mathcal{O}(n\sqrt{m})$	$\mathcal{O}(\sqrt{m})$
INTERLEAVE (ours)	$\mathcal{O}(n^2)$	$\mathcal{O}(\log n)$

A theoretical analysis of INTERLEAVE reveals that it requires the same amount of symbolic operations and symbolic space as BASIC, namely, $\mathcal{O}(n^2)$ symbolic operations and $\mathcal{O}(\log n)$ symbolic space for an MDP with n vertices and m edges. However, an empirical analysis showcases that INTERLEAVE is faster than previous symbolic MEC decomposition algorithms. Following the format of [8], we provide an implementation of the INTERLEAVE algorithm in the STORM probabilistic model checker. We perform an experimental evaluation of INTERLEAVE, comparing it to the BASIC and LOCKSTEP algorithms on 368 benchmarks from the Quantitative Verification Benchmark Set (QVBS) [12]. In contrast to the theoretical complexities in Table 1, we show that INTERLEAVE is the fastest symbolic MEC Decomposition algorithm on QVBS, solving 19 more benchmarks than the closest other algorithm (BASIC) given the same timeout (240 s) and achieving an average speedup of 3.81x on the 149 that both algorithms were able to solve.

Outline: We begin with preliminaries in Sect. 2. Section 3 explains the MEC decomposition and SCC decomposition algorithms BASIC and SKELETON, respectively. Section 4 describes our algorithm, its correctness argument, and complexity analysis. Finally, Sect. 5 presents the empirical evaluation.

2 Preliminaries

2.1 Markov Decision Process (MDP)

A *Markov Decision Process* (MDP) is given by a tuple $\mathcal{M} = (S, A, d_{\text{init}}, \delta)$ where S is a finite, non-empty set of states, A is a finite set of actions, $d_{\text{init}} : S \to [0, 1]$ is an initial probability distribution over states i.e. $\Sigma_{s \in S} d_{\text{init}}(s) = 1$, and $\delta : S \times A \times S \to [0, 1]$ specifies the transition distributions for each state and each action i.e. $\Sigma_{s' \in S} \delta(s, \alpha, s') \in \{0, 1\}$ for all $s \in S, \alpha \in A$. We say that an action $\alpha \in A$ is *enabled* in state $s \in S$ if $\Sigma_{s' \in S} \delta(s, \alpha, s') = 1$ (or, equivalently, if $\exists s' \in S . \delta(s, \alpha, s') > 0$). For an action set $A' \subseteq A$ and state $s \in S$, the set of actions in A' which are enabled in s is denoted by $A'[s]$. Wlog, we assume that every state has at least one enabled action, i.e., $A[s] \neq \emptyset$ for all $s \in S$ and every action is enabled in some state, i.e., $\bigcup_{s \in S} A[s] = A$.

The underlying graph of an MDP $\mathcal{M} = (S, A, d_{\text{init}}, \delta)$ is given by the labelled directed graph $G(\mathcal{M}) = (V, E)$ where $V = S$, $E = \{(s, \alpha, s') \in S \times A \times S \mid$

$\delta(s, \alpha, s') > 0\}$. A *strongly connected component (SCC)* in an MDP is given by a strongly connected component in its underlying graph. I.e. a set of vertices $T \subseteq S$ is strongly connected in MDP $\mathcal{M}$ if (a) for all $s, t \in T$ there is a (labelled) path from s to t in T and (b) there does not exist a $T' \subseteq S$ such that $T \subset T'$ and for all $s', t' \in T'$ there is a path from s' to t'.

2.2 Maximal End-Component (MEC)

A *sub-MDP* of an MDP $\mathcal{M}$ is a tuple (T, π) where $T \subseteq S$ is a non-empty set of states and $\pi : T \to 2^A$ such that (a) $\emptyset \neq \pi(s) \subseteq A[s]$ for all $s \in T$ and (b) for all $s \in T, \alpha \in \pi(s)$ and $s' \in S$, if $\delta(s, \alpha, s') > 0$, then $s' \in T$. We refer to the last condition as *self-containment*. The underlying graph of a sub-MDP refers to the labelled directed graph obtained from all edge transitions in the sub-MDP. Formally, the underlying graph $G(T, \pi) = (V, E)$ of a sub-MDP (T, π) is defined as $V = T$ and $E = \{(s, \alpha, s') \in T \times A \times T \mid \alpha \in \pi(s) \wedge \delta(s, \alpha, s') > 0\}$.

The *state-action pair set* of a sub-MDP (T, π) is given by $\mathsf{sa}(T, \pi) = \{(s, \alpha) \in T \times A \mid \alpha \in \pi(s)\}$. A sub-MDP (T_1, π_1) of $\mathcal{M}$ is said to be *included in* another sub-MDP (T_2, π_2) of $\mathcal{M}$, denoted $(T_1, \pi_1) \subseteq (T_2, \pi_2)$ if $T_1 \subseteq T_2$, and, for each $s \in T_1$, $\pi_1(s) \subseteq \pi_2(s)$.

An *end-component* of an MDP $\mathcal{M}$ is a sub-MDP (T, π) such that for all $s, t \in T$, there is a sequence $s_0, \alpha_0, s_1, \alpha_1 \ldots, s_n \in T$ such that $s_0 = s$, $s_n = t$, $\alpha_i \in \pi(s_i)$ and $\delta(s_i, \alpha_i, s_{i+1}) > 0$ for all $i \in \{0, n-1\}$. In other words, an end-component is a sub-MDP such that there is a labeled path between every two states in the sub-MDP.

An end-component (T, π) of an MDP $\mathcal{M}$ is *maximal* if it is maximal with respect to sub-MDP inclusion in $\mathcal{M}$, i.e., there is no end component (T', π') of $\mathcal{M}$ such that $(T, \pi) \subseteq (T', \pi')$ and $(T, \pi) \neq (T', \pi')$. In other words, a maximal end-component is a maximal set of state-action pairs of the MDP that are self-contained and strongly connected. It is known that every state (and thus, every state-action pair) belongs to at most one MEC [1]. We denote the MEC of a state $s \in S$, if it exists, by $\mathsf{MEC}_{\mathcal{M}}(s)$. Similarly, we denote the set of MECs of a set of states $S' \subseteq S$ by $\mathsf{MECs}_{\mathcal{M}}(S') = \{\mathsf{MEC}_{\mathcal{M}}(s) \mid s \in S'$ and s is contained in an $\mathsf{MEC}\}$. We denote the set of MECs of all states in $\mathcal{M}$ by $\mathsf{MECs}(\mathcal{M})$.

Definition 1 (MEC Decomposition). *Given an MDP $\mathcal{M}$, the problem of MEC decomposition is to compute the set of all MECs $\mathsf{MECs}(\mathcal{M})$ of $\mathcal{M}$.*

It is known that every MDP has a unique MEC decomposition. MEC decomposition is known to be solvable in polynomial time in the number of states and actions in the MDP [7].

2.3 Symbolic Representation

The symbolic representation of an MDP $\mathcal{M}$ is given by a symbolic representation of its underlying labeled graph. The underlying graph $G = (V, E)$ is represented using two *Binary Decision Diagrams* (BDDs) [3], one for the vertices V and another for the (labeled) edge relation $E \subseteq V \times A \times V$.

Each symbolic operation corresponds to a primitive operation in a BDD library such as CUDD [16]. In this paper, we allow basic set-based symbolic operations. Namely, a unit symbolic operation consists of a single union, intersection, complementation, cross-product, exists, or forall operation on sets. We also consider two special operations Pre and Post to compute the predecessor and successor sets in a graph as unit operations since they correspond to a single $\exists$ BDD operation. Formally, given a labeled graph $G = (V, E)$ the predecessor of a set of vertices $U \subseteq V$ is given by $\mathsf{Pre}(U, G) = \{v \in V \mid \exists u, \alpha . (v, \alpha, u) \in E$ and $u \in U\}$. Similarly, the successor of a set of vertices $U \subseteq V$ is given by $\mathsf{Post}(U, G) = \{v \in V \mid \exists u, \alpha . (u, \alpha, v) \in E$ and $u \in U\}$. Finally, we consider the $\mathsf{Pick}(S)$ operation which returns an arbitrary vertex $v \in S$ and the $|S|$ operation which returns the cardinality of S.

Symbolic space is defined as the maximum number of BDDs present at any one instance during the execution of an algorithm. Since BDDs represent sets, we compute symbolic space in terms of the maximum number of sets present at any instance during the execution of an algorithm.

3 BASIC Symbolic MEC Decomposition

We begin by describing the state-of-the-art symbolic algorithm for MEC decomposition BASIC [6]. We begin by defining few algorithmic concepts essential to symbolic algorithms for MEC decomposition in Sect. 3.1, followed by a description of BASIC in Sect. 3.2.

3.1 Essential Concepts for Symbolic MEC Decomposition

Essential Non-primitive Operations. We introduce two essential non-primitive operations that will be used extensively in BASIC and in our improved algorithm INTERLEAVE, namely ROut and Attr.

Definition 2 (ROut of a state set in a sub-MDP). *Let (T, π) be a sub-MDP and $U \subseteq T$. The* random out *of U in (T, π), denoted by $\mathsf{ROut}_{(T,\pi)}(U)$, is defined as the set of state-action pairs in (T, π) which can go outside U. Formally,*

$$\mathsf{ROut}_{(T,\pi)}(U) = \{(s, \alpha) \in U \times A \mid \alpha \in \pi(s) \wedge \exists s' \in (T \setminus U) . (\delta(s, \alpha, s') > 0)\}$$

Definition 3 (Attractor of a state-action pair set in a sub-MDP). *Let (T, π) be a sub-MDP and $X \subseteq \mathsf{sa}(T, \pi)$ be a state-action pair set. The* attractor *of X in (T, π), denoted by $\mathsf{Attr}_{(T,\pi)}(X)$, is given by the tuple $(S', X') = \left(\bigcup_{i \in \mathbb{N}} S_i, \bigcup_{i \in \mathbb{N}} X_i \right)$ where*

- *For $i = 0$,*
  - $X_0 = X$
  - $S_0 = \{s \in T \mid \forall \alpha \in \pi(s) . ((s, \alpha) \in X_0)\}$

- *For $i > 0$,*
  - $X_i = X_{i-1} \cup \{(s, \alpha) \in \mathsf{sa}(T, \pi) \mid \exists s' \in S_{i-1} . (\delta(s, \alpha, s') > 0)\}$.
  - $S_i = S_{i-1} \cup \{s \in T \mid \forall \alpha \in \pi(s) . ((s, \alpha) \in X_i)\}$.

Both ROut and Attr can be implemented using $\exists$ and other basic set operations in a straightforward manner from their definitions. Complete details of their implementations can be found in Algorithms 3, 4 in Appendix 1 of the extended version.[1]

SCC Symbolic Decomposition Algorithm SKELETON. We present a high-level view of a symbolic SCC computation algorithm called SKELETON.

We recall some basic definitions. The *forward-reachable set* of a state v in a directed graph $G = (V, E)$ is the set of states that are reachable from v. Similarly, the *backward-reachable set* of a state v is the set of states from which there is a path to v. For a vertex v, the forward-reachable and backward-reachable sets can be computed as the fixed points of $\mathsf{Pre}(\{v\}, G)$ and $\mathsf{Post}(\{v\}, G)$, respectively.

SKELETON is a recursive algorithm. Given as input a directed graph (V, E) and a start vertex v, SKELETON computes the SCC of v (denoted by C_v) by first computing the forward-reachable set of v (denoted by F_v) and then computing the backward-reachable set of vertices that are also forward-reachable. It outputs this SCC C_v and partitions the rest of the graph into two induced subgraphs, with vertex sets $F_v \backslash C_v$ and $V \backslash F_v$. The SCCs of these subgraphs can be computed independently, so SKELETON calls itself on both of these subgraphs recursively, if their vertex sets are non-empty.

3.2 BASIC **Algorithm Description**

BASIC is essentially the symbolic version of the classical algorithm for MEC decomposition when the MDP is given explicitly [7]. The algorithm closely follows the definition of an MEC. Observe that an MEC can be seen as a strongly-connected subgraph in the underlying graph which is also self-contained. Then, the algorithm is described as follows: Let (T, π) be a sub-MDP. All the MECs of this sub-MDP can be computed using the following symbolic algorithm: First compute all SCC using SKELETON algorithm. Once all SCCs have been obtained, evaluate each SCC for self-containment as follows: If the SCC is self-contained, return the SCC as an MEC. Otherwise remove state-action pairs that violate self-containment from the SCC and recurse on the remaining component. This algorithm requires $\mathcal{O}(n^2)$ symbolic operations and $\mathcal{O}(\log n)$ symbolic space [5,6].

We claim that BASIC does some redundant work. To see why, observe that BASIC calls SKELETON to get an SCC decomposition, then removes vertices and edges that violate self-containment from those SCCs, then performs SCC decompositions on the remaining components, and so on. Now, during the SCC computation, when SKELETON recurses on $(V \setminus F_v)$, there could be edges crossing from $V \setminus F_v$ to F_v. Let (s, α) be one such state-action pair. We claim that (s, α)

---

[1] https://arxiv.org/abs/2505.20748.

cannot be present in any MEC. By contradiction, suppose (s, α) were present in an MEC. Then, first note that the MEC must be disjointed from F_v. This is because if every MEC is a connected-component and there cannot be any connected component spanning F_v and $V \setminus F_v$ as there is no path from F_v to $V \setminus F_v$ (Recall F_v is the forward-reachable set of v – it is a fixed point). Hence, the MEC must be contained entirely in $V \setminus F_v$. But this is not possible, since we have assumed that a target state of (s, α) goes to F_v. Hence, (s, α) must not be present in any MEC. Therefore, such state-action pairs can be removed as soon as the sets F_v and $V \setminus F_v$ are made available as part of the SCC decomposition. Instead, BASIC will remove these state-action pairs only after all SCCs have been created. As a result, these redundant state-action pairs will keep getting processed in every SCC computation, causing unproductive work.

Our algorithm INTERLEAVE will eliminate this redundant work. Instead of creating all SCCs first, then removing state-action pairs that cross SCCs, we will remove state-action pairs that cross between $V \setminus F_v$ and F_v as soon as possible. Infact, in Lemma 3 we will show that we can remove all of $\mathsf{Attr}_{(T,\pi)}(\mathsf{ROut}_{(T,\pi)}(V \setminus F_v))$ as soon as the set $V \setminus F_v$ is made available. Hence, interleaving SCC computation with eager elimination of states and state-action pairs that will not be present in any MEC can reduce much redundant work.

4   INTERLEAVE Algorithm

The INTERLEAVE algorithm enhances MEC decomposition by interleaving the removal of unnecessary state-action pairs with SCC decomposition to avoid redundant work that BASIC executes. This integration ensures removals happen at the earliest possible point, avoiding redundant work. We first present a detailed description of the algorithm's operation, followed by an illustrative example of its execution. We then prove its correctness and analyze its complexity.

4.1   Algorithm Description and Illustration

Overview: Given an MDP $\mathcal{M}$, algorithm INTERLEAVE takes as input (a). a graph $G = (V, E) = G(T, \pi)$ where (T, π) is a sub-MDP of $\mathcal{M}$ and (b) either a singleton set $\{v\}$ where $v \in V$ is a vertex in T or v_{arb}, denoting an arbitrary start vertex. The algorithm requires as a precondition that the sub-MDP (T, π) is *MEC-closed*, meaning that for each vertex in T, its MEC (if it exists) must be fully contained within the sub-MDP. This MEC-closure property ensures the soundness of computing MECs independently on the sub-MDP. We provide a formal treatment of MEC-closed sub-MDPs in Sect. 4.2. If INTERLEAVE is invoked with v_{arb}, we arbitrarily pick a state v from T and use $\{v\}$ as the input singleton set. Given these inputs, the algorithm outputs the graphs of all MECs of states in T. Therefore, when interested in computing all MECs of an MDP $\mathcal{M}$, we invoke INTERLEAVE with $G = G(\mathcal{M})$ and v_{arb}.

Suppose INTERLEAVE is passed with $\{v\}$, INTERLEAVE partitions the graph into three subgraphs whose MECs it can independently compute (recursively).

Algorithm 1. MEC-Decomp-Interleave($V, E, \{v\} = v_{\text{arb}}$)

Input: $(V, E) = G(T, \pi)$ for some sub-MDP (T, π) of some MDP $\mathcal{M} = (S, A, d_{\text{init}}, \delta)$ and (optionally), a start vertex $v \in V$. For the initial call, $\{v\} = v_{\text{arb}}$.

Output: The set of graphs of $\text{MECs}_{\mathcal{M}}(T)$, i.e., $\{G(T', \pi') \mid (T', \pi') \in \text{MECs}_{\mathcal{M}}(T)\}$.

1: **if** $\{v\} = v_{\text{arb}}$ **then** $\{v\} \leftarrow \text{Pick}(V)$
2: $C_v, F_v, \{v'\} \leftarrow \text{SCC-Fwd-NewStart}(\{v\}, V, E)$
3: // Call on the SCC C_v
4: $(U_1, X_1) \leftarrow \text{Attr}(\text{ROut}(C_v, V, E), V, E)$ $\triangleright \text{Attr}_{(T,\pi)}(\text{ROut}_{(T,\pi)}(C_v))$
5: **if** $X_1 = \emptyset$ **then**
6: $\quad\downarrow \quad (C_v, E \cap (C_v \times A \times C_v))$ is an MEC
7: **else**
8: $\quad$ $E_1 \leftarrow E \setminus (X_1 \times V)$ $\triangleright$ *Remove the state-action pairs in X_1 from E.*
9: $\quad$ $V_1 \leftarrow C_v \setminus U_1$ $\triangleright$ *Remove the states in U_1 from C_v.*
10: $\quad$ **if** $V_1 \neq \emptyset$ **then** MEC-Decomp-Interleave($V_1, E_1 \cap (V_1 \times A \times V_1), v_{\text{arb}}$)
11: // Call on $F_v \setminus C_v$
12: $V_2 \leftarrow (F_v \setminus C_v)$
13: **if** $V_2 \neq \emptyset$ **then** MEC-Decomp-Interleave($V_2, E \cap (V_2 \times A \times V_2), \{v'\}$)
14: // Call on $V \setminus F_v$
15: $(U_3, X_3) \leftarrow \text{Attr}(\text{ROut}(V \setminus F_v, V, E), V, E)$ $\triangleright \text{Attr}_{(T,\pi)}(\text{ROut}_{(T,\pi)}(V \setminus F_v))$
16: $E_3 \leftarrow E \setminus (X_3 \times V)$ $\triangleright$ *Remove the state-action pairs in X_3 from E.*
17: $V_3 \leftarrow (V \setminus F_v) \setminus U_3$ $\triangleright$ *Remove the states in U_3 from $V \setminus F_v$.*
18: **if** $V_3 \neq \emptyset$ **then** MEC-Decomp-Interleave($V_3, E_3 \cap (V_3 \times A \times V_3), v_{\text{arb}}$)

The vertex partitions are - the SCC of v (call it C_v), the set $F_v \setminus C_v$ where F_v the forward-reachable set of v, and $V \setminus F_v$. Recall that the inputs to the recursive calls need to be (graphs of) MEC-closed sub-MDPs. The MEC-closed bit is ensured because these three partitions have disjoint sets of SCCs and since an MEC is strongly connected, no two states in different SCCs can be in the same MEC (proven formally in Sect. 4.2). To ensure each subgraph represents a sub-MDP (which, recall, can't have outgoing state-action pairs), we remove the ROut of its vertex set (and Attr(ROut)) before recursing (removing vertices and edges earlier to avoid wasted work). This also provides the base-case for our recursion. If we find an SCC C_v whose ROut is empty, we output it as an MEC. Termination is guaranteed because the subgraphs we recurse on always have at least one edge less than the input and we don't recurse on an empty subgraph.

Details: Algorithm 1 presents a formal description of the INTERLEAVE algorithm. Given a graph $G = (V, E) = G(T, \pi)$ and a (given or arbitrarily chosen) start vertex $v \in V$, we call Algorithm 2 SCC-Fwd-NewStart($\{v\}, V, E$) to compute the SCC of v (C_v), the forward-reachable set of v (F_v) and a vertex v' at maximum distance from v in G. Then, we deal with three vertex partitions - C_v, $(F_v \setminus C_v)$ and $(V \setminus F_v)$. Note that these could be handled in any order as the

---

Algorithm 2. SCC-Fwd-NewStart($\{v\}, V, E$)

Input: A singleton vertex set $\{v\}$ ($v \in V$) and a labelled graph $G = (V, E)$.
Output: The SCC of v in G, the set of vertices reachable from v, and a vertex at maximum distance from v.

1: $F_v, \{v'\} \leftarrow$ Fwd-NewVertex($\{v\}, V, E$)
2: $C_v \leftarrow \{v\}$.
3: **while** ($\mathsf{Pre}(C_v, (V, E)) \cap F_v \not\subseteq C_v$ **do**
4:     $C_v \leftarrow C_v \cup (\mathsf{Pre}(C_v, (V, E)) \cap F_v)$
5: **return** $C_v, F_v, \{v'\}$

---

three recursive calls are all independent of each other (we will use this fact to ensure efficient space complexity in Theorem 4).

Lines 4–10 handle C_v. We compute $\mathsf{Attr}_{(T,\pi)}(\mathsf{ROut}_{(T,\pi)}(C_v))$, which returns a set of states U_1 and a set of state-action pairs X_1. If $X_1 = \emptyset$ (which, from the definition of ROut and Attr, can only happen if $\mathsf{ROut}_{(T,\pi)}(C_v) = \emptyset$), then we output the subgraph induced by C_v as an MEC. Otherwise, we remove all states in U_1 from C_v, remove all edges with state-action pairs in X_1 from E, and recurse on the remaining induced subgraph (if it is non-empty). Lemma 2 will prove that none of the state-action pairs removed in this step can be present in any MEC. Lemma 5 will show that the induced subgraph belong to a MEC-closed sub-MDP of the original MDP $\mathcal{M}$, enabling recursion on the subgraph.

Lines 12–13 handle $(F_v \setminus C_v)$. Lemma 4 will show that the ROut of this set is always empty. Therefore, we can recurse on this subgraph directly (if it is non-empty) without removing any vertices or edges. We pass the vertex v' computed previously as the start vertex for this recursive call. We adopt this optimization from [10]. To see the benefit we get from passing a start vertex v', suppose $v_0 = v, \ldots, v_k = v'$ is a shortest path from v to v'. Note that computing the forward-reachable set of v requires $\mathcal{O}(k)$ symbolic operations (all vertices must be discovered within k Post calls in Fwd-NewVertex since v' is at a maximum distance), so we can charge $\mathcal{O}(1)$ operations to each v_i. Then, in the recursive call on $F_v \setminus C_v$, when we compute $F_{v'}$, we are guaranteed that only those v_is will be in $F_{v'}$ which are also in $C_{v'}$. So we will not charge the same vertices again in the immediate next call, except when they are in the SCC we compute. While this does not change the complexity of the algorithm, this optimization has shown to have empirical benefits.

Finally, lines 15–18 deal with $(V \setminus F_v)$. We compute $\mathsf{Attr}_{(T,\pi)}(\mathsf{ROut}_{(T,\pi)}(V \setminus F_v))$, which returns a set of states U_3 and a set of state-action pairs X_3. We remove the state-action pairs in X_3 from E, remove the states in U_3 from $(V \setminus F_v)$, and recurse on the remaining induced subgraph (if it's non-empty). Similar to the case of C_v, Lemma 3 and Lemma 7 will show that none of the state-action pairs removed can be present in an MEC and that the induced subgraph belongs to a MEC-closed sub-MDP fo the original MDP $\mathcal{M}$.

Algorithm 2 is a formal description of the SCC-Fwd-NewStart($\{v\}, V, E$) function. It calls Fwd-NewVertex($\{v\}, V, E$) to get the forward-reachable set of v

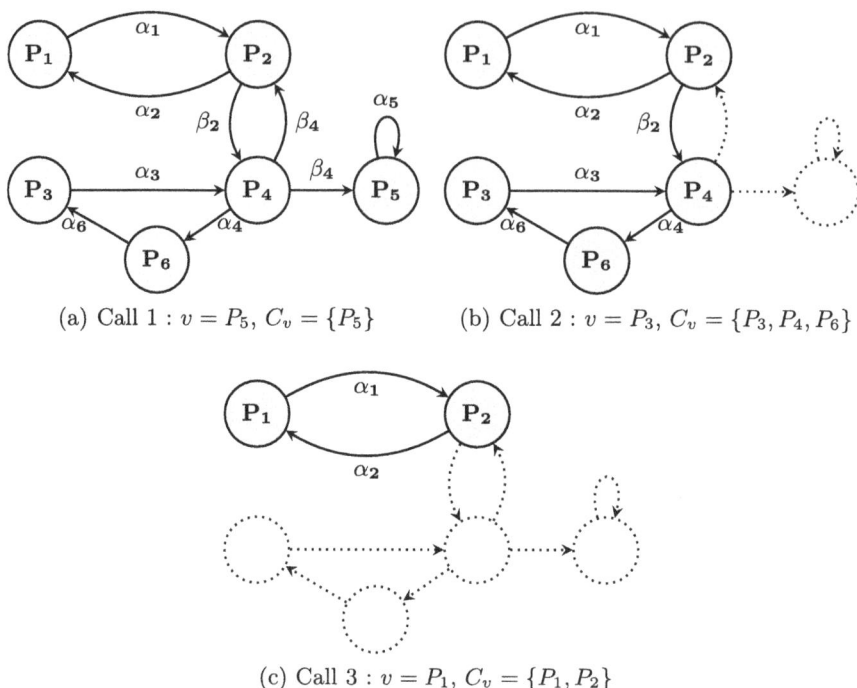

(a) Call 1 : $v = P_5$, $C_v = \{P_5\}$ (b) Call 2 : $v = P_3$, $C_v = \{P_3, P_4, P_6\}$

(c) Call 3 : $v = P_1$, $C_v = \{P_1, P_2\}$

Fig. 1. Example Execution of INTERLEAVE: (C_v (SCC of v) *in blue*), ($V \setminus F_v$ *in green*)

(F_v) and a vertex v' at maximum distance from v. Then, by repeatedly performing Pre operations and intersecting with F_v, it iteratively computes the set
of backward-reachable vertices from v which are also forward-reachable from it,
or in other words, the SCC of v. The Fwd-NewVertex($\{v\}, V, E$) function computes the fixed point of Post($., (V, E)$) on $\{v\}$. This fixed-point is returned as
the forward-reachable set of v, and any vertex added in the last iteration can be
returned as a vertex v' at maximum distance from v. Refer to Algorithm 5 in
Appendix 1 of the extended version for details.[2]

Example Execution: We compare the executions of INTERLEAVE and BASIC
on the example MDP given in Fig. 1.

Figure 1a shows the first call in INTERLEAVE. Here $v = P_5$ is picked as the
starting vertex. We compute $C_v = \{P_5\}$ (blue), $F_v \setminus C_v = \emptyset$, and $V \setminus F_v =$
$\{P_1, P_2, P_3, P_4, P_6\}$ (green). Since ROut(C_v, V, E) $= \emptyset$, it is output as an MEC
(with edges $\{(P_5, \alpha_5, P_5)\}$).

Figure 1b shows the next call. ROut($V \setminus F_v, V, E$) $= \{(P_4, \beta_4)\}$ (and its Attr is
the same) is removed from the graph before the recursive call is made on $V \setminus F_v$.
The subgraph passed to the recursive call consists of the solid vertices and edges.

---

[2] https://arxiv.org/abs/2505.20748.

$v = P_3$ is picked as the vertex to start from. $C_v = \{P_3, P_4, P_6\}$ is computed (blue), $F_v \setminus C_v = \emptyset$ and $V \setminus F_v = \{P_1, P_2\}$ (green). Since $\mathsf{ROut}(C_v, V, E) = \emptyset$, it is output as an MEC (with edges $\{(P_3, \alpha_3, P_4), (P_4, \alpha_4, P_6), (P_6, \alpha_6, P_3)\}$).

Figure 1c shows the final call. $\mathsf{ROut}(V \setminus F_v, V, E) = \{(P_2, \beta_2)\}$ (and its Attr is the same) is removed from the graph before the recursive call is made on $V \setminus F_v$. The subgraph passed to the recursive call consists of the solid vertices and edges. $v = P_1$ is picked as the vertex to start from. $C_v = \{P_1, P_2\}$ is computed (blue), $F_v \setminus C_v = \emptyset$ and $V \setminus F_v = \emptyset$. Since $\mathsf{ROut}(C_v, V, E) = \emptyset$, it is output as an MEC (with edges $\{(P_1, \alpha_1, P_2), (P_2, \alpha_2, P_1)\}$).

Consider what BASIC does on this example. It first calls SKELETON. Assuming SKELETON starts from the same $v = P_5$, it computes $C_v = \{P_5\}$ (same as INTERLEAVE's first step). Then **when SKELETON removes the SCC $\{P_5\}$ and recurses on $(V \setminus F_v)$, it doesn't know that β_4 will be removed later by BASIC.** So it outputs the entire induced subgraph with $\{P_1, P_2, P_3, P_4, P_6\}$ as an SCC. After processing $\{P_5\}$ and outputting it as an MEC, when BASIC processes this SCC, it identifies (P_4, β_4) in the ROut and removes it. Then it calls SKELETON again, which does the same as steps 2 and 3 of INTERLEAVE and outputs $\{P_3, P_4, P_6\}$ and $\{P_1, P_2\}$ as SCCs, which BASIC outputs as MECs. The work that SKELETON does to compute the subgraph $\{P_1, P_2, P_3, P_4, P_6\}$ as an SCC for BASIC is wasted, and INTERLEAVE avoids it by removing (P_4, β_4) early as part of the SCC computation.

4.2   Correctness Argument

We begin by formally defining an *MEC-closed sub-MDP* (which was used in the precondition for INTERLEAVE).

Definition 4 (MEC-closed sub-MDP). *A sub-MDP (T, π) is called MEC-closed if for every state $s \in T$, $\mathsf{MEC}_{\mathcal{M}}(s)$, if it exists, satisfies $\mathsf{MEC}_{\mathcal{M}}(s) \subseteq (T, \pi)$.*

To prove the correctness of our algorithm (i.e. it outputs all the MECs of any MEC-closed sub-MDP passed to it), we will require the following three types of results. We will prove some and omit others which have similar proofs. Detailed proofs for all of them can be found in Appendix 2 of the extended version.[3]

- Whenever we output a subgraph as an MEC, it is actually an MEC. [Soundness, Theorem 1]
- All vertices and state-action pairs that are removed cannot be part of an MEC [Lemmas 1-3]
- The recursive calls satisfy the preconditions, i.e., the subgraphs passed are graphs of MEC-closed sub-MDPs of $\mathcal{M}$. [Lemmas 5-7]

For all the results to come, let (T, π) be an MEC-closed sub-MDP of MDP $\mathcal{M} = (S, A, d_{\mathsf{init}}, \delta)$ and $(V, E) = G(T, \pi)$. Consider the execution of MEC-Decomp-Interleave$(V, E, \{v\})$ where $\{v\} = v_{\mathsf{arb}}$ or $v \in V$. If $\{v\} = v_{\mathsf{arb}}$, let $s \in V$ be the vertex picked on line 1. Otherwise, let $s = v$.

---

[3] https://arxiv.org/abs/2505.20748.

Soundness. To prove soundness, we want to establish that everytime the algorithm outputs a subgraph, the subgraph is an MEC. For this, we observe that Algorithm 1 produces an output only when when $X_1 = \emptyset$. Therefore, we prove the following:

Theorem 1 (Soundness). *If $X_1 = \emptyset$, then $(C_s, E \cap (C_s \times A \times C_s)) = G(\mathsf{MEC}_{\mathcal{M}}(s))$.*

Proof Sketch.

From the algorithm, we know $(U_1, X_1) = \mathsf{Attr}_{(T,\pi)}(\mathsf{ROut}_{(T,\pi)}(C_s))$. From the definition of Attr, if $X_1 = \emptyset$, then we must have $\mathsf{ROut}_{(T,\pi)}(C_s) = \emptyset$. Now, the subgraph $(C_s, E \cap (C_s \times A \times C_s))$ (call it $G[C_s]$) is strongly-connected, has no outgoing state-action pairs, and has at least one edge (because s must have an outgoing edge for the input to be the graph of a valid sub-MDP). So it is an end-component. Further, since the input sub-MDP is MEC-closed, the MEC of s is contained in G. It is also contained in $G[C_s]$ since an MEC is strongly connected. As $G[C_s]$ is an end-component that contains a maximal end component, we must have $G[C_s] = G(\mathsf{MEC}_{\mathcal{M}}(s))$. ∎

All that is Removed is Redundant. Lemma 1 asserts that if a set of state-action pairs cannot be a part of any MEC, then its attractor cannot be a part of any MEC either. This justifies the optimization to remove $\mathsf{Attr}(\mathsf{ROut})$ instead of just ROut.

Lemma 1. *Let $X \subseteq \mathsf{sa}(T,\pi)$ be a state-action pair set such that for all $(T',\pi') \in \mathsf{MECs}(\mathcal{M})$, $\mathsf{sa}(T',\pi') \cap X = \emptyset$. Suppose $\mathsf{Attr}_{(T,\pi)}(X) = (S', X')$. Then, for all $(T',\pi') \in \mathsf{MECs}(\mathcal{M})$, $T' \cap S' = \emptyset$ and $\mathsf{sa}(T',\pi') \cap X' = \emptyset$.*

Proof Sketch. Let $(T',\pi') \in \mathsf{MECs}(\mathcal{M})$. From the definition of Attr, we have $(S', X') = \mathsf{Attr}_{(T,\pi)}(X) = (\bigcup_{i \in \mathbb{N}} S_i, \bigcup_{i \in \mathbb{N}} X_i)$. We will show by induction on i that for all $i \in \mathbb{N}$, $T' \cap S_i = \emptyset$ and $\mathsf{sa}(T',\pi') \cap X_i = \emptyset$. For the base case $i = 0$, $S_0 = \emptyset$ (implies $T' \cap S_0 = \emptyset$) and $X_0 = X$ (implies $\mathsf{sa}(T',\pi') \cap X_0 = \emptyset$ by assumption) by definition of Attr.

For the induction step, we need to show that if (the states of) S_i and (the state-action pairs of) X_i can't be in the MEC (T',π'), then S_{i+1} and X_{i+1} can't either. We show both of these by contradiction. First, assume there is some state $s' \in S_{i+1} \cap T'$. Since $S_i \cap T' = \emptyset$, we have $s' \in S_{i+1} \setminus S_i$. From the definition of Attr, this implies all state-action pairs of s' are in X_i. But it must have at least one state-action pair in (T',π') (by defn. of MEC), contradicting the I.H. that $\mathsf{sa}(T',\pi') \cap X_i = \emptyset$. A similar argument can show that $X_{i+1} \cap \mathsf{sa}(T',\pi') = \emptyset$. Please refer to Appendix 2 in the extended version for details. ∎

We use Lemma 1 to prove that no state-action pair returned by $(U_1, X_1) = \mathsf{Attr}_{(T,\pi)}(\mathsf{ROut}_{(T,\pi)}(C_s))$ is present in MEC, and therefore can be safety removed:

Lemma 2. *For any $(T',\pi') \in \mathsf{MECs}(\mathcal{M})$, $T' \cap U_1 = \emptyset$ and $\mathsf{sa}(T',\pi') \cap X_1 = \emptyset$.*

Proof. We know, from the algorithm, that $(U_1, X_1) = \mathsf{Attr}_{(T,\pi)}(\mathsf{ROut}_{(T,\pi)}(C_s))$, where C_s is the SCC of s. Because of lemma 1, we only need to show that for any $(T', \pi') \in \mathsf{MECs}(\mathcal{M})$, $\mathsf{sa}(T', \pi') \cap \mathsf{ROut}_{(T,\pi)}(C_s) = \emptyset$. Proof is by contradiction. Assume that there is some MEC (T', π') and $(s', \alpha) \in \mathsf{sa}(T', \pi') \cap \mathsf{ROut}_{(T,\pi)}(C_s)$.

Since $(s', \alpha) \in \mathsf{ROut}_{(T,\pi)}(C_s)$, there is a state $t \in (T \setminus C_s)$ such that $\delta(s', \alpha, t) > 0$. By the definition of an MEC, this implies $t \in T'$ too. So s' and t can reach each other in (T', π'). As $(T', \pi') \subseteq (T, \pi)$ (from the assumption that (T, π) is MEC-closed), they can reach other in (T, π) too, contradicting the fact that $t \notin C_s$. ∎

Similarly, we show that all state-action pairs returned by $(U_3, X_3) = \mathsf{Attr}_{(T,\pi)}(\mathsf{ROut}_{(T,\pi)}(C_s))$ are redundant:

Lemma 3. *For any* $(T', \pi') \in \mathsf{MECs}(\mathcal{M})$, $T' \cap U_3 = \emptyset$ *and* $\mathsf{sa}(T', \pi') \cap X_3 = \emptyset$.

Proof. The proof is similar to Lemma 2's proof and is omitted (see Appendix 2 in the extended version for the full proof).[4] ∎

Last but not the least, we show that we cannot eliminate anything from $F_s \setminus C_s$.

Lemma 4. $\mathsf{ROut}_{(T,\pi)}(F_s \setminus C_s) = \emptyset$.

Proof. Assume, for the sake of contradiction, that there is some $(s_1, \alpha) \in \mathsf{ROut}_{(T,\pi)}(F_s \setminus C_s)$. From the definition of ROut, there is some $s_2 \in (T \setminus (F_s \setminus C_s)) = ((T \setminus F_s) \uplus C_s)$ such that $\delta(s_1, \alpha, s_2) > 0$. First note that $s_2 \in F_s$ since $s_1 \in F_s$ and there is an edge (labelled α) from s_1 to s_2. So we must have $s_2 \in C_s$. But then, there is a path from s_2 to s, and thus from s_1 to s. Combined with $s_1 \in F_s$, this means $s_1 \in C_s$, contradicting the fact that $(s_1, \alpha) \in \mathsf{ROut}_{(T,\pi)}(F_s \setminus C_s)$. ∎

Induced Subgraphs and MEC-closed sub-MDPs of $\mathcal{M}$. The following proves that the subgraph induced by removing the attractor of the random-out of C_s is an MEC-closed sub-MDP:

Lemma 5. *If* $X_1 \neq \emptyset$ *and* $V_1 \neq \emptyset$, *then* $(V_1, E_1 \cap (V_1 \times A \times V_1)) = G(T_1, \pi_1)$ *for some MEC-closed sub-MDP* (T_1, π_1).

Proof Sketch. We define (T_1, π_1) as $T_1 = V_1$ and for all $v \in V_1$, $\pi_1(v) = \{\alpha \in A \mid \exists u \in V_1 \text{ s.t. } (v, \alpha, u) \in E_1\}$. By definition, $G(T_1, \pi_1) = (V_1, E_1 \cap (V_1 \times A \times V_1))$. Recall that $V_1 = C_s \setminus U_1$ and $E_1 = E \setminus (X_1 \times V)$, where $(U_1, X_1) = \mathsf{Attr}_{(T,\pi)}(\mathsf{ROut}(C_s, (T, \pi)))$.

Now we need to prove two claims. First, (V_1, π_1) is a sub-MDP. Every state in V_1 has an action in π_1 because otherwise all its state-action pairs are in X_1, which means it's in U_1 by definition of Attr, contradicting the fact that it's in $V_1 = C_s \setminus U_1$. Similarly, for any $s' \in V_1$ and $\alpha \in \pi_1(s')$, (s', α) cannot go outside V_1 because if it reaches U_1, then $(s', \alpha) \in X_1$ by definition of Attr, and if it

---

[4] https://arxiv.org/abs/2505.20748.

reaches $(T \setminus C_s)$, then $(s', \alpha) \in \mathsf{ROut}_{(T,\pi)}(C_s)$ and thus in X_1. Second, we need to show that (V_1, π_1) is MEC-closed. This follows from the fact that (T, π) is MEC-closed, C_s is an SCC (MECs are strongly-connected) and lemma 2 $(U_1, X_1$ can't be a part of any MEC). See Appendix 2 in the extended version for details.[5]
∎

For $F_s \setminus C_s$, we show that the induced graph is an MEC-closed sub-MDP. Recall, the random-out for this partition is empty, hence we retain the entire partition:

Lemma 6. *If $V_2 \neq \emptyset$, then $(V_2, E \cap (V_2 \times A \times V_2)) = G(T_2, \pi_2)$ for some MEC-closed sub-MDP (T_2, π_2).*

Finally, the subgraph induced by removing the attractor of the random-out of $V \setminus F_s$ is an MEC-closed sub-MDP:

Lemma 7. *If $V_3 \neq \emptyset$, then $(V_3, E_3 \cap (V_3 \times A \times V_3)) = G(T_3, \pi_3)$ for some MEC-closed sub-MDP (T_3, π_3).*

Correctness. Finally, we are ready to prove the correctness of Algorithm 1 `INTERLEAVE`.

Theorem 2 (Correctness). *Let $\mathcal{M} = (S, A, d_{\mathsf{init}}, \delta)$ be an MDP, (T, π) be an MEC-closed sub-MDP of $\mathcal{M}$ and $G(T, \pi) = (V, E)$. `MEC-Decomp-Interleave`$(V, E, \{v\})$ where $\{v\} = v_{\mathsf{arb}}$ or $v \in V$ outputs the graphs of all MECs in $\mathsf{MECs}_{\mathcal{M}}(T)$.*

Proof Sketch. If $\{v\} = v_{\mathsf{arb}}$, let $s \in V$ be the vertex picked on line 1. Otherwise, let $s = v$. Proof is by strong induction on the number of edges in $G(T, \pi) = (V, E)$. **Base Case $(|E| = 1)$:** Since each state in an MDP must have at least one action, we must have $(V, E) = (\{s\}, \{(s, \alpha, s)\})$. This is also what our algorithm outputs and is the MEC of s because (T, π) is MEC-closed.

Induction Step $(|E| = k + 1)$: If $X_1 = \emptyset$, then from Theorem 1, we know that the algorithm outputs the MEC of all states in C_s. If $X_1 \neq \emptyset$ and $V_1 = \emptyset$, then it vacuously outputs all the MECs of V_1. If $X_1, V_1 \neq \emptyset$, then we apply Lemma 5 and the induction hypothesis to get that it outputs all the MECs of V_1. In all cases, since the states in U_1 don't have an MEC (Lemma 2) and $V_1 = C_s \setminus U_1$, the algorithm outputs all the MECs of C_s. Similarly, we apply Lemma 6 (resp. Theorem 7) and the induction hypothesis to get that the algorithm outputs all the MECs of $V_2 = (F_s \setminus C_s)$ (resp. V_3). Then, for V_3, we apply Lemma 3 to say that it outputs all the MECs of $V_3 \cup U_3 = (V \setminus F_s)$. Putting together C_s, $(F_s \setminus C_s)$ and $(V \setminus F_s)$, we get that the algorithm outputs all the MECs of V. ∎

---

[5] https://arxiv.org/abs/2505.20748.

4.3   Complexity Analysis

Since symbolic operations are more expensive than non-symbolic operations, symbolic time is defined as the number of symbolic operations in a symbolic algorithm. Previous literature [5,6] focuses only on the number of Pre/Post operations in a symbolic algorithm. We additionally include $\exists$ operations. Like in all previous algorithms, the number of basic set operations in INTERLEAVE is asymptotically at most the number of Pre/Post/$\exists$ operations. Symbolic space is defined as the maximum number of sets (regardless of the size of the sets) stored by a symbolic algorithm at any point of time.

Theorem 3. *For an MDP* $\mathcal{M} = (S, A, d_{\mathsf{init}}, \delta)$, *and* $(V, E) = G(\mathcal{M})$, *MEC-Decomp-Interleave(V, E, v_{arb}) performs* $\mathcal{O}(|S|^2 \cdot |A|)$ *symbolic operations.*

Proof. There are two kinds of Pre/Post/$\exists$ operations. The first kind are the $\exists$ operations in the ROut and Attr computations on lines 4 and 15. Each such operation discovers at least one new state or state-action pair that is then removed from the graph and never seen again (see Algorithms 3, 4 in Appendix 1 of the extended version for details).[6] So over the entire algorithm the cost of these is $\mathcal{O}(|S| + |S| \cdot |A|)$ symbolic operations. The second kind are those in the SCC-Fwd-NewStart computation. For a graph with k vertices, these can be at most $2k$ (k Post calls for forward and k Pre calls for backward). Now, if you look at the tree of recursive calls, the top-level cost is $\leq 2|S|$ (recall $V = S$). At the second level, the cost is $\leq 2(|V_1|+|V_2|+|V_3|) \leq 2(|C_v|+|F_v \setminus C_v|+|V \setminus F_v|) = 2|S|$. The same is true for every level. There can be at most $(|S|+|S| \cdot |A|)$ levels since the number of states and/or state-action pairs decreases by at least one in every recursive call. So the number of symbolic operations is $\mathcal{O}(|S| \cdot (|S| + |S| \cdot |A|)) = \mathcal{O}(|S|^2 \cdot |A|)$. ∎

Theorem 4. *For an MDP* $\mathcal{M} = (S, A, d_{\mathsf{init}}, \delta)$, *and* $(V, E) = G(\mathcal{M})$, *MEC-Decomp-Interleave(V, E, v_{arb}) uses* $\mathcal{O}(\log |S|)$ *symbolic space.*

Proof. Note that each recursive call, excluding the space used by its children, only stores $\mathcal{O}(1)$ number of sets simultaneously. Thus, symbolic space is just the maximum depth of recursive calls reached throughout the algorithm. We use the fact that MEC-Decomp-Interleave is tail-recursive and the three calls can be made in any order. After the first two recursive calls have returned, the memory stored by the current call can be deleted before making the third recursive call. Now, the three calls should be made in increasing order of the sizes of the vertex sets $|V_1|, |V_2|, |V_3|$. The first 2 sizes must be $< 2p/3$. So on both branches, the vertex set size becomes at least $2/3$ of the previous. Therefore, the maximum depth that can be reached in the first two recursive calls is $\log_{\frac{3}{2}} |S| = \mathcal{O}(\log |S|)$. ∎

The complexity of MEC decomposition algorithms in prior work are given in terms of parameters $n = |S| \cdot |A|$ and $m = |S|^2 \cdot |A|$ (see Table 1). The corollary

---

[6] https://arxiv.org/abs/2505.20748.

below is immediate from Theorem 3 and Theorem 4 and presents the complexity of INTERLEAVE in those parameters for a fair comparison of algorithms:

Corollary 1. *Let* $\mathcal{M} = (S, A, d_{\text{init}}, \delta)$ *be an MDP,* $(V, E) = G(\mathcal{M})$ *and* n, m *be as defined above. Then* MEC-Decomp-Interleave(V, E, v_{arb}) *performs* $\mathcal{O}(n^2)$ *symbolic operations and uses* $\mathcal{O}(\log n)$ *symbolic space.*

Complexity of other state-of-the-art MEC decomposition approaches is given in Table 1. We see that INTERLEAVE has the same complexity of BASIC, warranting an extended empirical evaluation to examine algorithmic performance.

5   Empirical Evaluation

The goal of the empirical analysis is to examine the performance of INTERLEAVE against existing state-of-the-art algorithms for MEC decomposition.

Experimental Setup. We compare our algorithm INTERLEAVE to two state-of-the-art symbolic algorithms for MEC decomposition, namely BASIC [7] and LOCKSTEP [6]. We use benchmarks from the *Quantitative Verification Benchmark Set (QVBS)* [12]. QVBS consists of 379 MDP benchmarks derived from probabilistic models and Markov automata. We use 368/379 of these benchmarks, eliminating 11 benchmarks as they are not supported by STORM.

We record the runtime and number of symbolic operations required by each tool on each benchmark. To evaluate the number of symbolic operations, we count every non-basic set operation such as exists. We choose to count these operations since they directly correspond to the number of Pre/Post operations, which are counted in the theoretical analysis of the number of symbolic operations.

The experiments measuring runtime and number of symbolic operations were performed on a machine equipped with an Intel(R) Xeon(R) CPU E5-2695 v2 processor running at 2.40GHz. The machine had 8 cores and 8 GB RAM. For the experiments measuring peak memory usage, we used a machine equipped with an AMD EPYC 7V13 Processor running at 2.50GHz. The machine had 24 cores and 220GB RAM. The memory limit for CUDD was set as 4 GB for each benchmark and each experiment was run with a timeout of 4 min.

Implementation Details. INTERLEAVE has been written in the STORM model checker. We choose the STORM platform since implementations of BASIC and LOCKSTEP are publicly available in a custom build of STORM [8,9]. Building on the STORM platform, therefore, ensures that all three algorithm share several commonalities, including using the same MDP graph representations, the same implementation for the SKELETON algorithm for symbolic SCC decomposition [10], the same library for symbolic operations (CUDD [16]), and so on. This enables a fair comparison of the tool's performance. The implementation code is open source and is available at https://github.com/Ramneet-Singh/

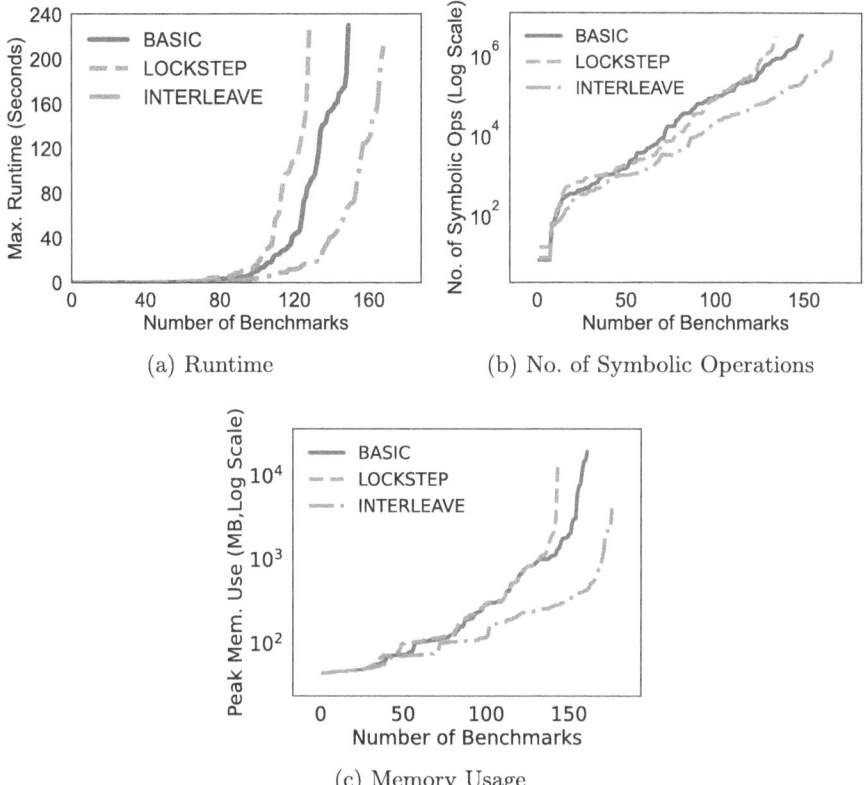

(a) Runtime

(b) No. of Symbolic Operations

(c) Memory Usage

Fig. 2. Cactus plots of performance measures

storm-masters-thesis/tree/stable. The full table of runtimes of each algorithm (BASIC, LOCKSTEP and INTERLEAVE) is available in the extended version (Table 2, Appendix 3).[7]

Observations and Inferences

INTERLEAVE Solves the Most Benchmarks. Figure 2 shows the cactus plots on the runtime of the three tools BASIC, LOCKSTEP and INTERLEAVE on the QVBS. Figure 2a shows that INTERLEAVE solves the most number of benchmarks by solving 168 benchmarks. We note that INTERLEAVE solves all 128 and 149 benchmarks solved by LOCKSTEP and BASIC, respectively. Hence, INTERLEAVE solves strictly more benchmarks than the other two tools.

INTERLEAVE Requires the Fewest Symbolic Operations. In stark contrast to the theoretical analysis, INTERLEAVE requires the fewest number of symbolic operations. Recall from Table 1 that BASIC requires $\mathcal{O}(n^2)$ symbolic operations,

---

[7] https://arxiv.org/abs/2505.20748.

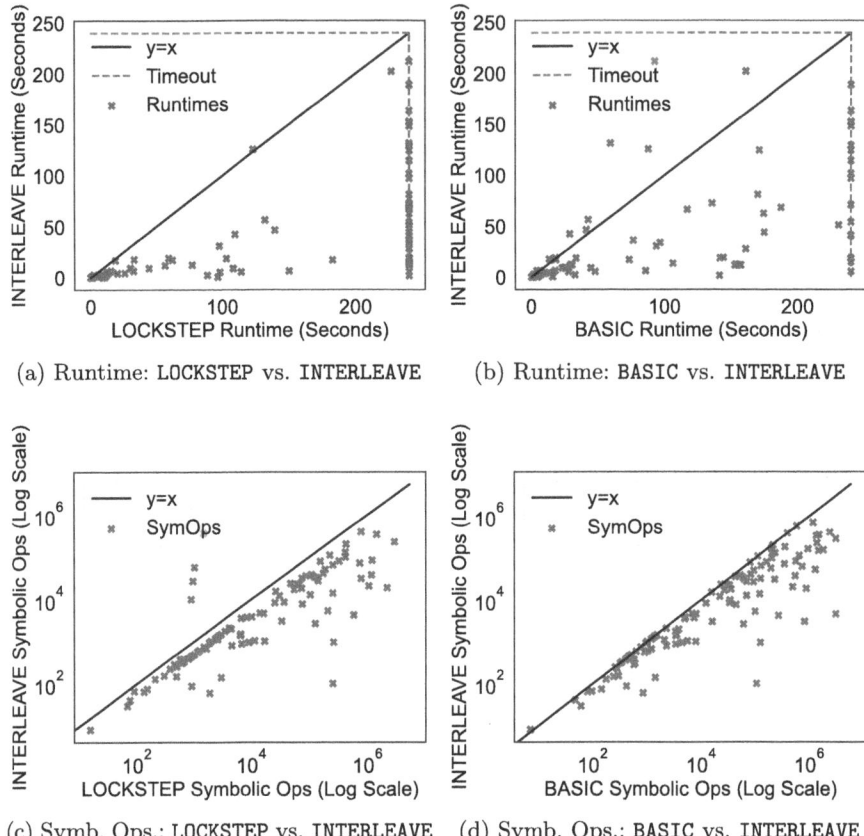

(a) Runtime: LOCKSTEP vs. INTERLEAVE   (b) Runtime: BASIC vs. INTERLEAVE

(c) Symb. Ops.: LOCKSTEP vs. INTERLEAVE   (d) Symb. Ops.: BASIC vs. INTERLEAVE

Fig. 3. Scatter plots of the runtime and number of symbolic operations

which is identical to those required by INTERLEAVE, while LOCKSTEP [6] requires $\mathcal{O}(n\sqrt{m})$ symbolic operations only. However, Fig. 2b shows that INTERLEAVE requires significantly fewer symbolic operations in practice. We attribute this to our interleaving approach that enables the elimination of several redundant operations that the other approaches would perform. This also explains the reduced runtime, as demonstrated in Fig. 2a, highlighting the practical advantages of our approach.

INTERLEAVE Uses the Least Memory. All three algorithms – BASIC, LOCKSTEP and INTERLEAVE have the same worst-case symbolic space complexity ($\mathcal{O}(\log n)$). However, Fig. 2c shows that INTERLEAVE's peak memory usage is significantly lower in practice. This is an important advantage, as memory is often a bottleneck for symbolic algorithms.

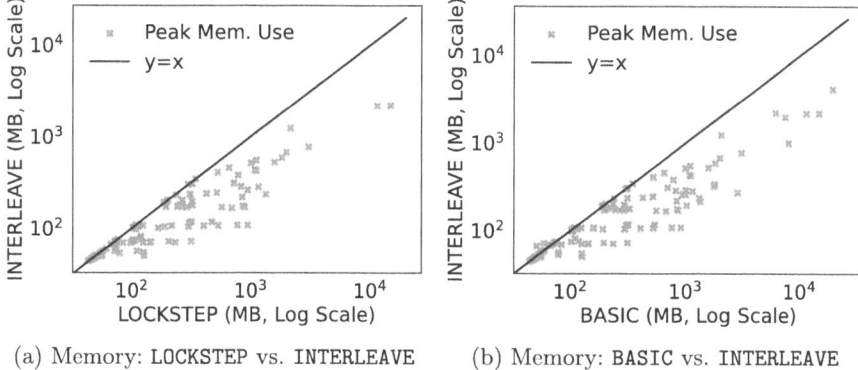

(a) Memory: LOCKSTEP vs. INTERLEAVE   (b) Memory: BASIC vs. INTERLEAVE

Fig. 4. Scatter plots of the peak memory usage

INTERLEAVE Outperforms on Individual Benchmarks. In order to compare tool performances on individual benchmarks, we analyze the scatter plots of INTERLEAVE vs BASIC and LOCKSTEP on runtime and the number of symbolic operations in Fig. 3.

The runtime plots (Fig. 3a and Fig. 3b) are on the 168 benchmarks that at least one algorithm solved within the timeout. The marks on the vertical/horizontal red lines show benchmarks where one of the algorithms timed out and the other did not. As noted earlier, INTERLEAVE strictly solves more benchmarks than the others. Out of 168, INTERLEAVE is slower than LOCKSTEP on 2 benchmarks and slower than BASIC on 24 benchmarks. On average, INTERLEAVE records an average speedup of 6.41 and 3.81 on the 128 and 149 benchmarks solved by LOCKSTEP and BASIC, respectively. The average speedup is computed as the mean of the inverse ratios of runtimes of both algorithms over all benchmarks which both solved.

The scatter plots for symbolic operations (Fig. 3c and Fig. 3d) are on all benchmarks that both algorithms solve within the timeout. The general trends are similar to those of runtime with INTERLEAVE performing fewer or the same number of operations on almost all benchmarks. This seems to correlate with the runtimes, though the difference in runtimes is more stark.

Similarly, Fig. 4a and Fig. 4b are on all benchmarks that both algorithms solve within the timeout. They show that INTERLEAVE has a lower or equal peak memory usage on almost all benchmarks.

INTERLEAVE Scales to Large MDPs. Figure 5 shows scatter plots of the runtime of each algorithm vs. the number of states, transitions, and branches in the MDP. These are on the 110 benchmarks (out of the 168 which at least one algorithm solved within timeout) for which the number of states, transitions, and branches are available in the QVBS. INTERLEAVE scales with each of these dimensions better than the other two algorithms, illustrated by the points to the far right of each graph where only INTERLEAVE was able to finish within the timeout.

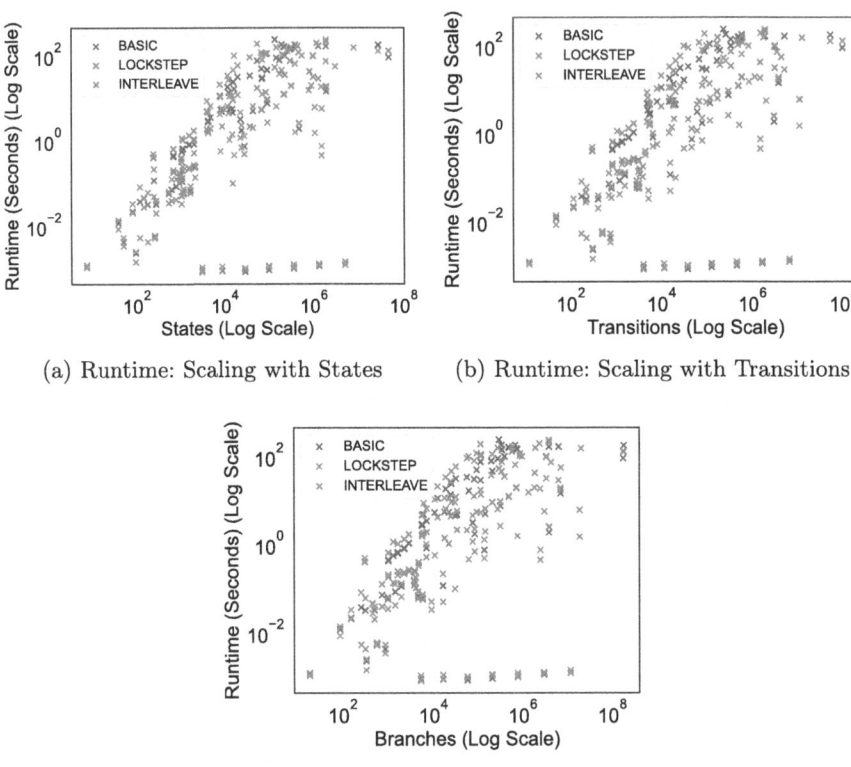

(a) Runtime: Scaling with States   (b) Runtime: Scaling with Transitions

(c) Runtime: Scaling with Branches

Fig. 5. Scatter plots of the runtime vs the number of states, transitions, branches

6   Concluding Remarks

We presented INTERLEAVE, a symbolic algorithm for MEC decomposition that interleaves redundant state-action pair removal with SCC decomposition. While matching the theoretical complexity of the prior BASIC algorithm, INTERLEAVE significantly improves practical performance, solving more QVBS benchmarks faster and with fewer symbolic operations than existing state-of-the-art algorithms.

Future work could explore alternative symbolic representations of MDPs (in theory and in practice) and algorithms designed to work with them. The effect of MEC decomposition algorithm performance on downstream task performance, and parallel or distributed implementations of INTERLEAVE are also promising directions.

Disclosure of Interests. The authors have no competing interests to declare that are relevant to the content of this paper.

References

1. Baier, C., Katoen, J.P.: Principles of Model Checking. MIT press, Cambridge (2008)
2. Baier, C., Klein, J., Leuschner, L., Parker, D., Wunderlich, S.: Ensuring the reliability of your model checker: interval iteration for Markov Decision Processes. In: Majumdar, R., Kunčak, V. (eds.) CAV 2017. LNCS, vol. 10426, pp. 160–180. Springer, Cham (2017). https://doi.org/10.1007/978-3-319-63387-9_8
3. Bryant, R.E.: Symbolic manipulation of boolean functions using a graphical representation. In: 22nd ACM/IEEE Design Automation Conference, pp. 688–694. IEEE (1985)
4. Chatterjee, K., Dvořák, W., Henzinger, M., Loitzenbauer, V.: Model and objective separation with conditional lower bounds: Disjunction is harder than conjunction. In: Proceedings of the 31st Annual ACM/IEEE Symposium on Logic in Computer Science, pp. 197–206 (2016)
5. Chatterjee, K., Dvořák, W., Henzinger, M., Svozil, A.: Symbolic time and space tradeoffs for probabilistic verification. In: 2021 36th Annual ACM/IEEE Symposium on Logic in Computer Science (LICS), pp. 1–13. IEEE (2021)
6. Chatterjee, K., Henzinger, M., Loitzenbauer, V., Oraee, S., Toman, V.: Symbolic algorithms for graphs and markov decision processes with fairness objectives. In: Chockler, H., Weissenbacher, G. (eds.) CAV 2018. LNCS, vol. 10982, pp. 178–197. Springer, Cham (2018). https://doi.org/10.1007/978-3-319-96142-2_13
7. De Alfaro, L.: Formal verification of probabilistic systems. Stanford university (1998)
8. Faber, F.: Comparison of Maximal End Component Decomposition Algorithms: Data and Code (2023). https://doi.org/10.5281/zenodo.8311805
9. Faber, F.: Comparison of Symbolic Maximal End Component Decomposition Algorithms (2023). https://felixfaber.dev/thesis.pdf. Accessed 21 June 2024
10. Gentilini, R., Piazza, C., Policriti, A., et al.: Computing strongly connected components in a linear number of symbolic steps. In: SODA, vol. 3, pp. 573–582. Citeseer (2003)
11. Haddad, S., Monmege, B.: Interval iteration algorithm for mdps and imdps. Theor. Comput. Sci. **735**, 111–131 (2018)
12. Hartmanns, A., Klauck, M., Parker, D., Quatmann, T., Ruijters, E.: The quantitative verification benchmark set. In: Vojnar, T., Zhang, L. (eds.) TACAS 2019. LNCS, vol. 11427, pp. 344–350. Springer, Cham (2019). https://doi.org/10.1007/978-3-030-17462-0_20
13. Hensel, C., Junges, S., Katoen, J.P., Quatmann, T., Volk, M.: The probabilistic model checker storm. Int. J. Softw. Tools Technol. Transf., 1–22 (2022)
14. Křetínský, J., Pérez, G.A., Raskin, J.F.: Learning-based mean-payoff optimization in an unknown mdp under omega-regular constraints. arXiv preprint arXiv:1804.08924 (2018)
15. Kwiatkowska, M., Norman, G., Parker, D.: PRISM 4.0: verification of probabilistic real-time systems. In: Gopalakrishnan, G., Qadeer, S. (eds.) CAV 2011. LNCS, vol. 6806, pp. 585–591. Springer, Heidelberg (2011). https://doi.org/10.1007/978-3-642-22110-1_47
16. Somenzi, F.: Cudd: Cu decision diagram package-release 2.4. 0. Univ. Colorado at Boulder **21** (2009)

Small Decision Trees for MDPs
with Deductive Synthesis

Roman Andriushchenko[1] , Milan Češka[1(✉)] , Sebastian Junges[2] ,
and Filip Macák[1]

[1] Brno University of Technology, Brno, Czech Republic
ceskam@fit.vut.cz
[2] Radboud University, Nijmegen, The Netherlands

Abstract. Markov decision processes (MDPs) describe decision making subject to probabilistic uncertainty. A classical problem on MDPs is to compute a policy, selecting actions in every state, that maximizes the probability of reaching a dedicated set of target states. Computing such policies in tabular form is efficiently possible via standard algorithms. However, for further processing by either humans or machines, policies should be represented concisely, e.g., as a decision tree. This paper considers finding (almost) optimal decision trees of minimal depth and contributes a deductive synthesis approach. Technically, we combine pruning the space of concise policies with an abstraction-refinement loop with an SMT-encoding that maps candidate policies into decision trees. Our experiments show that this approach beats the state-of-the-art solver using an MILP encoding by orders of magnitude. The approach also pairs well with heuristic approaches that map a fixed policy into a decision tree: for an MDP with 1.5M states, our approach reduces the size of the given tree by 90%, while sacrificing only 1% of the optimal performance.

1 Introduction

Markov decision processes (MDPs) are the ubiquitous model to describe sequential decision making under uncertainty: the outcomes of nondeterministic actions are determined by a probability distribution over the successor states. MDP policies resolve the nondeterminism and describe for each state which action to take. A classical synthesis task in MDPs is to compute a policy that maximizes a given objective, such as: *Given a set of goal states, find a maximizing policy*, i.e. a policy ensuring that the goal is reached with the maximal probability. These policies are efficiently computed by probabilistic model checkers such as STORM [24] or Prism [29] or can be approximated using (deep) reinforcement learning techniques [25,37]. These techniques apply to huge MDPs that are concisely represented, e.g. in the PRISM language. The result is a policy represented either in tabular form, mapping states to an action, or as a neural network. While the tabular form is often prohibitively large for further analysis by machines or a human, neural networks are hard to analyze despite the

© The Author(s) 2025
R. Piskac and Z. Rakamarić (Eds.): CAV 2025, LNCS 15932, pp. 169–192, 2025.
https://doi.org/10.1007/978-3-031-98679-6_8

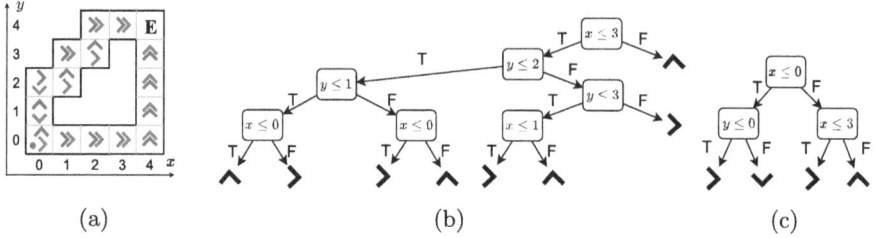

Fig. 1. (a) A simple slippery maze. The goal is to lead the robot placed in the lower left corner (the red dot) towards the exit cell while minimizing the number of steps. Red arrowheads illustrate the optimal policy that achieves a value of 12.8 (expected steps). Blue arrowheads illustrate a sub-optimal policy that achieves a value of 13.3. (b) The smallest DT implementing the optimal policy has depth 4. (c) The smallest DT implementing the sub-optimal policy has only depth 2. (Color figure online)

tremendous progress in neural network verification. This observation has motivated the search for concise representations of policies, in particular in the form of programs [10, 40] or decision trees (DTs) [9, 38, 41]. *The main contribution of this paper is an approach to synthesize policies that are optimal within a class of small DTs.*

Illustrative Example. Consider a simple grid-world maze as in Fig. 1. The agent starts at the bottom left and wants to reach the exit marked **E**. It can move in the four cardinal directions, and each action has a 10% probability of transitioning into an unintended neighboring cell. Consequently, every state is reachable under every policy. When moving in a direction blocked by a wall, the agent bumps into the wall and remains in the same cell. E.g., in the cell $(x = 1, y = 2)$ moving to the right (as the blue policy does) means the agent will with high probability stay in the same cell but there is a small probability that it slips into the cell above. STORM computes an optimal (in this example, unique) policy that ensures reaching the exit in an expected 12.8 steps (the policy visualized by the red arrowheads). To represent this policy as a DT (using predicates that compare variables to constants) requires a tree of depth at least 4 (see Fig. 1b). Alternatively, we may ask: What is the optimal expected number of steps to reach the exit among all policies that can be represented as a DT of depth 2? The answer is 13.3 realized by the policy visualized by the blue arrowheads. The corresponding DT is shown in Fig. 1c. This policy aims to avoid the 'staircase' in the left upper corner and then takes sub-optimal actions within that staircase.

Problem Setup. We call a policy *k-implementable*, if there is a DT of depth k (and with a particular class of predicates) that represents the policy. The first problem studied in the literature, *the mapping problem*, asks whether a given tabular policy is k-implementable for any fixed k. Solving this problem then allows us to find the smallest DT, measured by depth, that implements this policy. The second problem studied, the *synthesis problem*, is to find a policy that is optimal with respect to some objective, such as reaching the goal state, and within the class of k-implementable policies. We want to highlight that the mapping problem assumes one fixed policy. Therefore, the mapping problem cannot find the minimal representation of *any* optimal policy. In particular, in our experiments, we show that we can find optimal policies that are 2-implementable, whereas the policy that STORM computes is not 5-implementable. The construction of optimal DTs is well-known to be NP-hard for different notions of optimality [22,30].

State-of-the-Art: Policy Mapping. Mapping policies into small, but not necessarily the smallest, DTs is prominently supported by the tools DTCONTROL [6] and Uppaal Stratego [7,16]. These tools approach the problem by *learning* small DTs by recursively splitting the tree based on ideas like information gain. The result is an approximation or exact representation of the original policy. Generally, these tools favor scalability over minimality.

State-of-the-Art: The Synthesis Problem. The tool OMDT [41] builds a monolithic MILP that encodes both the structural constraints on the policy (being k-implementable) and the constraint that the policy achieves the optimal value (using the standard LP formulation for maximal discounted rewards). This LP-based approach encounters the same scalability as (MI)LP-based MDP model checking approaches face, e.g., in [2,17–19].

Our Approach: Abstraction Refinement with SMT-Based Mapping. Inspired by encodings of DTs in propositional formulas [34], we encode the set of k-implementable trees in an SMT formula over the bounded integers and with linear inequalities. Using an SMT solver allows us to determine if there is a k-implementable tree representing the given policy. Moreover, the encoding allows us to design an abstraction-refinement loop that avoids solving the synthesis problem in one shot. Our approach takes a set of k-implementable policies and abstracts them to search for an optimal policy in a larger class of policies. If this policy is not improving over the best k-implementable policy found so far, it abandons the search here. Otherwise, by solving the mapping problem, it tests whether this optimal policy is k-implementable. If yes, we can abandon the search here and store the policy as our best policy so far. Otherwise, the policy is *spurious*, and the search is recursively invoked on smaller subsets of k-implementable policies.

Example 1. We present a conceptual version of our routine on the example given above, see Fig. 1. To find an optimal 2-implementable policy, we would first search for an optimal memoryless policy σ. This policy is better than the previously found policy (we can e.g. initialize this policy as a random tree). Using the mapping problem, σ is spurious. We can now split and independently search for the best k-implementable policy that goes up in the initial state and for the best k-implementable policy that goes right in the initial state. We observe that these sub-classes can be overapproximated by memoryless deterministic policies on two sub-MDPs of the original MDP.

Effective Abstraction Refinement. We introduce a novel abstraction-refinement loop DTPAYNT that analyzes the spurious policies to split in an informed way. Compared to an abstraction-refinement loop for finite state controllers in POMDPs [2], the set of k-implementable policies is highly irregular and a policy can be represented by many different trees. To overcome this problem, we use an unsatisfiable core UC witnessing that the given policy is not k-implementable. We introduce a *harmonization* technique that analyzes UC and finds two trees that serve as good approximations of the policy and, most importantly, they differ in one parameter that provides a good heuristic on how to construct the subsets of k-implementable policies. The proposed refinement procedure further-more entails the ability to first learn a k-tree before learning a $k+1$-tree.

Relation to Partially Observable MDPs. Finding optimal k-implementable poli-cies can be phrased as finding a colouring of states and for every colour an action. This reformulation clarifies a connection to the synthesis for memoryless observation-based policies POMDPs [2,28,31]. Usually, in POMDPs, one cannot pick the colouring of the states, but such variations have been investigated in [15,27]. However, contrary to those settings, in DTs, the state colouring cannot be arbitrary but must be implementable with a DT.

Contributions. We propose DTPAYNT, an abstraction-refinement loop that itera-tively invokes an SMT-based routine to search for DTs with maximum value among all DTs up to the given depth. DTPAYNT significantly outperforms OMDT [41], the state-of-the-art tool solving the same problem using a MILP encoding. In contrast to DTCONTROL, a prominent tool for policy mapping, DTPAYNT is able to effectively control the trade-offs between the size and qual-ity of the resulting DTs. For example, for the *consensus* protocol, DTPAYNT finds a DT with 10 inner nodes, which is about 38 times smaller than the DT found by DTCONTROL, while it achieves 93% of the optimal performance. DTPAYNT can scale to MDPs with hundreds of thousands of states, provided that a small DT with the desired performance exists. Finally, DTPAYNT can be used to reduce large DTs: for a variant of a *cmsa* model with 1.5M states, we reduce the num-ber of inner nodes in the DT constructed by DTCONTROL from 236 to 22 while sacrificing less than 1% of the performance.

2   Background and Problem Statement

A *distribution* over a countable set A is a function $\mu\colon A \to [0,1]$ s.t. $\sum_a \mu(a){=}1$. The set $Distr(A)$ contains all distributions over A.

Definition 1 (MDP). *A* Markov decision process (MDP) *is a tuple* $M = (S, s_0, Act, P)$ *with a finite set* S *of states, an initial state* $s_0 \in S$, *a finite (indexed) set* Act *of actions, and a partial transition function* $P\colon S \times Act \nrightarrow Distr(S)$.

For an MDP M, we define the *available actions* in $s \in S$ as $Act(s) := \{\alpha \in Act \mid P(s,\alpha) \neq \bot\}$; we denote $P(s,\alpha,s') := P(s,\alpha)(s')$. An MDP with $|Act(s)| = 1$ for each $s \in S$ is a *Markov chain (MC)*; we denote MCs as tuples (S, s_0, P). A (deterministic, memoryless) *policy* is a function $\sigma\colon S \to Act$ with $\sigma(s) \in$

$Act(s)$ for all $s \in S$. The set Σ^M denotes the policies for MDP M. A policy $\sigma \in \Sigma^M$ induces the MC $M^\sigma = (S, s_0, P^\sigma)$ where $P^\sigma(s) = P(s, \sigma(s))$. A *partial* (deterministic, memoryless) policy is a function $\sigma \colon S \nrightarrow Act$.

Specifications. We consider indefinite-horizon reachability and expected reward properties as well as discounted (infinite-horizon) total reward objectives [36]. To simplify the exposition, we formalize our approach only for the *maximal reachability probability*[1]. Formally, let $M = (S, s_0, P)$ be an MC, and let $G \subseteq S$ be a set of *goal states*. Let $\mathbb{P}[M, s \models \Diamond G]$ denote the probability of reaching (some state in) G from state $s \in S$. Let $\mathbb{P}[M \models \Diamond G]$ denote $\mathbb{P}[M, s_0 \models \Diamond G]$. For MDPs, specifications are taken over the best and worst possible resolution of the non-determinism. Assume MDP $M = (S, s_0, Act, P)$. The maximal reachability probability of G from state s_0 in M is $\mathbb{P}_{\max}[M \models \Diamond G] := \sup_{\sigma \in \Sigma^M} \mathbb{P}[M^\sigma \models \Diamond G]$. We denote $V(\sigma) := \mathbb{P}[M^\sigma \models \Diamond G]$ as the *value* of policy σ. An optimal policy that maximizes the value is denoted with σ^*. The value of MDP is defined as $V(M) = V(\sigma^*)$. Details are given in [8].

2.1   Representing Policies as Decision Trees

Symbolic MDPs. We aim to represent policies in MDPs symbolically. Inspired by the PRISM language [29], we assume a finite set of bounded integer variables $\mathcal{V}$, and thus states are mappings $s \colon \mathcal{V} \to \mathbb{Z}$. *State predicates* are inequalities of the form $v \leq b$ with $v \in \mathcal{V}$ and $b \in \mathbb{Z}$; the set of such predicates is denoted $\Psi_{\mathcal{V}}$. A state s *satisfies* a predicate $v \leq b$ iff $s(v) \leq b$; we denote this with $s \models (v \leq b)$.

The Random Action. To concisely represent policies, it is convenient to allow a policy to take some dedicated *arbitrary* action. We explicitly create this arbitrary action α_{rand} for every state which uniformly selects one of the (available) actions. Formally, we define $M' = (S, s_0, Act', P')$ with $Act'(s) = Act(s) \cup \{\alpha_{\text{rand}}\}$, $P'(s, \alpha_{\text{rand}}, s') = \frac{1}{|Act(s)|} \sum_{\alpha \in Act(s)} P(s, \alpha, s')$. Henceforth, we assume that MDP $M' = M$, i.e., that every MDP contains an action α_{rand}. This is sound for the specifications considered in this paper: it holds that the optimal value is achievable by a memoryless deterministic policy σ^* as per [35, Thm 7.9.1].

Corollary 1 (Proof in [5, App. A.1]) *Given an MDP M, its modification M' defined above, and the considered specifications, it holds that $V(M) = V(M')$.*

Any policy in MDP M' can be mimicked by a (randomizing) policy in M.

Remark 1 (Interpretability of random action). Adding the random action makes it explicit that a policy may randomly pick either available action. Sometimes, having this opportunity makes for more concise policies. A possible downside is that the policy in M' may not reflect a memoryless deterministic policy in M.

Trees. A (binary) *tree* is a tuple $T = (n_0, N, L, l, r)$ with the *root node* n_0, the set N of *inner nodes*, the set L of *leaf nodes*, and functions $l, r \colon N \to N \cup L$

---

[1] Our implementation supports all the aforementioned specifications.

defining the *left* and *right successors* of the inner nodes, respectively. A *path* (of length k) in a tree T is a sequence $\pi = n_0 \ldots n_k$ of nodes s.t. $\forall 0 < i \leq k : n_i \in \{l(n_{i-1}), r(n_{i-1})\}$. Path π is *complete* if it ends in a leaf node. The *depth* of T is the length of its longest path.

Definition 2 (Decision tree). *Assume an MDP* $M = (S, s_0, Act, P)$ *defined over the set* $\mathcal{V}$. *A* decision tree *(DT) for* M *is a tuple* $\mathcal{T} = (T, \gamma, \delta)$ *where (i)* T *is a binary tree, (ii) predicate function* $\gamma \colon N \to \Psi_{\mathcal{V}}$ *assigns to inner nodes a state predicate, and (iii) action function* $\delta \colon L \to Act$ *assigns to leaf nodes an action.*

We lift the notions of inner and leaf nodes, paths and depths of trees to DTs. DTs of depth k are further denoted as k-DTs.

Definition 3 (Corresponding states). *The set* $\mathsf{st}^{\mathcal{T}}(n)$ *of states that corresponds to a node* n *is recursively defined as follows:* $\mathsf{st}^{\mathcal{T}}(n_0) = S$, $\mathsf{st}^{\mathcal{T}}(l(n)) = \{s \in \mathsf{st}^{\mathcal{T}}(n) \mid s \models \gamma(n)\}$, *and* $\mathsf{st}^{\mathcal{T}}(r(n)) = \{s \in \mathsf{st}^{\mathcal{T}}(n) \mid s \not\models \gamma(n)\}$.

Note that the sets $\{\mathsf{st}^{\mathcal{T}}(n) \mid n \in L\}$ represent a partition of S. Thus, we can define $\mathsf{leaf}^{\mathcal{T}}(s)$ as the unique leaf node $n \in L$ such that $s \in \mathsf{st}^{\mathcal{T}}(n)$.

Definition 4 (Induced policy). *The DT* $\mathcal{T}$ *induces policy* $\sigma_{\mathcal{T}} \colon S \to Act$ *with* $\sigma_{\mathcal{T}}(s) = \delta(\mathsf{leaf}^{\mathcal{T}}(s))$ *if* $\delta(\mathsf{leaf}^{\mathcal{T}}(s)) \in Act(s)$ *and* $\sigma_{\mathcal{T}}(s) = \alpha_{\mathrm{rand}}$ *otherwise. The value* $V(\mathcal{T})$ *of the DT* $\mathcal{T}$ *is defined as the value of* $\sigma_{\mathcal{T}}$.

Example 2. Consider an MDP presented in Fig. 1 and a DT $\mathcal{T}_c$ depicted in Fig. 1c. Assume a state $s \in S$ with $s(x) = 4$ and $s(y) = 3$. Then, $\mathsf{leaf}^{\mathcal{T}}(s)$ is the rightmost node of $\mathcal{T}_c$ and thus $\mathcal{T}_c$ induces policy $\sigma_{\mathcal{T}_c}$ where $\sigma_{\mathcal{T}_c}(s) = up$.

Remark 2 (Fallback action interpretability). Our approach can synthesize a DT that assigns an action that is not available at a given state, in which case we use the random action as a fallback. This setup avoids that the DT must precisely capture when an action is available and allows for smaller DTs. Note that the information which actions are available is usually also accessible in another format (e.g. masks or shields heavily used in reinforcement learning settings).

2.2   Problem Statement

This paper's key problem is to find a decision tree with maximum value (e.g. reachability probability) among all decision trees up to the given depth.

> **Bounded-depth synthesis problem**: Given MDP M and bound k, find a DT $\mathcal{T}$ of depth up to k with maximum value.

Akin to [41], we are interested in anytime synthesis: the faster we find a DT that achieves a high value, the better. This is a variant of widely studied a *policy mapping problem* [6,12,21,32,38]: find a DT inducing a given fixed policy (typically a pre-computed policy that maximizes reachability). In contrast, in the bounded-depth synthesis problem, we seek the best DT up to the given depth.

3   Solving the Fixed-Tree Policy Mapping Problem

In this section, we construct an SMT-based subroutine that solves a *fixed-tree policy mapping problem*, a variant of the policy mapping that searches over a set of DTs having the same topology. Additionally, we consider the construction of a witness that explains why a policy cannot be represented as such a DT. We start with *tree templates* representing a blueprint of the set of DTs.

Definition 5 (Tree template). *Assume an MDP $M = (S, s_0, Act, P)$ defined over the set $\mathcal{V}$. A tree template for M is a tuple $\mathbb{T} = (T, \Gamma, \Delta)$ where (i) T is a binary tree, (ii) $\Gamma \colon N \to 2^{\Psi_{\mathcal{V}}}$ assigns to inner nodes a set of state predicates, and (iii) $\Delta \colon L \to 2^{Act}$ assigns to leaf nodes subset of actions.*

A tree template encodes (or instantiates) a set of DTs and, thus, a set of policies.

Definition 6 (Instantitation). *Template $\mathbb{T} = (T, \Gamma, \Delta)$ instantiates DT $\mathcal{T} = (T, \gamma, \delta)$, written $\mathcal{T} \in \mathbb{T}$, if $\gamma(n) \in \Gamma(n)$ for all $n \in N$ and $\delta(n) \in \Delta(n)$ for all $n \in L$. A policy σ is* contained in template $\mathbb{T}$*, written $\sigma \in \mathbb{T}$, if there exists a tree $\mathcal{T} \in \mathbb{T}$ that induces σ; in such a case, we say that σ is $\mathbb{T}$-implementable (via $\mathcal{T}$).*

3.1   SMT Encoding

Let's assume a fixed tree template $\mathbb{T}$. In this subsection, we present an SMT formula over the theory of quantifier-free linear integer arithmetic that is satisfiable iff a (partial) policy σ is $\mathbb{T}$-implementable. To this end, we first reparameterize the decision trees and templates in terms of integer-valued variables.

Parameterization. We assume that the set of state variables $\mathcal{V} = \{v_i\}_{i=1}^{|\mathcal{V}|}$ is ordered and the actions are integers $Act \subseteq \mathbb{Z}$ and are ordered. Observe that any state predicate $v_i \leq b$ can be described by a pair of integers i, b. Therefore, the predicate function $\gamma \colon N \to \Psi_{\mathcal{V}}$ of a DT can be expressed using two integer-valued functions: the *variable selection function* $\mathcal{D} \colon N \to \{1, \ldots, |\mathcal{V}|\}$ and the *bound selection function* $\mathcal{B} \colon N \to \mathbb{Z}$. Then, the predicate function $\gamma_{\mathcal{D}, \mathcal{B}}$ associated with $\mathcal{D}, \mathcal{B}$ is defined as $\gamma_{\mathcal{D}, \mathcal{B}}(n) := (v_{\mathcal{D}(n)} \leq \mathcal{B}(n))$. Likewise, with the *action selection function* $\mathcal{A} \colon L \to Act$, we can define action function $\delta_{\mathcal{A}}$ where $\delta_{\mathcal{A}}(n) := \mathcal{A}(n)$.

Definition 7 (Parameterization). *Given $\mathbb{T}$ and functions $\mathcal{D}$, $\mathcal{B}$ and $\mathcal{A}$ as above. The* parameterization *$f = (\mathcal{D}, \mathcal{B}, \mathcal{A})$ is* contained in $\mathbb{T}$ *if the DT $(T, \gamma_{\mathcal{D}, \mathcal{B}}, \delta_{\mathcal{A}}) \in \mathbb{T}$; we write $\mathbb{T}(f)$ to denote this DT. The value $V(f)$ of f is the value $V(\mathbb{T}(f))$.*

Towards an SMT encoding, we introduce the variables $\mathcal{X}^{\mathbb{T}} = \{\mathcal{B}_n, \mathcal{D}_n \mid n \in N\} \cup \{\mathcal{A}_n \mid n \in L\}$ such that $\mathcal{B}_n$ encodes the value of $\mathcal{B}(n)$, etc. We write $f(x)$ to denote the value of any variable $x \in \mathcal{X}^{\mathbb{T}}$.

While parameterization f allows us to generate a DT $\mathbb{T}(f)$ from a template, a *set of parameterizations* allows us to generate restrictions of the template.

Definition 8 (Parameterization set). *Given a template* $\mathbb{T}$, *a (rectangular) set of parameterizations is a function* $\mathcal{F}\colon \mathcal{X}^{\mathbb{T}} \to 2^{\mathbb{Z}}$ *where, for any* $n \in N$, *it holds that* $\mathcal{F}(\mathcal{D}_n) \subseteq \{1, \ldots, |\mathcal{V}|\}$, $\mathcal{F}(\mathcal{B}_n) \subseteq \mathbb{Z}$ *and for any* $n \in L$, $\mathcal{F}(\mathcal{A}_n) \subseteq Act$. *Parameterization* f *belongs to set* $\mathcal{F}$, *denoted* $f \in \mathcal{F}$, *if* $f(x) \in \mathcal{F}(x)$ *for any variable* $x \in \mathcal{X}^{\mathbb{T}}$. *We write* $\mathbb{T}(\mathcal{F})$ *for the template that contains exactly the DTs* $\mathbb{T}(f)$ *with* $f \in \mathcal{F}$.

Encoding. We present an encoding that checks for a given $\mathcal{F}$ whether a (partial) policy σ is $\mathbb{T}(\mathcal{F})$-implementable. In the encoding below, we assume that σ is a partial policy where $\sigma(s) = \bot$ if $s \in G$ or s is unreachable in M^σ. The formula $\mathsf{pol}(\mathcal{F}, \sigma)$ uses the variables from $\mathcal{X}^{\mathbb{T}}$ and abstractly is a conjunction of (1) $\mathsf{dom}(\mathcal{F})$, which limits possible parameterizations to $\mathcal{F}$, and (2) $\mathsf{act}_{s,\sigma(s)}$, which ensures that the tree represents σ in every state.

$$\mathsf{pol}(\mathcal{F}, \sigma) := \quad \mathsf{dom}(\mathcal{F}) \wedge \bigwedge_{s \in S, \sigma(s) \neq \bot} \mathsf{act}_{s,\sigma(s)}.$$

We explain the individual constraints below.

Contained in a Template. $\mathsf{dom}(\mathcal{F})$ is a constraint that limits the variables to ensure that a DT is contained in $\mathbb{T}(\mathcal{F})$

$$\mathsf{dom}(\mathcal{F}) := \bigwedge_{x \in \mathcal{X}^{\mathbb{T}}} x \in \mathcal{F}(x)$$

State-Representing Leaf. Before we discuss expressing the correct policy, we match the leaves of the DT with states. Recall that a DT partitions the state space S into $\{\mathsf{st}^{\mathcal{T}}(n) \mid n \in L\}$. In a tree template, this partitioning depends on the choice of f, i.e. on the choice of $\mathcal{B}$ and $\mathcal{D}$. We create a formula $\mathsf{sel}_{s,n}(f)$ that is true iff $s \in \mathsf{st}^{\mathbb{T}(f)}(n)$. First, for the unique path $n_0, \ldots, n_k$ from root to leaf $n = n_k$, we define the relation $\bowtie_i^n$ such that $\bowtie_i^n := \leq$ if $n_{i+1} = l(n_i)$ and $\bowtie_i^n := >$ if $n_{i+1} = r(n_i)$. The formula $\mathsf{sel}_{s,n}$ is then given by:

$$\mathsf{sel}_{s,n} := \quad \bigwedge_{i=0}^{k-1} \bigwedge_{j=1}^{|\mathcal{V}|} \quad (j = \mathcal{D}_{n_i}) \to \big(s(v_j) \bowtie_i^n \mathcal{B}_{n_i}\big).$$

Action-Choice. For the state s to take action α in a DT, it must hold that the (unique) leaf n that represents state s picks this action α. The randomized action α_{rand} can also be picked when this leaf selects an unavailable action.

$$\mathsf{act}_{s,\alpha} := \bigwedge_{n \in L} \mathsf{sel}_{s,n} \to \mathsf{act}_{s,\alpha,n}, \quad \text{using}$$

$$\mathsf{act}_{s,\alpha,n} := \begin{cases} \mathcal{A}_n = \alpha & \text{if } \alpha \neq \alpha_{\mathrm{rand}} \\ \mathcal{A}_n \in \{\alpha_{\mathrm{rand}}\} \cup Act \backslash Act(s) & \text{otherwise} \end{cases}$$

Correctness. A parameterization f satisfying $\mathsf{pol}(\mathcal{F}, \sigma)$ is denoted as $f \models \mathsf{pol}(\mathcal{F}, \sigma)$.

Theorem 1. (Proof in [5, App. A.2]) *Assume a parameterization* f, *a set of parameterizations* $\mathcal{F}$, *and a policy* $\sigma \in \Sigma^M$. *Then* $f \models \mathsf{pol}(\mathcal{F}, \sigma)$ *iff* $f \in \mathcal{F}$ *and forall* $s \in S, \sigma(s) \neq \bot$ *implies* $\sigma(s) = \sigma_{\mathbb{T}(f)}$.

3.2   Diagnosing Non-implementable Policies

Unsatisfiable Cores. For further usage, we want to examine why $\mathsf{pol}(\mathcal{F}, \sigma)$ is unsatisfiable. The conjunction $\mathsf{pol}(\mathcal{F}, \sigma)$ is essentially a set of domain constraints and a set of action-choice constraints. An *unsatisfiable core* [11] is a natural way of explaining why $\mathsf{pol}(\mathcal{F}, \sigma)$ cannot be satisfied by using a subset of the constraints. The computation of unsatisfiable cores is supported by existing SMT solvers, e.g. by Z3 [33]. An unsatisfiable core UC is simply a subset of parameters and state-leaf constraints that make $\mathsf{pol}(\mathcal{F}, \sigma)$ unsatisfiable.

Definition 9 (Unsatisfiable core). *An unsatisfiable core for $\mathcal{F}$ and σ is a pair $\mathsf{UC} = (\mathcal{X}^{\mathsf{UC}} \subseteq \mathcal{X}^{\mathbb{T}}, SP^{\mathsf{UC}} \subseteq S \times L)$ s.t. the following formula is unsatisfiable*

$$\mathsf{pol}^{\mathsf{UC}}(\mathcal{F}, \sigma) := \bigwedge_{x \in \mathcal{X}^{\mathsf{UC}}} x \in \mathcal{F}(x) \wedge \bigwedge_{s,n \in SP^{\mathsf{UC}}} \mathsf{act}_{s,\sigma(s),n}.$$

The set of critical states for $\mathcal{F}$ and σ is $S^{\mathsf{UC}} := \{s \in S \mid \exists n : (s, n) \in SP^{\mathsf{UC}}\}$.

In our experiments, SP^{UC} is often much smaller than $S \times L$: In fact, it is not uncommon that SP^{UC} contains only two elements.

   Given a subset $S' \subseteq S$ and a policy σ, we define the *restriction* $\sigma_{\downarrow S'}$ of σ on S' as $\sigma_{\downarrow S'}(s) = \sigma(s)$ if $s \in S'$ and $\sigma_{\downarrow S'}(s) = \bot$ otherwise. The following proposition asserts that the set of critical states witnesses the non-implementability of σ.

Proposition 1. *Let S^{UC} be critical states for $\mathcal{F}$ and σ. The partial policy $\sigma_{\downarrow S^{\mathsf{UC}}}$ is not $\mathbb{T}(\mathcal{F})$-implementable.*

Remark 3. $\mathsf{pol}(\mathcal{F}, \sigma)$ can have multiple unsatisfiable cores and thus multiple sets of critical states. We prefer critical states where the policy choice also critically affects the value, similar to [12]. Assume that the state space $S = \{s_i\}_{i=1}^{|S|}$ is ordered. Instead of deducing critical states from $\mathsf{pol}(\mathcal{F}, \sigma)$, we deduce them from $\mathsf{dom}(\mathcal{F}) \wedge \bigwedge_{i=1}^{m} \mathsf{act}_{s_i, \sigma(s_i)}$ where m is the smallest state index that makes the formula unsatisfiable. We use a breadth-first search from the initial state[2].

Harmonising Parameterizations. The set of critical states S^{UC} identifies which state decisions $\sigma(s)$, $s \in S^{\mathsf{UC}}$, are incompatible with $\mathbb{T}(\mathcal{F})$, i.e. make $\sigma_{\downarrow S^{\mathsf{UC}}}$ not $\mathbb{T}(\mathcal{F})$-implementable. To gain another insight into this incompatibility, we reverse the question and ask what makes $\mathbb{T}(\mathcal{F})$ incompatible with $\sigma_{\downarrow S^{\mathsf{UC}}}$. Since there is no one parameterization $f \in \mathcal{F}$ s.t. $\sigma_{\mathbb{T}(f)} = \sigma$, we seek two parameterizations f_1, f_2 that differ in only one variable assignment and where policies $\sigma_{\mathbb{T}(f_1)}, \sigma_{\mathbb{T}(f_2)}$ *together* describe σ on the set S^{UC}. We now formalize this concept.

Definition 10 (Harmonizing parameterizations). *Let σ be a policy that is not $\mathbb{T}(\mathcal{F})$-implementable. Parameterizations $f_1, f_2 \in \mathcal{F}$ are called harmonizing for σ if $\exists! x \in \mathcal{X}^{\mathbb{T}} : f_1(x) \neq f_2(x)$ and for any state $s \in S^{\mathsf{UC}}$, $\sigma(s) \in \{\sigma_{\mathbb{T}(f_1)}(s), \sigma_{\mathbb{T}(f_2)}(s)\}$. The variable x above is the harmonizing variable.*

---

[2] We tested various other orders, but this one seemed to be the most robust.

Encoding. We provide an SMT encoding that yields harmonizing parameterizations. Intuitively, we seek two trees, one from the original tree template $\mathbb{T}$ (encoded with the original variables $\mathcal{X}^{\mathbb{T}}$), and the other from the identical tree template $\mathbb{T}'$ (encoded with the primed variables $\mathcal{X}^{\mathbb{T}'}$). We first describe the requirement for the two trees to differ in at most one variable, using the fact that $\mathcal{X}^{\mathbb{T}}$ and $\mathcal{X}^{\mathbb{T}'}$ are ordered similarly and using an auxiliary integer variable h to encode the index of the harmonizing variable:

$$\mathsf{harm}(\mathcal{F}) := \bigwedge\nolimits_{1 \leq i \leq |\mathcal{X}^{\mathbb{T}}|} h \neq i \;\rightarrow\; x_i = x'_i.$$

The primed variables are associated with the identical set $\mathcal{F}'$ of parameterizations: $\mathcal{F}'(x') = \mathcal{F}(x)$. Then, the encoding is given by:

$$\mathsf{pol}^H(\mathcal{F}, \sigma) := \mathsf{dom}(\mathcal{F}) \wedge \mathsf{dom}(\mathcal{F}') \wedge \mathsf{harm}(\mathcal{F}) \wedge \bigwedge\nolimits_{s \in S^{\mathsf{UC}}} \left(\mathsf{act}_{s,\sigma(s)} \vee \mathsf{act}'_{s,\sigma(s)} \right)$$

using dom as above and $\mathsf{act}'_{s,\sigma(s)}$ is identical to $\mathsf{act}_{s,\sigma(s)}$ except every occurrence of variables $\mathcal{D}_n, \mathcal{B}_n, \mathcal{A}_n$ is replaced with their primed counterpart.

Theorem 2. (Proof in [5, App. A.3]) *Assume parameterizations f_1, f_2, two (identical) sets of parameterizations $\mathcal{F}, \mathcal{F}'$, a policy σ that is not $\mathbb{T}(\mathcal{F})$-impelementable, and an evaluation $f_h \in \mathbb{Z}$ of the variable h. Then $f_h, f_1, f_2 \models \mathsf{pol}^H(\mathcal{F}, \sigma)$ iff f_1, f_2 are harmonizing for σ via a harmonizing variable $x_{f_h} \in \mathcal{X}^{\mathbb{T}}$.*

4   Fixed-Tree Synthesis Problem

We now shift our focus to the fixed-tree synthesis problem: given template $\mathbb{T}$, we seek for a DT $\mathcal{T} \in \mathbb{T}$ with the highest value $V(\mathcal{T})$. We first show the NP-hardness of this problem. Afterwards, we outline our abstraction refinement approach.

4.1   Problem Complexity

The complexity of fixed-tree synthesis problem follows from the result of [30], which showed that finding optimal decision trees (in terms of size) is NP-complete.

Theorem 3. (Proof in [5, App. A.4]) *The decision variant of the fixed-tree synthesis problem is NP-hard.*

Our proof follows similar principles to the proof in [30]. Here we provide the main idea of the reduction, for full proof refer to [5, App. A.4]. The proof is a reduction from the Exact Cover by 3-sets (X3C) problem to the problem of deciding whether there exists a decision tree of depth k for MDP M that implements a policy that reaches a goal state with probability above 0.5. The X3C problem is a known NP-Complete problem which asks whether for some set U and set $T = \{T_1, T_2, \ldots, T_j\}$ where $|T_i| = 3$ and $T_i \subseteq U$ there exists an exact

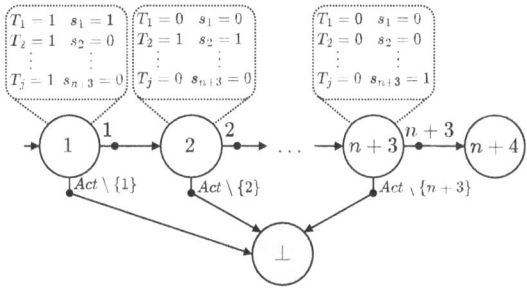

Fig. 2. MDP construction for the reduction from X3C problem.

cover $T' \subseteq T$. The main idea is to create an MDP where the states correspond to the elements of the set U for X3C, such that in every state of the MDP exactly one unique action progresses towards the goal state $n + 4$ while the rest of the actions lead to a sink state as shown in Fig. 2. This means that a DT that reaches a goal state with probability above 0.5 needs to distinguish all states of the MDP. There are two types of state variables in this MDP: 1) those that correspond to the sets in T which have a value of 1 when $x \in T_i$ and 2) variables for each state which have a value of 1 only in one unique state. In [5, App. A.4] we show that for such an MDP there exists a DT of depth $k = |U|/3 + 2$ that reaches the goal state if and only if there exists an exact cover T'.

4.2   Abstraction Refinement

Due to the finiteness of the state space S and the variable set $\mathcal{V}$, the number of variable valuations is finite as well. Thus, we consider a finite number of bound selection functions: $\mathcal{B}(n) \in \{s(v) \mid s \in S, v \in \mathcal{V}\}$. We use $\mathcal{F}^{\mathbb{T}}$ to denote the largest finite set of such parameterizations for $\mathbb{T}$. The following definition introduces an abstraction that overapproximates the set of policies induced by described by $\mathcal{F}$.

Definition 11 (Family-MDP). *Assume an MDP $M = (S, s_0, Act^M, P)$, a tree template $\mathbb{T}$ and a family $\mathcal{F} \subseteq \mathcal{F}^{\mathbb{T}}$. An $\mathcal{F}$-MDP is an MDP $M(\mathcal{F}) = (S, s_0, Act, P')$ where $P'(s, \alpha) = P(s, \alpha)$ if $\exists f \in \mathcal{F} : \sigma_{\mathbb{T}(f)}(s) = \alpha$ and $P(s, \alpha) = \bot$ otherwise.*

An $\mathcal{F}$-MDP $M(\mathcal{F})$ is a sub-MDP of M where action α is enabled in state s only if at least some DT $\mathbb{T}(f)$, $f \in \mathcal{F}$, induces a policy that associates s with α. We create this family-MDP by checking the satisfiability of $\mathsf{dom}(\mathcal{F}) \wedge \mathsf{act}_{s,\alpha}$ for every state-action pair. The following proposition asserts that the set of policies for $M(\mathcal{F})$ includes all policies obtained from $\mathbb{T}$ using assignments from $\mathcal{F}$.

Proposition 2. *Let $\mathcal{F} \subseteq \mathcal{F}^{\mathbb{T}}$. Then $\forall f \in \mathcal{F} : \sigma_{\mathbb{T}(f)} \in \Sigma^{M(\mathcal{F})}$.*

We stress that $M(\mathcal{F})$ is an abstraction, i.e. $\Sigma^{M(\mathcal{F})}$ may contain policies that are not $\mathbb{T}(\mathcal{F})$-implementable.

Algorithm 1: Recursive DT construction

Input : MDP M, goal set G, tree template $\mathbb{T}$

Output: DT $\mathbb{T}(f)$ s.t. $f \in \arg\max_{f \in \mathcal{F}^{\mathbb{T}}} V(f)$

---

1   $\mathfrak{F} \leftarrow \text{STACK}(), \mathfrak{F}.\text{PUSH}(\mathcal{F}^{\mathbb{T}}), f_{best} = \varnothing, V_{best} = -\infty$

2   **while** $\mathfrak{F} \neq \emptyset$ **do**

3      $\mathcal{F} \leftarrow \mathfrak{F}.\text{POP}()$

4      $M(\mathcal{F}) \leftarrow \text{BUILDFAMILYMDP}(M, \mathbb{T}, \mathcal{F})$ ▷ applying Def. 11

5      $\sigma, V(\sigma) \leftarrow \text{MODELCHECK}(\mathbb{P}_{\max}[M(\mathcal{F}) \models \Diamond G])$

6   **if** $V(\sigma) \leq V_{best}$ **then continue**

7   **if** $f \models \text{pol}(\mathcal{F}, \sigma)$ **then** $f_{best} \leftarrow f, V_{best} \leftarrow V(\sigma)$, **continue**

8      $\mathcal{X}^{\text{UC}}, SP^{\text{UC}} \leftarrow \text{UNSATCORE}(\text{pol}(\mathcal{F}, \sigma))$ ▷ applying Remark 3 and Def. 9

9   **if** $f_h, f_1, f_2 \models \text{pol}^H(\mathcal{F}, \sigma)$ **then**   ▷ according to Sec. 3.2

10   **for** $f \in \{f_1, f_2\}$ **do**

11 | **if** $V(f) > V_{best}$ **then** $f_{best} \leftarrow f, V_{best} \leftarrow V(f)$

12         $\mathcal{F}_1, \mathcal{F}_2 \leftarrow \text{SPLITINFORMED}(\mathcal{F}, f_h, f_1, f_2)$

13   **else** $\mathcal{F}_1, \mathcal{F}_2 \leftarrow \text{SPLITARBITRARY}(\mathcal{F}, \mathcal{X}^{\text{UC}})$

14      $\mathfrak{F}.\text{PUSH}(\mathcal{F}_1), \mathfrak{F}.\text{PUSH}(\mathcal{F}_2)$

15 **return** $\mathbb{T}(f)$ ▷ applying Def. 7

We propose an abstraction-refinement-based approach to synthesize a tree from a given template that maximizes the value among all trees in the template. The basic idea is borrowed from [14]. For a given family $\mathcal{F}$ (starting from $\mathcal{F}^{\mathbb{T}}$), an abstraction $M(\mathcal{F})$ is built that allows either prune the family from the search space or splitting the family into smaller subfamilies that are recursively analyzed. In order to prune family $\mathcal{F}$, we compute the maximizing policy σ for (sub-)MDP $M(\mathcal{F})$ and either show that no $f \in \mathcal{F}$ has a better value than the current optimum or that σ is $\mathbb{T}$-implementable using SMT encoding from above, updating the optimum. Otherwise, we will divide and conquer $\mathcal{F}$ by partitioning it. We guide the partitioning using harmonization.

The approach is summarized in Algorithm 1. On l.1, we start with a stack $\mathfrak{F}$ of sub-families, initially containing $\mathcal{F}^{\mathbb{T}}$, and initialize the running optimum f_{best} and its value V_{best}. In every iteration, we pop a family $\mathcal{F}$ from the stack, build the corresponding $M(\mathcal{F})$ and compute the policy σ that maximizes $\mathbb{P}[M(\mathcal{F}) \models \Diamond G]$ (ll. 3–5). If its value $V(\sigma)$ is worse than V_{best}, then no assignment in $\mathcal{F}$ induces a tree with a better value, and thus this family is pruned from the search space (l.6). Otherwise, we solve the SMT formula $\text{pol}(\mathcal{F}, \sigma)$ to check whether σ is $\mathbb{T}$-implementable. If $f \in \mathcal{F}$ is a parameter assignment s.t. $\sigma_{\mathbb{T}(f)} = \sigma$, we update the running optimum and prune the family (l.7). Otherwise, on ll.8–13 we split $\mathcal{F}$ into sub-families $\mathcal{F}_1, \mathcal{F}_2$ and push these onto the stack $\mathfrak{F}$ (l.14).

Theorem 4. *Algorithm 1 is sound and complete.* Proof in [5, App. A.5].

Any nontrivial splitting makes Algorithm 1 terminate: the number $|\mathcal{F}^{\mathbb{T}}|$ of parameterizations is finite and, in the worst case, a nontrivial splitting yields a family with a single assignment f, in which case $M(\{f\})$ is an MC with only one policy $\sigma_{\mathbb{T}(f)}$ and the SMT formula $\mathsf{pol}(\{f\}, \sigma_{\mathbb{T}(f)})$ is satisfiable with parameter assignment f. However, even for a tree template of small depth, the number of template instantiations is insurmountable, and thus, a proper splitting strategy should yield sub-families that can be pruned as soon as possible.

To deal with enormous design spaces, the abstraction refinement framework of [14] successfully used the notion of inconsistent variables (holes), where a split was made on a hole for which the optimizing policy wanted to pick multiple values. In our framework, the harmonising variable x_h plays the role of this inconsistent hole, and therefore, on l.8, we extract the unsatisfiable core (see Remark 3) and solve the SMT formula $\mathsf{pol}^H(\mathcal{F}, \sigma)$, as described in Sect. 3.2. Assume the formula is SAT with the harmonising variable x_h and f_1, f_2 is the corresponding pair of trees that differ in the value of x_h. We then split $\mathcal{F}$ into subfamilies $\mathcal{F}_1, \mathcal{F}_2$ by splitting the domain $\mathcal{F}(x_h)$ s.t. $f_1(x_h) \in \mathcal{F}_1(x_h)$ and $f_2(x_h) \in \mathcal{F}_2(x_h)$; if x_h is a variable encoding bound selection function $\mathcal{B}_n$, then its domain (initially, an interval) is split into two sub-intervals. The idea here is to build in subsequent iterations sub-MDPs $M(\mathcal{F}_1), M(\mathcal{F}_2)$ that do not contain σ, although this cannot always be guaranteed. Otherwise, if the harmonising formula is unsatisfiable, we split the family arbitrarily on some parameter from $\mathcal{X}^{\mathsf{UC}}$. We remark that during our experiments, the harmonising formula was practically always satisfiable. Additionally, on ll.10–11 we update the value of V_{best} based on the values $V(f_1), V(f_2)$. Empirically, this leads to a mildly better performance.

Bounded-Depth Synthesis. Even for modest values of k, Algorithm 1 cannot explore all parameter assignments. Finding good assignments early can accelerate abstraction refinement [1,14] as it prunes sub-optimal families faster. Thus, when searching for the optimal k-tree, it can be beneficial to first go through families of 0-, 1-, 2-trees, etc., where good values are easier to find. This idea inspired the *bounded-depth mode* of our abstraction refinement approach that proceeds as follows. We iteratively use Algorithm 1 on templates of trees of depths $0, 1, \ldots, k_{\max}$; in each iteration, we keep the current optimum f_{best} and its value V_{best} and use it in subsequent iterations. To ensure that the algorithm reaches depth $k_{\max}$, we run Algorithm 1 on lower depths $0, 1, \ldots, k_{\max}-1$ with a timeout, that we empirically choose to be $t/(2 \cdot k_{\max})$, such that at least 50% of the given time is dedicated to the search on depth $k_{\max}$.

Tree Hints. Having (partially) explored a family of $(k-1)$-trees, we can accelerate the search for the best k-tree even further by first looking at k-trees that mimic a good $(k-1)$-tree $\mathcal{T}_{k-1}$. Our abstraction-refinement approach on families naturally supports this idea: before running Algorithm 1 with a stack containing the whole family $\mathcal{F}^{\mathbb{T}_k}$ for a tree template $\mathbb{T}_k$ of depth k, we can first make it look within the family $\mathcal{F}'$ of assignments that mimic $\mathcal{T}_{k-1}$. Intuitively, $\mathcal{F}' \subset \mathcal{F}^{\mathbb{T}_k}$ describes all k-trees that, in the inner nodes on the first $k-1$ levels, behave according to $\mathcal{T}_{k-1}$, and behave arbitrarily on the last k-th level as well as in the leaves. Putting family $\mathcal{F}'$ on top of the stack prioritizes the search for the best k-tree within this family, increasing the chance of finding good k-trees early.

Tree Post-processing. We perform two steps to remove redundant nodes. First, we remove every node $n \in N \cup L$ for which $\mathsf{st}^T(n) = \emptyset$, that is, no state $s \in S$ can take a path to n. Second, if for a node $n \in N$ it holds that $l(n), r(n) \in L$ and $\delta(l(n)) = \delta(r(n))$, i.e. the children are leaves selecting the same action, then both children are removed, and n becomes a leaf associated with this action.

5   Experimental Evaluation

In the experimental evaluation, we investigate the performance of the proposed synthesis algorithm DTPAYNT. DTPAYNT is an algorithm that solves the bounded-depth synthesis problem (with an explicit timeout) using abstraction refinement in a bounded-depth mode using tree hints as described in Sect. 4.2. DTPAYNT is implemented on top of PAYNT [3] and STORM [24], utilising Z3 [33] to solve SMT queries. The implementation and all the considered benchmarks are publicly available[3]. Our evaluation focuses on the following four questions:

Q1: *Does* DTPAYNT *outperform* OMDT [41] *that is based on a MILP formulation? Can* DTPAYNT *scale to more complex MDPs?*

Q2: *Does* DTPAYNT *provide a good trade-off between value and size of the synthesized trees compared to* DTCONTROL [6]*?*

Q3: *Can* DTPAYNT *handle huge MDPs having up to 1M states?*

Q4: *Can we use* DTPAYNT *as a reduction procedure for large DTs?*

Setting. The timeout (TO) for all experiments was 20 min[4]. All the experiments were run on a machine equipped with AMD EPYC 9124 16-core Processor and 380GB RAM. Each method was run on a single CPU core.

Benchmarks. In order to answer the questions Q1 and Q2, we consider three types of benchmarks: (1) The 11 models from OMDT [41] using expected discounted rewards. (2) The standard MDP benchmarks from the QComp evaluation [13] with 8 models with state variables defined. Since OMDT requires discounted-reward specifications, we derived such specifications for these QComp models. (3) Two fully observable variants of the classical *maze* [23] problem with a discounted-reward specifications. Information about the models is reported in [5, App. B]. In order to perform a fair comparison of the tools, we modify the models as follows: (1) We equip all the models with the action α_{rand} that uniformly selects the available actions (recall Definition 4). (2) We ensure that in every state, all actions in *Act* are available[5], as it is required by the available implementation of OMDT. We note that, in theory, the approach proposed in [41] can handle MDPs where not every action is available in every state, however, there is currently no implementation which supports this. Also note that this modification effectively makes the synthesis task on these models more difficult. We group the benchmarks into two categories: (1) *smaller models* with

---

[3] https://doi.org/10.5281/zenodo.15228774.

[4] Based on our preliminary experiments as well as the results from [41].

[5] The actions added to the original QComp models behave as α_{rand}.

the number of choices ($|S| \cdot |Act|$) below 3k and (2) *larger models* with up to 10k states and 175k choices. Overall, we have 10 smaller models and 11 larger models.

Q1: Comparison with *OMDT*

We consider the bounded-depth synthesis problem and compare DTPAYNT with OMDT. We performed a comparison including all benchmarks and tree depths up to $k = 8$. The comparison therefore includes $21 \cdot 8 = 168$ instances.

Results. Figure 3 shows two scatter plots that visualize the normalized values of the best k-DTs found by DTPAYNT and OMDT. The values are normalized such that 0 corresponds to a uniform random policy and 1 to an optimal MDP policy. The uniform random policy can be represented with a 0-DT that chooses the action α_{rand}[6]. Note that the normalized value 1.0 represents the value of the optimal MDP strategy, which might not be reachable for a given synthesis problem with bounded depth. We split the results according to the size of the MDP and the depth k to highlight the scalability advantage of DTPAYNT over OMDT. Detailed statistics for the experiments are reported in [5, App. C].

On the Smaller Models, Both Tools Perform Very Similarly. With growing k, both tools produce DTs with an increasing performance that gets close to the optimal value. OMDT finds slightly better DTs on two models: *lake-12* and *sys-2*.

On the Majority of the Larger Models, DTPAYNT Outperforms OMDT Significantly. In fact, there is no larger model in our data set where OMDT performs better at any depth k. OMDT is only able to keep up with DTPAYNT on

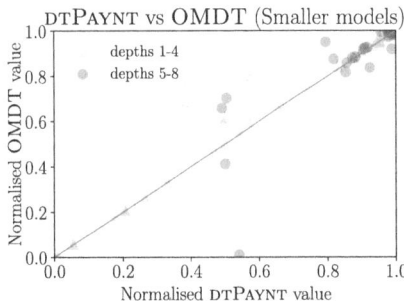
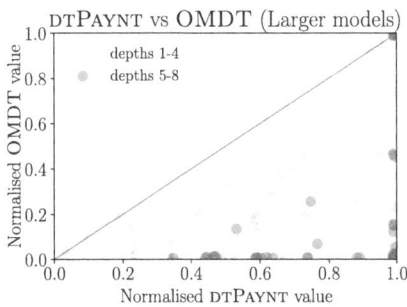

Fig. 3. Comparison on the bounded-depth synthesis problem for Q1. The scatter plot shows the normalized values of the best k-DTs found in the 20-min timeout. A point (x, y) shows the value of the best k-DT found by DTPAYNT (the x-value) and OMDT (the y-value) for a specific model and a specific depth k. Points below the diagonal shows the synthesis problems where DTPAYNT outperforms OMDT. The plot on the left compares performance on smaller models (less than 3k choices), and the plot on the right compares performance on larger models.

---

[6] Note that this value is not a strict lower bound on the worst policy.

the model *inventory* and for smaller k on *firewire-3*. On the other models, the performance gap is significant. The greatest difference was observed on models *resource*, *pnueli* and *csma* where DTPAYNT is able to find a tree with value within 1% of the optimum while OMDT struggles to improve on the best 0-DT. Another observation is that with increasing k, DTPAYNT mostly improves, but OMDT struggles even more to find good DTs. This can be seen by the higher occurrence of the green dots at the bottom of the plot. These results clearly demonstrate the scalability advantage of DTPAYNT compared to OMDT.

Runtimes. In most cases, both tools reach the 20-min timeout: DTPAYNT is not able to completely explore all DTs up to the given depth; OMDT is not able to reduce the gap between the lower and upper bound in the underlying MILP below the given precision. However, we observe (see [5, Fig. 6] in [5, App. C.1]) that typically DTPAYNT finds better DTs significantly faster.

Conclusion. For simple synthesis problems (smaller MDPs or depths), our approach is competitive with the monolithic MILP formulation. For larger models, solving MILP is no longer tractable while DTPAYNT is able to find high-quality DTs and keep its performance even for higher values of k. This clearly demonstrates the significant advantage of DTPAYNT over OMDT.

Q2: Size and Value Trade-off Comparison with dtControl

DTCONTROL, in contrast to OMDT and DTPAYNT, solves the policy mapping problem; it takes a policy σ and constructs a DT representing σ. It favors scalability over minimality, i.e., it does not search for the smallest DT representing σ. Thus, DTCONTROL excels in finding a DT representing the given optimal policy even for large MDPs. In this section, we demonstrate the key advantage of DTPAYNT: it is able to effectively control the trade-offs between the size and value of the resulting DTs at the cost of scalability.

Setting. Figure 4 reports the trade-offs achieved by DTs of different depths compared to the DT produced by DTCONTROL. The figure contains results for 13 models (out of the 21 models) that demonstrate the key observations we made; complete results can be found in [5, App. C]. As before, the timeout for each experiment (model and depth) is 20 min. The upper part compares the normalized values achieved by the particular DTs produced by DTPAYNT. The lower part of Fig. 4 compares the sizes of DTs (the number of inner nodes). Recall that DTPAYNT optimizes the depth, and thus, the number of inner nodes can be larger than in DTCONTROL, although the depth of the DT is smaller.

Preprocessing for DTCONTROL . In order to provide a fair comparison, we perform the following preprocessing of the policy σ for DTCONTROL: we remove from its tabular representation the states in the goal set G and the states that

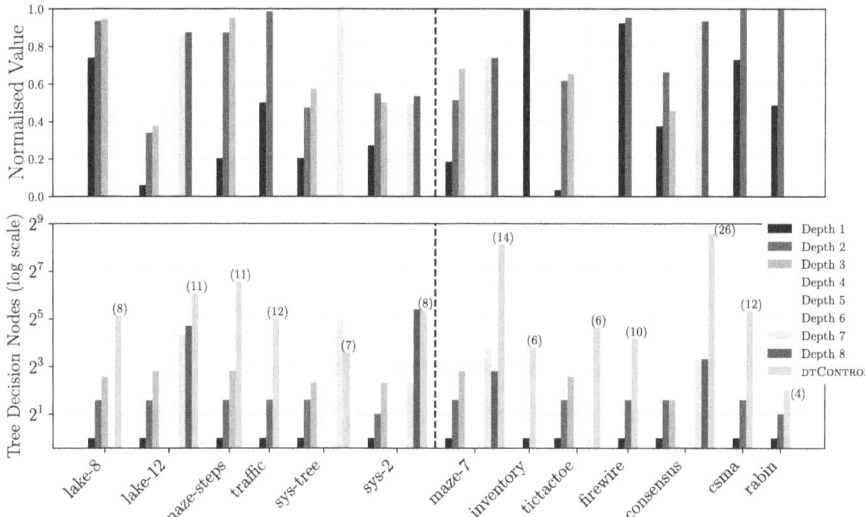

Fig. 4. The plot shows the trade-off between the value and size of the DTs found by DTPAYNT and DTCONTROL. The left part contains smaller models, and the right part contains larger ones. The upper part shows the normalized values of the synthesized DTs (the same normalization as in Q1). DTCONTROL maps an optimal policy with the value 1 (not shown). The lower part shows the number of inner nodes using a logarithmic scale. We report the performance of DTPAYNT for depths 1 to 8 (if a DT with a normalized value above 0.95 is obtained, we exclude the subsequent depths on the given model to simplify the plot). Numbers in brackets above the DTCONTROL bars denote the depth of the DT.

are unreachable in M^σ. This helps DTCONTROL to find significantly (5–10 times in some cases) smaller DTs. DTPAYNT performs this simplification implicitly.

Results. On the majority of the models, DTPAYNT finds DTs that provides good trade-offs between the size and value. On the models *inventory, csma* and *rabin*, DTPAYNT finds a DT that achieves the optimal value, while the number of inner nodes is reduced by 2 times (for *rabin*) up to 16 times (for *inventory*) compared to the DTs constructed by DTCONTROL. On the other 6 models, DTPAYNT is able to find a DT with a normalized value better than 0.9 while producing a more compact DT compared to DTCONTROL. These DTs are, on average, 3-5 times smaller. The most interesting trade-off can be observed on the model *consensus*, where the DT produced by DTPAYNT is 38-times smaller (note that the bottom plot in Fig. 4 uses logarithmic scale) while its normalized value is above 0.93. On the models *sys-tree* and *tictactoe*, DTPAYNT finds a DT that achieves the optimal value, but it has more inner nodes compared to the one from DTCONTROL. For the models where good DTs require depth $k \geq 8$, such as *lake-12, sys-2* and *maze-7*, DTPAYNT is not capable of finding a DT that achieves a value close to 1, but it still provides a reasonable trade-off. In the case of *maze-7*, DTPAYNT finds a 25 times smaller DT that achieves normalized value 0.76.

Runtimes. The runtimes for DTCONTROL are less than 2 s for all benchmarks. While DTPAYNT usually finds the best DT long before the 20-min timeout is reached, it would still benefit from a longer timeout for larger depths.

Conclusions. We show the advantages and limitations of using DTPAYNT in comparison to DTCONTROL. While DTPAYNT iteratively performs analysis of the underlying MDP and solves complicated SMT queries that hinder the scalability, it is able, in contrast to DTCONTROL, to effectively explore alternative policies. This is essential for constructing smaller and thus more explainable DTs.

Q3: Scalability of dtPaynt on Very Large MDPs

The goal of the experiment is to demonstrate that DTPAYNT can handle much larger MDPs than those considered in Q1 and Q2 provided that a small DT with the desired performance exists. There are generally three reasons why small DTs suffice: (1) The optimal policy induces only a very small MC, and thus the optimal DT needs to encode the decision only for a small subset of states. (2) In many states, there is only one available action, and thus the optimal DT does not need to encode decisions in these states. (3) In many states, playing the random action α_{rand} that uniformly selects one of the available actions is sufficient to obtain the optimal performance. DTPAYNT, in contrast to OMDT and DTCONTROL, naturally leverages all three features; recall Definition 4 (induced policy) and our SMT encoding. Note that the experimental setting in Q1 and Q2 was designed with the goal of providing a fair comparison among the tools, and this advantage of DTPAYNT was not fully exploited.

Setting. We consider MDPs with up to 1M states. We take MDPs from the QComp benchmark set and scale them up using their parameters. We run DTPAYNT for depths 0 to 4. Table 1 reports selected results that demonstrate the key observations within Q3. We compare the results with DTCONTROL that maps the optimal policy σ^*. To provide a fair comparison, we exclude from σ^* the unreachable states (as in Q2) and states where only one action is available (such states were not in Q2). We report the size of the pre-processed policy as $|\sigma_{rel}^*|$[7].

Results. Except for the *ij-20* model, the pre-processing drastically reduces the size of σ^*. The optimal DTs thus need to encode significantly less state compared to the size of S. For the first two models, DTPAYNT finds a 0-DT with the optimal value. It selects a single action $\alpha \neq \alpha_{rand}$ and exploits the fact that playing α_{rand} in the states where $\alpha \notin Act(s)$ is optimal. Although trivial policies suffice in these two models, they showcase the ability of DTPAYNT to steer towards simpler policies, while DTCONTROL returns very complicated DTs despite the pre-processing. Note that the QComp benchmark contains several other synthesis problems where simple randomization is sufficient. In the other models in the

---

[7] $|\sigma_{rel}^*|$ can be further reduced, at the expense of precision, by considering only states with a high probability of being visited [12]. We left this idea for future work.

Table 1. This table presents selected results of the synthesis for large MDPs. It shows the normalized values (as before), the number of inner nodes and the time it took to find the DTs. $|\sigma^*_{rel}|$ is the size of the preprocessed policy σ^*.

model	$|S|$	choices	DTPAYNT			DTCONTROL		
			value	nodes	time	$|\sigma^*_{rel}|$	nodes	time
ij-20	1M	10M	1	0	547 s	624k	393k	210 s
pnueli-zuck-5	308k	1.7M	1	0	103 s	2395	1258	1 s
firewire-f-36	212k	479k	1	14	531 s	376	12	1 s
pacman-30	853k	1.1M	0.76	6	1360 s	673	144	1 s
firewire-t-3-600	1.1M	1.5M	0.85	8	3135 s	1147	12	1 s

table, the randomization is not optimal. For the *firewire-f-36* model, DTPAYNT finds an optimal DT with a depth lower than DTCONTROL (4 vs. 7), but it has two more inner nodes. For the last two models, DTPAYNT finds DTs that achieve a reasonable performance while being smaller (24-fold for *pacman-30*) compared to the DTs produced by DTCONTROL.

Conclusions. DTPAYNT is able to find small DTs with a good performance even for very large MDPs with hundreds of thousands of states. In some cases, it finds optimal DTs that are smaller than the DTs constructed by DTCONTROL.

Q4: Using dtPaynt as a Reduction Procedure for Large DTs

Finally, we discuss an alternative use of DTPAYNT that demonstrates its broader applicability even to MDPs that require large DTs. The main idea is that DTPAYNT can be used as a procedure for minimizing decision trees by analyzing individual sub-trees in a DT and trying to find an adequate smaller alternative for a given sub-tree. We give a short and simple outline below. For a more detailed discussion on this use of DTPAYNT, refer to our follow-up paper [4].

Using DTPAYNT *in a Compositional Manner.* We take a large DT $\mathcal{T}$ representing an optimal policy for the given MDP and investigate whether DTPAYNT can find a smaller variant of this DT. Therefore, we consider $\mathcal{T}$ and its sub-tree $\mathcal{T}_n$ given by an inner node n in $\mathcal{T}$ (i.e. n is the root of $\mathcal{T}_n$). We build a tree template $\mathbb{T}_n$ by fixing all nodes outside $\mathcal{T}_n$ to coincide with $\mathcal{T}$. For the nodes in $\mathcal{T}_n$, we define Γ and Δ as in Definition 5. The size of the sub-tree $\mathcal{T}_n$ indeed determines the size of $\mathbb{T}_n$, and also the complexity of the synthesis problem: $\mathbb{T}_n$ defines a partial policy and thus induces a (possibly much smaller) subset of states that has to be considered in the synthesis process. DTPAYNT can straightforwardly take $\mathbb{T}_n$ and synthesize a new smaller tree $\mathcal{T}'_n$ to replace $\mathcal{T}_n$ in $\mathcal{T}$ to reduce the total number of inner nodes. We can allow a certain error with respect to the optimal policy to increase the possible reduction. This process can be applied iteratively on different sub-trees on the original DT $\mathcal{T}$.

Setting. We consider two more complex variants of the models from Q1 and Q2: i) *consensus-Q4* has only 23k states, but the DT found by DTCONTROL has depth 19 and 841 inner nodes; ii) *csma-Q4* has 1.5M states and the DT found by DTCONTROL has depth 19 and 236 nodes. In both cases, DTPAYNT fails to find a small DT with a reasonable performance. To obtain a smaller DT with almost optimal value, we take the DT $\mathcal{T}$ produced by DTCONTROL and iteratively run DTPAYNT on templates induced by all sub-trees of $\mathcal{T}$ of depth 7 (and consequently on depth 6 if all sub-trees of depth 7 were processed). We allow an *absolute error* of 1% with respect to the optimal policy.

Results. For the *consensus-Q4* model, DTPAYNT analyzed in 1 h 54 different sub-trees and found 37 smaller sub-trees that were used to replace the original ones in $\mathcal{T}$. The resulting DT has a depth of 16 and 452 inner nodes, signifying a 46% decrease in size, while its normalized value is 0.99. For the *csma-Q4* model, DTPAYNT analyzed in 30 min 34 different sub-trees and found 24 smaller sub-trees. The resulting DT has depth 6 and 22 inner nodes, signifying a 90% decrease in size, while its normalized value is 0.99.

Conclusions. Although the scalability of DTPAYNT itself is limited if a deep tree is needed to achieve the desired quality of the resulting policy, we demonstrate that DTPAYNT can be effectively used to reduce the size of large DTs even in large MDPs. Thus DTPAYNT provides an important contribution towards the automated construction of near-optimal smaller DTs for complex problems.

6   Related Work

The related work in learning [6] and MILP-based synthesis [41] of decision trees as well as in deductive controller synthesis [2] is discussed in the introduction.

Learning Concise Representation of Neural Policies. With the boom of explainable reinforcement learning, various methods for learning concise representations of neural policies have been proposed. Imitation learning methods such as VIPER [9] extract a DT from a more complex teacher policy using a supervised learning paradigm. As shown in [41], imitating a complex policy using a small DT can lead to poor performance as the limited capacity of the DT is used ineffectively. A different approach for overcoming this limitation has been recently proposed in [38]. The authors introduce a new type of MDP (so-called iterative bounding MDP) where each policy corresponds to a DT policy for the base MDP. Especially for small DTs, this approach significantly outperforms VIPER. A different line of work focuses on learning a programmatic representation of policies using an oracle in the form of neural policy. In the seminal paper [40], the authors showed how to search over programmatic policies that minimize the distance from the oracle. More recently, a fast distillation method that uses regularized oblique trees to produce tree programs that fits neural oracle has been proposed [26].

Beyond DTs. Recently, alternative representations of policies in MDPs have been studied. In [10], the authors establish a tight connection between program-level construction of strategies resolving nondeterminism in probabilistic programs and finding good policies in (countably infinite) MDPs. This enables a direct construct of programmatic policies. A different line of work introduces templates of decision diagrams using hierarchical control structures with under-specified entities to encapsulate and reuse common decision-making patterns [20]. In contrast to our templates used to effectively reason about sets of DTs, the hierarchical decision diagrams aim at a more concise and explainable representation of the policies.

7 Conclusion

We present DTPAYNT, a novel approach to synthesize small DTs providing good trade-offs between quality and size. Our experiments demonstrate clear advantages with respect to the state-of-the-art. In the future, we will investigate how to improve the scalability: (1) exploit counterexamples [39] in the synthesis of DTs, (2) symbiotically combine DTPAYNT with DTCONTROL in a more efficient synthesis loop to improve over the ideas in Q4, and (3) construct the DTs only for a subset of most relevant states as in [12].

Acknowledgments. 🌐 This work has been executed under the project VASSAL: "Verification and Analysis for Safety and Security of Applications in Life" funded by the European Union under Horizon Europe WIDERA Coordination and Support Action/Grant Agreement No. 101160022 and the NWO VENI Grant ProMiSe (222.147). This work has been also funded by the Czech Science Foundation grant GA23-06963S (VESCAA) and the IGA VUT project FIT-S-23-8151.

Disclosure of Interests. The authors have no competing interests to declare that are relevant to the content of this article.

References

1. Andriushchenko, R., Češka, M., Junges, S., Katoen, J.P.: Inductive synthesis for probabilistic programs reaches new horizons. In: TACAS. LNCS, vol. 12651, pp. 191–209. Springer (2021)
2. Andriushchenko, R., Češka, M., Junges, S., Katoen, J.P.: Inductive synthesis of finite-state controllers for POMDPs. In: UAI, vol. 180, pp. 85–95. PMRL (2022)
3. Andriushchenko, R., Češka, M., Junges, S., Katoen, J.P., Stupinský, Š.: PAYNT: a tool for inductive synthesis of probabilistic programs. In: CAV. LNCS, vol. 12759, pp. 856–869. Springer (2021)
4. Andriushchenko, R., Češka, M., Chakraborty, D., Junges, S., Křetinský, J., Macák, F.: Symbiotic local search for small decision tree policies in MDPs. In: UAI (to appear) (2025)

190 R. Andriushchenko et al.

5. Andriushchenko, R., Češka, M., Junges, S., Macák, F.: Small decision trees for MDPs with deductive synthesis (2025). https://arxiv.org/abs/2501.10126
6. Ashok, P., Jackermeier, M., Křetínský, J., Weinhuber, C., Weininger, M., Yadav, M.: dtcontrol 2.0: explainable strategy representation via decision tree learning steered by experts. In: TACAS. LNCS, vol. 12652, pp. 326–345. Springer (2021)
7. Ashok, P., Křetínský, J., Larsen, K.G., Le Coënt, A., Taankvist, J.H., Weininger, M.: SOS: safe, optimal and small strategies for hybrid Markov decision processes. In: QEST, pp. 147–164. Springer (2019)
8. Baier, C., de Alfaro, L., Forejt, V., Kwiatkowska, M.: Model checking probabilistic systems. In: Handbook of Model Checking, pp. 963–999. Springer (2018)
9. Bastani, O., Pu, Y., Solar-Lezama, A.: Verifiable reinforcement learning via policy extraction. In: Advances in Neural Information Processing Systems, vol. 31 (2018)
10. Batz, K., Biskup, T.J., Katoen, J.P., Winkler, T.: Programmatic strategy synthesis: resolving nondeterminism in probabilistic programs. Proc. ACM Program. Lang. 8(POPL), 2792–2820 (2024)
11. Biere, A., Heule, M., van Maaren, H.: Handbook of Satisfiability, vol. 185. IOS Press (2009)
12. Brázdil, T., Chatterjee, K., Chmelík, M., Fellner, A., Křetínský, J.: Counterexample explanation by learning small strategies in Markov decision processes. In: CAV, pp. 158–177. Springer (2015)
13. Budde, C.E., et al.: On correctness, precision, and performance in quantitative verification: QComp 2020 competition report. In: ISoLA, pp. 216–241. Springer (2020)
14. Češka, M., Jansen, N., Junges, S., Katoen, J.P.: Shepherding hordes of Markov chains. In: TACAS. LNCS, vol. 11428, pp. 172–190. Springer (2019)
15. Chatterjee, K., Chmelik, M., Topcu, U.: Sensor synthesis for pomdps with reachability objectives. In: ICAPS, pp. 47–55. AAAI Press (2018)
16. David, A., Jensen, P.G., Larsen, K.G., Mikučionis, M., Taankvist, J.H.: Uppaal stratego. In: TACAS, pp. 206–211. Springer (2015)
17. Dehnert, C., Jansen, N., Wimmer, R., Ábrahám, E., Katoen, J.P.: Fast debugging of PRISM models. In: ATVA. LNCS, vol. 8837, pp. 146–162. Springer (2014)
18. Delgrange, F., Katoen, J.P., Quatmann, T., Randour, M.: Simple strategies in multi-objective MDPs. In: TACAS, pp. 346–364. Springer (2020)
19. Drager, K., Forejt, V., Kwiatkowska, M., Parker, D., Ujma, M.: Permissive controller synthesis for probabilistic systems. Log. Methods Comput. Sci. 11 (2015)
20. Dubslaff, C., Klös, V., Päßler, J.: Template decision diagrams for meta control and explainability. In: XAI, pp. 219–242. Springer (2024)
21. Gupta, U.D., Talvitie, E., Bowling, M.: Policy tree: adaptive representation for policy gradient. In: AAAI, vol. 29 (2015)
22. Hancock, T., Jiang, T., Li, M., Tromp, J.: Lower bounds on learning decision lists and trees. Inf. Comput. 126(2), 114–122 (1996)
23. Hauskrecht, M.: Incremental methods for computing bounds in partially observable Markov decision processes. In: AAAI/IAAI, pp. 734–739 (1997)
24. Hensel, C., Junges, S., Katoen, J., Quatmann, T., Volk, M.: The probabilistic model checker Storm. Int. J. Softw. Tools Technol. Transf. 24(4), 589–610 (2022)

25. Junges, S., Jansen, N., Dehnert, C., Topcu, U., Katoen, J.: Safety-constrained reinforcement learning for MDPs. In: TACAS. LNCS, vol. 9636, pp. 130–146. Springer (2016)
26. Kohler, H., Delfosse, Q., Akrour, R., Kersting, K., Preux, P.: Interpretable and editable programmatic tree policies for reinforcement learning. Preprint arXiv:2405.14956 (2024)
27. Konsta, A.M., Lluch Lafuente, A., Matheja, C.: What should be observed for optimal reward in POMDPs? In: CAV, pp. 373–394. Springer (2024)
28. Kumar, A., Zilberstein, S.: History-based controller design and optimization for partially observable MDPs. In: ICAPS, pp. 156–164. AAAI Press (2015)
29. Kwiatkowska, M., Norman, G., Parker, D.: PRISM 4.0: verification of probabilistic real-time systems. In: CAV. LNCS, vol. 6806, pp. 585–591. Springer (2011)
30. Laurent, H., Rivest, R.L.: Constructing optimal binary decision trees is np-complete. Inf. Process. Lett. **5**(1), 15–17 (1976)
31. Li, Y., Yin, B., Xi, H.: Finding optimal memoryless policies of POMDPs under the expected average reward criterion. Eur. J. Oper. Res. **211**(3), 556–567 (2011)
32. Likmeta, A., Metelli, A.M., Tirinzoni, A., Giol, R., Restelli, M., Romano, D.: Combining reinforcement learning with rule-based controllers for transparent and general decision-making in autonomous driving. Robot. Auton. Syst. **131**, 103568 (2020)
33. de Moura, L., Bjørner, N.: Z3: an efficient SMT solver. In: TACAS, pp. 337–340. Springer (2008)
34. Narodytska, N., Ignatiev, A., Pereira, F., Marques-Silva, J.: Learning optimal decision trees with SAT. In: IJCAI, pp. 1362–1368. AAAI Press (2018)
35. Puterman, M.L.: Markov Decision Processes: Discrete Stochastic Dynamic Programming. Wiley Series in Probability and Statistics, Wiley (1994)
36. Puterman, M.L.: Markov Decision Processes: Discrete Stochastic Dynamic Programming. Wiley (2014)
37. Sutton, R.S., Barto, A.G.: Reinforcement Learning: An Introduction. MIT Press (2018)
38. Topin, N., Milani, S., Fang, F., Veloso, M.: Iterative bounding MDPs: learning interpretable policies via non-interpretable methods. In: AAAI, vol. 35, pp. 9923–9931 (2021)
39. Češka, M., Hensel, C., Junges, S., Katoen, J.P.: Counterexample-guided inductive synthesis for probabilistic systems. Form. Asp. Comput. **33**(4–5), 637–667 (2021)
40. Verma, A., Murali, V., Singh, R., Kohli, P., Chaudhuri, S.: Programmatically interpretable reinforcement learning. In: ICML, vol. 80, pp. 5052–5061. PMLR (2018)
41. Vos, D., Verwer, S.: Optimal decision tree policies for Markov decision processes. In: IJCAI, pp. 5457–5465 (2023)

Approximating Fixpoints of Approximated Functions

Paolo Baldan[1]([⊠]) ⓘ, Sebastian Gurke[2] ⓘ, Barbara König[2] ⓘ,
Tommaso Padoan[3] ⓘ, and Florian Wittbold[2] ⓘ

[1] Dipartimento di Matematica "Tullio Levi-Civita",
Università di Padova, Padua, Italy
baldan@math.unipd.it

[2] Universität Duisburg-Essen, Duisburg, Germany

{sebastian.gurke,barbara_koenig,florian.wittbold}@uni-due.de

[3] Università di Trieste, Trieste, Italy
tommaso.padoan@units.it

Abstract. Fixpoints are ubiquitous in computer science and when dealing with quantitative semantics and verification one often considers least fixpoints of (higher-dimensional) functions over the non-negative reals. We show how to approximate the least fixpoint of such functions, focusing on the case in which they are not known precisely, but represented by a sequence of approximating functions that converge to them. We concentrate on monotone and non-expansive functions, for which uniqueness of fixpoints is not guaranteed and standard fixpoint iteration schemes might get stuck at a fixpoint that is not the least. Our main contribution is the identification of an iteration scheme, a variation of Mann iteration with a dampening factor, which, under suitable conditions, is shown to guarantee convergence to the least fixpoint of the function of interest. We then argue that these results are relevant in the context of model-based reinforcement learning for Markov decision processes, showing how the proposed iteration scheme instantiates and allows us to derive convergence to the optimal expected return. More generally, we show that our results can be used to iterate to the least fixpoint almost surely for systems where the function of interest can be approximated with given probabilistic error bounds, as it happens for probabilistic systems which can be explored via sampling.

Keywords: Fixpoints · Approximation · Mann iteration · MDPs

1 Introduction

Fixpoints are fundamental in computer science as they arise as a natural way of providing a meaning to inductive and recursive definitions. When dealing with systems or programming languages embodying quantitative aspects, such as probability, time, or cost, we are often led to consider fixpoints of functions associating states with real values. Fixpoints also occur in optimization methods

R. Piskac and Z. Rakamarić (Eds.): CAV 2025, LNCS 15932, pp. 193–215, 2025.
https://doi.org/10.1007/978-3-031-98679-6_9

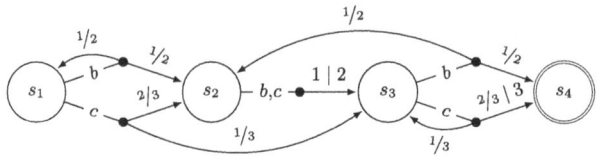

Fig. 1. A Markov decision process

where one typically determines solutions that are stable under suitable transformations. For instance, in probabilistic systems such as finite Markov decision
processes (MDPs) [5], the expected payoff or the likelihood of satisfying a property can be characterized as a (least) fixpoint, from which one can then derive
optimal policies.

The aim of this paper is to develop a theory of fixpoints for functions that
are not completely known but can be approximated. Estimating fixpoints of
unknown functions is a common task in computer science. In the aforementioned
optimization setting, a standard framework is the one in which the parameters
of a dynamic system of interest (e.g. probabilities, rewards, costs) are partially
unknown and can only be estimated by experimenting with the system. This is
exactly what happens in reinforcement learning, a branch of machine learning
that is intended to provide methods for learning optimal policies for an agent in
order to maximize rewards in an unknown dynamic environment.

We exemplify our motivations by focusing on MDPs and (a variant of) the
Dyna-Q algorithm [25,37,38]. Consider the MDP M in Fig. 1 with state set
$S = \{s_1, s_2, s_3, s_4\}$. In each state $s \in S$, the agent can choose an action a from
an action set $A = \{b, c\}$. Performing an action $a \in A$ in state s yields a successor
state s' with a probability $T(s, a, s')$ and results in reward $R(s, a, s')$ (in the
picture, arrows are labelled $T(s, a, s') \mid R(s, a, s')$; if a reward is 0, the vertical
line and the number 0 are omitted). Rewards can be discounted by a factor
$\gamma < 1$ so that rewards obtained in the future are valued less than immediate
rewards.

A typical aim is to determine a policy for the agent which maximises the
expected return. The expected return (also called payoff or total reward) $q(s, a)$
at state s taking action a can be naturally expressed by means of a recursive
equation, the so-called Bellman equation

$$q(s, a) = \sum_{s' \in S} T(s, a, s')(R(s, a, s') + \gamma \cdot \max_{a' \in A} q(s', a')) \tag{1}$$

stating that $q(s, a)$ coincides with the (discounted) expected returns based on
the successor states. If we denote by $g_M \colon \mathbb{R}^{S \times A} \to \mathbb{R}^{S \times A}$ the operator associated with the MDP, defined by $g_M(q)(s, a) = \sum_{s' \in S} T(s, a, s')(R(s, a, s') + \gamma \cdot$
$\max_{a' \in A} q(s', a'))$, the equation reduces to $q = g_M(q)$ and the maximal expected
reward is the least fixpoint of g_M (unique when $\gamma < 1$ and thus g_M contractive).

Various techniques have been devised for determining such fixpoints. However, in reinforcement learning, the MDP describes the interaction with an envi-

ronment that is unknown or only partially known. In particular, the probabilities $T(s, a, s')$ of arriving in s' after choosing action a in state s can only be estimated, e.g., by sampling. In fact, a natural approach consists in interacting with the model and record how many times one arrives in each state s', after choosing action a in s. If we denote by $N(s, a, s')$ this number, then $T(s, a, s')$ can be estimated as $N(s, a, s')/\sum_{s''} N(s, a, s'')$. Clearly, as we proceed and the number of interactions increases, we can expect to obtain better and better approximations of the MDP. For instance, the Dyna-Q algorithm starts from arbitrary values. At each step, the model is sampled and updated, and then also the values $q(s, a)$ are updated by taking a weighted sum of the previously computed value and the (γ-discounted) expectation of the return according to Eq. (1) (either for selected pairs or for all pairs, the variant that we consider here) according to the following schema:

$$q(s, a) := (1 - \alpha) \cdot q(s, a) + \alpha \cdot \sum_{s' \in S} T(s, a, s')(R(s, a, s') + \gamma \cdot \max_{a' \in A} q(s', a')) \quad (2)$$

which, using function g_M, becomes $q := (1 - \alpha) \cdot q + \alpha \cdot g_M(q)$. The weighted sum makes the update more conservative, with a value of α closer to 0 giving more relevance to the past knowledge. As the number of samplings increases, better approximations of the MDP are obtained, leading to better q-values.

Several other model-based algorithms use variations of this scheme, where the updates (determining the value vector and the optimal policy) and the exploration of the model are interleaved [25,31]. Model-free versions, such as Q-learning [40] or SARSA [36], do not explicitly build a model of the MDP.

The schema (2) above resembles iteration algorithms for determining the fixpoint of the function $g_M \colon \mathbb{R}^{S \times A} \to \mathbb{R}^{S \times A}$ associated to the MDP. When $\alpha = 1$, we obtain Kleene iteration which converges to the least fixpoint for monotone functions over a complete lattice, starting the iteration from the least element. In general, it corresponds to a Mann iteration [6] which, under suitable hypotheses, converges to a fixpoint of a continuous function starting from any initial state. The twist here is that the function f is not fixed, but can only be approximated, since the probabilities $T(s, a, s')$ (and possibly also the rewards $R(s, a, s')$) change and will be updated during the iteration.

Aim of the Paper. Our aim is to develop a fixpoint theory of approximated functions of which the scenario above is a special case. There is a large body of work guaranteeing the existence of fixpoints for certain classes of functions and providing methods for computing them. This includes, for instance, Banach's fixpoint theorem for contractive functions over complete metric spaces [4], Knaster-Tarski theorem for monotone functions over complete lattices [39] that is frequently employed in computer science, and Kleene iteration [14].

There is much less work on how to compute (least) fixpoints for a function which is not known exactly, but can only be obtained by a sequence of subsequently better approximations. As we will see, developing such a theory is relatively simple when the functions of interest are contractions (or power contractions) whose (repeated) application decreases the distance of two vectors by

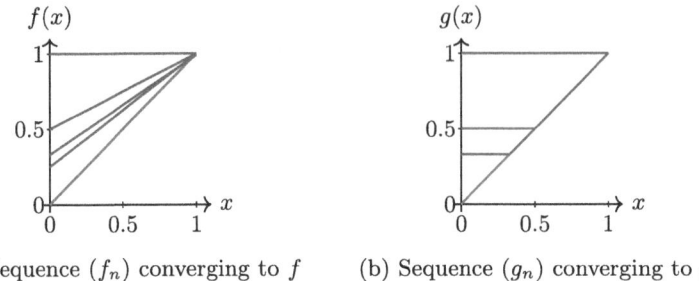

(a) Sequence (f_n) converging to f (b) Sequence (g_n) converging to g

Fig. 2. Problems in determining least fixpoints of approximated functions.

a factor $\gamma < 1$. This happens, for instance, for reinforcement learning in the discounted case (cf. the proof of correctness of Q-learning [40] based on stochastic approximation theory [7]). However, in this paper, we are also and, actually, mostly interested in the non-discounted case ($\gamma = 1$) where the functions are just non-expansive (the distance of two vectors after function application is bounded by their original distance) and the aim is to determine their least fixpoints. We remark that working on the non-discounted case is sometimes the only appropriate choice, e.g., when the reward represents the likelihood of eventually satisfying a given property.

We will concentrate on functions that are monotone and non-expansive with respect to the supremum norm. Besides policy computation for MDPs, a number of other applications consider value vectors which can be characterized as (least) fixpoints of functions of this kind, e.g., computing bisimilarity metrics [1], solving (simple) stochastic games [12,26], or model-checking quantitative logics on probabilistic systems [24,30].

Least Fixpoints of Simple Functions are not Easy to Compute. As a warm up, we consider some simple examples showing that computing the least fixpoint of an approximated function is non-trivial. Let $f \colon \mathbb{R}_{\geq 0} \to \mathbb{R}_{\geq 0}$ be a non-expansive and monotone function over the non-negative reals. A non-expansive function is also continuous. Moreover, if it has a fixpoint, it has a least fixpoint μf which can be computed by Kleene iteration, that is, the sequence $0, f(0), f^2(0), \dots$ converges to μf. Now, assume that f is not known exactly, but can only be approximated via a sequence of functions f_n converging to f. One might think that Kleene iteration can be easily adapted to deal with this situation. We provide some examples showing that, instead, non-trivial problems arise.

Example 1.1 (Non-continuity of the least fixpoint operator). Take $f, f_n \colon [0,1] \to [0,1]$, $n \in \mathbb{N}$, with $f_n(x) = \frac{1}{n} + (1 - \frac{1}{n}) \cdot x$, $f(x) = x$, as depicted in Fig. 2a.

The least (and only) fixpoint of each approximation f_n is 1, while the least fixpoint of f is 0. Hence, $\lim_{n \to \infty} \mu f_n = 1 \neq 0 = \mu f$, i.e., the least fixpoint operator is non-continuous. In particular, trying to obtain an approximation of the least fixpoint of f by naively performing a Kleene iteration on any fixed approximation f_n is doomed to fail, as we will always converge to 1 instead of 0.

Example 1.2 (Kleene over improving approximations fails). Take $g, g_n \colon [0,1] \to [0,1]$ with $g_n(x) = \frac{1}{n}$ if $x \leq \frac{1}{n}$, $g_n(x) = x$ otherwise, and $g(x) = x$, as depicted in Fig. 2b. In this case, $\lim_{n \to \infty} \mu g_n = 0 = \mu g$, hence the sequence of least fixpoints of the approximations will converge to the least fixpoint of g. But imagine that we want to reuse intermediate results once we have obtained a better approximating function. This is what is done in reinforcement learning where one alternates sampling and iteration of the estimated value function. In this scenario, this would mean that we have already obtained an approximation of μg, based on a Kleene iteration with some g_n. This will, however, over-estimate the least fixpoint of g by $1/n$ and further iterating on the previously obtained approximation of μg with "better" functions g_m $(m > n)$ will never decrease it.

Example 1.3 (Approximations might not have fixpoints). Let $h, h_n \colon \mathbb{R}_{\geq 0} \to \mathbb{R}_{\geq 0}$ where $h_n(x) = x + 1/n$ and $h(x) = x$. Here, functions h_n have no fixpoint while the least fixpoint of h is 0. We want to be able to compute μh even in such cases.

A Fixpoint Theory for Approximated Functions. As a first option, one could think of confining the attention to contractive or power contractive functions, where the problem mentioned above do not occur. This, however, would restrict applicability to probabilistic systems that have some form of stopping condition which typically produce functions of this kind (e.g. MDPs without end components) or force the use of a discount factor.

Another option would be to restart the (Kleene) fixpoint iteration from scratch for each newly obtained approximation f_n, a technique, called *resetting* in the paper, which resembles certainty equivalent methods in reinforcement learning [28]. Even when this approach is viable, it precludes the reuse of approximations obtained in a previous step, making it very inefficient and inadequate in scenarios where live value estimates are required.

We propose a solution that does neither: we allow non-expansive functions and interleave sampling and fixpoint iteration, which allows us to continue from previously computed approximations. The central idea is to combine the fixpoint iteration with a dampening factor that can be seen as a form of discount factor that "vanishes" over time. It is inspired by work in [27] which, however, does not apply to our setting since it does not deal with approximations. Furthermore, it puts stronger restrictions on the iteration parameters and the space where the functions are defined, preventing its use for the applications we have in mind.

To be more precise, given a function f over d-tuples of positive reals we propose what we call a *dampened Mann iteration*:

$$x_{n+1} = (1 - \beta_n) \cdot (\alpha_n \cdot x_n + (1 - \alpha_n) \cdot f(x_n)) \qquad (3)$$

The genesis of this recursion scheme can be explained as follows: As a first step the right-hand side of a simple Kleene-iteration is replaced, as in the case of Dyna-Q, with a weighted sum $\alpha \cdot x_n + (1 - \alpha) \cdot f(x_n)$ for some parameter α. Next, we allow this parameter to be potentially different in every step, i.e. for a fixed sequence (α_n) in the unit interval we consider the sequence generated by the recursion $x_{n+1} := \alpha_n \cdot x_n + (1 - \alpha_n) \cdot f(x_n)$. Recursion schemes of this form are called Mann iterations and can in some cases be used to improve convergence properties of the generated sequence to a larger class of functions f than only contractive functions. Indeed, one of the more elementary results on Mann iterations states that if $f\colon [a, b] \to [a, b]$ is any continuous function on a bounded interval, then choosing a parameter sequence (α_n) with $\alpha_n \to 1$ and $\sum_n (1 - \alpha_n) = \infty$ guarantees that the corresponding Mann iteration always converges to some fixed point of f for any choice of initial value $x_0 \in [a, b]$ [9].

There are many results that guarantee the (weak) convergence of a Mann iteration in more general spaces under more restrictive assumptions on the function f and/or other assumptions on the parameter sequences [6,16]. The existing results in the literature are, however, not directly applicable to the problem we want to solve since the assumptions on the surrounding space are often too restrictive and, more importantly, since we specifically want to find the *least fixed point* of a function. Note that a Mann iteration that starts on some fixed point x_0 of f which is not the least will get stuck there forever. For the notion of a least fixed point to be well-defined we, on the other hand, will – unlike most literature on Mann iterations we are aware of – always assume that the map f is monotone with respect to the pointwise order.

To be able to always guarantee the convergence to the least fixed point and also to deal with approximations later on, we add – as a last step – the dampening factor $(1 - \beta_n)$ to the iteration scheme.

Depending on the setting, we will require conditions on the coefficients α_n, they must either converge to 0 (Mann-Kleene scheme) or to a value strictly less than 1 (relaxed Mann-Kleene scheme). This is combined with a sequence $(1 - \beta_n)$ of dampening factors such that $\lim_{n \to \infty} \beta_n = 0$ and $\sum_n \beta_n = \infty$. The first condition ensures that we dampen less and less during the iteration so that we converge to a Mann iteration, while the second condition guarantees that the dampening factors always have enough "power" left to decrease an over-approximation to the least fixpoint.

We will show that, for a fixed non-expansive and monotone function f, this form of iteration converges to the least fixpoint of f starting from every point in the domain. We will also identify sufficient conditions so that the scheme works when in (3) function f is replaced by f_n, a sequence of approximations converging to f. The resulting theory will allow to treat the case of MDPs, possibly non-discounted and with end-components.

For more general probabilistic systems which can be explored by sampling, we will show how to iterate to the least fixpoint by making sure that the functions are sampled "fast enough": using the law of large numbers and Bernstein's inequality, one can estimate the probability that the functions f_n are close enough to f after some sampling. Then, based on the Borel-Cantelli lemma, we can give an algorithm which guarantees convergence to the least fixpoint almost surely.

In summary, the main contributions of our work are:

- The definition of an iteration scheme, referred to as dampened Mann iteration, which converges to the least fixpoint of a given non-expansive and monotone function f from any starting point (Sect. 3).
- The identification of various sufficient conditions for applying such iteration scheme in a setting where the function f is unknown and can only be approximated via a sequence of functions f_n converging to it (Sect. 4).
- The instantiation of dampened Mann iteration to the computation of the maximal expected return for MDPs where the model is unknown and explored via sampling (Sect. 5).
- The instantiation of dampened Mann iteration to systems where the function of interest can be approximated with given probabilistic error bounds (this includes various probabilistic systems which can be explored via sampling) (Sect. 5.4).

We view this work as an important step towards extending fixpoint theory to deal with scenarios arising from machine learning and data-driven applications.

An extended version of the paper with full proofs of the results and some additional material is available as [3].

2   Preliminaries and Notation

We introduce some basic notions and notation on finite-dimensional real spaces and Markov decision processes [5], that will be our main application.

2.1   Finite-Dimensional Real Spaces

We denote by $\mathbb{R}_{\geq 0}$ the set of non-negative reals, by $\mathbb{N}_0$ and $\mathbb{N}$ the sets of naturals with and without 0, respectively. For sets X, Y, we will denote by Y^X the set of functions $f\colon X \to Y$. If X is finite, we will identify Y^X with the set of vectors $Y^{|X|}$. For $x \in \mathbb{R}^d$, we will write $(x)^i \in \mathbb{R}$ for its i-th component and, by abuse of notation, we will sometimes identify $x \in \mathbb{R}$ with the vector $(x, \dots, x) \in \mathbb{R}^d$.

We equip $\mathbb{R}^d$ with the *supremum norm* defined as $\|x\| = \sup\{|(x)^i| \mid i \in \{1, \dots, d\}\}$ for $x \in \mathbb{R}^d$ and extended to functions $f\colon A \to B$, where $A, B \subseteq \mathbb{R}^d$ by $\|f\| = \sup_{x \in A} \|f(x)\| \in [0, \infty]$. Given $x \in \mathbb{R}^d$, we denote by $|x|$ the vector in $\mathbb{R}^d_{\geq 0}$ defined by $(|x|)^i = |(x)^i|$. Note that $\|x\| = \||x|\|$.

For $x, y \in \mathbb{R}^d$, we write $x \leq y$ for the pointwise (partial) order, i.e., $(x)^i \leq (y)^i$ for all $i \in \{1, \dots, d\}$. A function $f \in Y^X$ with $X, Y \subseteq \mathbb{R}^d$ is *monotone* if, for all $x, x' \in X$, we have that $x \leq x'$ implies $f(x) \leq f(x')$. A *fixpoint* of $f\colon X \to X$ is $x \in X$ such that $f(x) = x$. The *set of fixpoints* of a function f is denoted by $\mathrm{Fix}(f)$ and, in case it exists, the *least fixpoint* of f is denoted by μf.

A function $f \in Y^X$ with $X, Y \subseteq \mathbb{R}^d$ is L-Lipschitz for a constant $L \in \mathbb{R}_{\geq 0}$ if, for all $x, x' \in X$, $\|f(x) - f(x')\| \leq L\|x - x'\|$. The function is *non-expansive* if it is 1-Lipschitz. It is *contractive* if it is q-Lipschitz for some $q < 1$, and it is a *power contraction* if there is some $n \in \mathbb{N}$ such that f^n, the n-fold composition of f, is a contraction. If $f\colon X \to X$ is a contraction (and, more generally, power contraction) with $X \subseteq \mathbb{R}^d$ closed (hence complete), by Banach's theorem, it has a unique fixpoint given by $\lim_{n \to \infty} f^n(x_0)$ where $x_0 \in X$ is arbitrary.

2.2   Markov Decision Processes

We will focus on Markov decision processes [5] in a non-discounted non-negative reward setting.

Definition 2.1 (Markov decision process). *A Markov decision process (MDP) is a tuple $M = (S, A, T, R)$ where S and A are the finite sets of states and actions. Moreover $T\colon S \times A \times S \to [0,1]$ provides the probability $T(s, a, s')$ of transitioning from state $s \in S$ to state $s' \in S$ when action $a \in A$ is chosen, in a way that $\sum_{s' \in S} T(s, a, s') \in \{0, 1\}$. When $\sum_{s' \in S} T(s, a, s') = 1$ we say that action a is* enabled *in s and we write $A(s)$ for the set of actions enabled in s. Finally, $R\colon S \times A \times S \to \mathbb{R}_{\geq 0}$ is a non-negative step-wise reward function. We let $F = F(M) := \{s \in S \mid A(s) = \emptyset\}$ and call it the set of* final states. *The Markov decision process is a Markov chain if, for all $s \in S$, we have $|A(s)| \leq 1$.*

The idea is that M describes an interactive system that, when in state s, transitions to another state s' with probability $T(s, a, s')$ based on an action $a \in A(s)$ chosen by an external agent. Possible strategies of the agent can be described by (positional) policies $\pi\colon S \backslash F \to A$ with $\pi(s) \in A(s)$ for any non-final state $s \in S \setminus F$. We denote the set of all such policies by $\Pi(M)$.

For MDPs, one is interested in finding a policy that optimizes the expected return. It should be noted that positional policies (as defined above) are sufficient for optimal behaviour in *finite* MDPs where the goal is to maximize the non-discounted total reward [32]. The essential step often lies in finding the (least) fixpoint of a so-called Bellman operator. In reinforcement learning, one often considers the state-action-value operator, discussed in the introduction, whose fixpoint gives the expected optimal return $q^*(s, a)$ at state s when taking action a. Alternatively, one can consider the state-value operator f_M whose fixpoint gives the expected optimal return $v^*(s)$ at state s. The two options are tightly related, e.g., $q^*(s, a) = \sum_{s' \in S} T(s, a, s') \cdot (R(s, a, s') + v^*(s'))$. Here we will focus on the state-value operator since it allows for a simpler presentation. As we are assuming a model-based scenario, approximations to the state-action values $q^*(s, a)$ can be retrieved using the above equation (with an appropriately close approximation of T).

Definition 2.2 (Bellman operator). *Given an MDP $M = (S, A, T, R)$, the (state-value) Bellman operator $f_M\colon \mathbb{R}_{\geq 0}^S \to \mathbb{R}_{\geq 0}^S$ is defined, for $v \in \mathbb{R}_{\geq 0}^S$, by*

$$f_M(v)(s) = \max_{a \in A(s)} \sum_{s' \in S} T(s, a, s')(R(s, a, s') + v(s')) \tag{4}$$

In contrast to the usually treated *discounted* case, the operator f_M is not necessarily contractive. Hence, it might have several fixpoints or might not have any fixpoint in $\mathbb{R}_{\geq 0}^S$, intuitively because the expected return might sum up to infinity. Hereafter, we will work with so-called *MDPs with finite value*, for which a fixpoint exists. In Sect. 5.3, they will be characterized as those MDPs where positive rewards are given only outside end-components. By a later result (Lemma 3.1), existence of a fixpoint for the Bellman operator implies the existence of a least fixpoint. For an MDP with finite value $M = (S, A, T, R)$, we let $v_M^* = \mu f_M$.

3 Dampened Mann Iteration for Known Functions

We define an iteration scheme for approximating, with arbitrary precision, the least fixpoint of monotone and non-expansive functions over the non-negative reals. It is a variation of Mann iteration [6] suitably modified in order to be "robust" with respect to perturbations in the computation with the introduction of a dampening factor [22,27]. In this section, we will focus on the case in which the function of interest is known and identify conditions which ensure convergence to the least fixpoint. The case in which the function can only be approximated will be discussed in the next section.

3.1 Dampened Mann Iteration Scheme

We start by clarifying the class of functions of interest in the paper.

Assumption 1. Given a *closed* and *convex* set $X \subseteq \mathbb{R}^d_{\geq 0}$ with $0 \in X$, where $d \in \mathbb{N}_0$ is a fixed arity, let $f \colon X \to X$ be *monotone* and *non-expansive* with $\mathrm{Fix}(f) \neq \emptyset$.

Note that, under the above assumption, if f is a (power) contraction, by Banach's theorem, it has a unique fixpoint, i.e., $\mathrm{Fix}(f) = \{\mu f\}$. Otherwise, if f is just non-expansive, the condition $\mathrm{Fix}(f) \neq \emptyset$ is non-trivial (e.g., the function $x \mapsto x + 1$ over $\mathbb{R}_{\geq 0}$ is monotone and non-expansive, but it has no fixpoints). However, when $\mathrm{Fix}(f) \neq \emptyset$, we can show that f also admits a least fixpoint μf.

Lemma 3.1 (Existence of least fixpoints). *Let $X \subseteq \mathbb{R}^d_{\geq 0}$ be a closed set with $0 \in X$ and let $f \colon X \to X$ be a monotone function with $\mathrm{Fix}(f) \neq \emptyset$. Then f has a least fixpoint μf. Moreover, if f is continuous then $\mu f = \sup_{n \in \mathbb{N}} f^n(0)$.*

Since our functions are non-expansive and thus continuous, by the lemma above, the least fixpoint can be obtained by iterating the function on 0, according to what is often called *Kleene iteration* (see, e.g. [14]). However, as noted in the introduction, Kleene iteration is not "robust" with respect to perturbations in the computation. For this, we introduce a variation of a Mann iteration scheme.

Definition 3.2 (Mann scheme/iteration). *A (dampened) Mann scheme $\mathcal{S} = ((\alpha_n)_{n \in \mathbb{N}_0}, (\beta_n)_{n \in \mathbb{N}_0})$ is a pair of parameter sequences in $[0, 1)$ such that*

$$\lim_{n \to \infty} \beta_n = 0, \tag{5}$$

$$\sum_{n \in \mathbb{N}_0} \beta_n = \infty \quad \text{(or equivalently,} \quad \prod_{n \in \mathbb{N}_0} (1 - \beta_n) = 0 \text{)}. \tag{6}$$

A Mann-Scheme is called a Mann-Kleene *scheme whenever* $\lim_{n \to \infty} \alpha_n = 0$ *and a* relaxed Mann-Kleene *scheme if* $\lim_{n \to \infty} \alpha_n < 1$.

Given a convex $X \subseteq \mathbb{R}^d_{\geq 0}$ with $0 \in X$, a Mann scheme $\mathcal{S}$ defines a sequence $(T_n^{\mathcal{S}})_{n \in \mathbb{N}_0}$ of operators $T_n^{\mathcal{S}} \colon X^X \times X \to X$ given by

$$T_n^{\mathcal{S}}(f, x) = (1 - \beta_n) \cdot (\alpha_n \, x + (1 - \alpha_n) f(x)).$$

Together with a sequence $(f_n)_{n \in \mathbb{N}_0}$ of functions $f_n \colon X \to X$ and an initial point $x_0 \in X$, it gives rise to a (dampened) Mann iteration $\mathcal{F} = (\mathcal{S}, (f_n), x_0)$, determining a sequence $(x_n^{\mathcal{F}})_{n \in \mathbb{N}_0}$ defined as

$$x_0^{\mathcal{F}} = x_0, \qquad x_{n+1}^{\mathcal{F}} = T_n^{\mathcal{S}}(f_n, x_n^{\mathcal{F}}).$$

Note that the iteration can start at any point (not just 0). This might look irrelevant in cases where the function of interest is known exactly, but it will be extremely useful when it can only be approximated.

Intuitively, when trying to approximate the least fixpoint, Condition (5) ensures that dampening eventually reduces – meaning that, in the long run, when we are close to the least fixpoint of f, we stay close to it. On the other hand, Condition (6) guarantees that at any stage there is still enough "dampening power" left to correct possible over-approximations. In the exact case, when $f_n = f$ for all n, this is needed for the iteration to be convergent for *all* initial points. In the approximated case, when (f_n) converges to f, dampening will be indispensable since over-approximations at some components can be introduced along the way.

3.2   Approximating the Fixpoint of Known Functions

For an approximation scheme to be reasonable, it should at least converge to the correct solution μf when we use the exact function f at every step. Hence, we first focus on the case in which $f_n = f$ for all $n \in \mathbb{N}_0$ and identify conditions which ensure convergence. By abuse of notation, we will sometimes identify f with the sequence (f_n) with $f_n = f$ for all $n \in \mathbb{N}_0$.

Definition 3.3 (Exact Mann scheme). *Let $\mathcal{S} = ((\alpha_n), (\beta_n))$ be a Mann scheme. We call it exact if for all $f \colon X \to X$ as in Assumption 1 and $x_0 \in X$, the sequence $(x_n^{\mathcal{F}})$ generated by the iteration $\mathcal{F} = (\mathcal{S}, f, x_0)$ converges to μf.*

One can prove that, for functions satisfying Assumption 1, even if the domain X might not be bounded, the sequence generated by a Mann scheme is bounded. However, in general, the sequence does not converge to the least fixpoint of f (and it might not converge at all) without additional restrictions on the parameters.

We next prove that convergence of the iteration to the least fixed point is ensured by working with Mann-Kleene schemes, i.e., Mann schemes satisfying

$$\lim_{n \to \infty} \alpha_n = 0. \tag{7}$$

Intuitively, Condition (7) implies that the iteration gets closer and closer to a Kleene iteration (in fact, when $\alpha_n \to 0$, the operator $T_n^{\mathcal{S}}(f, \cdot)$ tends to f).

Canonical choices of the parameters for obtaining a Mann-Kleene scheme are $\beta_n = 1/n$ and either $\alpha_n = 1/n$ as well or $\alpha_n = 0$ constantly. In the sequel we sometimes start at x_n with $n > 0$ rather than x_0 to ensure that all parameters are well-defined, particular when they are based on fractions such as $1/n$.

Theorem 3.4 (Approximating the fixpoint of known functions). *Every Mann-Kleene scheme $\mathcal{S}$ is exact.*

Although so far we have only considered the case in which $f_n = f$ for every $n \in \mathbb{N}_0$, Theorem 3.4 already yields a significant improvement to the usual Kleene approximation, where one sets $x_{n+1} = f(x_n)$: The Mann-Kleene iteration with a non-expansive function converges to the least fixpoint of f for *every* starting point x_0 and not just for $x_0 = 0$.

With some additional effort one can prove convergence also for relaxed Mann-Kleene schemes where Condition (7) $\alpha_n \to 0$ is relaxed to $\alpha_n \to \alpha < 1$. This for instance allows to set $\alpha_n = \alpha \in [0, 1)$.

Corollary 3.5 (Convergence for relaxed Mann-Kleene). *Every relaxed Mann-Kleene scheme is exact.*

Theorem 3.4 and Corollary 3.5 above instantiate to our main application scenario, i.e., finding the optimal value function of an MDP M and imply that, given a (relaxed) Mann-Kleene scheme $\mathcal{S}$, the iterations $\mathcal{F} = (\mathcal{S}, f_M, v_0)$ yields a converging sequence $x_n^{\mathcal{F}} \to v_M^*$ for all initial values v_0, q_0. In fact, the domain $X = \mathbb{R}_{\geq 0}$ is closed and the Bellman operator f_M is monotone, non-expansive and admit fixpoints (since we work with MDPs with finite value).

4   Approximated Fixpoints of Approximated Functions

In this section, we are, more generally, interested in the least fixpoint of a function f under the assumption that we can get access only to a sequence (f_n) of approximations converging to f.

Assumption 2. Given a closed and convex set $X \subseteq \mathbb{R}_{\geq 0}^d$ with $0 \in X$ where $d \in \mathbb{N}_0$ is a fixed arity, let (f_n) be a sequence of monotone and non-expansive functions $f_n \colon X \to X$, pointwise converging to $f \colon X \to X$ with $\mathrm{Fix}(f) \neq \emptyset$.

Note that, under Assumption 2, also f is guaranteed to be monotone and non-expansive. Furthermore, a standard result from analysis ensures that, given a sequence (f_n) of L-Lipschitz functions, $f_n \colon X \to X$, with $X \subseteq \mathbb{R}^d$ compact, if the sequence converges to a function f, then the convergence is uniform. Therefore, if we consider the function sequence (f_n) only on a compact subset of X, we can assume w.l.o.g. that it converges uniformly. Indeed, in the sequel we will often show that the sequences generated by Mann iterations are bounded and use this fact to restrict to a bounded and thus compact domain $X \subseteq \mathbb{R}_{\geq 0}^d$.

Now, given an iteration scheme $\mathcal{S}$ that is exact, i.e., which works when iterating the exact function, a naive idea to construct a sequence of approximations (x_n) of the least fixpoint of the target function f might be to perform *resetting*, i.e., to restart the iteration in each step and calculate x_k as $T_{n_k}^{\mathcal{S}}(f_k, T_{n_k-1}^{\mathcal{S}}(f_k, \ldots T_0^{\mathcal{S}}(f_k, x_0) \ldots))$, namely approximate μf by iterating appropriately many times with an approximation f_k sufficiently close to f.

However, as already noted, the least fixpoint operator μ is not continuous for non-expansive functions, i.e., the sequence μf_n might not converge to μf (see Example 1.1). Even worse, the approximations might not even have a fix-point (see Example 1.3). Hence, simply choosing an approximation f_n sufficiently close to f, and iterating with it, will not guarantee to get close to μf.

In the rest of this section we show that, under suitable assumptions, damp-ened Mann schemes, which instead avoid restarting and properly reuse previous iterates, work in the approximated setting given by Assumption 2. Here, Condi-tion (6) on the dampening parameters (β_n) is essential – even when the iteration starts from 0 (bottom value) – as the approximations f_n constantly introduce errors, possibly causing over-approximations which need to be "dampened".

One can show that the least fixpoint μf of the target function serves as an asymptotic lower bound for all relaxed Mann-Kleene schemes.

Lemma 4.1. *Under Assumption 2, given a relaxed Mann-Kleene scheme $\mathcal{S}$ and arbitrary $x_0 \in X$, consider the iteration $\mathcal{F} = (\mathcal{S}, (f_n), x_0)$. If $(x_n^{\mathcal{F}})$ is bounded, we have $\liminf_{n \to \infty} x_n^{\mathcal{F}} \geq \mu f$.*

Moreover, restricting to the one-dimensional case, i.e., for functions $f_n : X \to X$ with $X \subseteq \mathbb{R}_{\geq 0}$, the condition $\mu f = \lim_{n \to \infty} \mu f_n$, ensures convergence for every (relaxed) Mann-Kleene scheme.

Theorem 4.2 (Approximated Mann-Kleene - one dimension). *Let $f, f_n : X \to X$ be as in Assumption 2 with $d = 1$, let $\mathcal{S}$ be a (relaxed) Mann-Kleene scheme, $x_0 \in X$, and consider the iteration $\mathcal{F} = (\mathcal{S}, (f_n), x_0)$. If $\mu f = \lim_{n \to \infty} \mu f_n$ then $(x_n^{\mathcal{F}})$ converges to μf.*

In the above result the hypothesis that $\lim_{n \to \infty} \mu f_n = \mu f$ is essential, wit-nessed by the example below.

Example 4.3 (Mann-Kleene iteration converging to the wrong value). Consider again Example 1.1 from the introduction, with $f, f_n : [0, 1] \to [0, 1]$ where $f(x) = x$ and $f_n(x) = (1 - 1/n) \cdot x + 1/n$ for $n \in \mathbb{N}$. We choose the Mann-Kleene scheme $\alpha_n = 0, \beta_n = 1/n$, and iterate starting with $x_1 = 0$. This generates a sequence $(x_n^{\mathcal{F}})$ such that $x_{n+1}^{\mathcal{F}} = \frac{n-1}{2n}$ and thus $x_n^{\mathcal{F}} \to 1/2 \neq 0 = \mu f$.

Theorem 4.2 does not generalise to the multidimensional case. As shown by the example below, there are Mann-Kleene schemes satisfying $\lim_{n \to \infty} \mu f_n = \mu f$ where iterating with the approximations does not even converge.

Example 4.4 (Mann-Kleene iteration diverging). Let $f : [0, 1]^2 \to [0, 1]^2$ be the flip map given by $f(x, y) = (y, x)$ and consider a sequence of maps $f_n : [0, 1]^2 \to [0, 1]^2$ as follows:

1. If n is even let $f_n = f$ and
2. if n is odd define f_n by $f_n(x, y) = (y \ominus \varepsilon_n, x \oplus \varepsilon_n)$ where $\varepsilon_n := 2/n$ and $\ominus, \oplus$ stand for truncated subtraction/addition in the interval $[0, 1]$.

Then, the maps f and f_n for $n \in \mathbb{N}$ are monotone and non-expansive. More-over, f_n converges (uniformly) to f and since $f_n(0, \varepsilon_n) = (0, \varepsilon_n)$ we also have $\lim_{n \to \infty} \mu f_n = \mu f = (0, 0)$.

However, if we choose the Mann-Kleene scheme $\mathcal{S} = ((\alpha_n), (1/n+1))$, with $\alpha_n = 0$ for all n, it is easy to check that the sequence $(x_n^{\mathcal{F}})$ generated by the iteration $\mathcal{F} = (\mathcal{S}, (f_n), (0, 1))$ (starting at index 1) is given, for $n > 1$, by

$$x_n^{\mathcal{F}} = \begin{cases} (\frac{n-2}{n}, 0) & \text{if } n \text{ is odd} \\ (0, \frac{n-1}{n}) & \text{if } n \text{ is even} \end{cases}$$

Thus, both $(1, 0)$ and $(0, 1)$ are cluster points of $(x_n^{\mathcal{F}})$. The sequence $(x_n^{\mathcal{F}})$ is not even asymptotically regular, i.e. $\|x_n^{\mathcal{F}} - x_{n+1}^{\mathcal{F}}\|$ does not converge to 0.

We provide a first positive result for the multidimensional case when the limit function f is a power contraction. Power contractions naturally arise in the study of MDPs. Hence this result will play an important role in Sect. 5.

Theorem 4.5 (Approximated Mann-Kleene - power contractions). *Let $f, f_n : X \to X$ be as in Assumption 2 with f a power contraction. Given a Mann-Kleene scheme $\mathcal{S}$ and $x_0 \in X$, consider the iteration $\mathcal{F} = (\mathcal{S}, (f_n), x_0)$.*
   Then, if $(x_n^{\mathcal{F}})$ is bounded, it converges to the unique fixpoint of f.

Next we come to one of our main results for general non-expansive functions. It provides sufficient conditions on the approximation sequence (f_n), ensuring that an exact Mann scheme converges to the least fixpoint when iterating with approximations. Note that it applies, in particular, to (relaxed) Mann-Kleene schemes which are known to be exact by Theorem 3.4 and Corollary 3.5.

Main Theorem 4.6 (Approximated Mann iteration). *Let $f, f_n : X \to X$ be as in Assumption 2, let $\mathcal{S}$ be an exact Mann scheme, $x_0 \in X$, and consider the iteration $\mathcal{F} = (\mathcal{S}, (f_n), x_0)$. Then $(x_n^{\mathcal{F}})$ converges to μf if either*

1. *the sequence (f_n) is monotone and $\mu f = \lim_{n \to \infty} \mu f_n$ or*
2. *the sequence (f_n) converges normally to f, i.e. $\sum_{n \in \mathbb{N}_0} \|f - f_n\| < \infty$.*

It is remarkable that under the assumption of normal convergence of (f_n) to f, the sequence $(x_n^{\mathcal{F}})$ converges to the correct solution even if $\lim_{n \to \infty} \mu f_n \neq \mu f$. Combining with estimates obtained in Theorem 3.4 one can even calculate error bounds ε_n (converging to 0) such that $\|x_n^{\mathcal{F}} - \mu f\| \leq \varepsilon_n$ for all $n \in \mathbb{N}_0$, provided that we can calculate such estimates for $\|f^n(0) - \mu f\|$.

Example 4.7. Consider again the sequence of functions (f_n) from Example 4.3. We observed that the Mann-Kleene iteration does not converge to the least fixpoint in this case. Indeed, (f_n) does not converge normally as $\|f_n - f\| = 1/n$.

However, let us consider a sped up sequence of approximations as to guarantee normal convergence, e.g., put $g_n = f_{n^2}$ and thus $\|g_n - f\| = 1/n^2$. If $(x_n^{\mathcal{G}})$ is the sequence generated from (g_n) by Theorem 4.6 we get $\lim_{n \to \infty} x_n^{\mathcal{G}} = \mu f = 0$.

Normal convergence intuitively expresses the fact that (f_n) converges sufficiently fast to f. In the context of a sampling-based approximation such as model-based reinforcement learning, this can be obtained by taking a sufficiently large number of samples. As discussed in Sect. 5.4, this number can be bounded using quantitative versions of the law of large numbers (Bernstein's inequality).

5   Value Functions of MDPs and Probabilistic Systems

5.1   MDP Sampling

We now come to our main application: approximating the optimal value functions of MDPs in a model-based reinforcement learning setting. We show that dampened Mann iteration on the Bellman operators of sampled MDPs always almost surely converges to the optimal value function for any Mann-Kleene scheme.

For an MDP $M = (S, A, T, R)$ we assume that the states, actions, and reward function are known to the agent, and that the transition function is learned through sampling in the following sense: For every state $s \in S$ and every action $a \in A(s)$, there is a family of independent discrete random variables $(X_n^{s,a})_{n \in \mathbb{N}}$ with range S defined on some probability space $(\Omega, \mathcal{A}, \mathbb{P})$ whose distributions are given by $\mathbb{P}[X_n^{s,a} = s'] = T(s, a, s')$.

We let T_n be the maximum likelihood approximation to T after performing n random experiments on each state-action pair, that means

$$T_n(s, a, s') := \frac{|\{i \in \{1, \dots, n\} \mid X_i^{s,a} = s'\}|}{n}.$$

Note that, in particular, we never over-estimate a probability 0, i.e.

$$T(s, a, s') = 0 \Rightarrow T_n(s, a, s') = 0 \qquad \text{for all } s, s' \in S, a \in A(s). \tag{8}$$

The n-th approximation of M is given by $M_n = (S, A, T_n, R)$ with f_n being the value iteration functions of M_n. By the law of large numbers, we then infer that $\mathbb{P}\left[\lim_{n \to \infty} T_n(s, a, s') = T(s, a, s')\right] = 1$ for all $s, s' \in S, a \in A(s)$. Hence the sequence (f_n) converges to the value iteration function f of M almost surely.

Assumption 3. Let $M = (S, A, T, R)$ be an MDP with finite value, let (M_n) be given by a sampling process as described above with $T_n \to T$. We denote by $f_n \colon \mathbb{R}_{\geq 0}^S \to \mathbb{R}_{\geq 0}^S$ and $f \colon \mathbb{R}_{\geq 0}^S \to \mathbb{R}_{\geq 0}^S$ the Bellman operators of M_n and M, respectively (see (1)).

Note that Assumption 3 implies Assumption 2. We can show that iterations based on a Mann scheme using MDP functions stay bounded. Still, Theorem 4.6 does not apply directly since approximations are obtained by a generic sampling process and thus convergence is neither monotone nor normal, in general. Still, we can conclude using a combination of the results about convergence in the "exact case" (Theorem 3.4) and for power contractions (Theorem 4.5). In order to state the result more abstractly and concisely, we give a name to Mann schemes satisfying the two mentioned properties.

Definition 5.1 (Regular Mann scheme). *A Mann scheme $\mathcal{S}$ is regular if*

1. *it is exact and*
2. *in the approximated setting (Assumption 2), the sequence $(x_n^{\mathcal{F}})$ generated by the iteration $\mathcal{F} = (\mathcal{S}, (f_n), x_0)$ converges to μf for all $x_0 \in X$, provided that it is bounded and f is a power contraction.*

By Theorem 3.4 and Theorem 4.5, all Mann-Kleene schemes are regular, while it is currently unknown whether all relaxed Mann-Kleene schemes are regular.

5.2 Simple MDPs

In general, the Bellman operators of MDPs are not contractions. We show that if we restrict to a suitable subclass MDPs, they are power contractions. To single out such class of MDPs, we recall the notion of (maximal) end-components [2,15].

Definition 5.2 (Maximal end-components, simple MDPs). *Let an MDP $M = (S, A, T, R)$ be given. A tuple (S', A') identifying a subprocess $M' = (S', A', T', R')$ with $T'(s, a, s') = T(s, a, s')$ for all $s, s' \in S', a \in A'(s)$ and $R' = R|_{S' \times A' \times S'}$ is called an end-component if the following conditions hold:*

- $F(M') = \emptyset$,
- *for all $s \in S', s' \in S\backslash S', a \in A'(s)$, we have $T(s, a, s') = 0$*
- *for all $s, s' \in S'$, there exists a path in M' from s to s'.[1]*

An end-component (S', A') is called maximal end-component (MEC) iff there exists no larger end-component (with respect to (pointwise) inclusion). We will write $\mathrm{MEC}(M)$ for the set of all maximal end-components of the MDP M.
We call an MDP M simple if $\mathrm{MEC}(M) = \emptyset$.

Intuitively, an end-component is a strongly connected subset S' of non-final states such that each state has an action giving probability zero of leaving S'.

We now show convergence of regular Mann schemes for simple MDPs. The proof proceeds by introducing a class of functions which we refer to as witness-bounded functions, and proving convergence of a regular Mann scheme for functions in this class. The result for simple MDPs follows by observing that the corresponding Bellman operators are witness-bounded. A property playing a prominent role is that the Bellman operator for simple MDPs is a power contraction, a result which is probably folklore (see e.g. [18]).

Theorem 5.3 (Convergence for simple MDPs). *Let M, M_n be MDPs as in Assumption 3. Given a regular Mann scheme $\mathcal{S}$ and an initial point $v \in \mathbb{R}_{\geq 0}^S$, consider the iteration $\mathcal{F} = (\mathcal{S}, (f_n), v)$. If M is simple, then $x_n^{\mathcal{F}} \to v_M^*$.*

---

[1] Given two states $s, t \in S$, a path from s to t is a sequence $s_0 = s, s_1, \ldots, s_k = t \in S$ and $a_1, \ldots, a_k \in A$ with $a_j \in A(s_{j-1})$ and $T(s_{j-1}, a_j, s_j) > 0$ for all $1 \leq j \leq k$.

5.3   General MDPs

When MDPs have end-components [2,11,20], the iteration functions are no longer power contractions, which implies that they might not admit fixpoints. As anticipated in Sect. 2.2, we will work under the assumption that all MDPs have finite value, i.e., the Bellman operator has a (finite) fixpoint and thus a least fixpoint. We observe here that MDPs with finite value can be naturally characterized as MDPs where no reward is given inside end-components. As observed later in Remark 5.9 this setting generalises MDPs with discounted return.

Lemma 5.4 (Characterising MDPs with finite value). *An MDP M has a finite value, i.e., its Bellman operator f_M has a (least) fixpoint, if and only if for all maximal end-components (S', A') and all $s \in S', a \in A'(s)$, and $s' \in S'$ with $T(s, a, s') > 0$, we have $R(s, a, s') = 0$.*

Still, the existence of multiple fixpoints, with the possibility of getting stuck at a fixpoint that is not the least, brings additional complications. An idea explored in the literature [11,20] is to work on an MDP obtained from the original one by quotienting each MEC into a single node. In order to deal with this quotient we need some notation. Given a function $r : S \to Q$, we define:

- *Reindexing*: $r^\bullet : \mathbb{R}_{\geq 0}^Q \to \mathbb{R}_{\geq 0}^S$ defined, for all $w \in \mathbb{R}_{\geq 0}^Q$, by $r^\bullet(w) = w \circ r$
- *Maximum*: $\max_r : \mathbb{R}_{\geq 0}^S \to \mathbb{R}_{\geq 0}^Q$ defined, for all $v \in \mathbb{R}_{\geq 0}^S$ and $e \in Q$ by $\max_r(v)(e) = \max\{v(s) \mid s \in \bar{S} \wedge r(s) = e\}$.

When dealing with quotients, it is convenient to work with MDPs $M = (S, A, T, R)$ where the action sets for different states are disjoint, i.e., for $s, s' \in S$ if $s \neq s'$ then $A(s) \cap A(s') = \emptyset$. It is clear that any MDP can be transformed into an equivalent MDP with disjoint action sets simply by relabelling the actions, without changing the value or Bellman function, whence we will, from now on, w.l.o.g., work under the disjointness assumption.

Definition 5.5 (Quotient MDP). *Let $M = (S, A, T, R)$ be an MDP with finite value. Let $\equiv$ denote the equivalence identifying states in the same MEC. Consider $r : S \to S/_\equiv$ defined by mapping each state to its equivalence class: $r(s) = [s]$. The quotient MDP is $M_r = (S_r, A_r, T_r, R_r)$ where $S_r = S/\equiv$, $A_r([s]) = \bigcup_{s' \in [s]} A(s')$. Moreover, for $s, s' \in S$, $a \in A(s)$:*

$$T_r([s], a, [s'])) = \sum_{s'' \in [s']} T(s, a, s'') \qquad R_r([s], a, [s']) = \frac{\sum_{s'' \in [s']} T(s, a, s') R(s, a, s')}{T_r([s], a, [s'])}.$$

The reduced quotient $\hat{M}_r$ is defined as the MDP derived from M_r by removing self-loops, i.e., modifying the definition of the set of enabled actions as follows:

$$\hat{A}_r([s]) = A_r([s]) \setminus \{a \in A_r([s]) \mid T_r([s], a, [s]) = 1\}.$$

and adapting $\hat{T}_r$ accordingly.

The quotient is an MDP with only singleton end-components, i.e., states with actions producing self-loops. Since the reduced quotient is obtained from the quotient by removing self-loops, it clearly has no end-components, allowing to reuse results from Sect. 5.2.

The following proposition restates results from [11, 20] on collapsing MECs.

Proposition 5.6 (Fixpoints of non-discounted MDPs). *Let M be an MDP with finite value. Let $\hat{M}_r$ be the reduced quotient. Then $v_M^* = r^\bullet(v_{\hat{M}_r}^*)$.*

We show that for the successive approximation of (the value iteration function of) an MDP by sampling as described above, the least fixpoints of the approximations always converge to the least fixpoint of the underlying MDP.

Theorem 5.7. *Under Assumption 3, we have $\lim_{n\to\infty} \mu f_n = \mu f$.*

Now, we can show that, also for general MDPs, a dampened Mann iteration based on a regular Mann scheme converges to the optimal value function.

Main Theorem 5.8 (Mann iteration over MDPs). *Let M, M_n be MDPs as in Assumption 3. Given a regular Mann scheme $\mathcal{S}$ and any $v \in \mathbb{R}_{\geq 0}^S$, consider the iteration $\mathcal{F}^a = (\mathcal{S}, (f_n), v)$, generating a sequence $(v_n^{\mathcal{F}^a})$. Then $\lim_{n\to\infty} v_n^{\mathcal{F}^a} = v_M^* = \mu f_M$.*

The proof first shows that μf_M serves as a lower bound to the limit of $(v_n^{\mathcal{F}^a})$, making use of the fact that the expected return for an MDP is the maximum of the expected return of the Markov chains over all possible policies. As, furthermore, any state in an end-component of a Markov chain has expected return 0, the iteration generated by their reduced quotients can serve as a lower bound to the iteration of interest, which together with the above observation yields μf as a lower bound. The crux of the proof is to show that μf also serves as an upper bound. Roughly the idea is to show that iterating on the quotient MDPs generates a sequence (v_n) over-approximating the actual sequence $(v_n^{\mathcal{F}^a})$. Using the fact that reduced quotients are simple MDPs one can build on the results of Sect. 5.2 to deduce that $\lim_{n\to\infty} v_n^{\mathcal{F}^a}$ is below μf_M.

Remark 5.9. In the context of (model-based) reinforcement learning, usually the discounted total reward criterion is used, that is the aim of the agent is to optimize the discounted total reward for some discount factor $\gamma < 1$, as described in Sect. 1. This setting yields some desirable properties, mainly that the resulting discounted Bellman operator is contractive, making the optimal value its unique fixpoint and always well-defined. It can also be motivated by interpreting it as a scenario in which the agent prefers an immediate reward over long-term rewards or where the system terminates at any step with probability $1 - \gamma$.

However, we remark that the discounted setting can be interpreted as a special case of the non-discounted one by adding a sink state which is reached by every state with probability $1 - \gamma$ (akin to its interpretation as a system that stops with probability $1 - \gamma$ in each step). Then the resulting MDP is not only simple in the sense of Definition 5.2 but its Bellman operators are,

---

Algorithm 1: Dampened Mann Iteration with Probabilistic Guarantees

---

1 **Input:** A map $n \mapsto f_n$ such that (f_n) uniformly converges to f almost surely.
   Parameters $\gamma_i, \delta_i \in \mathbb{R}_{\geq 0}$ such that $\gamma_i > 0$ and $\sum_{i \in \mathbb{N}} \gamma_i < \infty$ (analogously for δ_i)
2 **Output:** A sequence (x_i) in $\mathbb{R}^d_{\geq 0}$
3 $x_0 := 0$;
4 $i := 0$;
5 **while** *true* **do**
6 $\quad$ Choose n_i such that $\mathbb{P}\big[\|f_{n_i} - f\| \geq \gamma_i\big] \leq \delta_i$;
7 $\quad$ $x_{i+1} := (1 - \beta_i) \cdot \big(\alpha_i \cdot x_i + (1 - \alpha_i) \cdot f_{n_i}(x_i)\big)$;
8 $\quad$ $i := i + 1$;
9 **end**

---

with slight modifications, also contractions whence we can apply Theorem 5.8 to derive convergence results. In particular, this gives a convergence result of simple versions of model-based algorithms such as the Dyna-Q algorithm [37,38] where we consider only full-sweep updates and no direct update step.

5.4 Reaching the Least Fixpoint by Fast Iteration

In the previous section we proved a convergence result for MDPs, approximated by sampling. It would be desirable to extend such results to more general settings involving probabilistic systems which are explored by sampling. Indeed, our results allow the formulation of a generic algorithm that can compute a sequence of values converging to the least fixpoint of f almost surely. This can be done in all cases where we can estimate the error $\|f_n - f\|$ at least with a certain probability. The procedure, reported in Algorithm 1, relies on a very simple idea: make sure algorithmically that the sequence (f_n) converges normally to f almost surely. The correctness of the procedure follows by the Borel-Cantelli Lemma [8].

Theorem 5.10. *For exact Mann schemes the sequence (x_i) produced by Algorithm 1 converges to the least fixpoint of f almost surely.*

The only precondition for the algorithm is that the indices n_i in line 6 can be chosen effectively. When the sequence (f_n) is generated by a sampling process as described above, this can often be done by using Bernstein's inequality [23] – a quantitative version of the law of large numbers. If we sample the transition probabilities $T_n(s, a, s')$ as detailed in Sect. 5.1, we can estimate the error as below, which allows us to computationally determine the indices needed in line 4 of the algorithm:

$$\mathbb{P}\big[|T_n(s, a, s') - T(s, a, s')| \geq \varepsilon\big] \leq 2e^{-2\varepsilon^2 n}$$

As an example, the described technique can be used to deal with (simple) stochastic games (This is fully detailed in the extended version of the paper [3]).

6 Conclusion

Related Work. There has been a significant amount of research on convergence properties of Mann iterations of non-expansive maps. However, most of the existing literature deals with the undampened case and only a single function f, i.e., with a scheme defined by $x_{n+1} = \alpha_n x_n + (1 - \alpha_n) f(x_n)$.

It is known [10] that in every Banach space and for every non-expansive f with at least one fixpoint this scheme produces a sequence which is f-asymptotically regular (i.e. $\|x_n - f(x_n)\| \to 0$) for all parameter sequences (α_n) with $\sum(1 - \alpha_n) = \infty$. In general the sequence does not need to converge. (Weak) convergence is shown under additional assumptions on the map f and/or the surrounding space in various places (see for example [6,16,34]).

Dampened versions similar to ours have been considered in [27] where the authors show convergence to a fixpoint under strong additional assumptions on the parameter sequences in a uniformly smooth Banach space and in [41] where convergence is shown for more general parameter sequences in Hilbert spaces.

Here, in addition, we deal with the case where the function f can only be approximated. Motivated by the applicability to MDPs, we consider the case of monotone non-expansive functions in finite-dimensional Banach spaces with the supremum norm, which are neither uniformly smooth nor Hilbert spaces. They are not even uniformly convex as is assumed e.g. in [34]. We also introduced a probabilistic setting and devised a generic algorithm, which applies in many situations and guarantees almost sure convergence to the least fixpoint of f.

As mentioned earlier, our work is inspired by the integration of reinforcement learning algorithms with fixpoint theory [28,31,36,40], and in particular by the Dyna-Q algorithm [25,37,38]. Reinforcement learning techniques are by now a central ingredient in machine learning and we plan to strengthen the foundations behind this method.

There is some similarity of our results to the theory of stochastic approximation [7,17,29], going back to [35], which has also been employed in the correctness proof of Q-learning [40]. Stochastic approximation deals with a root finding problem where the function contains an error term with expected value zero. In that line of work, the function itself is stochastic with known expected value, while we separate the (approximated) fixpoint theory from the probabilistic setting by checking that we converge almost surely via sampling. More importantly, the focus in stochastic approximation is to consider either contractions (with unique fixpoints) or convergence to *some* fixpoint, while the case of convergence to the *least* fixpoint is not treated. Hence there is no machinery for leaving a fixpoint once it is reached, such as we have by employing a dampening factor.

In order to obtain our results on MDPs, the notion of end-components is quite fundamental. For an introduction to end-components see [2], while the connection of non-uniqueness of fixpoints of MDP functions to end-components was exploited in [11,20] in order to compute the correct expected return by collapsing maximal end components. In [11] the authors assume – as we do – that MDPs are not known exactly but are sampled. They present a different solution by collapsing maximal end-components, which is unnecessary in our approach.

Numerical Experiments. We made several numerical experiments that are reported in the extended version [3]. For unknown functions the outcome can be summarized as follows: in terms of precision, the results are comparable to "resetting", where – for some n – we perform the iteration from 0 with the current approximation f_n. Compared to our suggested form of iteration, resetting has the disadvantage that the results vary highly with the quality of the current approximation and that intermediate results are not available.

Future Work. For future work we are in particular interested in the case of parameter sequences where α_n converges to one and the question is whether we can still guarantee convergence to μf. This would be interesting, since such parameters are for instance used in the context of Q-learning [40]. Our long-term aim is to devise a fixpoint theory of approximated functions for which a large number of reinforcement learning algorithms are special cases. Here we concentrated on model-based reinforcement learning, for model-free reinforcement learning we need a theory that allows updates with a sampled value rather than with the current best approximation and we plan to work with the weaker assumption that the limit-average of the functions f_n converges to f (rather than the functions themselves). This has some overlap to stochastic approximation theory as discussed above, even though we do not consider stochastic functions. Hence we plan to partially build on the results obtained in that area.

To properly match reinforcement learning algorithms we will look into chaotic and asynchronous iteration [13,19] where one can iterate at different speeds at various states. This is useful when traversing an MDP or stochastic system, making updates on-the-fly and locally when better estimates are obtained.

We will also investigate how to iterate to the greatest fixpoint rather than the least, either by dualizing or adapting ideas from [22,27] on iterating to the fixpoint closest to a given value. Including rewards from different domains, such as negative rewards, is also a direction of future work.

We plan to identify more cases where approximated fixpoint iteration works out of the box. For instance, we mentioned that simple stochastic games are covered by the results in Sect. 5.4, but there we needed a way to enforce fast convergence. We will investigate whether the case of simple stochastic games (and related applications) works with the standard iteration scheme. Due to Example 4.4 it is clear that this will not be true for all approximated functions, but we plan to find requirements weaker than the current ones.

Moreover we will further look into error estimates, making guarantees of the form "with probability p the error is below ε". In the case of MDPs, even when they are known exactly, determining upper/lower bounds and thus error estimates already requires some non-trivial techniques, such as the results in [20, 21,33]. It is our aim to generalize these results to the case where the probabilities associated to the MDP are not known exactly and, in this case, we expect to obtain probabilistic error estimates.

Acknowledgements. This work is partially supported by the European Union – NextGenerationEU under the National Recovery and Resilience Plan (NRRP) - Call PRIN 2022 PNRR - Project P2022HXNSC "Resource Awareness in Programming: Algebra, Rewriting, and Analysis" and by the Deutsche Forschungsgemeinschaft (DFG, German Research Foundation) – project number 434050016 (SpeQt).

Disclosure of Interests. The authors have no competing interests to declare that are relevant to the content of this article.

References

1. Bacci, G., Bacci, G., Larsen, K.G., Mardare, R.: On-the-fly exact computation of bisimilarity distances. Log. Methods Comput. Sci. **13**(2:13), 1–25 (2017)
2. Baier, C., Katoen, J.-P.: Principles of Model Checking. MIT Press (2008)
3. Baldan, P., Gurke, S., König, B., Padoan, T., Wittbold, F.: Approximating fixpoints of approximated functions (2025). arXiv:2501.08950
4. Banach, S.: Sur les opérations dans les ensembles abstraits et leur application aux équations intégrales. Fundam. Math. **3**(1), 133–181 (1922)
5. Bellman, R.: A Markovian decision process. J. Math. Mech. **6**(5), 679–684 (1957)
6. Berinde, V.: Iterative Approximation of Fixed Points. Lecture Notes in Mathematics, vol. 1912. Springer (2007)
7. Bertsekas, D.P., Tsitsiklis, J.N.: Neuro-Dynamic Programming. Athena Scientific, Belmont, Massachusetts (1996)
8. Billingsley, P.: Probability and Measure. Wiley Series in Probability and Mathematical Statistics, 3rd edn. Wiley, New York (1995)
9. Borwein, D., Borwein, J.: Fixed point iterations for real functions. J. Math. Anal. Appl. **157**(1), 112–126 (1991)
10. Borwein, J., Reich, S., Shafrir, I.: Krasnoselski-Mann iterations in normed spaces. Can. Math. Bull. **35**(1), 21–28 (1992)
11. Brázdil, T., et al.: Verification of Markov decision processes using learning algorithms. In: Cassez, F., Raskin, J.-F. (eds.) ATVA 2014. LNCS, vol. 8837, pp. 98–114. Springer, Cham (2014). https://doi.org/10.1007/978-3-319-11936-6_8
12. Condon, A.: The complexity of stochastic games. Inf. Comput. **96**(2), 203–224 (1992)
13. Cousot, P.: Asynchronous iterative methods for solving a fixed point system of monotone equations in a complete lattice. Research report R.R. 88, Laboratoire IMAG, Université scientifique et médicale de Grenoble, Grenoble, France (1977)
14. Cousot, R., Cousot, P.: Constructive versions of Tarski's fixed point theorems. Pac. J. Math. **82**(1), 43–57 (1979)
15. de Alfaro, L.: Formal Verification of Probabilistic Systems. Ph.D. thesis, Stanford University (1997)
16. Dong, Q.-L., Cho, Y.J., He, S., Pardalos, P.M., Rassias, T.M.: The Krasnosel'skiĭ-Mann Iterative Method Recent Progress and Applications. SpringerBriefs in Optimization, 1st edn. Springer, Cham (2022)
17. Duflo, M.: Random Iterative Models. Number 34 in Applications of Mathematics – Stochastic Modelling and Applied Probability. Springer (1991). Translated by Stephen S. Wilson

18. Eaton, J.H., Zadeh, L.A.: Optimal pursuit strategies in discrete-state probabilistic systems. J. Basic Eng. **84**(1), 23–29 (1962)
19. Frommer, A., Szyld, D.B.: On asynchronous iterations. J. Comput. Appl. Math. **123**(1), 201–216 (2000). Numerical Analysis 2000. Vol. III: Linear Algebra
20. Haddad, S., Monmege, B.: Interval iteration algorithm for MDPs and IMDPs. Theoret. Comput. Sci. **735**, 111–131 (2018)
21. Hartmanns, A., Kaminski, B.L.: Optimistic value iteration. In: Lahiri, S.K., Wang, C. (eds.) CAV 2020. LNCS, vol. 12225, pp. 488–511. Springer, Cham (2020). https://doi.org/10.1007/978-3-030-53291-8_26
22. He, S., Zhu, W.: A modified Mann iteration by boundary point method for finding minimum-norm fixed point of nonexpansive mappings. Abstr. Appl. Anal. **2013** (2013). Article ID 768595
23. Hoeffding, W.: Probability inequalities for sums of bounded random variables. J. Am. Stat. Assoc. **58**(301), 13–30 (1963)
24. Huth, M., Kwiatkowska, M.: Quantitative analysis and model checking. In: Proceedings of LICS 1997. IEEE (1997)
25. Kaelbling, L.P., Littman, M.L., Moore, A.W.: Reinforcement learning: a survey. J. Artif. Intell. Res. **4**, 237–285 (1996)
26. Kelmendi, E., Krämer, J., Křetínský, J., Weininger, M.: Value iteration for simple stochastic games: stopping criterion and learning algorithm. In: Chockler, H., Weissenbacher, G. (eds.) CAV 2018. LNCS, vol. 10981, pp. 623–642. Springer, Cham (2018). https://doi.org/10.1007/978-3-319-96145-3_36
27. Kim, T.-H., Hong-Kun, X.: Strong convergence of modified Mann iterations. Nonlinear Anal. Theory Methods Appl. **61**(1), 51–60 (2005)
28. Kumar, P.R., Varaiya, P.: Stochastic Systems. Society for Industrial and Applied Mathematics, Philadelphia (2015)
29. Kushner, H.J., Clark, D.S.: Stochastic Approximation Methods for Constrained and Unconstrained Systems. Number 26 in Applied Mathematical Sciences. Springer (1978)
30. Mio, M., Simpson, A.: Łukasiewicz μ-calculus. Fund. Inform. **150**(3–4), 317–346 (2017)
31. Moore, A.W., Atkeson, C.G.: Prioritized sweeping: reinforcement learning with less data and less time. Mach. Learn. **13**, 103–130 (1990)
32. Puterman, M.L.: Markov Decision Processes: Discrete Stochastic Dynamic Programming. Wiley Series in Probability and Statistics. Wiley (1994)
33. Quatmann, T., Katoen, J.-P.: Sound value iteration. In: Chockler, H., Weissenbacher, G. (eds.) CAV 2018. LNCS, vol. 10981, pp. 643–661. Springer, Cham (2018). https://doi.org/10.1007/978-3-319-96145-3_37
34. Reich, S.: Weak convergence theorems for nonexpansive mappings in banach spaces. J. Math. Anal. Appl. **67**(2), 274–276 (1979)
35. Robbins, H., Monro, S.: A stochastic approximation method. Ann. Math. Stat. **22**(3), 400–407 (1951)
36. Rummery, G.A., Niranjan, M.: On-line Q-learning using connectionist systems, vol. 37. University of Cambridge, Department of Engineering Cambridge, UK (1994)
37. Sutton, R.S.: Dyna, an integrated architecture for learning, planning, and reacting. SIGART Bull. **2**(4), 160–163 (1991)
38. Sutton, R.S.: Planning by incremental dynamic programming. In: Proceedings of ML 1991 (Conference on Machine Learning), pp. 353–357. Morgan Kaufmann (1991)
39. Tarski, A.: A lattice-theoretical fixpoint theorem and its applications. Pac. J. Math. **5**, 285–309 (1955)

40. Christopher, J.: Watkins and Peter Dayan. Q-learning. Mach. Learn. **8**, 279–292 (1992)
41. Yao, Y., Zhou, H., Liou, Y.-C.: Strong convergence of a modified Krasnoselski-Mann iterative algorithm for non-expansive mappings. J. Appl. Math. Comput. **29**, 383–389 (2008)

StatWhy: Formal Verification Tool for Statistical Hypothesis Testing Programs

Yusuke Kawamoto[1]([✉]) [iD], Kentaro Kobayashi[1,2] [iD], and Kohei Suenaga[3] [iD]

[1] National Institute of Advanced Industrial Science and Technology (AIST),
Tokyo, Japan
yusuke.kawamoto@aist.go.jp
[2] University of Tsukuba, Ibaraki, Japan
[3] Kyoto University, Kyoto, Japan

Abstract. Statistical methods have been widely misused and misinterpreted in various scientific fields, raising significant concerns about the integrity of scientific research. To mitigate this problem, we propose a tool-assisted method for formally specifying and automatically verifying the correctness of statistical programs. In this method, programmers are required to annotate the source code of the statistical programs with the requirements for these methods. Through this annotation, they are reminded to check the requirements for statistical methods, including those that cannot be formally verified, such as the distribution of the unknown true population. Our software tool StatWhy automatically checks whether programmers have properly specified the requirements for the statistical methods, thereby identifying any missing requirements that need to be addressed. This tool is implemented using the Why3 platform to verify the correctness of OCaml programs that conduct statistical hypothesis testing. We demonstrate how StatWhy can be used to avoid common errors in various statistical hypothesis testing programs.

Keywords: Formal verification · Hypothesis testing · Program verification · Why3 platform

1 Introduction

Statistical techniques have been essential for acquiring scientific knowledge from data in various academic fields. In particular, an increasing number of researchers have used *statistical hypothesis testing* [2,11] to derive scientific conclusions from datasets. However, these statistical methods have been widely misused and misinterpreted, raising significant concerns about the integrity of scientific research [7,24]. For example, the notion of *statistical significance*, assessed by calculating *p-values*, has been widely misused and misinterpreted [32].

The artifact of the paper is available at https://github.com/fm4stats/statwhy and https://zenodo.org/records/13991312.

R. Piskac and Z. Rakamarić (Eds.): CAV 2025, LNCS 15932, pp. 216–230, 2025.
https://doi.org/10.1007/978-3-031-98679-6_10

For this reason, various guidelines for statistical analyses [25,31] have been proposed to improve the quality and reproducibility of scientific research. However, owing to the absence of a formal language to describe procedures, we need to manually refer to these guidelines, written in natural language. As a result, the correctness of statistical analyses has not been checked automatically.

To mitigate these problems, we propose a new method for the formal specification and automatic verification of statistical program correctness. Specifically, programmers are required to annotate their source code with the requirements for the statistical methods and the interpretations of the analysis results. Then, our tool StatWhy automatically checks whether these requirements and interpretations are correctly annotated. For example, StatWhy can verify whether a p-value is correctly calculated in a program, thus preventing p-value hacking, i.e., a technique to manipulate statistical analyses to obtain a lower p-value.

The goal of StatWhy stems from the nature of statistics: many requirements for statistical methods cannot be proven mathematically because they are usually properties of an unknown true population that analysts seek to estimate from sampled data. For example, many statistical hypothesis testing methods require a population to follow a normal distribution. Since analysts cannot prove this requirement mathematically, they are responsible for judging whether the population appears to follow a normal distribution, possibly using their background knowledge about the population. For this reason, StatWhy asks analysts to explicitly write down the requirements for statistical methods—typically, the assumptions that they make about the population distributions—as an annotation in their source code. Then, the analysts are reminded to check these requirements empirically and approximately using their background knowledge.

To design StatWhy, we use the framework of belief Hoare logic (BHL) [17,19] and provide constructs to make writing statistical programs easier, as well as libraries for the specification of various hypothesis testing methods. For the implementation of this tool, we rely on the Why3 platform [8] to handle practical programming languages and to automatically discharge verification conditions using external SMT solvers.

Although the current implementation of StatWhy focuses on statistical hypothesis testing, the approach is not limited to a specific branch of statistics. Rather, it can be applied to any situation where the usage of statistical methods in programs needs to be checked. In future versions of the tool, we will include additional statistical methods beyond hypothesis testing.

Contributions. Our main contributions are summarized as follows:

1. We propose a new tool-assisted method for formally specifying and automatically verifying statistical programs (i.e., programs that perform hypothesis testing and calculate statistics under certain assumptions about an unknown population). This method requires programmers to annotate their source code with the requirements and the interpretations of statistical analyses, which makes a statistical procedure verifiable and explainable.
2. We implemented a software tool StatWhy based on our verification method. Given a program as input, StatWhy automatically verifies whether a program-

mer has correctly annotated it with the requirements for statistical hypothesis testing and the interpretation of the test results. StatWhy is available with a range of examples and comprehensive documentation [16].

3. We demonstrate how StatWhy can be used to avoid common errors in various popular statistical hypothesis testing methods.

To the best of our knowledge, StatWhy appears to be the first tool to automatically verify the requirements for the appropriate use of hypothesis tests. This work represents the first step in building a framework for specifying and verifying the integrity of scientific conclusions based on statistical analyses.

Related Work. *Logic for Statistics.* Several studies on modal logic have been proposed to express statistical properties [13,18]. The work on statistical epistemic logic (StatEL) [13–15] is the first attempt to construct a modal logic to describe statistical properties of hypothesis testing. They introduce a belief modality weaker than S5 and interpret it in a Kripke model where an accessibility relation is defined using a statistical distance between possible worlds. However, these logics cannot reason about the procedures of statistical methods.

Belief Hoare Logic. Belief Hoare logic (BHL) [17,19] is a program logic with an epistemic modality for statistical belief. Using this logic, we can derive the correctness of a hypothesis testing program (Sect. 2). Our verification tool, StatWhy, uses BHL as its theoretical foundation to produce a proof tree for the correctness of hypothesis testing programs within the tool. To develop StatWhy, we implemented several constructs specific to BHL using the WhyML language— the intermediate language used within Why3 framework. This allows verification conditions generated by StatWhy to be discharged by off-the-shelf SMT solvers.

Program Verification Tools. Various tools used for specifying the preconditions and postconditions of each function and statically verifying their correctness; for example, Frama-C [6] for C programs; Dafny [22] for imperative programs that compile to Boogie [21]; ESC/Java [9] and KeY [1] for Java programs. To the best of our knowledge, no attempt has been made to apply these tools for verifying the correct usage of statistical methods in programs.

The Verification Frameworks Used in Our Tool. StatWhy is implemented as an extension of Cameleer [29], a verifier for OCaml programs built on top of the Why3 framework [8]. Cameleer works as a translator from OCaml to the simple functional programming language WhyML. The translated WhyML code is then verified by Why3. StatWhy extends Cameleer to verify the correctness of hypothesis testing programs written in OCaml by incorporating the constructs and inference rules of BHL.

Verification of Statistical Algorithms. From a broader perspective, a number of studies have investigated the numerical accuracy of statistical algorithms [23], the formal verification of randomized algorithms [20,26], and the PAC verification [10,28] for approximately checking the correctness of statistical algorithms. Furthermore, formal methods have been used to verify a certain guarantee of the correctness of statistical machine learning models [30]. However, no prior work has provided a formal method tool for specifying or verifying the correct usage of statistical methods rather than the correctness of statistical algorithms.

Plan of the paper. The rest of the paper is organized as follows. In Sect. 2, we review basic notions in hypothesis testing and belief Hoare logic (BHL). In Sects. 3 and 4, we present StatWhy's design and implementation, respectively. In Sect. 5, we show examples of StatWhy being applied to common errors in hypothesis testing. In Sect. 6, we present our final remarks.

2   Background

Statistical hypothesis testing [2,11] is a method for inferring information about an unknown population x from a dataset y that has been sampled from the population x. In a hypothesis test, the *null hypothesis* φ_0 is a claim that we wish to test, while the *alternative hypothesis* φ_1 is a claim that we will accept if the null hypothesis is rejected. The goal of a hypothesis test is to determine whether we have sufficient evidence to reject the null hypothesis φ_0 in favor of the alternative hypothesis φ_1.

Example 1 (t-test for a population mean). For a population x following a normal distribution with an unknown mean, the *t-test for the population mean* is a hypothesis test to check whether the unknown mean $\mathsf{mean}(x)$ differs from a certain value μ_0 specified in the null hypothesis.

In the t-test, we want to show the alternative hypothesis $\varphi_1 \overset{\text{def}}{=} (\mathsf{mean}(x) \neq \mu_0)$ by rejecting the null hypothesis $\varphi_0 \overset{\text{def}}{=} (\mathsf{mean}(x) = \mu_0)$. First, we calculate the *t-test statistic* from a dataset y: $t(y) := \frac{\mathsf{mean}(y) - \mu_0}{s/\sqrt{n}}$ where n is the sample size of y and s is a sampled standard deviation, i.e., $s \overset{\text{def}}{=} \sqrt{\frac{\sum_{i=1}^{n}(y_i - \mathsf{mean}(y))^2}{n-1}}$. This statistic is compared to Student's t-distribution with $n - 1$ degrees of freedom (i.e., the distribution of the t-statistic $t(y)$ when y is normally distributed). Specifically, we calculate the *p-value*: $\Pr_{d \sim N(\mu, \sigma^2)^n}[\, |t(d)| > |t(y)| \,]$ under the null hypothesis φ_0. For a smaller p-value, the dataset y is far from what we expect under the null hypothesis that $\mathsf{mean}(x) = \mu_0$. Hence, in the t-test, if the p-value is smaller than a certain threshold (e.g., 0.05), we reject the null hypothesis φ_0 and accept the alternative hypothesis φ_1, i.e., $\mathsf{mean}(x) \neq \mu_0$.

We remark that this t-test requires that the population x should follow a normal distribution. If this requirement is not satisfied, the use of the t-test is inappropriate and its result may be incorrect. Therefore, analysts need to check this requirement in some way. Since they cannot mathematically prove this requirement on the unknown population x, they use their background knowledge about the population x and check approximately whether the dataset y at hand (rather than the unknown population x itself) follows a normal distribution.

Belief Hoare logic (BHL) [17,19] is a program logic equipped with epistemic modal operators for the statistical beliefs acquired via hypothesis testing. The epistemic modal logic used in BHL is defined by:

$$\varphi ::= \eta(u_1, \ldots, u_n) \mid \neg\varphi \mid \varphi \wedge \varphi \mid \mathbf{K}\varphi \mid \mathbf{K}^{\leq\epsilon}_{y,A}\,\varphi$$

for a predicate symbol η, terms $u_1, \ldots, u_n$, a dataset y, a hypothesis test A, and a p-value ϵ. The knowledge modality $\mathbf{K}$ is defined in the S5 modal logic system with axioms T, 4, and 5. Intuitively, $\mathbf{K}\varphi$ represents that we know φ. The epistemic possibility $\mathbf{P}$ is defined as usual by $\mathbf{P}\varphi \overset{\text{def}}{=} \neg\mathbf{K}\neg\varphi$. $\mathbf{K}^{\leq\epsilon}_{y,A}\,\varphi$ represents that by a hypothesis test A on a dataset y, we believe φ with a p-value $\alpha \leq \epsilon$.

The semantics of this epistemic logic is based on a Kripke model [17,19]. The satisfaction of an epistemic formula φ in a possible world w is denoted by $w \models \varphi$ and is defined straightforwardly in a Kripke model where each possible world is equipped with a test history that is updated by performing hypothesis tests.

In the framework of BHL, we express a procedure for hypothesis testing as a program C using a programming language. Then, we use epistemic modal logic to describe the requirements for the hypothesis tests as a precondition formula, e.g., $\psi_{\mathsf{pre}} \overset{\text{def}}{=} y \leftsquigarrow N(\mu_0, \sigma^2) \wedge \mathbf{P}\varphi_1 \wedge \kappa_\emptyset$, where the atomic formula $y \leftsquigarrow N(\mu, \sigma^2)$ represents that a dataset y is sampled from the population that follows a normal distribution $N(\mu, \sigma^2)$ with an unknown mean μ and an unknown variance σ^2. The modal formula $\mathbf{P}\varphi$ represents that, before conducting the hypothesis test, we have the *prior belief* that the alternative hypothesis φ *may be* true. The formula $\kappa_\emptyset$ represents that no hypothesis test has been conducted previously.

The statistical belief we acquire from the hypothesis test is specified as a *postcondition* formula, e.g., $\varphi_{\mathsf{post}} \overset{\text{def}}{=} \mathbf{K}^{\leq 0.05}_{y,A}\varphi_1$, representing that by a hypothesis test A on the dataset y, we believe φ with a p-value $\alpha \leq 0.05$. Since the result of the hypothesis test may be wrong, we use the statistical belief modality $\mathbf{K}^{\leq 0.05}_{y,A}$ instead of the knowledge modality $\mathbf{K}$.

Finally, we combine all the above and describe the whole statistical inference as a *judgment* $\Gamma \vdash \{\psi_{\mathsf{pre}}\}\, C\, \{\varphi_{\mathsf{post}}\}$, representing that whenever the precondition ψ_{pre} is satisfied, the execution of the program C results in the satisfaction of the postcondition φ_{post}. By deriving this judgment using derivation rules in BHL, we conclude that the program C for the statistical inference results in the statistical belief φ_{post} whenever the requirement ψ_{pre} is satisfied.

BHL has been applied only to pen-and-paper analyses of a few simple examples of statistical hypothesis testing in previous work [17,19] and has not yet been used to build a computer-aided verification tool.

3   The Design of StatWhy

3.1   Running Examples

Simple Example. We present the main idea of our formal specification and automated verification method using the program in Fig. 1. This

```
let p = exec_ttest_1samp t_n 1.0 d Two
(*@ requires  sampled d t_n
    ensures  (World (!st) interp) |= StatB p fmlA *)
```

Fig. 1. An OCaml program that calls a t-test command for a mean of a population.

program shows an OCaml source code that executes a command
`exec_ttest_1samp` for the one-sample t-test (Example 1 in Sect. 2) with an
alternative hypothesis `fmlA` (e.g., representing `mean(t_n) != 1.0`).

To specify the requirements and the interpretation of this t-test command, a
programmer writes the precondition in the `requires` clause and the postcondition in the `ensures` clause using the specification language Gospel [5].

In this code, `sampled` is a predicate defined in WhyML, and the precondition
`sampled d t_n` expresses that the dataset `d` has been sampled from a population that has a normal distribution type `t_n` with an unknown mean and an
unknown variance. In the WhyML implementation of BHL, a dataset is implemented as a record with a field storing the distribution type of the population.

The postcondition `(World (!st) interp) |= StatB p fmlA` represents the
interpretation of the result of the hypothesis test. Specifically, we obtain a *statistical belief*—denoted by the logical formula `StatB p fmlA`—that an alternative hypothesis `fmlA` holds with a p-value `p`, in the possible world (`World (!st)`
`interp`) equipped with the record `st` of all hypothesis tests executed so far. This
postcondition encodes the satisfaction of the epistemic formula $w \models \mathbf{K}_{y,A}^{\leq \mathrm{p}}$ `fmlA`
in the world w in the Kripke model addressed in Sect. 2.

By applying StatWhy to this source code, the program verification fails
because other requirements are missing in the precondition. However, since Why3
finds the failure to discharge the verification conditions corresponding to such
requirements, the tool user can easily find out the missing requirements.

We remark that the specification of `exec_ttest_1samp` is defined in StatWhy
using WhyML so that it (1) checks the requirements for the hypothesis test in
the precondition, (2) asserts the conclusion implied by the hypothesis test in the
postcondition, and (3) updates the test history `st` with the test result (Fig. 2).

```
val exec_ttest_1samp (p:population) (mu:real) (y:dataset (list real)) (alt:alternative):real
  ...
  requires {
   match p with
   | (NormalD _ _) -> sampled y p /\ ... /\
     match alt with
     | Two -> (World !st interp) |= Possible ((mean p) <' (const_term mu)) /\
              (World !st interp) |= Possible ((mean p) >' (const_term mu)) ...
  }
  ensures {
   pvalue result /\
   let h = match alt with
     | Two -> (mean p) $!= (const_term mu) ...
   end in !st = Cons ("ttest_1samp", h, Eq result) !(old st)
  }
```

Fig. 2. The specification of `exec_ttest_1samp`

In the `requires`-clause, the two-tailed (`TWO`) t-test requires the prior belief
that both tails $\mathrm{mean}(p) < \mu$ and $\mathrm{mean}(p) > \mu$ are possible. In the `ensures`-
clause, the test result consisting of the test name, the hypothesis `h`, and the
p-value `result` is added to the test history `st`. This specification of the two-
tailed t-test encodes an instance of the following inference rule in BHL [17,19]:

$$\frac{\Gamma \models \psi \to (\varpi \wedge \mathbf{P}\varphi_L \wedge \mathbf{P}\varphi_U)}{\Gamma \vdash \{\psi \wedge \kappa_\emptyset\} \; \alpha := f_A(y) \; \{\psi \wedge \kappa_{y,A} \wedge \mathbf{K}^\alpha_{y,A}(\varphi_L \vee \varphi_U)\}} \quad \text{(Two-HT)}$$

where the precondition ψ includes the assumption ϖ on the population distribution and the prior beliefs on the two tails $\mathbf{P}\varphi_L$ and $\mathbf{P}\varphi_U$; the postcondition updates the empty test history $\kappa_\emptyset$ to the history $\kappa_{y,A}$ recording the test result.

P-**Value Hacking.** Figure 3 is another example presenting how StatWhy detects an error in the code conducting the *p-value hacking* (a.k.a. *data dredging*), a technique to manipulate statistical analyses to obtain a lower p-value.

```
let ex_hack trial1 trial2 =
  let p1 = exec_ttest_1samp ppl_new 1.0 trial1 Two in
  let p2 = exec_ttest_1samp ppl_new 1.0 trial2 Two in
  let p = min p1 p2 in (* This is INCORRECT *)
  (p1, p2, p)
(*@ (p1, p2, p) = ex_hack trial1 trial2
  requires
    is_empty (!st) /\ sampled trial1 ppl_new /\ sampled trial2 ppl_new /\
    (World (!st) interp) |= Possible h_new_l /\ (World (!st) interp) |= Possible h_new_u
  ensures
    (Leq p = compose_pvs h_new !st
      && (World !st interp) |= StatB (Leq p) h_new) *)
```

Fig. 3. An OCaml program that performs the p-value hacking.

In this program, we execute a t-test `exec_ttest_1samp` on a dataset `trial1` and another on another dataset `trial2`. Given the p-values `p1` and `p2` for these two t-tests, we should report `p1 + p2` as the p-value of these experiments. However, this program reports only the experiment showing the lower p-value (i.e., `min p1 p2`) by ignoring the other showing higher p-value. By ensuring that all hypothesis tests are described in the program, StatWhy can automatically check whether the p-values are correctly calculated, thus preventing p-value hacking.

We remark that in the precondition, the atomic expression `is_empty (!st)` with the dereference operator '`!`' represents that the test history `st` is empty; i.e., no hypothesis test has performed before. The expression `sampled trial1 ppl_new` represents that the dataset `trial1` is sampled from a population `ppl_new`. For specific predicates such as `is_empty` and `sampled`, we can use abbreviated expressions where "`(World !st interp) |= `" is omitted for the sake of simplicity. In the postcondition, `compose_pvs h_new !st` obtains the correct p-value from the test history `st`, which is found to be different from the p-value `p` incorrectly calculated in this program.

3.2   More Details on Specifications

The latest version of StatWhy can automatically verify the correctness of specifications written in the WhyML language [8]. It can also verify programs written in the subset of OCaml supported by Cameleer [29], a verifier for OCaml programs. Specifically, Cameleer covers the core OCaml language except for several features, including object-oriented programming, generalized algebraic data types (GADTs), and polymorphic variants.

StatWhy requires minimal modifications to the source code. Programmers need to insert annotations into the OCaml program to describe the requirements and interpretations for hypothesis testing. More specifically, a requirement (respectively, interpretation) for a hypothesis testing command is expressed as a logical formula written in the Gospel language [5], representing a precondition (respectively, postcondition) for the command.

To describe these annotations in Gospel, we introduce types for *terms*, *atomic formulas*, and *logical formulas* of belief Hoare logic (BHL) as follows.

```
type term = RealT real_term | PopulationT population | ...
type atomic_formula = Pred psymb (list term)
type formula = Atom atomic_formula | Not formula
             | Conj formula formula | Disj formula formula
             | Possible formula | Know formula | StatB pvalue formula | ...
```

where a term can express a real number and a population; an atomic formula consists of a predicate symbol (e.g., `is_normal`) and a list of terms; a formula is built using `Possible`, `Know`, and `StatB`, each corresponding to the modal epistemic operators $\mathbf{P}$, $\mathbf{K}$, and $\mathbf{K}_{y,A}^{\leq\epsilon}$, respectively, shown in Sect. 2.

In the WhyML grammar, an atomic expression is of the form `World (!st) interp |= formula` representing that the formula `formula` is satisfied in the possible world equipped with the test history `st` (i.e., the record of all hypothesis tests executed so far) and the interpretation `interp` of private-variables in the Kripke model for BHL [17,19]. For the non-modal formulas using only specific predicates (e.g., `is_empty` or `sampled`), we allow an abbreviation that can omit "`World (!st) interp |=`" from an expression. We can also use function symbols (e.g., `mean` and `ppl`) to simplify expressions.

For clarity in hypothesis testing specifications, programmers can use abbreviation operators. Since hypothesis testing programs often involve repeated comparisons among multiple groups of data, StatWhy provides a set of folding operations to simplify the repetition of similar conditions in specifications. In particular, folding operators can be used to briefly describe the iteration of the hypothesis tests that compare all combinations of groups in multiple comparison.

```
use ocamlstdlib.Stdlib
let function p =
  [@vc:white_box]
  (begin
     requires { sampled d t_n }
     returns { p -> (World (!st) interp) |= (StatB p fmlA) }
     exec_ttest_1samp t_n 1.0 d Two
  end)
```

Fig. 4. A WhyML program calling a *t*-test command for a mean of a population.

3.3   Verification of Statistical Programs

To verify a given OCaml program, StatWhy first transforms it into a program written in the WhyML language [8]. This preprocessing is performed using our extension of Cameleer [29], a static verifier for OCaml. For example, the OCaml program in Fig. 1 is transformed into the WhyML program in Fig. 4.

Next, StatWhy proves the correctness of a WhyML program using the Why3 platform [8]. Specifically, the tool internally synthesizes a proof tree using the proof rules of Belief Hoare logic and derives the verification condition for the program. Then, it automatically discharges these conditions by using external SMT solvers, e.g., CVC5 [3] or Z3 [27]. If the verification succeeds, StatWhy outputs a proof tree that attests to the correctness of the program. If the verification fails or times out, the tool reports the failure. Even in that case, the tool users can identify any missing or incorrect requirements and interpretations for statistical methods so that they can re-specify the requirements and interpretations.

The verification process using StatWhy guarantees the following correctness. If StatWhy successfully verifies a program, for any function f defined as let f d1 ... dn = e, annotated with a precondition ψ_{pre} and a postcondition φ_{post}, the judgment $\{\psi_{\text{pre}}\}\ [v_1/\text{d1}, \ldots, v_n/\text{dn}]\ e\ \{\varphi_{\text{post}}\}$ holds for any value v_i of type di, assuming the soundness of the Why3 framework. By the soundness of BHL, if the expression e is evaluated under the environment satisfying the precondition ψ_{pre}, then the resulting environment satisfies the postcondition φ_{post}.

We remark that StatWhy focuses on automatically verifying the *procedure* and the *annotations* in a statistical program by assuming the correctness of the implementation of each hypothesis testing method used in the procedure as a subroutine. In other words, our automated verification tool only checks that a program correctly uses hypothesis testing functions. Technically, StatWhy checks whether the preconditions and the postconditions of hypothesis testing functions are satisfied when the program calls these functions as subroutines. By using StatWhy, programmers are encouraged to pay attention to the requirements, the interpretations, and the choices of hypothesis testing methods.

We also remark that StatWhy verifies a statistical program only under the assumption that all requirements about an unknown true population are satisfied (e.g., a population follows a normal distribution). Thus, such an assumption needs to be checked externally; for instance, the analysts are responsible for judging whether the population appears to approximately follow the normal distribution[1], possibly using background knowledge about the population.

4   The Implementation of StatWhy

In this section, we explain and discuss the implementation of the StatWhy tool. More details on the tool is available in the user documentation [16].

---

[1] There are hypothesis testing methods for checking the normality approximately. Such tests are applied to the *dataset* (instead of the actual *population*) and cannot prove the normality of the population mathematically.

4.1   The Architecture of StatWhy

Figure 5 shows the architecture of StatWhy. To specify the requirements and interpretations of hypothesis tests as preconditions and postconditions, StatWhy has modules for real number arithmetic, basic statistics, and individual hypothesis testing commands (e.g., t-test) that cover most of the popular hypothesis testing methods [12]. To reason about the interpretation of hypothesis testing, the tool also has modules for BHL [17,19], an epistemic logic with statistical belief explained in Sect. 2, and for the record of the hypothesis tests performed so far.

Since the goal of our verification tool is to ensure the correct usage of the hypothesis testing methods in programs, the StatWhy tool reasons about p-values in hypothesis testing, which requires basic reasoning about probabilities. Specifically, we extended Cameleer so that it can access the real number arithmetic formalized in Why3 standard library, and added basic statistics functions (e.g., mean) and their lemmas.

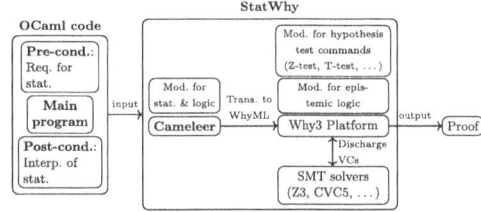

Fig. 5. The architecture of the StatWhy tool.

To reason about p-values appearing in epistemic formulas in simplifying verification conditions, we added Why3 lemmas about the composition of p-values under multiple-tests and about the comparisons between p-values. With these lemmas in the StatWhytool, we avoid the need for SMT solvers to handle probability computations, while maintaining the soundness and correctness in the statistical context.

To accept OCaml programs as input, StatWhy internally calls our extension of Cameleer [29] to translate an OCaml program to a WhyML program. Then the tool verifies a WhyML program by using the Why3 platform.

4.2   Extension of Cameleer

The programs given to StatWhy share several peculiar features. For example, StatWhy specifications often involve repeated comparisons among multiple groups of data, which are expressed using folding operations. Furthermore, the programs often involve the array structure of records of hypothesis tests executed so far. We have found that SMT solvers often get stuck if we try to discharge the verification conditions that involve such folding operations.

To improve the performance of StatWhy, we implemented a custom proof strategy—a combination of proof tactics and transformations—that exploits these characteristics of hypothesis testing programs to accelerate the proof search. Our strategy first applies Why3's default proof strategies (e.g., `split_vc` for splitting conjunctive verification conditions into smaller ones and `compute_in_goal` for applying computations and simplifications to proof goals).

```
let cmp_with_existing_drugs d_new d_drug1 d_drug2 =
  let p_drug1 = exec_ttest_ind_eq ppl_new ppl_drug1 (d_new, d_drug1) Up in
  let p_drug2 = exec_ttest_ind_eq ppl_new ppl_drug2 (d_new, d_drug2) Up in
  p_drug1 +. p_drug2
(*@ p = testing d_new d_drug1 d_drug2
    requires
      is_empty (!st) /\ non_paired d_new d_drug1 /\ non_paired d_new d_drug2 /\
      sampled d_new ppl_new /\ sampled d_drug1 ppl_drug1 /\ sampled d_drug2 ppl_drug2 /\
      (World (!st) interp) |= Possible h_new_drug1 /\
      (World (!st) interp) |= Not (Possible h_new_drug1_c) /\
      (World (!st) interp) |= Possible h_new_drug2 /\
      (World (!st) interp) |= Not (Possible h_new_drug2_c)
    ensures
      (Leq p) = compose_pvs (Disj h_new_drug1 h_new_drug2) !st &&
      (World !st interp) |= StatB (Leq p) (Disj h_new_drug1 h_new_drug2) *)
```

Fig. 6. An OCaml program that performs multiple comparison.

Table 1. The execution times (sec) for verifying hypothesis testing programs with practical numbers of disjunctive (OR) and conjunctive (AND) hypotheses.

#hypotheses	2	3	4	5	6	7	8	9	10
OR	8.77	8.89	8.84	8.94	9.01	9.01	9.04	9.16	9.23
AND	8.82	8.72	8.86	8.98	8.95	9.03	9.11	9.17	9.46

These invocations of the proof strategies are interleaved with calls to SMT solvers, whose timeouts are set to small values. If these applications of the default proof strategies fail to discharge the VCs, then we apply aggressive transformation strategies that unfold the definitions of the functions and predicates defined in StatWhy.

These extensions are implemented as follows. We added WhyML modules for StatWhy to the standard library of Why3 at the installation of our extension of Cameleer. We also extended Cameleer so that Uterm, the module for OCaml untyped terms, and Why3ocaml_driver, the module for translation from OCaml to WhyML, can handle floating-point numbers. We also extended the Why3 plugins provided by Cameleer by adding plugin/cameleerBHL.ml and modifying plugin/plugin_cameleer.ml to handle the algebraic data types in StatWhy.

5   Case Studies on Common Errors in Hypothesis Testing

We present examples to demonstrate how StatWhy can be used to avoid common errors in a variety of popular hypothesis testing programs.

Multiple Comparison Problems. Analysts occasionally make mistakes in computing the p-value in comparing more than two groups, which is called a *multiple comparison problem* [4].

Let us consider an experiment comparing the efficacy of a new drug with that of two existing drugs drug1 and drug2. We conduct two one-tailed t-tests: one comparing the new drug with drug1 and another with drug2. Then the alternative hypotheses h_new_drug1 and h_new_drug2 for these tests represent that the new drug has a better efficacy than drug1 and drug2, respectively. For the p-values p_1 and p_2 of these two tests, the p-value p for the combined test with the disjunctive hypothesis h_new_drug1 $\vee$ h_new_drug2 satisfies $p \leq p_1 + p_2$, which is known as *Bonferroni correction*. In contrast, the p-value p for the conjunctive hypothesis h_new_drug1$\wedge$h_new_drug2 satisfies $p \leq \min(p_1, p_2)$.

StatWhy can automatically check that the program in Fig. 6 correctly calculates the p-value of the disjunctive hypothesis Disj h_new_drug1 h_new_drug2.

Table 2. The execution times (sec) for various multiple comparison methods. #groups (respectively, #comparisons) represents the (practical) number of groups (respectively, combinations of groups) compared in the testing.

Test methods	Metric	#groups					
		2	3	4	5	6	7
Tukey's HSD test	Times (sec)	0.37	9.09	9.33	9.81	15.27	16.39
	#comparisons	1	3	6	10	15	21
Dunnett's test	Times (sec)	0.48	8.98	9.17	9.61	9.62	9.77
	#comparisons	1	2	3	4	5	6
Williams' test	Times (sec)	0.48	8.90	9.04	9.16	9.23	9.58
	#comparisons	1	2	3	4	5	6
Steel-Dwass' test	Times (sec)	0.44	9.05	9.43	9.76	15.10	16.24
	#comparisons	1	3	6	10	15	21
Steel's test	Times (sec)	0.49	8.79	8.92	9.11	9.43	9.74
	#comparisons	1	2	3	4	5	6

Scalability of StatWhy. We evaluated the scalability of the performance of the program verification using StatWhy to (i) the complex hypotheses and (ii) the larger number of compared groups. For the evaluation, we conducted experiments on a MacBook Pro with Apple M2 Max CPU and 96 GB memory using the external SMT solver cvc5 1.0.6.

Table 1 shows the execution times for StatWhy to verify hypothesis testing programs for practical numbers of disjunctive/conjunctive hypotheses. These experiments took roughly the same amount of time for a larger number of hypotheses. Table 2 provides the execution times for the most common multiple comparison methods described in standard textbooks. The numbers of groups compared in the experiments are practical but challenging, as the number of comparisons grows rapidly with the number of groups. The verification of these programs is efficient, since our proof strategy (Sect. 4) accelerates the proof search for programs with folding operations and test histories.

6   Conclusion

We proposed a tool-assisted method for formally specifying and automatically verifying the correctness of statistical programs. In particular, we presented the StatWhy tool for automatically checking whether the programmers have properly specified the requirements and the interpretations of the statistical methods.

In future work, we will extend StatWhy to verify the procedures for power analyses and interval estimation and to deal with other types of statistical methods and other programming languages, e.g., a subset of Python. We also plan to work on the formal verification of the correctness of the implementation of each hypothesis testing function called from statistical software as a subroutine.

Acknowledgments. The authors are supported by JSPS KAKENHI Grant Number JP24K02924, Japan. Yusuke Kawamoto is supported by JST, PRESTO Grant Number JPMJPR2022, Japan. Kohei Suenaga is supported by JST CREST Grant Number JPMJCR2012, Japan.

Disclosure of Interests. The authors have no competing interests to declare that are relevant to the content of this article.

References

1. Ahrendt, W., Beckert, B., Bubel, R., Hähnle, R., Schmitt, P.H., Ulbrich, M.: Deductive Software Verification - The KeY Book - From Theory to Practice, Lecture Notes in Computer Science, vol. 10001. Springer (2016). https://doi.org/10.1007/978-3-319-49812-6
2. Arbuthnot, J.: An argument for divine providence, taken from the constant regularity observ'd in the births of both sexes. Philos. Trans. Roy. Soc. London **27**(328), 186–190 (1710). https://doi.org/10.1098/rstl.1710.0011
3. Barbosa, H., et al.: cvc5: a versatile and industrial-strength SMT solver. In: TACAS 2022. LNCS, vol. 13243, pp. 415–442. Springer, Cham (2022). https://doi.org/10.1007/978-3-030-99524-9_24
4. Bretz, F., Hothorn, T., Westfall, P.: Multiple Comparisons Using R. Chapman and Hall/CRC (2010). https://doi.org/10.1201/9781420010909
5. Charguéraud, A., Filliâtre, J.-C., Lourenço, C., Pereira, M.: GOSPEL—providing OCaml with a formal specification language. In: ter Beek, M.H., McIver, A., Oliveira, J.N. (eds.) FM 2019. LNCS, vol. 11800, pp. 484–501. Springer, Cham (2019). https://doi.org/10.1007/978-3-030-30942-8_29
6. Cuoq, P., Kirchner, F., Kosmatov, N., Prevosto, V., Signoles, J., Yakobowski, B.: Frama-C - a software analysis perspective. In: Eleftherakis, G., Hinchey, M., Holcombe, M. (eds.) SEFM 2012. LNCS, vol. 7504, pp. 233–247. Springer, Heidelberg (2012). https://doi.org/10.1007/978-3-642-33826-7_16
7. Fernandes-Taylor, S., Hyun, J.K., Reeder, R.N., Harris, A.H.: Common statistical and research design problems in manuscripts submitted to high-impact medical journals. BMC. Res. Notes **4**(1), 304 (2011). https://doi.org/10.1186/1756-0500-4-304
8. Filliâtre, J.-C., Paskevich, A.: Why3 — where programs meet provers. In: Felleisen, M., Gardner, P. (eds.) ESOP 2013. LNCS, vol. 7792, pp. 125–128. Springer, Heidelberg (2013). https://doi.org/10.1007/978-3-642-37036-6_8

9. Flanagan, C., Leino, K., Lillibridge, M., Nelson, G., Saxe, J.B., Stata, R.: PLDI 2002: extended static checking for Java. ACM SIGPLAN Not. **48**(4S), 22–33 (2013). https://doi.org/10.1145/2502508.2502520

10. Goldwasser, S., Rothblum, G.N., Shafer, J., Yehudayoff, A.: Interactive proofs for verifying machine learning. In: Lee, J.R. (ed.) Proceedings of the 12th Innovations in Theoretical Computer Science Conference (ITCS 2021). Leibniz International Proceedings in Informatics (LIPIcs), vol. 185, pp. 41:1–41:19. Schloss Dagstuhl – Leibniz-Zentrum für Informatik, Dagstuhl, Germany (2021). https://doi.org/10.4230/LIPIcs.ITCS.2021.41

11. Hogg, R.V., McKean, J.W., Craig, A.T.: Introduction to mathematical statistics. Pearson Education India (2013)

12. Kanji, G.K.: 100 Statistical Tests. Sage (2006)

13. Kawamoto, Y.: Statistical epistemic logic. In: Alvim, M.S., Chatzikokolakis, K., Olarte, C., Valencia, F. (eds.) The Art of Modelling Computational Systems: A Journey from Logic and Concurrency to Security and Privacy. LNCS, vol. 11760, pp. 344–362. Springer, Cham (2019). https://doi.org/10.1007/978-3-030-31175-9_20

14. Kawamoto, Y.: Towards logical specification of statistical machine learning. In: Ölveczky, P.C., Salaün, G. (eds.) SEFM 2019. LNCS, vol. 11724, pp. 293–311. Springer, Cham (2019). https://doi.org/10.1007/978-3-030-30446-1_16

15. Kawamoto, Y.: An epistemic approach to the formal specification of statistical machine learning. Softw. Syst. Model. **20**(2), 293–310 (2020). https://doi.org/10.1007/s10270-020-00825-2

16. Kawamoto, Y., Kobayashi, K., Suenaga, K.: User Documentation for StatWhy v.1.2 (2025). https://github.com/fm4stats/statwhy

17. Kawamoto, Y., Sato, T., Suenaga, K.: Formalizing statistical beliefs in hypothesis testing using program logic. In: Proceedings of KR 2021, pp. 411–421 (2021). https://doi.org/10.24963/kr.2021/39

18. Kawamoto, Y., Sato, T., Suenaga, K.: Formalizing statistical causality via modal logic. In: Proceedings of JELIA 2023. Lecture Notes in Computer Science, vol. 14281, pp. 681–696. Springer (2023). https://doi.org/10.1007/978-3-031-43619-2_46

19. Kawamoto, Y., Sato, T., Suenaga, K.: Sound and relatively complete belief Hoare logic for statistical hypothesis testing programs. Artif. Intell. **326**, 104045 (2024). https://doi.org/10.1016/J.ARTINT.2023.104045

20. Kozen, D.: A probabilistic PDL. J. Comput. Syst. Sci. **30**(2), 162–178 (1985). https://doi.org/10.1016/0022-0000(85)90012-1

21. Leino, K.R.M.: This is Boogie 2. Manuscript KRML **178**(131), 9 (2008)

22. Leino, K.: Dafny: an automatic program verifier for functional correctness. In: Clarke, E.M., Voronkov, A. (eds.) LPAR 2010. LNCS (LNAI), vol. 6355, pp. 348–370. Springer, Heidelberg (2010). https://doi.org/10.1007/978-3-642-17511-4_20

23. Lesage, J.P., Simon, S.D.: Numerical accuracy of statistical algorithms for microcomputers. Comput. Stat. Data Anal. **3**, 47–57 (1985). https://doi.org/10.1016/0167-9473(85)90057-X

24. Makin, T.R., de Xivry, J.: Science forum: ten common statistical mistakes to watch out for when writing or reviewing a manuscript. Elife **8**, e48175 (2019)

25. Moher, D., et al.: Consort 2010 explanation and elaboration: updated guidelines for reporting parallel group randomised trials. Int. J. Surg. **10**(1), 28–55 (2012)

26. Morgan, C., McIver, A., Seidel, K.: Probabilistic predicate transformers. ACM Trans. Program. Lang. Syst. **18**(3), 325–353 (1996). https://doi.org/10.1145/229542.229547

27. de Moura, L., Bjørner, N.: Z3: an efficient SMT solver. In: Ramakrishnan, C.R., Rehof, J. (eds.) TACAS 2008. LNCS, vol. 4963, pp. 337–340. Springer, Heidelberg (2008). https://doi.org/10.1007/978-3-540-78800-3_24

28. Mutreja, S., Shafer, J.: Pac verification of statistical algorithms. In: Neu, G., Rosasco, L. (eds.) Proceedings of Thirty Sixth Conference on Learning Theory. Proceedings of Machine Learning Research, vol. 195, pp. 5021–5043. PMLR (2023)

29. Pereira, M., Ravara, A.: Cameleer: a deductive verification tool for OCaml. In: Silva, A., Leino, K. (eds.) CAV 2021. LNCS, vol. 12760, pp. 677–689. Springer, Cham (2021). https://doi.org/10.1007/978-3-030-81688-9_31

30. Seshia, S.A., Sadigh, D., Sastry, S.S.: Toward verified artificial intelligence. Commun. ACM **65**(7), 46–55 (2022). https://doi.org/10.1145/3503914

31. Von Elm, E., Altman, D.G., Egger, M., Pocock, S.J., Gøtzsche, P.C., Vandenbroucke, J.P.: The strengthening the reporting of observational studies in epidemiology (strobe) statement: guidelines for reporting observational studies. Bull. World Health Organ. **85**, 867–872 (2007)

32. Wasserstein, R.L., Lazar, N.A.: The ASA statement on p-values: context, process, and purpose. Am. Stat. **70**(2), 129–133 (2016). https://doi.org/10.1080/00031305.2016.1154108

Assessing the Quality of Binomial Samplers: A Statistical Distance Framework[*]

Uddalok Sarkar[1]([✉]) [iD], Sourav Chakraborty[1] [iD], and Kuldeep S. Meel[2,3] [iD]

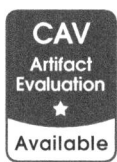

[1] Indian Statistical Institute, Kolkata, India
uddaloksarkar@gmail.com
[2] Georgia Institute of Technology, Atlanta, USA
[3] University of Toronto, Toronto, Canada

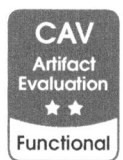

Abstract. Randomized algorithms depend on accurate sampling from probability distributions, as their correctness and performance hinge on the quality of the generated samples. However, even for common distributions like Binomial, exact sampling is computationally challenging, leading standard library implementations to rely on heuristics. These heuristics, while efficient, suffer from approximation and system representation errors, causing deviations from the ideal distribution. Although seemingly minor, such deviations can accumulate in downstream applications requiring large-scale sampling, potentially undermining algorithmic guarantees. In this work, we propose statistical distance as a robust metric for analyzing the quality of Binomial samplers, quantifying deviations from the ideal distribution. We derive rigorous bounds on the statistical distance for standard implementations and demonstrate the practical utility of our framework by enhancing APSEst, a DNF model counter, with improved reliability and error guarantees. To support practical adoption, we propose an interface extension that allows users to control and monitor statistical distance via explicit input/output parameters. Our findings emphasize the critical need for thorough and systematic error analysis in sampler design. As the first work to focus exclusively on Binomial samplers, our approach lays the groundwork for extending rigorous analysis to other common distributions, opening avenues for more robust and reliable randomized algorithms.

1 Introduction

Randomization stands as a cornerstone of computer science, permeating algorithm design from the field's earliest days to its cutting-edge developments. From Quicksort [20], one of the most widely used algorithms, to modern cryptographic protocols, randomization has proven indispensable in achieving efficiency and functionality that deterministic approaches struggle to match. While the fundamental question of whether randomization offers additional computational power over determinism remains open, randomized algorithms have established themselves as the preferred choice in numerous domains, including data structures [42], hash functions [11], and probabilistic data structures [6].

---

[*] The full version of the paper is available at https://arxiv.org/abs/2506.12061.

ⓒ The Author(s) 2025
R. Piskac and Z. Rakamarić (Eds.): CAV 2025, LNCS 15932, pp. 231–253, 2025.
https://doi.org/10.1007/978-3-031-98679-6_11

At the heart of every randomized algorithm lies its ability to sample from probability distributions. The algorithm's correctness and performance guarantees intrinsically depend on the quality of these samples. For instance, a hash table's performance relies on the uniformity of its hash function's output distribution, while a Monte Carlo algorithm's accuracy depends on the fidelity of its random sampling process. This fundamental reliance on sampling has led to the development of sophisticated sampling algorithms implemented as standard library functions across programming languages.

While specialized techniques exist for generating high-quality samples from certain distributions [29], these approaches typically circumvent direct probability mass computation through transformations of basic random processes. However, such techniques remain constrained to specific distributions exhibiting particular mathematical properties. In practice, standard library implementations predominantly rely on transformed rejection sampling [22,24], which necessitates explicit probability mass computation. These computations entail multiple arithmetic operations and specialized function evaluations, including factorial and logarithm computations, thereby introducing approximation errors at each step. The accumulation of these errors can significantly impact the statistical properties of the generated samples, potentially compromising the theoretical guarantees of algorithms that depend on them.

In this work, we focus on analyzing standard library implementations of Binomial samplers, which are largely based on transformed rejection sampling techniques [22,23,24]. These implementations require computation of Binomial distribution probability mass, denoted by $b_{n,p}(k)$, necessitating approximations of factorial terms [33], logarithmic computations [9], and various arithmetic operations. While such approximations enable efficient sampling, they introduce systematic deviations from the ideal Binomial distribution that current implementations neither quantify nor report to users. These deviations can accumulate and potentially trigger cascading failures in downstream applications [4,49]. Despite the widespread adoption of these libraries, there exists no documentation providing precise analysis of accumulated errors.

The primary research problem we address is: *how to develop a rigorous methodology to analyze the errors in existing samplers to provide meaningful measurement of their impact on downstream applications?* This question is particularly pertinent given the increasing reliance on randomized algorithms in critical applications, where understanding and quantifying sampling errors becomes crucial for ensuring system reliability and correctness.

Our first contribution is a rigorous framework for analyzing the quality of existing samplers through the lens of statistical distance. We advocate statistical distance as a theoretically sound metric for quantifying sampler quality, owing to its fundamental property of indistinguishability. Let p and q be two probability distributions with statistical distance at most η, i.e., $d_{TV}(p, q) \leq \eta$. Then, for any statistical test T (even computationally unbounded), the probability of distinguishing between samples from p and q is bounded by η. This fundamental property has profound implications for sampler quality analysis: if a sampler's output distribution has a statistical distance η from the ideal distribution, then the downstream application cannot experience an error greater than η, regardless of its computational sophistication. Building on this theoretical foundation, we present a detailed analysis of state-of-the-art implementations, deriving concrete bounds on their deviation from the ideal distributions through careful decomposition of numerical approximation errors. We propose an extension to sampler interfaces that exposes statistical distance as an input/output parameter, enabling users to control and monitor the sampling accuracy.

To demonstrate the practical utility of our theoretical framework, we present a comprehensive case study in the context of DNF model counting. We show how our quality measures can be integrated into APSEst, a state-of-the-art DNF counter that relies heavily on Binomial sampling. By incorporating our error bounds into the APSEst's analysis framework, we provide the first implementation that offers both scalability and rigorous error guarantees. This integration not only enhances the reliability of the counter but also establishes a blueprint for how sampler quality analysis can be systematically incorporated into broader algorithmic frameworks. Our empirical evaluation demonstrates that this enhanced implementation maintains the efficiency of existing approaches while providing substantially stronger theoretical guarantees.

We believe our work highlights a fundamental challenge in randomized computation: the need for rigorous analysis of sampler implementations to establish precise error bounds and enhance trust in randomized algorithms. While we have focused on Binomial samplers as a crucial first step, the theoretical framework we develop for analyzing sampling error propagation, combined with our practical demonstration in DNF counting, establishes a foundation for future research. A natural direction for future investigation would be the analysis of other standard distributions such as Poisson, Normal, and Beta distributions, each presenting its own unique challenges in implementation and error analysis. Our approach of integrating error analysis into algorithmic frameworks opens new avenues for developing robust randomized algorithms that maintain both theoretical guarantees and practical efficiency. This work will likely motivate the broader community to examine and enhance the reliability of randomized computation implementations, particularly in the context of standard library functions that serve as building blocks for numerous algorithms.

Organisation In section 2, we present the necessary preliminaries and an overview of related concepts that lay the foundation for the rest of the paper. In section 3, we explore related work on error analysis in computational programs and the evaluation of sampler quality. Section 4 outlines our proposal for using statistical distance as a quality metric for samplers, along with the motivation behind this approach. Section 5 offers a detailed discussion on standard Binomial samplers, including our theoretical results, correctness proofs, and error analysis. In section 6, we include a case study on using our sampler to count the number of solutions of a Boolean formula in the Disjunctive Normal Form. Finally, in section 7, we discuss the limitations of our work and future directions.

2   Preliminaries

In this work, we are interested in probability distributions over discrete sets and their samplers. A probability distribution, or simply, a distribution (denoted by p) on a discrete set Ω is a mapping $\mathsf{p} : \Omega \to [0,1]$ such that $\sum_{x \in \Omega} \mathsf{p}(x) = 1$. We define $\mathsf{p}(A) = \sum_{x \in A} \mathsf{p}(x)$ for any $A \subseteq \Omega$. A uniform distribution, or uniform randomness over a set Ω is defined as $\mathsf{p}(x) = \frac{1}{|\Omega|}$ for all $x \in \Omega$. We use the notation $\mathsf{b}_{n,p}$ to denote the Binomial distribution with parameters n and p, which is given by $\mathsf{b}_{n,p}(k) = \binom{n}{k} p^k (1-p)^{n-k}$ for $k \in [0,n]$.

Recall that a Turing Machine (TM) is a theoretical model of computation defined as a tuple $(Q, \Sigma, \Gamma, \sqcup, \Delta, s_0, F)$, where Q is a finite set of states, $\Sigma \subseteq \Gamma \setminus \{\sqcup\}$ is the input alphabet, Γ is the tape alphabet, $\sqcup \in \Gamma$ is the blank symbol, $\Delta : Q \times \Gamma \to Q \times \Gamma \times \{L, R\}$ is the transition function, $s_0 \in Q$ is the initial state, and $F \subseteq Q$ is the set of final states [21]. A natural extension of a Turing Machine is a Turing Transducer [34], which, in addition to the input and work tapes, has a separate write-only output tape. A Transducer computes a function $f : \{0,1\}^* \to \{0,1\}^*$, and the output is the content of the output tape when the machine halts. A Probabilistic Turing Machine (PTM) is a Turing Machine that, in addition to the input tape, has access to a read-only random tape filled with an infinite sequence of random bits [1]. On a given input $x \in \{0,1\}^*$ and for each fixed random string $u \in \{0,1\}^\infty$, the machine's behavior is deterministic. A probabilistic Transducer is defined analogously as a PTM equipped with an output tape. It computes an output string $M(x; u)$ for each fixed u, and writes it on the output tape.

A randomized algorithm $\mathcal{A}$ is modeled as a probabilistic Transducer. On input x and a source of randomness, the output of the algorithm $\mathcal{A}(x; u)$ is written on the output tape of the corresponding Transducer. Consequently, $\mathcal{A}$ defines a distribution over outputs depending on the randomness. While this definition assumes that the random bits are drawn from the uniform distribution, we allow randomized algorithms to access randomness from arbitrary distributions. The ability to sample from arbitrary distributions is without loss of generality, since any distribution can be simulated using uniformly random bits. An example of a randomized algorithm is a sampler Samp_p for a distribution p. Given a source of uniform randomness u, the sampler outputs a sample from p, that is, for all $x \in \Omega$, $\mathrm{Pr}_u(\mathsf{Samp}_\mathsf{p} \text{ outputs } x) = \mathsf{p}(x)$. Conversely, a sampler induces an associated probability distribution p from which it draws samples.

2.1   Approximating Factorials

Lanczos Approximation [33] is a widely used method to approximate the factorials with remarkable accuracy. For a fixed value of t, g, and a positive integer $n \geq 1$, the Lanczos approximation of $n!$, denoted by $\mathsf{Fact}^{\mathsf{Lancz}}(n)$, is defined as, $\mathsf{Fact}^{\mathsf{Lancz}}(n) = \sqrt{2\pi} \left(n + g + \frac{1}{2}\right)^{n+\frac{1}{2}} e^{-(n+g+\frac{1}{2})} A_{t,g}(n)$. The polynomial $A_{t,g}(n)$ contains t terms. The accuracy of the approximation depends on the number of terms t in its expansion, as well as on the constant g. Here g is any real constant such that $g + \frac{1}{2} > 0$. The parameters g and t affect the accuracy and convergence rate of the Lanczos approximation, where larger t improves accuracy at the cost of higher computational resources.

In the Lanczos approximation, a uniform error bound [41] can be established, which provides a measure of how closely the Lanczos approximation approximates the factorial function for all relevant inputs. Given t, g the uniform error bound $\zeta_{t,g}$ of the approximation is defined by, $\zeta_{t,g} = \sup_{n \in \mathbb{N}} \left| n! - \mathsf{Fact}^{\mathsf{Lancz}}(n) \right|$. Let $\zeta = \sqrt{\frac{\pi}{e}} \cdot |\zeta_{t,g}|$. The relative error can be bounded as follows [41],

$$\frac{|n! - \mathsf{Fact}^{\mathsf{Lancz}}(n)|}{n!} \leq \zeta \tag{1}$$

2.2   Multiple-precision Arithmetic

Given a working precision $\beta > 0$, the set of all definable numbers in this context is expressed as $\mathbb{F} = \left\{ w \cdot 2^e \; : \; \frac{1}{2} \leq |w| \leq 1 \text{ and } e \in \mathbb{Z} \right\}$ [48,38,27]. Here e is an integer denoting the exponent, and the $\mathrm{ulp}(x) = 2^{e-\beta}$, where ulp denotes the unit in the last place [48]. Let $\mathbf{rnd} : \mathbb{R} \to \mathbb{F}$ be the rounding function that rounds a real number to the nearest definable number. The corresponding relative errors are bounded by $\frac{|\mathbf{rnd}(x) - x|}{|x|} \leq \varepsilon$, for $x \neq 0$, where $\varepsilon = \frac{1}{2^\beta}$, is referred to as the *unit round-off* [48,38,27].

We define a set of operations by *basic operations* for which it is possible to directly compute the correct rounding of the result [17]. These operations are $\{+, -, \times, /, \sqrt{\ }\}$. For any two numbers $x, y \in \mathbb{R}$, the following bound holds:

$$|(\mathbf{rnd}(x) \circledast \mathbf{rnd}(y)) - (x * y)| \leq \varepsilon \cdot |x * y| \tag{2}$$

where $* \in \{+, -, \times, /\}$, and, $\circledast$ is the corresponding operation in $\mathbb{F}$. Same bound holds for $\sqrt{x}$ [27]. For n real numbers $x_1, x_2, \ldots, x_n$, the computed sum $\hat{s} := \mathbf{rnd}(x_1) \oplus \mathbf{rnd}(x_2) \oplus \ldots \oplus \mathbf{rnd}(x_n)$, regardless of the order of computation, deviates from the exact sum $s = \sum_{i=1}^{n} x_i$ by at most following bound [27],

$$|\hat{s} - s| \leq n\varepsilon \sum_{i=1}^{n} |x_i| \tag{3}$$

The basic operations are the building blocks for other advanced operations, such as logarithms, exponentials, and trigonometric functions.

2.3   Approximate Computation of Logarithm

Logarithm computation is generally approximated using the Taylor series. However, for high precision, *arithmetic-geometric-mean (AGM)* [9] is used. Let us consider two sequences $\{w_n\}, \{z_n\}$ of positive real numbers such that, $w_{n+1} = \frac{w_n + z_n}{2}, z_{n+1} = \sqrt{w_n \cdot z_n}$. These two sequences converge to the common limit and are denoted by $AGM(w_0, z_0)$.

For $x \in \mathbb{F}$ represented as $x = w \cdot 2^e$, we define the function exponent$(x) = e$. To compute $\log(x)$ using the *AGM* method, an integer m is computed such that $x2^m > 2^{\beta/2}$. The algorithm then evaluates $AGM(1, 4/s)$ and computes the logarithm as

$$\mathsf{Log}(x) = \frac{\pi}{2AGM(1, 4/s)} - m \log 2$$

In the MPFR library [48], the value of m is fixed as $m = \left\lceil \frac{\beta + 3}{2} \right\rceil - \text{exponent}(x)$. This choice of m ensures that $s = x2^m$ lies within the range $[2^{\beta/2}, 2^{\beta}]$. The following lemma provides an error bound for the AGM method.

Lemma 1 (Prop. 2 of [9]). *For the function AGM, the following holds for any $s \geq 4$:* $\left| \frac{\pi}{2AGM(1, 4/s)} - \log(s) \right| \leq \frac{64}{s^2}(10 + |\log s|)$.

Let Log be the function that computes the logarithm using the AGM method. Since, for $\beta > 8$, we have $3 \log(s) > 10$ and $2^{\beta/2} \leq s \leq 2^{\beta}$, we make the following conclusion:

$$|\mathsf{Log}(x) - \log(x)| \leq \frac{178\beta}{2^{\beta}} \tag{4}$$

We will use the notation $\tau = \frac{178\beta}{2^{\beta}}$ as the additive error bound for the logarithm approximation in the rest of the paper. Note that, $\tau = \mathcal{O}(\varepsilon)$. A similar error bound can be derived for the Taylor series method as well [7,8].

Evaluating the logarithm of the factorial, rather than the factorial itself, is the standard technique. The function $\mathsf{LogFactorial}$ computes the logarithm of the factorial using the Lanczos approximation with fixed parameters t and g.

$$\mathsf{LogFactorial}(k) = \frac{1}{2}\mathsf{Log}(2\pi) + \left(k + \frac{1}{2}\right)\mathsf{Log}\left(k + g + \frac{1}{2}\right)$$
$$- \left(k + g + \frac{1}{2}\right) + \mathsf{Log}\left(A_{t,g}(k)\right) \tag{5}$$

3   Related Work

The impact of computational approximations has been a longstanding concern in the literature. Considerable effort has been devoted to designing samplers that generate samples with arbitrary precision and provably no deviation from the original distribution, a concept referred to as *exact sampling*. This line of work dates back to Von Neumann and has been further developed in studies such as [29], which propose arbitrarily precise algorithms for sampling from distributions like the normal and exponential. The core idea involves employing a random process that efficiently generates a sample x with probability e^{-x}. Remarkably, this algorithm achieves an expected runtime of $\mathcal{O}(1)$.

Similarly, significant attention has been given to designing exact Binomial samplers [14,16] as well. The approach in [14] employs the geometric distribution to generate Binomial samples but requires $\mathcal{O}(np)$ time. More recent advances by

[16] achieve $\mathcal{O}(\sqrt{n})$ time complexity. Their approach involves efficiently accessing $b_{n,1/2}$ and leveraging its samples, combined with the binary representation of p, to generate samples from $b_{n,p}$.

Constant time sampling algorithms for binomial distributions are categorized under the framework of *transformed rejection sampling* [15,44,22,28]. These algorithms achieve a sampling time complexity of $\mathcal{O}(1)$, but at the cost of approximations. This is because the framework needs to evaluate the probability mass function, which is computationally expensive unless approximated.

The impact of numerical accuracy on computational programs has been extensively studied. Significant research has been conducted to analyze errors in arithmetic operations [10,26,25,27,43]. Recently, [5] and [8] have explored how these errors affect the performance of functions such as log-sum-exp and softmax. These studies underscore the critical need to account for the inherent numerical errors when designing algorithms and assessing their practical performance.

Finally, statistical distance has been widely recognized as a key measure of sampler quality. For instance, a series of works [12,35,40,39,2,32,3] focus on designing tests to determine the quality of samplers in terms of the statistical distance between the sampler and the target distribution.

4   Statistical Distance as Quality Metric

Since exact sampling from distributions such as Binomial is computationally expensive for most parameters of interest, the standard libraries rely on approximations to achieve practical efficiency. While these approximations significantly reduce time complexity, they introduce deviation from the actual distribution, effectively causing the samples to come from a distribution different from the intended one. Therefore, we need to focus on a fundamental question: *how do we make systems that rely on samplers trustworthy?*

Simply ignoring these deviations is not advisable, as they can have cascading effects that compromise the correctness of the entire system. Often, a user designs a randomized algorithm $\mathcal{A}$ to solve a particular problem, with an upper bound δ on its failure probability. If $\mathcal{A}$ relies on a standard Binomial sampler without knowledge of the sampler's quality, the program may experience a higher failure rate due to approximations in the underlying samplers.

Our proposal immediately raises the question: how should one measure the quality of the sampler? To this end, we first focus on the fact that the objective of the measurement of quality is to allow the end user to quantify the impact of the usage of the sampler. There are several metrics, such as KL-divergence, statistical distance, and Hellinger distance, that have been proposed in the literature focused on probability distributions that seek to quantify the distance between two probability distributions. In this regard, a natural question is to ask what distance metric we should choose. To this end, we propose the usage of statistical distance (Definition 1) as the metric to report the quality.

Definition 1 (Statistical Distance). *Suppose two distributions* p, q *are defined over the set* Ω. *The Statistical Distance (denoted by* d_{TV}*) between* p *and* q *is defined by,* $d_{TV}(p,q) = \frac{1}{2}\sum_{x\in\Omega}|p(x) - q(x)| = \sup_{A\subseteq\Omega} p(A) - q(A)$.

Our proposal for statistical distance stems from its ability to allow end users to derive the worst-case bounds on the behavior of the system in a *black-box* manner. Formally, this follows from the folklore lemma below, for which we provide a proof for completeness.

Lemma 2. *Let* $\mathcal{A}$ *be a randomized algorithm that uses randomness from a source distribution* p, *and let* Bad *be an event in the output of* $\mathcal{A}$. *If* p *is replaced by another distribution* q, *then the probability of the event* Bad *is bounded by the statistical distance between:*

$$\left|\Pr_{r\sim p}(\mathcal{A}(x;r) \in \mathsf{Bad}) - \Pr_{r\sim q}(\mathcal{A}(x;r) \in \mathsf{Bad})\right| \leq d_{TV}(p,q)$$

Proof. Let $B \subseteq \Omega$ be the set of random strings (or, numbers) that trigger the event Bad. Then, we have $\left|\Pr_{r\sim p}(\mathcal{A}(x;r) \in \mathsf{Bad}) - \Pr_{r\sim q}(\mathcal{A}(x;r) \in \mathsf{Bad})\right| = |p(B) - q(B)|$. Using the definition of statistical distance (definition 1), $|p(B) - q(B)| \leq \sup_{A\subseteq\Omega} p(A) - q(A) = d_{TV}(p,q)$. □

Note that the lemma above imposes no restrictions on $\mathcal{A}$ or the event Bad, highlighting the power of statistical distance as a metric. In particular, if $d_{TV}(p,q)$ is small, then the end user can be confident in bounding the overall impact on the program. We give a general recipe of how to incorporate statistical distance in the implementation of randomized algorithms.

4.1   Integrating Statistical Distance Analysis in Applications

The correctness of randomized algorithms typically relies on access to exact samples from a target distribution p. However, in practice, algorithms must use samplers that draw from an approximate distribution q, potentially compromising their theoretical guarantees. We propose a systematic framework for incorporating these approximations while maintaining rigorous error bounds through minimal modifications to existing algorithms and their analyses.

Algorithm Modification Let $\mathcal{A}$ be a randomized algorithm that requires samples from distribution p. We modify $\mathcal{A}$ to explicitly track and bound the accumulated error from using an approximate sampler as follows:

1. Introduce an error budget parameter δ_1 representing the maximum allowable error due to sampling approximations.
2. Initialize an error accumulator δ' to track the statistical distance:

$$\delta' \leftarrow 0.$$

3. For each sampler invocation, update the accumulated error:

$$\delta' \leftarrow \delta' + d_{TV}(p, q)$$

where $d_{TV}(p, q)$ is the pre-computed statistical distance bound.
4. If δ' exceeds the budget ($\delta' > \delta_1$), abort execution.

Analysis Modification Let δ_2 denote the original error probability of algorithm $\mathcal{A}$ assuming access to exact samples from p. After incorporating the sampling approximation error δ_1, the total error probability δ is bounded by:

$$\delta \leq \delta_1 + \delta_2$$

This framework maintains theoretical guarantees while transparently accounting for sampling approximations. The modifications are minimal and the analysis remains straightforward. We demonstrate an end-to-end integration of this approach through a case study in section 6.

An alternative approach would be to directly analyze algorithm $\mathcal{A}$ with respect to the approximate distribution q. However, this presents several challenges. The target distribution p often possesses mathematically convenient properties that facilitate analysis, while the implementation-specific q may lack such properties, making direct analysis intractable. Furthermore, updates to the underlying sampler implementation would inevitably necessitate re-analysis of every dependent algorithm.

Our framework enables separation of concerns: algorithm designers can conduct analysis assuming access to the idealized distribution p, while library developers focus on bounding the statistical distance between p and their implementation q. The errors can then be composed as shown above, providing rigorous bounds with minimal modification to existing analyses.

4.2 Proposal for Extending Sampler Interfaces

To enable seamless integration of our statistical distance framework, we propose extending the interface of existing samplers by incorporating two new components (see fig. 1): (1) an input parameter δ_{in} that allows users to specify the maximum allowable statistical distance from the ideal distribution, and (2) an output parameter δ_{out} that reports the actual statistical distance achieved during sampling. These additions give users fine-grained control over the sampler. By setting δ_{in}, users can explicitly define their tolerance for the statistical distance, while δ_{out} enables real-time monitoring of the sampler's performance. The fine-grained control offered by our interface allows users to make informed decisions about the trade-off between accuracy and performance.

5 Analysis of Standard Binomial Samplers

This section examines standard Binomial sampling algorithms and their inherent errors. We first present the standard Binomial sampling algorithm and then analyze the bounds on the statistical distance between the actual distribution and the distribution from which the sampler draws the samples.

```
def BinSamp(n, p):                    def BinSamp(n, p, delta_in):
    """                                   """
    Input:      n, p                      Input:      n, p, delta_in
    Output:     sample                    Output:     sample, delta_out
    """                                   """

    ...                                   ...
```

Fig. 1: Early (left) and new (right) sampler interfaces. The new version includes statistical distance control via `delta_in` and `delta_out`.

5.1   Standard Binomial Sampling Algorithms

This section describes the standard Binomial sampling algorithms commonly used in practice, with particular attention given to Python's implementation. These samplers rely on the method of *transformed rejection sampling* which combines two well-established sampling techniques: (1) inverse transform sampling and (2) rejection sampling. Rejection sampling requires existence of an, *easy to sample from*, hat distribution h such that for all $k \in [n]$, $b_{n,p}(k) < \alpha h(k)$ for some $\alpha > 0$, known as *rejection rate*. Inverse transform sampling generates samples from h. Suppose the cumulative distribution of h is denoted by $\mathcal{H}$. Because $\mathcal{H}$ is a cumulative distribution therefore, its inverse $\mathcal{H}^{-1}$ is well defined. To get a sample from h, a uniform random variable u is generated, and correspondingly the sample $k = \lfloor \mathcal{H}^{-1}(u) \rfloor$ is computed. From the principles of inverse transform sampling, we can show that $k \sim h$. The next step involves rejection sampling. After generating k, another uniform random sample v is generated from $[0, 1]$. The sample is rejected if $v > \frac{b_{n,p}(k)}{\alpha h(k)}$, else k is returned.

Among the various Binomial sampling algorithms, the choice of the (inverse) hat distribution $\mathcal{H}^{-1}(u)$ is a key difference. For example, Hörmann [22] considered the following definitions of hat distribution[4] for $-0.5 \leq u \leq 0.5$, which has high acceptance probabilities for Binomial distributions over varied n, p.

$$\mathcal{H}^{-1}(u) = \left(\frac{2\lambda_{n,p}}{(1/2 - |u|)} + \mu_{n,p} \right) u + \nu_{n,p}, \quad h^{-1}(u) = \frac{\lambda_{n,p}}{(1/2 - |u|)^2} + \mu_{n,p}$$

The parameters $\lambda_{n,p}, \mu_{n,p}, \nu_{n,p}$ depend on the parameters of Binomial distribution n, p. Specifically, in Hörmann's algorithm, the corresponding parameters were chosen to be: $\lambda_{n,p} = -0.05878 + 0.062744\sqrt{np(1-p)} + 0.01p$, $\mu_{n,p} = 1.15 + 2.53\sqrt{np(1-p)}$, $\nu_{n,p} = np + 0.5$. Importantly, our results are not restricted to any specific choice of hat distribution. Instead, we consider any arbitrary hat distribution h and its inverse $\mathcal{H}^{-1}$ that satisfy the conditions of transformed rejection sampling and involve a constant number of basic arithmetic operations. Therefore, for simplicity and readability, we omit the explicit details of $\mathcal{H}$ and h

---

[4] Since $(\mathcal{H}^{-1})'(u) = \frac{1}{h(k)}$, we use the notation $h^{-1}(u) = \frac{1}{h(k)}$ directly for simplicity.

in the rest of the paper. We will refer to $\mathcal{H}^{-1}$ as the 'inverse function' and h as the 'hat function' or 'hat distribution'.

The expected runtime of these algorithms is proportional to the rejection rate α, and therefore, the runtime is independent of the parameters of the distribution. These algorithms require computing the rejection ratio $r_k = \frac{\mathsf{b}_{n,p}(k)}{\alpha \mathsf{h}(k)}$. But computing this ratio, especially evaluating $\mathsf{b}_{n,p}(k)$ exactly, can be as expensive as exponential in the number of bits. Therefore, an easily computable approximation $\widetilde{r}_k$ is often obtained to achieve fast scalable practical algorithms. Usually, due to scalability purposes, the logarithm of the rejection ratio $\log r_k$ is computed rather than directly computing r_k, which again suffers from other approximation errors due to log computation. Therefore, these algorithms lack sampling exactly from the distribution.

Python implementation of Binomial Sampler Standard implementations of Binomial samplers, such as those available in libraries like the GNU Scientific Library (GSL) [18], are designed to work with 64-bit floating-point numbers. Similarly, Python's standard libraries and NumPy [19], provide an implementation of Hörmann's algorithm for up to the 64-bit floating-point range. Notably, starting from Python version 3.12, this algorithm has also been integrated into the standard random library of Python, offering support for higher precision computations (though still constrained by the arithmetic computational limits of Python's standard library).

Algorithm 1 presents an abstraction of the standard implementation Binomial Sampler. Consistent with the current Python implementation, we assume that the BinSamp algorithm uses the Lanczos approximation to compute the logarithm of the factorial function. To employ the Lanczos approximation, the algorithm uses LogFactorial as described in eq. (5). This is one of the most widely used implementations of the Binomial sampling algorithm in practice. We adopt it as a benchmark for developing our error bounds. For clarity, we denote the distribution generated by Python's standard library implementation of Algorithm 1 as $\mathsf{b}_{n,p}^{\mathsf{BinSamp}}$, as opposed to the notation $\mathsf{b}_{n,p}$, which refers to the Binomial distribution with parameters n, p.

5.2 Our Findings

We begin by stating the main theorem of our paper, followed by the supporting lemmas that are used to establish the theorem.

Theorem 1. *Let the precision of the context be $\beta \geq \max(2\lceil \log_2 n \rceil, \lceil -\log_2 p \rceil)$, and let $\mathsf{b}_{n,p}^{\mathsf{BinSamp}}$ denote the distribution from which BinSamp samples are drawn. The statistical distance between $\mathsf{b}_{n,p}^{\mathsf{BinSamp}}$ and $\mathsf{b}_{n,p}$ is given by:*

$$\mathsf{d}_{\mathsf{TV}}\left(\mathsf{b}_{n,p}, \mathsf{b}_{n,p}^{\mathsf{BinSamp}}\right) \leq (1110\beta + 3cp + c + \alpha c)n\varepsilon + 15\zeta + o(\varepsilon)$$

Where c is a constant determined by the inverse function pair $(\mathcal{H}, \mathsf{h})$, α is the rejection rate, ζ denotes the uniform error bound due to the Lanczos's approx-

---

Algorithm 1: BinSamp(n, p)

Input : Parameters n, p
Output: Sample k

1 Initialize inverse-function-pair $(\mathcal{H}, \mathsf{h})$
2 Initialize rejection parameter α
3 $l_n \leftarrow \mathsf{LogFactorial}(n)$
4 **while** *True* **do**
5       $v \leftarrow$ uniform random samples within $[0, 1]$
6       $u \leftarrow$ uniform random samples within $[-0.5, 0.5]$
7       $k \leftarrow \lfloor \mathcal{H}^{-1}(u) \rfloor$
8       $l_k \leftarrow \mathsf{LogFactorial}(k)$, $l_{nk} \leftarrow \mathsf{LogFactorial}(n - k)$
9       $l_v \leftarrow l_n \ominus l_k \ominus l_{nk} \oplus k \otimes \mathsf{Log}(p) \oplus (n - k) \otimes \mathsf{Log}(1 - p) \oplus \mathsf{Log}(\mathsf{h}^{-1}(u)) \ominus \mathsf{Log}(\alpha)$
10   **if** $\mathsf{Log}(v) \leq l_v$ **then**
11 | **return** k

---

imation, ε *represents the unit round off error* $\frac{1}{2^\beta}$, *and* $o(\varepsilon)$ *denotes the higher order terms in* ε.

The sources of deviations are categorized into two types of errors: (1) **E1**, which arises from errors in transformed rejection sampling caused by inaccuracies in the computation of $\lfloor \mathcal{H}^{-1}(u) \rfloor$ in line 7 of Algorithm 1; and (2) **E2**, which refers to errors in the computation of the rejection ratio, accumulating throughout lines 3, 8, and 9 of Algorithm 1. We will bound the effects of these two errors independently and then combine them to get our main theorem.

Analysis of E1: The error **E1** arises from inaccuracies in the inverse transform sampling, specifically due to deviations in the hat distribution h caused by basic arithmetic operations. The key challenge stems from the inverse sampling procedure evaluating $\mathcal{H}^{-1}(u)$ for a uniform random sample u. Since evaluating $\mathcal{H}^{-1}(u)$ requires basic arithmetic operations, the inverse sampling component may produce an incorrect output k', different from the intended value $k \neq k'$ and thereby deviating h into a modified distribution $\tilde{\mathsf{h}}$.

For $\beta > 2 \log_2 \lceil n \rceil$, we show that the possible values of k' are limited to $\{k - 1, k, k + 1\}$. Through careful analysis of the probabilities of k' being $k - 1$ or $k + 1$, we show that these probabilities are bounded by $\mathcal{O}(k\varepsilon)$. This leads to the bound on $\tilde{\mathsf{h}}(k)$ which is stated in the following lemma:

Lemma 3. *Suppose* $\tilde{\mathsf{h}}$ *is the deviated version of the hat distribution* h *due to the error in the computation of* $\mathcal{H}^{-1}(u)$. *Then, if the error is distributed uniformly over the range* $[-\varepsilon_\mathcal{H}, \varepsilon_\mathcal{H}]$ *and* $\varepsilon_\mathcal{H} \leq \frac{1}{2}$, *then for any* $k \in [n]$, $(1 - \varepsilon_\mathcal{H}(3k + 1))\mathsf{h}(k) \leq \tilde{\mathsf{h}}(k) \leq (1 + w_k \varepsilon_\mathcal{H}(k + 2))\mathsf{h}(k)$ *where,* $w_k = \max\left(\frac{\mathsf{h}(k-1)}{\mathsf{h}(k)}, \frac{\mathsf{h}(k+1)}{\mathsf{h}(k)} \right)$

Analysis of E2: The error **E2** stems from inaccuracies in the rejection ratio computation, which are influenced by factorial approximations, basic arithmetic operations, and log computation approximations. Specifically, the rejection ratio error originates from three primary sources: (1) errors introduced by factorial approximations, (2) errors and approximations in basic arithmetic operations and log computation during the rejection ratio computation. Both of these errors contribute to the error in the rejection ratio computation. The computed rejection ratio in line 9 of Algorithm 1 is denoted as $\widetilde{r}_k$, specifically, $\widetilde{r}_k = \frac{b_{n,p}^{\mathsf{BinSamp}}(k)}{\alpha h(k)}$.

Since Python's standard library uses the Lanczos approximation for log computations, we bound the relative error of factorial approximation using the corresponding error bound of the Lanczos approximation (see section 2.1 for details). To bound E2, we also need to understand the relative error in basic arithmetic operations and additive error bounds for logarithm approximations (see section 2.2 for details). By combining these error bounds, we establish a relative error bound for the rejection ratio, formalized in the following lemma.

Lemma 4. *Let r_k denote the actual rejection ratio, defined as $r_k = \frac{b_{n,p}(k)}{\alpha h(k)}$, and let $\widetilde{r}_k$ denote the computed rejection ratio, defined as $\widetilde{r}_k = \frac{b_{n,p}^{\mathsf{BinSamp}}(k)}{\alpha h(k)}$, for any k in $[n]$. Then, for any $k \in [0, n]$, we have:*

$$\left| \frac{\widetilde{r}_k}{r_k} - 1 \right| \leq (1110n + 2540)\beta\varepsilon + 14\varepsilon \log\left(h(k)\right) + 15\zeta + o(\varepsilon)$$

By combining the error bounds from both the rejection ratio computation and hat distribution deviation, we obtain the final bound on the statistical distance, as stated in Theorem 1.

5.3   Detailed Technical Analysis

We start by proving the main theorem of our paper using Lemma 3 and Lemma 4.

Proof (of theorem 1). Without loss of generality, assume $h(-1) = h(n+1) = b_{n,p}(-1) = b_{n,p}(n+1) = 0$ and $r_{-1} = r_{n+1} = 1$. Let us define the event accept as the event such that a sample k is sampled by the sampler. In BinSamp a sample drawn from $\widetilde{h}$ is accepted with probability $\widetilde{r}_k$. Therefore, the acceptance probability is given by, $\Pr(\mathsf{accept}) = \sum_{k=0}^{n} \Pr(\mathsf{accept}|k)\Pr(k) = \sum_{k=0}^{n} \widetilde{r}_k \widetilde{h}(k)$. Substituing the lower bounds for $\widetilde{r}_k$, $\widetilde{h}(k)$ from Lemma 4 and Lemma 3 we get:

$$\Pr(\mathsf{accept}) \geq \sum_{k=0}^{n} (1 - (1110n + 2540)\beta\varepsilon - 14\varepsilon \log\left(h^{-1}(u)\right) - 15\zeta - o(\varepsilon))$$

$$(1 - (3k+1)\varepsilon_{\mathcal{H}})r_k h(k)$$

$$\geq \sum_{k=0}^{n} (1 - (1110n + 2540)\beta\varepsilon - 14\varepsilon \log\left(h^{-1}(u)\right) - 15\zeta - o(\varepsilon))$$

$$(1 - (3k+1)\varepsilon_{\mathcal{H}})\frac{b_{n,p}(k)}{\alpha}$$

To complete the lower bound we first observe that,

$$\sum_{k=0}^{n} \log(\mathsf{h}^{-1}(u))\mathsf{b}_{n,p}(k) = \sum_{k=0}^{n} \log\left(\frac{\mathsf{b}_{n,p}(k)}{\mathsf{h}(k)}\right)\mathsf{b}_{n,p}(k) - \sum_{k=0}^{n} \log(\mathsf{b}_{n,p}(k))\mathsf{b}_{n,p}(k).$$

Given that $\frac{\mathsf{b}_{n,p}(k)}{\mathsf{h}(k)} \leq \alpha$ for all k, and that the entropy of Binomial distribution satisfies $\mathbb{E}[-\log(\mathsf{b}_{n,p}(k))] \leq \frac{1}{2}\log_2(2\pi e np(1-p))$, we conclude that

$$\sum_{k=0}^{n} \log(\mathsf{h}^{-1}(u))\mathsf{b}_{n,p}(k) \leq \alpha + \frac{1}{2}\log_2(2\pi e np(1-p)).$$

Thus we can lower bound acceptance probability $\Pr(\mathsf{accept})$ as follows,

$$\Pr(\mathsf{accept}) \geq \left(1 - (1110n + 2554)\beta\varepsilon - 14\alpha\varepsilon + \log\left(\mathsf{h}^{-1}(u)\right) - 15\zeta\right.$$
$$\left. -(3np+1)\varepsilon_{\mathcal{H}} - o(\varepsilon)\right) \cdot \frac{1}{\alpha}$$

Therefore, the probability of observing a point k under the sampler's output distribution is given by $\mathsf{b}_{n,p}^{\mathsf{BinSamp}}(k) = \Pr(k|\mathsf{accept})$. Applying Bayes' rule we get, $\mathsf{b}_{n,p}^{\mathsf{BinSamp}}(k) = \frac{\Pr(\mathsf{accept}|k)\Pr(k)}{\Pr(\mathsf{accept})} = \frac{\widetilde{r}_k\widetilde{\mathsf{h}}(k)}{\Pr(\mathsf{accept})}$. By using the upper bound of $\widetilde{r}_k$, from Lemma 4,

$$\mathsf{b}_{n,p}^{\mathsf{BinSamp}}(k) \leq \frac{1 + (1110n + 2540)\beta\varepsilon + 14\varepsilon\log\left(\mathsf{h}^{-1}(u)\right) + 15\zeta + o(\varepsilon)}{1 - (1110n + 2554)\beta\varepsilon - 15\zeta - (3np+1)\varepsilon_{\mathcal{H}} - o(\varepsilon)} \cdot \alpha r_k\widetilde{\mathsf{h}}(k)$$
$$\leq \left(1 + (2220n + 5080)\beta\varepsilon + 28\varepsilon\log\left(\mathsf{h}^{-1}(u)\right) + 30\zeta\right.$$
$$\left. + (6np+2)\varepsilon_{\mathcal{H}} + o(\varepsilon)\right) \cdot \frac{\mathsf{b}_{n,p}(k)\widetilde{\mathsf{h}}(k)}{\mathsf{h}(k)}$$

The last inequality follows from assuming $(1110n + 2540)\beta\varepsilon + (3np+1)\varepsilon_{\mathcal{H}} + 14\varepsilon\log\left(\mathsf{h}^{-1}(u)\right) + 15\zeta + o(\varepsilon) \leq \frac{1}{2}$. Next we bound the ratio $\frac{\widetilde{\mathsf{h}}(k)}{\mathsf{h}(k)}$ using Lemma 3,

$$\mathsf{b}_{n,p}^{\mathsf{BinSamp}}(k) \leq \left(1 + (2220n + 5080)\beta\varepsilon + 28\varepsilon\log\left(\mathsf{h}^{-1}(u)\right) + 30\zeta\right.$$
$$\left. + (6np+2)\varepsilon_{\mathcal{H}} + o(\varepsilon)\right) \cdot (1 + w_k\varepsilon_{\mathcal{H}}(k+2)) \cdot \mathsf{b}_{n,p}(k)$$
$$\leq \left(1 + (2220n + 5080)\beta\varepsilon + 28\varepsilon\log\left(\mathsf{h}^{-1}(u)\right) + 30\zeta + (6np+2)\varepsilon_{\mathcal{H}} + \right.$$
$$\left. w_k\varepsilon_{\mathcal{H}}(k+2) + o(\varepsilon)\right) \cdot \mathsf{b}_{n,p}(k)$$

Where $w_k = \max\left(\frac{\mathsf{h}(k-1)}{\mathsf{h}(k)}, \frac{\mathsf{h}(k+1)}{\mathsf{h}(k)}\right)$. Since $r_k \leq 1$, it follows that $\mathsf{h}(k) \geq \frac{\mathsf{b}_{n,p}(k)}{\alpha}$ and $\mathsf{h}(k+1) = \frac{\mathsf{b}_{n,p}(k+1)}{\alpha r_{k+1}}$. This implies $\frac{\mathsf{h}(k+1)}{\mathsf{h}(k)} \leq \frac{\mathsf{b}_{n,p}(k+1)}{\mathsf{b}_{n,p}(k)r_{k+1}}$. Similarly, we have $\frac{\mathsf{h}(k-1)}{\mathsf{h}(k)} \leq \frac{\mathsf{b}_{n,p}(k-1)}{\mathsf{b}_{n,p}(k)r_{k-1}}$. Combining these, w_k can be upper bounded as follows,

$$w_k = \max\left(\frac{\mathsf{h}(k-1)}{\mathsf{h}(k)}, \frac{\mathsf{h}(k+1)}{\mathsf{h}(k)}\right) \leq \max\left(\frac{\mathsf{b}_{n,p}(k-1)}{\mathsf{b}_{n,p}(k)r_{k-1}}, \frac{\mathsf{b}_{n,p}(k+1)}{\mathsf{b}_{n,p}(k)r_{k+1}}\right)$$

This yields the following bound: $w_k \mathsf{b}_{n,p}(k) \leq \max\left(\frac{\mathsf{b}_{n,p}(k-1)}{r_{k-1}}, \frac{\mathsf{b}_{n,p}(k+1)}{r_{k+1}}\right)$. Thus, $w_k \mathsf{b}_{n,p}(k) \leq \max\left(\mathsf{h}(k-1), \mathsf{h}(k+1)\right) \leq \mathsf{h}(k-1) + \mathsf{h}(k+1)$. Using this bound, we can upper bound the sum $\sum_{k=0}^{n} w_k \varepsilon_{\mathcal{H}}(k+2) \mathsf{b}_{n,p}(k)$ as follows,

$$\sum_{k=0}^{n} w_k \varepsilon_{\mathcal{H}}(k+2) \mathsf{b}_{n,p}(k) \leq \alpha \varepsilon_{\mathcal{H}} \sum_{k=0}^{n} (k+2)\left(\mathsf{h}(k-1) + \mathsf{h}(k+1)\right)$$
$$\leq 2\alpha \varepsilon_{\mathcal{H}}(n+2)$$

The last inequality follows from the fact that $k \leq n$, $\sum_{i=0}^{n-1} \mathsf{h}(i) \leq 1$ and $\sum_{i=1}^{n} \mathsf{h}(i) \leq 1$. Therefore, the statistical distance between the sampler's distribution and the Binomial distribution is given by,

$$d_{\mathsf{TV}}(\mathsf{b}_{n,p}^{\mathsf{BinSamp}}, \mathsf{b}_{n,p}) = \frac{1}{2} \sum_{k=0}^{n} \left| \mathsf{b}_{n,p}^{\mathsf{BinSamp}}(k) - \mathsf{b}_{n,p}(k) \right|$$

$$\leq \frac{1}{2} \sum_{k=0}^{n} \left| (2220n + 5080)\beta\varepsilon + 28\varepsilon \log\left(\mathsf{h}^{-1}(u)\right) + 30\zeta + (6np+2)\varepsilon_{\mathcal{H}} \right.$$
$$\left. + 2\alpha\varepsilon_{\mathcal{H}}(n+2) + o(\varepsilon) \right| \cdot \mathsf{b}_{n,p}(k)$$
$$\leq (1110n + 2554)\beta\varepsilon + 14\alpha\varepsilon + 15\zeta + (3np+1)\varepsilon_{\mathcal{H}} + \alpha\varepsilon_{\mathcal{H}}(n+2) + o(\varepsilon)$$
$$= (1110\beta + 3cp + c + \alpha c)n\varepsilon + 15\zeta + o(\varepsilon)$$

This completes the proof.   □

Error in Inverse Transform Sampling In this subsection, we analyze the error introduced during the inverse transform sampling process which arises from the arithmetic operations involved in evaluating the inverse hat function $\mathcal{H}^{-1}(u)$. Instead of assuming a specific hat distribution, we argue that for any hat distribution, the multiplicative error introduced during the computation of $\mathcal{H}^{-1}(u)$ is multiplicatively bounded by $\varepsilon_{\mathcal{H}} := c\varepsilon$, where $c > 0$ depends on the number of basic arithmetic operations[5] $*$ used in $\mathcal{H}^{-1}$ with $* \in \{+, -, \times, /, \sqrt{}\}$. Consequently, the computed value of $\mathcal{H}^{-1}(u)$ in line 7 of BinSamp falls within the range $[(1 - \varepsilon_{\mathcal{H}})\mathcal{H}^{-1}(u), (1 + \varepsilon_{\mathcal{H}})\mathcal{H}^{-1}(u)]$. To model the impact of the error we assume it to be uniformly distributed over the range $[-\varepsilon_{\mathcal{H}}, \varepsilon_{\mathcal{H}}]$. While a Gaussian distribution might seem like a natural choice for such errors, the uniform distribution offers a more conservative approach. Among all zero-mean Gaussian like distributions with bounded support, the uniform distribution has the heaviest tails within its support. This characteristic makes it suitable for handling errors in the worst-case scenario. In particular, if the mean of the error is centered at $\mathcal{H}^{-1}(u)$, then assuming a uniform distribution for the error allows us to upper bound deviations in $\mathsf{h}(k)$ more conservatively. This ensures that our bounds remain valid even under pessimistic error assumptions. We restate the Lemma 3 for completness and provide its proof in the full version.

---

[5] For most practical hat functions, we typically have $c \leq 100$, which implies that $\varepsilon_{\mathcal{H}} \leq \frac{1}{2}$ when the precision parameter $\beta > 8$.

Lemma 3. *Suppose* $\widetilde{h}$ *is the deviated version of the hat distribution* h *due to the error in the computation of* $\mathcal{H}^{-1}(u)$. *Then, if the error is distributed uniformly over the range* $[-\varepsilon_{\mathcal{H}}, \varepsilon_{\mathcal{H}}]$ *and* $\varepsilon_{\mathcal{H}} \leq \frac{1}{2}$, *then for any* $k \in [n]$, $(1-\varepsilon_{\mathcal{H}}(3k+1))h(k) \leq \widetilde{h}(k) \leq (1 + w_k \varepsilon_{\mathcal{H}}(k + 2))h(k)$ *where,* $w_k = \max\left(\frac{h(k-1)}{h(k)}, \frac{h(k+1)}{h(k)}\right)$

Error in Rejection Ratio Computation In this subsection, we will analyze the impact of factorial approximations, basic arithmetic operations, and log computation approximations on the rejection sampling process. Before proceeding further, we introduce the notation $b_{n,p}^{\text{Inter}}$, which we refer to it as the *intermediate distribution*, where only the factorial computations are approximated. The key result of this subsection is Lemma 4, whose proof builds on two auxiliary lemmas: one addressing errors from arithmetic and log approximations, and another handling factorial approximation. Proofs are deferred to the full version due to space constraints.

Lemma 5. *Let* r_k^{Inter} *denotes the ratio* $r_k^{\text{Inter}} = \frac{b_{n,p}^{\text{Inter}}(k)}{\alpha h(k)}$, *and let* $\widetilde{r}_k$ *denote the computed rejection ratio, defined as* $\widetilde{r}_k = \frac{b_{n,p}^{\text{BinSamp}}(k)}{\alpha h(k)}$, *for any* k *in* $[n]$. *Then, for all* $k \in [n]$, $\left|\frac{\widetilde{r}_k}{r_k^{\text{Inter}}} - 1\right| \leq (1110n + 2540)\beta\varepsilon + 14\varepsilon \log(h(k)) + o(\varepsilon)$

Lemma 6. *For all* $k \in [n]$, $(1-15\zeta)b_{n,p}(k) \leq b_{n,p}^{\text{Inter}}(k) \leq (1+15\zeta)b_{n,p}(k)$, *where* ζ *denotes the uniform error bound due to the Lanczos approximation and* $b_{n,p}^{\text{Inter}}$ *denotes the intermediate distribution.*

For completeness, we restate the Lemma 4 whose proof follows by combining Lemma 5 and Lemma 6.

Lemma 4. *Let* r_k *denote the actual rejection ratio, defined as* $r_k = \frac{b_{n,p}(k)}{\alpha h(k)}$, *and let* $\widetilde{r}_k$ *denote the computed rejection ratio, defined as* $\widetilde{r}_k = \frac{b_{n,p}^{\text{BinSamp}}(k)}{\alpha h(k)}$, *for any* k *in* $[n]$. *Then, for any* $k \in [0, n]$, *we have:*

$$\left|\frac{\widetilde{r}_k}{r_k} - 1\right| \leq (1110n + 2540)\beta\varepsilon + 14\varepsilon \log(h(k)) + 15\zeta + o(\varepsilon)$$

6   Case Study: DNF Counting

This case study demonstrates how our proposed bounds on the statistical distance between the sampler and the Binomial distribution can be easily integrated into practical tools. To demonstrate the applicability of these bounds, we utilize them in conjunction with an off-the-shelf Binomial sampler to implement the DNF Counting algorithm APSEst [37].

A DNF formula is a disjunction of conjunctions of literals, where each conjunction (clause) represents a set of conditions. For example, $(x_1 \wedge \neg x_2) \vee$

$(x_2 \wedge \neg x_3)$ is a DNF formula with clauses like $(x_1 \wedge \neg x_2)$. A DNF formula $\varphi := \varphi_1 \vee \ldots \vee \varphi_m$ has m clauses, and the number of its solutions is denoted as $|sol(\varphi)|$. The problem of counting the $|sol(\varphi)|$ for a DNF formula φ is #P-hard. To address this challenge, various Fully Polynomial-Time Randomized Approximation Schemes (FPRAS) have been developed [30,31,13]. Given a DNF formula φ and tolerance and confidence parameters $\varepsilon, \delta \in [0, 1]$, these FPRAS return $\widehat{n} \in [(1 - \varepsilon)|sol(\varphi)|, (1 + \varepsilon)|sol(\varphi)|]$ with probability at least $(1 - \delta)$.

The most recent progress in sampling-based DNF counting FPRAS is embodied by the algorithm APSEst [37]. Given a DNF formula φ, the APSEst returns an ε multiplicative approximation of $|sol(\varphi)|$ with high probability. The algorithm maintains a bucket $\mathcal{X}$ to keep sampled solutions from DNF clauses and, also, a probability parameter p such that, for any solution σ of φ, σ belongs to $\mathcal{X}$ with probability p. To achieve this goal, the algorithm removes all the elements σ from bucket $\mathcal{X}$ if σ satisfies φ_i. The algorithm next samples new solutions from φ_i. To determine the number of solutions, the APSEst asks for a sample N_i from Binomial distribution $\mathsf{b}_{|sol(\varphi_i)|, p}$ and adds N_i many new satisfying assignments of φ_i to $\mathcal{X}$. If the bucket overflows, the algorithm keeps on removing elements uniformly from the bucket until the bucket size falls under the threshold. The end goal of APSEst is to output the ratio $\frac{|\mathcal{X}|}{p}$ which is a good estimate of $|sol(\varphi)|$.

Since APSEst heavily relies on the Binomial sampler, the theoretical guarantees of APSEst are contingent on the quality of the Binomial sampler. This case study illustrates how our results allow users to maintain the theoretical guarantees of APSEst. Computing bounds on $\mathsf{d_{TV}}$ between the Binomial distribution and the sampler, users can adjust the confidence parameter δ in APSEst to account for errors from the underlying Binomial sampler, thereby ensuring correctness with theoretical guarantees.

Algorithm Modification We demonstrate how easily the APSEst algorithm can be modified to incorporate our statistical distance bounds. We denote this modified version as APSEst2, detailed in algorithm 2, with highlighted modifications. The primary difference between APSEst and APSEst2 lies in handling the confidence parameter δ to account for the errors due to the underlying binomial sampler. Therefore, APSEst2 takes another parameter $\kappa \in [0, 1]$ to adjust the error budget for the sampler, such that, $\kappa\delta$ is the error budget for the sampler and $(1 - \kappa)\delta$ is the error budget for the algorithm. If the accumulated error due to the sampler exceeds the error budget, APSEst2 halts immediately and returns Fail. The user can restart the algorithm using a larger value of κ to accommodate an increased error budget.

Analysis Modification We now illustrate how simply the analysis of APSEst can be modified to APSEst2. Recall that we are concerned with the event: $\frac{|\mathcal{X}|}{p} \notin (1 \pm \varepsilon)|sol(\varphi)|$, which we will refer to as Bad. Note that, $\delta_1 = \kappa\delta$ is the error budget for the sampler and $\delta_2 = (1 - \kappa)\delta$ is the error budget for the algorithm. By the correctness guarantee of APSEst, $\mathrm{Pr}_{\mathsf{b}_{n,p}}(\mathsf{Bad}) \leq \delta_2$. During the execution of APSEst2, if the algorithm invokes the sampler t times with parameters n_i, p_i,

---

Algorithm 2: APSEst2($\varphi, \varepsilon, \delta, \kappa$)

(The modifications from APSEst to APSEst2 are highlighted)

---

1 $\delta_1 \leftarrow \kappa\delta$

2 $\delta_2 \leftarrow (1 - \kappa)\delta$

3 Initialize $T \leftarrow \left(\frac{\log(4/\delta_2) + \log m}{\varepsilon^2} \right)$

4 Initialize $p \leftarrow 1$, $\mathcal{X} \leftarrow \emptyset$

5 $\delta' \leftarrow 0$

6 for $i = 1$ *to* m **do**

7   **for** *all* $\sigma \in \mathcal{X}$ **do**

8   **if** $\sigma \vDash \varphi_i$ **then**

9   remove σ from $\mathcal{X}$

10 $N_i \leftarrow \mathsf{BinSamp}(|sol(\varphi_i)|, p)$

11 $\delta' \leftarrow \delta' + \delta^i_{|sol(\varphi_i)|, p}$

12   **if** $\delta' > \delta_1$ **then**

13   **return** Fail

14   Add N_i distinct random solutions of ϕ_i to $\mathcal{X}$

15   **while** $|\mathcal{X}| > T$ **do**

16 $p = p/2$

17   Throw away each element of $\mathcal{X}$ with probability $\frac{1}{2}$

18 Output $\frac{|\mathcal{X}|}{p}$

---

then from Lemma 2, we have

$$\Pr_{\mathsf{b}^{\mathsf{BinSamp}}_{n,p}} (\mathsf{Bad}) \leq \Pr_{\mathsf{b}_{n,p}} (\mathsf{Bad}) + \sum_{i=1}^{t} \mathsf{d_{TV}}(\mathsf{b}_{n_i,p_i}, \mathsf{b}^{\mathsf{BinSamp}}_{n_i,p_i})$$

Suppose during the execution, the computed $\mathsf{d_{TV}}$ bounds using Theorem 1 are given by $\delta^1_{n_1,p_1}, \delta^2_{n_2,p_2}, \ldots, \delta^t_{n_t,p_t}$ such that $\delta' = \sum_{i=1}^{t} \delta^i_{n_i,p_i}$. Therefore, if APSEst2 does not halt then $\Pr_{\mathsf{b}^{\mathsf{BinSamp}}_{n,p}}(\mathsf{Bad}) \leq \Pr_{\mathsf{b}_{n,p}}(\mathsf{Bad}) + \sum_{i=1}^{t} \mathsf{d_{TV}}(\mathsf{b}_{n,p}, \mathsf{b}^{\mathsf{BinSamp}}_{n,p}) \leq \delta_2 + \delta' \leq \delta_2 + \delta_1 \leq \delta$. Thus, by the correctness of APSEst the count returned by APSEst2 is within the ε error bound. If APSEst2 halts and returns Fail, this implies that the error budget of the sampler has been exceeded.

6.1 Experimental Setup and Evaluation Results

We conducted accuracy experiments following the methodology of [46] to assess the reliability of the counts returned by APSEst2. Specifically, we compared the counts from APSEst2 with those from Ganak [45], an exact counting tool. We used a comprehensive benchmark suite from [46] to evaluate the performance and accuracy of the algorithms. This suite consists of DNF formulas with the number of variables ranging from 100 to 700 and clause counts ranging from 30 to 700. Following prior work [46,36,47], we adopted the standard settings for the tolerance parameter ($\varepsilon = 0.8$) and the confidence parameter ($\delta = 0.36$),

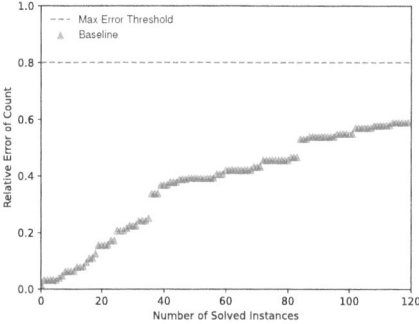

Fig. 2: Accuracy experiment results for APSEst2. The red line represents the tolerance factor ($\varepsilon = 0.8$).

which are commonly used in both model counting competitions and practical applications. Finally, we set κ to 0.5.

Summary of Results Our observations reveal that APSEst2 delivers counts that are nearly as precise as the exact counts obtained from Ganak, as demonstrated in fig. 2. The y-axis of fig. 2 represents the relative error of the counts, with the tolerance parameter ($\varepsilon = 0.8$) marked by a red straight line, while the x-axis represents the instances. We observed that for all instances, APSEst2 computed counts within the tolerance, demonstrating high accuracy.

Figure 3 presents the reported errors δ' of the Binomial sampler during the execution of APSEst2. The left plot presents the reported errors for individual instances, while the right plot groups the average error by the number of clauses in the DNF formula. Across our benchmark suite, the errors remain around 10^{-6}. The error increases with the number of clauses as the number of calls to the Binomial sampler increases. Notably, we observe a 10-fold increase in error when the number of clauses grows from 30 to 700.

The results suggest that APSEst2 is capable of providing highly reliable approximations of counts across a diverse range of DNF instances, maintaining accuracy within the predefined error margin despite its simple design. The integration of our statistical distance bounds into the algorithm allows users to effectively manage the error budget, ensuring that the algorithm remains robust and reliable even in the presence of approximation errors from the underlying Binomial sampler.

7 Conclusion

In this work, we first identified the sources of deviation in the practical implementations of standard binomial samplers. We observed that exact sampling from distributions is infeasible in practice due to high runtime overhead; thus, implementations inevitably introduce deviations. Accordingly, we proposed the

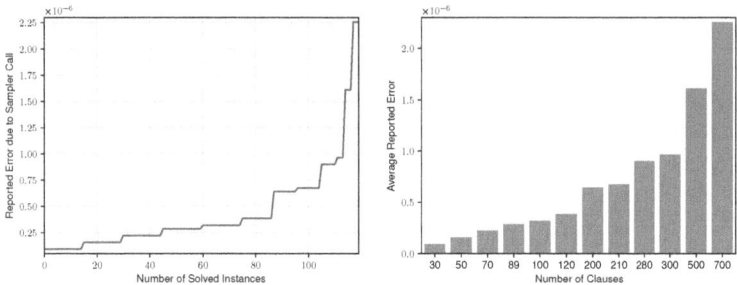

Fig. 3: Left: Reported errors (δ') by `APSEst2` for individual instances. Right: Average error grouped by the number of clauses in the DNF formula, showing a clear upward trend as formula size increases.

usage of statistical distance as the quality metric owing to its ability to allow end users to obtain sound bounds on the *bad* events. We also presented a case study demonstrating the minimal effort required by system designers to incorporate the reported deviation bounds into their systems.

Limitations and Future Work While our current work establishes a foundational framework, there are several limitations and opportunities for future enhancement. The current analysis relies on several simplifying assumptions—for instance, uniformity in the error distribution—which may not hold in more general settings. Additionally, the reported bounds are not yet tight and can be refined for greater accuracy, making this an important avenue for further research. Moreover, the principles of quality measurement can be extended to samplers for other distributions. Developing a general framework for error reporting across various types of samplers would be a valuable contribution to the field. Finally, proposing efficient sampling scheme that can achieve the desired statistical distance with minimal overhead is an open problem that warrants further investigation.

Acknowledgments. Part of this research is supported by DCSW-TAC Project ACMU-24/VPP (SC). Meel acknowledges the support of the Natural Sciences and Engineering Research Council of Canada (NSERC), funding reference number RGPIN-2024-05956. Sarkar acknowledges the support of Google PhD Fellowship. Part of the research was conducted while Sarkar was at the University of Toronto. Computations were performed on the Niagara supercomputer at the SciNet HPC Consortium. SciNet is funded by Innovation, Science and Economic Development Canada; the Digital Research Alliance of Canada; the Ontario Research Fund: Research Excellence; and the University of Toronto.

Disclosure of Interests. The authors declare that they have no competing interests.

References

1. Arora, S., Barak, B.: Computational complexity: a modern approach. Cambridge University Press (2009)
2. Banerjee, A., Chakraborty, S., Chakraborty, S., Meel, K.S., Sarkar, U., Sen, S.: Testing of horn samplers. In: AISTATS (2023)
3. Bhattacharyya, R., Chakraborty, S., Pote, Y., Sarkar, U., Sen, S.: Testing self-reducible samplers. In: AAAI (2024)
4. Binder, K., Heermann, D.W., Binder, K.: Monte Carlo simulation in statistical physics, vol. 8. Springer (1992)
5. Blanchard, P., Higham, D.J., Higham, N.J.: Accurately computing the log-sum-exp and softmax functions. IMA Journal of Numerical Analysis **41**(4), 2311–2330 (2021)
6. Bloom, B.H.: Space/time trade-offs in hash coding with allowable errors. Communications of the ACM **13**(7), 422–426 (1970)
7. Bonnot, P., Boyer, B., Faissole, F., Marché, C., Rieu-Helft, R.: Formally verified bounds on rounding errors in concrete implementations of logarithm-sum-exponential functions. Tech. rep., Inria (2023)
8. Bonnot, P., Boyer, B., Faissole, F., Marché, C., Rieu-Helft, R.: Formally verified rounding errors of the logarithm sum exponential function. In: FMCAD. pp. 251–260. TU Wien Academic Press (2024)
9. Borwein, J.M., Borwein, P.B.: The arithmetic-geometric mean and fast computation of elementary functions. SIAM review **26**(3), 351–366 (1984)
10. Brent, R., Percival, C., Zimmermann, P.: Error bounds on complex floating-point multiplication. Mathematics of Computation **76**(259), 1469–1481 (2007)
11. Carter, J.L., Wegman, M.N.: Universal classes of hash functions. In: STOC (1977)
12. Chakraborty, S., Meel, K.S.: On testing of uniform samplers. In: AAAI (2019)
13. Chakraborty, S., Meel, K.S., Vardi, M.Y.: Algorithmic improvements in approximate counting for probabilistic inference: From linear to logarithmic sat calls. In: IJCAI. pp. 3569–3576 (2016)
14. Devroye, L.: Generating the maximum of independent identically distributed random variables. Computers & Mathematics with Applications **6**(3), 305–315 (1980)
15. Devroye, L.: Nonuniform random sample generation. Handbooks in operations research and management science **13**, 83–121 (2006)
16. Farach-Colton, M., Tsai, M.T.: Exact sublinear binomial sampling. Algorithmica **73**, 637–651 (2015)
17. Fousse, L., Hanrot, G., Lefèvre, V., Pélissier, P., Zimmermann, P.: Mpfr: A multiple-precision binary floating-point library with correct rounding. ACM Transactions on Mathematical Software (TOMS) **33**(2), 13–es (2007)
18. Galassi, M., Davies, J., Theiler, J., Gough, B., Jungman, G., Alken, P., Booth, M., Rossi, F., Ulerich, R.: GNU scientific library. Network Theory Limited Godalming (2002)
19. Harris, C.R., Millman, K.J., van der Walt, S.J., Gommers, R., Virtanen, P., Cournapeau, D., Wieser, E., Taylor, J., Berg, S., Smith, N.J., Kern, R., Picus, M., Hoyer, S., van Kerkwijk, M.H., Brett, M., Haldane, A., del Río, J.F., Wiebe, M., Peterson, P., Gérard-Marchant, P., Sheppard, K., Reddy, T., Weckesser, W., Abbasi, H., Gohlke, C., Oliphant, T.E.: Array programming with NumPy. Nature **585**, 357–362 (2020)
20. Hoare, C.A.R.: Algorithm 64: quicksort. Communications of the ACM **4**(7), 321 (1961)

21. Hopcroft, J.E., Motwani, R., Ullman, J.D.: Introduction to automata theory, languages, and computation. Acm Sigact News **32**(1), 60–65 (2001)
22. Hörmann, W.: The generation of binomial random samples. Journal of statistical computation and simulation **46**(1-2), 101–110 (1993)
23. Hörmann, W., Derflinger, G.: The transformed rejection method for generating random variables, an alternative to the ratio of uniforms method. Communications in Statistics-Simulation and Computation **23**(3), 847–860 (1994)
24. Hörmann, W., Leydold, J., Derflinger, G., Hörmann, W., Leydold, J., Derflinger, G.: Transformed density rejection (tdr). Automatic Nonuniform Random Variate Generation pp. 55–111 (2004)
25. Jeannerod, C.P., Kornerup, P., Louvet, N., Muller, J.M.: Error bounds on complex floating-point multiplication with an fma. Mathematics of Computation **86**(304), 881–898 (2017)
26. Jeannerod, C.P., Rump, S.M.: Improved error bounds for inner products in floating-point arithmetic. SIAM Journal on Matrix Analysis and Applications **34**(2), 338–344 (2013)
27. Jeannerod, C.P., Rump, S.M.: On relative errors of floating-point operations: optimal bounds and applications. Mathematics of computation **87**(310), 803–819 (2018)
28. Kachitvichyanukul, V., Schmeiser, B.W.: Binomial random sample generation. Communications of the ACM **31**(2), 216–222 (1988)
29. Karney, C.F.: Sampling exactly from the normal distribution. ACM Transactions on Mathematical Software (TOMS) **42**(1), 1–14 (2016)
30. Karp, R.M., Luby, M.: Monte-carlo algorithms for enumeration and reliability problems. In: FOCS (1983)
31. Karp, R.M., Luby, M., Madras, N.: Monte-carlo approximation algorithms for enumeration problems. Journal of algorithms **10**(3), 429–448 (1989)
32. Kumar, G., Meel, K.S., Pote, Y.: Tolerant testing of high-dimensional samplers with subcube conditioning. In: AISTATS (2025)
33. Lanczos, C.: A precision approximation of the gamma function. Journal of the Society for Industrial and Applied Mathematics, Series B: Numerical Analysis **1**(1), 86–96 (1964)
34. Meduna, A., Meduna, A.: Turing transducers. Automata and Languages: Theory and Applications pp. 833–887 (2000)
35. Meel, K.S., Pote, Y.P., Chakraborty, S.: On testing of samplers. NeurIPS (2020)
36. Meel, K.S., Shrotri, A.A., Vardi, M.Y.: Not all fprass are equal: demystifying fprass for dnf-counting. Constraints **24**, 211–233 (2019)
37. Meel, K.S., Vinodchandran, N., Chakraborty, S.: Estimating the size of union of sets in streaming models. In: PODS. pp. 126–137 (2021)
38. Muller, J.M., Muller, J.M.: Elementary functions. Springer (2006)
39. Pote, Y., Meel, K.S.: On scalable testing of samplers. NeurIPS (2022)
40. Pote, Y.P., Meel, K.S.: Testing probabilistic circuits. NeurIPS (2021)
41. Pugh, G.R.: An analysis of the Lanczos gamma approximation. Ph.D. thesis, University of British Columbia (2004)
42. Pugh, W.: Concurrent maintenance of skip lists. Citeseer (1990)
43. Rump, S.M., Ogita, T., Oishi, S.: Accurate floating-point summation part i: Faithful rounding. SIAM Journal on Scientific Computing **31**(1), 189–224 (2008)
44. Schmeiser, B., Kachitvichyanukul, V.: Poisson random sample generation. Research memorandum pp. 81–4 (1981)
45. Sharma, S., Roy, S., Soos, M., Meel, K.S.: Ganak: A scalable probabilistic exact model counter. In: IJCAI. vol. 19, pp. 1169–1176 (2019)

46. Soos, M., Aggarwal, D., Chakraborty, S., Meel, K.S., Obremski, M.: Engineering an efficient approximate dnf-counter. In: IJCAI. pp. 2031–2038 (2023)
47. Soos, M., Meel, K.S.: Bird: engineering an efficient cnf-xor sat solver and its applications to approximate model counting. In: Proceedings of the AAAI Conference on Artificial Intelligence. vol. 33, pp. 1592–1599 (2019)
48. The MPFR Team: The mpfr library: Algorithms and proofs, `https://www.mpfr.org/algorithms.pdf/`
49. Thomopoulos, N.T.: Essentials of Monte Carlo simulation: Statistical methods for building simulation models. Springer Science & Business Media (2012)

Robust Probabilistic Bisimilarity
for Labelled Markov Chains

Syyeda Zainab Fatmi[1]($\boxtimes$) (iD), Stefan Kiefer[1] (iD), David Parker[1] (iD),
and Franck van Breugel[2] (iD)

[1] University of Oxford, Oxford, UK
{syyeda.fatmi,stefan.kiefer,david.parker}@cs.ox.ac.uk
[2] York University, Toronto, Canada
franck.van.breugel@lassonde.yorku.ca

Abstract. Despite its prevalence, probabilistic bisimilarity suffers from
a lack of robustness under minuscule perturbations of the transition
probabilities. This can lead to discontinuities in the probabilistic bisimilarity distance function, undermining its reliability in practical applications where transition probabilities are often approximations derived
from experimental data. Motivated by this limitation, we introduce the
notion of robust probabilistic bisimilarity for labelled Markov chains,
which ensures the continuity of the probabilistic bisimilarity distance
function. We also propose an efficient algorithm for computing robust
probabilistic bisimilarity and show that it performs well in practice, as
evidenced by our experimental results.

Keywords: (probabilistic) model checking · labelled Markov chain ·
probabilistic bisimilarity · behavioural pseudometric

1 Introduction

In the analysis and verification of probabilistic systems, one of the foundational
concepts is identifying and merging system states that are behaviorally indis-
tinguishable. Kemeny and Snell [22] introduced the notion of lumpability for
Markov chains and it was adapted to the setting of labelled Markov chains by
Larsen and Skou [25], known as probabilistic bisimulation. State-of-the-art probabilistic verification tools [18, 24] implement a variety of methods for minimizing
the state space of the system by collapsing probabilistically bisimilar states. This
can significantly improve verification efficiency in some cases [21].

However, due to the sensitivity of behavioural equivalences to small changes
in the transition probabilities, Giacalone et al. [16] proposed using behavioural
pseudometrics to capture the behavioural similarity of states in a probabilistic
system. Instead of classifying states as either equivalent or inequivalent, the
pseudometric maps each pair of states to a real value in the unit interval, thus also
quantifying the behavioral difference between non-equivalent states. Behavioural
pseudometrics have been studied in the context of systems biology [32], games [5],
planning [8] and security [4], among others.

© The Author(s) 2025
R. Piskac and Z. Rakamarić (Eds.): CAV 2025, LNCS 15932, pp. 254–275, 2025.
https://doi.org/10.1007/978-3-031-98679-6_12

In probabilistic verification, the most widely studied example of such a behavioural pseudometric is the *probabilistic bisimilarity distance*. It generalizes probabilistic bisimilarity quantitatively; in particular, the distance between two states is zero if and only if they are probabilistically bisimilar. The probabilistic bisimilarity distance was introduced by Desharnais et al. [10], based on a real-valued semantics for Larsen and Skou's probabilistic modal logic [25]. A formula φ of this logic maps any state s to a number $[\![\varphi]\!](s) \in [0,1]$. The probabilistic bisimilarity distance between two states s,t can be characterized as $\delta(s,t) = \sup_\varphi |[\![\varphi]\!](s) - [\![\varphi]\!](t)| \in [0,1]$, where φ ranges over all formulas. The lower the distance between two states, the more similar their behaviour. As shown by Van Breugel and Worrell [3], the probabilistic bisimilarity distance can also be characterized as a fixed point of a function (we use this definition in this paper).

However, as pointed out by Jaeger et al. [19], probabilistic bisimilarity distances are sometimes not continuous, leading to unexpected and abrupt changes in behaviour between two states when the transition probabilities are perturbed. Since the probabilities of the labelled Markov chain are usually obtained experimentally and, therefore, are often an approximation [13,27,28,30,31], the lack of robustness of probabilistic bisimilarity is a serious drawback. This inconsistency undermines the reliability of probabilistic bisimilarity as a measure of system equivalence and can be particularly problematic when used in practical applications where approximate models are prevalent.

Example 1. Consider Fig. 1a on page 6. When $\varepsilon = 0$, states h_0 and h_1 are probabilistically bisimilar; i.e., their distance $\delta_0(h_0,h_1)$ equals 0 (the subscript of δ indicates ε). For $\varepsilon > 0$ we have $\delta_\varepsilon(h_0,h_1) > 0$; i.e., h_0 and h_1 are no longer bisimilar. However, when ε is small then $\delta_\varepsilon(h_0,h_1)$ is small. In fact, one can show that $\delta_\varepsilon(h_0,h_1) \leq 2\varepsilon$, which implies that $\lim_{\varepsilon \to 0} \delta_\varepsilon(h_0,h_1) = 0$. This means that in this example, the distance is continuous in ε. One may say that states h_0, h_1 are not only probabilistically bisimilar, but also robustly so, in that they remain "almost" bisimilar when the transition probabilities are perturbed. Intuitively, states h_0 and h_1 behave similarly even for small positive ε: both states carry a blue label and perform a geometrically distributed number of self-loops (about two in expectation) before transitioning to state t.

Example 2. Consider Fig. 1b on page 6. When $\varepsilon = 0$, states h_2 and h_3 are probabilistically bisimilar; i.e., their distance $\delta_0(h_2,h_3)$ equals 0. But for any $\varepsilon > 0$ we have $\delta_\varepsilon(h_2,h_3) = 1$; i.e., h_2 and h_3 behave "maximally" differently in terms of the probabilistic bisimilarity distance. We have $\lim_{\varepsilon \to 0} \delta_\varepsilon(h_2,h_3) = 1$; so, in this example, the distance is discontinuous in ε. One may say that although states h_2, h_3 are probabilistically bisimilar, they are not robustly so, because upon perturbing the transition probabilities the behaviour of h_3 changes completely. For any positive ε, state h_2 remains in a self-loop forever, whereas h_3 eventually reaches the (red-labelled) state t_3 with probability 1. Since reachability properties are at the heart of probabilistic model checking, it may be unsafe to merge states h_2 and h_3 if the transition probabilities are not known precisely.

In this paper, we address this issue by introducing the notion of *robust probabilistic bisimilarity* for labelled Markov chains. Robust probabilistic bisimilarity is a particular probabilistic bisimulation, implying that robust probabilistic bisimilarity is a subset of probabilistic bisimilarity. Crucially, we show that our definition ensures the continuity of the probabilistic bisimilarity distance function. This means that for any two states that are robustly probabilistically bisimilar, their probabilistic bisimilarity distance remains small even after small perturbations of any transition probabilities. Note that it is easy to see that the distance from [12] is robust in this sense; on the other hand, states with very small distance in terms of [12] can have very different long-term behaviour, as in Example 2.

Secondly, we develop a polynomial-time algorithm for computing robust probabilistic bisimilarity. It is suitable for large-scale verification tasks, opening the door to checking probabilistic models from the literature for (lack of) robustness of their probabilistic bisimilarity relation. Thus, one can identify pairs of states that may be dangerous to merge if the transition probabilities are not known precisely. We present experimental results on the applicability and efficiency of an implementation of our algorithm on models from the Quantitative Verification Benchmark Set (QVBS) [17] and the examples included in the Java PathFinder extension jpf-probabilistic [14].

The rest of the paper is structured as follows. Section 2 introduces the model of interest, namely a labelled Markov chain, and probabilistic bisimilarity. In Sect. 3, we formally define probabilistic bisimilarity distances and further examine how the bisimilarity distance changes when the transition function is varied. Section 4 describes robust probabilistic bisimilarity and demonstrates that it ensures the continuity of the bisimilarity distance function. In Sect. 5, we present a polynomial-time algorithm for computing robust probabilistic bisimilarity. Section 6 reports experimental results on the algorithm's implementation. Finally, Sect. 7 concludes the paper and discusses directions for future research. The full version of this paper, found in [15], includes omitted proofs and further details.

2   Labelled Markov Chains and Probabilistic Bisimilarity

In this section, we present some fundamental concepts that underpin this paper.

Let X be a nonempty finite set. A function $\mu : X \to [0,1]$ is a *subprobability distribution* on X if $\sum_{x \in X} \mu(x) \leq 1$. We denote the set of subprobability distributions on X by $\mathcal{S}(X)$. For $\mu \in \mathcal{S}(X)$ and $A \subseteq X$, we often write $\mu(A)$ instead of $\sum_{x \in A} \mu(x)$. For a distribution $\mu \in \mathcal{S}(X)$ we define the *support* of μ by $\mathrm{support}(\mu) = \{ x \in X \mid \mu(x) > 0 \}$. A subprobability distribution μ on X is a *probability distribution* if $\mu(X) = 1$. We denote the set of probability distributions on X by $\mathcal{D}(X)$.

A *Markov chain* is a pair $\langle S, \tau \rangle$ consisting of a finite set S of states and a transition probability function $\tau : S \to \mathcal{D}(S)$. A *labelled Markov chain* is a tuple $\langle S, L, \tau, \ell \rangle$ where $\langle S, \tau \rangle$ is a Markov chain, L is a finite set of labels and $\ell : S \to L$

is a labelling function. A *path* in a Markov chain $\langle S, \tau \rangle$ is a sequence of states $s_0, s_1, s_2 \ldots$ such that $s_i \in S$ and $\tau(s_i)(s_{i+1}) > 0$ for all $i \geq 0$.

For the remainder, we fix a labelled Markov chain $\langle S, L, \tau, \ell \rangle$, and we will study perturbations of the transition probability function τ.

For all $\mu, \nu \in \mathcal{D}(X)$, the set $\Omega(\mu, \nu)$ of *couplings* of μ and ν is defined by

$$\Omega(\mu, \nu) = \{ \omega \in \mathcal{D}(X \times X) \mid \forall x \in X : \omega(x, X) = \mu(x) \wedge \omega(X, x) = \nu(x) \}.$$

We write $\omega(x, X)$ for $\sum_{y \in X} \omega(x, y)$.

Definition 1. *An equivalence relation $R \subseteq S \times S$ is a probabilistic bisimulation (or just bisimulation) if for all $(s, t) \in R$, $\ell(s) = \ell(t)$ and there exists $\omega \in \Omega(\tau(s), \tau(t))$ such that* support$(\omega) \subseteq R$. *States s and t are* bisimilar, *denoted $s \sim t$, if $(s, t) \in R$ for some bisimulation R.*

If $|\ell(S)| = 1$ then $\sim = S \times S$. In the remainder, we assume that the labelled Markov chain contains states with different labels, that is, $|\ell(S)| \geq 2$. Hence, we also have that $|S| \geq 2$.

Definition 1 [20, Definition 4.3] differs from the standard definition [25, Definition 6.3] which defines a bisimulation as an equivalence relation $R \subseteq S \times S$ such that for all $(s, t) \in R$, $\ell(s) = \ell(t)$ and for all R-equivalence classes C, $\tau(s)(C) = \tau(t)(C)$, where $\tau(s)(C) = \sum_{t \in C} \tau(s)(t)$. Nevertheless, an equivalence relation R is a bisimulation by Definition 1 if and only if it is a bisimulation as per the standard definition (see [20, Theorem 4.6]).

3   Probabilistic Bisimilarity Distances

Definition 2. *The* probabilistic bisimilarity distance *(or just bisimilarity distance), $\delta_\tau : S \times S \to [0, 1]$, is the least fixed point of the function $\Delta_\tau : (S \times S \to [0, 1]) \to (S \times S \to [0, 1])$ defined by*

$$\Delta_\tau(d)(s, t) = \begin{cases} 1 & \text{if } \ell(s) \neq \ell(t) \\ \displaystyle\inf_{\omega \in \Omega(\tau(s), \tau(t))} \sum_{u, v \in S} \omega(u, v) \, d(u, v) & \text{otherwise.} \end{cases}$$

Intuitively, the smaller the distance between two states, the more similar they behave.

Theorem 1 ([11, Theorem 4.10]). *For all s, $t \in S$, $s \sim t$ if and only if $\delta_\tau(s, t) = 0$.*

Quantitative μ-calculus [1,23,26] is an expressive modal logic that uses fixed point operators to define properties of transition systems. It supports the concise representation of a wide range of properties, including reachability, safety, and the probability of satisfying a general ω-regular specification. We use the syntax described in [5], except that we use the operator next instead of pre_1 and pre_2. Let $q\mu$ denote the set of quantitative μ-calculus formulae, then a formula $\varphi \in q\mu$ maps states to a numerical value within $[0, 1]$, that is, $[\![\varphi]\!] : S \to [0, 1]$. The bisimilarity distances can be characterized in terms of the quantitative μ-calculus [5, Equation 2.3] as $\delta_\tau(s, t) = \sup_{\varphi \in q\mu} |[\![\varphi]\!](s) - [\![\varphi]\!](t)|$.

3.1   Examples

We now investigate how the bisimilarity distance changes when the transition function varies. In the following, let $\varepsilon \in [0, \frac{1}{2}]$. Define τ_ε as shown in Fig. 1. For example, $\tau_{1/6}(h_5)(t_5) = \frac{2}{3}$. Then $\tau_\_ : [0, \frac{1}{2}] \to (S \to \mathcal{D}(S))$ and $\delta_{\tau_\_} : [0, \frac{1}{2}] \to (S \times S \to [0,1])$.

Example 3. Consider Fig. 1a. As ε increases, h_1 becomes more biased and the distance between h_0 and h_1 increases proportionally. One can show that $\delta_{\tau_\varepsilon}(h_0, h_1) = \frac{\varepsilon}{0.5+\varepsilon} \leq 2\varepsilon$. Note that if ε is small then the distance is also small and $\lim_{\varepsilon \to 0} \delta_{\tau_\varepsilon}(h_0, h_1) = 0$.

The formula $\varphi = \mu V. \text{next}(tails \vee V) \ominus 0.5$ distinguishes the states h_0 and h_1 the most, that is $\delta_{\tau_\varepsilon}(h_0, h_1) = \frac{\varepsilon}{0.5+\varepsilon} = |[\![\varphi]\!](h_0) - [\![\varphi]\!](h_1)|$. The quantifier μ denotes the least fixed point of the recursive formula involving the variable V. Intuitively, a state satisfies V if the next state is *tails* or satisfies V with probability greater than a half. More precisely, considering state h_1, $[\![\varphi]\!](h_1)$ is the expected value of $\max([\![\varphi]\!](s), [\![tails]\!](s)) - \frac{1}{2}$, where s denotes the random successor state of h_1. Then, $[\![\varphi]\!](h_1)$ evaluates to $\sum_{n=0}^{\infty} \varepsilon(\frac{1}{2} - \varepsilon)^n = \frac{\varepsilon}{0.5+\varepsilon}$. Each summand in the series represents the probability of reaching state t in $n + 1$ steps, starting from state h_1, with 0.5 subtracted at each step. On the other hand, $[\![\varphi]\!](h_0) = 0$.

Example 4. In Fig. 1b, when $\varepsilon = 0$, the states h_2 and h_3 are bisimilar with $\delta_{\tau_0}(h_2, h_3) = 0$. However, if $\varepsilon > 0$, then $\delta_{\tau_\varepsilon}(h_2, h_3) = 1$. This difference is evident when considering the probability of eventually reaching a state labelled with *tails* when starting in h_2 compared to h_3. In the first Markov chain, $[\![\Diamond tails]\!] = 0$, while in the second Markov chain, $[\![\Diamond tails]\!] = 1$. This property can be expressed as the quantitative μ-calculus formula $\mu V. \text{next}(tails \vee V)$. This example was also presented in [19].

Example 5. The first Markov chain in Fig. 1c represents fair coin flips, while the second Markov chain represents potentially biased coin flips. When $\varepsilon = 0$, the states h_4 and h_5 are bisimilar with $\delta_{\tau_0}(h_4, h_5) = 0$. However, if $\varepsilon > 0$, one can show that $\delta_{\tau_\varepsilon}(h_4, h_5) = 1$. Intuitively, this is because small differences in probabilities can compound and lead to qualitative differences in the long-run behaviour.

Let us illustrate this. Assume that a point is awarded each time the coin lands on *tails* and a point is deducted each time it lands on *heads*. Let us examine the limit behaviour of the Markov chains. Observe that the Markov chains behave like a random walk on the integer number line, $\mathbb{Z}$, starting at 0. At each step, the first Markov chain goes up by one with probability $\frac{1}{2}$ and down by one with probability $\frac{1}{2}$. On the other hand, at each step, the second Markov chain goes up by one with probability $\frac{1}{2} + \varepsilon$ and down by one with probability $\frac{1}{2} - \varepsilon$. Let $Y_1, Y_2, Y_3, \ldots$ be the sequence of independent random variables, where Y_i denotes the ith step taken by the random walk, with $Y_i = 1$ for a step up and $Y_i = -1$ for a step down. Define $S_n = \sum_{i=1}^{n} Y_i$. In the first Markov chain, $P(\liminf_{n \to \infty} S_n = -\infty) = 1$ and $P(\limsup_{n \to \infty} S_n = \infty) = 1$, by the Hewitt-Savage zero-one law [7, Example 5.19]. In contrast, in the second Markov chain,

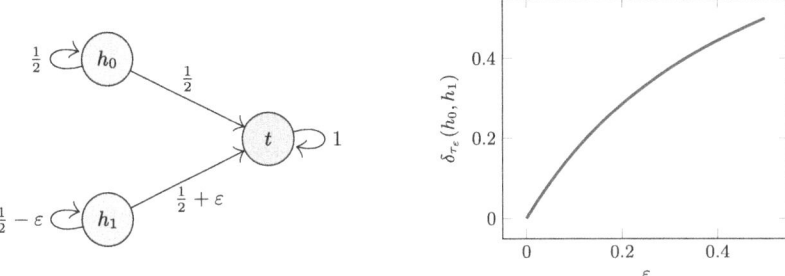

(a) Repeated tosses of a fair coin (top) and a biased coin (bottom) until each lands on tails.

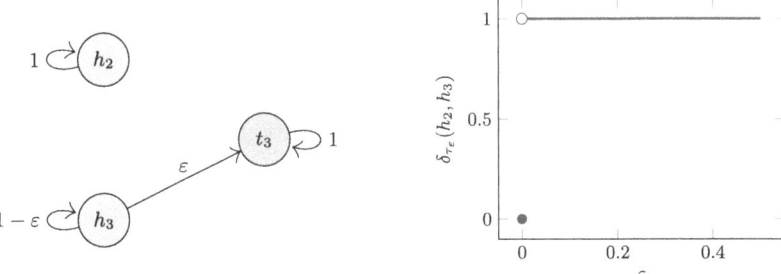

(b) Single toss of a rigged coin (top) and repeated tosses of an extremely biased coin until it lands on tails (bottom).

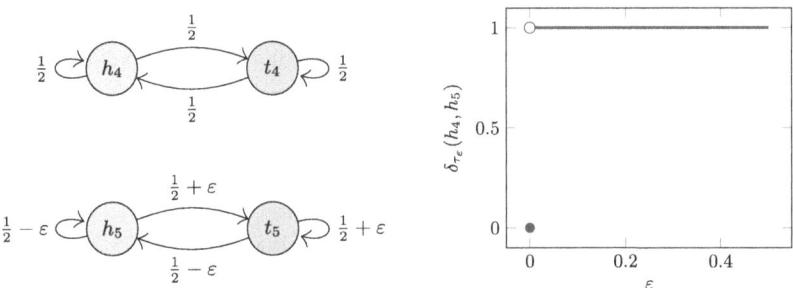

(c) Repeated tosses of a fair coin (top) and a biased coin (bottom).

Fig. 1. Various examples featuring fair and biased coins. States labeled with *heads* are shown in blue, while states labeled with *tails* are shown in red. (Color figure online)

we have $P(\lim_{n\to\infty} S_n = \infty) = 1$, by the law of large numbers [29]. Thus, in the first Markov chain, with equal chances of gaining or losing points at each step, the random walk almost surely oscillates infinitely. In contrast, in the second Markov chain, the upward bias introduced by $\varepsilon > 0$ guarantees that the total number of points will eventually diverge to $+\infty$.

We see that small changes in the transition probabilities can lead to significant changes in the behaviour and, thus, in the distances between states. This example is similar to the one presented in [19].

In the remainder, we conservatively assume that the transition function can be varied arbitrarily, that is, changes to the transition function are not restricted to specific transitions with constrained variables as in the examples. Also, different from [19], the changes might "add transitions." Therefore, we are interested in the continuity of the function $\delta\_(s,t) : (S \to \mathcal{D}(S)) \to [0,1]$. See [15, Appendix A] for the metric on distributions $S \to \mathcal{D}(S)$ used here.

The bisimilarity distance function $\delta\_(s,t)$ is *lower semi-continuous* at τ if for any sequence $(\tau_n)_n$ converging to τ we have $\liminf_n \delta_{\tau_n}(s,t) \geq \delta_\tau(s,t)$ and *upper semi-continuous* at τ if we have $\limsup_n \delta_{\tau_n}(s,t) \leq \delta_\tau(s,t)$. Lastly, $\delta\_(s,t)$ is *continuous* at τ if it is both upper semi-continuous and lower semi-continuous at τ.

The examples in Fig. 1 suggest that the bisimilarity distance function $\delta\_$ is lower semi-continuous at τ. Indeed the following proposition shows that this holds in general, even allowing for arbitrary modifications of τ.

Proposition 1. *For all s, $t \in S$, the function $\delta\_(s,t) : (S \to \mathcal{D}(S)) \to [0,1]$ is lower semi-continuous at τ, that is, if $(\tau_n)_n$ converges to τ then $\liminf_n \delta_{\tau_n}(s,t) \geq \delta_\tau(s,t)$.*

In Fig. 1c, the bisimilarity distance function is not upper semi-continuous. Specifically, $\limsup_{\epsilon \to 0} \delta_{\tau_\epsilon}(h_4,h_5) = 1$, while $\delta_{\tau_0}(h_4,h_5) = 0$. As a result, small perturbations of τ cause a jump in the distance from 0 to 1. The main goal of this paper is to characterize and identify the continuity of the bisimilarity distance function for bisimilar pairs of states.

The following subsets of $S \times S$ play a key role in the subsequent discussion.

Definition 3. *The sets S_Δ^2, $S_{0,\tau}^2$, S_1^2, $S_{?,\tau}^2$, and $S_{0?}^2$ are defined by*

$$S_\Delta^2 = \{ (s,s) \mid s \in S \}$$
$$S_{0,\tau}^2 = \{ (s,t) \in S \times S \mid s \neq t \wedge s \sim t \}$$
$$S_1^2 = \{ (s,t) \in S \times S \mid \ell(s) \neq \ell(t) \}$$
$$S_{?,\tau}^2 = (S \times S) \setminus (S_\Delta^2 \cup S_{0,\tau}^2 \cup S_1^2)$$
$$S_{0?}^2 = S_{0,\tau}^2 \cup S_{?,\tau}^2$$

The first four sets form a partition of $S \times S$. Observe that the sets $S_{0,\tau}^2$ and $S_{?,\tau}^2$ depend on τ and may, therefore, change when we perturb τ, whereas the sets S_Δ^2 and S_1^2 stay the same. Note that $S_{0?}^2 = (S \times S) \setminus (S_\Delta^2 \cup S_1^2)$. Hence, this set also stays the same if we perturb τ. Furthermore, note that $\sim = S_\Delta^2 \cup S_{0,\tau}^2$ and for all $(s,t) \in S_1^2$, we have $\delta_\tau(s,t) = 1$.

Definition 4. *Let $\tau : S \to \mathcal{D}(S)$. The set $\mathcal{P}_\tau$ of policies for τ is defined by*

$$\mathcal{P}_\tau = \left\{ P : S \times S \to \mathcal{D}(S \times S) \,\middle|\, \begin{array}{l} \forall (s,t) \in S_\Delta^2 \cup S_{0?}^2 : P(s,t) \in \Omega(\tau(s), \tau(t)) \\ \forall (s,t) \in S_1^2 : \text{support}(P(s,t)) = \{(s,t)\} \end{array} \right\}.$$

Note that a policy $P \in \mathcal{P}_\tau$ induces a Markov chain $\langle S \times S, P \rangle$. The subscript τ is omitted when clear from the context. The following proposition characterizes δ_τ in terms of policies.

Proposition 2. *For all s, $t \in S$, $\delta_\tau(s,t) = \min\limits_{P \in \mathcal{P}} \gamma_P$, where γ_P is the probability with which (s,t) reaches S_1^2 in $\langle S \times S, P \rangle$.*

Proof Sketch. The proof follows from [2, Theorem 10.15] and [6, Theorem 8]. □

Example 6. Consider the labelled Markov chain in Fig. 1a when $\varepsilon = \frac{1}{8}$. Then the probability with which (h_0, h_1) reaches S_1^2 for any policy $P \in \mathcal{P}$ is $\geq \frac{1}{5}$. Any policy P such that $P(h_0, h_1) = \{(h_0, h_1) \mapsto \frac{3}{8}, (h_0, t) \mapsto \frac{1}{8}, (t, t) \mapsto \frac{1}{2}\}$ achieves the minimum probability of $\frac{1}{5}$. The Markov chain induced by such a policy P is illustrated in Fig. 2. Thus, $\delta_{\tau_\varepsilon}(h_0, h_1) = \frac{1}{5}$.

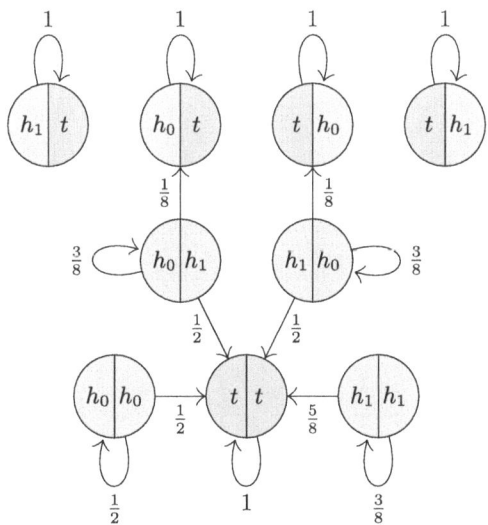

Fig. 2. The Markov chain $\langle S \times S, P \rangle$ induced by the policy P such that (h_0, h_1) reaches S_1^2 with probability $\frac{1}{5}$.

4 Robust Probabilistic Bisimilarity

We aim to define a notion of robust bisimilarity which is a bisimulation that is robust against perturbations of the transition function τ. As we will see in Theorem 2 below, the following definition fulfills this requirement.

Definition 5. Robust probabilistic bisimilarity *(or just robust bisimilarity), denoted $\simeq$, is defined for s, $t \in S$ as $s \simeq t$ if there exists a policy $P \in \mathcal{P}$ such that (s,t) reaches S_Δ^2 with probability 1 in $\langle S \times S, P \rangle$.*

Lemma 1. *Robust bisimilarity, $\simeq$, is a bisimulation.*

Proof Sketch. Clearly, $\simeq$ is reflexive and symmetric. We prove in [15, Appendix] that $\simeq$ is transitive as well and, therefore, an equivalence relation.

Let $s, t \in S$ such that $s \simeq t$. Let $P \in \mathcal{P}$ be the policy such that (s, t) reaches S_Δ^2 with probability 1 in $\langle S \times S, P \rangle$. Then, it follows from the definition of $\mathcal{P}$ that $(s, t) \notin S_1^2$. Thus, $\ell(s) = \ell(t)$.

Let $\omega = P(s, t)$, $u, v \in S$ and $(u, v) \in \text{support}(\omega)$. Hence, $\omega(u, v) > 0$ and (u, v) is reachable from (s, t). Therefore, (u, v) must reach S_Δ^2 with probability 1 in $\langle S \times S, P \rangle$. Consequently, $u \simeq v$. As a result, $\text{support}(\omega) \subseteq \simeq$.   □

Therefore, $\simeq \subseteq \sim$ and, by Theorem 1, for any $s, t \in S$ such that $s \simeq t$ we have $\delta_\tau(s, t) = 0$.

Example 7. In Fig. 1a, when $\varepsilon = 0$, then $h_0 \simeq h_1$, since there exists a policy $P \in \mathcal{P}$ such that (h_0, h_1) reaches $(t, t) \in S_\Delta^2$ with probability 1 in $\langle S \times S, P \rangle$. Indeed, take $P(h_0, h_1) = \{(h_0, h_1) \mapsto \frac{1}{2}, (t, t) \mapsto \frac{1}{2}\}$ as shown in Fig. 3. Hence, $h_0 \simeq h_1$. Note, however, that $h_2 \not\simeq h_3$ and $h_4 \not\simeq h_5$.

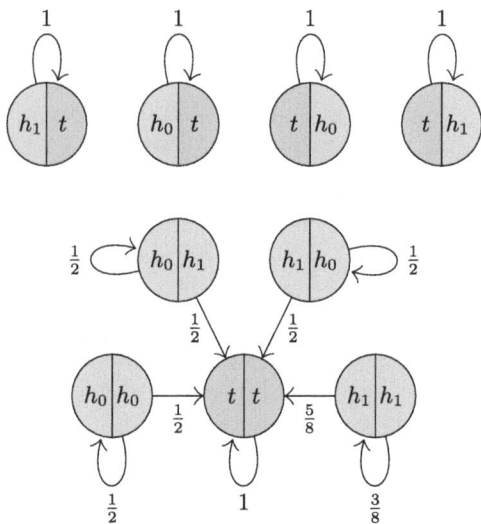

Fig. 3. The Markov chain $\langle S \times S, P \rangle$ induced by the policy P such that (h_0, h_1) reaches S_Δ^2 with probability 1.

The following theorem provides the rationale behind the term robust bisimilarity. It establishes that for all robust bisimilar pairs of states, small perturbations of τ result in a correspondingly small change in the distance between them.

Theorem 2. *For all $s, t \in S$, if $s \simeq t$ then the function $\delta_{-}(s,t) : (S \to \mathcal{D}(S)) \to$ $[0,1]$ is continuous at τ, that is, for any sequence $(\tau_n)_n$ converging to τ we have $\lim_n \delta_{\tau_n}(s,t) = 0$.*

Proof Sketch. To build some intuition behind this theorem, we first outline the underlying idea. Let $P \in \mathcal{P}$ be the policy such that (s,t) reaches S_Δ^2 with probability 1 in $\langle S \times S, P \rangle$. Then, for some k, the probability of (s,t) reaching S_Δ^2 within k steps is almost one, say $1 - x$, where $x > 0$ is a small value. When the transition function τ is perturbed by a small ε, there is a policy P' such that the transitions in $\langle S \times S, P' \rangle$ differ from those in $\langle S \times S, P \rangle$ only by a small $\varepsilon' > 0$. Therefore, (s,t) still reaches S_Δ^2 with high probability in $\langle S \times S, P' \rangle$.

To argue the last point in slightly more detail, observe that if $\varepsilon > 0$ is small enough so that $(1 - \varepsilon')^k \geq 1 - x$ then the probability, say p, of any individual path of length at most k from (s,t) to S_Δ^2 remains at least $(1 - x) \cdot p$ after the perturbation. It follows that the probability of *all* paths of length at most k from (s,t) to S_Δ^2 remains at least $(1 - x) \cdot (1 - x) \geq 1 - 2x$ after the perturbation.

In [15, Appendix], we provide a different, formal proof using matrix norms. There we construct a graph consisting of the closed communication classes of $\langle S \times S, P \rangle$ that are reachable from (s,t). Let $P_n \in \mathcal{P}_{\tau_n}$. We then show that for all closed communication classes C reachable from (s,t) and for all pairs $(u,v) \in C$, it holds that $\lim_n \gamma_{P_n}(u,v) = \gamma_P(u,v) = 0$, by induction on the length of a longest path from C.

By Proposition 2, we have $\lim_n \delta_{\tau_n}(s,t) \leq \lim_n \gamma_{P_n}(s,t)$. Using the above result, we conclude that $\lim_n \delta_{\tau_n}(s,t) \leq \gamma_P(s,t) = 0$. $\square$

Towards an algorithm for computing $\simeq$, let us develop another characterization of robust bisimilarity. Given a policy $P \in \mathcal{P}$, we say that a set $R \subseteq S \times S$ *supports* a path $(u_1, v_1) \ldots (u_n, v_n)$ in $\langle S \times S, P \rangle$ if for all $1 \leq i \leq n$ we have $(u_i, v_i) \in R$ and support$(P(u_i, v_i)) \subseteq R$.

Definition 6. *A robust bisimulation is a bisimulation $R \subseteq S \times S$ such that for all $(s,t) \in R$, there exists a policy $P \in \mathcal{P}$ such that R supports a path from (s,t) to S_Δ^2 in $\langle S \times S, P \rangle$.*

Proposition 3. *Robust bisimilarity, $\simeq$ is a robust bisimulation.*

Proof Sketch. By Lemma 1, $\simeq$ is a bisimulation. Let $P \in \mathcal{P}$ be the policy such that (s,t) reaches S_Δ^2 with probability 1 in $\langle S \times S, P \rangle$. Observe that for all (u,v) reachable from (s,t), (u,v) must reach S_Δ^2 with probability 1 in $\langle S \times S, P \rangle$. Consequently, support$(P(s,t)) \subseteq \simeq$. In fact, $\simeq$ supports a path from (s,t) to S_Δ^2 in $\langle S \times S, P \rangle$, and we can conclude that $\simeq$ is a robust bisimulation. $\square$

Proposition 4. *For any robust bisimulation $R \subseteq S \times S$, we have $R \subseteq \simeq$.*

Proof Sketch. We construct a policy $P \in \mathcal{P}$ such that for every $(s,t) \in R$, R supports a path from (s,t) to S_Δ^2 in $\langle S \times S, P \rangle$ and for all $(s,t) \in S_\Delta^2$, support$(P(s,t)) \subseteq S_\Delta^2$. Note that P is designed to simultaneously ensure that all pairs in R have an R-supported path to S_Δ^2 in $\langle S \times S, P \rangle$. It follows from a standard result in Markov chain theory that all $(s,t) \in R$ reach S_Δ^2 with probability 1 in $\langle S \times S, P \rangle$. $\square$

It follows from Propositions 3 and 4 that $\simeq$, that is, robust bisimilarity, is the greatest robust bisimulation. This is analogous to ordinary bisimulation, where bisimilarity is the greatest bisimulation.

5 Algorithm

In this section, we present an efficient algorithm to compute robust bisimilarity; see Algorithm 1. The algorithm relies on the following properties of any robust bisimulation R:

1. for every $(s,t) \in R$ there exists a policy P such that R supports a path from (s,t) to S_Δ^2 in $\langle S \times S, P \rangle$,
2. R is an equivalence relation, and
3. R is a bisimulation.

Robust bisimilarity is the greatest relation with these properties. More formally, we define a function, Refine, such that robust bisimilarity is the greatest fixed point of Refine.

Algorithm 1: Computing robust bisimilarity for labelled Markov chains

---

Input: A labelled Markov chain with a finite set S of states and a transition probability function $\tau : S \to \mathcal{D}(S)$, and the set of pairs of bisimilar states $\sim = S_{0,\tau}^2 \cup S_\Delta^2$

Output: The set of pairs of robustly bisimilar states $R = \simeq$

1 $R \leftarrow \sim$
2 **repeat**
3      $R_{\mathrm{old}} \leftarrow R$
4      $R \leftarrow \mathrm{Refine}(R)$ /* see Algorithm 2 */
5 **until** $R = R_{\mathrm{old}}$
6 **return** R

For any L, U with $L \subseteq U \subseteq S \times S$, write $[L, U] = \{\, R \subseteq S \times S \mid L \subseteq R \subseteq U \,\}$ and $[L, U]_\mathcal{B} = \{\, R \in [L, U] \mid R \text{ is a bisimulation } \}$.

- The function Filter : $[S_\Delta^2, \sim]_\mathcal{B} \to [S_\Delta^2, \sim]$ is defined as
  Filter$(R) = \{\, (s,t) \in R \mid \exists P \in \mathcal{P} \text{ such that } R \text{ supports a path from } (s,t) \text{ to } S_\Delta^2 \text{ in } \langle S \times S, P \rangle \,\}$.
- The function Prune : $[S_\Delta^2, \sim] \to [S_\Delta^2, \sim]$ is defined as
  Prune$(R) = \{\, (s,t) \in R \mid \forall (t,u) \in R : (s,u) \in R \wedge \forall(u,s) \in R : (u,t) \in R \,\}$.
- The function Bisim : $[S_\Delta^2, \sim] \to [S_\Delta^2, \sim]_\mathcal{B}$ is defined as
  Bisim(R) is the largest bisimulation R' with $R' \subseteq R$.
  Given an equivalence relation R, Bisim(R) can be computed in polynomial time (see [15, Proposition 24]).
- Lastly, the function Refine : $[S_\Delta^2, \sim]_\mathcal{B} \to [S_\Delta^2, \sim]_\mathcal{B}$ is defined as
  Refine$(R) = $ Bisim(Prune(Filter(R))).

Proposition 5. Bisim *and* Filter *are monotone with respect to* $\subseteq$. *However,* Prune *is not.*

Proof Sketch. A counterexample for Prune is as follows. Let $S = \{s, t, u\}$, $A = \{(s, s), (t, t), (u, u), (s, t), (t, s)\}$ and $B = \{(s, s), (t, t), (u, u), (s, t), (t, s), (t, u), (u, t)\}$. A and B are symmetric and reflexive and, thus, can be visualized as an undirected graph as shown in Fig. 4. Observe that $A \subseteq B$, however, $\text{Prune}(A) = A \not\subseteq \text{Prune}(B) = \{(s, s), (t, t), (u, u)\}$. □

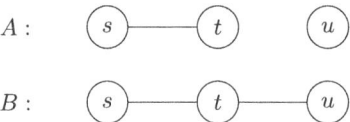

Fig. 4. Graph visualization of the relations A and B used in the proof of Proposition 5.

Note that Algorithm 1 is not a typical fixed point iteration, since we do not know whether Refine is monotone.

Algorithm 2: Refine

Input: A set $R \in [S_\Delta^2, \sim]_\mathcal{B}$
Output: Refine(R)
1 $R \leftarrow \text{Filter}(R)$ /* see Algorithm 3 */
2 $R \leftarrow \text{Prune}(R)$ /* see Algorithm 4 */
3 $R \leftarrow \text{Bisim}(R)$
4 **return** R

Proposition 6. *Any relation $R \subseteq S \times S$ is a robust bisimulation if and only if it is a fixed point of* Refine.

Proof Sketch. Let $R \subseteq S \times S$. Assume that R is a robust bisimulation. By definition, $\text{Refine}(R) \subseteq R$. Since R is a robust bisimulation, $R \subseteq \text{Refine}(R)$.

Assume that R is a fixed point of Refine, then R is a bisimulation and for every $(s, t) \in R$ there exists a policy P such that R supports a path from (s, t) to S_Δ^2 in $\langle S \times S, P \rangle$. Therefore, R is a robust bisimulation. □

It follows from Propositions 4 and 6 that every fixed point of Refine is a subset of $\simeq$. Furthermore, by Propositions 3 and 6, $\simeq$ is a fixed point of Refine. Therefore, $\simeq$ is the greatest fixed point of Refine.

Let $Q \subseteq S \times S$ and $s, t, u, v \in S$. We use the following notation below: $\text{Post}((s, t)) = \text{support}(\tau(s)) \times \text{support}(\tau(t))$ and $\text{Pre}(Q) = \{ (s, t) \in S \times S \mid \text{Post}((s, t)) \cap Q \neq \varnothing \}$.

Algorithm 3: Filter

    Input: A set $R \in [S_\Delta^2, \sim]_\mathcal{B}$
    Output: Filter(R)
1 $Q \leftarrow S_\Delta^2$
2 $n \leftarrow 0$
3 **repeat**
4     $Q_{\text{old}} \leftarrow Q$
5   **foreach** $(s,t) \in (R \cap \text{Pre}(Q_{\text{old}})) \setminus Q_{\text{old}}$ **do**
6         $Q \leftarrow Q \cup \{(s,t)\}$
7   **end**
8     $n \leftarrow n + 1$
9 **until** $Q = Q_{\text{old}}$
10 **return** Q

Algorithm 4: Prune

    Input: A set $Q \in [S_\Delta^2, \sim]$
    Output: Prune(Q)
1 $E \leftarrow Q$
2 **foreach** $(s,t) \in Q$ **do**
3   **foreach** $u \in S : (t,u) \in Q$ **do**
4   **if** $(s,u) \notin Q$ **then**
5             $E \leftarrow E \setminus \{(s,t),(t,u)\}$
6   **end**
7   **end**
8 **end**
9 **return** E

Proposition 7. *Given $R \in [\simeq, \sim]_\mathcal{B}$, for all (s,t), $(t,u) \in$ Filter(R), if $s \simeq t$ or $t \simeq u$ then $(s,u) \in$ Filter(R).*

Proof Sketch. We show that if $t \simeq u$ then $(s,u) \in$ Filter(R). The case $s \simeq t$ is similar. Write $s_1 = s$ and $t_1 = t$ and $u_1 = u$.

The idea behind the proof is that since Filter(R) $\subseteq R$, we have (s,t), $(t,u) \in R$. Since R is an equivalence relation, $(s,u) \in R$. We define a policy $P \in \mathcal{P}$ such that for all $(s,t) \in R \cap S_{0?}^2$, support($P(s,t)$) = Post($(s,t)$) $\cap R$. We then show that since $(s,t) \in$ Filter(R), there exists a path $(s_1,t_1), \ldots, (s_n,t_n)$ in $\langle S \times S, P \rangle$, where $s_n = t_n$.

Assume that $(t,u) \in \simeq$. Recall that $\simeq$ is a bisimulation. Since $t_1, \ldots, t_n$ is a path in the original Markov chain $\langle S, \tau \rangle$, there is also a path $u_1, \ldots, u_n$ in $\langle S, \tau \rangle$ such that $(t_i, u_i) \in \simeq$ for all $1 \le i \le n$. Since $\simeq \subseteq R$, there exists a path $(t_1, u_1), \ldots, (t_n, u_n)$ in $\langle S \times S, P \rangle$. Note that $(s_i, u_i) \in R$ for all $1 \le i \le n$. Hence, there exists a path $(s_1, u_1), \ldots, (s_n, u_n) = (t_n, u_n)$ in $\langle S \times S, P \rangle$. See Fig. 5.

Since $(t_n, u_n) \in \simeq$, we know that (t_n, u_n) reaches S_Δ^2 with probability 1. Therefore, there is a path $(t_n, u_n), \ldots, (t_m, u_m)$, with $t_m = u_m$ in $\langle S \times S, P \rangle$ and $(t_i, u_i) \in \simeq$ for all $n \le i \le m$. Thus, there exists paths $(s_1, u_1), \ldots, (s_n, u_n)$ and

$(t_n, u_n), \ldots, (t_m, u_m)$ in $\langle S \times S, P \rangle$, with $(s_n, u_n) = (t_n, u_n)$. By the definition of P, R supports the same path in $\langle S \times S, P \rangle$. Hence, $(s, u) \in \text{Filter}(R)$.   □

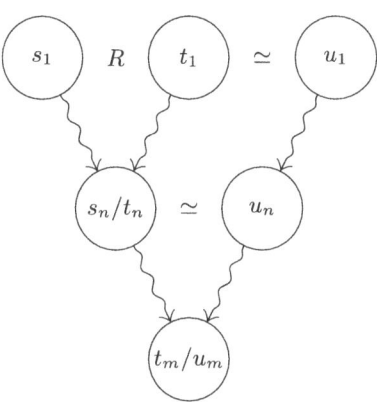

Fig. 5. Illustration of the proof of Proposition 7.

Proposition 7 allows us to prove the following proposition.

Proposition 8. $R \in [\simeq, \sim]_{\mathcal{B}}$ *is a loop invariant of Algorithm 1.*

Proof Sketch. R is initialized to $\sim$, so the loop invariant holds before the loop.

Assume that the loop invariant holds before an iteration of the loop. Since $\simeq \subseteq R$, Filter is monotone and $\simeq$ is a fixed point of Refine, we have that $\simeq$ is a subset of $\text{Filter}(R)$.

If $s \simeq t$, then $(s, t) \in \text{Filter}(R)$. Then, by Proposition 7, for all $(t, u) \in \text{Filter}(R)$ we have $(s, u) \in \text{Filter}(R)$ and for all $(u, s) \in \text{Filter}(R)$ we have $(u, t) \in \text{Filter}(R)$. Hence, $(s, t) \in \text{Prune}(\text{Filter}(R))$, and we have that $\simeq$ is a subset of $\text{Prune}(\text{Filter}(R))$.

Bisim is monotone, therefore, $\simeq$ is a subset of $\text{Bisim}(\text{Prune}(\text{Filter}(R)))$ and $\text{Refine}(R)$. By the definition of Bisim, $\text{Refine}(R) \in [\simeq, \sim]_{\mathcal{B}}$. Thus, the loop invariant is maintained in each iteration of the loop.   □

Using the loop invariant established in Proposition 8, we can now prove the correctness of Algorithm 1.

Theorem 3. *Algorithm 1 computes the set* $\simeq$.

Proof Sketch. It is immediate from the definitions of Bisim, Filter and Prune that $\text{Refine}(R) \subseteq R$ holds for all $R \subseteq S \times S$. By Proposition 8, $\simeq \subseteq R$, thus, it computes a fixed point of Refine greater than or equal to $\simeq$. Since $\simeq$ is the greatest fixed point of Refine, we can conclude that Algorithm 1 computes $\simeq$.   □

In [15, Proposition 27], we show that Algorithm 1 has a time complexity of $\mathcal{O}(n^6)$, where $n = |S|$. The computational bottleneck is the function Filter.

6   Experiments

To evaluate the efficiency and usefulness of our robust bisimilarity algorithm, we implemented it in the widely used probabilistic model checker PRISM [24], an open-source tool providing quantitative verification and analysis of several types of probabilistic models, including labelled Markov chains.

6.1   Implementation

PRISM's implementation of the traditional (i.e., non-robust) bisimilarity algorithm, Bisim, is a standard partition-refinement approach which uses the signature-based method of Derisavi [9]. The initial partition is based on the labelling of the states. Let Π be the current partition and E_Π be the set of equivalence classes in Π. Then the new partition is computed as $\{\,(s,t) \in \Pi \mid \forall B \in E_\Pi : \tau(s)(B) = \tau(t)(B)\,\}$.

We implemented Algorithm 1 in Java as part of PRISM's explicit-state model checking engine. Each state and equivalence class (referred to as a block) is represented by an integer ID. The current partition of the state space is tracked by an array that is indexed by state IDs and contains the corresponding block IDs. To store the list of successors for each state, we use a map. Bisim is run on the input Markov chain to obtain the set of bisimilar states.

The function Filter first constructs R from the current partition and initializes Q to S_Δ^2. In our approach, R is implemented as an array indexed by block IDs, with each block containing a list of states. Conversely, Q is implemented as an array indexed by state IDs, with each state storing the set of states related to it. Predecessors of Q in R are added to Q until a fixed point is reached. A pair of states $(s,t) \in R \setminus Q$ is a predecessor of Q if they have some successors that are related in Q. Specifically, there must exist successors s' and t' of s and t, respectively, such that $t' \in Q[s']$ and vice versa.

Prune constructs a new partition of the state space by grouping states in the same block if they have the same neighbourhood in Q, that is, they are related to the same states. In other words, s and t are placed in the same block if $Q[s] = Q[t]$ holds. Bisim is then called with the current partition passed as the initial partition. This process continues until no further refinement is possible, resulting in the set of robustly bisimilar states. Finally, the minimized Markov chain is constructed.

6.2   Experimental Setup

We evaluated our algorithm by applying it to all (discrete-time) labelled Markov chains from the Quantitative Verification Benchmark Set (QVBS) [17], a comprehensive collection of probabilistic models which is designed as a benchmark suite for quantitative verification and analysis tools and is the foundation of the Quantitative Verification Competition (QComp), which compares the performance, versatility, and usability of such tools.

For an additional source of models, we also use jpf-probabilistic [14]. Java PathFinder (JPF) [33] is the most popular model checker for Java code, and the JPF extension jpf-probabilistic provides Java implementations of sixty randomized algorithms [14]. As shown in [14], JPF, extended by jp-probabilistic and jpf-label, can be used in tandem with PRISM to check properties of these algorithms and supplement JPF's qualitative results with quantitative information. A description of the subset of these algorithms utilized in our study is provided in [15, Appendix J].

In order to explore both the benefits and the efficiency of our algorithm, we run both the robust and traditional bisimilarity algorithms on all models. For the latter, we use PRISM's existing implementation, in order to provide a comparable implementation. Our experiments were run on a MacBook with an M1 chip and 16GB memory, and with the Java virtual machine limited to 8GB.

6.3   Results

Table 1 shows results for all benchmarks where the minimized models obtained by traditional bisimilarity and robust bisimilarity differ. These are of particular interest because they are instances where our algorithm identifies that a model minimized in traditional fashion may not be robust. In fact, in all benchmarks we have checked, we have observed that the distance between pairs of states that are not robustly bisimilar is discontinuous. This leads us to the conjecture that for bisimilar states, robust bisimilarity is also a necessary condition for continuity. The property used for each benchmark dictates the labelling used for the model. In the table, *Min* denotes the number of states in the minimized model and *Time* denotes the amount of time taken (in seconds) to compute bisimilarity.

The results are promising, since robust bisimilarity, although (unsurprisingly) slower than traditional bisimilarity, remains practical across a wide range of standard benchmarks. Table 2 displays some of the largest models per benchmark along with the time required to compute robust bisimilarity. The longest time recorded is about 50 min for the *crowds* benchmark. This may be due to the fact that the *crowds* benchmark has many non-robustly bisimilar pairs of states, which we believe makes the benchmark harder. Other benchmarks, e.g. *brp (p4)*, point in a similar direction.

The complete set of experiments includes 170 models, of which 160 are aggregated in Table 3. This table presents the average percentage increase in both the state space of the minimized model and the computation time for robust bisimilarity compared to traditional bisimilarity. The *crowds* benchmark exhibits the largest average percentage increase for both metrics. The reported values may seem large, however, it is important to note that the traditional bisimilarity algorithm required a maximum of 2.14 seconds per model in this table.

Furthermore, robust bisimilarity was successfully computed in less than a minute for 152 models (over 89%). Of the total set of models, the remaining 10 (approximately 6%), listed in Table 4, could only be minimized using traditional bisimilarity, as the robust bisimilarity computation ran out of available memory

Table 1. The results of the benchmarks for which the minimized models differ.

Benchmark			Bisimilarity		Robust Bisimilarity	
Name (prop.)	Parameters	States	Min	Time	Min	Time
brp (p1)	N=32 MAX=2	1349	646	0.036	901	0.054
	MAX=3	1766	871	0.043	1127	0.062
	MAX=4	2183	1096	0.051	1353	0.068
	MAX=5	2600	1321	0.058	1579	0.075
	N=64 MAX=2	2693	1286	0.080	1797	0.105
	MAX=3	3526	1735	0.084	2247	0.119
	MAX=4	4359	2184	0.103	2697	0.130
	MAX=5	5192	2633	0.132	3147	0.167
brp (p4)	N=32 MAX=2	1349	10	0.012	711	3.690
	MAX=3	1766	12	0.013	937	6.291
	MAX=4	2183	14	0.018	1163	9.331
	MAX=5	2600	16	0.021	1389	13.952
	N=64 MAX=2	2693	10	0.017	1415	27.299
	MAX=3	3526	12	0.015	1865	45.031
	MAX=4	4359	14	0.016	2315	69.949
	MAX=5	5192	16	0.018	2765	102.941
crowds	CS=5 TR=3	1198	41	0.018	505	0.231
(positive)	TR=4	3515	61	0.021	1484	1.304
	TR=5	8653	81	0.038	3659	7.575
	TR=6	18817	101	0.071	7969	34.765
	CS=10 TR=3	6563	41	0.024	2320	8.296
	TR=4	30070	61	0.078	10524	196.233
	TR=5	111294	81	0.190	38770	2946.840
oscillators	T=6 N=3	57	28	0.007	38	0.009
(power)	T=8 N=6	1717	1254	0.037	1255	0.037
	N=8	6436	5148	0.100	5149	0.122
oscillators	T=6 N=3	57	28	0.007	38	0.008
(time)	T=8 N=6	1717	1254	0.032	1255	0.036
	N=8	6436	5148	0.111	5149	0.115
set isolation	U=13 ST=3	8196	19	0.029	27	21.885
(good sample)	ST=4	8196	20	0.029	26	24.325
	ST=5	8196	21	0.032	25	24.330
	ST=6	8196	22	0.031	24	25.162

Table 2. Models with the maximum state space per benchmark.

Benchmark			Robust Bisimilarity	
Name	Property	States	Min States	Time
crowds	positive	111294	38770	2946.84
egl	messages	115710	131	153.01
herman	steps	32768	612	25.29
oscillators	power	24311	17877	0.42

Table 3. Summary of all benchmarks with the change due to robust bisimilarity.

Benchmark			Average % Increase	
Name	Property	Instances	States	Time
brp	p1	12	27.93	28.95
	p2	12	7.76	80.54
	p4	12	9193.43	142193.57
crowds	positive	7	12306.72	273258.24
egl	messages	6	-	20693.83
erdös-rényi model	connected	18	-	799.07
fair biased coin	heads	9	-	0.00
has majority element	incorrect	24	-	16.08
herman	steps	7	-	297.99
leader-sync	elected & time	18	-	518.98
haddad-monmege	target	3	-	0.00
oscillators	power & time	14	5.12	11.73
pollards factorization	input	8	-	0.00
queens	success	6	-	1193.93
set isolation	good sample	4	25.06	79035.95
Total		160	1231.68	25589.22

before completion. This issue occurred with all instances of the *nand* benchmark and half of the instances of the *egl* benchmark.

Ultimately, robust bisimilarity proves feasible for large models, despite needing more resources than traditional bisimilarity. Furthermore, it offers a more reliable method of determining equivalence, which can be particularly beneficial in mission-critical applications, which require a higher level of precision.

Table 4. Models for which robust bisimilarity results in an `OutOfMemoryError`.

Benchmark				Bisimilarity	
Name	Property	Parameters		States	Min States	Time
crowds	positive	CS=10	TR=6	352535	101	0.57
egl	messages	N=5	L=8	156670	171	0.87
	unfair	N=5	L=2	33790	229	0.10
			L=4	74750	469	0.26
			L=6	115710	709	0.40
			L=8	156670	949	0.70
nand	reliable	N=20	K=1	78332	39982	0.81
			K=2	154942	102012	1.89
			K=3	231552	164042	3.67
queens	success		N=10	23492	527	0.08

7 Conclusions and Future Work

To address the lack of robustness of probabilistic bisimilarity, we have introduced the concept of robust bisimilarity for labelled Markov chains. Robust bisimilarity ensures that the distance function remains continuous even under perturbations of transition probabilities. Additionally, we have presented a computationally efficient algorithm, with experimental results demonstrating that robust bisimilarity is plausible for large-scale verification tasks.

Our work opens new avenues for future exploration. First, a logical characterization of robust bisimilarity could provide deeper insights. Second, while we have established in Theorem 2 that robust bisimilarity is a sufficient condition for continuity, we conjecture that for bisimilar states, robust bisimilarity is in fact also a necessary condition for continuity. We also aim to define continuity for non-bisimilar state pairs, to complete the theoretical characterization of robustness. Thirdly, in [19] it was shown that when the distances are discounted (i.e., differences that manifest themselves later count less), the distance function becomes continuous. This raises the question: can we identify the properties for which the discontinuity is relevant? The examples suggest that these are long-term properties. Finally, we plan to investigate specific types of perturbations of the transition probabilities, such as those that do not introduce new transitions, preserving the graph structure, as seen in Figs. 1a and 1c, unlike the perturbation shown in Fig. 1b which adds a new transition.

Acknowledgments. This research was supported in part by the Clarendon Fund and by the Natural Sciences and Engineering Research Council of Canada.

Disclosure of Interests. The authors have no competing interests to declare that are relevant to the content of this article.

References

1. de Alfaro, L., Majumdar, R.: Quantitative solution of omega-regular games. In: Vitter, J.S., Spirakis, P.G., Yannakakis, M. (eds.) Proceedings of the 33rd Annual Symposium on Theory of Computing, Heraklion, Crete, Greece, pp. 675–683. ACM (2001)
2. Baier, C., Katoen, J.P.: Principles of Model Checking. The MIT Press, Cambridge (2008)
3. van Breugel, F., Worrell, J.: Towards quantitative verification of probabilistic transition systems. In: Orejas, F., Spirakis, P.G., van Leeuwen, J. (eds.) Proceedings of the 28th International Colloquium on Automata, Languages and Programming, Crete, Greece. LNCS, vol. 2076, pp. 421–432. Springer (2001)
4. Cai, X., Gu, Y.: Measuring anonymity. In: Bao, F., Li, H., Wang, G. (eds.) Proceedings of the 5th International Conference on Information Security Practice and Experience, Xi'an, China. LNCS, vol. 5451, pp. 183–194. Springer (2009)
5. Chatterjee, K., de Alfaro, L., Majumdar, R., Raman, V.: Algorithms for game metrics (full version). Log. Methods Comput. Sci. **6**(3) (2010)
6. Chen, D., van Breugel, F., Worrell, J.: On the complexity of computing probabilistic bisimilarity. In: Birkedal, L. (ed.) Proceedings of the 15th International Conference on Foundations of Software Science and Computational Structures, Tallinn, Estonia. LNCS, vol. 7213, pp. 437–451. Springer (2012)
7. Çınlar, E.: Probability and Stochastics. Graduate Texts in Mathematics, vol. 261. Springer, New York (2011)
8. Comanici, G., Precup, D.: Basis function discovery using spectral clustering and bisimulation metrics. In: Burgard, W., Roth, D. (eds.) Proceedings of the 25th AAAI Conference on Artificial Intelligence, San Francisco, California, USA, pp. 325–330. AAAI Press (2011)
9. Derisavi, S.: Signature-based symbolic algorithm for optimal Markov chain lumping. In: Proceedings of the 4th International Conference on the Quantitative Evaluation of Systems, Edinburgh, Scotland, UK, pp. 141–150. IEEE Computer Society (2007)
10. Desharnais, J., Gupta, V., Jagadeesan, R., Panangaden, P.: Metrics for labeled Markov systems. In: Baeten, J.C.M., Mauw, S. (eds.) Proceedings of the 10th International Conference on Concurrency Theory, Eindhoven, The Netherlands. LNCS, vol. 1664, pp. 258–273. Springer (1999)
11. Desharnais, J., Gupta, V., Jagadeesan, R., Panangaden, P.: Metrics for labelled Markov processes. Theoret. Comput. Sci. **318**(3), 323–354 (2004)
12. Desharnais, J., Laviolette, F., Tracol, M.: Approximate analysis of probabilistic processes: logic, simulation and games. In: Proceedings of the 5th International Conference on the Quantitative Evaluation of Systems, Saint-Malo, France, pp. 264–273. IEEE Computer Society (2008)
13. Eastman, J.R., He, J.: A regression-based procedure for Markov transition probability estimation in land change modeling. Land **9**(11) (2020)
14. Fatmi, S.Z., Chen, X., Dhamija, Y., Wildes, M., Tang, Q., van Breugel, F.: Probabilistic model checking of randomized Java code. In: Laarman, A., Sokolova, A. (eds.) Proceedings of the 27th International Symposium on Model Checking Software, SPIN. LNCS, vol. 12864, pp. 157–174. Springer (2021)

15. Fatmi, S.Z., Kiefer, S., Parker, D., van Breugel, F.: Robust probabilistic bisimilarity for labelled Markov chains. CoRR (2025). https://doi.org/10.48550/arXiv.2505.15290

16. Giacalone, A., Jou, C., Smolka, S.A.: Algebraic reasoning for probabilistic concurrent systems. In: Broy, M., Jones, C.B. (eds.) Proceedings of the Working Conference on Programming Concepts and Methods, North-Holland, Sea of Galilee, Israel, pp. 443–458 (1990)

17. Hartmanns, A., Klauck, M., Parker, D., Quatmann, T., Ruijters, E.: The quantitative verification benchmark set. In: Vojnar, T., Zhang, L. (eds.) Proceedings of the 25th International Conference on Tools and Algorithms for the Construction and Analysis of Systems, Prague, Czech Republic. LNCS, vol. 11427, pp. 344–350. Springer (2019)

18. Hensel, C., Junges, S., Katoen, J., Quatmann, T., Volk, M.: The probabilistic model checker storm. Int. J. Softw. Tools Technol. Transfer 24(4), 589–610 (2022)

19. Jaeger, M., Mao, H., Larsen, K.G., Mardare, R.: Continuity properties of distances for Markov processes. In: Norman, G., Sanders, W.H. (eds.) Proceedings of the 11th International Conference on Quantitative Evaluation of Systems, Florence, Italy. LNCS, vol. 8657, pp. 297–312. Springer (2014)

20. Jonsson, B., Larsen, K.: Specification and refinement of probabilistic processes. In: Proceedings of the 6th Annual Symposium on Logic in Computer Science, Amsterdam, The Netherlands, pp. 266–277. IEEE (1991)

21. Katoen, J., Kemna, T., Zapreev, I.S., Jansen, D.N.: Bisimulation minimisation mostly speeds up probabilistic model checking. In: Proceedings of the 13th International Conference on Tools and Algorithms for the Construction and Analysis of Systems. LNCS, vol. 4424, pp. 87–101. Springer (2007)

22. Kemeny, J.G., Snell, J.L.: Finite Markov Chains. Springer, Heidelberg (1960)

23. Kozen, D.: A probabilistic PDL. In: Johnson, D.S., et al. (eds.) Proceedings of the 15th Annual Symposium on Theory of Computing, Boston, Massachusetts, USA, pp. 291–297. ACM (1983)

24. Kwiatkowska, M., Norman, G., Parker, D.: PRISM 4.0: verification of probabilistic real-time systems. In: Gopalakrishnan, G., Qadeer, S. (eds.) Proceedings of the 23rd International Conference on Computer Aided Verification, Snowbird, Utah, USA. LNCS, vol. 6806, pp. 585–591. Springer (2011)

25. Larsen, K., Skou, A.: Bisimulation through probabilistic testing. In: Proceedings of the 16th Annual ACM Symposium on Principles of Programming Languages, Austin, TX, USA, pp. 344–352. ACM (1989)

26. McIver, A., Morgan, C.: Abstraction, Refinement and Proof for Probabilistic Systems. Monographs in Computer Science. Springer (2004)

27. Mizutani, D., Lethanh, N., Adey, B.T., Kaito, K.: Improving the estimation of Markov transition probabilities using mechanistic-empirical models. Front. Built Environ. 3, 58 (2017)

28. Olariu, E., Cadwell, K.K., Hancock, E., Trueman, D., Chevrou-Severac, H.: Current recommendations on the estimation of transition probabilities in Markov cohort models for use in health care decision-making: a targeted literature review. ClinicoEcon. Outcomes Res. 9, 537–546 (2017)

29. Spitzer, F.: Principles of Random Walk. Graduate Texts in Mathematics. Springer, New York (1964)

30. Srivastava, T., Latimer, N.R., Tappenden, P.: Estimation of transition probabilities for state-transition models: a review of NICE appraisals. Pharmacoeconomics 39(8), 869–878 (2021)

31. Tang, Q., van Breugel, F.: Algorithms to compute probabilistic bisimilarity distances for labelled Markov chains. In: Meyer, R., Nestmann, U. (eds.) Proceedings of the 28th International Conference on Concurrency Theory, Berlin, Germany. LIPIcs, vol. 85, pp. 27:1–27:16. Schloss Dagstuhl - Leibniz-Zentrum für Informatik (2017)
32. Thorsley, D., Klavins, E.: Approximating stochastic biochemical processes with Wasserstein pseudometrics. IET Syst. Biol. **4**, 193–211 (2010)
33. Visser, W., Havelund, K., Brat, G., Park, S., Lerda, F.: Model checking programs. Autom. Softw. Eng. **10**(2), 203–232 (2003)

Accelerating Markov Chain Model Checking: Good-for-Games Meets Unambiguous Automata

Yong Li[1,2] , Soumyajit Paul[2] , Sven Schewe[2] , and Qiyi Tang[2(✉)]

[1] Key Laboratory of System Software (Chinese Academy
of Sciences) and SKLCS, Institute of Software,
Chinese Academy of Sciences, Beijing,
People's Republic of China
liyong@ios.ac.cn

[2] University of Liverpool, Liverpool, UK
{yong.li3,soumyajit.paul,sven.schewe,qiyi.tang}@liverpool.ac.uk

Abstract. Good-for-Games (GfG) automata require that their nondeterminism can be resolved on-the-fly, while unambiguous automata guarantee that no word has more than one accepting run. These two mutually exclusive ways of restricted nondeterminism play their roles independently in Markov chain model checking (MCMC) for almost a decade but synthesising them seems hopeless: an automaton that is both GfG and unambiguous is essentially deterministic. This work breaks this perception by combining the strengths of unambiguity with the GfG co-Büchi minimisation recently proposed by Abu Radi and Kupferman. More precisely, this combination allows us to turn unambiguous automata to certain types of probabilistic automata that can be used for MCMC. The resulting automata can be exponentially smaller, and we have provided a family of automata exemplifying this state space reduction, which translates into a significant acceleration of MCMC.

Keywords: Unambiguous Büchi automata · Good-for-games automata · Markov chains · Probabilistic model checking

1 Introduction

Markov chains are widely used across numerous application domains, including computer science, engineering, operations research, and the modelling of population growth and behaviour. Verifying Markov chains against ω-regular properties, such as Linear Temporal Logic (LTL) specifications [9] and Linear Dynamic Logic (LDL) [7], has long been the one exemption to the rule that automata are a perfect tool for the analysis of Markovian models. The automata suitable for Markov chain model checking (MCMC) have to restrict their nondeterminism in some way [9]. We consider two known types of restricted nondeterminism for MCMC in this paper, namely good-for-games (GfG) and unambiguous variants.

© The Author(s) 2025
R. Piskac and Z. Rakamarić (Eds.): CAV 2025, LNCS 15932, pp. 276–298, 2025.
https://doi.org/10.1007/978-3-031-98679-6_13

These two types of automata have been applied in MCMC independently for almost a decade.

GfG automata [17] have the ability to resolve nondeterministic choices on-the-fly. That is, a strategy exists for the automaton to generate an accepting run transition by transition, even when an accepting word is given letter by letter, such that the resolution of the nondeterminism does not depend on the future. Klein et al. [20] first proved that GfG automata can be used in probabilistic model checking, and thus in MCMC. Despite this, GfG automata have not been widely adopted in state of the art tools for verifying ω-regular properties, such as ePMC [13], PRISM [22], and IscasMC [15], due to the lack of effective constructions of GfG automata.

Unambiguous automata have been more successful in MCMC than GfG automata. Unambiguous automata restrict the nondeterminism by guaranteeing that every word has at most one accepting run. Unambiguity has gained traction in MCMC when Couvreur et al. [10] developed a polynomial-time algorithm to model check against separated Büchi automata - a class of Büchi automata that have disjoint languages from every pair of states. This reduced the complexity of automata-based LTL model checking down to PSPACE, matching its lower bound [9]. Recently, Baier et al. [5] have developed an NC approach to model check against a more general and succinct class of automata than separated Büchi automata called *unambiguous Büchi automata* (UBAs) [8]. Different to GfG automata, there is also a rich set of sources of UBAs from LTL [19,24], and LDL [23].

Furthermore, unambiguity retains the expressive power of Büchi automata: UBAs can recognise all ω-regular languages [8], while GfG Büchi (or co-Büchi) automata only accept the languages recognised by their deterministic counterparts [17,21]. On one hand, unambiguity retains the expressive power of the ω-regular languages, but poses challenges in minimisation reduction of the automata. On the other hand, GfGness loses expressive power, but transition-based GfG co-Büchi can benefit from a recent polynomial-time minimisation construction [1]. Both types of restricted nondeterminism have been independently studied for MCMC. A natural question arises: *can we combine the strengths of unambiguity and GfGness for MCMC?* A trivial attempt would be to consider unambiguous GfG automata, which actually can be made deterministic by removing unreachable and unproductive states (cf. [6] for details). That is, we would not only lose expressive power in this attempt, but would also have to determinise the automaton.

Contributions. This work is the *first* successful effort to synergise unambiguity and GfGness. We first show that, when the input UBA is deterministic, we can directly apply the GfG co-Büchi minimisation construction to the deterministic automaton. We then prove that the resultant minimised automaton is *stochastically resolvable*, meaning that we can turn it into a probabilistic automaton by resolving the nondeterminism randomly such that the probabilistic automaton accepts (resp. rejects) every word from the input automaton's language (resp. its complement language) with probability one. This specific probabilistic automaton is well-suited for MCMC. The case for nondeterministic UBA, however, is more challenging because the GfG minimisation algorithm does not work directly on general UBAs. We address this challenge by proposing an algorithm that accommodates both GfGness and unambiguity for MCMC (Sect. 4). Furthermore, we provide a family of UBAs for which our proposed minimisation reduction can reduce the state space exponentially. Empirical evaluations on selected benchmarks show that our algorithm significantly accelerates MCMC, thus making our contribution a valuable addition to the existing portfolio of MCMC techniques.

Related Work. Other known types of automata suitable for MCMC are limit-deterministic Büchi automata with mild constraints [14,26] and a more general class called good-for-MDPs (GfM) automata [16,25]. We note that GfM-ness is a generalisation of GfGness and minimising GfM Büchi automata is PSPACE-hard [25]. Therefore, we do not consider GfM automata in this work. Klein et al. [20] used the algorithm in [17] to construct GfG automata from LTL, which are even larger than their deterministic counterparts. This highlights the need for more efficient methods for constructing GfG automata.

The efficient minimisation algorithm of [1] only works for GfG co-Büchi automata. Our work bypasses this limit and allows for using GfG co-Büchi minimisation in MCMC against all ω-regular properties. Baier et al. [5] also work on MCMC against UBAs. Thanks to our reduction algorithm for UBAs, our model checking algorithm can be (possibly exponentially) more efficient than theirs for certain properties.

Organisation of the Paper. We discuss the preliminaries in Sect. 2. In Sect. 3, we present an alternative approach for model checking Markov chains against DBA specifications using GfG automata. Section 4 introduces our algorithm for model checking Markov chains against UBA specifications via GfG automata. Next, in Sect. 5, we present a case study on a family of UBAs, where our reduction achieves exponential state-space savings, followed by implementation details and experimental results demonstrating the better scalability of our algorithm compared to existing UBA model checking methods. Finally, we conclude in Sect. 6.

2   Preliminaries

Automata. A nondeterministic automaton is a tuple $\mathcal{A} = (\Sigma, Q, \delta, q_0, \alpha)$ where Σ is the alphabet, Q is a finite set of states, $q_0 \in Q$ is the initial state, $\delta : Q \times \Sigma \mapsto 2^Q$ is the transition function and $\alpha \subseteq Q \times \Sigma \times Q$ is a set of transitions for describing a transition-based acceptance condition. The transition function δ induces a transition relation $\Delta_{\mathcal{A}} \subseteq Q \times \Sigma \times Q$, where for every two states $p, q \in Q$ and letter $a \in \Sigma$, we have that $(p, a, q) \in \Delta_{\mathcal{A}}$ iff $q \in \delta(p, a)$. When it is clear from the context, we omit the subscript $\mathcal{A}$ and directly write Δ. We also extend δ to sets and words in a usual way, by letting $\delta(S, a) = \bigcup_{q \in S} \delta(q, a)$, $\delta(S, \epsilon) = S$ and $\delta(S, u \cdot a) = \delta(\delta(S, u), a)$, where $u \in \Sigma^*$, $a \in \Sigma$ and ϵ is the empty word. Let $\delta^\alpha(p,a) = \{q \mid (p,a,q) \in \alpha\}$ and $\delta^{\bar{\alpha}}(p,a) = \{q \mid (p,a,q) \notin \alpha\}$. We use the terms α-transitions and $\bar{\alpha}$-transitions to refer to transitions in α and in $\Delta \setminus \alpha$, respectively.

A word $w \in \Sigma^\omega$ is an infinite sequence of letters in Σ. A run of a word $w = a_0a_1\cdots \in \Sigma^\omega$ in $\mathcal{A}$ is an infinite sequence $\rho = p_0p_1\cdots \in Q^\omega$ of states such that $p_0 = q_0$ and $\forall i \in \mathbb{N}$, $p_{i+1} \in \delta(p_i, a_i)$. A run ρ is accepted by $\mathcal{A}$ if it satisfies the acceptance condition α. We consider both Büchi and co-Büchi acceptance conditions to determine which runs should be accepted. We say that a run ρ satisfies the Büchi acceptance condition if, for infinitely many $i \in \mathbb{N}$, $(p_i, a_i, p_{i+1}) \in \alpha$, while ρ satisfies the co-Büchi acceptance condition if we only have $(p_i, a_i, p_{i+1}) \in \alpha$ for finitely many i. The language of $\mathcal{A}$, denoted by $\mathcal{L}(\mathcal{A})$, is the set of all words w with at least one accepting run. For $q \in Q$, let $\mathcal{A}^q$ be the automaton obtained from $\mathcal{A}$ by setting q as the initial state.

We write $\overline{\mathcal{L}}$ for the complement language of $\mathcal{L}$, that is, $\overline{\mathcal{L}} = \Sigma^\omega \setminus \mathcal{L}$. We say that two states $p, q \in Q$ are equivalent, denoted $p \sim_{\mathcal{A}} q$, if $\mathcal{L}(\mathcal{A}^p) = \mathcal{L}(\mathcal{A}^q)$. Let u be a finite word and L be an ω-language. We define the right language of u as $u^{-1}L = \{w \in L \mid uw \in L\}$.

We say that $\mathcal{A}$ is *deterministic* if, for all $q \in Q, a \in \Sigma$, we have $|\delta(q,a)| \le 1$. $\mathcal{A}$ is said to be *unambiguous* if there is *at most* one accepting run in $\mathcal{A}$ for every word $w \in \Sigma^\omega$. $\mathcal{A}$ is said to have a *diamond* if there exist two states $q, q' \in Q$ and a finite word $w \in \Sigma^*$, such that w has two different runs from q to q' in $\mathcal{A}$. Otherwise, $\mathcal{A}$ is called *diamond-free*. An unambiguous automaton can be made diamond-free in polynomial time. We use DBA/NBA/UBA for deterministic/nondeterministic/unambiguous Büchi automata and DCA/NCA for deterministic/nondeterministic co-Büchi automata.

An automaton $\mathcal{A}$ is called *good-for-games* (GfG) [17][1] if there is a strategy function $f : \Sigma^* \mapsto Q$ such that, for every accepting word $w = a_0a_1\cdots$, the run $\rho_f = f(\epsilon)f(a_0)\cdots f(a_0\cdots a_i)\cdots$ is an accepting run. We usually represent a strategy function as a resolver automaton $\mathcal{R} = (\mathbb{M}, \mathrm{m}_0, g)$, where $\mathbb{M}$ is the set of memory states of the resolver, $\mathrm{m}_0 \in \mathbb{M}$ is the initial memory state and $g : \mathbb{M} \times Q \times \Sigma \mapsto \mathbb{M} \times Q$ is the *deterministic* transition function that selects the successor for a state $q \in Q$ and $a \in \Sigma$. As usual, we also extend g to words such that $g(\mathrm{m}_0, q_0, ua) = g(g(\mathrm{m}_0, q_0, u), a)$ for all $u \in \Sigma^*$ and $a \in \Sigma$, where $(\mathrm{m}_0, q_0) = g(\mathrm{m}_0, q_0, \epsilon)$. Consequently, for all finite words $u_1, u_2 \in \Sigma^*$, if $g(\mathrm{m}_0, q_0, u_1) = g(\mathrm{m}_0, q_0, u_2)$, then $f(u_1) = f(u_2)$.

In [1], a polynomial-time algorithm is presented that, given a GfG-NCA $\mathcal{A}$, computes a minimal GfG-NCA $\mathcal{A}'$ such that $\mathcal{L}(\mathcal{A}') = \mathcal{L}(\mathcal{A})$. The minimal GfG-NCA $\mathcal{A}'$ satisfies several important properties. For instance, $\mathcal{A}'$ is semantically deterministic, meaning that, for a state $q \in Q$ in $\mathcal{A}'$ and a letter $a \in \Sigma$, all the a-successors of q (i.e., all states in $\delta(q,a)$) are equivalent. $\mathcal{A}'$ is also *safe deterministic*, meaning all transitions are deterministic *or* α-transitions. That is, for every state $q \in Q$ and letter $a \in \Sigma$, we have that $|\delta(q,a)| \le 1$ *or* $\delta^\alpha(q,a) = \delta(q,a)$.

---

[1] For ω-automata, GfG automata are equivalent to history-deterministic automata.

Components. Let $G = (V, E)$ be a directed graph. For $C \subseteq V$ and $E' \subseteq E$ let (C, E') denote a subgraph of G where every edge in E' lies within C. A component (C, E') is a strongly connected subgraph of G, i.e., for every two vertices $u, v \in C$, there is a path from u to v via E'. A strongly connected component (SCC) (C, E') of G is a maximal, strongly connected subgraph of G, i.e., there does not exist a strongly connected subgraph of G, (C', E''), such that $C \subsetneq C'$ or $E' \subsetneq E''$. An SCC (C, E) is called a *bottom* SCC (BSCC) if there is no path in G from any $u \in C$ to another SCC (C', E'). The automaton $\mathcal{A}$ induces a directed graph $G_{\mathcal{A}} = (V, E)$ with $V = Q$, and $(p, q) \in E$ iff for some $a \in \Sigma$, $q \in \delta(p, a)$. The SCCs (or components) of $\mathcal{A}$ are in fact those of $G_{\mathcal{A}}$. A *safe* component of $\mathcal{A}$ is an SCC of the graph $G_{\mathcal{A}}^{\bar{\alpha}} = (Q, E^{\bar{\alpha}})$, where $(p, q) \in E^{\bar{\alpha}}$ iff there exists a letter $a \in \Sigma$ such that $q \in \delta^{\bar{\alpha}}(p, a)$.

Markov Chains and Probability Measures. For a finite set S, we denote column vectors by boldface letters such as $\mathbf{x} \in \mathbb{R}^S$, and write $\mathbf{x}^{\mathsf{T}}$ for the transpose (a row vector) of $\mathbf{x}$; in particular, $\mathbf{1} \in \{1\}^S$ and $\mathbf{0} \in \{0\}^S$ are column vectors whose entries are all 1 and 0, respectively. We denote the vector entry for $s \in S$ as $\mathbf{x}(s)$ and write $\mathbf{x}_C$ for the restriction of $\mathbf{x}$ to $C \subseteq S$. Let $\mathrm{Distr}(S)$ be the set of all probability distributions on S. We denote the Dirac distribution concentrated at some $s \in S$ by ι_s.

We consider Markov chains where transitions are labelled with letters from the alphabet Σ of the automaton. A *labelled Markov chain* (LMC) is a tuple $\mathcal{M} = \langle S, \Sigma, M, s_0 \rangle$ where S is a finite and non-empty set of states, the alphabet is Σ (labels), $M : \Sigma \to [0, 1]^{S \times S}$ is the transition function such that $\sum_a M(a)$ is stochastic[2] and $s_0 \in S$ is the initial state. $\mathcal{M}$ can be perceived as a labelled weighted graph (WG) with S as the set of states and for $a \in \Sigma$, $M(a) \in [0, 1]^{S \times S}$ is the weighted adjacency matrix corresponding to transitions with label a. A labelled path $\pi = s_0 a_0 s_1 a_1 s_2 \ldots$ in $\mathcal{M}$ generates the word $w(\pi) = a_0 a_1 \ldots$. We can talk about probability measures of measurable subsets of Σ^ω in the σ-algebra generated by basic cylinder sets. For a finite word $x = a_0, \ldots, a_n$, the cylinder set $Cyl(x) = x\Sigma^\omega$ is the set of all infinite words with x as prefix. The probability measure of the set $Cyl(x)$ is given by $Pr(Cyl(x)) = \iota_{s_0}{}^{\mathsf{T}} M(a_0) M(a_1) \ldots M(a_n) \mathbf{1}$. Essentially, $Pr(Cyl(x))$ is the probability that x is generated by a path of length n in $\mathcal{M}$. This can be extended to all measurable sets generated by the cylinder sets in the standard way. In particular ω-regular languages are measurable sets. Given $\mathcal{M}$ and an ω-regular language $\mathcal{L}$, let $Pr_{\mathcal{M}}(\mathcal{L})$ be the probability that a word generated randomly by $\mathcal{M}$ is in $\mathcal{L}$. We omit $\mathcal{M}$ when it is clear from context. For an automaton state $q \in Q$ and a state $s \in S$ in $\mathcal{M}$, $Pr_s(\mathcal{L}(\mathcal{A}^q))$ is the probability that a word generated by $\mathcal{M}$ is in the language $\mathcal{L}(\mathcal{A}^q)$. We require the LMC be *separated*. This means that for any two distinct states s, s', and for any word $w \in \Sigma^*$, if there exists a run from s on w, then there does not exist a run from s' on w, and vice versa. This is a mild constraint. As demonstrated in [5], we can satisfy this requirement by making the name of each state part of the alphabet. Alternatively, since we have

---

[2] A nonnegative matrix is stochastic (resp. substochastic) if each row is stochastic (resp. substochastic), that is, each row adds up to exactly one (resp. at most one).

letters on transitions, we can make the name of the state part of the letter on each outgoing transition.

We also consider general weighted graphs W over the state space S and matrix W. For $C, D \subseteq S$ we write $W^{C,D}$ for the submatrix of W obtained by deleting the rows not indexed by C and the columns not indexed by D. Similarly, we write $W^{(C,E)}$, where (C, E) is an SCC in the graph of the submatrix of $W^{C,C}$.

In this paper we are interested in the MCMC problem: given an LMC $\mathcal{M}$ and a UBA $\mathcal{U}$ with initial states s_0 and q_0, respectively, we want to compute the probability $Pr_{s_0}(\mathcal{L}(\mathcal{U}^{q_0}))$. In the following, we begin with the DBA specifications in Sect. 3, and then proceed to the more involved UBA specifications in Sect. 4.

3   Model Checking Against DBAs

Let $\mathcal{M} = (S, \Sigma, M, s_0)$ be an LMC and $\mathcal{D} = (\Sigma, Q, \delta, q_0, \alpha)$ be a complete deterministic automaton. The classic MCMC algorithm first builds the product LMC $\mathcal{D} \times \mathcal{M}$ and then computes the probability of reaching the set K, denoted $Pr_{\mathcal{D} \times \mathcal{M}}(\Diamond K)$, where K is the set of all states in the *accepting BSCCs* of $\mathcal{D} \times \mathcal{M}$. Accepting BSCCs of $\mathcal{D} \times \mathcal{M}$ are BSCCs with at least one edge whose projection onto $\mathcal{D}$ lies in α. The probability $Pr_{\mathcal{M}}(\mathcal{L}(\mathcal{D}))$ is equal to the reachability probability of accepting BSCCs in $\mathcal{D} \times \mathcal{M}$.

In this section, we propose an alternative procedure to compute this probability by leveraging GfG automata minimisation. Our main idea is to construct an intermediate *probabilistic automaton* (PA) that preserves the language of $\mathcal{D}$ and analyse its product with $\mathcal{M}$. A PA $\mathcal{P} = (\Sigma, Q, \delta, q_0, \alpha)$ is a nondeterministic automaton equipped with a randomised transition function $\delta : Q \times \Sigma \mapsto \text{Distr}(Q)$, where from state q with letter a, transition to q' is taken with probability $\delta(q, a)(q')$. We often abuse the notation by writing $\delta(q, a)$ to denote its support. Each word $w \in \Sigma^\omega$ induces a probability measure $Pr_{\mathcal{P}}^w$ on Q^ω in the usual way. The probability that $\mathcal{P}$ accepts w, denoted by $Pr_{\mathcal{P}}(w)$, is the probability measure of all accepting runs of w on $\mathcal{P}$, that is, $Pr_{\mathcal{P}}(w) = Pr_{\mathcal{P}}^w(\{\pi \mid \pi \text{ is an accepting run of } w\})$. For a detailed introduction to PAs, please refer to [3].

Moreover, we require our PAs to be $0/1$-*PA*. A PA $\mathcal{P}$ is $0/1$-*PA* if, for any word $w \in \Sigma^\omega$, we have either $Pr_{\mathcal{P}}(w) = 1$ or $Pr_{\mathcal{P}}(w) = 0$. For a $0/1$-*PA* $\mathcal{P}$, and with a slight abuse of notation, we say that a word w is accepted by $\mathcal{P}$ (i.e., $w \in \mathcal{L}(\mathcal{P})$) if $Pr_{\mathcal{P}}(w) = 1$. In this paper, we focus on $0/1$-*PAs* that accept ω-regular languages.

In general, a $0/1$-*PA* $\mathcal{P}$ may accept a non-ω-regular language [3, Example 4.2.1]. Note that for some $w \notin \mathcal{L}(\mathcal{P})$, there may exist accepting runs in $\mathcal{P}$, but the probability measure of such accepting runs is 0. Additionally, we assume that $\mathcal{P}$ is complete, meaning that for all $w \in \Sigma^\omega$, we have $Pr_{\mathcal{P}}^w(\{\pi \mid \pi \text{ is a run over } w\}) = 1$.

Given an LMC $\mathcal{M}$, and state s in $\mathcal{M}$, let $Pr_s(\mathcal{L}(\mathcal{P}^q))$ be the probability that a random word generated in $\mathcal{M}$ starting from s lies in $\mathcal{L}(\mathcal{P}^q)$. We will first describe how we can compute the probabilities $Pr_s(\mathcal{L}(\mathcal{P}^q))$ by solving a system of linear equations on the product of $\mathcal{P}$ and $\mathcal{M}$. Given a 0/1-PA $\mathcal{P} = (\Sigma, Q, \delta, q_0, \alpha)$, we define the product $\mathcal{P} \times \mathcal{M} = (\Sigma, Q \times S, \delta_\otimes, \langle q_0 s_0 \rangle, \alpha_\otimes)$ where $Q \times S$ is the set of states, $\langle q_0 s_0 \rangle \in Q \times S$ is the initial state, $\alpha_\otimes \subseteq \Delta_{\mathcal{P} \times \mathcal{M}}$ is the set of α-transitions of $\mathcal{P} \times \mathcal{M}$ such that $(\langle qs \rangle, a, \langle q's' \rangle) \in \alpha_\otimes$ if $(q, a, q') \in \alpha$, and $\delta_\otimes : (Q \times S) \times \Sigma \mapsto \mathrm{Distr}(Q \times S)$ is the transition function such that $\delta_\otimes(\langle qs \rangle, a)(\langle q's' \rangle) = M(a)(s, s') \cdot \delta(q, a)(q')$ for all $\langle qs \rangle, \langle q's' \rangle \in Q \times S$ and $a \in \Sigma$.

The definition of the product can be easily adapted when $\mathcal{M}$ is a weighted graph. We show in Proposition 2 that $\mathcal{P}$ can be used to model check $\mathcal{M}$ by analysing the product $\mathcal{P} \times \mathcal{M}$. The product $\mathcal{P} \times \mathcal{M}$ can be effectively represented by the matrix $B_\otimes \in \mathbb{R}^{(Q \times S) \times (Q \times S)}$, where $B_\otimes(\langle qs \rangle, \langle q's' \rangle) = \sum_{a \in \Sigma} \delta_\otimes(\langle qs \rangle, a)(\langle q's' \rangle)$ for all $\langle qs \rangle, \langle q's' \rangle \in Q \times S$.

It is not hard to see that the matrix $B_\otimes$ is stochastic and $\mathcal{P} \times \mathcal{M}$ is a Markov chain. The linear equation system in Eq. (1) has a unique solution, denoted by χ. A proof of uniqueness can be found in [4, Theorem 10.19]. The value $\chi(\langle qs \rangle)$ precisely represents the probability of $\langle qs \rangle$ reaching an accepting BSCC.

$$\mathbf{x} = B_\otimes \mathbf{x}$$
$$\text{for all states } c \text{ in accepting BSCCs} \quad \mathbf{x}(c) = 1$$
$$\text{for all states } c \text{ in rejecting BSCCs} \quad \mathbf{x}(c) = 0 \tag{1}$$

Now we establish some useful properties of 0/1-PAs: they are semantically deterministic and can be complemented by simply negating the acceptance condition, similar to deterministic automata.

Lemma 1. *Let $\mathcal{P}$ be a 0/1-PA.*

(1) For any $a \in \Sigma$, $q \in Q$ and $q_1, q_2 \in \delta(q, a)$, we have $\mathcal{L}(\mathcal{P}^{q_1}) = \mathcal{L}(\mathcal{P}^{q_2})$.
(2) Let $\mathcal{P}'$ be the PA obtained by negating the acceptance condition. Then $\mathcal{P}'$ is also a 0/1-PA. Moreover, $\mathcal{L}(\mathcal{P}') = \overline{\mathcal{L}(\mathcal{P})}$.

Using Lemma 1(1), we show:

Proposition 2. *Let $\mathcal{M}$ be an LMC, and $\mathcal{P}$ be a 0/1-PA recognising the DBA language L. Then $Pr_s(\mathcal{L}(\mathcal{P}^q)) = \chi(\langle qs \rangle)$ for all $\langle qs \rangle \in Q \times S$. In particular, $Pr_\mathcal{M}(L) = Pr_{\mathcal{M} \times \mathcal{P}}(\Diamond K)$ where K is the set of all states in the accepting BSCCs of $\mathcal{P} \times \mathcal{M}$.*

Proposition 2 is a simple yet effective generalisation of existing similar standard result for deterministic automata [4] since DBAs and DCAs can be seen as 0/1-PAs by transitioning to the only successor with probability one.

Our source of 0/1-PA is a property satisfied by the minimised GfG-NCA automata in [1] called *stochastic resolvability*. Stochastically resolvable automata can be turned into language-preserving 0/1-PAs by resolving nondeterminism using good (positional) *stochastic resolvers*. A good stochastic resolver $R : Q \times \Sigma \mapsto \mathrm{Distr}(Q)$ for nondeterministic automaton $\mathcal{A}$ is simply a randomised transition function that turns $\mathcal{A}$ into a 0/1-PA, denoted by $\mathcal{A} \times R$, such that $\mathcal{L}(\mathcal{A}) = \mathcal{L}(\mathcal{A} \times R)$. A stochastic resolver is said to be uniform when for every q and a, $R(q, a)$ is the uniform distribution over $\delta(q, a)$.

With the preparations above, we now propose the following steps to model check an LMC $\mathcal{M}$ against a DBA $\mathcal{D}$: (1) regard (complete) DBA $\mathcal{D}$ as a DCA $\mathcal{C}$, (2) minimise $\mathcal{C}$ to a GfG-NCA $\mathcal{G}$ using [1], (3) resolve the nondeterminism by random choices and obtain a 0/1 PA $\mathcal{P}$ with Büchi acceptance condition s.t. $\mathcal{L}(\mathcal{D}) = \mathcal{L}(\mathcal{P})$, (4) compute the product $\mathcal{P} \times \mathcal{M}$, and (5) calculate the reachability probability of accepting BSCCs by solving Eq. (1). The 0/1-PA $\mathcal{P}$ is expected to be smaller than $\mathcal{D}$ to make our approach more efficient compared to the classic MCMC against DBAs.

The main observation is that the minimal GfG-NCA $\mathcal{G}$ produced by [1] has a very simple good stochastic resolver R, the uniform stochastic resolver. This makes $\mathcal{G}$ a stochastically resolvable automaton. Then, by Lemma 1(2), we can obtain a 0/1-PA of $\mathcal{L}(\mathcal{D})$ by interpreting the α-transitions as accepting in $\mathcal{G}$.

Lemma 3. *Let $\mathcal{G}$ be an NCA that is semantically deterministic and safe deterministic and let R be a uniform stochastic resolver for $\mathcal{G}$. Then, the PA $\mathcal{G} \times R$ with Büchi acceptance condition is a 0/1-PA. Also, $\mathcal{L}(\mathcal{G} \times R) = \mathcal{L}(\mathcal{D})$.*

We sketch our proof idea as follows. Let $w \in \Sigma^\omega$. First, assume that $w \in \mathcal{L}(\mathcal{D})$, i.e., $w \notin \mathcal{L}(\mathcal{G})$. It immediately follows that $Pr_{\mathcal{G} \times R}(w) = 1$ since all runs of $\mathcal{G}$ over w are rejecting. Now we assume that $w \notin \mathcal{L}(\mathcal{D})$, i.e. $w \in \mathcal{L}(\mathcal{G}) = \mathcal{L}(\mathcal{C})$. Since $\mathcal{G}$ is safe deterministic, every accepting run of $\mathcal{G}$ over a word $w \in \mathcal{L}(\mathcal{C})$ will eventually get trapped in a deterministic safe component. Therefore, the probability measure of every accepting run of $\mathcal{G}$ over w is positive because as soon as the run enters the deterministic safe component, all visited transitions have probability one. Assume by contradiction that $Pr_{\mathcal{G} \times R}(w) = Pr_{\mathcal{G} \times R}^w(\{\pi \mid \pi \text{ is rejecting run over } w \text{ in } \mathcal{G}\}) > 0$. This means that there exists a state $q \in \delta(q_0, u)$ such that the probability measure of rejecting runs of w' in $\mathcal{G}$ from q is 1 where $w = uw'$. However, since $\mathcal{G}$ is semantically deterministic and $w \in \mathcal{L}(\mathcal{G})$, we have $w' \in \mathcal{L}(\mathcal{G}^q)$. This indicates that there is a run of $\mathcal{G}$ over w' from q that goes to a deterministic safe component and stays there. But then this entails that the probability measure of accepting runs over w' in $\mathcal{G}$ from q is positive, leading to contradiction. Hence, $Pr_{\mathcal{G} \times R}(w) = 0$. We can conclude that $\mathcal{G}$ is stochastically resolvable and $\mathcal{L}(\mathcal{D}) = \mathcal{L}(\mathcal{G} \times R)$.

Let $\mathcal{P} = \mathcal{G} \times R$ where R is the uniform stochastic resolver for $\mathcal{G}$. With Lemma 3 and Proposition 2, our main result of this section immediately follows.

Theorem 4. *Given an LMC $\mathcal{M}$ and a DBA $\mathcal{D}$, we have $Pr_{\mathcal{M}}(\mathcal{L}(\mathcal{D})) = \chi(q_0)$ where q_0 is the initial state of $\mathcal{P} \times \mathcal{M}$ and χ is the unique solution of the linear equation system Eq. (1).*

According to [20], GfG automata can be used to model check LMCs by constructing the product of $\mathcal{M}$ and $\mathcal{G}$, where the nondeterminism in $\mathcal{G}$ is resolved by incorporating additional actions. This process yields a product Markov decision process (MDP) rather than a Markov chain. The probability $Pr_{\mathcal{M}}(\mathcal{L}(\mathcal{D}))$ can then be expressed as one minus the maximum satisfiability of $\mathcal{L}(\mathcal{G})$ within the resulting MDP. Nonetheless, our algorithm still provides some advantage in this context, as it reduces the computational complexity from solving a linear programming problem for MDPs to solving a linear system of equations for LMCs. Beyond this advantage, the MCMC algorithm against DBA specifications paves the way towards our primary objective—MCMC against UBA specifications.

4   Model Checking Against UBAs

The DBA languages cannot express all ω-regular properties. This section considers UBAs, which can represent all ω-regular properties, as specifications. Our MCMC algorithm against UBAs leverages similar idea for the DBA case which also constructs a PA $\mathcal{P}$ using the minimisation algorithm in [1]. The first challenge we face here is that the minimisation construction only works on GfG-NCAs but our input automaton $\mathcal{U}$ is unambiguous. If we assume that $\mathcal{U}$ is both GfG and unambiguous, then the automaton is essentially deterministic[3] [6, Proposition 9]; this again will lose expressiveness.

We address the first challenge by determinising the UBA $\mathcal{U}$ with auxiliary letters. That is, we make the nondeterministic choices explicit by marking each choice with different fresh letters. This way, we obtain a complete DBA $\mathcal{D}$ over an extended alphabet Σ', and regard it as a DCA $\mathcal{C}$. Since $\mathcal{C}$ is deterministic, we can again compute a minimal GfG-NCA $\mathcal{G}$ accepting $\mathcal{L}(\mathcal{C})$. Clearly, $\mathcal{G}$ has a positional stochastic resolver according to Lemma 3. However, $\mathcal{G}$ is defined over Σ', which is different than the alphabet Σ in the LMC $\mathcal{M}$. Our second challenge is how to define the product of $\mathcal{M}$ and $\mathcal{P}$. To resolve this, we turn $\mathcal{M}$ into a weighted graph $\mathcal{W}$ over Σ' in a way that the product $\mathcal{G} \times \mathcal{W}$ can guide $\mathcal{G}$ to obtain a positional stochastic resolver, yielding the product $\mathcal{P} \times \mathcal{W}$. When we map Σ' back to Σ in the product $\mathcal{P} \times \mathcal{W}$, we can still calculate the correct probability $Pr_{\mathcal{M}}(\mathcal{L}(\mathcal{U}))$.

Let $\mathcal{M} = (S, \Sigma, M, s_0)$ be the given LMC and $\mathcal{U} = (\Sigma, Q, \delta, q_0, \alpha)$ the given UBA. We dedicate the rest of this section to describe in detail how we address the two challenges above and present our new MCMC algorithm.

4.1   Product Construction

We first describe our determinisation approach for $\mathcal{U}$. This approach preserves the underlying graph of $\mathcal{U}$ but modifies the alphabet along with providing means to recover the original language. In theory, we can obtain a DBA $\mathcal{D} = \langle \Sigma', Q, q_0, \delta_{\mathcal{D}}, \alpha_{\mathcal{D}} \rangle$ over new alphabet $\Sigma' \subseteq \Sigma \times \mathbb{N}$ from $\mathcal{U}$, using any map $\mathbf{p} : \Delta_{\mathcal{U}} \mapsto \Delta_{\mathcal{D}}$ such that any two transitions (q_1, a, q_1'), (q_1, a, q_2') in $\Delta_{\mathcal{U}}$ with $q_1' \neq q_2'$, are mapped by $\mathbf{p}$ to transitions in $\Delta_{\mathcal{D}}$ with $\langle a, i \rangle$ and $\langle a, j \rangle$, that is, two distinct labels from Σ'. This gives a natural projection map $\mathbf{p}^{-1} : \Sigma' \mapsto \Sigma$, that is, $\mathbf{p}^{-1}(\langle a, i \rangle) = a$ for all $\langle a, i \rangle \in \Sigma'$, which can be naturally extended to infinite words and languages.

---

[3] GfG unambiguous automata are determinisable by pruning, meaning they can be seen as deterministic automata with additional transitions on top.

For a given state $q \in Q$, a letter $a \in \Sigma$, without loss of generality we can assume an ordering on the successors states $\delta(q, a)$, i.e. $\delta(q, a) = \{q'_0, \cdots, q'_h\}$. We define $\mathbf{p}((q, a, q'_i)) = (q, a', q'_i)$ where $a' = \langle a, i \rangle \in \Sigma'$. With $\alpha_{\mathcal{D}} = \mathbf{p}(\alpha_{\mathcal{U}})$, it is easy to see that $\mathcal{L}(\mathcal{U}) = \mathbf{p}^{-1}(\mathcal{L}(\mathcal{D}))$. Essentially in the transitions of $\mathcal{D}$ we have encoded the information regarding which successor was taken in $\mathcal{U}$.

Hence a word in $\mathcal{L}(\mathcal{D})$ uniquely determines its origin word in $\mathcal{L}(\mathcal{U})$ obtained by applying $\mathbf{p}^{-1}$. This gives us the following crucial observation on how $\mathcal{D}$ retains information on the unambiguity of $\mathcal{U}$.

Lemma 5. *For two distinct words* $w_1, w_2 \in \mathcal{L}(\mathcal{D})$, *it always holds that* $\mathbf{p}^{-1}(w_1) \neq \mathbf{p}^{-1}(w_2)$.

We assume $\mathcal{D}$ is complete and can also be read as a DCA $\mathcal{C}$ with $\mathcal{L}(\mathcal{C}) = \overline{\mathcal{L}(\mathcal{D})}$.

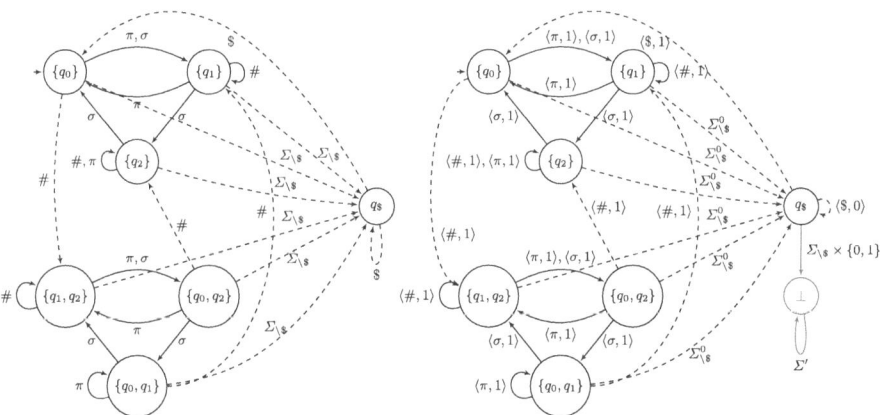

Fig. 1. Left: An example UBA $\mathcal{U}_3$ with alphabet $\Sigma = \{\pi, \sigma, \#, \$\}$; let $\Sigma_{\backslash \$} = \{\pi, \sigma, \#\}$. The dashed transitions are α-transitions which are accepting for Büchi automata. **Right**: Determinise the UBA one the left into a complete DBA with $\Sigma' = \Sigma \times \{0, 1\}$. Let $\Sigma^0_{\backslash \$} = \Sigma_{\backslash \$} \times \{0\}$.

Example 6. The UBA $\mathcal{U}_3$ (shown on the left of Fig. 1) belongs to a family of UBAs $\{\mathcal{U}_i\}_i$ for which our algorithm produces an exponentially smaller product. Since there are at most two nondeterministic choices at every state in $\mathcal{U}_3$, we can resolve the nondeterminism with a boolean variable. A value of 0 (false) will direct transitions to the state $q_\$$, whereas a value of 1 will take the transition that doesn't lead to $q_\$$. The result is a DBA $\mathcal{D}_3$ over $\Sigma' = \Sigma \times \{0, 1\}$; see the right of Fig. 1. Since we will later treat $\mathcal{D}_3$ as a DCA accepting the complement language, we make it complete by adding a new sink state $\bot$. Specifically, we add non-accepting $\langle \$, 0 \rangle$- and $\langle \$, 1 \rangle$-transitions from q to $\bot$ for $q \in 2^{\{q_0, q_1, q_2\}}$ and for the missing letters from $q_\$$ to $\bot$, and a non-accepting self-loop on $\bot$ for all letters in Σ'. Transitions from $q \in 2^{\{q_0, q_1, q_2\}}$ to $\bot$ are omitted in the figure.

The projection $\mathbf{p}^{-1}$, which maps every letter of Σ' to a letter of Σ, is defined as follows: $\mathbf{p}^{-1}(\langle a, i \rangle) = a$ for all $a \in \Sigma$ and $i \in \{0, 1\}$. $\qquad \square$

By applying the minimisation algorithm from [1] on $\mathcal{C}$, we obtain a minimal GfG-NCA $\mathcal{G} = \langle \Sigma', Q_{\mathcal{G}}, q_{0_{\mathcal{G}}}, \delta_{\mathcal{G}}, \alpha_{\mathcal{G}} \rangle$ that recognises the same language as $\mathcal{C}$. Let R be a uniform stochastic resolver for $\mathcal{G}$. By Lemma 3, the PA $\mathcal{P}$ with a Büchi acceptance condition, defined as $\mathcal{P} = \mathcal{G} \times R$, is a 0/1-PA, and its language satisfies $\mathcal{L}(\mathcal{P}) = \mathcal{L}(\mathcal{D})$. Formally, $\mathcal{P}$ differs from $\mathcal{G}$ only in its transition function, which is given by $\delta_{\mathcal{P}}(q, a)(q') = \frac{1}{|\delta_{\mathcal{G}}(q,a)|}$ for all $(q, a, q') \in \Delta_{\mathcal{G}}$. We have:

Lemma 7. $\mathcal{L}(\mathcal{U}) = \mathbf{p}^{-1}(\mathcal{L}(\mathcal{D})) = \mathbf{p}^{-1}(\mathcal{L}(\mathcal{P}))$.

Being a 0/1-PA, $\mathcal{P}$ also enjoys the properties given in Lemma 1. That is, $\mathcal{P}$ is semantically deterministic and can be complemented by simply complementing the acceptance condition. To show that $\mathcal{P}$ can be used to model check LMCs, we first establish additional properties of $\mathcal{P}$ concerning its projected languages over Σ. Firstly, since $\mathcal{P}$ is semantically deterministic, for $\langle a, i \rangle \in \Sigma'$ and a state q in $\mathcal{P}$, projected languages of two $\langle a, i \rangle$-successors of q would also be the same. Secondly, let $\langle a, i \rangle, \langle a, j \rangle \in \Sigma'$ be two distinct letters. Let $q \in Q_{\mathcal{G}}$ be a reachable state, and $q_1 \in \delta_{\mathcal{P}}(q, \langle a, i \rangle)$ and $q_2 \in \delta_{\mathcal{P}}(q, \langle a, j \rangle)$ be two successors. Since q is reachable, for some $w \in \Sigma'^*$ having a run from initial state to q, we have $w\langle a, i \rangle \mathcal{L}(\mathcal{P}^{q_1}) \cup w\langle a, j \rangle \mathcal{L}(\mathcal{P}^{q_2}) \subseteq \mathcal{L}(\mathcal{P}) = \mathcal{L}(\mathcal{D})$. From Lemma 5 it follows that $\mathbf{p}^{-1}(\mathcal{L}(\mathcal{P}^{q_1})) \cap \mathbf{p}^{-1}(\mathcal{L}(\mathcal{P}^{q_2})) = \emptyset$. Hence we have the following lemma.

Lemma 8. Let $q \in Q_{\mathcal{G}}$, $\langle a, i \rangle$ and $\langle a, j \rangle$ be two different letters in Σ'. We have:

(1) for all states $q_1, q_2 \in \delta_{\mathcal{P}}(q, \langle a, i \rangle)$, it holds that $\mathbf{p}^{-1}(\mathcal{L}(\mathcal{P}^{q_1})) = \mathbf{p}^{-1}(\mathcal{L}(\mathcal{P}^{q_2}))$
(2) for states $q_1 \in \delta_{\mathcal{P}}(q, \langle a, i \rangle)$ and $q_2 \in \delta_{\mathcal{P}}(q, \langle a, j \rangle)$, it holds that $\mathbf{p}^{-1}(\mathcal{L}(\mathcal{P}^{q_1})) \cap \mathbf{p}^{-1}(\mathcal{L}(\mathcal{P}^{q_2})) = \emptyset$.

Example 9. Consider the complete DBA $\mathcal{D}_3$ in Example 6. We now read it as a DCA $\mathcal{C}_3$. Since DCAs are GfG, we can apply the algorithm from [1] to obtain a minimal GfG-NCA $\mathcal{G}_3$; see left of Fig. 2. We then turn the NCA into a 0/1-PA $\mathcal{P}$ by turning all transitions to randomised ones. Note that ignoring the probabilities and projecting Σ' down to Σ does *not* result in an automaton that is either unambiguous or diamond-free. E.g. $\#\#\$$ creates three paths from q_0 back to q_0, and $(\#\#\$)^\omega$ has an uncountable set of accepting runs. □

Lemma 8 is a key result of this paper, enabling us to combine good-for-gameness and unambiguity without losing the expressive power of ω-regular languages. The main idea is to leverage the good-for-game properties to resolve nondeterminism in the outer layer of the language over Σ', while exploiting the unambiguity inherent in the inner layer of the language over Σ. This is facilitated by the mapping function $\mathbf{p}$.

To align the LMC $\mathcal{M}$ with the alphabet Σ' of $\mathcal{P}$, we transform $\mathcal{M}$, originally defined over Σ, into a weighted graph (WG) $\mathcal{W}$ with alphabet Σ'. Let $\mathcal{W} = \langle S, \Sigma', W, s_0 \rangle$, where $W(a) = M(\mathbf{p}^{-1}(a))$ for all $a \in \Sigma'$.

Example 10. The LMC $\mathcal{M} = \langle S, \Sigma, M, s \rangle$ generates infinite words over $\Sigma = \{\sigma, \pi, \#, \$\}$ uniformly at random, with a single state s and $M(a)(s, s) = \frac{1}{4}$ for

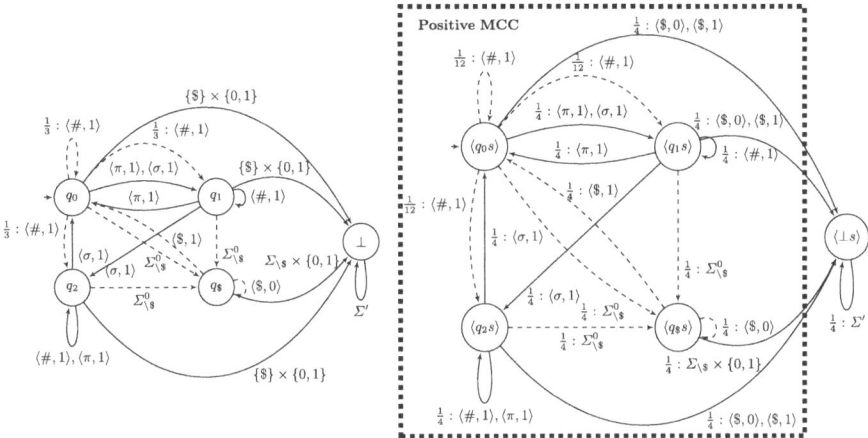

Fig. 2. Left: Read the complete DBA in Example 6 as a DCA and minimise it into a GfG-NCA $\mathcal{G}_3$ using the algorithm from [1]. The fractions in orange should be disregarded when reading it as an NCA. We then turn it into a 0/1-PA $\mathcal{P}$ by applying a stochastic resolver on $\mathcal{G}_3$. **Right**: The product of the GfG-NCA $\mathcal{G}_3$ and the WG $\mathcal{W}$ (or the PA $\mathcal{P}$ and the WG $\mathcal{W}$). There is one positive MCC in this product which is highlighted in thick dashed box.

all $a \in \Sigma$ (see left of the figure below). Since there is only one state in the LMC, it is obviously separated. Transforming $\mathcal{M}$ into a WG $\mathcal{W} = \langle S, \Sigma', W, s \rangle$ over $\Sigma' = \Sigma \times \{0,1\}$ preserves the state space, and $W(a')(s,s) = \frac{1}{4}$ for all $a' \in \Sigma'$ (see right of the figure below). □

$$\rightarrow \left(s \right) \circlearrowright \frac{1}{4} : a \in \Sigma \qquad\qquad \rightarrow \left(s \right) \circlearrowright \frac{1}{4} : a' \in \Sigma'$$

With both challenges being addressed, we are ready to define the product WG $\mathcal{P} \times \mathcal{W} = (\Sigma', Q_\otimes, \delta_{\mathcal{P} \times \mathcal{W}}, \langle q_{0\mathcal{G}} s_0 \rangle, \alpha_\otimes)$, the state space $Q_\otimes$ of which is equal to $Q_{\mathcal{G}} \times S$. As usual, $(\langle qs \rangle, a, \langle q's' \rangle) \in \alpha_\otimes$ if $(q, a, q') \in \alpha_{\mathcal{G}}$.

This product can actually be seen as the product of $\mathcal{P}$ and $\mathcal{M}$ where there is a transition from $\langle qs \rangle$ to $\langle q's' \rangle$ over a letter $a \in \Sigma'$ if $M(\mathbf{p}^{-1}(a))(s,s') > 0$ and $(q, a, q') \in \Delta_{\mathcal{P}}$. It is important to use the maps $\mathbf{p}$ and $\mathbf{p}^{-1}$ in the model checking procedure to associate the language $\mathcal{L}(\mathcal{D})$ with the language $\mathcal{L}(\mathcal{U})$, in particular, deriving the corresponding linear equations.

We define the matrix $B_\otimes \in \mathbb{R}^{Q_\otimes \times Q_\otimes}$, where $B_\otimes(\langle qs \rangle, \langle q's' \rangle) = \sum_{a \in \Sigma'} \delta_{\mathcal{P} \times \mathcal{W}}(\langle qs \rangle, a)(\langle q's' \rangle)$ for all $\langle qs \rangle, \langle q's' \rangle \in Q_\otimes$. Unlike the matrix in Eq. (1), the matrix $B_\otimes$ here may not be stochastic. We conclude this subsection by constructing the basic linear equation system $\boldsymbol{x} = B_\otimes \boldsymbol{x}$ to compute the probability $Pr_\mathcal{M}(\mathcal{L}(\mathcal{U}))$. Hereafter, we use $\chi(\langle qs \rangle)$ to denote the probability $Pr_s(\mathbf{p}^{-1}(\mathcal{L}(\mathcal{P}^q)))$ for simplicity. Based on the relationship between the languages of automata (Lemma 7), we have $\chi(\langle q_{0\mathcal{G}} s_0 \rangle) = Pr_{s_0}(\mathbf{p}^{-1}(\mathcal{L}(\mathcal{P}))) = Pr_{s_0}(\mathcal{L}(\mathcal{U})) = Pr_\mathcal{M}(\mathcal{L}(\mathcal{U}))$. Using Lemma 8 and that the LMC is separated, we have the following.

Proposition 11. *Let $\mathcal{M}$ be an LMC and $\mathcal{U}$ be a UBA. The vector $\boldsymbol{\chi}$ satisfies $\boldsymbol{x} = B_\otimes \boldsymbol{x}$.*

Proposition 11 only provides a basic linear equation system, but it does not answer the following two questions: how to identify accepting components, and how to make sure that the obtained linear equation system has a unique solution. We address these questions in the remainder of this section.

4.2   Analysing MCCs of the Product

In the DBA case, we add additional equations—one for each BSCC—to ensure a unique solution (cf. Eq. (1)). Since the underlying matrix is stochastic, it is straightforward that, for any state in a BSCC, if an outgoing transition labelled with a belongs to the BSCC, then all other outgoing transitions labelled with a must also be within the BSCC; otherwise, the SCC is transient. In the UBA case, however, since the matrix $B_\otimes$ may *not* be stochastic, rather than looking at BSCCs, we focus on the components of $\mathcal{P} \times \mathcal{W}$ that are *closed* and *maximal*, which we refer to as maximal closed components (MCCs). We call a component (C, E) closed if, for any state $q \in C$ and any letter $a \in \Sigma'$, either *all* or *none* of a-successors of q lie in C, i.e. $\delta(q, a) \subseteq C$ or $\delta(q, a) \cap C = \emptyset$. A closed component (C, E) is maximal if there does not exist a closed component (C', E') such that $C \subsetneq C'$ or $E \subsetneq E'$. Algorithm 1 computes MCCs efficiently.[4]

Algorithm 1: MCC Computation

---

1 **repeat**
2 | compute SCCs of $\mathcal{P} \times \mathcal{W}$;
3 | **if** *there exist an SCC (C, E), a state $\langle qs \rangle \in C$ and a letter $a \in \Sigma'$ such that $(\langle qs \rangle, a, \langle q's' \rangle) \in \Delta_{\mathcal{P} \times \mathcal{W}}$ and $\langle qs \rangle, \langle q's' \rangle$ belong to different SCCs*
4 | **then**
5 | | remove all transitions labelled with a from $\langle qs \rangle$ in C;
6 **until** *no further changes.*

An MCC (C, E) is called *positive* if it is accepting, meaning that it contains some accepting transition, and *recurrent* if there exists a positive solution $\mathbf{x}$ to the following linear equation system: $B_\otimes^{(C,C)} \mathbf{x} = \mathbf{x}$ and $\mathbf{x}(c) = \mathbf{x}(d)$ for all $c, d \in C$ such that c and d can be reached simultaneously from some state by the same word. States c and d are language equivalent when $\mathcal{P} \times \mathcal{W}$ is interpreted as a Büchi automaton, which entails from Lemma 8. In case the underlying matrix $B_\otimes$ is stochastic, the positive MCCs are accepting BSCCs. Thus, in the DBA case, all accepting BSCCs are positive MCCs.

---

[4] MCC is closely related to maximal end components (MECs) in Markov decision processes (MDPs). Algorithm 1 is an adaption to MCC of the standard algorithm for computing MECs in MDPs, see e.g. [4, Algorithm 47].

For a state $\langle qs \rangle$ in $\mathcal{P} \times \mathcal{W}$ that cannot reach a positive MCC, the probability $\chi(\langle qs \rangle)$ is zero. Consequently, we can add the equations $\boldsymbol{x}(\langle qs \rangle) = 0$ to our linear equation system for all such states $\langle qs \rangle$ that cannot reach a positive MCC.

Proposition 12. *For a state $\langle qs \rangle$ of $\mathcal{P} \times \mathcal{W}$ that cannot reach a positive MCC, we have $\chi(\langle qs \rangle) = 0$.*

We can also show that the probability that the UBA $\mathcal{U}$ accepts a word randomly generated by the LMC $\mathcal{M}$ is positive if, and only if, a positive MCC exists in $\mathcal{P} \times \mathcal{W}$. Hence, for qualitative model checking, it suffices to check whether there is a positive MCC.

Proposition 13. *(Qualitative MCMC) $Pr_{\mathcal{M}}(\mathcal{L}(\mathcal{U})) > 0$ iff the product $\mathcal{P} \times \mathcal{W}$ has a positive MCC.*

For positive MCCs (C, E) of $\mathcal{P} \times \mathcal{W}$, the key observation is that each positive MCC includes all transitions within it and can, therefore, be referred to simply as C. This also entails that the projection of a positive MCC onto the states of the LMC is a BSCC of the LMC. Moreover, there exist sets called cuts that can be used to compute the values $\chi(\langle qs \rangle)$ for the states $\langle qs \rangle$. Cuts were introduced in [5] for MCMC against UBA specifications. Intuitively, these cuts are subsets $K \subseteq C$ of states with pairwise disjoint languages over Σ, such that almost all words have an accepting run starting from some state $q \in K$. We denote the transition function of $\mathcal{P} \times \mathcal{W}$ over Σ by $\delta_\otimes : Q_\otimes \times \Sigma \to 2^{Q_\otimes}$, defined as follows: $q' \in \delta_\otimes(q, a)$ if and only if there exists $a' \in \Sigma'$ such that $\mathbf{p}^{-1}(a') = a$ and $\delta_{\mathcal{P} \times \mathcal{W}}(q, a')(q') > 0$. For an MCC C, we write $\delta_\otimes^C$ to denote the restriction of $\delta_\otimes$ to C.

A subset $K \subseteq C$ is a *cut* for a positive MCC C if it satisfies the following conditions: (1) $K \subseteq \delta_\otimes(c, v)$ for some $c = \langle qs \rangle \in C$ and $v \in \Sigma^*$, (2) $\delta_\otimes(K, w) \neq \emptyset$ for all $w \in \Sigma^*$ such that w can be generated in $\mathcal{M}$ from some s where $\langle qs \rangle \in K$, and (3) all states in K are language disjoint.[5]

Given a cut $K \subseteq C$, we call its characteristic vector $\mu_C \in \{0, 1\}^C$ a *cut vector*, that is, $\mu_C(k) = 1$ iff $k \in K$. A cut can be computed in polynomial time in the size of the positive MCC C using Algorithm 2. Our cut computation is inspired by [5]; however, our algorithm additionally accounts for language equivalence of states, $\sim_{\mathcal{P} \times \mathcal{W}}$ where $\mathcal{P} \times \mathcal{W}$ is read as a Büchi automaton, mainly because the product $\mathcal{P} \times \mathcal{W}$ is neither unambiguous nor diamond-free (cf. Example 9).

The following lemma summarises the key properties of cuts that we will need.

Lemma 14. *Let C be a positive MCC. Then*

(1) C has a cut $K \subseteq C$ and $\mu_C^\mathsf{T} \chi_C = 1$, that is, $\sum_{k \in K} \chi(k) = 1$.
(2) One can compute a cut K for C in polynomial time.

---

[5] The cuts defined in [5] did not require (3), as any set K satisfying (1) would automatically satisfy (3) in their product due to its unambiguity and diamond-freeness.

Algorithm 2: Computing a cut K of a positive MCC (C, E)

---
1 $c \in C$ (c can be any state in C);
2 $w := \varepsilon$ (the empty word);
3 **while** $\exists v \in \Sigma^*$ and $d \not\sim_{\mathcal{P} \times \mathcal{W}} c$ with $\{c, d\} \subseteq \delta_\otimes^C(c, v)$ and $\delta_\otimes^C(d, w) \neq \emptyset$ **do**
4 $\quad \lfloor \; w := vw;$
5 return $K = \delta_\otimes^C(c, w)/{\sim_{\mathcal{P} \times \mathcal{W}}}.$

Now, we are ready to present the complete linear equation system:

$$\mathbf{x} = B_\otimes \mathbf{x}$$
$$\text{for all positive MCCs } C \text{ of } \mathcal{P} \times \mathcal{W}: \quad \boldsymbol{\mu}_C^\mathsf{T} \mathbf{x}_C = 1$$
$$[\text{where } \boldsymbol{\mu}_C \text{ is a cut vector for the positive MCC } C]$$
$$\text{for all states } c \text{ that cannot reach a positive MCC:} \quad \mathbf{x}(c) = 0 \qquad (2)$$

By combining Propositions 11, 12, and 13, and Lemma 14, we can demonstrate that Eq. (2) has a unique solution $\boldsymbol{v}$, which corresponds to χ. Consequently, we can prove Algorithm 3, which summarises our approach to model checking LMCs against UBA specifications, correctly computes the satisfying probability.

Theorem 15. *(Quantitative MCMC) Given an LMC $\mathcal{M}$ and a UBA $\mathcal{U}$, the linear equation system Eq. (2) has a unique solution $\boldsymbol{v}$. Moreover, we have $\boldsymbol{v} = \chi$, and thus $Pr_\mathcal{M}(\mathcal{L}(\mathcal{U})) = \boldsymbol{v}(q_0)$, where q_0 denotes the initial state in $\mathcal{P} \times \mathcal{W}$.*

Algorithm 3: Summary of the overall algorithm

---
1 Determinise the UBA $\mathcal{U}$ into a complete DBA $\mathcal{D}$ on the new alphabet Σ'; Read $\mathcal{D}$ as a DCA $\mathcal{C}$;
2 Obtain the minimal GfG-NCA $\mathcal{G}$ which is language equivalent to $\mathcal{C}$ by running the algorithm in [1] ;
3 Turn the LMC $\mathcal{M}$ into a WG $\mathcal{W}$ on Σ';
4 Obtain a 0/1-PA $\mathcal{P}$ by applying a positional stochastic resolver on $\mathcal{G}$;
5 Build the product $\mathcal{P} \times \mathcal{W}$, and denote the underlying matrix as $B_\otimes$;
6 return $\chi(q_0)$ where q_0 is the initial state of $\mathcal{P} \times \mathcal{W}$ and χ is the unique solution of the linear equation system Eq. (2).

Example 16. The product of the PA $\mathcal{P}$ in Example 9 and the WG $\mathcal{W}$ in Example 10 is shown on the right of Fig. 2. There is a single accepting MCC (C, E) highlighted in this product, which consists of all four states of the product $\langle q_0 s \rangle, \langle q_1 s \rangle, \langle q_2 s \rangle, \langle q_\$ s \rangle$ and all transitions between them. We have $B_\otimes^{(C,C)} \mathbf{x} = \mathbf{x}$ and $\mathbf{x}(\langle q_0 s \rangle) = \mathbf{x}(\langle q_1 s \rangle) = \mathbf{x}(\langle q_2 s \rangle)$, which indicates that this MCC is recurrent.

Thus, the probability is positive that the given UBA $\mathcal{U}_3$ accepts a word randomly generated by the LMC $\mathcal{M}$. This is indeed the case, as the probability is $\frac{3}{4}$. This is because the probability that a randomly generated word in $\mathcal{M}$ has finitely many \$ is 0. And among the words containing infinitely many \$, the set of words rejected by the UBA $\mathcal{U}_3$ is exactly $\{\$w \mid w \in \Sigma^\omega\}$ - all ω-words that start with \$. These words are generated by the LMC $\mathcal{M}$ with a probability of $\frac{1}{4}$. The probability is determined by adding an equation for the *cut* of the positive MCC, $\mu_C^\mathsf{T} \boldsymbol{x}_C = 1$, and an equation $\boldsymbol{x}(\langle \perp s \rangle) = 0$ for states that cannot reach a positive MCC. A cut $K = \{\langle q_i s \rangle, \langle q_\$ s \rangle\}$ for any $i \in \{0, 1, 2\}$, thus a cut vector, can be computed by running Algorithm 2. □

Correctness Proofs. For proof of correctness, we establish the existence of a good and fair resolver $\mathcal{R}$ for the product $\mathcal{G} \times \mathcal{W}$. This enables the construction of the product WG $\mathcal{G} \times \mathcal{W} \times \mathcal{R}$ over Σ' and $\mathcal{B}_{\otimes'}$ over Σ.

The product $\mathcal{G} \times \mathcal{W}$ differs from $\mathcal{P} \times \mathcal{W}$ only in terms of its transition function. The resolver is termed *good* for $\mathcal{G} \times \mathcal{W}$ because, for every word $w \in \mathcal{L}(\mathcal{G})$ generated by $\mathcal{W}$, the run of $\mathcal{G} \times \mathcal{W} \times \mathcal{R}$ on w visits an α-transition only finitely often. It is *fair* as, for every ω-word $w = a_0 a_1 \cdots$, if a transition $(\langle qsm \rangle, a, \langle q's'm' \rangle) \in \Delta_{\mathcal{G} \times \mathcal{W} \times \mathcal{R}}$ has been visited infinitely often, then, for all transitions $(\langle qs \rangle, a, \langle q''s' \rangle) \in \Delta_{\mathcal{G} \times \mathcal{W}}$, some transition $(\langle qsm'' \rangle, a, \langle q''s'm''' \rangle) \in \Delta_{\mathcal{G} \times \mathcal{W} \times \mathcal{R}}$ must be visited infinitely often as well. In our approach, the stochastic resolver takes the place of the good and fair resolver. It is *good* since it "preserves" the language of $\mathcal{U} \times \mathcal{M}$ when projecting $\mathcal{P} \times \mathcal{W}$ back to the original alphabet, and it is *fair* in the sense that if an a-transition of a state is taken infinitely often, then all its a-transitions must be taken infinitely often with probability one.

The final product WG, $\mathcal{B}_{\otimes'}$ over Σ, is both diamond-free and unambiguous, enabling us to adapt the algorithm from [5] for both qualitative and quantitative model checking. This allows us to use the structural similarity between $\mathcal{B}_{\otimes'}$ and $\mathcal{P} \times \mathcal{W}$ to establish the correctness of our approach. The full proof is presented in the full version.

5   Experiments

In this section, we present experimental results from our implementation of our algorithm for model checking LMCs against UBAs and compare our implementation against the one in [5]. Section 5.1 describes results validating exponential speed-up of our algorithm using a family of UBAs, for which the resulting automata are exponentially smaller after GfG minimisation. Section 5.2 compares the sizes of automata before and after automata transformation with benchmarks from [5], highlighting how our proposed algorithm effectively reduces the state sizes of automata across these benchmarks.

5.1   Case Study: A Family of UBAs with Exponential Gain

We substantiate our claims of exponential speed up in Markov chain model checking by providing a family of UBAs for which our algorithm produces an exponentially smaller product graph in the final stage of the algorithm. The UBA $\mathcal{U}_3$ in this family is illustrated on the left of Fig. 1, while the GfG-NCA $\mathcal{G}_3$ is on the left of Fig. 2.

Theorem 17. *There exists a family of UBAs* $\{\mathcal{U}_n\}_{n\geq 2}$ *with* $|\mathcal{U}_n| = \Omega(2^n)$ *such that the GfG automata* $\mathcal{G}_n$ *produced as a sub-routine of Algorithm 3 has size* $O(n)$.

Below, we define this family of UBAs and then give a brief description of the languages they accept. The construction of these UBAs are inspired from the family of DCAs in [21]. A UBA $\mathcal{U}_n = (\Sigma, Q_n, \delta_n, \{q_0\}, \alpha_n)$ over the alphabet $\Sigma = \{\sigma, \pi, \#, \$\}$ with initial state $\{q_0\}$ in the family consists of

- set of states $Q_n = \{q_\$\}\cup 2^{B_n}$ for $B_n = \{q_0, \ldots, q_{n-1}\}$;
- the transition function δ_n producing the set of transitions $\Delta_n \subseteq Q_n \times \Sigma \times Q_n$:
  σ: $(P, \sigma, P')\in\Delta_n$ for $P' = \{q_{(i+1) \mod n} \mid q_i \in P\}$,
  π: $(P, \pi, P')\in\Delta_n$ for $P' = \{q_i \mid q_i\in P \wedge i\geq 2\} \cup \{q_{(i+1) \mod 2} \mid q_i\in P \wedge i<2\}$,
  $\#$: $(P, \#, P')\in\Delta_n$ for P' is $\{q_1, \ldots, q_{n-1}\}$ if $P = \{q_0\}$ and $P\backslash\{q_0\}$ otherwise,
  $\$$: $(P, a, q_\$)\in\Delta_n$ $\forall P\in 2^{B_n}, a\in\Sigma_{\backslash\$}$ and $(q_\$, \$, \{q_0\}), (q_\$, \$, q_\$)\in\Delta_n$;
- the set of transitions $\alpha_n \subseteq \Delta_n$ describing the acceptance condition: $\alpha_n = \{(P_1, \#, P_2)\subseteq\Delta_n \mid q_0\in P_1\} \cup \{(P, a, q_\$) \mid P\in 2^{B_n}\} \cup \{(q_\$, \$, \{q_0\}), (q_\$, \$, q_\$)\}$.

Similar to [21], each letter in Σ represents an action performed using an infinite set of tokens and a set B_n of n boxes. Initially, each box has exactly one token. σ moves tokens cyclically, i.e. moves token from q_i to $q_{(i+1) \mod n}$ for every i; π swaps the tokens in boxes q_0 and q_1; $\#$ discards the token in box q_0, replacing with a new one; and $\$$ discards tokens from all boxes and replaces with new ones. The language $\mathcal{L}(\mathcal{U}_n)$ is the set of all infinite sequences of actions such that any token present in some box at any instance is eventually discarded. The automaton $\mathcal{U}_n$ operates by tracking tokens within possible sets of boxes using states $P \subseteq 2^{B_n}$ or by predicting a $\$$ action through the designated state $q_\$$. More details and proofs can be found in the full version.

Implementation and Experiments. We have implemented a probabilistic model-checking procedure for LMCs and UBA specifications using the algorithm described in Sect. 4. This implementation extends the probabilistic model checker PRISM [22]. This enables a comparison with the implementation of the algorithm presented in [5, Section 8], which we refer to as PRISM UBA. All experiments were carried out on a computer with one Apple M3 8-core CPU with 16 GB of RAM running MacOS and a time limit of 30 min. Our implementation consists of two components: the first is a stand-alone tool that performs UBA determinisation and GfG-NCA minimisation (lines 1–2 of Algorithm 3), and the second is our model-checking algorithm (starting from line 3 of Algorithm 3), which takes the GfG-NCA generated by the first component and the input LMC. The first component is implemented in C++ and built on top of the Spot automata library [12]: it takes as input a UBA in HOA format [2], determinises the UBA to a DCA using the approach from Sect. 4.1, minimises the DCA using [1], and outputs the minimal GfG-NCA in HOA format.

Similar to PRISM UBA, the second component is also based on the explicit engine of PRISM, where the Markov chain is represented explicitly. Our implementation supports direct verification against a path specification given by a UBA provided in the HOA format [2]. For the linear algebra parts of the algorithms, we use the COLT library [18], as also used in [5].

Table 1. Comparison of PRISM UBA from [5] (rank-based) and our algorithm for model checking against a family of UBAs ($n \in \{3, \ldots, 8\}$) on a randomly generated LMC with 20 states. The table shows the number of states in the automata, product sizes, and model checking times (t_{total}). For our algorithm, t_{total} includes t_{tr} (UBA determinisation and GfG minimisation, lines 1–2 of Algorithm 3) and t_{mc} (model checking the minimal GfG automaton, starting at line 3). A dash ('-') indicates a timeout (30 min) or a stack overflow (1 GB).

n	PRISM UBA [5]			Our Algorithm				
	UBA	Product	t_{total}	GfG	Product	t_{total}	t_{tr}	t_{mc}
3	7	100	0.324 s	5	100	0.384 s	0.052 s	0.332 s
4	15	200	0.882 s	6	120	0.434 s	0.021 s	0.413 s
5	31	400	7.220 s	7	140	0.471 s	0.077 s	0.394 s
6	63	800	87.527 s	8	160	0.513 s	0.059 s	0.454 s
7	127	1600	1201.652 s	9	180	0.583 s	0.117 s	0.466 s
8	255	3200	-	10	200	0.513 s	0.102 s	0.411 s

We consider direct model checking against UBA specifications, where the UBAs are taken from the family described earlier in this section. The experiments were conducted on a simple randomly generated LMC. Table 1 presents the results for $n \in \{3, \ldots, 8\}$, obtained with a timeout of 30 min and a stack size of 1 GB. These results demonstrate that, for this family of UBAs, our algorithm is competitive with the UBA model checking algorithm from [5], particularly for $n \geq 4$, as highlighted in the table. Notably, PRISM UBA becomes unsuccessful for $n \geq 8$, unable to model check against the UBAs due to the immense size of the products. In contrast, our algorithm successfully scales to larger instances within a reasonable time for model checking. We are aware of a more efficient iterative version of the PRISM-UBA algorithm proposed in [5, Section 8.1]. We believe that a similar iterative optimisation could be applied to our algorithm as well, which we leave for future work.

5.2 Additional Benchmarks

Here we consider benchmarks from [5] and report whether the GfG minimisation step reduces the size of automata, since reduction in the number of states in the input UBA accelerates the subsequent model-checking procedure.

Complete and Nearly-Complete UBAs. First, we consider the two families of parametrised UBAs, the complete and the nearly-complete UBAs benchmarks, from [5, Section 8.2]. Our minimisation algorithm usually achieves a significant reduction in the number of states, often cutting the state count by more than half. The following table compares the sizes of UBAs and the GfG automata, where k is a parameter for the two families of UBAs.

	Complete UBAs				Nearly-complete UBAs		
k	UBA	GfG	t_{tr}	k	UBA	GfG	t_{tr}
5	193	96	0.121 s	5	193	94	0.122 s
6	449	192	0.126 s	6	449	190	0.126 s
7	1025	384	0.215 s	7	1025	382	0.251 s
8	2305	768	1.119 s	8	2305	766	1.070 s
9	5121	1536	8.160 s	9	5121	1534	8.179 s

LTL Specifications for Bounded Retransmission Protocol. Next, we consider the two LTL properties described in [5, Section 8.3] for the bounded retransmission protocol (BRP) model in the PRISM benchmark suite [22]. BRP concerns a single message transmission and retrying for a bounded number of times in case of an error. The first formula is $\varphi^k = (\neg ack\_received)\mathcal{U} \ retransmit \wedge (\neg ack\_received \, \mathcal{U}^{=k} \ ack\_received)$, where $a \, \mathcal{U}^{=k} \, b$ stands for $a \wedge \neg b \wedge \bigcirc(a \wedge \neg b) \wedge \cdots \wedge \bigcirc^{k-1}(a \wedge \neg b) \wedge \bigcirc^k b$. φ^k ensures that the message was retransmitted k steps before acknowledgement. The second formula is $\psi^k = (msg\_send \rightarrow (ack\_send \wedge \Diamond^{\leq k} ack\_received))$, where $\Diamond^{\leq k}$ denotes $a \vee \bigcirc(a \vee \bigcirc(\cdots \vee \bigcirc a))$ (repeated k times). ψ^k ensures that for every message sent, the receiver of the message sends an acknowledgement, and this acknowledgement is received within the next k steps.

For both benchmarks, using Spot 2.12.1 (the version used for our experiments), we observed that after some value of k, the generated UBAs were very large, whereas the GfG automata obtained from our minimisation step were significantly smaller. For example, for $k = 14$ in the first LTL family, the UBA produced by Spot 2.12.1 had 6,147 states on our macOS machine whereas our tool obtained GfG with only 16 states. For $k = 12$ in the second LTL family, the UBA had 8,452 states, while our tool obtained a GfG automaton with 159 states within a few seconds. Thus, the advantage of our model-checking algorithm over [5] becomes clear when the UBAs are significantly reduced after some value of k. In fact, the first BRP LTL formulas define a classic family of languages where DBAs can be exponentially larger than the corresponding UBAs where minimal UBAs for k should have $k+2$ states. Our minimisation approach for $k = 14$ gives GfG automaton with 16 (i.e. $k+2$) states, matching the size of the minimal UBA. We note that [5] used Spot 2.7, and also reported that the UBA had size 16 for $k = 14$. This then demonstrates that our algorithm is not only effective but also more robust across different tool choices.

6   Conclusion

We have synergised two recent advancements in the efficient verification of Markov chains: facilitating unambiguous Büchi automata and minimising GfG-NCAs [1]. These two classes of automata are very surprising candidates for obtaining synergistic effects, because they generalise deterministic automata in very different ways. Unambiguous automata guarantee the uniqueness of an accepting run, which has been at the heart of the approach to use them in model checking Markov chains [5]. Broadly speaking, it allows for *not* resolving the nondeterminism and to still measure the accepting paths. This heavily relies on two things: one is that this is the only nondeterminism to consider (which is why it does not work for MDPs), and the other is that the path to acceptance is narrow, allowing for only a single accepting run of the automaton on every word of the Markov chain in the target language.

It is fair to say that GfG nondeterminism is the polar opposite. It needs to be resolvable *on-the-fly* and we need to choose between transitions to various language equivalent states. Locally—i.e., on any finite prefix of a run—all of these transitions can be taken; broadly speaking, one could say that it depends on the path to acceptance being broad: having infinitely many accepting runs for a word is the norm. To justify the term polar opposite further, these two restrictions of nondeterminism are mutually exclusive ways to generalise deterministic automata in that unambiguous GfG automata are essentially deterministic (cf. [6]).

The second big difference between these classes is that UBAs recognise all ω-regular languages, while GfG-NCA can only recognise co-Büchi languages. We have shown that these concepts can nevertheless be brought together in an intricate construction, where the nondeterminism of the automaton is resolved randomly. When interpreting the probabilistic transitions as nondeterministic, the resulting PA is not guaranteed to be unambiguous. Yet, the resulting probabilities can be used in MCMC and retain the full expressive power of UBAs.

This allows us to reduce the state space of a UBA in polynomial time, where the target is not normally a UBA, and the optimisation step minimises a DCA as a GfG-NCA, an exponentially more succinct automata class [21]. We believe that our algorithm can further speed up model checking against LTL [5,11], LDL and weak alternating automata [23], and UBAs in general, especially when the input LMCs are large, as is often the case with real-world models.

Acknowledgments. We would like to thank the anonymous reviewers for their suggestions that helped improve the paper. This work has been supported in part by the Engineering and Physical Sciences Research Council (EPSRC) through grant EP/X03688X/1 and EP/X042596/1, ISCAS Basic Research (Grant Nos. ISCAS-JCZD-202406, ISCAS-JCZD-202302), CAS Project for Young Scientists in Basic Research (Grant No. YSBR-040), and ISCAS New Cultivation Project ISCAS-PYFX-202201.

Disclosure of Interests. The authors have no competing interests.

References

1. Abu Radi, B., Kupferman, O.: Minimization and canonization of GFG transition-based automata. Log. Methods Comput. Sci. **18**(3), 16:1–16:33 (2022). https://doi.org/10.46298/LMCS-18(3:16)2022

2. Babiak, T., et al.: The Hanoi omega-automata format. In: Kroening, D., Păsăreanu, C.S. (eds.) Computer Aided Verification, pp. 479–486. Springer, Cham (2015)

3. Baier, C., Größer, M., Bertrand, N.: Probabilistic ω-automata. J. ACM **59**(1), 1:1–1:52 (2012). https://doi.org/10.1145/2108242.2108243

4. Baier, C., Katoen, J.: Principles of Model Checking. MIT Press (2008)

5. Baier, C., Kiefer, S., Klein, J., Müller, D., Worrell, J.: Markov chains and unambiguous automata. J. Comput. Syst. Sci. **136**, 113–134 (2023). https://doi.org/10.1016/J.JCSS.2023.03.005

6. Boker, U., Kupferman, O., Skrzypczak, M.: How deterministic are good-for-games automata? In: Lokam, S.V., Ramanujam, R. (eds.) 37th IARCS Annual Conference on Foundations of Software Technology and Theoretical Computer Science, FSTTCS 2017, Kanpur, India, 11–15 December 2017. LIPIcs, vol. 93, pp. 18:1–18:14. Schloss Dagstuhl - Leibniz-Zentrum für Informatik (2017). https://doi.org/10.4230/LIPICS.FSTTCS.2017.18

7. Bustan, D., Rubin, S., Vardi, M.Y.: Verifying omega-regular properties of Markov chains. In: Alur, R., Peled, D.A. (eds.) Computer Aided Verification, 16th International Conference, CAV 2004, Boston, MA, USA, 13–17 July 2004, Proceedings. LNCS, vol. 3114, pp. 189–201. Springer (2004). https://doi.org/10.1007/978-3-540-27813-9_15

8. Carton, O., Michel, M.: Unambiguous Büchi automata. Theor. Comput. Sci. **297**(1–3), 37–81 (2003). https://doi.org/10.1016/S0304-3975(02)00618-7

9. Courcoubetis, C., Yannakakis, M.: The complexity of probabilistic verification. J. ACM **42**(4), 857–907 (1995). https://doi.org/10.1145/210332.210339

10. Couvreur, J., Saheb, N., Sutre, G.: An optimal automata approach to LTL model checking of probabilistic systems. In: Vardi, M.Y., Voronkov, A. (eds.) Logic for Programming, Artificial Intelligence, and Reasoning, 10th International Conference, LPAR 2003, Almaty, Kazakhstan, 22–26 September 2003, Proceedings. LNCS, vol. 2850, pp. 361–375. Springer (2003). https://doi.org/10.1007/978-3-540-39813-4_26

11. Duret-Lutz, A., Lewkowicz, A., Fauchille, A., Michaud, T., Renault, E., Xu, L.: Spot 2.0 - a framework for LTL and omega-automata manipulation. In: Artho, C., Legay, A., Peled, D. (eds.) Automated Technology for Verification and Analysis - 14th International Symposium, ATVA 2016, Chiba, Japan, 17–20 October 2016, Proceedings. LNCS, vol. 9938, pp. 122–129 (2016). https://doi.org/10.1007/978-3-319-46520-3_8

12. Duret-Lutz, A., et al.: From Spot 2.0 to Spot 2.10: what's new? In: Proceedings of the 34th International Conference on Computer Aided Verification (CAV 2022). LNCS, vol. 13372, pp. 174–187. Springer (2022). https://doi.org/10.1007/978-3-031-13188-2_9

13. Fu, C., et al.: EPMC gets knowledge in multi-agent systems. In: Finkbeiner, B., Wies, T. (eds.) Verification, Model Checking, and Abstract Interpretation - 23rd International Conference, VMCAI 2022, Philadelphia, PA, USA, 16–18 January 2022, Proceedings. LNCS, vol. 13182, pp. 93–107. Springer (2022). https://doi.org/10.1007/978-3-030-94583-1_5

14. Hahn, E.M., Li, G., Schewe, S., Turrini, A., Zhang, L.: Lazy probabilistic model checking without determinisation. In: Aceto, L., de Frutos-Escrig, D. (eds.) 26th International Conference on Concurrency Theory, CONCUR 2015, Madrid, Spain, 1–4 September 2015. LIPIcs, vol. 42, pp. 354–367. Schloss Dagstuhl - Leibniz-Zentrum für Informatik (2015). https://doi.org/10.4230/LIPICS.CONCUR.2015.354

15. Hahn, E.M., Li, Y., Schewe, S., Turrini, A., Zhang, L.: ISCASMC: a web-based probabilistic model checker. In: Jones, C.B., Pihlajasaari, P., Sun, J. (eds.) FM 2014: Formal Methods - 19th International Symposium, Singapore, 12–16 May 2014. Proceedings. LNCS, vol. 8442, pp. 312–317. Springer (2014). https://doi.org/10.1007/978-3-319-06410-9_22

16. Hahn, E.M., Perez, M., Schewe, S., Somenzi, F., Trivedi, A., Wojtczak, D.: Good-for-MDPs automata for probabilistic analysis and reinforcement learning. In: Biere, A., Parker, D. (eds.) Tools and Algorithms for the Construction and Analysis of Systems - 26th International Conference, TACAS 2020, Held as Part of the European Joint Conferences on Theory and Practice of Software, ETAPS 2020, Dublin, Ireland, 25–30 April 2020, Proceedings, Part I. LNCS, vol. 12078, pp. 306–323. Springer (2020). https://doi.org/10.1007/978-3-030-45190-5_17

17. Henzinger, T.A., Piterman, N.: Solving games without determinization. In: Ésik, Z. (ed.) Computer Science Logic, 20th International Workshop, CSL 2006, 15th Annual Conference of the EACSL, Szeged, Hungary, 25–29 September 2006, Proceedings. LNCS, vol. 4207, pp. 395–410. Springer (2006). https://doi.org/10.1007/11874683_26

18. Hoschek, W.: The Colt distribution: open source libraries for high performance scientific and technical computing in Java (2002). http://nicewww.ccrn.ch/hoschek/colt/index.htm

19. Jantsch, S., Müller, D., Baier, C., Klein, J.: From LTL to unambiguous Büchi automata via disambiguation of alternating automata. Formal Methods Syst. Des. **58**(1–2), 42–82 (2021). https://doi.org/10.1007/S10703-021-00379-Z

20. Klein, J., Müller, D., Baier, C., Klüppelholz, S.: Are good-for-games automata good for probabilistic model checking? In: Dediu, A., Martín-Vide, C., Sierra-Rodríguez, J.L., Truthe, B. (eds.) Language and Automata Theory and Applications - 8th International Conference, LATA 2014, Madrid, Spain, 10–14 March 2014. Proceedings. LNCS, vol. 8370, pp. 453–465. Springer (2014). https://doi.org/10.1007/978-3-319-04921-2_37

21. Kuperberg, D., Skrzypczak, M.: On determinisation of good-for-games automata. In: Halldórsson, M.M., Iwama, K., Kobayashi, N., Speckmann, B. (eds.) Automata, Languages, and Programming - 42nd International Colloquium, ICALP 2015, Kyoto, Japan, 6–10 July 2015, Proceedings, Part II. LNCS, vol. 9135, pp. 299–310. Springer (2015). https://doi.org/10.1007/978-3-662-47666-6_24

22. Kwiatkowska, M., Norman, G., Parker, D.: PRISM 4.0: verification of probabilistic real-time systems. In: Gopalakrishnan, G., Qadeer, S. (eds.) Proceedings of the 23rd International Conference on Computer Aided Verification (CAV 2011). LNCS, vol. 6806, pp. 585–591. Springer (2011)

23. Li, Y., Schewe, S., Vardi, M.Y.: Singly exponential translation of alternating weak Büchi automata to unambiguous Büchi automata. Theor. Comput. Sci. **1006**, 114650 (2024). https://doi.org/10.1016/J.TCS.2024.114650

24. Rohde, G.S.: Alternating automata and the temporal logic of ordinals. Ph.D. thesis, University of Illinois at Urbana-Champaign (1997)

25. Schewe, S., Tang, Q., Zhanabekova, T.: Deciding what is good-for-MDPs. In: Pérez, G.A., Raskin, J. (eds.) 34th International Conference on Concurrency Theory, CONCUR 2023, Antwerp, Belgium, 18–23 September 2023. LIPIcs, vol. 279, pp. 35:1–35:16. Schloss Dagstuhl - Leibniz-Zentrum für Informatik (2023). https://doi.org/10.4230/LIPICS.CONCUR.2023.35

26. Sickert, S., Esparza, J., Jaax, S., Kretínský, J.: Limit-deterministic Büchi automata for linear temporal logic. In: Chaudhuri, S., Farzan, A. (eds.) Computer Aided Verification - 28th International Conference, CAV 2016, Toronto, ON, Canada, 17–23 July 2016, Proceedings, Part II. LNCS, vol. 9780, pp. 312–332. Springer (2016). https://doi.org/10.1007/978-3-319-41540-6_17

Neural Networks

Floating-Point Neural Networks are Provably Robust Universal Approximators

Geonho Hwang[1] (ID), Wonyeol Lee[2] (ID), Yeachan Park[3] (ID), Sejun Park[4(✉)] (ID), and Feras Saad[5] (ID)

[1] GIST, Gwangju, Republic of Korea
hgh2134@gist.ac.kr
[2] POSTECH, Pohang, Republic of Korea
wonyeol.lee@postech.ac.kr
[3] Sejong University, Seoul, Republic of Korea
ychpark@sejong.ac.kr
[4] Korea University, Seoul, Republic of Korea
sejun.park000@gmail.com
[5] Carnegie Mellon University, Pittsburgh, PA, USA
fsaad@cmu.edu

Abstract. The classical universal approximation (UA) theorem for neural networks establishes mild conditions under which a feedforward neural network can approximate a continuous function f with arbitrary accuracy. A recent result shows that neural networks also enjoy a more general *interval* universal approximation (IUA) theorem, in the sense that the abstract interpretation semantics of the network using the interval domain can approximate the direct image map of f (i.e., the result of applying f to a set of inputs) with arbitrary accuracy. These theorems, however, rest on the unrealistic assumption that the neural network computes over infinitely precise real numbers, whereas their software implementations in practice compute over finite-precision floating-point numbers. An open question is whether the IUA theorem still holds in the floating-point setting.

This paper introduces the first IUA theorem for *floating-point* neural networks that proves their remarkable ability to *perfectly capture* the direct image map of any rounded target function f, showing no limits exist on their expressiveness. Our IUA theorem in the floating-point setting exhibits material differences from the real-valued setting, which reflects the fundamental distinctions between these two computational models. This theorem also implies surprising corollaries, which include (i) the existence of *provably robust* floating-point neural networks; and (ii) the *computational completeness* of the class of straight-line programs that use only floating-point additions and multiplications for the class of all floating-point programs that halt.

Keywords: Neural networks · Robust machine learning · Floating point · Universal approximation · Abstract interpretation

---

G. Hwang and W. Lee—Equal contribution.

The full version of this article is at https://doi.org/10.48550/arXiv.2506.16065.

R. Piskac and Z. Rakamarić (Eds.): CAV 2025, LNCS 15932, pp. 301–326, 2025.
https://doi.org/10.1007/978-3-031-98679-6_14

1   Introduction

Background. Despite the remarkable success of neural networks on diverse tasks, these models often lack *robustness* and are subject to adversarial attacks. Slight perturbations to the network inputs can cause the network to produce significantly different outputs [23,63], raising serious concerns in safety-critical domains such as healthcare [18], cybersecurity [57], and autonomous driving [16].

These issues have brought about significant advances in new algorithms for *robustness verification* [2,34,42], which prove the robustness of a given network; and *robust training* [24,48,56,68], which train a network to be provably robust. But despite these advances, provably robust networks do not yet achieve state-of-the-art accuracy [38]. For example, on the CIFAR-10 image classification benchmark, non-robust networks achieve over 99% accuracy, whereas the best provably robust networks achieve less than 63% [37]. This performance gap has prompted researchers to explore whether there exists fundamental limits on the *expressiveness* of provably robust networks that restrict their accuracy [3].

Surprisingly, it has been proven that no such fundamental limit exists. Informally, for any continuous function $f : \mathbb{R}^d \to \mathbb{R}$ and compact set $\mathcal{K} \subset \mathbb{R}^d$, there exists a neural network $g : \mathbb{R}^d \to \mathbb{R}$ whose robustness properties are "sufficiently close" to those of f over $\mathcal{K}$ and easily provable using abstract interpretation [10] over the interval domain. This result, known as the *interval universal approximation* (IUA) theorem [4,66], generalizes the classical universal approximation (UA) theorem [12,27] from pointwise-values to intervals, and confirms that provably robust networks do not suffer from a fundamental loss of expressive power.

Key Challenges. The IUA theorem in [4,66] overlooks a critical aspect of real-world computation, which is the use of *floating-point arithmetic* instead of real arithmetic. It assumes that neural networks and interval analyses operate on arbitrary real numbers with exact operations. In reality, numerical implementations of neural networks use floating-point numbers and operations [22, §4.1], sometimes with extremely low-precision to speed-up performance [14,29]. This discrepancy means that the existing IUA theorem does not directly apply to neural networks that are implemented in software and actually used in practice.

To our knowledge, no prior work has studied the robustness and expressiveness properties of floating-point neural networks or established an IUA theorem for them. The unique complexities of floating-point arithmetic introduce daunting challenges to any such theoretical study. For example, floating-point numbers are discretized and bounded, and their operations have rounding errors that become infinite in cases of overflow. Whereas the IUA proof over reals requires very large real numbers for network weights or intermediate computations, these values cannot be represented as floats. Naively rounding reals to floats causes approximation errors that invalidate many steps of the IUA proofs in [4,66].

This Work. We formally study the IUA theorem over floating point, as a step toward bridging the theory and practice of provably robust neural networks.

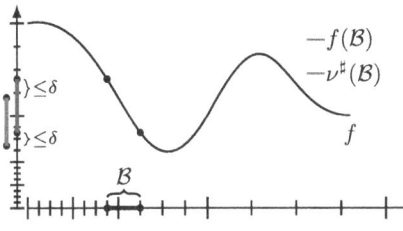 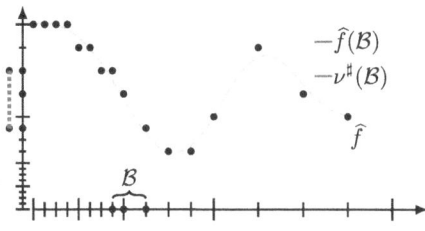

(a) $f : \mathbb{R}^d \to \mathbb{R}$ is a continuous target function; $\nu : \mathbb{R}^d \to \mathbb{R}$ is a neural network.

(b) $\widehat{f} : \overline{\mathbb{F}}^d \to \overline{\mathbb{F}}$ is a rounded target function; $\nu : \overline{\mathbb{F}}^d \to \overline{\mathbb{F}}$ is a neural network.

Fig. 1. Illustration and comparison of the IUA theorems. (a) In the real-valued setting, the neural network abstract interpretation $\nu^\sharp$ forms a δ-approximation to the image map of f. (b) In the floating-point setting, $\nu^\sharp$ exactly computes the upper and lower points of the image map of f: $\nu^\sharp(\mathcal{B}) = [\min \widehat{f}(\mathcal{B}), \max \widehat{f}(\mathcal{B})] \cap \overline{\mathbb{F}}$.

We first formulate a floating-point analog of the IUA theorem, considering the details of floating point. Let $f : \mathbb{R}^d \to \mathbb{R}$ be a target function to approximate. Since all floating-point neural networks are functions between floating-point values, they can at-best approximate the rounded version $\widehat{f} : \overline{\mathbb{F}}^d \to \overline{\mathbb{F}}$ of f over floats, where $\overline{\mathbb{F}}$ denotes the set of all floats. The floating-point version of the IUA theorem asks the following: is there a floating-point neural network $\nu : \overline{\mathbb{F}}^d \to \overline{\mathbb{F}}$ whose *interval semantics* is arbitrarily close to the *direct image map* of the rounded target $\widehat{f}$ over $[-1, 1]^d$? More formally, this property means that for any $\delta > 0$, there exists a neural network ν such that for all boxes $\mathcal{B} \subseteq [-1, 1]^d \cap \overline{\mathbb{F}}^d$,

$$\left| \min \nu^\sharp(\mathcal{B}) - \min \widehat{f}(\mathcal{B}) \right| \leq \delta, \qquad \left| \max \nu^\sharp(\mathcal{B}) - \max \widehat{f}(\mathcal{B}) \right| \leq \delta. \qquad (1)$$

In Eq. (1), $\nu^\sharp(\mathcal{B})$ is the result of abstract interpretation of $\mathcal{B}$ under ν (using the interval domain), and $\widehat{f}(\mathcal{B}) := \left\{ \widehat{f}(\mathbf{x}) \mid \mathbf{x} \in \mathcal{B} \right\} \subset \mathbb{R}$ is the image of $\mathcal{B}$ under $\widehat{f}$.

We prove that the IUA theorem holds for floating-point networks, despite all their numerical complexities. In particular, we show that for *any* target function f and a *large* class of activation functions σ, including most practical ones (e.g., ReLU, GELU, sigmoid), it is possible to find a floating-point network ν with σ whose interval semantics *exactly* matches the direct image map of the rounded target $\widehat{f}$ over $[-1, 1]^d \cap \overline{\mathbb{F}}^d$ (Fig. 1). This result implies that no fundamental limit exists on the expressiveness of provably robust floating-point neural networks.

Our result is considerably different from the previous IUA theorem over the reals in three key aspects. The previous theorem considers continuous target functions; requires a restricted class of so-called squashable activation functions; and finds networks that are arbitrarily close to target functions. In contrast, our result considers arbitrary target functions; allows almost all activation functions used in practice; and find networks that are precisely equal to (rounded) target functions. Our IUA theorem even holds for the *identity* activation function, which is not the case for the traditional IUA or UA theorems over real numbers, because any network that uses the identity activation is affine over the reals.

As a corollary of our main theorem, we prove the following existence of provably robust floating-point neural networks: given an ideal floating-point classifier $\widehat{f}$ (not necessarily a neural network) that is robust (not necessarily provably robust), we can find a floating-point neural network ν that is *identical* to $\widehat{f}$ and is *provably* robust with interval analysis. We also prove a nontrivial result about "floating-point completeness", as an unexpected byproduct of the main theorem. Specifically, we show that the class of straight-line floating-point programs that use only floating-point $+$ and $\times$ operations is *floating-point interval-complete*: it can simulate *any* terminating floating-point program that takes finite floats as input and returns arbitrary floats as output. The same statement holds under the interval semantics. To our knowledge, no prior work has identified such a small yet powerful class of floating-point programs, suggesting that this corollary is of significant independent interest to the extensive floating-point literature.

Contributions. This article makes the following contributions:

- We formalize a *floating-point* analog of the *interval universal approximation* (IUA) theorem, to bridge the theory and practice of *provably robust* neural networks (Sect. 2, Sect. 3). It asks if there is a floating-point network whose interval semantics is close to the direct image map of a given target function.
- We prove the floating-point version of the IUA theorem does hold, for *all* target functions and a *broad* class of activation functions that includes most of the activations used in practice (Sect. 3.1, Sect. 3.2, Sect. 5). This shows no fundamental limit exists on the expressiveness of provably robust networks over floats.
- We rigorously analyze the essential differences between the previous IUA theorem over reals and our IUA theorem over floats (Sect. 3.3). Unlike real-valued networks, floating-point networks can *perfectly* capture the behavior of *any* rounded target function, even with the *identity* activation function.
- We prove that if there exists an ideal robust floating-point classifier, then one can always find a *provably* robust floating-point network that makes *exactly* the same prediction as the classifier (Sect. 4.1).
- We prove that the set of straight-line floating-point programs with only $(+, \times)$ is *floating-point interval-complete*: it can simulate *any* terminating floating-point programs that take finite inputs and return finite/infinite outputs, under the usual floating-point semantics and interval semantics (Sect. 4.2).

2   Preliminaries

This section introduces floating-point arithmetic (Sect. 2.1), neural networks that compute over floating-point numbers (Sect. 2.2), and interval analysis for neural networks (Sect. 2.3). Throughout the paper, we define $\mathbb{N}$ to be the set of positive integers and let $[n] := \{1, \ldots, n\}$ for each $n \in \mathbb{N}$.

2.1 Floating Point

Floating-Point Numbers. Let $E, M \in \mathbb{N}$. The set of *finite* floating-point numbers with E-bit exponent and $(M+1)$-bit significand is typically defined by

$$\mathbb{F}_M^E := \left\{ (-1)^b \times (s_0.s_1 \ldots s_M)_2 \times 2^e \mid b, s_i \in \{0,1\}, e \in \{\mathfrak{e}_{\min}, \ldots, \mathfrak{e}_{\max}\} \right\}, \quad (2)$$

where $\mathfrak{e}_{\min} := -2^{E-1} + 2$ and $\mathfrak{e}_{\max} := 2^{E-1} - 1$ [52]. The set of *all* floating-point numbers, including non-finite ones, is then defined by $\overline{\mathbb{F}}_M^E := \mathbb{F}_M^E \cup \{-\infty, +\infty, \bot\}$, where $\bot$ denotes NaN (i.e., not-a-number). For brevity, we call a floating-point number simply a *float*, and write $\mathbb{F}_M^E$ and $\overline{\mathbb{F}}_M^E$ simply as $\mathbb{F}$ and $\overline{\mathbb{F}}$. In this paper, we assume $E \geq 5$ and $2^{E-1} \geq M \geq 3$, which hold for nearly all practical floating-point formats, including bfloat16 [1] and all the formats defined in the IEEE-754 standard [31] such as float16, float32, and float64.

We introduce several notations and terms related to finite floats. First, we define three key constants: the *smallest* positive float $\omega := 2^{\mathfrak{e}_{\min}-M}$, the *largest* positive float $\Omega := 2^{\mathfrak{e}_{\max}}(2 - 2^{-M})$, and the *machine epsilon* $\varepsilon := 2^{-M-1}$. Next, consider a finite float $x \in \mathbb{F}$. We call x a *subnormal* number if $0 < |x| < 2^{\mathfrak{e}_{\min}}$, and a *normal* number otherwise. The *exponent* and *significand* of x are defined by $\mathfrak{e}_x := \max\{\lfloor \log_2 |x| \rfloor, \mathfrak{e}_{\min}\} \in [\mathfrak{e}_{\min}, \mathfrak{e}_{\max}]$ and $\mathfrak{s}_x := |x|/2^{\mathfrak{e}_x} \in [0, 2)$. We use $\mathfrak{s}_{x,0}, \ldots, \mathfrak{s}_{x,M}$ to denote the binary expansion of $\mathfrak{s}_x$, i.e., $(\mathfrak{s}_{x,0}.\mathfrak{s}_{x,1} \ldots \mathfrak{s}_{x,M})_2 = \mathfrak{s}_x$ with $\mathfrak{s}_{x,i} \in \{0,1\}$. The *predecessor* and *successor* of x in $\mathbb{F}$ are written as $x^- := \max\{y \in \overline{\mathbb{F}} \setminus \{\bot\} \mid x > y\}$ and $x^+ := \min\{y \in \overline{\mathbb{F}} \setminus \{\bot\} \mid x < y\}$.

Floating-Point Operations. We define the *rounding function* $\mathrm{rnd} : \mathbb{R} \cup \{-\infty, +\infty\} \to \overline{\mathbb{F}}$ as follows: $\mathrm{rnd}(x) := -\infty$ if $x \in [-\infty, -\Omega - c]$, $\mathrm{rnd}(x) := \arg\min_{y \in \mathbb{F}} |y - x|$ if $x \in (-\Omega - c, \Omega + c)$, and $\mathrm{rnd}(x) := +\infty$ if $x \in [\Omega + c, +\infty]$, where $c := 2^{\mathfrak{e}_{\max}}\varepsilon$ and $\arg\min$ breaks ties by choosing a float y with $\mathfrak{s}_{y,M} = 0$. This function corresponds to the rounding mode "round to nearest (ties to even)", which is the default rounding mode in the IEEE-754 standard [31].

The floating-point *arithmetic operations* $\oplus, \ominus, \otimes : \overline{\mathbb{F}} \times \overline{\mathbb{F}} \to \overline{\mathbb{F}}$ are defined via the rounding function: for finite floats $x, y \in \mathbb{F}$, $x \oplus y := \mathrm{rnd}(x + y)$, $x \ominus y := \mathrm{rnd}(x - y)$, and $x \otimes y := \mathrm{rnd}(x \times y)$. We omit the definition for non-finite operands because they are unimportant in this paper, except that $x \oplus 0 = x \ominus 0 = x$ for all $x \in \{-\infty, +\infty\}$. For the full definition, refer to the IEEE-754 standard [31].

We introduce two more floating-point operations: $\mathrm{aff}_{W,\mathbf{b}}$ and $\mathrm{rnd}(f)$. First, we define the floating-point *affine transformation*: for a matrix $W = (w_{i,j})_{i \in [m], j \in [n]} \in \mathbb{F}^{m \times n}$ and a vector $\mathbf{b} = (b_1, \ldots, b_m) \in \mathbb{F}^m$, $\mathrm{aff}_{W,\mathbf{b}} : \overline{\mathbb{F}}^n \to \overline{\mathbb{F}}^m$ is defined by

$$\mathrm{aff}_{W,\mathbf{b}}(x_1, \ldots, x_n) := \left(\left(\bigoplus_{j=1}^n x_j \otimes w_{1,j} \right) \oplus b_1, \ldots, \left(\bigoplus_{j=1}^n x_j \otimes w_{m,j} \right) \oplus b_m \right). \quad (3)$$

Here, $\bigoplus$ denotes the floating-point summation defined in the left-associative way: $\bigoplus_{i=1}^n y_i := (\cdots((y_1 \oplus y_2) \oplus y_3) \cdots) \oplus y_n$, where the order of $\oplus$ is important

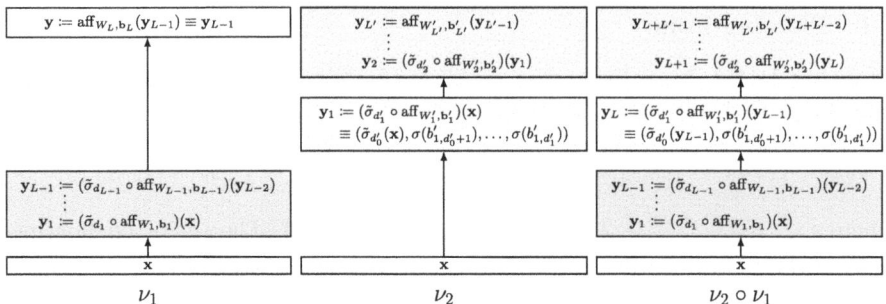

Fig. 2. Illustrations of a network ν_1 without the last affine layer (left), a network ν_2 without the first affine layer (middle), and their composition $\nu_2 \circ \nu_1$ (right). Note that $\mathrm{aff}_{W_1',\mathbf{b}_1'} \circ \mathrm{aff}_{W_L,\mathbf{b}_L} = \mathrm{aff}_{W_1',\mathbf{b}_1'}$ is a floating-point affine transformation.

because $\oplus$ is not associative. Next, we define the *correctly rounded version* of a real-valued function. For $f : \mathbb{R} \to \mathbb{R}$, the function $\mathrm{rnd}(f) : \overline{\mathbb{F}} \to \overline{\mathbb{F}}$ is defined by

$$\mathrm{rnd}(f)(x) := \begin{cases} \mathrm{rnd}(f(x)) & \text{if } x \in (-\infty, +\infty) \\ \mathrm{rnd}\left(\lim_{t \to x} f(t)\right) & \text{if } x \in \{-\infty, +\infty\} \wedge \lim_{t \to x} f(t) \in \mathbb{R} \cup \{-\infty, +\infty\} \\ \bot & \text{otherwise.} \end{cases} \quad (4)$$

2.2 Neural Networks

A neural network typically refers to a composition of affine transformations and activation functions. Formally, for $L \in \mathbb{N}$ and $\sigma : \overline{\mathbb{F}} \to \overline{\mathbb{F}}$, we call a function ν a *depth-L σ-neural network* (or a *neural network*) if ν is defined by

$$\nu : \overline{\mathbb{F}}^{d_0} \to \overline{\mathbb{F}}^{d_L}, \quad \nu := \mathrm{aff}_{W_L,\mathbf{b}_L} \circ \tilde{\sigma}_{d_{L-1}} \circ \mathrm{aff}_{W_{L-1},\mathbf{b}_{L-1}} \circ \cdots \circ \tilde{\sigma}_{d_1} \circ \mathrm{aff}_{W_1,\mathbf{b}_1} \quad (5)$$

for some $d_\ell \in \mathbb{N}$, $W_\ell \in \mathbb{F}^{d_\ell \times d_{\ell-1}}$, and $\mathbf{b}_\ell \in \mathbb{F}^{d_\ell}$, where $\tilde{\sigma}_n : \overline{\mathbb{F}}^n \to \overline{\mathbb{F}}^n$ is the coordinatewise application of σ. Here, L denotes the number of layers, σ the floating-point activation function, d_0 and d_L the input and output dimensions, d_ℓ the number of hidden neurons in the ℓ-th layer ($\ell \in [L-1]$), and W_ℓ and $\mathbf{b}_\ell$ the parameters of the floating-point affine transformation in the ℓ-th layer ($\ell \in [L]$). We emphasize that a neural network in this paper is a function over *floating-point* values, defined in terms of *floating-point* activation function and arithmetic. For instance, a depth-1 neural network is a floating-point affine transformation.

Let ν be a neural network defined as Eq. (5). We say ν is *without the last affine layer* if $d_L = d_{L-1}$, W_L is the identity matrix, and $\mathbf{b}_L = \mathbf{0}$. Similarly, we say ν is *without the first affine layer* if $d_1 \geq d_0$, W_1 is a rectangular diagonal matrix whose diagonal entries are all 1, and $b_{1,i} = 0$ for all $i \in [d_0]$. The two definitions are not perfectly symmetric due to some technical details arising in our proofs. We note that a neural network can be constructed by composing networks without the first/last affine layer(s) and arbitrary networks (Fig. 2). For example, consider arbitrary networks $\nu_1 : \overline{\mathbb{F}}^{n_0} \to \overline{\mathbb{F}}^{n_1}$ and $\nu_4 : \overline{\mathbb{F}}^{n_3} \to \overline{\mathbb{F}}^{n_4}$, a network without the first affine layer $\nu_2 : \overline{\mathbb{F}}^{n_1} \to \overline{\mathbb{F}}^{n_2}$, and a network without the first and last affine layers $\nu_3 : \overline{\mathbb{F}}^{n_2} \to \overline{\mathbb{F}}^{n_3}$. It is easily verified that the function $\nu : \overline{\mathbb{F}}^{n_0} \to \overline{\mathbb{F}}^{n_4}$ specified by $\nu(\mathbf{x}) = (\nu_4 \circ \cdots \circ \nu_1)(\mathbf{x})$ denotes a network, whose definition in the form of Eq. (5) can be obtained by "merging" the last layer of ν_1 and the first layer of ν_2, etc.

2.3   Interval Semantics

Interval analysis [11,50] is a technique for analyzing the behavior of numerical programs soundly and efficiently, based on abstract interpretation [10]. It uses intervals to overapproximate the ranges of inputs and expressions, and propagates them through a program to overapproximate the output range. Interval analysis has been used to establish the robustness of practical neural networks [19,24,33,43]. It can overapproximate the output range of a network over perturbed inputs, which is required to prove robustness; and it runs efficiently by performing only simple computations, which is required to analyze large-scale networks.

Interval Domain and Operations. We formalize interval analysis for neural networks as follows. We first define the *interval domain*

$$\mathbb{I} := \{\langle a, b \rangle \mid a, b \in \overline{\mathbb{F}} \setminus \{\bot\} \text{ with } a \leq b\} \cup \{\top\}, \tag{6}$$

on which interval analysis operates. Here, $\langle a, b \rangle$ abstracts the floating-point interval $[a, b] \cap \overline{\mathbb{F}}$, and $\top$ abstracts the entire floating-point set $\overline{\mathbb{F}}$ including $\bot$. The concrete semantics of an *abstract interval* $\mathcal{I} \in \mathbb{I}$ and an *abstract box* $\mathcal{B} = (\mathcal{I}_1, \ldots, \mathcal{I}_d) \in \mathbb{I}^d$ are defined through the *concretization function* γ, where

$$\gamma : \cup_{d=1}^{\infty} \mathbb{I}^d \to \cup_{d=1}^{\infty} 2^{\overline{\mathbb{F}}^d}, \quad \gamma(\mathcal{I}) := \begin{cases} [a, b] \cap \overline{\mathbb{F}} & \text{if } \mathcal{I} = \langle a, b \rangle \\ \overline{\mathbb{F}} & \text{if } \mathcal{I} = \top \end{cases}, \quad \gamma(\mathcal{B}) := \prod_{i=1}^{d} \gamma(\mathcal{I}_i). \tag{7}$$

We say that an abstract box $\mathcal{B} \in \mathbb{I}^d$ *is in* a set $\mathcal{S} \subseteq \mathbb{R}^d$ if $\gamma(\mathcal{B}) \subseteq \mathcal{S}$.

For any function $\phi : \overline{\mathbb{F}}^d \to \overline{\mathbb{F}}$ over floats (which is not a neural network or a floating-point affine transformation), the *interval operation* $\phi^{\sharp} : \mathbb{I}^d \to \mathbb{I}$ extends ϕ to the interval domain as follows:

$$\phi^{\sharp}(\mathcal{B}) := \begin{cases} \langle \min \mathcal{S}, \max \mathcal{S} \rangle & \text{if } \bot \notin \mathcal{S} \\ \top & \text{if } \bot \in \mathcal{S} \end{cases}, \quad \text{where } \mathcal{S} := \phi(\gamma(\mathcal{B})). \tag{8}$$

In the special case that $\phi = \odot \in \{\oplus, \ominus, \otimes\}$ is a floating-point arithmetic operation, the above definition (using infix notation) is equivalent to the following:

$$\langle a, b \rangle \odot^{\sharp} \langle c, d \rangle := \begin{cases} \langle \min \mathcal{S}, \max \mathcal{S} \rangle & \text{if } \bot \notin \mathcal{S} \\ \top & \text{if } \bot \in \mathcal{S} \end{cases}, \quad \text{where } \mathcal{S} := \begin{Bmatrix} a \odot c, a \odot d, \\ b \odot c, b \odot d \end{Bmatrix}, \tag{9}$$

and $\odot^\sharp$ returns $\top$ if at least one of its operands is $\top$.[1] We remark that $\odot^\sharp$ can be efficiently computed, and so can $\phi^\sharp$ when $\phi : \overline{\mathbb{F}} \to \overline{\mathbb{F}}$ is piecewise-monotone with finitely many pieces, which holds for the correctly rounded versions of widely-used activation functions (e.g., ReLU, GELU, sigmoid). We then define the *interval affine transformation* $\mathrm{aff}^\sharp_{W,\mathbf{b}} : \mathbb{I}^n \to \mathbb{I}^m$, which extends its floating-point counterpart $\mathrm{aff}_{W,\mathbf{b}} : \overline{\mathbb{F}}^n \to \overline{\mathbb{F}}^m$: $\mathrm{aff}^\sharp_{W,\mathbf{b}}(\mathcal{I}_1, \ldots, \mathcal{I}_n) :=$ $\left(\left(\bigoplus_{j=1}^{n}{}^\sharp \mathcal{I}_j \otimes^\sharp \langle w_{i,j}, w_{i,j} \rangle\right) \oplus^\sharp \langle b_i, b_i \rangle\right)_{i=1}^{m}$, where $\bigoplus^\sharp$ is the interval summation which uses $\oplus^\sharp$ instead of $\oplus$.

Interval Semantics. The *interval semantics* $\nu^\sharp : \mathbb{I}^{d_0} \to \mathbb{I}^{d_L}$ of a neural network $\nu : \overline{\mathbb{F}}^{d_0} \to \overline{\mathbb{F}}^{d_L}$ is defined as the result of interval analysis on ν:

$$\nu^\sharp := \mathrm{aff}^\sharp_{W_L, \mathbf{b}_L} \circ \tilde{\sigma}^\sharp_{d_{L-1}} \circ \mathrm{aff}^\sharp_{W_{L-1}, \mathbf{b}_{L-1}} \circ \cdots \circ \tilde{\sigma}^\sharp_{d_1} \circ \mathrm{aff}^\sharp_{W_1, \mathbf{b}_1}, \tag{10}$$

where ν is assumed to be defined as Eq. (5) and $\tilde{\sigma}^\sharp_n : \mathbb{I}^n \to \mathbb{I}^n$ is the coordinate-wise application of $\sigma^\sharp : \mathbb{I} \to \mathbb{I}$. It is easily verified that the interval semantics is sound with respect to the floating-point semantics:

$$\nu\left(\gamma\left(\mathcal{B}\right)\right) \subseteq \gamma\left(\nu^\sharp(\mathcal{B})\right) \qquad (\mathcal{B} \in \mathbb{I}^{d_0}). \tag{11}$$

That is, the result of interval analysis $\nu^\sharp(\mathcal{B}) \in \mathbb{I}^{d_L}$ subsumes the set of all possible outputs of the network ν when the input is in the concrete box $\gamma\left(\mathcal{B}\right) \subseteq \overline{\mathbb{F}}^{d_0}$.

3 Interval Universal Approximation Over Floats

This section presents our main result on interval universal approximation (IUA) for floating-point neural networks. We first introduce conditions on activation functions for our result (Sect. 3.1), and then formally describe our result under these conditions (Sect. 3.2). We then compare our IUA theorem over floats with existing IUA theorems over reals, highlighting several nontrivial differences (Sect. 3.3).

3.1 Conditions on Activation Functions

Our IUA theorem is for floating-point neural networks that use activation functions satisfying the following conditions (Fig. 3).

Condition 1. *An activation function* $\sigma : \overline{\mathbb{F}} \to \overline{\mathbb{F}}$ *satisfies the following conditions:*

---

[1] This definition of $\odot^\sharp$ differs slightly from the standard definition, as $\odot^\sharp$ uses "round to nearest" mode (implicit in $\odot$), whereas the more common mode is "round downward/upward" (e.g., $\langle a, b \rangle \oplus^\sharp \langle c, d \rangle := \langle a \oplus_\downarrow c, b \oplus_\uparrow d \rangle$) [26, Section 5]. This choice is due to different goals to achieve: our definition overapproximates floating-point operations (e.g., $\oplus$), while the usual one overapproximates exact operations (e.g., $+$).

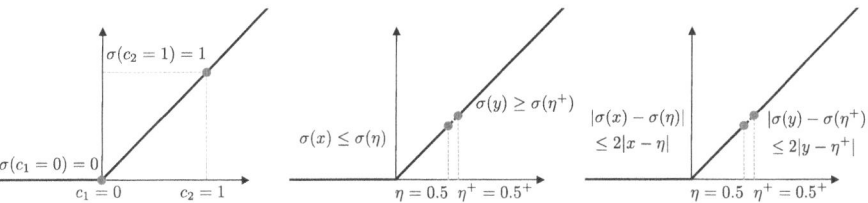

Fig. 3. Illustration of the first (left), second (middle), and third (right) conditions in Condition 1 for the ReLU activation function: $\sigma(x) := \max\{x, 0\}$ for $x \in \overline{\mathbb{F}}$.

(C1) *There exist $c_1, c_2 \in \mathbb{F}$ such that $\sigma(c_1) = 0$, $|\sigma(c_2)| \in [\frac{\varepsilon}{2} + 2\varepsilon^2, \frac{5}{4} - 2\varepsilon]$, $\max\{|c_1|, |c_2|\} \geq 2^{\mathfrak{e}_{\min}+1}$, and $\sigma(x)$ lies between $\sigma(c_1)$ and $\sigma(c_2)$ for all x between c_1 and c_2, where ε is the machine epsilon (see Sect. 2.1).*

(C2) *There exists $\eta \in \mathbb{F}$ with $|\eta| \in [2^{\mathfrak{e}_{\min}+5}, 4-8\varepsilon]$ and $|\sigma(\eta)|, |\sigma(\eta^+)| \in [2^{\mathfrak{e}_{\min}+5}, 2^{\mathfrak{e}_{\max}-6} \cdot |\eta|]$ such that for any $x, y \in \mathbb{F}$ with $x \leq \eta < \eta^+ \leq y$,*

$$\sigma(x) \leq \sigma(\eta) < \sigma(\eta^+) \leq \sigma(y) \quad \text{or} \quad \sigma(x) \geq \sigma(\eta) > \sigma(\eta^+) \geq \sigma(y). \qquad (12)$$

(C3) *There exists $\lambda \in [0, 2^{\mathfrak{e}_{\max}-7} \cdot \min\{|\sigma(\eta)|, 2^{M+3}\}]$ such that for any $x, y \in \mathbb{F}$ with $x \leq \eta < \eta^+ \leq y$,*

$$|\sigma(x) - \sigma(\eta)| \leq \lambda|x - \eta| \quad \text{and} \quad |\sigma(y) - \sigma(\eta^+)| \leq \lambda|y - \eta^+|. \qquad (13)$$

The condition (C1) states that the activation function σ can output the exact zero (i.e., $\sigma(c_1)$) and some value whose magnitude is approximately in $[\frac{\varepsilon}{2}, \frac{5}{4}]$ (i.e., $\sigma(c_2)$); and its output is within $\sigma(c_1)$ and $\sigma(c_2)$ for all inputs between c_1 and c_2. The condition (C2) states that there exists some *threshold* η such that $\sigma(x)$ is either smaller or greater than $\sigma(\eta)$ or $\sigma(\eta^+)$, depending on whether x is on the left or right side of η. This condition holds automatically for all monotone activation functions that are non-constant on either $[2^{\mathfrak{e}_{\min}+5}, 4-8\varepsilon] \cap \mathbb{F}$ or $[-4 + 8\varepsilon, -2^{\mathfrak{e}_{\min}+5}] \cap \mathbb{F}$. The condition (C3) states that σ does not increase or decrease too rapidly from η and η^+, which implies that $\sigma(x)$ is finite for all finite floats $x \in \mathbb{F}$.

While Condition 1 is mild, verifying whether practical activation functions over floats satisfy Condition 1 can be cumbersome. Floating-point activation functions are typically implemented in complicated ways [7,44,51] (e.g., by intermixing floating-point operations with integer/bit-level operations and if-else branches), which makes it challenging to rigorously analyze such implementations [17,36]. To bypass this issue, we focus on the correctly rounded version $\sigma : \overline{\mathbb{F}} \to \overline{\mathbb{F}}$ of a real-valued activation function $\rho : \mathbb{R} \to \mathbb{R}$ (i.e., $\sigma(x) := \mathrm{rnd}(\rho(x))$), when verifying Condition 1. Correctly rounded versions of elementary mathematical functions have been actively developed in several software libraries [13,39,40,58,72].

Under the correct rounding assumption, we provide an easily verifiable sufficient condition for activation functions on reals that can be used to verify Condition 1 for their rounded versions. The proof of Lemma 1 is in §B.1.

Lemma 1. *For any activation function* $\rho : \mathbb{R} \to \mathbb{R}$*, the correctly rounded activation* $\mathrm{rnd}(\rho) : \overline{\mathbb{F}} \to \overline{\mathbb{F}}$ *satisfies Condition 1 if the following conditions hold:*

(C1′) *There exist* $c_1', c_2' \in \mathbb{F}$ *such that* $|\rho(c_1')| \leq \frac{\omega}{2}$, $|\rho(c_2')| \in [\frac{\varepsilon}{2} + 2\varepsilon^2, \frac{5}{4} - 2\varepsilon]$, $\max\{|c_1'|, |c_2'|\} \geq 2^{e_{\min}+1}$*, and* $\rho(x)$ *lies between* $\rho(c_1')$ *and* $\rho(c_2')$ *for all* x *between* c_1' *and* c_2'*, where* ω *is the smallest positive float (see Sect. 2.1).*

(C2′) *There exists* $\delta \in \mathbb{R}$ *with* $|\delta| \in [\frac{3}{8}, \frac{7}{8}]$ *such that*
- *for all* $x, y \in \mathbb{R}$ *satisfying* $x \leq \delta - \frac{1}{8} < \delta + \frac{1}{8} \leq y$,

$$\rho(x) \leq \rho(\delta - \tfrac{1}{8}) < \rho(\delta + \tfrac{1}{8}) \leq \rho(y) \quad \text{or} \quad \rho(x) \geq \rho(\delta - \tfrac{1}{8}) > \rho(\delta + \tfrac{1}{8}) \geq \rho(y),$$

- $|\rho(x)| \in [\frac{1}{4}, 1]$ *and* $|\rho(x) - \rho(y)| > \frac{1}{8}|x - y|$ *for all* $x, y \in [\delta - \frac{1}{8}, \delta + \frac{1}{8}]$.

(C3′) ρ *is* λ*-Lipschitz continuous for some* $\lambda \in [0, \frac{1}{5} \cdot 2^{e_{\max}-9}]$.

The Conditions (C1′)–(C3′) in Lemma 1 correspond to the Conditions (C1)–(C3) in Condition 1. The Condition (C1′), corresponding to (C1), can be easily satisfied since modern activation functions are piecewise-monotone and either zero at zero (e.g., ReLU, GELU, softplus, tanh) or close to zero at $-\Omega$ or Ω (e.g., sigmoid). The Condition (C2′) roughly states the existence of $\delta \in \mathbb{R}$ satisfying the following: (i) $\rho(\delta - \frac{1}{8})$ and $\rho(\delta + \frac{1}{8})$ are lower/upper bounds of ρ on $(-\infty, \delta - \frac{1}{8})$ and $(\delta + \frac{1}{8}, \infty)$; and (ii) ρ is bounded and strictly monotone on $[\delta - \frac{1}{8}, \delta + \frac{1}{8}]$. This condition guarantees the existence of $\eta \in \mathbb{F}$ in (C2). The Condition (C3′), corresponding to (C3), can also be easily satisfied since $\lambda < 3$ for most practical activation functions. We note that Lemma 1 gives sufficient but not necessary conditions for a correctly rounded activation function to satisfy Condition 1.

The following corollary uses Lemma 1 to show that many prominent activation functions satisfy Condition 1. Its proof is in §B.2.

Corollary 1. *The correctly rounded implementations of the* ReLU, LeakyReLU, GELU, ELU, Mish, softplus, sigmoid, *and* tanh *activations satisfy Condition 1.*

3.2   Main Result

We are now ready to present our IUA theorem over floating-point arithmetic.

Theorem 1. *Let* $\sigma : \overline{\mathbb{F}} \to \overline{\mathbb{F}}$ *be an activation function satisfying Condition 1.*[2] *Then, for any target function* $f : \mathbb{R}^d \to \mathbb{R}$*, there exists a* σ*-neural network* $\nu : \overline{\mathbb{F}}^d \to \overline{\mathbb{F}}$ *such that*

$$\gamma\left(\nu^{\sharp}(\mathcal{B})\right) = \left[\min \widehat{f}\left(\gamma(\mathcal{B})\right), \max \widehat{f}\left(\gamma(\mathcal{B})\right)\right] \cap \overline{\mathbb{F}} \tag{14}$$

---

[2] Condition 1 is sufficient for Theorem 1 but not necessary. E.g., Theorem 1 still holds under 8-bit floats (both E4M3 and E5M2 formats [46]) for the ReLU activation function; this corresponds to the case where (C1) and (C2) hold but (C3) is violated.

for $\widehat{f} = \mathrm{rnd}(f) : \overline{\mathbb{F}}^d \to \overline{\mathbb{F}}^d$ and for all abstract boxes $\mathcal{B}$ in $[-1, 1]^d$.[3]

Theorem 1 states that for any activation function $\sigma : \overline{\mathbb{F}} \to \overline{\mathbb{F}}$ satisfying Condition 1 and any target function $f : \mathbb{R}^d \to \mathbb{R}$, there exists a σ-network ν whose interval semantics *exactly computes* the upper and lower points of the direct image map of the rounded target $\widehat{f} : \overline{\mathbb{F}}^d \to \overline{\mathbb{F}}$ on $[-1, 1]^d \cap \mathbb{F}^d$. A special case of our IUA Theorem 1 is the following universal approximation (UA) theorem for floating-point neural networks:

$$\nu(\mathbf{x}) = \widehat{f}(\mathbf{x}) \qquad\qquad (\mathbf{x} \in [-1, 1]^d \cap \mathbb{F}^d). \qquad (15)$$

That is, floating-point neural networks using an activation function satisfying Condition 1 can represent any function $\widehat{f} : [-1, 1]^d \cap \mathbb{F}^d \to \mathbb{F} \cup \{-\infty, +\infty\}$; or the rounded version of any real function $f : [-1, 1]^d \to \mathbb{R}$. Moreover, Theorem 1 easily extends to any target function $f : \mathbb{R}^d \to \mathbb{R}^{d'}$ with multiple outputs.

As previous IUA results assume exact operations over reals, they do not extend to our setting of floating-point arithmetic (due to rounding errors, overflow, NaNs, discreteness, boundedness, etc.). As a simple example of these issues, consider the following subnetwork, which is used in the IUA proof of [4]:

$$\mu(x, y) = \frac{1}{2} \left(\mathrm{ReLU}(x + y) - \mathrm{ReLU}(-x - y) - \mathrm{ReLU}(x - y) - \mathrm{ReLU}(y - x) \right).$$

This subnetwork returns $\min\{x, y\}$ if all operations are exact. However, it does not under floating-point arithmetic due to the rounding error: if $(+, \times)$ is replaced by $(\oplus, \otimes)$, then $\mu(x, y) = 0 \neq \varepsilon = \min\{x, y\}$ for $x = 1$ and $y = \varepsilon$.

In addition, the network construction in [66, Theorem 4.10] requires multiplying a large number z that depends on the target error and the activation function, to the output of some neuron. However, because $\mathbb{F}$ is bounded and floating-point operations are subject to overflow, the number z and the result of the multiplication are not guaranteed to be within $\mathbb{F}$ when using a small target error (e.g., less than ω) or when using common activations functions (e.g., ReLU, softplus). To bypass these issues, we carefully analyze rounding errors and design a network without infinities in the intermediate layers, when proving Theorem 1.

We present the proof outline of Theorem 1 in Sect. 5, and the full proof in §D–§F. We implemented the proof (i.e., our network construction) in Python and made it available at https://github.com/yechanp/floating-point-iua-theorem.

3.3 Comparison With Existing Results Over Reals

Theorem 1, which gives an IUA theorem over floats, has notable differences from previous IUA theorems over the reals [4, Theorem 1.1]; [66, Theorem 3.7].

---

[3] In the literature on universal approximation theorems, it is typically assumed that the inputs are in $[0, 1]$ or in a compact subset of $\mathbb{R}$ (e.g., [4,12,66,69]). Since the inputs are often normalized to $[-1, 1]$, we focus the theoretical analysis on $[-1, 1]^d$.

One difference is the class of target functions and the desired property of networks. Previous IUA theorems find a network that *sufficiently approximates* the direct image map of a *continuous* target function (i.e., $\delta > 0$ in Eq. (1)). In contrast, our IUA theorem finds a network that *exactly computes* the direct image map of an *arbitrary* rounded target function (i.e., $\delta = 0$ in Eq. (1)). This difference arises from the domains of the functions being approximated: the real-valued setting considers functions f over $[-1,1]^d$ (or a compact $\mathcal{K} \subset \mathbb{R}^d$); the floating-point setting considers functions $\widehat{f}$ over $[-1,1]^d \cap \mathbb{F}^d$.

- Since $[-1,1]^d$ is uncountable, exactly computing the direct image map of f requires a network to fit *uncountably* many input/output pairs and related box/interval pairs. This task is difficult to achieve, and indeed, recent works [3,5,47] prove that it is theoretically unachievable even for simple target functions (e.g., continuous piecewise linear functions).
- Since $[-1,1]^d \cap \mathbb{F}^d$ is finite, exactly computing the direct image map of $\widehat{f}$ requires a network to fit *finitely* many input/output and box/interval pairs. Our result proves that, despite all the complexities of floating-point computation, this task can be achieved for any rounded target function.

Another key difference is the class of activation functions. There are real-valued activation functions $\rho, \rho' : \mathbb{R} \to \mathbb{R}$ such that previous IUA theorems *cannot* hold for ρ but our IUA theorem *does* hold for $\mathrm{rnd}(\rho) : \overline{\mathbb{F}} \to \overline{\mathbb{F}}$; and vice versa for ρ'.

- An example of ρ is the *identity* function: $\rho(x) = x$. No classical IUA or UA theorem can hold for ρ, since all *real-valued* ρ-networks $\mu : \mathbb{R}^d \to \mathbb{R}$ are *affine over the reals* (i.e., there exists $A \in \mathbb{R}^{1 \times d}$ and $b \in \mathbb{R}$ such that $\mu(\mathbf{x}) = A\mathbf{x} + b$ for all $\mathbf{x} \in \mathbb{R}^d$). In contrast, our IUA theorem does hold for $\mathrm{rnd}(\rho)$, because $\mathrm{rnd}(\rho)$ satisfies all the conditions in Lemma 1 (with constants $c_1' = 0$, $c_2' = 1$, $\delta = 1/2$, and $\lambda = 1$). This counterintuitive result is made possible because *floating-point* $\mathrm{rnd}(\rho)$-networks $\nu : \overline{\mathbb{F}}^d \to \overline{\mathbb{F}}$ can be *non-affine over the reals* (i.e., there may not exist $A \in \mathbb{R}^{1 \times d}$ and $b \in \mathbb{R}$ such that $\nu(\mathbf{x}) = A\mathbf{x} + b$ for all $\mathbf{x} \in \mathbb{F}^d$). This non-affineness arises from rounding errors: some floating-point affine transformations $\mathrm{aff}_{W,\mathbf{b}}$ are not actually affine over the reals due to rounding errors. An interesting implication of this result is discussed in Sect. 4.2.
- An example of ρ' is any function that is non-decreasing on $\mathbb{R}$, is constant on $[-\Omega, \Omega]$, and satisfies $\lim_{x \to -\infty} \rho'(x) < \lim_{x \to +\infty} \rho'(x)$, where the two limits exist in $\mathbb{R}$. The real-valued IUA theorem holds for ρ', because ρ' satisfies the condition in [66, Definition 2.3]. However, no floating-point IUA or UA theorem can hold for $\mathrm{rnd}(\rho')$, because all $\mathrm{rnd}(\rho')$-networks $\nu : \overline{\mathbb{F}} \to \overline{\mathbb{F}}$ must be monotone if its depth is 1, and must satisfy $\nu(0) = \nu(\omega)$ otherwise. The monotonicity holds when the depth is 1 since $\oplus, \otimes$ are monotone when an operand is a constant; and $\nu(0) = \nu(\omega)$ holds otherwise since $x \otimes a \oplus b \in [-\Omega, \Omega]$ for all $x \in \{0, \omega\}$ and $a, b \in \mathbb{F}$, and $\mathrm{rnd}(\rho')$ is constant on $[-\Omega, \Omega] \cap \mathbb{F}$.

4   Implications of IUA Theorem Over Floats

This section presents two important implications of our IUA theorem, on provable robustness and "floating-point completeness". We first prove the existence of a provably robust floating-point network, given an ideal robust floating-point classifier (Sect. 4.1). We then prove that floating-point $+$ and $\times$ are sufficient to simulate all halting programs that return finite/infinite floats when given finite floats (Sect. 4.2).

4.1   Provable Robustness of Neural Networks

Consider the task of classifying floating-point inputs $\mathbf{x} \in \mathcal{X}$ (e.g., images of objects) into $n \in \mathbb{N}$ classes (e.g., categories of objects), where $\mathcal{X} := [-1, 1]^d \cap \mathbb{F}^d$ denotes the space of inputs throughout this subsection. For this task, a function $f : \mathcal{X} \to \mathbb{F}^n$ is often viewed as a classifier in the following sense: f predicts $\mathbf{x}$ to be in the i-th class ($i \in [n]$), where $i := \mathrm{class}(f(\mathbf{x}))$ and $\mathrm{class} : \mathbb{F}^n \to [n]$ is defined by $\mathrm{class}(y_1, \ldots, y_n) := \arg\max_{i \in [n]} y_i$ with an arbitrary tie-breaking rule.

A typical robustness property of a classifier f is that f should predict the same class for all neighboring inputs under the ℓ_∞ distance [38]. We formalize this notion of *robust* classifiers in a way similar to [66, Definition A.4].

Definition 1. *Let $\delta > 0$ and $\mathcal{D} \subseteq \mathcal{X}$. A classifier $f : \mathcal{X} \to \mathbb{F}^n$ is called δ -robust on $\mathcal{D}$ if for all $\mathbf{x}_0 \in \mathcal{D}$, $\mathbf{y}, \mathbf{y}' \in f(\mathcal{N}_\delta(\mathbf{x}_0))$ implies $\mathrm{class}(\mathbf{y}) = \mathrm{class}(\mathbf{y}')$, where $\mathcal{N}_\delta(\mathbf{x}_0) := \{\mathbf{x} \in \mathcal{X} \mid \|\mathbf{x}_0 - \mathbf{x}\|_\infty \leq \delta\}$ and $\|\cdot\|_\infty$ denotes the ℓ_∞ -norm.*

Neural networks have been widely used as classifiers, but establishing the robustness properties of practical networks as in Definition 1 is intractable due to the enormous number of inputs to be checked (i.e., $|\mathcal{N}_\delta(\mathbf{x}_0)| \gg 1$ when $d \gg 1$). Instead, these properties have been proven often by using interval analysis, as mentioned in Sect. 2.3. We formalize the notion of such *provably robust* networks under interval analysis, in a way similar to [66, Definition A.5].

Definition 2. *Let $\delta > 0$ and $\mathcal{D} \subseteq \mathcal{X}$. A neural network $\nu : \overline{\mathbb{F}}^d \to \overline{\mathbb{F}}^n$ is called δ -provably robust on $\mathcal{D}$ if for all $\mathbf{x}_0 \in \mathcal{D}$, $\mathbf{y}, \mathbf{y}' \in \gamma(\nu^\sharp(\mathcal{B}))$ implies $\mathrm{class}(\mathbf{y}) = \mathrm{class}(\mathbf{y}')$, where $\mathcal{B} \in \mathbb{I}^d$ denotes the abstract box such that $\gamma(\mathcal{B}) = \mathcal{N}_\delta(\mathbf{x}_0)$.*

Under these definitions, we prove that given an ideal robust classifier f, we can always find a neural network ν (i) whose robustness property is *exactly* the same as that of f and is easily provable using only interval analysis, and (ii) whose predictions are *precisely* equal to those of f.

Theorem 2. *Let $f : \mathcal{X} \to \mathbb{F}^n$ be a classifier that is δ-robust on $\mathcal{D}$, and $\sigma : \overline{\mathbb{F}} \to \overline{\mathbb{F}}$ be an activation function satisfying Condition 1. Then, there exists a σ-neural network $\nu : \overline{\mathbb{F}}^d \to \overline{\mathbb{F}}^n$ that is δ-provably robust on $\mathcal{D}$ and makes the same prediction as f on $\mathcal{D}$ (i.e., $\mathrm{class}(\nu(\mathbf{x})) = \mathrm{class}(f(\mathbf{x}))$ for all $\mathbf{x} \in \mathcal{D}$).*

Proof Sketch. We show this (i) by applying Theorem 1 to n target functions that are constructed from f, and (ii) by using the following observation: the network constructed in the proof of Theorem 1 has depth not depending on a target function (when d is fixed). The full proof is in §C.1.   □

4.2 Floating-Point Interval-Completeness

To motivate our result, we recall the notion of Turing completeness. A computation model is called *Turing-complete* if for every Turing machine T, there exists a program in the model that can simulate the machine [6,35,49]. Extensive research has established the Turing completeness of numerous computation models: from untyped λ-calculus [8,64] and μ-recursive functions [9,20], to type systems (e.g., Haskell [67], Java [25]) and neural networks over the rationals (e.g., RNNs [59], Transformers [54]). These results identify simpler computation models as powerful as Turing machines, and shed light on the computational power of new models.

We ask an analogous question for *floating-point* computations instead of *binary* computations, where the former is captured by floating-point programs and the latter by Turing machines. That is, which small class of floating-point programs can simulate all (or nearly all) floating-point programs?

Formally, let $\mathcal{F}$ be the set of all terminating programs that take finite floats and return finite or infinite floats, where these programs can use any floating-point constants/operations (e.g., $-\infty$, $\otimes$) and language constructs (e.g., if-else, while). Then, $\mathcal{F}$ semantically denotes the set of all functions from $\mathbb{F}^n$ to $(\mathbb{F} \cup \{-\infty, +\infty\})^m$ for all $n, m \in \mathbb{N}$, because each such function can be expressed with if-else branches and floating-point constants. For this class of programs, we define the notion of *(interval-)simulation* and *floating-point (interval-)completeness* as follows.

Definition 3. *Let $P, Q \in \mathcal{F}$ be programs with arity n. We say Q simulates P if $Q(\mathbf{x}) = P(\mathbf{x})$ for all $\mathbf{x} \in \mathbb{F}^n$, where $P(\mathbf{x})$ denotes the concrete semantics of P on $\mathbf{x}$. We say Q interval-simulates P if $\gamma(Q^\sharp(\mathcal{B})) = [\min P(\gamma(\mathcal{B})), \max P(\gamma(\mathcal{B}))] \cap \overline{\mathbb{F}}$ for all abstract boxes $\mathcal{B}$ in $\mathbb{F}^n$, where $Q^\sharp(\mathcal{B})$ denotes the interval semantics of Q on $\mathcal{B}$.*

Definition 4. *We say a class of programs $\mathcal{G} \subseteq \mathcal{F}$ is floating-point (interval-) complete if for every $P \in \mathcal{F}$, there exists $Q \in \mathcal{G}$ such that Q (interval-) simulates P.*

We prove that a surprisingly small class of programs is floating-point interval-complete (so floating-point complete). In particular, we show that only floating-point addition, multiplication, and constants are sufficient to interval-simulate *all* halting programs that output finite/infinite floats when given finite floats.

Theorem 3. *$\mathcal{F}_{\oplus,\otimes} \subset \mathcal{F}$ is floating-point interval-complete, where $\mathcal{F}_{\oplus,\otimes}$ denotes the class of straight-line programs that use only $\oplus$, $\otimes$, and floating-point constants.*

Proof Sketch. We show this by extending the key lemma used in the proof of Theorem 1: there exist σ-networks that capture the direct image maps of indicator functions over $[-1,1]^n \cap \mathbb{F}^n$ (Lemma 2). In particular, we prove that $[-1,1]^n \cap \mathbb{F}^n$ can be extended to $\mathbb{F}^n$ if σ is the identity function. The full proof is in §C.2. □

To our knowledge, this is the first non-trivial result on floating-point (interval-) completeness. This result is an extension of our IUA theorem (Theorem 1) for the identity activation function σ_{id}, in that floating-point interval-completeness considers the input domain $\mathbb{F}^n$ (not $[-1,1]^n \cap \mathbb{F}^n$) and $\mathcal{F}_{\oplus,\otimes}$ includes all σ_{id}-networks (but no other σ-networks). Theorem 3, however, *cannot* be extended to the input domain $(\mathbb{F} \cup \{-\infty, +\infty\})^n$ (instead of $\mathbb{F}^n$), since no program in $\mathcal{F}_{\oplus,\otimes}$ can represent a non-constant function that maps an infinite float to a finite float—this is because $\oplus$ and $\otimes$ do not return finite floats when applied to $\pm\infty$.

5   Proof of IUA Theorem Over Floats

We now prove Theorem 1 by constructing a σ-neural network that computes the upper and lower points of the direct image map of a rounded target function $\widehat{f}$. For $a, b \in \mathbb{R}$, we let $[a,b]_\mathbb{F} := [a,b] \cap \mathbb{F}$ and $\mathbb{I}_{[a,b]} := \{\mathcal{I} \in \mathbb{I} \mid \gamma(\mathcal{I}) \subseteq [a,b]\}$. With this notation, $(\mathbb{I}_{[a,b]})^d$ is the set of all abstract boxes in $[a,b]^d$.

We start with defining indicator functions for a set of floating-point values and for an abstract box, which play a key role in our proof.

Definition 5. *Let $d \in \mathbb{N}$. For $\mathcal{S} \subseteq \overline{\mathbb{F}}^d$, we define $\iota_\mathcal{S} : \overline{\mathbb{F}}^d \to \overline{\mathbb{F}}$ as $\iota_\mathcal{S}(\mathbf{x}) := 1$ if $\mathbf{x} \in \mathcal{S}$, and $\iota_\mathcal{S}(\mathbf{x}) := 0$ otherwise. For $a \in \mathbb{F}$, we define $\iota_{>a} : \overline{\mathbb{F}} \to \overline{\mathbb{F}}$ by $\iota_{\{x>a \mid x\in\mathbb{F}\}}$, and define $\iota_{\geq a}, \iota_{<a}, \iota_{\leq a}$ analogously. For $\mathcal{C} \in \mathbb{I}^d$, we define $\iota_\mathcal{C} : \overline{\mathbb{F}}^d \to \overline{\mathbb{F}}$ by $\iota_{\gamma(\mathcal{C})}$.*

Our proof of Theorem 1 consists of two parts. We first show the existence of σ-networks that precisely compute indicator functions under the interval semantics. We then construct a σ-network stated in Theorem 1 by composing the σ-networks for indicator functions and using the properties of indicator functions.

Both parts of our proof are centered around a new property of activation functions, which we call "$([a,b]_\mathbb{F}, \eta, K, L_\phi, L_\psi)$-separability" and define as follows.

Definition 6. *We say that $\sigma : \overline{\mathbb{F}} \to \overline{\mathbb{F}}$ is $([a,b]_\mathbb{F}, \eta, K, L_\phi, L_\psi)$-separable for $a, b, \eta, K \in \mathbb{F}$ and $L_\phi, L_\psi \in \mathbb{N}$ if the following hold:*

- *For every $z \in [a,b]_\mathbb{F}$, there exist depth-L_ϕ σ-networks $\phi_{\leq z}, \phi_{\geq z} : \overline{\mathbb{F}} \to \overline{\mathbb{F}}$ without the last affine layer such that $\phi_{\leq z}^\sharp = (K\iota_{\leq z})^\sharp$ and $\phi_{\geq z}^\sharp = (K\iota_{\geq z})^\sharp$ on $\mathbb{I}_{[a,b]}$.*
- *There exists a depth-L_ψ σ-network $\psi_{>\eta} : \overline{\mathbb{F}} \to \overline{\mathbb{F}}$ without the first and last affine layers such that $\psi_{>\eta}^\sharp = (K\iota_{>\eta})^\sharp$ on $\mathbb{I}_{[a,b]}$.*

G. Hwang et al.

The first condition in Definition 6 ensures the existence of σ-networks that perfectly implement scaled indicator functions $K\iota_{\leq z}$ and $K\iota_{\geq z}$ under the interval semantics, for all $z \in [a, b]_{\mathbb{F}}$. Since these networks should have the same depth L_ϕ without the last affine layer, a function $\nu : \overline{\mathbb{F}}^n \to \overline{\mathbb{F}}$ defined, e.g., by

$$\nu(x_1, \ldots, x_n) = \left(\overset{n}{\underset{i=1}{\sum}} \alpha \otimes \phi_{\leq z_i}(x_i) \right) \oplus \beta \tag{16}$$

denotes a depth-L_ϕ σ-network for any $z_i \in [a, b]_{\mathbb{F}}$ and $\alpha, \beta \in \mathbb{F}$. The second condition in Definition 6 guarantees that another scaled indicator function $K\iota_{>\eta}$ can be precisely implemented by a depth-L_ψ σ-network $\psi_{>\eta}$ without the first and last affine layers. This implies, e.g., that $\psi_{>\eta} \circ \nu$ denotes a depth-$(L_\phi + L_\psi - 1)$ σ-network, where ν denotes the network presented in Eq. (16).

Using the separability property, we can formally state the two parts of our proof as Lemmas 2 and 3. Theorem 1 is a direct corollary of the two lemmas. We present the proofs of Lemmas 2 and 3 in the next subsections (Sect. 5.1 and 5.2).

Lemma 2. *Suppose that* $\sigma : \overline{\mathbb{F}} \to \overline{\mathbb{F}}$ *satisfies Condition 1 with constants* $c_2, \eta \in \mathbb{F}$. *Then,* σ *is* $([-1, 1]_{\mathbb{F}}, \eta, K, L_\phi, L_\psi)$*-separable for some* $L_\phi, L_\psi \in \mathbb{N}$, *where* η *and* $K := \sigma(c_2)$ *satisfy* $|\eta| \in [2^{\mathfrak{e}_{\min}+5}, 4 - 8\varepsilon]$ *and* $|K| \in [\frac{\varepsilon}{2} + 2\varepsilon^2, \frac{5}{4} - 2\varepsilon]$.

Lemma 3. *Suppose that* $\sigma : \overline{\mathbb{F}} \to \overline{\mathbb{F}}$ *is* $([a, b]_{\mathbb{F}}, \eta, K, L_\phi, L_\psi)$*-separable for some* $a, b, \eta, K \in \mathbb{F}$ *and* $L_\phi, L_\psi \in \mathbb{N}$ *with* $|\eta| \in [2^{\mathfrak{e}_{\min}+5}, 4 - 8\varepsilon]$ *and* $|K| \in [\frac{\varepsilon}{2} + 2\varepsilon^2, \frac{5}{4} - 2\varepsilon]$. *Then, for every* $d \in \mathbb{N}$ *and function* $h : \overline{\mathbb{F}}^d \to \overline{\mathbb{F}} \setminus \{\bot\}$, *there exists a* σ*-neural network* $\nu : \overline{\mathbb{F}}^d \to \overline{\mathbb{F}}$ *such that* $\nu^\sharp(\mathcal{B}) = h^\sharp(\mathcal{B})$ *for all abstract boxes* $\mathcal{B}$ *in* $[a, b]^d$.

To prove Lemma 2, we construct a σ-network for the scaled indicator function $K\iota_{\geq z}$ in two steps. We first construct a σ-network that maps all inputs smaller than z to some point x_1, and all other inputs to another point $x_2 \neq x_1$ (Lemma 4 and 6), where we exploit round-off errors to obtain such "contraction" (Lemma 17 in §F). We then map x_1 to c_1 and x_2 to c_2, and apply σ to the result so that the final network maps all inputs smaller than z to $\sigma(c_1) = 0$ and all other inputs to $\sigma(c_2) = K$ (Lemma 5). We construct σ-networks for $K\iota_{\leq z}$ and $K\iota_{>\eta}$ analogously.

To prove Lemma 3, we construct σ-networks for the scaled indicator functions of every box in $([a, b]_{\mathbb{F}})^d$ (Lemma 7) and every subset of $([a, b]_{\mathbb{F}})^d$ (Lemma 8), using the indicator functions constructed in Lemma 2. We construct the final σ-network (i.e., universal interval approximator) as a floating-point linear combination of the σ-networks that represent the scaled indicator functions of the level sets of the target function (Lemma 9).

5.1 Proof of Lemma 2

To prove Lemma 2, we assume that the activation function $\sigma : \overline{\mathbb{F}} \to \overline{\mathbb{F}}$ satisfies Condition 1 with some constants $c_1, c_2, \eta \in \mathbb{F}$. By Condition 1, the constants

η and $K := \sigma(c_2)$ clearly satisfy the range condition in Lemma 2. Hence, it remains to show the $([-1,1]_{\mathbb{F}}, \eta, K, L_\phi, L_\psi)$-separability of σ for some $L_\phi, L_\psi \in \mathbb{N}$. This requires us to construct σ-networks $\psi_{>\eta}$ and $\phi_{\leq z}, \phi_{\geq z}$ for every $z \in [-1,1]_{\mathbb{F}}$ such that $\psi_{>\eta}^\sharp = (K\iota_{>\eta})^\sharp$, $\phi_{\leq z}^\sharp = (K\iota_{\leq z})^\sharp$, and $\phi_{\geq z}^\sharp = (K\iota_{\geq z})^\sharp$ on $\mathbb{I}_{[-1,1]}$ (Definition 6).

We first construct $\psi_{>\eta}$ using Lemmas 4 and 5 (Fig. 4). The proofs of these lemmas, presented in §D.1 and §D.2, rely heavily on (C1)–(C3) of Condition 1.

Lemma 4. *There exists a σ-network $\mu : \overline{\mathbb{F}} \to \overline{\mathbb{F}}$ without the first affine layer such that $\mu^\sharp(\langle -\Omega, \eta \rangle) = \langle \eta, \eta \rangle$, $\mu^\sharp(\langle \eta^+, \Omega \rangle) = \langle \eta^+, \eta^+ \rangle$, and $\mu^\sharp(\langle -\Omega, \Omega \rangle) = \langle \eta, \eta^+ \rangle$.*

Lemma 5. *Let (θ, θ') be either (c_1, c_2) or (c_2, c_1). Then, there exists a depth-2 σ-network $\tau_{\theta,\theta'} : \overline{\mathbb{F}} \to \overline{\mathbb{F}}$ without the first affine layer such that $\tau_{\theta,\theta'}^\sharp(\langle \eta, \eta \rangle) = \langle \theta, \theta \rangle$, $\tau_{\theta,\theta'}^\sharp(\langle \eta^+, \eta^+ \rangle) = \langle \theta', \theta' \rangle$, and $\tau_{\theta,\theta'}^\sharp(\langle \eta, \eta^+ \rangle) = \langle \min\{\theta, \theta'\}, \max\{\theta, \theta'\} \rangle$.*

Lemma 4 states that we can construct a σ-network μ without the first affine layer, whose interval semantics maps all finite (abstract) intervals left of η to the singleton interval $\langle \eta, \eta \rangle$, all finite intervals right of η^+ to $\langle \eta^+, \eta^+ \rangle$, and all the remaining finite intervals to $\langle \eta, \eta^+ \rangle$. Similarly, Lemma 5 shows that there exists a σ-network $\tau_{\theta,\theta'}$ without the first affine layer, whose interval semantics maps $\langle \eta, \eta \rangle$ to $\langle \theta, \theta \rangle$, $\langle \eta^+, \eta^+ \rangle$ to $\langle \theta', \theta' \rangle$, and $\langle \eta, \eta^+ \rangle$ to the interval between θ and θ'. By composing these networks with σ, we construct $\psi_{>\eta}$ as

$$\psi_{>\eta} := \sigma \circ \tau_{c_1,c_2} \circ \mu. \tag{17}$$

This function $\psi_{>\eta}$ is a σ-network without the first and last affine layers, since τ_{c_1,c_2} are μ are without the first affine layer. Moreover, $\psi_{>\eta}^\sharp = (K\iota_{>\eta})^\sharp$ on $\mathbb{I}_{[-1,1]}$ by the aforementioned properties of τ_{c_1,c_2} and μ, and by the next properties of σ from Condition 1 of Condition 1: $\sigma(c_1) = 0$, $\sigma(c_2) = K$, and $\sigma(x)$ lies between them for all x between c_1 and c_2. Lastly, we choose L_ψ as the depth of $\psi_{>\eta}$.

We next construct $\phi_{\leq z}$ and $\phi_{\geq z}$ using Lemma 6 (Fig. 4). The proof of this lemma is provided in §D.3.

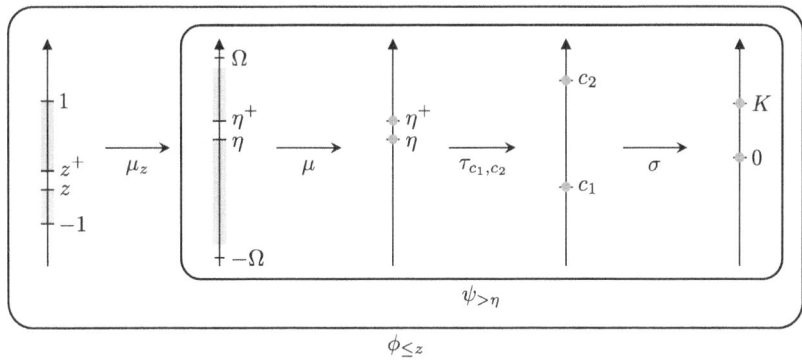

Fig. 4. Illustration of networks μ, τ_{c_1,c_2}, μ_z (Lemmas 4–6) and $\psi_{>\eta}$, $\phi_{\leq z}$ (Eqs. (17) and (18)), assuming (b) in Lemma 6. A box/dot denotes an abstract interval.

Lemma 6. *Let $z \in \mathbb{F}$ with $|z| \leq 1^+$. Then, there exists a depth-1 σ-network $\mu_z : \overline{\mathbb{F}} \to \overline{\mathbb{F}}$ such that one of the following holds.*

(a) $\gamma(\mu_z^\sharp(\langle -1, z \rangle)) \subset [-\Omega, \eta]$ and $\gamma(\mu_z^\sharp(\langle z^+, 1 \rangle)) \subset [\eta^+, \Omega]$.
(b) $\gamma(\mu_z^\sharp(\langle -1, z \rangle)) \subset [\eta^+, \Omega]$ and $\gamma(\mu_z^\sharp(\langle z^+, 1 \rangle)) \subset [-\Omega, \eta]$.

Lemma 6 ensures the existence of a depth-1 σ-network μ_z, whose interval semantics maps $\langle -1, z \rangle$ and $\langle z^+, 1 \rangle$ to an interval left of η and an interval right of η^+. By composing μ_z with the previous networks $\tau_{\theta, \theta'}$ and μ, we construct $\phi_{\leq z}$ as

$$\phi_{\leq z} := \begin{cases} \sigma \circ \tau_{c_2, c_1} \circ \mu \circ \mu_z & \text{if (a) holds in Lemma 6} \\ \sigma \circ \tau_{c_1, c_2} \circ \mu \circ \mu_z & \text{if (b) holds in Lemma 6.} \end{cases} \tag{18}$$

By a similar argument used above, the function $\phi_{\leq z}$ is a σ-network without the last affine layer, and it satisfies the desired equation: $\phi_{\leq z}^\sharp = (K \iota_{\leq z})^\sharp$ on $\mathbb{I}_{[-1,1]}$. We construct $\phi_{\geq z}$ analogously, but using μ_{z^-} instead of μ_z. Since the depths of $\phi_{\leq z}$ and $\phi_{\geq z}$ are identical for all z, we denote this depth by L_ϕ. This completes the construction of $\psi_{>\eta}$, $\phi_{\leq z}$, and $\phi_{\geq z}$, finishing the proof of Lemma 2.

5.2   Proof of Lemma 3

To prove Lemma 3, we assume that the activation function σ is $([a, b]_{\mathbb{F}}, \eta, K, L_\phi, L_\psi)$-separable for some $\eta, K \in \mathbb{F}$ with $|\eta| \in [2^{e_{\min}+5}, 4 - 8\varepsilon]$ and $|K| \in [\frac{\varepsilon}{2} + 2\varepsilon^2, \frac{5}{4} - 2\varepsilon]$. Given this, we construct a σ-network whose interval semantics exactly computes that of the target function $h : \overline{\mathbb{F}}^d \to \overline{\mathbb{F}} \setminus \{\bot\}$ for all abstract boxes in $[a, b]^d$. In our construction, we progressively implement the following functions using σ-networks: (i) scaled indicator functions of arbitrary boxes, (ii) scaled indicator functions of arbitrary sets, and (iii) the target function.

We first construct a σ-network $\tilde{\nu}_{\mathcal{B}}$, for any abstract box $\mathcal{B}$ in $[a, b]^d$, that implements the scaled indicator function $K \iota_{\mathcal{B}}$ under the interval semantics.

Lemma 7. *For any $\mathcal{B} \in (\mathbb{I}_{[a,b]})^d$, there exists a depth-$L$ σ-network $\tilde{\nu}_{\mathcal{B}} : \overline{\mathbb{F}}^d \to \overline{\mathbb{F}}$ without the last affine layer such that $\tilde{\nu}_{\mathcal{B}}^\sharp = (K \iota_{\mathcal{B}})^\sharp$ on $(\mathbb{I}_{[a,b]})^d$, where $L := L_\phi + (L_\psi - 1)(\lceil \log_{2M} d \rceil + 1)$.*

In the proof of Lemma 7, we design $\tilde{\nu}_{\mathcal{B}}$ using the networks $\psi_{>\eta}$, $\phi_{\leq z}$, and $\phi_{\geq z}$ constructed in Sect. 5.1. Specifically, for an abstract box $\mathcal{B} = (\langle a_1, b_1 \rangle, \ldots, \langle a_d, b_d \rangle)$, we define a σ-network $\tilde{\nu}_i : \overline{\mathbb{F}} \to \overline{\mathbb{F}}$ as

$$\tilde{\nu}_i(x) := \psi_{>\eta}((\alpha \otimes \phi_{\geq a_i}(x)) \oplus (\alpha \otimes \phi_{\leq b_i}(x)) \oplus \beta), \tag{19}$$

where $\alpha, \beta \in \mathbb{F}$ are constants such that $\beta \leq \eta$, $(\alpha \otimes K) \oplus \beta \leq \eta$, and $(\alpha \otimes K) \oplus (\alpha \otimes K) \oplus \beta > \eta$. Then, we can show that $\tilde{\nu}_i^\sharp = (K \iota_{\langle a_i, b_i \rangle})^\sharp$ on $\mathbb{I}_{[a,b]}$. When d is small (e.g., $d \leq 2^{M+1}$), we construct $\tilde{\nu}_{\mathcal{B}}$ using $\tilde{\nu}_i$ and $\psi_{>\eta}$, as follows:

$$\tilde{\nu}_{\mathcal{B}}(x_1, \ldots, x_d) := \psi_{>\eta}\left(\left(\bigoplus_{i=1}^{d} \alpha' \otimes \tilde{\nu}_i(x_i)\right) \oplus \beta'\right), \tag{20}$$

where $\alpha', \beta' \in \mathbb{F}$ are suitably chosen so that $\tilde{\nu}_{\mathcal{B}}^{\sharp} = (K \iota_{\mathcal{B}})^{\sharp}$ on $(\mathbb{I}_{[a,b]})^d$. When d is large (e.g., $d > 2^{M+1}$), this construction does not work since $\bigoplus_{i=1}^{d} \alpha' \otimes \tilde{\nu}_i(x_i)$ may not be computed as we want due to rounding errors (e.g., $\bigoplus_{i=1}^{n} 1 = 2^{M+1} < n$ for all $n > 2^{M+1}$). In such a case, we construct $\tilde{\nu}_{\mathcal{B}}$ hierarchically using more layers, but based on a similar idea. A rigorous proof of Lemma 7, including the proof that appropriate $\alpha, \alpha', \beta, \beta' \in \mathbb{F}$ exist, is presented in §E.1

Using $\tilde{\nu}_{\mathcal{B}}$, we next construct a σ-network $\tilde{\nu}_{\mathcal{S}}$, for any set $\mathcal{S}$ in $([a,b]_{\mathbb{F}})^d$, whose interval semantics computes that of the scaled indicator function $K \iota_{\mathcal{S}}$.

Lemma 8. *Suppose that for any $\mathcal{B} \in (\mathbb{I}_{[a,b]})^d$, there exists a depth-$L$ σ-network $\tilde{\nu}_{\mathcal{B}}$ without the last affine layer such that $\tilde{\nu}_{\mathcal{B}}^{\sharp} = (K \iota_{\mathcal{B}})^{\sharp}$ on $(\mathbb{I}_{[a,b]})^d$. Then, for any $\mathcal{S} \subseteq ([a,b]_{\mathbb{F}})^d$, there exists a depth-$(L + L_{\psi} - 1)$ σ-network $\tilde{\nu}_{\mathcal{S}} : \overline{\mathbb{F}}^d \to \overline{\mathbb{F}}$ without the last affine layer such that $\tilde{\nu}_{\mathcal{S}}^{\sharp} = (K \iota_{\mathcal{S}})^{\sharp}$ on $(\mathbb{I}_{[a,b]})^d$.*

In the proof of Lemma 8, we construct $\tilde{\nu}_{\mathcal{S}}$ using $\tilde{\nu}_{\mathcal{B}}$ and $\psi_{>\eta}$, as follows:

$$\tilde{\nu}_{\mathcal{S}}(\mathbf{x}) := \psi_{>\eta}\left(\left(\bigoplus_{\mathcal{B} \in \mathcal{T}} \alpha'' \otimes \tilde{\nu}_{\mathcal{B}}(\mathbf{x})\right) \oplus \eta\right), \tag{21}$$

where $\mathcal{T}$ denotes the collection of all abstract boxes in $\mathcal{S}$, and $\alpha'' \in \mathbb{F}$ is a constant such that $\eta < (\bigoplus_{i=1}^{n} \alpha'' \otimes K) \oplus \eta < \infty$ for all $n \geq 1$. We remark that it is possible to make the summation not overflow even for a large n, by cleverly exploiting the rounding errors from $\oplus$. With a proper choice of α'', we can further show that $\tilde{\nu}_{\mathcal{S}}^{\sharp} = (K \iota_{\mathcal{S}})^{\sharp}$ on $(\mathbb{I}_{[a,b]})^d$. A formal proof of Lemma 8 is given in §E.2.

Using $\tilde{\nu}_{\mathcal{S}}$, we finally construct a σ-network that coincides, under the interval semantics, with the target function h over $([a,b]_{\mathbb{F}})^d$. This result (Lemma 9) and the above results (Lemma 7 and 8) directly imply Lemma 3.

Lemma 9. *Assume that for any $\mathcal{S} \subseteq ([a,b]_{\mathbb{F}})^d$, there exists a depth-$L'$ σ-network $\tilde{\nu}_{\mathcal{S}}$ without the last affine layer such that $\tilde{\nu}_{\mathcal{S}}^{\sharp} = (K \iota_{\mathcal{S}})^{\sharp}$ on $(\mathbb{I}_{[a,b]})^d$. Then, for any $h : \overline{\mathbb{F}}^d \to \overline{\mathbb{F}} \setminus \{\bot\}$, there exists a σ-network $\nu : \overline{\mathbb{F}}^d \to \overline{\mathbb{F}}$ such that $\nu^{\sharp} = h^{\sharp}$ on $(\mathbb{I}_{[a,b]})^d$.*

We now illustrate the main idea of the proof of Lemma 9. For a simpler argument, we assume that h is non-negative; the proof for the general case is similar (see §E.3). Let $0 = z_0 < z_1 < \cdots < z_n = +\infty$ be all non-negative floats (except $\bot$) in increasing order, and let $\mathcal{S}_i := \{\mathbf{x} \in ([a,b]_{\mathbb{F}})^d \mid h(\mathbf{x}) \geq z_i\}$ be the level set of h for z_i. Under this setup, we construct ν using $\tilde{\nu}_{\mathcal{S}_i}$, as follows:

$$\nu(\mathbf{x}) := \bigoplus_{i=1}^{m} \alpha_i \otimes \tilde{\nu}_{\mathcal{S}_i}(\mathbf{x}), \tag{22}$$

where $m \in \mathbb{N} \cup \{0\}$ and $\alpha_i \in \mathbb{F}$ are chosen so that $z_m = \max\{h(\mathbf{x}) \mid \mathbf{x} \in ([a,b]_{\mathbb{F}})^d\}$ and $\alpha_i \otimes K \approx z_i - z_{i-1}$ for all $i \in [m]$. If $\alpha_i \otimes K$ is close enough to $z_i - z_{i-1}$, then the floating-point summation $\bigoplus_{i=1}^{k} \alpha_i \otimes K$ is exactly equal to the exact summation $\sum_{i=1}^{k} z_i - z_{i-1} = z_k$ for all $k \in [m]$, by the rounding errors of $\oplus$. Using this observation, we can show that $\nu(\mathbf{x}) = h(\mathbf{x})$ for all $\mathbf{x} \in ([a,b]_{\mathbb{F}})^d$, and more importantly, $\nu^{\sharp} = h^{\sharp}$ on $(\mathbb{I}_{[a,b]})^d$. The full proof of Lemma 9 is in §E.3.

6   Related Work

Universal Approximation. Universal approximation theorems for neural networks are widely studied in the literature, which include results for feedforward networks [12,27,28,55], convolutional networks [71], residual networks [41], and transformers [70]. With the advent of low-precision computing for neural networks (e.g., 8-bit E5M2, 8-bit E4M3 [46,65]; float16 [45]; bfloat16 [1]), there has been growing interest among researchers in characterizing their expressiveness power in this setting. New UA theorems for "quantized" neural networks, which use finite-precision network parameters with *exact* real arithmetic, have been studied in [15,21]. These networks differ from the floating-point networks considered in this work, because our networks use *inexact* floating-point arithmetic.

To the best of current knowledge, [30,53] are the only works that study UA theorems for floating-point neural networks. [53] proves UA theorems for ReLU and step activation functions. Our IUA Theorem 1, by virtue of Eq. (15), is a strict generalization of [53] in two senses: (i) it applies to a much broader class of activations that satisfy Condition 1, which subsumes ReLU and step functions; and (ii) it provides a result for abstract interpretation via interval analysis, of which the pointwise approximation considered in [53] is a special case. Concurrent with this article, [30] generalizes [53] to support a wider range of activation functions and larger input domains. Our Theorem 1 partially subsumes [30] in that it is a result for interval approximation, whereas [30] considers only pointwise approximation. Conversely, a special case of our Theorem 1 for pointwise approximation (i.e., Eq. (15)) is subsumed by [30] in that it applies to smaller classes of activation functions and input domains.

Interval Universal Approximation. The first work to establish an IUA theorem for neural networks used interval analysis with the ReLU activation [4], which was later extended to the more general class of so-called "squashable" activation functions [66]. Whereas these previous IUA theorems assume the neural network can compute over arbitrary real numbers with infinitely precise real arithmetic, the IUA result (Theorem 1) in this work applies to "machine-implementable" neural networks that use floating-point numbers and operations. To the best our knowledge, no previous work has established an IUA theorem for floating-point neural networks. These different computational models lead to substantial differences in both the proof methods (cf. Sect. 3.2 and 5) and the specific technical results—Sect. 3.3 gives a detailed discussion of how Theorem 1 differs from previous IUA and robustness results [4, Theorem 1.1]; [66, Theorem 3.7].

Provable Robustness. There is an extensive literature on robustness verification and robust training for neural networks, which is surveyed in, e.g., [4, Chapter 1]; [38,60]. Notable methods among these works are [61,62], which verify the robustness of a neural network using abstract interpretation with the zonotope and polyhedra domains for a restricted class of activations, and are sound with respect to floating-point arithmetic. Compared to these methods, our contribution is a theoretical result on the inherent expressiveness of provably robust floating-point networks under the interval domain for a broad class of activation functions, rather than new verification algorithms or abstract domains. Indeed, our existence result directly applies to the zonotope and polyhedra domains, as they are more precise than the interval domain. More specific IUA theorems tailored to these domains may yield more compact constructions that witness the existence of a provably robust floating-point neural network. Recently, [32] shows that even if a neural network is provably robust over real arithmetic, it can be non-robust over floating-point arithmetic and remain vulnerable to adversarial attacks. This highlights the importance of establishing robustness in the floating-point setting.

Acknowledgments. G. Hwang and Y. Park were supported by Korea Institute for Advanced Study (KIAS) Individual Grants AP092801 and AP090301, via the Center for AI and Natural Sciences at KIAS. G. Hwang was also supported by National Research Foundation of Korea (NRF) Grants RS-2025-00515264 and RS-2024-00406127, funded by the Korea Ministry of Science and ICT (MSIT); and the Gwangju Institute of Science and Technology (GIST) Global University Project in 2025. Y. Park was also supported by the Sejong University faculty research fund in 2025. S. Park was supported by the Korea Institute of Information & Communications Technology Planning & Evaluation (IITP) Grant RS-2019-II190079, funded by the Korea MSIT; the Information Technology Research Center (IITP-ITRC) Grant IITP-2025-RS-2024-00436857, funded by the Korea MSIT; and the Culture, Sports, and Tourism R&D Program through the Korea Creative Content Agency (KOCCA) Grants RS-2024-00348469 and RS-2024-00345025, funded by the Korea Ministry of Culture, Sports and Tourism (MCST) in 2024. W. Lee and F. Saad were supported by the United States National Science Foundation (NSF) under Grant No. 2311983 and funds from the Computer Science Department at Carnegie Mellon University. Any opinions, findings, and conclusions or recommendations expressed in this material are those of the authors and do not necessarily reflect the views of the funding agencies.

Disclosure of Interests. The authors have no competing interests to declare that are relevant to the content of this article.

References

1. Abadi, M., et al.: TensorFlow: large-scale machine learning on heterogeneous distributed systems. arXiv 1603.04467 (2016). https://doi.org/10.48550/arXiv.1603.04467
2. Albarghouthi, A.: Introduction to neural network verification (2021). https://doi.org/10.48550/arXiv.2109.10317
3. Baader, M.: Expressivity of certified neural networks. Ph.D. thesis, ETH Zurich, Zurich, Switzerland (2024). https://doi.org/10.3929/ETHZ-B-000677199

4. Baader, M., Mirman, M., Vechev, M.T.: Universal approximation with certified networks. In: Proceedings of the International Conference on Learning Representations (2020). https://doi.org/10.48550/arXiv.1909.13846

5. Baader, M., Müller, M.N., Mao, Y., Vechev, M.T.: Expressivity of ReLU-networks under convex relaxations. In: Proceedings of the International Conference on Learning Representations (2024). https://openreview.net/forum?id=awHTL3Hpto

6. Barak, B.: Introduction to Theoretical Computer Science (2023). https://introtcs.org

7. Beebe, N.: The Mathematical-Function Computation Handbook: Programming Using the MathCW Portable Software Library. Springer (2017). https://doi.org/10.1007/978-3-319-64110-2

8. Church, A.: A set of postulates for the foundation of logic. Ann. Math. **34**(4), 839–864 (1933). https://doi.org/10.2307/1968702

9. Church, A.: An unsolvable problem of elementary number theory. Am. J. Math. **58**(2), 345–363 (1936). https://doi.org/10.2307/2371045

10. Cousot, P., Cousot, R.: Abstract interpretation: a unified lattice model for static analysis of programs by construction or approximation of fixpoints. In: Proceedings of the ACM Symposium on Principles of Programming Languages, pp. 238–252 (1977). https://doi.org/10.1145/512950.512973

11. Cousot, P., Cousot, R.: Static determination of dynamic properties of generalized type unions. In: Proceedings of an ACM Conference on Language Design for Reliable Software, pp. 77–94 (1977). https://doi.org/10.1145/800022.808314

12. Cybenko, G.: Approximation by superpositions of a sigmoidal function. Math. Control Sig. Syst. **2**(4), 303–314 (1989). https://doi.org/10.1007/BF02551274

13. Daramy-Loirat, C., et al.: CR-LIBM: a library of correctly rounded elementary functions in double-precision. Research Report ENSL-01529804, Laboratoire de l'Informatique du Parallèlisme, December 2006. https://ens-lyon.hal.science/ensl-01529804

14. Dettmers, T., Pagnoni, A., Holtzman, A., Zettlemoyer, L.: QLoRA: efficient fine-tuning of quantized LLMs. In: Proceedings of the International Conference on Neural Information Processing Systems (2023). https://doi.org/10.5555/3666122.3666563

15. Ding, Y., Liu, J., Xiong, J., Shi, Y.: On the universal approximability and complexity bounds of quantized ReLU neural networks. In: International Conference on Learning Representations (2019). https://doi.org/10.48550/arXiv.1802.03646

16. Eykholt, K., et al.: Robust physical-world attacks on deep learning visual classification. In: Proceedings of the IEEE Conference on Computer Vision and Pattern Recognition, pp. 1625–1634 (2018). https://doi.org/10.1109/CVPR.2018.00175

17. Faissole, F., de Lamarlière, P.G., Melquiond, G.: End-to-end formal verification of a fast and accurate floating-point approximation. In: Proceedings of the International Conference on Interactive Theorem Proving, pp. 14:1–14:18 (2024). https://doi.org/10.4230/LIPIcs.ITP.2024.14

18. Finlayson, S.G., Bowers, J.D., Ito, J., Zittrain, J.L., Beam, A.L., Kohane, I.S.: Adversarial attacks on medical machine learning. Science **363**(6433), 1287–1289 (2019). https://doi.org/10.1126/science.aaw4399

19. Gehr, T., Mirman, M., Drachsler-Cohen, D., Tsankov, P., Chaudhuri, S., Vechev, M.T.: AI2: safety and robustness certification of neural networks with abstract interpretation. In: Proceedings of the IEEE Symposium on Security and Privacy, pp. 3–18 (2018). https://doi.org/10.1109/SP.2018.00058

20. Gödel, K.: On undecidable propositions of formal mathematics systems (Notes by Kleene, S.C., Rosser, J.B.) Institute for Advanced Study (1934). https://albert.ias.edu/20.500.12111/7996
21. Gonon, A., Brisebarre, N., Gribonval, R., Riccietti, E.: Approximation speed of quantized versus unquantized ReLU neural networks and beyond. IEEE Trans. Inf. Theory **69**(6), 3960–3977 (2023). https://doi.org/10.1109/TIT.2023.3240360
22. Goodfellow, I.J., Bengio, Y., Courville, A.C.: Deep Learning. MIT Press (2016). http://www.deeplearningbook.org/
23. Goodfellow, I.J., Shlens, J., Szegedy, C.: Explaining and harnessing adversarial examples. In: Proceedings of the International Conference on Learning Representations (2015). https://doi.org/10.48550/arXiv.1412.6572
24. Gowal, S., et al.: Scalable verified training for provably robust image classification. In: Proceedings of the IEEE International Conference on Computer Vision, pp. 4841–4850 (2019). https://doi.org/10.1109/ICCV.2019.00494
25. Grigore, R.: Java generics are Turing complete. In: Proceedings of the ACM Symposium on Principles of Programming Languages, pp. 73–85 (2017). https://doi.org/10.1145/3093333.3009871
26. Hickey, T.J., Ju, Q., van Emden, M.H.: Interval arithmetic: from principles to implementation. J. ACM **48**(5), 1038–1068 (2001). https://doi.org/10.1145/502102.502106
27. Hornik, K., Stinchcombe, M., White, H.: Multilayer feedforward networks are universal approximators. Neural Netw. **2**(5), 359–366 (1989). https://doi.org/10.1016/0893-6080(89)90020-8
28. Hornik, K., Stinchcombe, M., White, H.: Universal approximation of an unknown mapping and its derivatives using multilayer feedforward networks. Neural Netw. **3**(5), 551–560 (1990). https://doi.org/10.1016/0893-6080(90)90005-6
29. Hubara, I., Courbariaux, M., Soudry, D., El-Yaniv, R., Bengio, Y.: Quantized neural networks: training neural networks with low precision weights and activations. J. Mach. Learn. Res. **18**(1), 6869–6898 (2017). https://doi.org/10.5555/3122009.3242044
30. Hwang, G., Park, Y., Lee, W., Park, S.: Floating-point neural networks can represent almost all floating-point functions. In: Proceedings of the International Conference on Machine Learning (2025)
31. Institute of Electrical and Electronics Engineers: IEEE Standard for Floating-Point Arithmetic (IEEE Std 754-2019). IEEE, Piscataway, NJ, USA (2019). https://doi.org/10.1109/IEEESTD.2019.8766229
32. Jin, J., Ohrimenko, O., Rubinstein, B.I.P.: Getting a-round guarantees: floating-point attacks on certified robustness. In: Proceedings of the Workshop on Artificial Intelligence and Security, pp. 53–64 (2024). https://doi.org/10.1145/3689932.3694761
33. Jovanovic, N., Balunovic, M., Baader, M., Vechev, M.T.: On the paradox of certified training. Trans. Mach. Learn. Res. (2022). https://doi.org/10.48550/arXiv.2102.06700
34. Katz, G., Barrett, C., Dill, D.L., Julian, K., Kochenderfer, M.J.: Reluplex: an efficient SMT solver for verifying deep neural networks. In: Majumdar, R., Kunčak, V. (eds.) CAV 2017. LNCS, vol. 10426, pp. 97–117. Springer, Cham (2017). https://doi.org/10.1007/978-3-319-63387-9_5
35. Kozen, D.: Automata and Computability. Springer (1997). https://doi.org/10.1007/978-1-4612-1844-9

36. Lee, W., Sharma, R., Aiken, A.: On automatically proving the correctness of math.h implementations. Proc. ACM Programm. Lang. **2**(POPL), 47:1–47:32 (2018). https://doi.org/10.1145/3158135
37. Li, L., Xie, T., Li, B.: Leaderboard for "SoK: certified robustness for deep neural networks" (2023). https://sokcertifiedrobustness.github.io/leaderboard/. Accessed 19 May 2025
38. Li, L., Xie, T., Li, B.: SoK: certified robustness for deep neural networks. In: Proceedings of the IEEE Symposium on Security and Privacy, pp. 1289–1310. IEEE Press (2023). https://doi.org/10.1109/SP46215.2023.10179303
39. Lim, J.P., Nagarakatte, S.: High performance correctly rounded math libraries for 32-bit floating point representations. In: Proceedings of the ACM Conference on Programming Languages Design and Implementation, pp. 359–374 (2021). https://doi.org/10.1145/3453483.3454049
40. Lim, J.P., Nagarakatte, S.: One polynomial approximation to produce correctly rounded results of an elementary function for multiple representations and rounding modes. Proc. ACM Programm. Lang. **6**(POPL), 1–28 (2022). https://doi.org/10.1145/3498664
41. Lin, H., Jegelka, S.: ResNet with one-neuron hidden layers is a universal approximator. In: Proceedings of the International Conference on Neural Information Processing Systems (2018). https://dl.acm.org/doi/10.5555/3327345.3327515
42. Liu, C., Arnon, T., Lazarus, C., Strong, C.A., Barrett, C.W., Kochenderfer, M.J.: Algorithms for verifying deep neural networks. Found. Trends Optim. **4**(3–4), 244–404 (2021). https://doi.org/10.1561/2400000035
43. Mao, Y., Müller, M.N., Fischer, M., Vechev, M.T.: Understanding certified training with interval bound propagation. In: Proceedings of the International Conference on Learning Representations (2024). https://doi.org/10.48550/arXiv.2306.10426
44. Markstein, P.: IA-64 and Elementary Functions: Speed and Precision. Hewlett-Packard Professional Books, Prentice Hall (2000)
45. Micikevicius, P., et al.: Mixed precision training. In: International Conference on Learning Representations (2018). https://doi.org/10.48550/arXiv.1710.03740
46. Micikevicius, P., et al.: FP8 formats for deep learning. arXiv 2209.05433 (2022). https://doi.org/10.48550/arXiv.2209.05433
47. Mirman, M., Baader, M., Vechev, M.T.: The fundamental limits of neural networks for interval certified robustness. Trans. Mach. Learn. Res. (2022). https://openreview.net/forum?id=fsacLLU35V
48. Mirman, M., Gehr, T., Vechev, M.T.: Differentiable abstract interpretation for provably robust neural networks. In: Proceedings of the International Conference on Machine Learning (2018). http://proceedings.mlr.press/v80/mirman18b.html
49. Moore, C., Mertens, S.: The Nature of Computation. Oxford University Press (2011). https://doi.org/10.1093/acprof:oso/9780199233212.001.0001
50. Moore, R.E., Kearfott, R.B., Cloud, M.J.: Introduction to interval analysis. Soc. Ind. Appl. Math. (2009). https://doi.org/10.1137/1.9780898717716
51. Muller, J.: Elementary Functions: Algorithms and Implementation, 3rd edn. Birkhäuser, Boston, MA (2016). https://doi.org/10.1007/978-1-4899-7983-4
52. Muller, J.M., et al.: Handbook of Floating-Point Arithmetic. Springer (2018). https://doi.org/10.1007/978-3-319-76526-6
53. Park, Y., Hwang, G., Lee, W., Park, S.: Expressive power of ReLU and step networks under floating-point operations. Neural Netw. (2024). https://doi.org/10.1016/j.neunet.2024.106297
54. Pérez, J., Barceló, P., Marinkovic, J.: Attention is Turing-complete. J. Mach. Learn. Res. **22**, 75:1–75:35 (2021). https://dl.acm.org/doi/10.5555/3546258.3546333

55. Pinkus, A.: Approximation theory of the MLP model in neural networks. Acta Numerica **8**, 143–195 (1999). https://doi.org/10.1017/S0962492900002919

56. Raghunathan, A., Steinhardt, J., Liang, P.: Semidefinite relaxations for certifying robustness to adversarial examples. In: Proceedings of the International Conference on Neural Information Processing Systems (2018). https://dl.acm.org/doi/10.5555/3327546.3327746

57. Rosenberg, I., Shabtai, A., Elovici, Y., Rokach, L.: Adversarial machine learning attacks and defense methods in the cyber security domain. ACM Comput. Surv. **54**(5) (2021). https://doi.org/10.1145/3453158

58. Sibidanov, A., Zimmermann, P., Glondu, S.: The CORE-MATH project. In: Proceedings of the IEEE Symposium on Computer Arithmetic, pp. 26–34 (2022). https://doi.org/10.1109/ARITH54963.2022.00014

59. Siegelmann, H., Sontag, E.: On the computational power of neural nets. J. Comput. Syst. Sci. **50**(1), 132–150 (1995). https://doi.org/10.1006/jcss.1995.1013

60. Singh, G.: Building trust and safety in artificial intelligence with abstract interpretation. In: Hermenegildo, M.V., Morales, J.F. (eds.) Static Analysis, pp. 28–38. Springer, Cham (2023). https://doi.org/10.1007/978-3-031-44245-2_3

61. Singh, G., Gehr, T., Mirman, M., Püschel, M., Vechev, M.T.: Fast and effective robustness certification. In: Proceedings of the International Conference on Neural Information Processing Systems (2018). https://dl.acm.org/doi/10.5555/3327546.3327739

62. Singh, G., Gehr, T., Püschel, M., Vechev, M.T.: An abstract domain for certifying neural networks. Proc. ACM Programm. Lang. **3**(POPL), 41:1–41:30 (2019). https://doi.org/10.1145/3290354

63. Szegedy, C., et al.: Intriguing properties of neural networks. In: Proceedings of the International Conference on Learning Representations (2014). https://doi.org/10.48550/arXiv.1312.6199

64. Turing, A.M.: On computable numbers, with an application to the Entscheidungsproblem. Proc. London Math. Soc. **s2-42**(1), 230–265 (1937). https://doi.org/10.1112/plms/s2-42.1.230

65. Wang, N., Choi, J., Brand, D., Chen, C.Y., Gopalakrishnan, K.: Training deep neural networks with 8-bit floating point numbers. In: Proceedings of the International Conference on Neural Information Processing Systems (2018). https://doi.org/10.5555/3327757.3327866

66. Wang, Z., Albarghouthi, A., Prakriya, G., Jha, S.: Interval universal approximation for neural networks. Proc. ACM Programm. Lang. **6**(POPL), 14.1–14.29 (2022). https://doi.org/10.1145/3498675

67. Wansbrough, K.: Instance declarations are universal (1998). http://www.lochan.org/keith/publications/undec.html

68. Wong, E., Kolter, J.Z.: Provable defenses against adversarial examples via the convex outer adversarial polytope. In: Proceedings of the International Conference on Machine Learning (2018). https://doi.org/10.48550/arXiv.1711.00851

69. Yarotsky, D.: Optimal approximation of continuous functions by very deep ReLU networks. In: Proceedings of the Conference on Learning Theory (2018). https://doi.org/10.48550/arXiv.1802.03620

70. Yun, C., Bhojanapalli, S., Rawat, A.S., Reddi, S., Kumar, S.: Are transformers universal approximators of sequence-to-sequence functions? In: Proceedings of the International Conference on Learning Representations (2020). https://doi.org/10.48550/arXiv.1912.10077

71. Zhou, D.X.: Universality of deep convolutional neural networks. Appl. Comput. Harmon. Anal. **48**(2), 787–794 (2020). https://doi.org/10.1016/j.acha.2019.06.004
72. Ziv, A., Olshansky, M., Henis, E., Retiman, A.: IBM accurate portable Mathlib (2001). https://github.com/dreal-deps/mathlib

A Formally Verified Robustness Certifier for Neural Networks

James Tobler[2], Hira Taqdees Syeda[1], and Toby Murray[1(✉)]

[1] University of Melbourne, Melbourne, Australia
toby.murray@unimelb.edu.au
[2] University of Queensland, Brisbane, Australia
james.tobler@uq.edu.au

Abstract. Neural networks are often susceptible to minor perturbations in input that cause them to misclassify. A recent solution to this problem is the use of globally-robust neural networks, which employ a function to certify that the classification of an input cannot be altered by such a perturbation. Outputs that pass this test are called *certified robust*. However, to the authors' knowledge, these certification functions have not yet been verified at the implementation level. We demonstrate how previous unverified implementations are exploitably unsound in certain circumstances. Moreover, they often rely on approximation-based algorithms, such as power iteration, that (perhaps surprisingly) do not guarantee soundness. To provide assurance that a given output is robust, we implemented and formally verified a certification function for globally-robust neural networks in Dafny. We describe the program, its specifications, and the important design decisions taken for its implementation and verification, as well as our experience applying it in practice.

1 Introduction

Neural networks are deployed in safety- and security-critical systems such as object recognition and malware classification. For these kinds of models, it is important to be able to trust their outputs. One important guarantee is that of *robustness*, motivated by the existence of *adversarial examples* [31]: that a small change to the model's input would not have caused it to produce a different output.

No useful classifier can be robust everywhere. For this reason, a common approach is to assure the robustness of individual model outputs. Certified robustness is a prominent approach for doing so, and includes techniques like randomised smoothing [5], those based on enforcing differential privacy [20], and those that leverage the certification procedure during model training [21].

Many of these methods come with pen-and-paper proofs of their soundness: theorems that provide a degree of confidence that an output will be robust

J. Tobler—This work was conducted while the author was employed at University of Melbourne.

R. Piskac and Z. Rakamarić (Eds.): CAV 2025, LNCS 15932, pp. 327–348, 2025.
https://doi.org/10.1007/978-3-031-98679-6_15

if it is certified as robust. However, for high-assurance applications of neural networks, pen-and-paper proofs fall short of the kinds of guarantees enjoyed by *formally verified* safety- and security-critical systems software. For example, separation kernels [27] and cryptographic implementations [4] enjoy *mechanised* proofs about their *implementations*.

So-called "code-level" guarantees are important to rule out both design- and implementation-level flaws that might otherwise compromise robustness.

This paper considers the question of how to provide formally verified guarantees of certified robustness. Doing so requires being able to overcome key challenges. The first challenge is that work on formally verified robustness considers primarily *local robustness*, which means that it can require symbolic reasoning to be performed for each output point or each perturbation bound that is to be certified as robust [26]. This limits the efficiency of output certification. The second challenge is the complexity of many local robustness verification or certification approaches. Formally verifying their implementations is prohibitive, as the effort required to formally verify a program's implementation is known to be about an order of magnitude higher than that to program it [17].

We overcome both of these challenges by designing a formally verified robustness certifier for dense ReLU neural networks, which is inspired by Leino et al.'s training method for globally robust neural networks [23]. In their work, a model's Lipschitz constants are estimated during training and used to maximise the model's robustness against the training set. These constants are also used at inference time to cheaply certify the robustness of individual outputs. We adapt this design to produce a formally verified robustness certifier that works in two stages: the first stage verifiably pre-computes Lipschitz upper bounds once-and-for-all, while the second stage is then executed for each model output to verifiably check its robustness against the Lipschitz upper bounds. Both stages have been formally verified in the industrial program verifier Dafny [22].

Along the way we uncovered soundness issues in the design (Sect. 6) and implementation (Sect. 2) of previous certified global robustness certifiers. We overcome these problems by adopting state-of-the-art algorithms for computing Lipschitz bounds [6], which we implement and formally verify, along with our certifier routine. In addition, because our verification applies to the code of our certifier, it rules out soundness issues caused by floating point rounding (see Sect. 2.3) in the certification function [14]. Some orthogonal residual floating-point issues remain with our certifier, which we describe later in Sect. 9.

This paper makes the following contributions:

- We design a verifiable certifier for robustness based on globally robust neural networks proposed by Leino et al. [23],
- We formalise its soundness as Dafny specifications for the corresponding top-level functions,
- We present the implementation of our design, including how it overcomes the soundness issues explained above,
- We formally verify our implementation in Dafny against its soundness specifications, obtaining a usefully applicable executable implementation.

We present a high-level overview of this paper's main contributions in Sect. 3. The top-level specifications of soundness we describe in Sect. 4. Key aspects of the implementation we discuss in Sect. 5 (the certification procedure), Sect. 6 (deriving operator norms), and Sect. 7 (positive square roots). Section 8 reports on our experience applying our certifier to practical globally-robust image classification models whose size is on par with recent work on verification of global robustness properties [15]. In Sect. 9, we consider our approach in relation to prior work and conclude. Some technical details is relegated to the appendices contained in the extended version of this paper [32].

2 Exploitable Vulnerabilities in a Robustness Certifier

We further motivate our work by describing a series of exploitable vulnerabilities we discovered in the robustness certifier implementation of Leino et al. [23]. All are ruled out by our verification. Two are implementation flaws (i.e., bugs) that we reported to the developers. The third results inevitably from the use of floating point arithmetic in their implementation, which our certifier eschews.

2.1 Incorrect Lipschitz Constant Computation

The first vulnerability arises due to a subtle bug in the implementation of the routine that calculates Lipschitz constants in Leino et al.'s implementation[1]. An adversary who is able to choose a model's initial weights can cause their certifier to incorrectly classify non-robust points as robust, even after robust model training from those initial weights.

This issue could be exploited, for example, by an adversary who posts a model online that purports to be accurate while enjoying a certain level of robustness. Anyone who attempts to use that model in conjunction with Leino et al.'s certifier can be mislead into believing the model really is as robust as it purports to be, when in fact its true robustness can be dramatically lower.

This vulnerability arises for models with small weights. To exploit it we trained an ordinary (non-robust) MNIST model, achieving an accuracy of 98.45%. We then repeatedly halved all weights in the second-to-last model layer while also doubling all weights in the model's final layer. Doing so does not meaningfully change the model's Lipschitz constants. However, after repeating this process for a number of iterations, Leino et al.'s implementation mistakenly computes very small, misleading Lipschitz constants that then cause it to mistakenly certify non-robust outputs as robust, even for large perturbation bounds $\epsilon = 1.58$. When evaluating this model on the 10,000 MNIST test points, their certifier mistakenly reports a *Verified Robust Accuracy* (VRA) measure [23] of 98.42%. VRA is the percentage of points that the model accurately classifies and that their certifier says are robust at $\epsilon = 1.58$. We were able to generate adversarial examples at $\epsilon = 1.58$ for 8,682 of the test points that Leino et al.'s certifier said were robust. Further information about this issue is in the extended version [32].

---

[1] https://github.com/klasleino/gloro/issues/8.

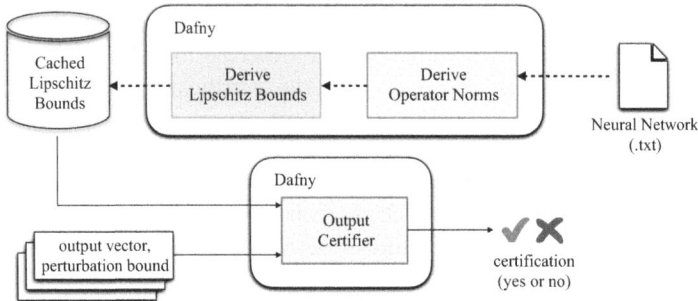

Fig. 1. An overview of the Dafny program. Lipschitz bounds are pre-computed and then reused as each model output is certified against a given perturbation bound.

2.2 Incorrect Certification

The second vulnerability results from a subtle error in their certification routine that, given the computed Lipschitz constants, certifies individual outputs[2]. An adversary who is able to supply specially crafted inputs to a model can cause Leino et al.'s certifier to mistakenly certify the model's output as robust.

This issue causes Leino et al.'s certifier to certify as robust any output vector whose individual elements are all equal. We validated that it can be exploited by an adversary who has white-box access to a model (i.e., knows the model architecture and weights). The adversary can simply perform a gradient descent search to find any input that produces the **0** output vector (whose elements are all zero), e.g., by using the mean absolute error (MAE) between the model's output and the target output vector **0** as the loss function.

We confirmed that this approach is able to find inputs that Leino et al.'s implementation will mistakenly certify as robust at *any* perturbation bound ϵ for the MNIST, Fashion MNIST, and CIFAR-10 models considered in this paper (see Sect. 8). Further information about this issue is in the extended version [32].

2.3 Floating Point Imprecision

The final issue arises due to floating point imprecision in Leino et al.'s implementation. This causes it to mistakenly compute Lipschitz constants of 0 for models with very tiny weights. It can be exploited using the same method as the issue in Sect. 2.1. Further information about this issue is in [32].

3 Overview

3.1 Robustness, Formally

For our purposes, a neural network N is a sequence of layers, represented by matrices $M_1, ..., M_n$. Each layer M_i can be *applied* to a vector $\mathbf{v}_i$ by taking

---

[2] https://github.com/klasleino/gloro/issues/9.

their matrix-vector product $M_i\mathbf{v}_i$. For all layers but the output layer M_n, the ReLU activation function R is then applied component-wise to the resulting vector, which we denote $R(M_i\mathbf{v}_i)$. To apply a neural network N with matrices $M_1, ..., M_n$ to an input vector $\mathbf{v}_1$, we simply apply each layer in-turn:

$$N(\mathbf{v}_1) = M_n\mathbf{v}_n \text{ where}$$
$$\mathbf{v}_{i+1} = R(M_i\mathbf{v}_i) \text{ for } 1 \leq i < n.$$

Let $\mathbf{v}[i]$ denote the ith component of $\mathbf{v}$. Formally, the output vector $N(\mathbf{v})$ is *robust* with respect to some perturbation bound ϵ if:

$$\forall \mathbf{u} : ||\mathbf{v} - \mathbf{u}|| \leq \epsilon \implies ArgMax(N(\mathbf{v})) = ArgMax(N(\mathbf{u})) \tag{1}$$

where $|| \cdot ||$ denotes the l_2 norm: $||\mathbf{v}|| = \sqrt{\sum_{i=1}^{|\mathbf{v}|} \mathbf{v}[i]^2}$. This condition guarantees that $\mathbf{v}$ is not an ϵ adversarial example [25].

3.2   The Global-Robustness Approach

Figure 1 illustrates our Dafny implementation of the global-robustness approach developed by Leino et al. [23] for certifying this condition. Distinctively, the approach involves deriving and caching *margin Lipschitz bounds* which can then be leveraged to efficiently certify any output vector against any perturbation bound. In our Dafny implementation, we generate margin Lipschitz bounds $L_{i,j}$ for distinct dimensions i, j of the neural network's output vector. These can be best described as upper bounds on the rate at which the difference between these two dimensions can change, relative to changes in the input vector. Formally, for a neural network N:

$$\forall \mathbf{v}, \mathbf{u} : \frac{|N(\mathbf{v})[j] - N(\mathbf{v})[i] - (N(\mathbf{u})[j] - N(\mathbf{u})[i])|}{||\mathbf{v} - \mathbf{u}||} \leq L_{i,j}$$

From this, follows:

$$\forall \mathbf{v}, \mathbf{u}, e : ||\mathbf{v} - \mathbf{u}|| \leq e \implies |N(\mathbf{v})[j] - N(\mathbf{v})[i] - (N(\mathbf{u})[j] - N(\mathbf{u})[i])| \leq eL_{i,j}$$

That is, $eL_{i,j}$ bounds the change in the difference between each pair of distinct components i, j in the output vector. Given this fact, we can prove the consequent of (1) by considering the maximum component $j = ArgMax(N(\mathbf{v}))$ and checking that the difference between it and each other component $i \neq j$ is greater than $eL_{i,j}$. Formally, we need to check that:

$$\forall i \neq j : N(\mathbf{v})[j] - N(\mathbf{v})[i] > eL_{i,j}$$

for each other component i in the output vector.

An important advantage of precomputing Lipschitz bounds is that they not only provide a way to efficiently certify outputs, but they also represent a global metric for the general robustness of the neural network. That is, neural networks with smaller Lipschitz bounds are robust for a broader range of outputs.

During training, Leino et al. [23] use an efficient method for estimating Lipschitz bounds to incorporate into the training objective the maximisation of the model's robustness against the training set. Unfortunately, the method that Leino et al. use for computing Lipschitz bounds is not guaranteed to be sound and is thus unsuitable to be implemented and verified in Dafny. Instead, we take advantage of the fact that our Dafny program is used after training has been completed, to verifiably pre-compute sound Lipschitz bounds for later use during output certification (i.e. that are used later at inference time). Therefore we can employ a sound but less efficient method to compute these bounds.

3.3 Deriving Lipschitz Bounds

To derive the Lipschitz bounds of our neural network, we first derive upper bounds on the operator norms of the first $n-1$ matrices. These can be thought of as Lipschitz bounds over the output vectors of the respective layers. Formally, the operator norm $||M||_{op}$ of matrix M satisfies by definition: $\forall \mathbf{v} : \frac{||M\mathbf{v}||}{||\mathbf{v}||} \leq ||M||_{op}$. By replacing $\mathbf{v}$ with $\mathbf{v}-\mathbf{u}$ and distributing the matrix-vector product, we observe that $||M||_{op}$ is a Lipschitz bound on multiplication by M:

$$\forall \mathbf{v}, \mathbf{u} : \frac{||M\mathbf{v} - M\mathbf{u}||}{||\mathbf{v} - \mathbf{u}||} \leq ||M||_{op} \tag{2}$$

The final step of applying a (non-output) layer is the component-wise application of the ReLU function R to the resulting vector. The function applied to each component is: $R(x) \mathrel{\hat{=}} max(0, x)$. Now note that for any two inputs to this function, the absolute difference in the outputs is less than or equal to the absolute difference in the inputs. Formally: $\forall x, y : |R(x) - R(y)| \leq |x - y|$. Hence, for any two vectors $\mathbf{w}, \mathbf{x}$ of equal length, the absolute difference between each component $|\mathbf{w}_i - \mathbf{x}_i|$ is the same or less after applying R to $\mathbf{w}_i$ and $\mathbf{x}_i$. Formally, by replacing x in the above with $\mathbf{w}_i$ and y with $\mathbf{x}_i$:

$$\forall i : |R(\mathbf{w}_i) - R(\mathbf{x}_i)| \leq |\mathbf{w}_i - \mathbf{x}_i|$$

Therefore, by applying R to each component in $\mathbf{w}, \mathbf{x}$, we reduce the distance in each dimension of the vector. We therefore decrease the distance overall: $||R(\mathbf{w}) - R(\mathbf{x})|| \leq ||\mathbf{w} - \mathbf{x}||$. Replacing $\mathbf{w}$ and $\mathbf{x}$ with $M\mathbf{v}$ and $M\mathbf{u}$: $||R(M\mathbf{v}) - R(M\mathbf{u})|| \leq ||M\mathbf{v} - M\mathbf{u}||$. And therefore, from (2):

$$\forall \mathbf{v}, \mathbf{u} : \frac{||R(M\mathbf{v}) - R(M\mathbf{u})||}{||\mathbf{v} - \mathbf{u}||} \leq ||M||_{op}$$

Hence, the operator norm of a matrix M is a Lipschitz bound on the application of a layer represented by M.

A Lipschitz bound over the output of the first $n-1$ layers of a neural network can therefore be derived as the product of their operator norms:

$$\prod_{i=1}^{n-1} ||M_i||_{op}. \tag{3}$$

When computing the output of neural network N, the value of the ith component of the output vector $\mathbf{v}_{n+1}$ is equal to the dot product of the input vector $\mathbf{v}_n$ to final matrix M_n, with the ith row in M_n. Hence, a margin Lipschitz bound on the difference between the jth and ith components can be derived by multiplying the product (3) by the operator norm of $M_n[j] - M_n[i]$ (where for matrix M we write $M[k]$ denote its kth row, indexed from 0). Because $M_n[j] - M_n[i]$ is a single vector, we prove in Dafny that (due to the Cauchy-Schwartz inequality) its operator norm can be efficiently bounded by its l_2 norm: $||M_n[j] - M_n[i]||$.

4 Top-Level Specification

This section details our encoding of the robustness condition in Dafny and the specifications our robustness certifier is verified against.

4.1 Types

For a type $\mathbf{t}$, the type $[\mathbf{t}]$ is the type of sequences of $\mathbf{t}$. Given a sequence x, we write $x[i]$ to denote the ith element of x (indexed from 0).

We define the type **Vector** to be a non-empty sequence of **reals**. These **reals** Dafny compiles to arbitrary-precision rationals, and ensure our certifier avoids the floating-point unsoundness issues of Leino et al.'s implementation that we identify in Sect. 2.3.

$$\mathbf{Vector} = \{v \in [\mathbf{real}] \mid |v| > 0\}$$

A matrix is a non-empty sequence of vectors with equal dimension:

$$\mathbf{Matrix} = \{M \in [\mathbf{Vector}] \mid |M| > 0$$
$$\wedge \, \forall i, j \in \mathbf{nat} \, . \, i < |M| \wedge j < |M| \implies |M[i]| = |M[j]|\}$$

We define each vector in a matrix to be a *row* of that matrix. We can define Dafny functions that return the number of rows and columns in a matrix:

$\quad$ **fun** $Rows(M : \mathbf{Matrix}) : \mathbf{nat} \,\,\widehat{=}\, |M| \qquad$ **fun** $Cols(M : \mathbf{Matrix}) : \mathbf{nat} \,\,\widehat{=}\, |M[0]|$

A neural network is a non-empty sequence of matrices where the number of rows in each matrix is equal to the number of the columns in the next:

$$\mathbf{NeuralNet} = \{N \in [\mathbf{Matrix}] \mid |N| > 0$$
$$\wedge \, \forall i \in \mathbf{nat} \, . \, i < |N| - 1 \implies Rows(N[i]) = Cols(N[i+1])\}$$

A vector is a compatible input to a neural network if and only if its dimension is compatible with multiplication by the first matrix:

$\quad$ **fun** $IsInput(v : \mathbf{Vector}, \, N : \mathbf{NeuralNet}) : \mathbf{bool} \,\,\widehat{=}\, |v| = Cols(N[0])$

Similarly, v is a compatible output of N if and only if its dimension is equal to that of the matrix-vector product of the final matrix and its input vector:

fun $IsOutput(v : \mathbf{Vector}, \, N : \mathbf{NeuralNet}) : \mathbf{bool} \,\,\widehat{=}\, |v| = Rows(N[|N| - 1])$

4.2   Modelling the Neural Network

The application of a neural network is modelled with the function *ApplyNN*, which makes use of the recursive helper *ApplyNNBody* that model the application of all layers but the final one:

> **fun** *ApplyNNBody*(N : **NeuralNet**, v : **Vector**) : **Vector** $\;\widehat{=}\;$
> **if** $|N| = 1$ **then** *ApplyLayer*($N[0], v$)
> **else** *ApplyLayer*($N[|N| - 1]$, *ApplyNNBody*($N[..|N| - 1], v$))
> **where** *IsInput*(v, N)

> **fun** *ApplyNN*(N : **NeuralNet**, v : **Vector**) : **Vector** $\;\widehat{=}\;$
> **if** $|N| = 1$ **then** *MVProduct*($N[0], v$)
> **else** *MVProduct*($N[|N| - 1]$, *ApplyNNBody*($N[..|N| - 1], v$))
> **where** *IsInput*(v, N)

The matrix-vector product *MVProduct* is defined in the extended version [32].

The application of a non-final layer *ApplyLayer* is defined to use the ReLU activation function. Note that the Dafny syntax $[x]$ for some variable x denotes a sequence only containing x, and that $+$ is sequence concatenation.

> **fun** *ApplyLayer*(M : **Matrix**, v : **Vector**) : **Vector** $\;\widehat{=}\;$
> *ApplyRelu*(*MVProduct*(M, v))
> **where** $|v| = Cols(M)$

> **fun** *ApplyRelu*(v : **Vector**) : **Vector** $\;\widehat{=}\;$ *Apply*($v, Relu$)

> **fun** *Apply*(v : **Vector**, f : real $\rightarrow$ real) : **Vector** $\;\widehat{=}\;$
> **if** $|v| = 1$ **then** $[f(v[0])]$ **else** $[f(v[0])] + Apply(v[1..], f)$

> **fun** *Relu*(x : real) : real $\;\widehat{=}\;$ **if** $x \geq 0$ **then** x **else** 0

4.3   Linear Algebra

Encoding the l_2 norm in Dafny requires building up a small set of basic mathematical functions:

> **fun** *L2*(v : **Vector**) : real $\;\widehat{=}\;$ *Sqrt*(*Sum*(*Apply*($v, Square$)))

The (positive) square root function cannot be defined directly and is therefore not compilable. However its properties can still be specified in Dafny. We do so by specifying it as a *ghost function* with postcondition ("**ensures**") annotations that precisely describe what it means for a real r to be the square root of a non-negative real x:

> **ghost fun** $Sqrt(x : \mathbf{real}) : (r : \mathbf{real})$
>
> > **ensures** $r \geq 0 \wedge r \cdot r = x$
>
> where $x \geq 0$

The *Sum* and *Square* functions are straightforward (see the extended version [32]).

For our definition of the robustness property, we additionally need to define vector subtraction and the *ArgMax* function:

> **fun** $Minus(v : \mathbf{Vector},\ u : \mathbf{Vector}) : \mathbf{Vector} \;\widehat{=}$
>
> > **if** $|v| = 1$ **then** $[v[0] - u[0]]$ **else** $[v[0] - u[0]] + Minus(v[1..], u[1..])$
>
> where $|v| = |u|$

> **fun** $ArgMax(s : \mathbf{Vector}) : \mathbf{nat} \;\widehat{=}$
>
> > **if** $|s| = 1$ **then** 0
> >
> > **else if** $s[ArgMax(s[..|s| - 1])] \geq s[|s| - 1]$ **then** $ArgMax(s[..|s| - 1])$
> >
> > **else** $|s| - 1$

Finally, for our convenience, we define a function that represents the distance between two vectors:

> **fun** $Distance(v : \mathbf{Vector},\ u : \mathbf{Vector}) : \mathbf{real} \;\widehat{=}\; L2(Minus(v, u))$
>
> where $|v| = |u|$

4.4   Robustness Definition

We can now define robustness in Dafny. For a given input vector v with output vector $v' = ApplyNN(N, v)$, we say v' is robust with respect to perturbation bound e if $Robust(v, v', e, N) = \mathbf{True}$, where:

> **fun** $Robust(v : \mathbf{Vector},\ v' : \mathbf{Vector},\ e : \mathbf{real}, N : \mathbf{NeuralNet}) : \mathbf{bool} \;\widehat{=}$
>
> > $\forall u \in \mathbf{Vector}\ .\ |v| = |u| \wedge Distance(v, u) \leq e$
> >
> > $\implies ArgMax(v') = ArgMax(ApplyNN(N, u))$
>
> where $IsInput(v, n) \wedge ApplyNN(N, v) = v'$

With global robustness certification, we can establish the robustness of an output vector irrespective of its input vector. That is, given an output vector v', a neural network N, and a perturbation bound e, our verified certifier says "Certified" only if Dafny can verify the assertion:

> **assert** $\forall v \in \mathbf{Vector}\ .\ IsInput(v, N) \wedge ApplyNN(N, v) = v'$
>
> > $\implies Robust(v, v', e, N)$

method *GenLipschitzBound*(N : **NeuralNet**, i : **nat**, k : **nat**, s : [**real**]) : (r : **real**)
  requires $|s| = |N| \wedge i < Rows(N[|N| - 1]) \wedge k < Rows(N[|N| - 1]) \wedge i \neq k$
  requires $\forall j \in$ **nat** . $j < |s| \implies s[j] \geq OpNorm(N[j])$
  ensures *IsMarginLipBound*(N, r, i, k)
{
  var $i := |N| - 1$
  var $d := Minus(N[|N| - 1][k], N[|N| - 1][i])$
  var $r := L2UpperBound(d)$
  while $i > 0$
    invariant $r \geq 0 \wedge IsMarginLipBound(N[i..], r, i, k)$
  {
    $i := i - 1$
    $r := s[i] * r$
  }
}

Fig. 2. Generating margin Lipschitz bounds in Dafny.

5   Verified Certification Procedure

As discussed in Sect. 3, for a neural network N composed of n matrices, a margin Lipschitz bound for the i, kth component-pair of the output vector can be derived by taking the product of the operator norms of the first $n - 1$ matrices, together with the operator norm of the difference between the kth and ith rows of the final matrix (bounded by its l_2 norm). We implement this computation in the Dafny method *GenLipschitzBound* in Fig. 2, which generates a Lipschitz bound for the i, kth component-pair in the output vector of a neural network N, given a sequence s containing the operator norms of all matrices in N. The conditions specified in the **requires** and **ensures** clauses state the precondition and postcondition of this method respectively.

fun *IsMarginLipBound*(N : **NeuralNet**, r : **real**, i : **nat**, k : **nat**) : **bool** $\hat{=}$
$\forall v \in$ **Vector**, $u \in$ **Vector** . *IsInput*(v, N) $\wedge$ *IsInput*(u, N)
    $\implies Abs($ *ApplyNN*(N, v)[k] $-$ *ApplyNN*(N, v)[i]$-$
        (*ApplyNN*(N, u)[k] $-$ *ApplyNN*(N, u)[i]))
    $\leq r \cdot Distance(v, u)$
where $i < |N[|N| - 1]| \wedge k < |N[|N| - 1]|$

The procedure begins by extracting the vector subtraction of the kth and ith rows of the final matrix in N and storing this vector difference in d. The upper bound of the l_2 norm of this new vector is then assigned to r. The final Lipschitz bound is then derived by taking the product of the first $|s| - 1$ elements of s, multiplied by r. The **invariant** annotation specifies while-loop's invariant.

The upper bound of the l_2 norm is computed by summing the squares of each vector element and then taking an upper bound of the square root (see Sect. 7 later). The operator norms in s are approximated using an iterative method described in Sect. 6.

To enable Dafny to verify the *GenLipschitzBound* method, we must first prove three facts. Firstly, that an upper bound of the l_2 norm of a vector is also an upper bound on the operator norm of the matrix that comprises just that vector. Secondly, that the operator norm bound of $M[k] - M[i]$ yields the margin Lipschitz bound for i, k for a single-layer neural network. These two facts establish that the invariant holds when the while-loop is entered. Thirdly, to prove that the loop's invariant is maintained, we must show that multiplying the margin Lipschitz bound by the operator norm bound for the matrix of the preceding layer yields the margin Lipschitz bound for the composition of that preceding layer and the subsequent part of the neural network. In Dafny, these facts are stated as *lemmas*, which are uncompiled Dafny methods wherein the **ensures** clause is verified against the **requires** clause with a proof in the method body. Essentially, the **requires** clauses state the lemma's assumptions and the **ensures** clause states its conclusion. The three lemmas corresponding to these three facts appear in Fig. 3. The proof of the first leverages the Cauchy-Schwartz inequality, which we axiomatise in Dafny.

With Lipschitz bounds generated and cached, the certification procedure is straightforward to implement and verify (though note that it is also easy to introduce subtle bugs in these kinds of routines, as we found in Leino et al.'s implementation as described in Sect. 2.2). Our certification method is shown in Fig. 4, where *AreLipBounds*(N, L) specifies that each $L[i][k]$ is a margin Lipschitz bound for components i, k of M, as specified by *IsMarginLipBound* above.

As discussed in Sect. 3, this involves checking that for each other component i in the output vector v', the difference between the maximum value of v' and $v'[i]$ is less than the product of the corresponding margin Lipschitz bound with the perturbation bound e.

6 Deriving Operator Norms

Matrix M's operator norm $||M||_{op}$ bounds how much it can "stretch" a vector:

$$||M||_{op} = \inf\{c \geq 0 \mid \forall \mathbf{v} . ||M\mathbf{v}|| \leq c||\mathbf{v}||\}$$

In Dafny, we encode this definition as in Fig. 5.

Unfortunately, operator norms cannot be derived directly and must be computed with iterative approximation. In Leino et al. [23], operator norms are derived using the *power method* [12]. For a given matrix M, this involves choosing a random initial vector $\mathbf{v}_1$ and applying the recurrence: $\mathbf{v}_{i+1} = M^T M \mathbf{v}_i$. The operator norm can then be derived as

$$\frac{||M\mathbf{v}_n||}{||\mathbf{v}_n||} \tag{4}$$

lemma *L2IsOpNormUpperBound*(s : **real**, m : **Matrix**)
   requires $|m| = 1$
   requires $s \geq L2(m[0])$
   ensures $s \geq OpNorm(m)$

lemma *OpNormIsMarginLipBound*(N : **NeuralNet**, m : **Matrix**,
                                           i : **nat**, k : **nat**, r : **real**)
   requires $|N| = 1$
   requires $i < |N[0]| \wedge k < |N[0]|$
   requires $m = [Minus(N[0][k], N[0][i])]$
   requires $r \geq OpNorm(m)$
   ensures *IsMarginLipBound*(N, r, i, k)

lemma *MarginRecursive*(N : **NeuralNet**, s : **real**, r : **real**, i : **nat**, k : **nat**,
                                 r' : **real**)
   requires $|N| > 1$
   requires $i < |N[|N| - 1]| \wedge k < |N[|N| - 1]|$
   requires $s \geq OpNorm(N[0])$
   requires *IsMarginLipBound*(N[1..], r, i, k)
   requires $r' = s \cdot r$
   requires $r \geq 0$
   ensures *IsMarginLipBound*(N, r', i, k)

Fig. 3. Lemmas used to prove Fig. 2.

for some suitably large n. In practice, intermediary normalisation is performed for each $\mathbf{v}_i$ to avoid overflow (though is easy to implement incorrectly; a bug here in Leino et al.'s implementation causes the vulnerability of Sect. 2.1).

Intuitively, this works because, as i increases, the direction of $\mathbf{v}_i$ converges to that of the maximum eigenvector of $M^T M$. This is the vector whose length is increased by the greatest factor when its product is taken with M.

There are a number of issues with the power method that make it unsuitable for formal verification in Dafny. One issue is that, if the random initial vector is orthogonal to the maximum eigenvector of $M^T M$, the algorithm may fail to converge. Furthermore, the method converges on the operator norm from *below*, since the result of the function in (4) applied to intermediary values of $\mathbf{v}_i$ is lower than that for the maximum eigenvector of $M^T M$, by definition.

For these reasons, our Dafny implementation takes advantage of a relatively new approach for approximating operator norms from *above*, called Gram iteration [6]. Unlike the power method, Gram iteration involves iterating on the matrix itself, rather than an initial starting vector. Let $M_0 = M$ be the initial

```
method Certify(v' : Vector, e : real, L : [[real]]) : (b : bool)
  ensures b ⟹ ∀v ∈ Vector,  N ∈ NeuralNet .
    IsInput(v, N) ∧ ApplyNN(N, v) = v' ∧ AreLipBounds(N, L)
      ⟹ Robust(v, v', e, N)
{
  var x := ArgMax(v')
  var i := 0
  b := True
  while i < |v'| {
    if i ≠ x {
      if L[i][x] · e ≥ v'[x] − v'[i] {
        b := False;
        break;
      }
    }
    i := i + 1;
  }
}
```

Fig. 4. Certification procedure implemented in Dafny.

matrix. Gram iteration involves applying the recurrence:

$$M_{i+1} = M_i^T M_i \qquad (5)$$

Then, for some suitably-large n, we derive an upper bound on the operator norm as: $\sqrt[2^n]{||M_n||_F}$, where $||\cdot||_F$ is the Frobenius norm, defined as:

$$||M||_F \triangleq \sqrt{\sum_{i=1}^{|M|} \sum_{j=1}^{|M[0]|} M[i][j]^2}.$$

This method relies on three key facts:

F1. $\sqrt{||M^T M||_{op}} = ||M||_{op}$.
F2. $||M||_{op} \leq ||M||_F$ for any real matrix M.
F3. As i increases, $||M_i||_F$ approaches $||M_i||_{op}$.

ghost fun *OpNorm*(M : **Matrix**) : (r : **real**)

   ensures $r \geq 0 \wedge$

   ($\forall v \in$ **Vector** . $|v| = Cols(M) \implies L2(MVProduct(M, v)) \leq r \cdot L2(v)) \wedge$

   $\neg \exists x \in$ **real** . $0 \leq x < r \wedge \forall v \in$ **Vector** . $|v| = Cols(M)$

      $\implies L2(MVProduct(M, v)) \leq x \cdot L2(v)$

Fig. 5. Defining operator norms in Dafny.

Gram iteration works by repeatedly taking the Gram matrix of M, as in (5), and then computing its Frobenius norm, which, due to fact **F2**, is an upper bound on its operator norm, but due to fact **F3**, is a very close approximation. Due to fact **F1**, we can then derive an upper bound on the operator norm of M by taking the square root n times. To enable verification, we encode facts **F1** and **F2** as axiomatic assumptions in Dafny.

Naively applying recurrence (5) quickly leads to having to compute matrix multiplication on very large numbers. Therefore, our implementation normalises the result on each iteration by dividing by the Frobenius norm and then truncating the result to 16 decimal places. Dividing by the Frobenius norm has a predictable impact on the matrix's operator norm, since $||M||_{op} \leq ||\frac{M}{x}||_{op} \cdot x$ for all $x > 0$. Truncation necessarily introduces errors into the resulting estimate of the matrix's operator norm. However, we can track and bound the error introduced. For a matrix M, let $Truncate(M)$ denote its truncation and define $E = M - Truncate(M)$ be the *error* introduced by truncation. Then, by Weyl's inequality, when M is a square, symmetric matrix (as all $M^T M$ are), we have $|\ ||M||_{op} - ||Truncate(M)||_{op}\ | \leq ||E||_{op}$ (since the operator norm is also the matrix's largest eigenvalue). Thus $||M||_{op} \leq ||Truncate(M)||_{op} + ||E||_{op}$. So, each Gram iteration computes

$$M_{i+1} = Truncate\left(\frac{M_i^T M_i}{||M_i^T M_i||_F}\right)$$

and we have $||M_i||_{op} \leq \sqrt{r_{i+1} \cdot (||M_{i+1}||_{op} + ||E_{i+1}||_{op})}$ where $r_{i+1} = ||M_i^T M_i||_F$ and $E_{i+1} = \left(\frac{M_i^T M_i}{||M_i^T M_i||_F}\right) - Truncate\left(\frac{M_i^T M_i}{||M_i^T M_i||_F}\right)$.

Our verified Dafny implementation of Gram iteration appears in Fig. 6.

This method accepts a matrix M and a natural number n which determines the number of iterations to apply. The return value r is verified to be an upper bound on the operator norm $OpNorm(M)$ as we have defined it in Dafny (as specified by the **ensures** postcondition annotation). For n iterations, the algorithm repeatedly redefines M to be its own Gram matrix, with normalisation and truncation as described above (taking care to avoid division by zero during normalisation). The implementation uses a specialised, optimised routine $MTM(M)$ for calculating $MMProduct(Transpose(M), M)$ (explained in the extended version [32]).

Returning to Fig. 6, the sequence a tracks quantities r and e corresponding to the scaling factor and error upper bound introduced by normalisation and truncation respectively. The return-variable ret is then set to a verified upper bound

method *GramIteration*(M : **Matrix**, n : **nat**) : (*ret* : **real**)
  ensures $ret \geq OpNorm(M)$
{
  var $i := 0$
  var $a := []$
  while $i \neq n$ {
    $M' := MTM(M)$
    $r := $ **if** $IsZeroMatrix(M')$ **then** 1 **else** $FrobeniusNormUpperBound(M')$
    $M, E := TruncateWithError(MatrixDiv(M', r))$
    $a := [(r, FrobeniusNormUpperBound(E)] + a$
    $i := i + 1$
  }
  $ret := FrobeniusNormUpperBound(M)$
  $ret := Expand(a, ret)$
}

function *Expand*(a : [(**real**, **real**)], v : **real**) **returns real**
  $Expand([], v) = v$
  $Expand((r, e) : a, v) = Expand(a, SqrtUpperBound(r \cdot (v + e)))$

Fig. 6. Gram iteration in Dafny. For an element x and sequence xs, we write $x : xs$ to denote the sequence whose head is x and whose tail is xs.

of the Frobenius norm of M, from which the verified upper bound of the operator norm is then computed by using the r and e terms to *expand* this quantity, via the *Expand* function. That function makes use of the *SqrtUpperBound* function for deriving upper bounds on square roots, discussed in the next section.

7 Generating Positive Square Roots

To derive upper bounds on square roots we implement a version of Heron's method (aka the Babylonian method), shown in Fig. 7. This is an ancient algorithm for deriving square roots, whose correctness proof is relatively straightforward and is guaranteed to generate an upper bound.

Our loop maintains the invariant $r \geq Sqrt(x)$, which holds upon entry due to the preceding ternary assignment to r. We then iterate until the desired precision is attained, or the maximum number of iterations is reached. These parameters are encoded as the global constants $SQRT\_ERR$ and $SQRT\_ITERATIONS$ (in our current implementation 10^{-11} and 2×10^6 respectively).

```
method SqrtUpperBound(x : real) : (r : real)
  requires x ≥ 0
  ensures Sqrt(x) ≤ r
{
  if x = 0 {
    return 0
  }
  r := if x < 1 then 1 else x
  i := 0
  while i < SQRT_ITERATIONS {
    r₀ := r
    r := (r + x/r)/2
    i := i + 1
    if r₀ - r ≤ SQRT_ERR {
      return r
    }
  }
  print "Warning: Sqrt algorithm terminated early."
}
```

Fig. 7. Heron's method for computing square root upper bounds in Dafny.

8   Applying the Certifier

After neural network training, our certifier is applied to compute safe Lipschitz bounds once-and-for-all. It is then repeatedly applied, having computed those bounds, to certify individual model outputs. The time required to certify each output vector v' is linear in the vector's length $|v'|$ and cheap: in the worst case it requires less than $2|v'|$ loads, $5|v'|$ comparisons, and $|v'|$ negations, subtractions, and multiplications each (Fig. 4), where each of these operations is performed over arbitrary-precision rationals (to which Dafny's **real**s are compiled). In practice, this means each individual output point requires approx. 8 milliseconds to certify (including text parsing, I/O and printing), *independent of the model size*. Alternative approaches report median certification times per individual output of anywhere from 10 milliseconds to 7.3 s [9, Table 2] on comparable models to those that we consider below.

Therefore, we seek to understand (1) to what degree our certifier computes useful (not too conservative) Lipschitz bounds, (2) how much computation is required to do so, and (3) whether it can be usefully applied. All reported experiments were carried out on a 2021 MacBook Pro (Model "MacBookPro18,3", 8 core Apple M1 Pro, 16 GB RAM, MacOS 15.2).

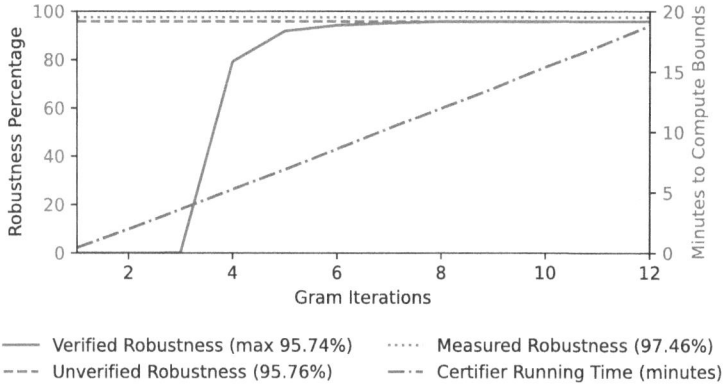

Fig. 8. Certifier performance on globally robust MNIST model ($\epsilon = 0.3$).

8.1 Certifier Performance

Figure 8 depicts performance results for our certifier, measuring the usefulness of the bounds it computes and the time required to compute them, for different numbers of Gram iterations (parameter n in Fig. 6). We evaluated this against a dense ReLU MNIST [19] model that comprises 8 hidden layers, each with 128 neurons. We note that this model has a comparable number of neurons to, and significantly more layers than, the MNIST models evaluated in Kabaha et al.'s recent work on verified global robustness properties [15] (discussed later in Sect. 9). We trained the model using the globally robust training method of Leino et al. [23], using the hyperparameters from the most closely related of their models [23, Table B.2, row 1] as detailed in the extended [32]. The model does not use bias terms (because our certifier specifications do not currently handle non-zero biases; see Sect. 9). Leino et al.'s training method produces a model with an extra output class "⊥" that is output whenever their certification procedure fails (i.e. decides that the model's answer was not robust). After training the model we discard the ⊥ output class to obtain an ordinary dense MNIST ReLU neural network, to which we apply our certifier to compute Lipschitz bounds. That neural network we then apply to the 10,000 MNIST test points, producing 10,000 output vectors. We then apply the certifier to those to determine the percentage certified robust at perturbation bound $\epsilon = 0.3$. Figure 8 reports this percentage (left axis) plus the time to compute the Lipschitz bounds (right axis).

We see that increasing Gram iterations produce tighter Lipschitz bounds. At 11+ iterations, we certify 95.74% of the 10,000 test points as robust.

To understand the quality of the Lipschitz bounds, we compare the percentage of test points that our verified certifier certifies as robust against the percentage of test points certified robust by Leino et al.'s unverified implementation [23], which we measure directly after training the globally robust model as the percentage of non-⊥ outputs when the model is applied to the 10,000 test points. We denote this measure the model's *Unverified Robustness* in Fig. 8. This percentage (95.76%) is just 0.02% points above that of our certifier.

We also empirically compute an upper bound on the model's true robustness against the 10,000 test points by carrying out various adversarial attacks on the model, including FGSM [11], the Momentum Method [7], and PGD [24], implemented using the Adversarial Robustness Toolbox [28]. For each of the original 10,000 test points x, this gives us a set $\{x'_1, x'_2, \ldots, x'_m\}$ of perturbed points where $||x - x'_i|| \leq \epsilon$. The model's *Measured Robustness* is then the proportion of points x for which *all* of the corresponding $x'_1, x'_2, \ldots, x'_m$ are classified identically to x. Our certifier's safe lower bound on the model's robustness is 1.72% points below this upper bound.

Thus our certifier produces safe robustness certifications that are extremely tight compared to unverified (and potentially unsound) bounds.

Our certifier's performance is linear in the number of Gram iterations, because of the normalisation and truncation applied during each Gram iteration to ensure that the sizes of the quantities involved remain roughly the same.

8.2   Practical Usefulness

Verified Robust Accuracy (VRA) measures the percentage of test points that a trained model correctly classifies and that are also certified robust. Achieving good VRA means that there exist useful models to which our certifier can be usefully applied. VRA also bounds a model's accuracy under ϵ-perturbations [25]. Table 1 summarises statistics for our certifier applied to globally robust models.

We evaluated it against the MNIST model described in Sect. 8.1 as well as against globally robust trained Fashion MNIST [33] and CIFAR-10 [18] models (trained with hyperparameters mimicking those of Leino et al. [23, Table B.2]; see the extended [32]). All of these models are dense models without bias terms and employing only ReLU activations, as required by our certifier. All are comparable in size to, if not significantly larger than, the corresponding models considered by Kabaha et al.'s state-of-the-art work on verified global robustness properties [15].

The resulting MNIST model with our certifier performs very close to the unverified and potentially unsound implementation of Leino et al. [23], with VRA within 0.01% points of their implementation applied to the same model. State-of-the-art (unverified) VRA for MNIST models at $\epsilon = 0.3$ is 95.7% [23] (for convolutional globally robust models employing MinMax [2] activations), which is just 0.3% points higher than what we were able to achieve.

Fashion MNIST is a more challenging machine learning task than MNIST. Our certifier can be usefully applied here as the results in Table 1 indicate. The 12-hidden layer, 1664-hidden neuron globally robust model we trained achieved 89.1% accuracy, which is on par with the accuracy typically achieved by (non-globally robust) Dense ReLU Fashion MNIST models [10]. At 12 g iterations our certifier was able to compute very useful Lipschitz bounds in just 20 min. Its safe robustness lower bound of 83.65% at $\epsilon = 0.25$ was within 0.05% points of that computed by Leino et al.'s unverified implementation. The resulting model and our certifier together achieved 79.54% VRA, just 0.03% points below the unverified estimate and 6% points *above* the (to our knowledge) best prior VRA for Fashion MNIST models at $\epsilon = 0.25$ [9].

CIFAR-10 is a more difficult image classification task than Fashion MNIST. We trained a 1536-hidden neuron model, whose first two hidden layers had 512 and 256 neurons respectively, to account for this extra difficulty. This model has twice the layers and 2.3× the neurons of the CIFAR-10 model considered by Kabaha et al. [15]. The accuracy of the resulting model was 57.7%, which is approx. 30% points lower than the most advanced globally robust CIFAR-10 models [13]. Even so, the increased size of this model's inputs ($\sim 4\times$ larger than for Fashion MNIST) means that our certifier takes hours rather than minutes to compute tight Lipschitz bounds. At 12 g iterations, the resulting VRA we obtain for $\epsilon = 0.141$ is 35.95%, which is just 0.22% points below that computed by Leino et al.'s unverified implementation. It is also ∼9% points *higher* than the (to our knowledge) best previously reported formally verified VRA for a CIFAR-10 model at $\epsilon = 0.1$ [9]. However, state-of-the-art (unverified) VRA for advanced CIFAR-10 models at $\epsilon = 0.141$ is 78.1% [13], which suggests that dense ReLU models may not have sufficient capacity to be trained to be both accurate and globally robust for CIFAR-10.

We conclude that our certifier can be practically applied to machine learning tasks for which dense ReLU robust models can be trained.

Table 1. Applying the certifier. *Hidden Neurons* describes the dense model architecture: $k \times [n]$ denotes k hidden layers, each with n neurons. The list $[n_1, n_2, \ldots, n_k]$ denotes k hidden layers where the ith hidden layer has n_i neurons. We use $+$ to denote composition of hidden layers. ϵ is the perturbation bound at which robustness was certified over the test set. *Gram* is the number of Gram iterations. *Time* is the time for our certifier to compute Lipschitz bounds. *VRA* is Verified Robust Accuracy. $y\%$ (-x) denotes percentage value y obtained from our certifier, which is x percentage points below the unverified estimate computed by Leino et al.'s implementation [23].

Dataset	Hidden Neurons	Accuracy	ϵ	Gram	Time (hh:mm:ss)	Verified Robustness	VRA
MNIST	$8 \times [128]$	98.4%	0.3	11	0:17:02	95.74% (−0.02)	95.40%(−0.01)
FashionMNIST	$[256]+$ $11 \times [128]$	89.1%	0.25	12	0:20:08	83.65% (−0.05)	79.54%(−0.03)
CIFAR-10	$[512, 256]+$ $6 \times [128]$	57.7%	0.141	12	19:02:32	46.12% (−0.30)	35.95%(−0.22)

9   Related and Future Work

In contrast to our approach, prior work on formally verified robustness guarantees for neural networks focuses on symbolic reasoning over the neural network itself [16,30] (see e.g. [26] for a survey). This has the disadvantage that the complexity of the symbolic reasoning scales with the size of the neural network.

Most of this work focuses on verifying local robustness, and requiring symbolic reasoning for each point that is to be certified. Like ours, the recent work of Kabaha et al. [15] instead focuses on verifying a global robustness property. Our work considers l_2 global robustness whereas Kabaha et al. consider instead a specialised robustness property, parameterised by an input perturbation function, that considers the robustness of a specific output class relative to the model's confidence about that class. Kabaha et al. employ mixed-integer programming and, like other approaches that also reason symbolically over the model, suffers similar symbolic scalability challenges [16, 26, 30].

Our approach in contrast avoids this symbolic scalability problem entirely. It is influenced by ideas from the field of formally verified *certifying computation* [1, 29]: rather than trying to formally verify a complex algorithm, we instead write and formally verify a checker that certifies the outputs of that algorithm. Thus symbolic reasoning complexity no longer scales with the size of the neural network but rather with the complexity of the certification program. In our case, we base our certifier on ideas from globally-robust neural networks [23], which we augment with sound methods for computing Lipschitz bounds [6], and all of which we formally verify in Dafny for the first time.

Our certifier's current implementation handles a relatively simple class of neural networks, namely dense feed-forward networks that use only the ReLU activation function. It also does not currently handle biases, but extending it to do so would be straightforward by extending our specification of neural network application *ApplyNN* (Sect. 4.2). We might be able to further improve our certifier's running time to compute Lipschitz bounds by avoiding compiling Dafny's **real**s to arbitrary precision rationals, instead compiling them to sound interval arithmetic [3]. Even so, our certifier is still usefully applicable (Sect. 8).

Extending it to convolutional neural nets may be possible in future, leveraging ideas of [6, 23]. A more interesting limitation of our approach relates to the top-level robustness specification (Sect. 4), which encodes neural network application with real-valued arithmetic. In reality, the neural network implementation will of course use floating point arithmetic [14]. Closing this gap is a key avenue for future research, where we might leverage deductive verification approaches to bounding floating point error [8].

Acknowledgements. Work supported by the joint CATCH MURI-AUSMURI.

Disclosure of Interests. The authors have no competing interests to declare that are relevant to the content of this article.

References

1. Alkassar, E., Böhme, S., Mehlhorn, K., Rizkallah, C.: Verification of certifying computations. In: Gopalakrishnan, G., Qadeer, S. (eds.) CAV 2011. LNCS, vol. 6806, pp. 67–82. Springer, Heidelberg (2011). https://doi.org/10.1007/978-3-642-22110-1_7

2. Anil, C., Lucas, J., Grosse, R.: Sorting out Lipschitz function approximation. In: International Conference on Machine Learning (ICML), pp. 291–301. PMLR (2019)
3. Brucker, A.D., Cameron-Burke, T., Stell, A.: Formally verified interval arithmetic and its application to program verification. In: Proceedings of the 2024 IEEE/ACM 12th International Conference on Formal Methods in Software Engineering (FormaliSE), pp. 111–121 (2024)
4. Chudnov, A., et al.: Continuous formal verification of amazon s2n. In: Chockler, H., Weissenbacher, G. (eds.) CAV 2018. LNCS, vol. 10982, pp. 430–446. Springer, Cham (2018). https://doi.org/10.1007/978-3-319-96142-2_26
5. Cohen, J., Rosenfeld, E., Kolter, Z.: Certified adversarial robustness via randomized smoothing. In: International Conference on Machine Learning (ICML), pp. 1310–1320. PMLR (2019)
6. Delattre, B., Barthélemy, Q., Araujo, A., Allauzen, A.: Efficient bound of Lipschitz constant for convolutional layers by Gram iteration. In: International Conference on Machine Learning (ICML), pp. 7513–7532. PMLR (2023)
7. Dong, Y., Liao, F., Pang, T., Su, H., Zhu, J., Hu, X., Li, J.: Boosting adversarial attacks with momentum. In: Proceedings of the IEEE Conference on Computer Vision and Pattern Recognition (CVPR), pp. 9185–9193 (2018)
8. Dross, C., Kanig, J.: Making proofs of floating-point programs accessible to regular developers. In: International Workshop on Numerical Software Verification, pp. 7–24. Springer, Heidelberg (2021). https://doi.org/10.1007/978-3-030-95561-8_2
9. Fromherz, A., Leino, K., Fredrikson, M., Parno, B., Pasareanu, C.S.: Fast geometric projections for local robustness certification. In: International Conference on Learning Representations (ICLR). OpenReview.net (2021). https://openreview.net/forum?id=zWy1uxjDdZJ
10. GitHub user vanajac: Hyperas on fashion-mnist - hyperparameter tuning for dense networks (2021). https://github.com/vanajac/fashion_mnist/blob/main/fashionMNIST.ipynb
11. Goodfellow, I.J., Shlens, J., Szegedy, C.: Explaining and harnessing adversarial examples. In: International Conference on Learning Representations (ICLR) (2015)
12. Gouk, H., Frank, E., Pfahringer, B., Cree, M.J.: Regularisation of neural networks by enforcing Lipschitz continuity. Mach. Learn. **110**(2), 393–416 (2021). https://doi.org/10.1007/S10994-020-05929-W
13. Hu, K., Leino, K., Wang, Z., Fredrikson, M.: A recipe for improved certifiable robustness. In: International Conference on Learning Representations (ICLR) (2024)
14. Jin, J., Ohrimenko, O., Rubinstein, B.I.: Getting a-round guarantees: floating-point attacks on certified robustness. In: Proceedings of the 2024 Workshop on Artificial Intelligence and Security, pp. 53–64 (2024)
15. Kabaha, A., Cohen, D.D.: Verification of neural networks' global robustness. Proc. ACM Program. Lang. **8**(OOPSLA1), 1010–1039 (2024)
16. Katz, G., Barrett, C., Dill, D.L., Julian, K., Kochenderfer, M.J.: Reluplex: an efficient SMT solver for verifying deep neural networks. In: Majumdar, R., Kunčak, V. (eds.) CAV 2017. LNCS, vol. 10426, pp. 97–117. Springer, Cham (2017). https://doi.org/10.1007/978-3-319-63387-9_5
17. Klein, G., et al.: Comprehensive formal verification of an OS microkernel. ACM Trans. Comput. Syst. (TOCS) **32**(1), 1–70 (2014)
18. Krizhevsky, A.: Learning multiple layers of features from tiny images. University of Toronto, Technical report (2009)
19. LeCun, Y., Bottou, L., Bengio, Y., Haffner, P.: Gradient-based learning applied to document recognition. Proc. IEEE **86**(11), 2278–2324 (1998)

20. Lecuyer, M., Atlidakis, V., Geambasu, R., Hsu, D., Jana, S.: Certified robustness to adversarial examples with differential privacy. In: IEEE Symposium on Security and Privacy, pp. 656–672. IEEE (2019)
21. Lee, S., Lee, J., Park, S.: Lipschitz-certifiable training with a tight outer bound. Adv. Neural Inf. Process. Syst. (NeurIPS) **33**, 16891–16902 (2020)
22. Leino, K.: Dafny: an automatic program verifier for functional correctness. In: Clarke, E.M., Voronkov, A. (eds.) LPAR 2010. LNCS (LNAI), vol. 6355, pp. 348–370. Springer, Heidelberg (2010). https://doi.org/10.1007/978-3-642-17511-4_20
23. Leino, K., Wang, Z., Fredrikson, M.: Globally-robust neural networks. In: International Conference on Machine Learning (ICML). Proceedings of Machine Learning Research, vol. 139, pp. 6212–6222. PMLR (2021). http://proceedings.mlr.press/v139/leino21a.html
24. Madry, A., Makelov, A., Schmidt, L., Tsipras, D., Vladu, A.: Towards deep learning models resistant to adversarial attacks. In: International Conference on Learning Representations (ICLR) (2018)
25. Mangal, R., et al.: Is certifying ℓ_p robustness still worthwhile? arXiv preprint arXiv:2310.09361 (2023)
26. Meng, M.H., et al.: Adversarial robustness of deep neural networks: a survey from a formal verification perspective. IEEE Trans. Depend. Secure Comput. (2022)
27. Murray, T., et al.: seL4: from general purpose to a proof of information flow enforcement. In: IEEE Symposium on Security and Privacy, pp. 415–429. IEEE (2013)
28. Nicolae, M.I., et al.: Adversarial Robustness Toolbox v1.0.0. arXiv preprint arXiv:1807.01069 (2018)
29. Rizkallah, C.: Verification of Program Computations. Ph.D. thesis, Saarland University (2015)
30. Singh, G., Gehr, T., Püschel, M., Vechev, M.: An abstract domain for certifying neural networks. Proc. ACM Program. Lang. **3**(POPL), 1–30 (2019)
31. Szegedy, C.: Intriguing properties of neural networks. arXiv preprint arXiv:1312.6199 (2013)
32. Tobler, J., Syeda, H.T., Murray, T.: A formally verified robustness certifier for neural networks (extended version) (2025). https://arxiv.org/abs/2505.06958
33. Xiao, H., Rasul, K., Vollgraf, R.: Fashion-MNIST: a novel image dataset for benchmarking machine learning algorithms. arXiv preprint arXiv:1708.07747 (2017)

Policy Verification in Stochastic Dynamical Systems Using Logarithmic Neural Certificates

Thom Badings[1,2]($\boxtimes$) , Wietze Koops[2,3,4], Sebastian Junges[2],
and Nils Jansen[2,5]

^{1} University of Oxford, Oxford, UK
thom.badings@cs.ox.ac.uk
^{2} Radboud University, Nijmegen, The Netherlands
^{3} Lund University, Lund, Sweden
^{4} University of Copenhagen, Copenhagen, Denmark
^{5} Ruhr-University Bochum, Bochum, Germany

Abstract. We consider the verification of neural network policies for discrete-time stochastic systems with respect to reach-avoid specifications. We use a learner-verifier procedure that learns a certificate for the specification, represented as a neural network. Verifying that this neural network certificate is a so-called reach-avoid supermartingale (RASM) proves the satisfaction of a reach-avoid specification. Existing approaches for such a verification task rely on computed Lipschitz constants of neural networks. These approaches struggle with large Lipschitz constants, especially for reach-avoid specifications with high threshold probabilities. We present two key contributions to obtain smaller Lipschitz constants than existing approaches. First, we introduce logarithmic RASMs (logRASMs), which take exponentially smaller values than RASMs and hence have lower theoretical Lipschitz constants. Second, we present a fast method to compute tighter upper bounds on Lipschitz constants based on weighted norms. Our empirical evaluation shows we can consistently verify the satisfaction of reach-avoid specifications with probabilities as high as 99.9999%.

1 Introduction

Feed-forward neural networks are widely used in reinforcement learning (RL) to represent policies for autonomous control systems operating in continuous and nonlinear environments [41,63,75]. To deploy such policies in safety-critical domains, it is crucial to provide guarantees about their (closed-loop) behavior [13]. The development of techniques that provide such guarantees is an ongoing research effort [37]. In this paper, we study (nonlinear) stochastic dynamical systems, which are ubiquitous in control theory [21,59] and AI [20,28] for modeling control tasks in uncertain environments. The operational model of such a

---

T. Badings and W. Koops—Equal contribution.

R. Piskac and Z. Rakamarić (Eds.): CAV 2025, LNCS 15932, pp. 349–375, 2025.
https://doi.org/10.1007/978-3-031-98679-6_16

discrete-time stochastic system (DTSS) is a Markov decision process (MDP) with a continuous state and action space, and with the transition function defined by stochastic difference equations. We aim to prove that a *reach-avoid specification* is satisfied, i.e., that the probability of reaching a set of goal states without visiting unsafe states is above some threshold [82]. More precisely, we study the following verification problem (see Fig. 1): Given a DTSS and a neural network policy for this DTSS, check whether the policy satisfies a given reach-avoid specification.

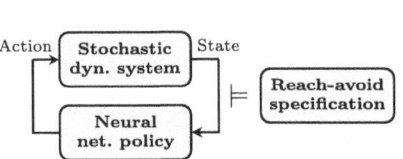

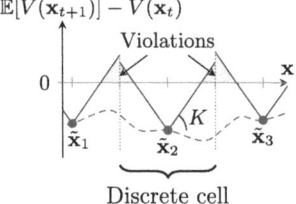

Fig. 1. We verify that a neural network policy deployed on a DTSS satisfies a reach-avoid specification.

Fig. 2. The verifier computes the expected decrease of a candidate RASM V on discrete states $\tilde{\mathbf{x}}_i$ and uses a Lipschitz constant K to generalize to all other states.

Certificate Functions. We follow the common paradigm of *verification by finding a certificate.* A certificate is a function satisfying conditions such that its *existence* implies satisfaction of a specification. Classical certificates include ranking functions [46] (to prove termination in program loops [25,71]) and Lyapunov functions (to prove stability in non-stochastic systems [59]). In this paper, we build upon ranking supermartingales [29,45], specifically *reach-avoid supermartingale* (RASM) certificates for DTSSes [95]. A RASM is a function from the system's states to real values which (among other conditions) must decrease *in expectation* at every step under the DTSS's dynamics. Hence, a RASM induces a *supermartingale* [72,89]. The existence of a RASM proves the satisfaction of a reach-avoid specification. Standard approaches to finding certificates mostly use optimization over restrictive templates, e.g., low-degree polynomials [77,81]. Thus, we follow the recent trend of representing certificates as neural networks instead [2,30,76,90,94] (collectively called *neural certificates* [38]).

Learner-Verifier Framework. An effective method to learn a RASM is to use a counterexample-guided framework as in Fig. 3. Such a framework iterates between (1) a *learner* that trains a neural network as a candidate certificate and (2) a *verifier* that either proves the validity of the candidate or returns counterexamples that disprove that the candidate is a RASM [3,31]. We initialize the learner with a policy (without guarantees) learned from any common RL algorithm. Then, the learner trains the neural network certificate and updates the (initial) policy based on counterexamples that it receives from the verifier.

Challenges in Verifying RASMs. Recall that the verifier in Fig. 3 must prove that the candidate RASM decreases in expectation with the DTSS's dynamics.

This *expected decrease condition* is shown by the blue line in Fig. 2, so we must show that this line is strictly negative in every state $\mathbf{x}$. Because the state space is continuous, existing RASM verifiers check conditions on a discretization of the state space (points $\tilde{\mathbf{x}}_1, \tilde{\mathbf{x}}_2, \tilde{\mathbf{x}}_3$ in Fig. 2) and use Lipschitz continuity of the policy and the RASM (with Lipschitz constant K in Fig. 2) to generalize to the entire state space.[1] However, this approach has two main limitations. First, specifications with very high threshold probabilities necessarily require RASMs with infeasibly large Lipschitz constants. Second, computing the (smallest) Lipschitz constant of a neural network exactly is intractable [86], so existing RASM verifiers use loose upper bounds instead. Consequently, applying the framework to safety-critical domains, where high levels of assurance are needed, remains elusive.

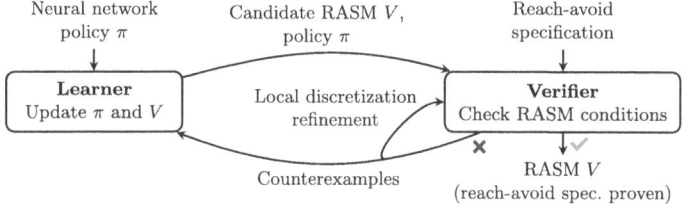

Fig. 3. Overview of the learner-verifier framework for finding a RASM.

Our Approach to Improving RASM Verifiers. In this paper, we propose novel techniques that address these two limitations in verifying RASMs represented as neural networks. Our method can verify reach-avoid specifications with threshold probabilities as high as 99.9999%, which is enabled by two key novel aspects:

1. **Logarithmic RASMs.** Instead of training the neural network to satisfy the RASM conditions from [95], we consider *the logarithm of these conditions.* Like a (standard) RASM, the resulting certificate, which we call a *logarithmic RASM* (or *logRASM*), proves the satisfaction of a reach-avoid specification. A logRASM takes exponentially smaller values than a RASM, leading to a lower theoretical Lipschitz constant of the certificate.
2. **Tighter bounds on Lipschitz constants.** We use *weighted norm systems* instead of standard norms to compute Lipschitz constants for neural networks. In combination with *averaged activation operators* [36], our method leads to significantly tighter global bounds on Lipschitz constants for neural networks. These better Lipschitz constants improve the performance of RASM verifiers without sacrificing the efficiency of the verifier.

We embed our techniques in the learner-verifier framework depicted in Fig. 3. We further accelerate the framework using a local refinement scheme for the verifier that only refines the discretization at points where necessary, similar to ideas

---

[1] For other neural certificates, different verifiers have been used, e.g., using satisfiability modulo theories (SMT) solving, which we discuss in the related work (Sect. 8).

from [14,65]. Specifically, when a discretized point violates the RASM conditions, we can determine if the violation could be mitigated by further refining that point. Following this intuition, we locally refine the discretization while avoiding unnecessary computations in cases where refinement cannot fix violations.

Contributions. In summary, we present novel techniques for verifying neural network policies in stochastic dynamical systems with reach-avoid specifications. Our approach combines the use of logarithmic RASMs as certificates with tighter upper bounds on Lipschitz constants of neural networks. Our experiments confirm that we can verify specifications with probability bounds orders of magnitude higher than the state-of-the-art.

2   Problem Statement

We study discrete-time stochastic (nonlinear dynamical) systems, which can be seen as a concise representation of MDPs with continuous state and action spaces:

Definition 1 (DTSS). *A* discrete-time stochastic system (DTSS) *is a tuple* $\mathcal{S} := \langle \mathcal{X}, \mathcal{X}_0, \mathcal{U}, \mathcal{N}, \mu, f \rangle$*, where* $\mathcal{X} \subseteq \mathbb{R}^d$ *is the (continuous) state space,* $\mathcal{X}_0 \subseteq \mathcal{X}$ *is a set of* initial states*,* $\mathcal{U} \subseteq \mathbb{R}^m$ *is the (continuous) action space,* $\mathcal{N} \subseteq \mathbb{R}^p$ *is the* noise space*,* $\mu \colon \mathcal{B}_\mathcal{N} \to [0,1]$ *is a probability measure* on the Borel σ-algebra $\mathcal{B}_\mathcal{N}$ on $\mathcal{N}$*, and* $f \colon \mathcal{X} \times \mathcal{U} \times \mathcal{N} \to \mathcal{X}$ *is the* transition function*.*

The stochasticity of a DTSS $\mathcal{S}$ is modeled by the probability space $(\mathcal{N}, \mathcal{B}_\mathcal{N}, \mu)$ (see, e.g., [42] for details). The state $\mathbf{x}_t$ of a DTSS is defined recursively over discrete steps $t \in \mathbb{N}_0$ as

$$\mathbf{x}_{t+1} = f(\mathbf{x}_t, \mathbf{u}_t, \omega_t), \quad \mathbf{x}_0 \in \mathcal{X}_0, \tag{1}$$

where $\omega_t \sim \mu$. An execution of the DTSS $\mathcal{S}$ is an infinite sequence $(\mathbf{x}_t, \mathbf{u}_t, \omega_t)_{t \in \mathbb{N}_0}$ of state-action-disturbance triples that satisfy Eq. 1 for all $t \in \mathbb{N}_0$.

Policy. A (memoryless deterministic) policy $\pi \colon \mathcal{X} \to \mathcal{U}$ chooses actions in a DTSS such that $\mathbf{u}_t := \pi(\mathbf{x}_t)$ in Eq. 1. Fixing a policy π and an initial state $\mathbf{x}_0 \in \mathcal{X}_0$ defines an *induced Markov process* in the probability space of all executions [21,73]. We denote the probability measure on this probability space by $\mathbb{P}^\pi_{\mathbf{x}_0}$.

Reach-Avoid Specification. For an induced Markov process, we want to evaluate the probability of reaching a *target set* $\mathcal{X}_T \subseteq \mathcal{X}$ before reaching an *unsafe set* $\mathcal{X}_U \subseteq \mathcal{X}$. Formally, this *reach-avoid probability* $\mathrm{Pr}^\pi_{\mathbf{x}_0}(\mathcal{X}_T, \mathcal{X}_U)$ is defined as

$$\mathrm{Pr}^\pi_{\mathbf{x}_0}(\mathcal{X}_T, \mathcal{X}_U) := \mathbb{P}^\pi_{\mathbf{x}_0}\{\exists t \in \mathbb{N}_0 \,:\, \mathbf{x}_t \in \mathcal{X}_T \wedge (\forall t' \in \{0, \ldots, t\} : \mathbf{x}_{t'} \notin \mathcal{X}_U)\}. \tag{2}$$

Intuitively, $\mathrm{Pr}^\pi_{\mathbf{x}_0}(\mathcal{X}_T, \mathcal{X}_U)$ is the probability that, from initial state $\mathbf{x}_0$, the system eventually reaches $\mathcal{X}_T$ while never reaching $\mathcal{X}_U$ before.

Definition 2 (Reach-avoid specification). *Given a DTSS as in Definition 1 and a policy π, a reach-avoid specification is a triple $\langle \mathcal{X}_T, \mathcal{X}_U, \rho \rangle$ and is satisfied if $\Pr_{\mathbf{x}_0}^{\pi}(\mathcal{X}_T, \mathcal{X}_U) \geq \rho$ for all $\mathbf{x}_0 \in \mathcal{X}_0$.*

Formal Problem. The following verification problem is central to this paper:

Problem 1 (Policy verification). *Given a DTSS $\mathcal{S}$ with a policy π, verify whether the reach-avoid specification $\langle \mathcal{X}_T, \mathcal{X}_U, \rho \rangle$ is satisfied.*

In this paper, we make the following standard assumptions [7,19,59]. These assumptions ensure that the reach-avoid probability is well-defined [21].

Assumption 1. *For a DTSS $\mathcal{S} = \langle \mathcal{X}, \mathcal{X}_0, \mathcal{U}, \mathcal{N}, \mu, f \rangle$, we assume that:*

1. *The transition function f and the policy π are Lipschitz continuous;*
2. *The sets $\mathcal{X}$, $\mathcal{X}_0$, $\mathcal{X}_T$, $\mathcal{X}_U$ and $\mathcal{U}$ are Borel measurable;*
3. *The sets $\mathcal{X}$ and $\mathcal{N}$ are compact (i.e., closed and bounded).*

3   Verifying Reach-Avoid Specifications Using RASMs

In this section, we fix a DTSS $\langle \mathcal{X}, \mathcal{X}_0, \mathcal{U}, \mathcal{N}, \mu, f \rangle$ as in Definition 1, a policy π, and a reach-avoid specification $\langle \mathcal{X}_T, \mathcal{X}_U, \rho \rangle$. We recap the certificate, called a *reach-avoid supermartingale* (RASM), and the verification procedure, proposed by [95] to solve Problem 1. This section deviates from [95] in one aspect (see Remark 1).

Definition 3 (RASM). *A continuous function $V \colon \mathcal{X} \to \mathbb{R}_{\geq 0}$ is a reach-avoid supermartingale* (RASM) *(for a fixed reach-avoid specification) if:*

1. Initial condition: $V(\mathbf{x}) \leq 1$ for all $\mathbf{x} \in \mathcal{X}_0$;
2. Safety condition: $V(\mathbf{x}) \geq \frac{1}{1-\rho}$ for all $\mathbf{x} \in \mathcal{X}_U$;
3. Expected decrease condition: *There exists $\epsilon > 0$ such that for all $\mathbf{x} \in \mathcal{X} \setminus \mathcal{X}_T$ with $V(\mathbf{x}) < \frac{1}{1-\rho}$, we have $\mathbb{E}_{\omega \sim \mu}\left[V(f(\mathbf{x}, \pi(\mathbf{x}), \omega))\right] \leq V(\mathbf{x}) - \epsilon$.*

A RASM V associates each state $\mathbf{x} \in \mathcal{X}$ with a non-negative value and decreases in expectation at every step in the dynamics. To reach an unsafe state from any initial state, the value $V(\mathbf{x}_t)$ needs to increase from at most 1 to at least $\frac{1}{1-\rho}$ along the execution. Since V decreases in expectation with every step, this happens with probability at most $1 - \rho$. This intuitively shows why the existence of a RASM implies that the reach-avoid specification in Problem 1 is satisfied:

Theorem 1 ([95], proof in [16, App. B.2]). *If there exists a RASM for the reach-avoid specification, then this specification is satisfied.*

3.1 Verifying RASMs by Discretization

Since the state space $\mathcal{X}$ is continuous, it is not feasible to check the conditions from Definition 3 on individual points $\mathbf{x} \in \mathcal{X}$. Instead, we check slightly stronger versions of the conditions from Definition 3 on a *discretization* of the state space into rectangular cells. Concretely, for a given *mesh size* $\tau > 0$, define $\mathrm{cell}_{\infty}^{\tau}(\mathbf{x}) = \{\mathbf{x}' : \|\mathbf{x} - \mathbf{x}'\|_{\infty} \leq \tau/d\}$, where $\|\cdot\|_{\infty}$ denotes the ∞-norm and d is the dimension of the state space $\mathcal{X} \subseteq \mathbb{R}^{d}$.[2] We allow different mesh sizes for cells around different centers $\mathbf{x}$. A discretization of $\mathcal{X}$ must cover $\mathcal{X}$ as follows:

Definition 4 (Discretization of $\mathcal{X}$). *A* discretization *of $\mathcal{X}$ is a finite set of points $\widetilde{\mathcal{X}}$ together with a mesh size $\tau_{\tilde{\mathbf{x}}}$ for each $\tilde{\mathbf{x}} \in \widetilde{\mathcal{X}}$ such that for every $\mathbf{x} \in \mathcal{X}$ there exists an $\tilde{\mathbf{x}} \in \widetilde{\mathcal{X}}$ such that $\mathbf{x} \in \mathrm{cell}_{\infty}^{\tau_{\tilde{\mathbf{x}}}}(\tilde{\mathbf{x}})$.*

Lipschitz Constants. To generalize results on a discretization to the full state space, we use Lipschitz continuity (using 1-norms). We say that L_g is a *Lipschitz constant* of a function g if $\|g(x) - g(x')\|_1 \leq L_g \|x - x'\|_1$ for all x, x' in the domain of g. All Lipschitz constants in this paper will be with respect to the 1-norm. Throughout the paper, we write L_f and L_{π} for the Lipschitz constants of the dynamics f and the policy π, respectively.

Conditions on the Discretization. We define a stronger version of the RASM conditions, such that the satisfaction of these stronger conditions on each point $\tilde{\mathbf{x}} \in \widetilde{\mathcal{X}}$ from a discretization of $\mathcal{X}$ implies the satisfaction of the conditions in Definition 3. Toward these conditions, we define for any $\tilde{\mathbf{x}} \in \widetilde{\mathcal{X}}$

$$V_{\min}(\tilde{\mathbf{x}}) = \min_{\mathbf{x} \in \mathrm{cell}_{\infty}^{\tau_{\tilde{\mathbf{x}}}}(\tilde{\mathbf{x}})} V(\mathbf{x}) \quad \text{and} \quad V_{\max}(\tilde{\mathbf{x}}) = \max_{\mathbf{x} \in \mathrm{cell}_{\infty}^{\tau_{\tilde{\mathbf{x}}}}(\tilde{\mathbf{x}})} V(\mathbf{x})$$

as the min/max of V within each $\mathrm{cell}_{\infty}^{\tau_{\tilde{\mathbf{x}}}}(\tilde{\mathbf{x}})$. Computing $V_{\min}(\tilde{\mathbf{x}})$ and $V_{\max}(\tilde{\mathbf{x}})$ analytically is in general not possible, but using interval bound propagation (IBP) [51] we can compute bounds $V_{\mathrm{LB}}(\tilde{\mathbf{x}})$ and $V_{\mathrm{UB}}(\tilde{\mathbf{x}})$ satisfying

$$V_{\mathrm{LB}}(\tilde{\mathbf{x}}) \leq V_{\min}(\tilde{\mathbf{x}}) \leq V(\tilde{\mathbf{x}}) \leq V_{\max}(\tilde{\mathbf{x}}) \leq V_{\mathrm{UB}}(\tilde{\mathbf{x}})$$

for all $\tilde{\mathbf{x}} \in \widetilde{\mathcal{X}}$. These bounds obtained from IBP are generally tighter than those computed using Lipschitz constants.

Discrete RASM. Concretely, the satisfaction of the conditions in Definition 3 is then implied by the following conditions on the discretization.

Definition 5 (Discrete RASM). *Let $V : \mathcal{X} \rightarrow \mathbb{R}_{\geq 0}$ be Lipschitz continuous with Lipschitz constant L_V. Let[3] $K = L_V L_f (L_{\pi} + 1)$ and let $\widetilde{\mathcal{X}}$ be a discretization with a mesh size $\tau_{\tilde{\mathbf{x}}}$ for each $\tilde{\mathbf{x}} \in \widetilde{\mathcal{X}}$. Then, V is a discrete RASM for $\widetilde{\mathcal{X}}$ if:*

1. Initial condition: $V_{\mathrm{UB}}(\tilde{\mathbf{x}}) \leq 1$ for all $\tilde{\mathbf{x}} \in \widetilde{\mathcal{X}}$ with $\mathrm{cell}_{\infty}^{\tau_{\tilde{\mathbf{x}}}}(\tilde{\mathbf{x}}) \cap \mathcal{X}_0 \neq \emptyset$.

---

[2] We divide by d in the definition of $\mathrm{cell}_{\infty}^{\tau}(\mathbf{x})$ to ensure that $\|\mathbf{x} - \mathbf{x}'\|_1 \leq \tau$ for all $\mathbf{x}' \in \mathrm{cell}_{\infty}^{\tau}(\mathbf{x})$, which we need later in Definition 5.

[3] In our implementation, we use a slightly improved definition of K; see [16, App. A.1].

2. Safety condition: $V_{\mathrm{LB}}(\tilde{\mathbf{x}}) \geq \frac{1}{1-\rho}$ for all $\tilde{\mathbf{x}} \in \widetilde{\mathcal{X}}$ with $\mathrm{cell}_\infty^{\tau_{\tilde{\mathbf{x}}}}(\tilde{\mathbf{x}}) \cap \mathcal{X}_U \neq \emptyset$.
3. Expected decrease condition:

$$\mathbb{E}_{\omega \sim \mu}\left[V(f(\tilde{\mathbf{x}}, \pi(\tilde{\mathbf{x}}), \omega))\right] < V_{\mathrm{LB}}(\tilde{\mathbf{x}}) - \tau_{\tilde{\mathbf{x}}} K \tag{3}$$

for all $\tilde{\mathbf{x}} \in \widetilde{\mathcal{X}}$ with $\mathrm{cell}_\infty^{\tau_{\tilde{\mathbf{x}}}}(\tilde{\mathbf{x}}) \cap (\mathcal{X} \setminus \mathcal{X}_T) \neq \emptyset$ and $V_{\mathrm{LB}}(\tilde{\mathbf{x}}) < \frac{1}{1-\rho}$.

Remark 1. We deviate slightly from [95], which instead uses $V(\tilde{\mathbf{x}}) - \tau(K + L_V)$ on the right-hand side of Eq. 3. Since IBP usually gives tighter bounds than Lipschitz continuity, our version of Eq. 3 is (slightly) easier to satisfy.

Verifying the conditions in Definition 5 is sufficient to show that V is a RASM:

Lemma 1 (proof in [16, App. B.3]). *Every discrete RASM is also a RASM.*

Computing the expected value in Eq. 3 exactly is generally infeasible. Instead, we bound this expectation from above by discretizing the noise space $\mathcal{N}$ into a collection of cells $\mathcal{C}$ (which is possible since $\mathcal{N}$ is compact), such that $\mathbb{E}_{\omega \sim \mu}\left[V(f(\tilde{\mathbf{x}}, \pi(\tilde{\mathbf{x}}), \omega))\right] \leq \sum_{C \in \mathcal{C}} \mathbb{P}(\omega \in C) \sup_{\omega \in C}\left[V(f(\tilde{\mathbf{x}}, \pi(\tilde{\mathbf{x}}), \omega))\right]$, where we again use IBP to upper bound $\sup_{\omega \in C}\left[V(f(\tilde{\mathbf{x}}, \pi(\tilde{\mathbf{x}}), \omega))\right]$ for each cell $C \in \mathcal{C}$.

Shape of a Discrete RASM. Finally, we make some remarks about the typical shape of a discrete RASM V, especially in the context where we try to minimize its Lipschitz constant K (to speed up verification). Since V is Lipschitz continuous, it is differentiable almost everywhere. Recall that the negative gradient vector $-\nabla V$ points in the direction that V decreases fastest. Due to the expected decrease condition, $-\nabla V$ will therefore typically roughly point in the direction the state moves under the dynamics. Moreover, since the expected decrease condition requires a fixed decrease of $\tau_{\tilde{\mathbf{x}}} K$, the slope $\|\nabla V\|$ will be roughly constant, at least in regions where the step size under the dynamics is roughly constant.

3.2   Challenges in Verifying RASMs

The existing verification procedure based on the discrete RASM conditions in Definition 5 is generally conservative and computationally expensive. The scalability of the procedure is especially limited by the large Lipschitz constant L_V of any RASM. Concretely, the initial condition in Definition 3 requires a value of at least $\frac{1}{1-\rho}$ in all $\mathbf{x} \in \mathcal{X}_U$, while the safety condition requires a value of at most 1 in all $\mathbf{x} \in \mathcal{X}_0$. Thus, these conditions on the RASM imply that

$$L_V \geq \frac{1}{\mathrm{dist}(\mathcal{X}_0, \mathcal{X}_U)}\left(\frac{1}{1-\rho} - 1\right),$$

where $\mathrm{dist}(\mathcal{X}_0, \mathcal{X}_U) = \inf_{(\mathbf{x}_0, \mathbf{x}_u) \in \mathcal{X}_0 \times \mathcal{X}_U} \|\mathbf{x}_0 - \mathbf{x}_u\|_1$ is the smallest distance between an initial and an unsafe state. Since a large L_V leads to a large K, verifying the conditions in Definition 5 requires a fine discretization (i.e., a discretization with small mesh size τ), which is hence computationally expensive.

Moreover, a higher L_V is required for specifications with a higher threshold probability ρ.

The limitations of large Lipschitz constants are exacerbated since the RASM V and policy π are neural networks. In particular, computing the (smallest) Lipschitz constant of a neural network exactly is intractable [86]. Hence, approaches such as [95] use loose upper bounds on these Lipschitz constants instead.

Concretely, our key contributions address these challenges by (1) taking the logarithm of the RASM conditions (Sect. 4), which reduces the lower bound on L_V to $\frac{1}{\text{dist}(\mathcal{X}_0, \mathcal{X}_U)} \log\left(\frac{1}{1-\rho}\right)$, and (2) computing tighter bounds on the Lipschitz constant of neural networks (Sect. 5).

4   Logarithmic RASMs

We now turn to our first main contribution, which is proposing the notion of *logarithmic RASMs*, and providing a less conservative method for checking that a function is a logarithmic RASM using a discretization. Our starting point is to take the (natural) logarithm of the RASM conditions in Definition 3:

Definition 6 (logRASM). *A continuous function $V : \mathcal{X} \to \mathbb{R}$ is a* logarithmic RASM (logRASM) *if:*

1. Initial condition: $V(\mathbf{x}) \leq 0$ *for all* $\mathbf{x} \in \mathcal{X}_0$;
2. Safety condition: $V(\mathbf{x}) \geq \log\left(\frac{1}{1-\rho}\right)$ *for all* $\mathbf{x} \in \mathcal{X}_U$;
3. Expected decrease condition: *There exists $\epsilon > 0$ such that for all $\mathbf{x} \in \mathcal{X} \setminus \mathcal{X}_T$ with $V(\mathbf{x}) < \log\left(\frac{1}{1-\rho}\right)$, we have $\log \mathbb{E}_{\omega \sim \mu}\left[\exp\left(V(f(\mathbf{x}, \pi(\mathbf{x}), \omega))\right)\right] \leq V(\mathbf{x}) - \epsilon$.*

The exponential of a logRASM is indeed a RASM:

Lemma 2 (proof in [16, App. B.4]). *If V is a logRASM, then $\exp(V)$ is a RASM.*

The threshold of the safety condition Definition 6 is only $\log\left(\frac{1}{1-\rho}\right)$, which is much smaller (and thus easier to satisfy) than $\frac{1}{1-\rho}$ in Definition 3. On the other hand, for the expected decrease condition we now have to bound $\log \mathbb{E}_{\omega \sim \mu}\left[\exp(V(\mathbf{x}_{t+1}))\right]$ in Definition 6, which by Jensen's inequality is always larger than the $\mathbb{E}_{\omega \sim \mu}\left[V(\mathbf{x}_{t+1})\right]$ in Definition 3, and thus the condition of Definition 6 is easier to satisfy. Nevertheless, in practice, the positive effect of the (exponentially) smaller threshold is larger.

Conditions on the Discretization. Next, we show how we can check that a function $V : \mathcal{X} \to \mathbb{R}$ is a logRASM by checking stronger conditions on a discretization.

Definition 7 (Discrete logRASM). *Let $V : \mathcal{X} \to \mathbb{R}$ be Lipschitz continuous with Lipschitz constant L_V. Let $K = L_V L_f (L_\pi + 1)$ and let $\widetilde{\mathcal{X}}$ be a discretization with mesh sizes $\tau_{\tilde{\mathbf{x}}}$. Then, V is a* discrete logRASM *for $\widetilde{\mathcal{X}}$ if the following hold:*

1. Initial condition: $V_{\text{UB}}(\tilde{\mathbf{x}}) \leq 0$ *for all $\tilde{\mathbf{x}} \in \widetilde{\mathcal{X}}$ with $\text{cell}_\infty^{\tau_{\tilde{\mathbf{x}}}}(\tilde{\mathbf{x}}) \cap \mathcal{X}_0 \neq \emptyset$.*

2. Safety condition: $V_{\mathrm{LB}}(\tilde{\mathbf{x}}) \geq \log\left(\frac{1}{1-\rho}\right)$ for all $\tilde{\mathbf{x}} \in \tilde{\mathcal{X}}$ with $\mathrm{cell}_\infty^{\tau\tilde{\mathbf{x}}}(\tilde{\mathbf{x}}) \cap \mathcal{X}_U \neq \emptyset$.
3. Expected decrease condition:

$$\log \mathbb{E}_{\omega \sim \mu}\Big[\exp\big(V(f(\tilde{\mathbf{x}}, \pi(\tilde{\mathbf{x}}), \omega))\big)\Big] < V_{\mathrm{LB}}(\tilde{\mathbf{x}}) - \tau_{\tilde{\mathbf{x}}} K \tag{4}$$

for all $\tilde{\mathbf{x}} \in \tilde{\mathcal{X}}$ such that $\mathrm{cell}_\infty^{\tau\tilde{\mathbf{x}}}(\tilde{\mathbf{x}}) \cap (\mathcal{X} \setminus \mathcal{X}_T) \neq \emptyset$ and $V_{\mathrm{LB}}(\tilde{\mathbf{x}}) < \log\left(\frac{1}{1-\rho}\right)$.

The following theorem is the main result of this section and shows that the existence of a discrete logRASM implies the existence of a RASM.

Theorem 2 (proof in[16, App. B.5]). *If V is a discrete logRASM for a discretization $\tilde{\mathcal{X}}$, then $\exp(V)$ is a RASM.*

We now sketch the proof of Theorem 2. The main difference compared to Lemma 1 lies in the expected decrease condition. To show that Eq. 4 implies the expected decrease condition in Definition 3 for $\exp(V)$, we first note that $V(f(\mathbf{x}, \pi(\mathbf{x}), \omega)) \leq V(f(\tilde{\mathbf{x}}, \pi(\tilde{\mathbf{x}}), \omega)) + \tau_{\tilde{\mathbf{x}}} K$ by Lipschitz continuity. Hence,

$$\begin{aligned}
\mathbb{E}_{\omega \sim \mu}\Big[\exp\big(V(f(\mathbf{x}, \pi(\mathbf{x}), \omega))\big)\Big] &\leq \mathbb{E}_{\omega \sim \mu}\Big[\exp\big(V(f(\tilde{\mathbf{x}}, \pi(\tilde{\mathbf{x}}), \omega)) + \tau_{\tilde{\mathbf{x}}} K\big)\Big] \\
&= e^{\tau_{\tilde{\mathbf{x}}} K} \mathbb{E}_{\omega \sim \mu}\Big[\exp\big(V(f(\tilde{\mathbf{x}}, \pi(\tilde{\mathbf{x}}), \omega))\big)\Big] \\
&< e^{\tau_{\tilde{\mathbf{x}}} K} e^{-\tau_{\tilde{\mathbf{x}}} K} \exp(V_{\mathrm{LB}}(\tilde{\mathbf{x}})) \leq \exp(V(\mathbf{x})).
\end{aligned}$$

Finally, we obtain the $-\epsilon$ in the expected decrease condition from Definition 3 using a compactness argument (see [16, App. B.5]), from which Theorem 2 follows.

The main contribution of Definition 7 and Theorem 2 lies in Eq. 4. Notably, proving that Eq. 4 is sufficient for showing that the expected decrease condition holds effectively exploits the *local* Lipschitz constant of exp, rather than the global Lipschitz constant of $\exp(V)$. Indeed, if we would directly adapt the proof of Lemma 1, we would obtain the condition

$$\mathbb{E}_{\omega \sim \mu}\Big[\exp\big(V(f(\tilde{\mathbf{x}}, \pi(\tilde{\mathbf{x}}), \omega))\big)\Big] < \exp(V_{\mathrm{LB}}(\tilde{\mathbf{x}})) - \tau_{\tilde{\mathbf{x}}} K' \tag{5}$$

where $K' = \frac{1}{1-\rho} K$ is a Lipschitz constant of $\exp(V)$, where we use that we can cap any RASM at $\frac{1}{1-\rho}$. The following lemma shows that our novel condition Eq. 4 is always a weaker (i.e., better) condition than Eq. 5.

Lemma 3 (proof in [16, App. B.6]). *Let $K' = \frac{1}{1-\rho} K > 0$. If $V_{\mathrm{LB}}(\tilde{\mathbf{x}}) < \log\left(\frac{1}{1-\rho}\right)$, then $\exp(V_{\mathrm{LB}}(\tilde{\mathbf{x}})) - \tau_{\tilde{\mathbf{x}}} K' < \exp(V_{\mathrm{LB}}(\tilde{\mathbf{x}}) - \tau_{\tilde{\mathbf{x}}} K)$.*

Example 1. As a concrete example, consider $\rho = 0.9999$, $K' = 20$, and $V_{\mathrm{LB}}(\tilde{\mathbf{x}}) = 5$. Then $\exp(V_{\mathrm{LB}}(\tilde{\mathbf{x}})) - \tau_{\tilde{\mathbf{x}}} K' \approx -51.6 < 145.5 \approx \exp(V_{\mathrm{LB}}(\tilde{\mathbf{x}}) - \tau_{\tilde{\mathbf{x}}} K)$, showing that Eq. 4 is much easier to satisfy than Eq. 5. To obtain a right hand side of 145.5 in Eq. 5 we would require $\tau_{\tilde{\mathbf{x}}} \approx 1.5 \cdot 10^{-5}$. Hence, our new approach allows a discretization that is more than 60 times coarser (in each dimension).

Shape of a Discrete logRASM. Although both a discrete RASM and the exponential of a discrete logRASM yield a RASM, they typically look quite different. Due to the fixed decrease of $\tau_{\tilde{\mathbf{x}}}K$ required by the expected decrease condition (4), also a discrete logRASM generally has a nearly constant slope $\|\nabla V\|$, similarly to a discrete RASM. However, a RASM V' has an exponentially larger Lipschitz constant K and thus an (exponentially) larger slope than a logRASM V. After taking the exponential, the RASM $\exp(V)$ has a similar slope as V' at points where V' and $\exp(V)$ are large, but $\exp(V)$ has a smaller slope at points where V' and $\exp(V)$ are small.

5 Tighter Lipschitz Constants for Neural Networks

Our second main contribution is a novel method to compute tighter Lipschitz constants for feed-forward neural networks. In particular, to obtain tighter *global* Lipschitz constants, we combine the use of *weighted 1-norms* defined by $\|x\| = \sum_i w_i |x_i|$ (for weights $w_i > 0$) with *averaged activation operators* [36].

We first provide some intuition on why using weighted norms leads to tighter Lipschitz constants. For the standard, unweighted norm, the Lipschitz constant provides the same upper bound on the change of a function in each direction. In contrast, weighted norms allow for different bounds in different directions. When composing functions (e.g., different neural network layers), the method with standard norm therefore assumes the same upper bound on the change in all directions, while our method accounts for the upper bound on each individual direction. Since these bounds are generally tighter for all but the maximal direction, our method computes tighter Lipschitz constants.

We consider feed-forward neural networks with linear layers:

Definition 8 (Neural network). *An $(n+1)$-layer (feed-forward) neural network with dimensions m_k $(0 \le k \le n)$ is a sequence of tuples $\mathcal{A} := (\langle A_k, b_k, R_k \rangle)_{k=1}^n$, where $A_k \in \mathbb{R}^{m_k \times m_{k-1}}$ are matrices,[4] $b_k \in \mathbb{R}^{m_k}$ are biases, and $R_k \colon \mathbb{R}^{m_k} \to \mathbb{R}^{m_k}$ are activation functions. The operator $T^{\mathcal{A}} \colon \mathbb{R}^{m_0} \to \mathbb{R}^{m_n}$ corresponding to $\mathcal{A}$ maps x_0 to x_n, where x_k is defined recursively by $x_k = R_k(A_k x_{k-1} + b_k)$ for $1 \le k \le n$.*

Assumption 2. *The Lipschitz constant of each activation function R_k is 1.*

Assumption 2 is satisfied by common activation functions such as ReLU, Softplus, tanh, and sigmoid. It is straightforward to generalize our results to any Lipschitz continuous activation functions, but we do not pursue this here. In the following, we use the notation introduced in Definition 8 for the components of the neural network.

---

[4] We use A rather than the standard W for the matrices of the neural network to avoid confusion with the weights from weighted norms.

5.1   Weighted Norms

A weighted 1-norm of dimension m is a function from $\mathbb{R}^m$ to $\mathbb{R}$ defined by $\|x\| = \sum_{i=1}^{m} w_i \|x_i\|$, where $w \in \mathbb{R}_{>0}^m$. By combining a weighted 1-norm for each layer of a neural network, we obtain a *weight system*.

Definition 9 (Weight system). *A weight system $\mathcal{W}$ for an $(n{+}1)$-layer neural network consists of a weighted 1-norm $\|x\|_{\mathcal{W}}^k = \sum_{i=1}^{m_k} w_i^k |x_i|$ for each layer $0 \leq k \leq n$, where $w^k \in \mathbb{R}_{>0}^{m_k}$ and $\max_i w_i^k = 1$.[5]*

Given weighted norms $\| \cdot \|_{\mathcal{W}}^k$ and $\| \cdot \|_{\mathcal{W}}^\ell$ on $\mathbb{R}^{m_k}$ and $\mathbb{R}^{m_\ell}$, we define the weighted norm for a matrix $M \in \mathbb{R}^{m_\ell \times m_k}$ as $\|M\|_{\mathcal{W}}^{k,\ell} = \sup \left\{ \frac{\|Mx\|_{\mathcal{W}}^\ell}{\|x\|_{\mathcal{W}}^k} \;\middle|\; x \in \mathbb{R}^{m_k}, x \neq 0 \right\}$. The next lemma shows how we compute $\|M\|_{\mathcal{W}}^{k,\ell}$ in practice.

Lemma 4 (proof in [16, App. B.7]). *Let $M \in \mathbb{R}^{m_\ell \times m_k}$ be a matrix with entries M_{ij}. Equip the space $\mathbb{R}^{m_k}$ with the norm $\|x\|_{\mathcal{W}}^k = \sum_{i=1}^{m_k} w_i^k |x_i|$, and the space $\mathbb{R}^{m_\ell}$ with the norm $\|x\|_{\mathcal{W}}^\ell = \sum_{i=1}^{m_\ell} w_i^\ell |x_i|$. Then the corresponding matrix norm satisfies $\|M\|_{\mathcal{W}}^{k,\ell} = \max\limits_{1 \leq j \leq m_k} \left[\frac{1}{w_j^k} \sum_{i=1}^{m_\ell} w_i^\ell |M_{ij}| \right]$.*

We now define the Lipschitz bound of a neural network for a weight system.

Definition 10 (Lipschitz bound). *The Lipschitz bound of a neural network $\mathcal{A}$ for a weight system $\mathcal{W}$ is $L_{\mathcal{A},\mathcal{W}} = \prod_{\ell=1}^{n} \|A_\ell\|_{\mathcal{W}}^{\ell-1,\ell}$.*

The Lipschitz bound $L_{\mathcal{A},\mathcal{W}}$ is indeed a Lipschitz constant of the operator $T^{\mathcal{A}}$:

Lemma 5 (proof in [16, App. B.8]). *Let $\mathcal{W}$ be a weight system. Then $L_{\mathcal{A},\mathcal{W}}$ is a Lipschitz constant of $T^{\mathcal{A}}$, i.e. $\|T^{\mathcal{A}}(x) - T^{\mathcal{A}}(x')\|_{\mathcal{W}}^n \leq L_{\mathcal{A},\mathcal{W}} \|x - x'\|_{\mathcal{W}}^0$ for all $x, x' \in \mathbb{R}^{m_0}$. If additionally $w_i^n = 1$ for all $1 \leq i \leq m_n$, then $L_{\mathcal{A},\mathcal{W}}$ is a Lipschitz constant of $T^{\mathcal{A}}$ for the standard (unweighted) 1-norm, i.e. $\|T^{\mathcal{A}}(x) - T^{\mathcal{A}}(x')\| \leq L_{\mathcal{A},\mathcal{W}} \|x - x'\|$ for all $x, x' \in \mathbb{R}^{m_0}$.*

By choosing the same unweighted norm for each layer, one may recover the Lipschitz bound from [83], which corresponds to the approach presented in [95]. We now show that choosing weights aptly can lead to smaller Lipschitz bounds:

Example 2. Consider a neural network with 3 layers (1 hidden layer), matrices $A_1 = \begin{pmatrix} 4 & -1 \\ -1 & 1 \end{pmatrix}$ and $A_2 = \begin{pmatrix} 1 & 2 \end{pmatrix}$, biases $b_1 = \begin{pmatrix} 0 \\ 0 \end{pmatrix}$ and $b_2 = 0$, and ReLU activation functions. Define a weight system $\mathcal{W}$ by $w_1^0 = 1$, $w_2^0 = \frac{1}{2}$, $w_1^1 = \frac{1}{2}$, $w_2^1 = 1$, and $w_1^2 = 1$. Then Lemma 4 yields $L_{\mathcal{A},\mathcal{W}} = \|A_1\|_{\mathcal{W}}^{0,1} \|A_2\|_{\mathcal{W}}^{1,2} = 3 \cdot 2 = 6$. In contrast, the Lipschitz bound from [83] is $\|A_1\| \|A_2\| = 5 \cdot 2 = 10$. While both approaches compute a bound of 2 corresponding to A_2, our approach using the weighted norms records that the effect of the first neuron is only $w_1^1 = \frac{1}{2}$ times $\|A_2\| = 2$, which in turn yields a tighter bound for A_1, namely 3 instead of

---

[5] We assume w.l.o.g. that the max. weight is 1: we may rescale all weights (and thus the Lipschitz bound).

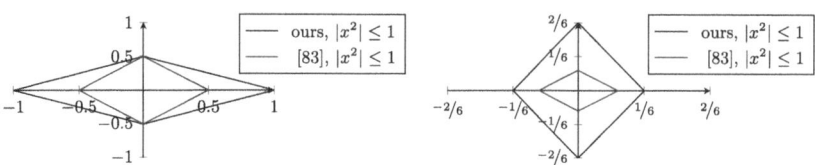

Fig. 4. On the left: The region such that we prove that the input x^1 of the hidden layer maps to output x^2 with $|x^2| \leq 1$. On the right: The region such that the input x^0 maps to output x^2 with $|x^2| \leq 1$. In black: our approach, in red: [83] (Color figure online).

Algorithm 1 Computing optimal weights.

Input: Output weights w^n for output layer n, matrices $A_k \in \mathbb{R}^{m_k \times m_{k-1}}$ $(1 \leq k \leq n)$ as in Def. 8.
Output: Input weights w^0 and a Lipschitz bound K such that (w^0, K) is optimal.
  for $\ell = n, \ldots, 1$ **do**
    $K_\ell \leftarrow \max\limits_{1 \leq j \leq m_{\ell-1}} \sum_{i=1}^{m_\ell} w_i^\ell |(A_\ell)_{ij}|$ ▷ Lipschitz constant $\|A_\ell\|_{\mathcal{W}}^{\ell-1,\ell}$ if $w_j^{\ell-1} = 1$ for all j
    for $j = 1, \ldots, m_{\ell-1}$ **do**
      $w_j^{\ell-1} \leftarrow \frac{1}{K_\ell} \sum_{i=1}^{m_\ell} w_i^\ell |(A_\ell)_{ij}|$ ▷ Smallest weight for which Lipschitz constant is K_ℓ
  return $w^0, \prod_{\ell=1}^{n} K_\ell$ ▷ Return input weights and Lipschitz bound K

---

5. We illustrate these better bounds for each layer in Fig. 4. For the first layer, we only get a better bound for one of the directions, but then using this, we get a better bound for both directions and hence a better Lipschitz constant for the second layer.

Next, we show how to compute a weight system $\mathcal{W}$ such that $L_{\mathcal{A},\mathcal{W}}$ is lowest among all weight systems, for given weights on the output layer.[6] We call such a weight system *optimal*. Observe that the Lipschitz bound decreases when the weights on the input layer increase. This observation motivates the following optimality criterion for weights, which is based on the product of the Lipschitz bound and the weights on the input layer.

Definition 11 (Optimality). *A weight system $\mathcal{W}$ is* optimal *for output weights w^n if the Lipschitz bound satisfies $L_{\mathcal{A},\mathcal{W}} w_j^0 \leq L_{\mathcal{A},\widetilde{\mathcal{W}}} \widetilde{w}_j^0$ for all $1 \leq j \leq m_0$ and all weight systems $\widetilde{\mathcal{W}}$ with output weights w^n, where $\widetilde{w}^0$ are the input weights of $\widetilde{\mathcal{W}}$.*

Lemma 6 (proof in [16, App. B.9]). *If $\mathcal{W}$ is optimal for output weights w^n, then $L_{\mathcal{A},\mathcal{W}} \leq L_{\mathcal{A},\widetilde{\mathcal{W}}}$ for all weight systems $\widetilde{\mathcal{W}}$ with output weights w^n.*

We now explain how Algorithm 1 computes an optimal weight system. Given weights w_i^ℓ for the space $\mathbb{R}^{m_\ell}$, we can set the normalized weights w_j^k in Lemma

---

[6] In practice, we set the weights on the output layer all to 1, since in the end we are interested in Lipschitz bounds for the unweighted 1-norm.

4 proportional to $\sum_{i=1}^{m_\ell} w_i^\ell |M_{ij}|$, which implies that the maximum in Lemma 4 is attained for all $1 \leq j \leq m_k$. Algorithm 1 starts from given output weights w_i^n and iteratively computes weights $w_j^{\ell-1}$ given weights w_i^ℓ in this way. Then the maximum in Lemma 4 is attained by all $1 \leq j \leq m_{\ell-1}$ for the matrix $M = A_\ell$.

Theorem 3 (Correctness of Algorithm 1; proof in [16, App. B.10]). *Let output weights w^n be given. Then the weights w_j^ℓ computed using Algorithm 1 are optimal for output weights w^n.*

In practice, we set the output weights $w_i^n = 1$ for all i. Then Algorithm 1 computes a Lipschitz constant of $T^{\mathcal{A}}$ for the unweighted 1-norm, cf. Lemma 5.

5.2   Averaged Activation Operators

Next, we explain how to combine weighted norms with *averaged activation operators* [18,36] to compute even tighter Lipschitz constants. Let $L_{T^{\mathcal{A}}}$ denote the Lipschitz constant of the neural network operator $T^{\mathcal{A}}$.

Definition 12. *An α-averaged activation operator $(0 < \alpha < 1)$ is an operator $R \colon \mathbb{R} \to \mathbb{R}$ that satisfies $R = (1-\alpha)\mathrm{Id} + \alpha Q$ for some $Q \colon \mathbb{R} \to \mathbb{R}$ with Lipschitz constant 1 and identity function Id.*

Since $\mathrm{ReLU}(x) = \frac{1}{2}x + \frac{1}{2}|x|$, the ReLU is $\frac{1}{2}$-averaged. For simplicity, we only use $\frac{1}{2}$-averaged activation operators. We extend a result of [36] to weighted norms:

Theorem 4 (proof in [16, App. B.11]). *Consider an $(n+1)$-layer network with $\frac{1}{2}$-averaged activation operators R_k. Let $\mathcal{W}$ be a corresponding weight system. Let $S_n = \{(k_1, k_2, \ldots, k_r) \in \mathbb{N}_0^r \mid 0 \leq r \leq n-1, 1 \leq k_1 < k_2 < \cdots < k_r \leq n-1\}$. Then, the Lipschitz constant $L_{T^{\mathcal{A}}}$ of the neural network operator $T^{\mathcal{A}}$ satisfies*

$$L_{T^{\mathcal{A}}} \leq \frac{1}{2^{n-1}} \sum_{(k_1, k_2, \ldots, k_r) \in S_n} \left[\prod_{\ell=1}^{r+1} \|A_{k_\ell} \ldots A_{k_{\ell-1}+1}\|_{\mathcal{W}}^{k_{\ell-1}, k_\ell} \right],$$

where we set $k_0 = 0$ and $k_{r+1} = n$.

For $n = 2$, this yields $L_{T^{\mathcal{A}}} \leq \frac{1}{2}\left(\|A_2 A_1\|_{\mathcal{W}}^{0,2} + \|A_2\|_{\mathcal{W}}^{1,2}\|A_1\|_{\mathcal{W}}^{0,1}\right)$, which (by the submultiplicativity of the matrix norm) is smaller than $\|A_1\|_{\mathcal{W}}^{1,2}\|A_0\|_{\mathcal{W}}^{0,1}$.

In the general case, the submultiplicativity of the matrix norm implies that each of the 2^{n-1} summands in the sum is at most $\prod_{\ell=1}^n \|A_\ell\|_{\mathcal{W}}^{\ell-1,\ell}$. Hence, the bound in Theorem 4 is (for given weights $\mathcal{W}$) tighter than the bound $\prod_{\ell=1}^n \|A_\ell\|_{\mathcal{W}}^{\ell-1,\ell}$. The intuition for the result is that for the 'identity part' of the averaged activation operator, we take the matrix product inside the matrix norm (which gives a smaller result than taking the product of the matrix norms).

The fact that Theorem 4 yields tighter bounds does not contradict the optimality in Theorem 3, since Theorem 3 only applies if the formula $\prod_{\ell=1}^n \|A_\ell\|_{\mathcal{W}}^{\ell-1,\ell}$ is used, while the bound in Theorem 4 is always smaller for given weights.

Example 3. Consider the network introduced in Example 2, for which we have $A_2 A_1 = \begin{pmatrix} 2 & 1 \end{pmatrix}$. Then just using averaged activation operators (as in [36]) yields a bound of $L_{T^A} \leq \frac{1}{2} \left(\|A_2 A_1\| + \|A_2\| \|A_1\| \right) = \frac{1}{2} (2 + 2 \cdot 5) = 6$, while using both weighted norms and averaged activation operators (Theorem 4) yields a bound of $L_{T^A} \leq \frac{1}{2} \left(\|A_2 A_1\|_{\mathcal{W}}^{0,2} + \|A_2\|_{\mathcal{W}}^{1,2} \|A_1\|_{\mathcal{W}}^{0,1} \right) = \frac{1}{2} (2 + 2 \cdot 3) = 4$.

6   Learner-Verifier Framework

Following [95], we implement our techniques from Sects. 4 and 5 in the learner-verifier framework from Fig. 3. Given an initial policy π (which we assume to be a neural network), the learner trains the certificate V to be a logRASM. The verifier checks whether V is a discrete logRASM (as per Definition 7), and thus whether $\exp(V)$ is a RASM. Checking these conditions involves the Lipschitz constants L_π and L_V, which we compute using our techniques from Sect. 5. We terminate and return the certificate V upon satisfaction of these conditions. If the conditions are not satisfied, the verifier either refines the discretization or returns counterexamples to the learner. As the learner also updates the policy π, we effectively solve the following problem:

Problem 2 (Policy synthesis). *Given a DTSS $\mathcal{S}$, compute a policy π such that the reach-avoid specification $\langle \mathcal{X}_T, \mathcal{X}_U, \rho \rangle$ is satisfied.*

Termination of the learner-verifier implies that we have solved Problem 2.

Verifier. Recall that the verifier checks the discrete logRASM conditions from Definition 7 on a discretization $\widetilde{\mathcal{X}}$ of the state space. When the verifier finds a point $\tilde{\mathbf{x}} \in \widetilde{\mathcal{X}}$ that violates these conditions, we either decrease the mesh size $\tau_{\tilde{\mathbf{x}}}$ of $\tilde{\mathbf{x}}$ (to try and mitigate the violation) or return $\tilde{\mathbf{x}}$ as a counterexample to the learner.

Local Refinement. Decreasing the mesh size $\tau_{\tilde{\mathbf{x}}}$ of the point $\tilde{\mathbf{x}}$ can only mitigate a violation if $\tilde{\mathbf{x}}$ is not a *hard violation* of the logRASM conditions. Hard violations are points $\tilde{\mathbf{x}} \in \widetilde{\mathcal{X}}$ that already suffice to prove that the current candidate certificate V is not a logRASM. For example, consider a point $\tilde{\mathbf{x}} \in \widetilde{\mathcal{X}} \cap \mathcal{X}_0$ that violates the discrete logRASM initial condition, i.e., $V_{\mathrm{UB}}(\tilde{\mathbf{x}}) > 0$. If the logRASM initial condition is also violated, i.e., $V(\tilde{\mathbf{x}}) > 0$, then V cannot be a logRASM, so $\tilde{\mathbf{x}}$ is a hard violation. We use an analogous argument for the other conditions.

We iteratively refine the discretization as long as *none of the violations* are hard violations, similar to common abstraction refinement schemes [35,40,85]. Specifically, we split the set $\mathrm{cell}_\infty^{\tau_{\tilde{\mathbf{x}}}}(\tilde{\mathbf{x}})$ associated with each (non-hard) violation $\tilde{\mathbf{x}}$ into multiple smaller cells whose mesh size $\tau_{\tilde{\mathbf{x}}}$ is reduced by a factor of $C \in (0, 1)$. In the context of supermartingale certificates, such refinements are also used by [14]. As a novel aspect, we observe that the reduction in $\tau_{\tilde{\mathbf{x}}}$ needed to mitigate a violation depends on the degree to which a condition is violated, so we use a different factor C for each violation. We discuss in [16, App. A.2] how we compute informed values for C. Importantly, the verifier only still needs to check the discrete logRASM conditions for the points associated with these new cells: points $\tilde{\mathbf{x}}$ that are not a violation cannot become a violation due to a discretization with a smaller mesh size $\tau_{\tilde{\mathbf{x}}}$.

Counterexamples. When the verifier finds at least one hard violation, we stop the refinement and return *all violations* $\widetilde{\mathcal{X}}' \subseteq \widetilde{\mathcal{X}}$ to the learner. These violations of the initial, safety, and expected decrease conditions are, respectively, added to three sets of counterexamples, denoted by C_0, C_{U}, and $C_{\mathbb{E}}$. However, if there are many violations, these counterexample sets become large. Thus, we implement these sets as buffers of a fixed size and, in each iteration, randomly replace a fixed fraction of the samples with new counterexamples.

Learner. The learner trains the certificate V and the policy π on a differentiable version of the logRASM conditions in Definition 6. The learner minimizes the loss function $\mathcal{L}(\pi, V) = \mathcal{L}_0(V) + \mathcal{L}_{\mathrm{U}}(V) + \alpha \cdot \mathcal{L}_{\mathbb{E}}(\pi, V)$, with hyperparameter $\alpha \in \mathbb{R}_{\geq 0}$, and where each term models a differentiable version of a logRASM condition:

$$\mathcal{L}_0(V) = \max_{\mathbf{x} \in P_0} \left\{ \max\{V(\mathbf{x}) + \varepsilon, 0\} \right\},$$

$$\mathcal{L}_{\mathrm{U}}(V) = \frac{1}{\log(\frac{1}{1-\rho})} \max_{\mathbf{x} \in P_{\mathrm{U}}} \left\{ \max \left\{ \log\left(\tfrac{1}{1-\rho}\right) - V(\mathbf{x}) \mid c, 0 \right\} \right\},$$

$$\mathcal{L}_{\mathbb{E}}(\pi, V) = \frac{1}{|P_{\mathbb{E}}|} \sum_{\mathbf{x} \in P_{\mathbb{E}}} \max \left\{ \log\left[\frac{1}{N} \sum_{\omega_i \sim d} \exp\left[V(f(\mathbf{x}, \pi(\mathbf{x}), \omega_i))\right] \right] - V(\mathbf{x}) + \tau K' + \varepsilon', 0 \right\}.$$

The points P_0, P_{U}, and $P_{\mathbb{E}}$ over which we check the conditions consist of randomly sampled points (which are freshly sampled each epoch) and the respective counterexamples C_0, C_{U}, and $C_{\mathbb{E}}$ returned by the verifier in previous iterations. The loss $\mathcal{L}_{\mathbb{E}}(\pi, V)$ approximates the expected decrease condition over a finite number N of noise samples, $\omega_i \sim d$. The terms $\varepsilon, \varepsilon' \in \mathbb{R}_{\geq 0}$ ensure that a loss of zero implies that the logRASM conditions are strictly satisfied at the points in the sets P_0, P_{U}, and $P_{\mathbb{E}}$. Finally, $K' = K + L_V = L_V(L_f(L_\pi + 1) + 1)$ is the Lipschitz constant of the function $\mathbf{x} \mapsto \log \mathbb{E}_{\omega \sim \mu}[\exp(V(f(\mathbf{x}, \pi(\mathbf{x}), \omega)))] - V(\mathbf{x})$, and τ is a *loss mesh* size chosen specifically for the problem.

7 Empirical Evaluation

We perform numerical experiments to answer the following questions about our techniques, implemented in the learner-verifier framework described in Sect. 6:

Q1: Can our methods be used to verify reach-avoid specifications with high probability bounds in challenging benchmarks?

Q2: Is our learner-verifier framework robust to deviations in the input policy?

Q3: How does our method for computing Lipschitz constants (Sect. 5) compare to other methods for computing Lipschitz constants of neural networks?

Setup. All experiments are run on a server running Debian, with an AMD Ryzen Threadripper PRO 5965WX CPU, 512 GB of RAM, and an NVIDIA GeForce RTX 4090 GPU. Our Python implementation uses JAX [24] (v0.4.26) with GPU acceleration. The policy and certificate neural networks both consist of 3 hidden layers of 128 neurons each. See [16, App. C.2] for all hyperparameters.

Q1. Verifying Reach-Avoid Specifications

We compare learner-verifier frameworks that implement different combinations of our verifier techniques: logRASM+Lip is our proposed verifier as described in Sect. 6 (i.e., using both logRASMs and improved Lipschitz bounds), logRASM only uses logRASMs, Lip only uses improved Lipschitz bounds, and the baseline uses neither. Since Lip and baseline train a (standard) RASM, these learner-verifiers use a different loss function (cf. [16, App. C.3]) based on the RASM conditions. The verifier in the baseline checks (except for Remark 1) the same discrete RASM conditions as in [95], but our learner-verifier framework differs in several algorithmic aspects. To obtain a fairer comparison between the cases, we use our own implementation as a baseline that we can also run on the same hardware. However, the baseline results are generally competitive with those in [95].

Benchmarks. We consider all benchmarks from [95] (linear-sys, pendulum, and collision-avoid), as well as a version of linear-sys with a more challenging layout. These four benchmarks have 2D state spaces. In addition, to assess the limits of our approach, we consider more challenging benchmarks with 3D and 4D state spaces. We consider reach-avoid specifications with different probability bounds ranging from $\rho = 0.8$ to 0.999999. We pretrain all policies with proximal policy optimization (PPO) [78] for 100,000 steps, which takes less than 30 seconds per instance (except for drone4D and planar-robot, which are trained for 1 and 10 million steps, respectively). We use a loss function that also penalizes high Lipschitz constants. For details on the benchmarks, we refer to [16, App. C.1].

Solving Problem 2. We show that our method reliably learns verified policies with only minor parameter tuning on individual benchmarks. Each instance is run on 10 seeds and is considered as failed when 3 or more seeds do not terminate within a 30 min timeout. We run our learner-verifier framework with the same hyperparameters across all 2D benchmarks; for the 3D and 4D benchmarks, we only slightly tune hyperparameters to adapt to these higher dimensions (see [16, App. C.2] for details). The average times required to find a valid (log)RASM are presented in Table 1 (excluding the time to train input policies). For all benchmarks, our new method is able to consistently verify (much) *higher probability bounds* ρ (99.9999% for all 2D benchmarks) at *lower run times* than the other learner-verifiers. The best bounds successfully verified by our baseline are slightly lower than the values from [95]. However, we use a lower timeout (30 min instead of 3 h) and consider an instance failed if $>2/10$ seeds failed, whereas [95] reports the highest bound successfully verified. Finally, the results for the 3D and 4D

Table 1. Average runtimes (in sec.) and st.dev. over 10 seeds (timeout of 30 min; d and m are the state and action space dimensions). See [16, App. C.2] for the hyperparameters. An instance is considered as failed if 3 or more seeds time out.

Benchmark	d	m	Learner-verifier	Probability bound ρ					
				0.8	0.9	0.99	0.999	0.9999	0.999999
linear-sys	2	1	logRASM+Lip (ours)	47±5	50±6	52±6	50±7	51±8	42±6
			logRASM	54±1	53±1	52±1	52±1	52±1	51±2
			Lip	45±3	42±5	79±18	180±66	545±117*	–
			baseline	88±10	89±4	308±157	699±224	–	–
linear-sys (hard layout)	2	1	logRASM+Lip (ours)	103±9	109±7	110±5	127±4	138±25	175±25*
			logRASM	283±40	386±73	668±151	–	–	–
			Lip	–	–	–	–	–	–
			baseline	–	–	–	–	–	–
pendulum	2	2	logRASM+Lip (ours)	77±10	71±2	85±2	99±11	107±11	137±43
			logRASM	226±23	229±26	216±13	221±30	239±28	218±7
			Lip	108±7	191±27	–	–	–	–
			baseline	721±168	–	–	–	–	–
collision-avoid	2	2	logRASM+Lip (ours)	69±1**	68±2	94±5	108±2	122±2	137±3
			logRASM	107±1	116±10	147±10	170±9	188±11	227±3
			Lip	117±6	152±12	391±42	–	–	–
			baseline	252±16**	–	–	–	–	–
triple-integrator	3	1	logRASM+Lip (ours)	793±180*	700±258	630±114	675±156	597±111	606±108
			logRASM	–	1394±148	1397±134**	–	1396±228	–
			Lip	1430±182**	–	–	–	–	–
			baseline	–	–	–	–	–	–
planar-robot	3	2	logRASM+Lip (ours)	326±44	380±89	341±58	341±94	491±99	–
			logRASM	720±262	–	–	–	–	–
			Lip	–	–	–	–	–	–
			baseline	–	–	–	–	–	–
drone4D	4	2	logRASM+Lip (ours)	665±282**	656±164	765±276*	873±124	–	–
			logRASM	–	–	–	–	–	–
			Lip	–	–	–	–	–	–
			baseline	–	–	–	–	–	–

* One timeout out of ten seeds; ** Two timeouts out of ten seeds.

benchmarks clearly show that our method scales to benchmarks that were out of reach for the baseline.

Learned logRASMs. Four logRASMs learned using our method are shown in Fig. 5. Especially the `linear-sys` (hard layout) benchmark requires a logRASM with a non-trivial shape, illustrating the usefulness of neural networks to represent certificates. For a RASM with the same bound of $\rho = 0.999999$, the learner would train the certificate to have values up to at least 10^6, which is required

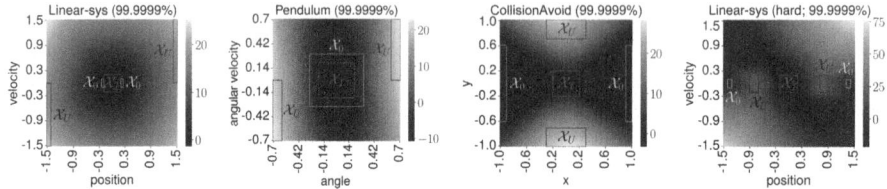

Fig. 5. The logRASMs learned using our new method (`logRASM+Lip`).

Table 2. Runtimes (in seconds) for verifying reach-avoid specifications (with probability $\rho = 0.999999$) on input policies trained with several RL algorithms for different numbers of steps (avgs. and st.dev. over 10 seeds; timeout of 30 min).

Benchmark	Steps	$\alpha = 10, \tau = 0.0005$				$\alpha = 0.1, \tau = 0.001$			
		TRPO	TQC	SAC	A2C	TRPO	TQC	SAC	A2C
linear-sys	1×10^4	55 ± 1	135 ± 37	143 ± 48	112 ± 32	86 ± 2	171 ± 1	167 ± 9	166 ± 14
	1×10^5	66 ± 18	180 ± 7	177 ± 18	115 ± 26	89 ± 9	185 ± 19	176 ± 5	170 ± 1
	1×10^6	67 ± 1	173 ± 3	170 ± 2	91 ± 43	109 ± 23	$334 \pm 276^*$	$338 \pm 193^*$	134 ± 46
linear-sys (hard layout)	1×10^4	192 ± 23	240 ± 3	245 ± 19	226 ± 31	170 ± 3	246 ± 41	242 ± 55	242 ± 20
	1×10^5	188 ± 3	245 ± 22	236 ± 3	238 ± 3	$237 \pm 16^{**}$	173 ± 19	163 ± 1	256 ± 40
	1×10^6	212 ± 39	314 ± 15	316 ± 18	219 ± 25	264 ± 34	–	–	261 ± 56
pendulum	1×10^4	$219 \pm 20^*$	206 ± 13	–	196 ± 21	365 ± 127	652 ± 312	543 ± 262	415 ± 184
	1×10^5	–	$279 \pm 42^{**}$	$295 \pm 66^{**}$	$193 \pm 24^*$	427 ± 180	708 ± 190	400 ± 161	447 ± 240
	1×10^6	$267 \pm 39^*$	–	–	–	525 ± 259	498 ± 194	334 ± 45	496 ± 251
collision- avoid	1×10^4	133 ± 7	194 ± 7	199 ± 7	197 ± 12	167 ± 18	175 ± 2	176 ± 3	183 ± 21
	1×10^5	101 ± 3	199 ± 7	198 ± 8	190 ± 13	95 ± 1	176 ± 2	178 ± 2	174 ± 2
	1×10^6	191 ± 28	246 ± 22	276 ± 30	194 ± 29	169 ± 16	–	–	170 ± 15

* One timeout out of ten seeds; ** Two timeouts out of ten seeds.

to satisfy the safety condition ($V(\mathbf{x}) \geq \frac{1}{1-\rho} = 10^6$). By contrast, the learned logRASMs in Fig. 5 only take values between -20 and 75, making them easier to learn.

Q2. Robustness to Input Policies

We consider the same benchmarks as in Table 1 (with $\rho = 0.999999$ and with our `logRASM+Lip` learner-verifier) but now pretrain input policies using the `Stable-Baselines3` [74] implementation of the RL algorithms TRPO, TQC, SAC, and A2C (with default parameters; see [16, App. C.1] for the loss functions) for either 10^4, 10^5 or 10^6 steps. Since we use these implementations unchanged, we now do not train for a lower Lipschitz constant (in contrast to the PPO-trained policies for Q1), but for a (state-based) reward function. Note that the RL reward maximization may not be able to fully capture the nature of a reach-avoid specification. Each instance is run on 10 seeds and is considered failed when 3 or more seeds do not terminate within 30 min.

The run times in Table 2 show that our method is generally agnostic to the policy training algorithm. We observe that training the policies longer tends to slightly increase the time to verify the policy, which can be a sign of over-training policies to maximize rewards. Moreover, the values of the hyperparameters α and τ in the loss function (cf. Sect. 6) influence the performance on individual benchmarks (e.g., we cannot reliably verify all `pendulum` policies for $\alpha = 10$, $\tau = 0.0005$). In conclusion, our method is reasonably robust against the input policy, but finding common hyperparameters for all benchmarks is difficult.

Q3. Comparison of Lipschitz Constants

We demonstrate the need for our efficient method to compute Lipschitz constants when solving Problems 1 and 2. We compare our techniques from Sect. 5 against the anytime algorithm LipBaB [22], a competitive solver for computing global Lipschitz constants, on the final policy and certificate networks (cf. [16, App. D]). Our method takes 0.2 s to compute a Lipschitz constant (and only 0.0002 s when already JIT-compiled). LipBaB returns a first Lipschitz constant after 0.5 s (which is, on average, 40% larger than ours) and requires usually more than 100 s to compute a better Lipschitz constant than ours. A typical benchmark requires 3–10 verifier iterations, each of which takes around 20 s, so better results from LipBaB may not outweigh the increase in verifier run time. For example, even just using LipBaB in the final verifier-iteration would, on most benchmarks, more than double the total runtimes from Table 1.

Discussion and Limitations

Beyond the mentioned scalability limitation (w.r.t. the dimension of the state space) in Q1, our experiments do not address the following: (1) We did not consider the robustness w.r.t. the loss functions used for pretraining and the learner. (2) We did not consider multiplicative RASMs as introduced in [96], although our results would also apply to these RASMs. (3) We did not consider using only IBP for the expected decrease condition. This would require piecewise linear under- and overapproximations of the dynamics as proposed by [66,67].

8   Related Work

Policy verification/synthesis for stochastic dynamical systems has largely been addressed using two approaches. The first is to generate a model-based [17,61,91, 93] or data-driven [52,55] abstraction (e.g., as a finite Markov decision process) and use probabilistic model checking on this abstraction. The second approach (which we take in this work) is to find a certificate function that implies the satisfaction of a specification. These approaches differ from typical objectives in constrained [8,11] and safe RL [10,19], which mostly focus on maximizing rewards while satisfying constraints on expected costs or safety in exploration [26,47].

Certificates are used in several areas, e.g., Lyapunov [39,59] and control barrier functions [12,33,64] in control, and ranking functions [25,46,71] in program analysis. For stochastic systems, the value of the certificate along trajectories needs to be a supermartingale [34,56,72]. Besides the RASMs [95,96] we build upon in this paper, [69] uses neural supermartingale certificates for continuous-time stochastic systems, and [6] proposes certificates for ω-regular properties in stochastic systems but makes restrictive assumptions to achieve a practical algorithm. Supermartingales are also used to analyze termination [5,9,29,32] and reachability [84] of probabilistic programs. Various recent papers represent such certificates as neural networks [2,30,38,76,90,94]. The resulting candidate certificate (i.e., the neural network) can be verified using satisfiability modulo theories (SMT) [1,4], branch-and-bound [65], or (like our approach) discretization and leveraging Lipschitz continuity [62,95]. Yet, all of these approaches are computationally expensive: SMT does not scale to large neural networks, whereas branch-and-bound and discretization do not scale with the state space dimension.

Neural Network Robustness and Lipschitz Constants

The use of Lipschitz constants as a measure of neural network stability and robustness was pioneered by [83], who propose the product of the Lipschitz constants of each layer as an upper bound for the Lipschitz constant of the network. This bound is fast to compute, but also very loose. Recently, there has been significant work in devising methods for computing tighter *global* and *local* Lipschitz constants. However, these methods are not designed for the large number of calls that our learner-verifier framework requires. Since the Lipschitz constant appears in the loss function, we need to recompute it for every batch and every epoch, leading to roughly 1,000 Lipschitz computations per learner-verifier iteration. Hence, even spending 20 ms on each Lipschitz computation would slow down our iterations by a factor two. Besides speed, another requirement is that the Lipschitz computation is differentiable, so that effects of weight updates on the Lipschitz constant are taken into account in the gradient of the loss function.

We now discuss why existing methods from the literature are (despite yielding tighter bounds on Lipschitz constants) less suited to our needs. Algorithms that compute global Lipschitz constants include LipBaB [44] and methods using semidefinite programming [22,87]. However, these methods are not differentiable, and have running times on the order of seconds per call. Methods for computing local Lipschitz constants include analytical bounds from [15], LiPopt [49], LipMIP [57], FastLin and FastLip [88], GenBaB [79], Recurjac [80,92]. The analytical methods from [15] are fast, but only apply relative to a fixed base point rather than within some region, which makes them unusable in our stochastic context. Out of the local methods, FastLin and FastLip [88] are the fastest, but running times of 5 ms per call are still too slow in our context for a local method.

We utilize results from [36] in Sect. 5.2, which is to our knowledge the only method (besides [83]) that can compute global Lipschitz constants sufficiently fast. We note that [68], which trains neural networks to certify the relation between two systems, also uses [36] to compute their Lipschitz constants (and could therefore improve their results by using the method proposed in this paper instead). Anisotropic certification [43] is similar to our weighted norms, but does not include an algorithm to compute optimal weights.

Besides approaches to bound Lipschitz constants, training networks to have a small Lipschitz constant is studied by [27,50,70]. However, for our purposes, we need an upper bound of the Lipschitz constant, and training a network to have a low Lipschitz constant does not guarantee that an upper bound for that Lipschitz constant computed with a particular method is also small. Another approach to neural network robustness is interval bound propagation (IBP), a technique to propagate interval inputs through neural networks [51]. Finally, a different line of research considers the adversarial robustness of neural networks [23,48,54,58, 60,83]. We refer to the survey articles [53,97] for a comprehensive overview of verification and robustness of neural networks.

9   Conclusion

We presented two contributions to improve the verification of policies in stochastic systems using reach-avoid supermartingales (RASMs). First, our logRASMs take exponentially lower values and hence have lower (theoretical) Lipschitz constants than (standard) RASMs. Second, we compute tight bounds on Lipschitz constants by integrating the novel idea of weighted norms with averaged activation operators. Our experiments show that our techniques allow the verification of reach-avoid specifications with much higher probability bounds than the state-of-the-art.

Future work includes generalizing our method for computing bounds on Lipschitz constants to broader classes of neural networks. In addition, while this work focuses on the verifier, improving the learner and the choice of counterexamples can improve the overall performance of the learner-verifier framework. Finally, we wish to investigate the robustness of the learner-verifier against perturbations in the system dynamics and the specification.

Acknowledgments. This research has been funded by the ERC Starting Grant 101077178 (DEUCE), the EPSRC grant EP/Y028872/1 (Mathematical Foundations of Intelligence: An "Erlangen Programme" for AI), the Wallenberg AI, Autonomous Systems and Software Program (WASP) funded by the Knut and Alice Wallenberg Foundation, the NWO Veni Grant ProMiSe (222.147), and the NWO grant NWA.1160.18.238 (PrimaVera).

Disclosure of Interests. The authors have no competing interests to declare that are relevant to the content of this article.

References

1. Abate, A., Ahmed, D., Edwards, A., Giacobbe, M., Peruffo, A.: FOSSIL: a software tool for the formal synthesis of Lyapunov functions and barrier certificates using neural networks. In: HSCC, pp. 24:1–24:11. ACM (2021)
2. Abate, A., Ahmed, D., Giacobbe, M., Peruffo, A.: Formal synthesis of Lyapunov neural networks. IEEE Control Syst. Lett. **5**(3), 773–778 (2021)
3. Abate, A., David, C., Kesseli, P., Kroening, D., Polgreen, E.: Counterexample guided inductive synthesis modulo theories. In: Chockler, H., Weissenbacher, G. (eds.) CAV 2018. LNCS, vol. 10981, pp. 270–288. Springer, Cham (2018). https://doi.org/10.1007/978-3-319-96145-3_15

4. Abate, A., Edwards, A., Giacobbe, M., Punchihewa, H., Roy, D.: Quantitative verification with neural networks. In: CONCUR. LIPIcs, vol. 279, pp. 22:1–22:18. Schloss Dagstuhl - Leibniz-Zentrum für Informatik (2023)
5. Abate, A., Giacobbe, M., Roy, D.: Learning probabilistic termination proofs. In: Silva, A., Leino, K. (eds.) CAV 2021. LNCS, vol. 12760, pp. 3–26. Springer, Cham (2021). https://doi.org/10.1007/978-3-030-81688-9_1
6. Abate, A., Giacobbe, M., Roy, D.: Stochastic omega-regular verification and control with supermartingales. In: Chockler, H., Weissenbacher, G. (eds.) CAV 2018. LNCS, vol. 14683, pp. 395–419. Springer, Cham (2024). https://doi.org/10.1007/978-3-031-65633-0_18
7. Abate, A., Prandini, M., Lygeros, J., Sastry, S.: Probabilistic reachability and safety for controlled discrete time stochastic hybrid systems. Automatica 44(11), 2724–2734 (2008)
8. Achiam, J., Held, D., Tamar, A., Abbeel, P.: Constrained policy optimization. In: ICML. Proceedings of Machine Learning Research, vol. 70, pp. 22–31. PMLR (2017)
9. Agrawal, S., Chatterjee, K., Novotný, P.: Lexicographic ranking supermartingales: an efficient approach to termination of probabilistic programs. Proc. ACM Program. Lang. 2(POPL), 34:1–34:32 (2018)
10. Alshiekh, M., Bloem, R., Ehlers, R., Könighofer, B., Niekum, S., Topcu, U.: Safe reinforcement learning via shielding. In: AAAI, pp. 2669–2678. AAAI Press (2018)
11. Altman, E.: Constrained Markov Decision Processes. Routledge (2021)
12. Ames, A.D., Xu, X., Grizzle, J.W., Tabuada, P.: Control barrier function based quadratic programs for safety critical systems. IEEE Trans. Autom. Control 62(8), 3861–3876 (2017)
13. Amodei, D., Olah, C., Steinhardt, J., Christiano, P.F., Schulman, J., Mané, D.: Concrete problems in AI safety. CoRR abs/1606.06565 (2016)
14. Ansaripour, M., Chatterjee, K., Henzinger, T.A., Lechner, M., Zikelic, D.: Learning provably stabilizing neural controllers for discrete-time stochastic systems. In: André, É, Sun, J. (eds.) ATVA 2023. LNCS, vol. 14215. Springer, Cham (2023). https://doi.org/10.1007/978-3-031-45329-8_17
15. Avant, T., Morgansen, K.A.: Analytical bounds on the local Lipschitz constants of ReLU networks. IEEE Trans. Neural Netw. Learn. Syst. (2023)
16. Badings, T., Koops, W., Junges, S., Jansen, N.: Policy verification in stochastic dynamical systems using logarithmic neural certificates (extended version). Technical report, CoRR, abs/2406.00826 (2025)
17. Badings, T.S., et al.: Robust control for dynamical systems with non-Gaussian noise via formal abstractions. J. Artif. Intell. Res. 76, 341–391 (2023)
18. Baillon, J.B., Bruck, R.E., Reich, S.: On the asymptotic behavior of nonexpansive mappings and semigroups in Banach spaces. Houston J. Math. 4, 1–9 (1978)
19. Berkenkamp, F., Turchetta, M., Schoellig, A.P., Krause, A.: Safe model-based reinforcement learning with stability guarantees. In: NIPS, pp. 908–918 (2017)
20. Bertsekas, D.: Reinforcement Learning and Optimal Control, vol. 1. Athena Scientific (2019)
21. Bertsekas, D.P., Shreve, S.E.: Stochastic Optimal Control: The Discrete-time Case. Athena Scientific (1978)
22. Bhowmick, A., D'Souza, M., Raghavan, G.S.: LipBaB: computing exact Lipschitz constant of ReLU networks. In: Farkaš, I., Masulli, P., Otte, S., Wermter, S. (eds.) ICANN 2021. LNCS, vol. 12894, pp. 151–162. Springer, Cham (2021). https://doi.org/10.1007/978-3-030-86380-7_13

23. Biggio, B., et al.: Evasion attacks against machine learning at test time. In: Blockeel, H., Kersting, K., Nijssen, S., Železný, F. (eds.) ECML PKDD 2013. LNCS (LNAI), vol. 8190, pp. 387–402. Springer, Heidelberg (2013). https://doi.org/10.1007/978-3-642-40994-3_25

24. Bradbury, J., et al.: JAX: composable transformations of Python+NumPy programs (2018). http://github.com/google/jax

25. Bradley, A.R., Manna, Z., Sipma, H.B.: Linear ranking with reachability. In: Etessami, K., Rajamani, S.K. (eds.) CAV 2005. LNCS, vol. 3576, pp. 491–504. Springer, Heidelberg (2005). https://doi.org/10.1007/11513988_48

26. Brunke, L., et al.: Safe learning in robotics: from learning-based control to safe reinforcement learning. Annu. Rev. Control. Robotics Auton. Syst. **5**, 411–444 (2022)

27. Bungert, L., Raab, R., Roith, T., Schwinn, L., Tenbrinck, D.: CLIP: cheap Lipschitz training of neural networks. In: Elmoataz, A., Fadili, J., Quéau, Y., Rabin, J., Simon, L. (eds.) SSVM 2021. LNCS, vol. 12679, pp. 307–319. Springer, Cham (2021). https://doi.org/10.1007/978-3-030-75549-2_25

28. Busoniu, L., de Bruin, T., Tolic, D., Kober, J., Palunko, I.: Reinforcement learning for control: performance, stability, and deep approximators. Annu. Rev. Control. **46**, 8–28 (2018)

29. Chakarov, A., Sankaranarayanan, S.: Probabilistic program analysis with martingales. In: Sharygina, N., Veith, H. (eds.) CAV 2013. LNCS, vol. 8044, pp. 511–526. Springer, Heidelberg (2013). https://doi.org/10.1007/978-3-642-39799-8_34

30. Chang, Y., Roohi, N., Gao, S.: Neural Lyapunov control. In: NeurIPS, pp. 3240–3249 (2019)

31. Chatterjee, K., Henzinger, T.A., Lechner, M., Zikelic, D.: A learner-verifier framework for neural network controllers and certificates of stochastic systems. In: Sankaranarayanan, S., Sharygina, N. (eds.) TACAS 2023. LNCS, vol. 13993, pp. 3–25. Springer, Cham (2023)

32. Chatterjee, K., Novotný, P., Zikelic, D.: Stochastic invariants for probabilistic termination. In: POPL, pp. 145–160. ACM (2017)

33. Choi, J.J., Castañeda, F., Tomlin, C.J., Sreenath, K.: Reinforcement learning for safety-critical control under model uncertainty, using control Lyapunov functions and control barrier functions. Rob. Sci. Syst. (2020)

34. Clark, A.: Control barrier functions for stochastic systems. Automatica **130**, 109688 (2021)

35. Clarke, E.M., Grumberg, O., Jha, S., Lu, Y., Veith, H.: Counterexample-guided abstraction refinement for symbolic model checking. J. ACM **50**(5), 752–794 (2003)

36. Combettes, P.L., Pesquet, J.C.: Lipschitz certificates for layered network structures driven by averaged activation operators. SIAM J. Math. Data Sci. **2**(2), 529–557 (2020)

37. Dalrymple, D., et al.: Towards guaranteed safe AI: a framework for ensuring robust and reliable AI systems. CoRR abs/2405.06624 (2024)

38. Dawson, C., Gao, S., Fan, C.: Safe control with learned certificates: a survey of neural Lyapunov, barrier, and contraction methods for robotics and control. IEEE Trans. Rob. **39**(3), 1749–1767 (2023)

39. De Queiroz, M.S., Dawson, D.M., Nagarkatti, S.P., Zhang, F.: Lyapunov-based control of mechanical systems. Springer Science & Business Media, Boston (2000). https://doi.org/10.1007/978-1-4612-1352-9

40. Dierks, H., Kupferschmid, S., Larsen, K.G.: Automatic abstraction refinement for timed automata. In: Raskin, J.-F., Thiagarajan, P.S. (eds.) FORMATS 2007.

LNCS, vol. 4763, pp. 114–129. Springer, Heidelberg (2007). https://doi.org/10. 1007/978-3-540-75454-1_10

41. Duan, Y., Chen, X., Houthooft, R., Schulman, J., Abbeel, P.: Benchmarking deep reinforcement learning for continuous control. In: ICML. JMLR Workshop and Conference Proceedings, vol. 48, pp. 1329–1338. JMLR.org (2016)

42. Durrett, R.: Stochastic Calculus: A Practical Introduction, 1st edn. CRC Press (1996)

43. Eiras, F., et al.: ANCER: anisotropic certification via sample-wise volume maximization. Trans. Mach. Learn. Res. **2022** (2022)

44. Fazlyab, M., Robey, A., Hassani, H., Morari, M., Pappas, G.J.: Efficient and accurate estimation of Lipschitz constants for deep neural networks. In: NeurIPS, pp. 11423–11434 (2019)

45. Fioriti, L.M.F., Hermanns, H.: Probabilistic termination: soundness, completeness, and compositionality. In: POPL, pp. 489–501. ACM (2015)

46. Floyd, R.W.: Assigning Meanings to Programs, pp. 65–81 (1993)

47. García, J., Fernández, F.: A comprehensive survey on safe reinforcement learning. J. Mach. Learn. Res. **16**, 1437–1480 (2015)

48. Gehr, T., Mirman, M., Drachsler-Cohen, D., Tsankov, P., Chaudhuri, S., Vechev, M.T.: AI2: safety and robustness certification of neural networks with abstract interpretation. In: IEEE Symposium on Security and Privacy, pp. 3–18. IEEE Computer Society (2018)

49. Gómez, F.L., Rolland, P., Cevher, V.: Lipschitz constant estimation of neural networks via sparse polynomial optimization. In: ICLR. OpenReview.net (2020)

50. Gouk, H., Frank, E., Pfahringer, B., Cree, M.J.: Regularisation of neural networks by enforcing Lipschitz continuity. Mach. Learn. **110**(2), 393–416 (2021)

51. Gowal, S., et al.: On the effectiveness of interval bound propagation for training verifiably robust models. CoRR abs/1810.12715 (2018)

52. Gracia, I., Laurenti, L., Jr., M.M., Abate, A., Lahijanian, M.: Temporal logic control for nonlinear stochastic systems under unknown disturbances (2024)

53. Huang, X., et al.: A survey of safety and trustworthiness of deep neural networks: verification, testing, adversarial attack and defence, and interpretability. Comput. Sci. Rev. **37**, 100270 (2020)

54. Huang, X., Kwiatkowska, M., Wang, S., Wu, M.: Safety verification of deep neural networks. In: Majumdar, R., Kunčak, V. (eds.) CAV 2017. LNCS, vol. 10426, pp. 3–29. Springer, Cham (2017). https://doi.org/10.1007/978-3-319-63387-9_1

55. Jackson, J., Laurenti, L., Frew, E.W., Lahijanian, M.: Strategy synthesis for partially-known switched stochastic systems. In: HSCC, pp. 6:1–6:11. ACM (2021)

56. Jagtap, P., Soudjani, S., Zamani, M.: Formal synthesis of stochastic systems via control barrier certificates. IEEE Trans. Autom. Control **66**(7), 3097–3110 (2021)

57. Jordan, M., Dimakis, A.G.: Exactly computing the local Lipschitz constant of ReLU networks. In: NeurIPS (2020)

58. Katz, G., Barrett, C., Dill, D.L., Julian, K., Kochenderfer, M.J.: Reluplex: an efficient SMT solver for verifying deep neural networks. In: Majumdar, R., Kunčak, V. (eds.) CAV 2017. LNCS, vol. 10426, pp. 97–117. Springer, Cham (2017). https:// doi.org/10.1007/978-3-319-63387-9_5

59. Khalil, H.K., Grizzle, J.W.: Nonlinear Systems, vol. 3. Prentice hall Upper Saddle River, NJ (2002)

60. Kurakin, A., Goodfellow, I.J., Bengio, S.: Adversarial examples in the physical world. In: ICLR (Workshop). OpenReview.net (2017)

61. Lahijanian, M., Andersson, S.B., Belta, C.: Formal verification and synthesis for discrete-time stochastic systems. IEEE Trans. Autom. Control **60**(8), 2031–2045 (2015)
62. Lechner, M., Zikelic, D., Chatterjee, K., Henzinger, T.A.: Stability verification in stochastic control systems via neural network supermartingales. In: AAAI, pp. 7326–7336. AAAI Press (2022)
63. Lillicrap, T.P., et al.: Continuous control with deep reinforcement learning. In: ICLR (Poster) (2016)
64. Lindemann, L., Dimarogonas, D.V.: Control barrier functions for signal temporal logic tasks. IEEE Control. Syst. Lett. **3**(1), 96–101 (2019)
65. Mathiesen, F.B., Calvert, S.C., Laurenti, L.: Safety certification for stochastic systems via neural barrier functions. IEEE Control. Syst. Lett. **7**, 973–978 (2023)
66. Mazouz, R., Mathiesen, F.B., Laurenti, L., Lahijanian, M.: Piecewise stochastic barrier functions. CoRR abs/2404.16986 (2024)
67. Mazouz, R., Muvvala, K., Ratheesh, A., Laurenti, L., Lahijanian, M.: Safety guarantees for neural network dynamic systems via stochastic barrier functions. In: NeurIPS (2022)
68. Nadali, A., Zhong, B., Trivedi, A., Zamani, M.: Transfer learning for control systems via neural simulation relations. CoRR abs/2412.01783 (2024)
69. Neustroev, G., Giacobbe, M., Lukina, A.: Neural continuous-time supermartingale certificates (2024). https://arxiv.org/abs/2412.17432
70. Pauli, P., Koch, A., Berberich, J., Kohler, P., Allgöwer, F.: Training robust neural networks using Lipschitz bounds. IEEE Control. Syst. Lett. **6**, 121–126 (2022)
71. Podelski, A., Rybalchenko, A.: A complete method for the synthesis of linear ranking functions. In: Steffen, B., Levi, G. (eds.) VMCAI 2004. LNCS, vol. 2937, pp. 239–251. Springer, Heidelberg (2004). https://doi.org/10.1007/978-3-540-24622-0_20
72. Prajna, S., Jadbabaie, A., Pappas, G.J.: A framework for worst-case and stochastic safety verification using barrier certificates. IEEE Trans. Autom. Control **52**(8), 1415–1428 (2007)
73. Puterman, M.L.: Markov Decision Processes: Discrete Stochastic Dynamic Programming. Wiley Series in Probability and Statistics, Wiley (1994)
74. Raffin, A., Hill, A., Gleave, A., Kanervisto, A., Ernestus, M., Dormann, N.: Stable-Baselines3: reliable reinforcement learning implementations. J. Mach. Learn. Res. **22**, 268:1–268:8 (2021)
75. Recht, B.: A tour of reinforcement learning: the view from continuous control. Annu. Rev. Control. Robotics Auton. Syst. **2**, 253–279 (2019)
76. Richards, S.M., Berkenkamp, F., Krause, A.: The Lyapunov neural network: adaptive stability certification for safe learning of dynamical systems. In: CoRL. Proceedings of Machine Learning Research, vol. 87, pp. 466–476. PMLR (2018)
77. Santoyo, C., Dutreix, M., Coogan, S.: A barrier function approach to finite-time stochastic system verification and control. Automatica **125**, 109439 (2021)
78. Schulman, J., Wolski, F., Dhariwal, P., Radford, A., Klimov, O.: Proximal policy optimization algorithms. CoRR abs/1707.06347 (2017)
79. Shi, Z., Jin, Q., Kolter, Z., Jana, S., Hsieh, C., Zhang, H.: Neural network verification with branch-and-bound for general nonlinearities. CoRR abs/2405.21063 (2024)
80. Shi, Z., Wang, Y., Zhang, H., Kolter, J.Z., Hsieh, C.: Efficiently computing local Lipschitz constants of neural networks via bound propagation. In: NeurIPS (2022)
81. Steinhardt, J., Tedrake, R.: Finite-time regional verification of stochastic nonlinear systems. In: Robotics: Science and Systems (2011)

82. Summers, S., Lygeros, J.: Verification of discrete time stochastic hybrid systems: a stochastic reach-avoid decision problem. Automatica **46**(12), 1951–1961 (2010)
83. Szegedy, C., et al.: Intriguing properties of neural networks. In: ICLR (Poster) (2014)
84. Takisaka, T., Oyabu, Y., Urabe, N., Hasuo, I.: Ranking and repulsing supermartingales for reachability in randomized programs. ACM Trans. Program. Lang. Syst. **43**(2), 5:1–5:46 (2021)
85. Tiwari, A., Khanna, G.: Series of abstractions for hybrid automata. In: Tomlin, C.J., Greenstreet, M.R. (eds.) HSCC 2002. LNCS, vol. 2289, pp. 465–478. Springer, Heidelberg (2002). https://doi.org/10.1007/3-540-45873-5_36
86. Virmaux, A., Scaman, K.: Lipschitz regularity of deep neural networks: analysis and efficient estimation. In: NeurIPS, pp. 3839–3848 (2018)
87. Wang, Z., et al.: On the scalability and memory efficiency of semidefinite programs for Lipschitz constant estimation of neural networks. In: ICLR (2024)
88. Weng, T., et al.: Towards fast computation of certified robustness for ReLU networks. In: ICML. Proceedings of Machine Learning Research, vol. 80, pp. 5273–5282. PMLR (2018)
89. Williams, D.: Probability with Martingales. Cambridge Mathematical Textbooks. Cambridge University Press (1991)
90. Wu, J., Clark, A., Kantaros, Y., Vorobeychik, Y.: Neural Lyapunov control for discrete-time systems. In: NeurIPS (2023)
91. Zamani, M., Esfahani, P.M., Majumdar, R., Abate, A., Lygeros, J.: Symbolic control of stochastic systems via approximately bisimilar finite abstractions. IEEE Trans. Autom. Control **59**(12), 3135–3150 (2014)
92. Zhang, H., Zhang, P., Hsieh, C.: RecurJac: an efficient recursive algorithm for bounding Jacobian matrix of neural networks and its applications. In: AAAI, pp. 5757–5764. AAAI Press (2019)
93. Zhang, L., She, Z., Ratschan, S., Hermanns, H., Hahn, E.M.: Safety verification for probabilistic hybrid systems. Eur. J. Control. **18**(6), 572–587 (2012)
94. Zhou, R., Quartz, T., Sterck, H.D., Liu, J.: Neural Lyapunov control of unknown nonlinear systems with stability guarantees. In: NeurIPS (2022)
95. Zikelic, D., Lechner, M., Henzinger, T.A., Chatterjee, K.: Learning control policies for stochastic systems with reach-avoid guarantees. In: AAAI, pp. 11926–11935. AAAI Press (2023)
96. Zikelic, D., Lechner, M., Verma, A., Chatterjee, K., Henzinger, T.A.: Compositional policy learning in stochastic control systems with formal guarantees. In: NeurIPS (2023)
97. Zühlke, M.M., Kudenko, D.: Adversarial robustness of neural networks from the perspective of Lipschitz calculus: a survey. ACM Comput. Surv. (2024)

StarV: A Qualitative and Quantitative Verification Tool for Learning-Enabled Systems

Hoang-Dung Tran[1(✉)], Sung Woo Choi[1], Yuntao Li[1], Qing Liu[1], Hideki Okamoto[2], Bardh Hoxha[2], and Georgios Fainekos[2]

[1] University of Florida, Gainesville, USA
{dungtran,sungwoo.choi,yli17,qliu1}@ufl.edu
[2] Toyota NA R&D, Ann Arbor, USA

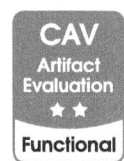

Abstract. This paper presents StarV, a new tool for verifying deep neural networks (DNNs) and learning-enabled Cyber-Physical Systems (Le-CPS) using the well-known star reachability. Distinguished from existing star-based verification tools such as NNV and NNENUM and others, StarV not only offers qualitative verification techniques using Star and ImageStar reachability analysis but is also the first tool to propose using ProbStar reachability for quantitative verification of DNNs with piecewise linear activation functions and Le-CPS. Notably, it introduces a novel ProbStar Temporal Logic formalism and associated algorithms, enabling the quantitative verification of DNNs and Le-CPS's temporal behaviors. Additionally, StarV presents a novel SparseImageStar set representation and associated reachability algorithm that allows users to verify deep convolutional neural networks and semantic segmentation networks with more memory efficiency. StarV is evaluated in comparison with state-of-the-art in many challenging benchmarks. The experiments show that StarV outperforms existing tools in many aspects, such as timing performance, scalability, and memory consumption.

Keywords: DNNs · cyber-physical systems · verification · tool

1 Introduction

Deep learning (DL) models have been adopted to tackle many real-world challenging problems such as image classification [1,41,90], natural language processing [50], and robotics [63]. However, it is well-known that deep learning models are vulnerable to adversarial attacks where a slightly change in the inputs may lead to unexpected output results [65]. Therefore, verification for learning-enabled systems (LES) built on DL technology becomes crucial to enable the use of DL models in safety-critical domains such as autonomous vehicles [48] and cancer diagnosis [78]. Extensive research efforts have been made in the last few years

---

H.-D. Tran, S.W. Choi, and Y. Li—Equal Contribution.

© The Author(s) 2025
R. Piskac and Z. Rakamarić (Eds.): CAV 2025, LNCS 15932, pp. 376–394, 2025.
https://doi.org/10.1007/978-3-031-98679-6_17

to deep neural network verification challenge [30, 42] as well as neural network control system verification [75] in which qualitative verification, i.e., providing SAT or UNSAT or UNKNOWN results, is the primary focus. While qualitative verification is crucial, quantitative verification with probabilistic results provides more information about the system's safety under probabilistic uncertainties. For example, if a system is unsafe, then what is the probability of safety violation? Additionally, physical uncertainties, such as those in sensing or actuating, are more naturally modeled in a probabilistic manner.

To fulfill the need for both qualitative and quantitative verification for LES, this paper introduces StarV, the first verification tool for deep learning models and learning-enabled cyber-physical systems (Le-CPS) that provides both qualitative and quantitative verification methods. For qualitative verification, StarV reimplements and optimizes star-based verification approaches [6, 12, 13, 34, 66, 68, 69, 73, 74]. **Notably, StarV introduces a new set representation called SparseImageStar**, a substantial improvement of ImageStar [66], and associated memory-efficient reachability algorithms to verify the robustness of very deep models like VGG networks [60] under thousand pixels attacks. Thanks to the SparseImageStar approach, StarV is currently the only tool that can verify the robustness of the VGG16 network with up to 3000-pixel attacks on a local computer. **For quantitative verification, StarV introduces ProbStar set representation** [11, 55, 72], a new variant of star set [7, 14], that allows the probabilistic modeling of uncertainties and the associated reachability algorithms for of deep neural networks with piecewise linear activation functions, e.g., ReLU, LeakyReLU, and Satlin and neural network control systems with linear plant dynamics. **Notably, StarV also introduces ProbStar Temporal Logic (ProbStarTL)** [70]**, a set-based formalism that enables the verification of LES's temporal properties using reachability analysis.** Thanks to ProbStarTL and associated verification algorithms, StarV is currently the only tool that can verify quantitatively the temporal properties of Le-CPS, such as a learning-based adaptive cruise control and emergency braking systems [68].

In summary, this paper provides a comprehensive overview of StarV and new features that users cannot find in individually published papers. It improves usability via multiple examples, case studies, and tutorials (in the user manual). This tool paper helps users quickly recognize all key features that can be used for their applications. Compared to individual published papers, there are many novelties and new technical contributions on 1) data structure, 2) reachability algorithms, 3) new activation functions support, and 4) new neural network architectures support. We also restructured the tool to make it more efficient and easier to use for future extensions. We highlight these novelties and new technical contributions in the following.

- **New data structures**: we implement new memory-efficient SparseStar and SparseImageStar data structures compared to the well-known Star and ImageStar.

- **New reachability algorithms**: we implemented new reachability algorithms on SparseStar and SparseImageStar data structures. We also implemented new quantitative reachability algorithms for massive linear systems using Krylov subspace method and probstar.
- **New activation functions**: For quantitative verification, we support new activation functions such as LeakyReLU, Satlin, and Satlins.
- **New network architectures**: StarV supports LSTM and GRU verification using new SparseStar reachability.
- **Improve Usability**: Installation instructions for local and Docker environments; Tutorials demonstrating key verification workflows; Example scripts for each supported network type; API documentation for extending the framework.

2 Related Work

Qualitative Verification of LES. Qualitative verification of learning-enabled systems (LES) has attracted the great attention of many researchers in recent years. In the area of open-loop LES (i.e., neural networks) verification, multiple approaches have been proposed, utilizing theories such as Satisfiability Modulo Theory (SMT) [2,37,38,85], optimization using mixed integer linear programming encoding [43], star reachability [6,73,74], facet-vertex incidence matrix [88,89], symbolic interval [81], semidefinite programming [19], abstract interpretation [54,61,92], input quantization [35], constraint-based [80], tree-based decomposition for incremental verification [79], certificate reuse [21] and relaxed convex programming [39], to name a few. There has also been significant effort in the development of efficient tools [6,15,20,22,38,46,77,86,88] (see [9] for more details). Closed-loop LES verification focuses on the safety of closed-loop neural network control systems under bounded input conditions, involving complex interactions between the neural network controller and the physical plant model [16,17,26–29,31,33,40,44,56,57,59,64,77,91]. Representative closed-loop LES verification frameworks include VeriSig [33], ReachNN [29], Sherlock [16], and NNV [67]. Recently, verification of perception-based control systems has attracted significant attention [47] and has been proven to be significantly challenging and time-consuming due to their large input space [24,26,32,52,56,64,89].

StarV reimplements and optimizes star-based reachability and qualitative verification algorithms for checking safety and robustness of a wide range of neural network architectures, such as feedforward neural networks (FFNNs) [73], recurrent neural networks (RNNs) [72], convolutional neural networks (CNNs) [66], and semantic segmentation networks (SSNs) [74], as well as neural network control systems (NNCS) [68]. Importantly, StarV tackles the memory consumption problem, a main bottleneck that reduces the scalability of reachability analysis and verification of very deep neural networks such as VGG16. To do that, we introduce SparseImageStar, a new set representation and associated reachability algorithms that allow memory-efficient verification of deep neural networks.

Using SparseImageStar method, we can verify the robustness of VGG16 with up to 3000-pixel attack on a local computer where popular tools like CROWN [92], Marabou [38], DeepPoly [61], and NNENUM [3] cannot.

Quantitative Verification of LES. Although important, quantitative verification for LES has attracted less attention from the community. Some quantitative verification methods verify *binary neural networks* with *quantized finite discrete inputs space* [8,58,93]. Some methods are proposed for the popular ReLU DNNs [18,23,45,51,53,83,84] with *continuous input space*. The first effort focuses on improving the sampling-based methods to certify neural networks' robustness under probabilistic uncertain inputs [45,53,83,84]. Although fast and scalable, these approaches do not provide a guarantee of output estimation for certification. The second effort focuses on probabilistic safety verification of ReLU networks with formal guarantee [18,23,71]. In the work by Fazlyab et al. [18], the authors investigate an ellipsoidal input space characterized by Gaussian random variables. They develop a method for propagating a confidence ellipsoid of the input through the neural network. By employing affine and quadratic constraints to approximate the nonlinear ReLU activation functions, they derive a confidence ellipsoid for the output. Furthermore, the safety of the original network can be established by analyzing the abstracted network using semidefinite programming techniques. In the work by Eric Goubault et al. [23], the authors introduce a new probabilistic abstraction named Zonotopic Dempster Shafer to construct tight overapproximation of the probabilistic outputs of a ReLU network using Interval Dempster Shafer arithmetic and probabilistic affine arithmetic. This approach can handle much more general classes of input uncertainties and provide guaranteed results.

StarV introduces ProbStar, a new set representation and associated quantitative reachability and verification algorithms for networks [71] with piecewise activation functions and neural network control systems (NNCS) with linear plant dynamics. It precisely estimates the safety violation probability of an LES under truncated Gaussian inputs distribution.

Verification of LES's Temporal Properties. The state-of-the-art techniques focus on safety, robustness, and fairness properties. There is a shortage of quantitative verification methods for complex temporal properties of Learning-enabled Systems (LES), specifically those that involve timing information. The neurosymbolic approach [25] is the first method developed to verify closed-loop LES with Signal Temporal Logic (STL) properties. This approach introduces a novel transformation technique, making the verification of temporal properties in closed-loop LES equivalent to performing reachability analysis of large feedforward neural networks.

StarV implements a method that is similar to the neurosymbolic approach [25] in that it also focuses on verifying temporal properties. However, we differentiate ourselves by introducing a new logic framework called ProbStarTL [70]. The semantics of this framework involve satisfying constraints on random variables, enabling us to precisely compute the probability of satisfaction. Additionally, our approach is more direct, as it does not require the transformation from STL to neural networks. This allows us to bypass the need for reachability analysis of large networks altogether. We highlight that neuroSymbolic approach uses the well-known signal temporal logic quantitative semantics to compute the robustness value of satisfaction (which can be any real number), while our Prob-StarTL has its own quantitative semantics defined based on reachable set signals to compute the probability of satisfaction (which is between 0 and 1).

3   Conceptual Overview and Core Features

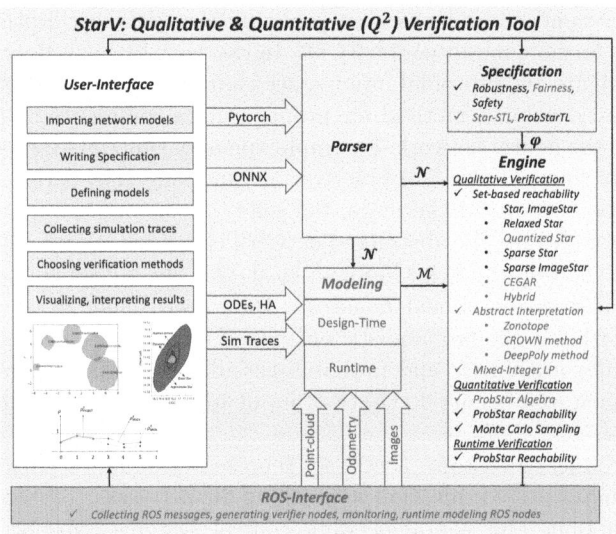

Fig. 1. A conceptual overview of StarV and core features (Features in blue color are under development). (Color figure online)

3.1   Conceptual Overview

StarV is an object-oriented toolbox developed in Python. Its conceptual overview and major features are depicted in Fig. 1. StarV aims to integrate popular and scalable verification approaches such as reachability-based [77], abstract interpretation [61,92], and mixed integer linear programming [43] so that users can choose appropriate techniques for their particular applications. It also aims to facilitate the adoption of formal methods in real robotic applications built on Robotic Operating Systems (ROS) [11,55].

Conceptually, StarV contains five modules, including a user interface, parser, specification and engine, and a ROS interface (under development). The user interface allows users to import a network model, write specifications, define a model, collect simulation traces, choose verification methods, and visualize and interpret verification results. The parser module currently supports automatic parsing of Pytorch and ONNX [49] models. StarV will construct corresponding internal models from these models for verification purposes. Users can also define their (StarV) models for verification using all supported layers or plant objects in StarV. The specification module allows users to specify the requirement for a LES. We fully support safety, robustness, and temporal properties (using Prob-StarTL). The fairness and Star temporal logic (StarTL) for deterministic input sets are under development. The modeling module supports users to construct a neural network control system at design time or runtime. At design time, users can construct an NNCS with a neural network controller and a physical plant model (ODEs or Hybrid Automaton). We are working on supporting the modeling of a complex learning-enabled CPS with multiple neural network components interacting with each other and with the physical world. At runtime, we plan to support perception-based runtime modeling in which the linear physical plant motion dynamics, e.g., human motion [55] or vehicle [11] will be obtained using only perception data in ROS, i.e., LiDAR and Camera Point-Cloud data. These works have been done but have not yet been fully integrated into StarV. The ROS interface will be developed in the future to support automatic generation of verifier, runtime modeling, and monitoring ROS nodes for robotic applications. The engine module is the core of StarV, which contains different set representations and multiple verification and reachability algorithms.

Verification Workflow and StarV's User Manual. The general verification workflow for using StarV is as follows. Firstly, the users construct an LES model object, whether a neural network using a generic neural network object or an NNCS object in StarV. Secondly, the users then specify the property as a safety, or robustness or temporal property using ProbStarTL. Thirdly, the users specify the input conditions as an input set, e.g., Star, ImageStar, or ProbStar, and provide verification parameters such as verification methods, the number of cores used for verification, the linear programming solver, and the number of time steps (for NNCS verification). Finally, the users execute the verification using the methods in the StarV LES object. Users can interpret and visualize reachable sets and verification results using the supported plot functions in StarV. **The detailed workflows for different LES can be found in StarV's user manual**.

3.2   Core Features

Table 1 summarizes StarV's core features, highlighting its novel features compared to the state-of-the-art. As we mentioned above, StarV reimplements and optimizes star-based verification approaches that have also been implemented in NNV [44,76] and NNENUM [3]. Therefore, in this section, we only highlight core features that are StarV's novel contributions compared to the state-of-the-art, specifically in addressing quantitative verification and memory and scalability problems in verifying deep CNNs.

Table 1. Overview of core features available in StarV. BN refers to batch normalization layers, FC to fully-connected layers, AvgPool to average pooling layers, Conv to convolutional layers, MaxPool to max-pooling layers, TC to transpose convolutional layers, and DC to dilated convolutional layers.

Feature	Supported
Neural Network Type	FFNN, CNN, SSN, Vanilla RNN, LSTM, GRU
Layers	MaxPool, Conv, BN, AvgPool, FC, TC, DC,
Activation functions	ReLU, Satlin, Sigmoid, Tanh, Leaky ReLU, Satlins
Plant dynamics (NNCS)	Linear ODE, Massive Linear ODE, Continuous & Discrete Time
Set Representation	Star, ImageStar, SparseStar, SparseImageStar, ProbStar
Qualitative Reach methods	exact, approx, relax, abs-dom
Quantitative Reach methods	exact, approx
Reachable set visualization	exact and over-approximation
Specification	Safety, Robustness, ProbStarTL Temporal Properties
Miscellaneous	Parallel computing, counterexample generation
Solver	Gurobi, GLPK
Import	Pytorch, ONNX

ProbStar Reachability [71]. StarV implements probstar reachability, which is built on a new set representation named probabilistic star (or shortly ProbStar), a variant of the well-known star set used in DNNs [6,66,73,74], and linear dynamical and hybrid systems verification [4,5,14]. A ProbStar is an affine mapping of a truncated multivariate Gaussian distribution that can be used to model probabilistic inputs and efficiently propagate them through the network to construct the reachable output set. The reachable output set (a union of probstars) is then used to verify a user-defined safety property in which the violation probability can be obtained efficiently. StarV supports exact quantitative verification, where the precise probability of safety violation is computed. It also supports approximate verification by filtering out reachable intermediate sets (in the layers) with probabilities lower than a user-predefined threshold. The exact verification algorithm is expensive as it explores all paths in reachability analysis. The over-approximate verification algorithm focuses on exploring paths with large probabilities, thus reducing the number of reachable sets involved and memory consumption in verification. Nevertheless, the over-approximate verification algorithm must filter intermediate ProbStars, which may be costly.

ProbStar Temporal Logic Verification [70]. StarV implements Probstar Temporal Logic (ProbStarTL), a formalism enabling quantitative verification of temporal properties of LES using probstar reachability analysis. ProbStarTL is defined on a (bounded-time) ProbStar signal (or ProbStar trace), a sequence of discrete, timed probstar reachable sets. The interpretation of ProbStarTL captures a symbolic representation of the set of LES traces that satisfy the specification. ProbStarTL supports two basic temporal operators: *always* ($\square$) and *eventually* ($\lozenge$). Since ProbStarTL is defined only over discrete-time and bounded-time intervals, the *until ($\mathcal{U}$)* operator is evaluated using the equivalent formula composed of the *always* ($\square$) and *eventually* ($\lozenge$) operators. The Prob-Star traces are constructed using exact or approximate ProbStar reachability algorithms, focusing on NNCS reachability with a feedforward neural network controlling a discrete linear plant model. In the future, we will extend the approach to verify temporal behaviors of networks handling time-series data, such as recurrent neural networks [72]. The verification of LES's temporal properties is done in two steps. First, we transform the user-defined ProbStar specification into a *abstract disjunctive normal form (ADNF)*, which is realized on the constructed reachable set traces to construct *computable disjunctive normal form (CDNF)*. The exact verification algorithm, while computationally expensive, calculates the exact satisfaction probability from the constructed CDNF. In contrast, the approximate verification algorithm, less expensive than the exact one, estimates only the lower and upper bounds of satisfaction probability from the CDNF.

ProbStar Reachability and Verification for Massive Linear Systems. StarV implements an efficient simulation-based probstar reachability method for massive linear systems based on the Krylov-subspace method proposed in [7]. However, with ProbStarTL [70], StarV allows users to quantitatively verify temporal behaviors of massive linear systems, a novel feature compared to the state-of-the-art, which supports only safety verification [4,5,7]. Our reachability analysis leverages state-space projection techniques to enhance memory efficiency and employs the Krylov subspace method in numerical simulation to optimize computation time at each discrete-time step. Additionally, our approach develops a robust quantitative verification algorithm based on ProbStarTL, which efficiently calculates the probability of satisfaction on a ProbStarTL specification, providing a way to quantify the system's temporal behaviors. We demonstrate the scalability and efficiency of our approach by successfully verifying nine large-scale linear systems, each with up to 10,000 dimensions.

SparseImageStar Reachability for CNNs. Verification of large CNNs, such as VGG16, with high-dimensional input like ImageNet presents significant challenges, particularly when computing resources are limited. To address these challenges, we develop SparseImageStar, a highly memory-efficient representation designed to handle pixel-level attacks involving up to 3000 pixels while ensuring scalability. This is accomplished by transforming multiple 3D RGB images into a column stack of flattened images in sparse matrix formats such as Coordinate (COO) and Compressed Sparse Row (CSR). However, this transformation disrupts the original spatial relationships. To mitigate this issue, we propose the indices-shifting technique that restores these spatial relationships without the need to revert the images to their original representation. Additionally, this technique enables SparseImageStar to operate at the feature map level rather than the pixel level. Leveraging this approach, we implement novel SpGEMM convolution and average pooling operations that directly operate on SparseImageStar, eliminating the need for feature extraction from the input, all while preserving both memory efficiency and scalability.

4   Evaluation

4.1   Qualitative Verification of LES

LSTM and GRU Verification. We evaluate MNIST LSTM, $\mathcal{L}_{15}$ and GRU, $\mathcal{G}_{15}$ RNNs with SparseStar against infinity norm attack such that $\bigwedge_{t=1}^{T_{max}} \|x_i'^t - x_i^t\|_\infty \leq \epsilon, T_{max} = 2$. SparseStar minimizes memory consumption by eliminating dependent basis vectors and storing linear constraints matrix in Compressed Sparse Column (CSC) format. SparseStar has the unique feature of reducing the number of predicates by their depth level, i.e., DR. We over-approximate LSTM and GRU layers as the combined activation operations in a new 3D geometric approach. In Fig. 2, SparseStar with LP solver('LP') proves the most robust cases for both networks, whereas with 'DR = 1' predicate reduction and 'EST' with estimate ranges, SparseStar proves the fewest cases due to the convex relation in return for improved scalability and memory consumption. The experiment is conducted on a computer with Intel Core i7-10700 CPU, 63.7 GiB Memory, 64-bit Ubuntu 18.04.6 LTS OS.

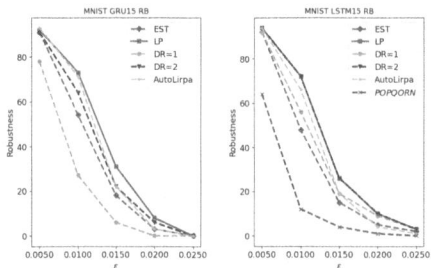

Fig. 2. $\mathcal{L}_{15}$ and $\mathcal{G}_{15}$ verification results. *'LP' proves the most robust cases.* AutoLirpa [86] proves as many robust cases as 'LP,' but it becomes more conservative as the epsilon becomes bigger. For $\mathcal{L}_{15}$, 'EST' proves more than AutoLirap for $\epsilon = 0.025$. POPQORN is the most conservative approach.

We evaluate SparseImageStar in CSR (SIM_{CSR}) and COO (SIM_{COO}) formats and ImageStar in StarV to compare with NNV for verifying the robustness of MNIST CNNs under brightening attacks. In Table 2, ImageStar in StarV is up to 2.66 $\times$, 6.85 $\times$, 6.94 $\times$ faster than NNV in Small, Medium, Large MNIST CNN networks, respectively. SIM_{CSR} is up to 2.82 $\times$, 8.45 $\times$, and 4.60 $\times$ faster

Table 2. Verification results of the MNIST CNN [66]. SIMs are up to 3.07 ×, 8.45 ×, 4.60 × faster than NNV in Small, Medium, Large networks, respectively.

	Robustness results (%)									Verification time (sec)								
	Small			Medium			Large			Small			Medium			Large		
	$\delta=0.005$	$\delta=0.01$	$\delta=0.015$	$\delta=0.005$	$\delta=0.01$	$\delta=0.015$	$\delta=0.005$	$\delta=0.01$	$\delta=0.015$	$\delta=0.005$	$\delta=0.01$	$\delta=0.015$	$\delta=0.005$	$\delta=0.01$	$\delta=0.015$	$\delta=0.005$	$\delta=0.01$	$\delta=0.015$
$d=250$ IM	87	87	87	99	99	99	99	99	99	0.135	0.195	0.195	0.143	0.220	0.345	0.190	0.284	0.395
SIM$_{csr}$	87	87	87	99	99	99	99	99	99	0.143	0.177	0.206	0.236	0.297	0.362	0.534	0.628	0.727
SIM$_{coo}$	87	87	87	99	99	99	99	99	99	0.166	0.194	0.216	0.274	0.375	0.454	0.693	0.865	1.032
NNV	87	87	87	99	99	99	99	99	99	0.207	0.327	0.469	0.433	1.210	2.179	0.546	1.208	2.178
$d=245$ IM	78	78	78	95	95	95	100	100	99	0.143	0.194	0.269	0.188	0.328	0.503	0.240	0.396	0.604
SIM$_{csr}$	78	78	78	95	95	95	100	100	99	0.168	0.221	0.255	0.281	0.387	0.542	0.619	0.770	0.965
SIM$_{coo}$	78	78	78	95	95	95	100	100	99	0.169	0.222	0.293	0.331	0.570	0.666	0.846	1.163	1.472
NNV	78	78	77	95	95	95	100	100	99	0.253	0.461	0.721	0.670	1.759	3.449	0.739	1.880	3.725
$d=240$ IM	73	73	73	90	90	88	99	99	99	0.149	0.242	0.372	0.236	0.424	0.863	0.288	0.496	0.784
SIM$_{csr}$	73	73	73	90	90	88	99	99	99	0.211	0.271	0.361	0.292	0.459	0.639	0.691	0.893	1.182
SIM$_{coo}$	73	73	73	90	90	88	99	99	99	0.222	0.248	0.322	0.370	0.602	0.963	1.008	1.353	1.842
NNV	73	72	71	90	89	88	99	99	99	0.335	0.642	0.989	0.906	2.653	5.400	0.942	2.333	5.445

than NNV in Small, Medium, Large networks, respectively, while SIM$_{COO}$ is up to 3.07 ×, 5.60 ×, 2.95 × faster than NNV. The substantial improvement is achieved due to the *indices-shifting technique* that allows our SparseImageStar and ImageStar to operate at the feature map level instead of the unscalable pixel level. The experiment is conducted on a computer with Intel Core i7-6950X CPU, 125.7 GB Memory, RTX 3090 GPU, and Ubuntu 20.04 LTS OS.

Robustness Verification of VGG16. We compare our SparseImageStar with NNV [76], DeepPoly [62], NNENUM [3], α, β-Crown [82,86,87,92], Marabou [85] by verifying the robustness of the VGG16 network from vnncomp2023 [10] under infinity norm attack with randomly selected $e \in [200, 3000]$ pixel attacks on the corn image with $\epsilon = 0.001/255$ perturbation. SIM$_{CSR}$ and SIM$_{COO}$ are the only two methods to verify all specifications without memory and scalability issues. SIM$_{CSR}$ is the fastest method: 1.15 ×, 1.24 × faster than NNENUM for c_0, c_2, respectively. For the spec 11 image, SIM methods require up to 38.91 MB, which is 18× memory efficient than ImageStar and NNV, which require up to 0.59 GB. The experiment is conducted on a computer with Intel Core i7-6950X CPU, 125.7 GB Memory, RTX 3090 GPU, and Ubuntu 20.04 LTS OS (Table 3, Fig. 3).

Table 3. SIM_{CSR} and SIM_{COO} are the only methods that verify all specifications without memory and scalability issues, with SIM_{CSR} being the fastest for VGG16 verification. 'O/M' and 'T/O' denote out-of-memory and time-out (12 h), respectively; e is the number of attacked pixels, and m is the number of predicates in the output reachable set (IM: StarV ImageStar; SIM: SparseImageStar).

			Original Network (seconds)							Relufied Network (seconds)				
Specs	e	Result	m	IM	SIM$_{CSR}$	SIM$_{COO}$	NNV	DeepPoly	Marabou	IM	NNV	NNENUM	α,β-CROWN	β-CROWN
c_0	200	UNSAT	358	O/M	612.5	871.2	O/M	O/M	T/O	O/M	O/M	744.02	T/O	26782.3
c_2	400	UNSAT	642	O/M	1089.4	1543.2	O/M	O/M	T/O	O/M	O/M	1354.75	T/O	T/O
c_4	1000	UNSAT	1613	O/M	2512.1	4076.5	O/M	O/M	T/O	O/M	O/M	T/O	T/O	T/O
c_6	3000	UNSAT	4871	O/M	7708.7	17362.4	O/M	O/M	T/O	O/M	O/M	O/M	T/O	T/O

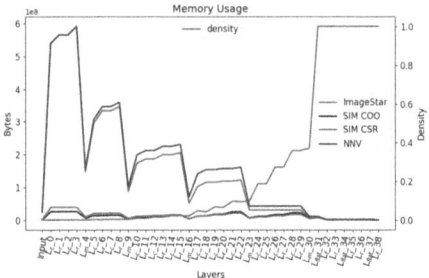

Fig. 3. *SIM methods require up to 38.91 MB, while ImageStar and NNV require up to 0.59 GB. SIM methods are 18 × more memory efficient in verifying the VGG16 with spec 11 image, which has l_∞ norm attack on 20 pixels.*

4.2 Quantitative Verification of LES

Quantitative Verification for ACASXu Networks. In this experiment, we assess our quantitative verification on unsafe ACASXu networks (properties P_2, P_3, and P_4) [6]) using 16 cores. Our approach computes violation bounds for 90 queries in roughly 24 h (query times: 5s–2hrs). Partial results are shown in Table 4, the approximate scheme ($p_f = 10^{-5}$) can speed up verification by up to $10\times$, though its upper bounds are sometimes conservative. Our results are consistent with NNV [77], Marabou [85], and NNenum [3]. While our method and NNV perform exhaustive counterexample searches and are slower, Marabou and NNenum stop after the first counterexample. Moreover, Monte Carlo sampling requires many samples, potentially leading to memory issues for low violation probabilities, highlighting the efficiency of our ProbStar approach. The experiment is conducted on a computer with Intel Core i7-6950X CPU, 125.7 GiB Memory, 64-bit Ubuntu 20.04.6 LTS OS.

Table 4. Quantitative verification results for unsafe ACASXu networks compared with MC sampling (10^7 samples) and qualitative tools. Notations: p_f (filtering probability), $\mathcal{O}$ (total output sets), $\mathcal{US} - \mathcal{O}$ (unsafe output sets), $\mathcal{C}$ (counter input sets), US-Prob-LB/US-Prob-UB (lower/upper bounds of violation probability), US-Prob-Min/US-Prob-Max (min/max unsafe probability over the infinite input space), I-Prob (input probability), and VT (verification time in seconds).

Quantitative Verification												Monte Carlo		Qualitative Verification		
Prop	Net	p_f	$\mathcal{O}$	$\mathcal{US} - \mathcal{O}$	$\mathcal{C}$	US-Prob-LB	US-Prob-UB	US-Prob-Min	US-Prob-Max	I-Prob	VT	US-Prob	VT	NNV	Marabou	NNenum
2	1-6	0	376352	80621	80621	9.07123e-06	9.07123e-06	9.07123e-06	0.0134354	0.986574	1287.45	4e-07	223.223	13739.970	166.58	1.5938
2	1-6	1e-05	4874	2662	2662	3.88239e-06	0.0538327	3.88239e-06	0.067259	0.986574	228.114					
3	1-7	0	500	500	500	0.986574	0.986574	0.986574	1	0.986574	7.52849	1	223.804	0.943	0.25	0.86683
3	1-7	1e-05	190	190	190	0.984972	0.985307	0.984972	0.998733	0.986574	6.635					
4	1-9	0	471	471	471	0.989244	0.989244	0.989244	1	0.989244	7.24032	1	209.705	1.176	0.31	0.86635
4	1-9	1e-05	142	142	142	0.989244	0.989244	0.989244	1	0.989244	5.38665					

Quantitative Verification of Temporal Properties of Le-ACC. We evaluate our approach to the learning-based adaptive cruise control (Le-ACC) system from the ARCH competition [36,77] in comparison with the NeuroSymbolic [25] approach with the network controller $N_{5 \times 20}$ for property φ_3 in [25]. Our ProbStarTL framework achieves safety guarantees similar to those of the NeuroSymbolic method but with substantially lower verification times. By decoupling reachability from property checking and computing satisfaction probabilities directly, our approach is significantly faster on the Le-ACC system, as shown in Table 5. The experiment is executed on an iMAC 3.8 GHz 8-Core Intell Core i7 with 128GB memory with a virtual 64-bit Ubuntu 20.04.4 LTS system.

Table 5. Verification results (robustness intervals) of NeuroSymbolic [25] are consistent with the proposed ProbStarTL verification results (probabilities of satisfaction). The proposed ProbStarTL verification approach is significantly faster than the NeuroSymbolic. *RS* is the verification result, *VT* is the verification time (in seconds), and *T* is the number of time steps.

CtrlNet	Method	$T = 10$		$T = 20$		$T = 30$		$T = 50$	
		RS	VT (sec)	RS	VT (sec)	RS	VT (sec)	RS	VT (sec)
$N_{5 \times 20}$	ProbStarTL	[0.9512, 0.9512]	1.7683	[0.9512, 0.9512]	5.892	[0.9512, 0.9512]	9.141	[0.9512, 0.9512]	29.0227
	NeuroSymbolic	[26.9067, 48.2244]	13.4654	[26.9067, 48.2244]	76.0396	[26.9067, 48.2244]	137.227	[24.0621, 44.3187]	356.74

5   Conclusions

We present StarV, a new qualitative and quantitative verification tool for LES. Our new tool reimplements and optimizes qualitative verification methods of the state-of-the-art for a wide range of network architectures. Notably, StarV includes a new set representation named SparseImageStar and SparseStar, as well as reachability and verification algorithms to improve memory efficiency and enhance the scalability of qualitative verification methods. Additionally, StarV introduces novel quantitative reachability and verification algorithms using ProbStar and ProbStarTL for neural networks with piecewise linear activation functions and NNCS. In the future, we will enhance StarV in the following aspects. Firstly, we will build a graphical, user-friendly interface and ROS interface for robotic applications. Secondly, we will develop Star Temporal Logic for verifying the temporal behaviors of LES with deterministic input sets. Thirdly, we will support fairness verification by developing hybrid and CEGAR reachability algorithms for LES. Fourthly, we will support the verification of complex LES with multiple neural network components and Large Language Model Verification by developing a Star/ProbStar algebra foundation and generic graph-based reachability algorithms. The key challenge in verifying complex LES with multiple neural network components is the complicated information flow (under uncertainties) inside the system. Therefore, tracking the dependencies of this information (represented as reachable sets) in multiple network components interacting with each other is crucial to constructing precise reachable sets for verification.

Additionally, scalability is also a main challenge for verifying complex Le-CPS (even in design time). Addressing these challenges is the focus of our future work. Finally, we will extend our integration to CROWN, DeepPoly, and MILP approaches.

Acknowledgments. This work is supported by the National Science Foundation (NSF) under grants NSF-CAREER-2441334, NSF-SLES-2331937, and NSF-FMitF-2220418. Any opinions, findings, conclusions, or recommendations expressed in this publication are those of the authors and do not necessarily reflect the views of NSF.

References

1. Affonso, C., Rossi, A.L.D., Vieira, F.H.A., de Leon Ferreira, A.C.P., et al.: Deep learning for biological image classification. Expert Syst. Appl. **85**, 114–122 (2017)
2. Amir, G., Wu, H., Barrett, C., Katz, G.: An SMT-based approach for verifying binarized neural networks. In: TACAS 2021. LNCS, vol. 12652, pp. 203–222. Springer, Cham (2021). https://doi.org/10.1007/978-3-030-72013-1_11
3. Bak, S.: nnenum: verification of ReLU neural networks with optimized abstraction refinement. In: Dutle, A., Moscato, M.M., Titolo, L., Muñoz, C.A., Perez, I. (eds.) NFM 2021. LNCS, vol. 12673, pp. 19–36. Springer, Cham (2021). https://doi.org/10.1007/978-3-030-76384-8_2
4. Bak, S., Duggirala, P.S.: HyLAA: a tool for computing simulation-equivalent reachability for linear systems. In: Proceedings of the 20th International Conference on Hybrid Systems: Computation and Control, pp. 173–178. ACM (2017)
5. Bak, S., Duggirala, P.S.: Simulation-equivalent reachability of large linear systems with inputs. In: Majumdar, R., Kunčak, V. (eds.) CAV 2017. LNCS, vol. 10426, pp. 401–420. Springer, Cham (2017). https://doi.org/10.1007/978-3-319-63387-9_20
6. Bak, S., Tran, H.-D., Hobbs, K., Johnson, T.T.: Improved geometric path enumeration for verifying ReLU neural networks. In: Lahiri, S.K., Wang, C. (eds.) CAV 2020. LNCS, vol. 12224, pp. 66–96. Springer, Cham (2020). https://doi.org/10.1007/978-3-030-53288-8_4
7. Bak, S., Tran, H.D., Johnson, T.T.: Numerical verification of affine systems with up to a billion dimensions. In: Proceedings of the 22nd ACM International Conference on Hybrid Systems: Computation and Control, pp. 23–32. ACM (2019)
8. Baluta, T., Shen, S., Shinde, S., Meel, K.S., Saxena, P.: Quantitative verification of neural networks and its security applications. In: Proceedings of the 2019 ACM SIGSAC Conference on Computer and Communications Security, pp. 1249–1264 (2019)
9. Brix, C., Bak, S., Liu, C., Johnson, T.T.: The fourth international verification of neural networks competition (VNN-comp 2023): summary and results. arXiv preprint arXiv:2312.16760 (2023)
10. Brix, C., Bak, S., Liu, C., Johnson, T.T.: The fourth international verification of neural networks competition (VNN-comp 2023): summary and results. arXiv:abs/2312.16760 (2023). https://api.semanticscholar.org/CorpusID:266572985
11. Brown, R., Nguyen, L.V., Xiang, W., Wolf, M., Tran, H.D.: Perception-based quantitative runtime verification for learning-enabled cyber-physical systems. In: 2025 the 16th ACM/IEEE International Conference on Cyber-Physical Systems (ICCPS), pp.1–11. ACM/IEEE (2025)

12. Choi, S.W., Ivashchenko, M., Nguyen, L.V., Tran, H.D.: Reachability analysis of sigmoidal neural networks. ACM Trans. Embed. Comput. Syst. **24**, 1–25 (2023)

13. Choi, S.W., et al.: Reachability analysis of recurrent neural networks. Hybrid Syst. Nonlinear Anal. **56**, 101581 (2025)

14. Duggirala, P.S., Viswanathan, M.: Parsimonious, simulation based verification of linear systems. In: Chaudhuri, S., Farzan, A. (eds.) CAV 2016. LNCS, vol. 9779, pp. 477–494. Springer, Cham (2016). https://doi.org/10.1007/978-3-319-41528-4_26

15. Duong, H., Li, L., Nguyen, T., Dwyer, M.: A DPLL (T) framework for verifying deep neural networks. arXiv preprint arXiv:2307.10266 (2023)

16. Dutta, S., Chen, X., Sankaranarayanan, S.: Reachability analysis for neural feedback systems using regressive polynomial rule inference. In: Proceedings of the 22nd ACM International Conference on Hybrid Systems: Computation and Control, pp. 157–168 (2019)

17. Everett, M., Habibi, G., Sun, C., How, J.P.: Reachability analysis of neural feedback loops. IEEE Access **9**, 163938–163953 (2021)

18. Fazlyab, M., Morari, M., Pappas, G.J.: Probabilistic verification and reachability analysis of neural networks via semidefinite programming. In: 2019 IEEE 58th Conference on Decision and Control (CDC), pp. 2726–2731. IEEE (2019)

19. Fazlyab, M., Morari, M., Pappas, G.J.: Safety verification and robustness analysis of neural networks via quadratic constraints and semidefinite programming. IEEE Trans. Autom. Control **16**, 1–5 (2020)

20. Ferlez, J., Khedr, H., Shoukry, Y.: Fast BATLLNN: fast box analysis of two-level lattice neural networks. In: Proceedings of the 25th ACM International Conference on Hybrid Systems: Computation and Control, pp. 1–11 (2022)

21. Fischer, M., Sprecher, C., Dimitrov, D.I., Singh, G., Vechev, M.: Shared certificates for neural network verification. In: Shoham, S., Vizel, Y. (eds.) Computer Aided Verification. CAV 2022. LNCS, vol. 13371, pp. 127–148. Springer, Cham (2022). https://doi.org/10.1007/978-3-031-13185-1_7

22. Girard-Satabin, J., Alberti, M., Bobot, F., Chihani, Z., Lemesle, A.: Caisar: a platform for characterizing artificial intelligence safety and robustness. arXiv preprint arXiv:2206.03044 (2022)

23. Goubault, E., Putot, S.: A zonotopic dempster-shafer approach to the quantitative verification of neural networks. In: Platzer, A., Rozier, K.Y., Pradella, M., Rossi, M. (eds.) Formal Methods. FM 2024. LNCS, vol. 14933, pp. 324–342. Springer, Cham (2024). https://doi.org/10.1007/978-3-031-71162-6_17

24. Habeeb, P., D'Souza, D., Lodaya, K., Prabhakar, P.: Interval image abstraction for verification of camera-based autonomous systems. IEEE Trans. Comput. Aided Des. Integr. Circuits Syst. **43**(11), 4310–4321 (2024)

25. Hashemi, N., Hoxha, B., Yamaguchi, T., Prokhorov, D., Fainekos, G., Deshmukh, J.: A neurosymbolic approach to the verification of temporal logic properties of learning-enabled control systems. In: Proceedings of the ACM/IEEE 14th International Conference on Cyber-Physical Systems (with CPS-IoT Week 2023), pp. 98–109 (2023)

26. Hsieh, C., Li, Y., Sun, D., Joshi, K., Misailovic, S., Mitra, S.: Verifying controllers with vision-based perception using safe approximate abstractions. IEEE Trans. Comput. Aided Des. Integr. Circuits Syst. **41**(11), 4205–4216 (2022)

27. Hu, H., Fazlyab, M., Morari, M., Pappas, G.J.: Reach-SDP: reachability analysis of closed-loop systems with neural network controllers via semidefinite programming. In: 2020 59th IEEE Conference on Decision and Control (CDC), pp. 5929–5934. IEEE (2020)

28. Huang, C., Fan, J., Chen, X., Li, W., Zhu, Q.: Polar: a polynomial arithmetic framework for verifying neural-network controlled systems. In: Bouajjani, A., Holík, L., Wu, Z. (eds.) Automated Technology for Verification and Analysis. ATVA 2022. LNCS, vol. 13505, pp. 414–430. Springer, Cham (2022). https://doi.org/10.1007/978-3-031-19992-9_27

29. Huang, C., Fan, J., Li, W., Chen, X., Zhu, Q.: Reachnn: Reachability analysis of neural-network controlled systems. arXiv preprint arXiv:1906.10654 (2019)

30. Huang, X., et al.: A survey of safety and trustworthiness of deep neural networks: Verification, testing, adversarial attack and defence, and interpretability. Comput. Sci. Rev. **37**, 100270 (2020)

31. Ivanov, R., Carpenter, T., Weimer, J., Alur, R., Pappas, G., Lee, I.: Verisig 2.0: verification of neural network controllers using Taylor model preconditioning. In: Silva, A., Leino, K. (eds.) CAV 2021. LNCS, vol. 12759, pp. 249–262. Springer, Cham (2021). https://doi.org/10.1007/978-3-030-81685-8_11

32. Ivanov, R., Carpenter, T.J., Weimer, J., Alur, R., Pappas, G.J., Lee, I.: Case study: verifying the safety of an autonomous racing car with a neural network controller. In: Proceedings of the 23rd International Conference on Hybrid Systems: Computation and Control, pp. 1–7 (2020)

33. Ivanov, R., Weimer, J., Alur, R., Pappas, G.J., Lee, I.: Verisig: verifying safety properties of hybrid systems with neural network controllers. In: Proceedings of the 22nd ACM International Conference on Hybrid Systems: Computation and Control, pp. 169–178 (2019)

34. Ivashchenko, M., Choi, S.W., Nguyen, L.V., Tran, H.D.: Verifying binary neural networks on continuous input space using star reachability. In: 2023 IEEE/ACM 11th International Conference on Formal Methods in Software Engineering (FormaliSE), pp. 7–17. IEEE (2023)

35. Jia, K., Rinard, M.: Verifying low-dimensional input neural networks via input quantization. In: Drăgoi, C., Mukherjee, S., Namjoshi, K. (eds.) SAS 2021. LNCS, vol. 12913, pp. 206–214. Springer, Cham (2021). https://doi.org/10.1007/978-3-030-88806-0_10

36. Johnson, T.T., Met al.: Arch-comp20 category report: artificial intelligence and neural network control systems (AINNCS) for continuous and hybrid systems plants. EPiC Ser. Comput. **74**, 107–173 (2020)

37. Katz, G., Barrett, C., Dill, D.L., Julian, K., Kochenderfer, M.J.: Reluplex: an efficient SMT solver for verifying deep neural networks. In: Majumdar, R., Kunčak, V. (eds.) CAV 2017. LNCS, vol. 10426, pp. 97–117. Springer, Cham (2017). https://doi.org/10.1007/978-3-319-63387-9_5

38. Katz, G., et al.: The Marabou framework for verification and analysis of deep neural networks. In: Dillig, I., Tasiran, S. (eds.) CAV 2019. LNCS, vol. 11561, pp. 443–452. Springer, Cham (2019). https://doi.org/10.1007/978-3-030-25540-4_26

39. Khedr, H., Ferlez, J., Shoukry, Y.: PEREGRiNN: penalized-relaxation greedy neural network verifier. In: Silva, A., Leino, K. (eds.) CAV 2021. LNCS, vol. 12759, pp. 287–300. Springer, Cham (2021). https://doi.org/10.1007/978-3-030-81685-8_13

40. Kochdumper, N., Schilling, C., Althoff, M., Bak, S.: Open-and closed-loop neural network verification using polynomial zonotopes. In: Rozier, K.Y., Chaudhuri, S. (eds.) NASA Formal Methods. NFM 2023. LNCS, vol. 13903, pp. 16–36. Springer, Cham (2023). https://doi.org/10.1007/978-3-031-33170-1_2

41. Krizhevsky, A., Sutskever, I., Hinton, G.E.: Imagenet classification with deep convolutional neural networks. In: Advances in Neural Information Processing Systems, pp. 1097–1105 (2012)

42. Liu, C., Arnon, T., Lazarus, C., Strong, C., Barrett, C., Kochenderfer, M.J.: Algorithms for verifying deep neural networks. Found. Trends Optim. **4**(3–4), 244–404 (2021). https://doi.org/10.1561/2400000035
43. Lomuscio, A., Maganti, L.: An approach to reachability analysis for feed-forward ReLu neural networks. arXiv preprint arXiv:1706.07351 (2017)
44. Lopez, D.M., Choi, S.W., Tran, H.D., Johnson, T.T.: NNV 2.0: the neural network verification tool. In: Enea, C., Lal, A. (eds.) Computer Aided Verification. CAV 2023. LNCS, vol. 13965, pp. 397–412. Springer, Cham (2023). https://doi.org/10.1007/978-3-031-37703-7_19
45. Mangal, R., Nori, A.V., Orso, A.: Robustness of neural networks: a probabilistic and practical approach. In: 2019 IEEE/ACM 41st International Conference on Software Engineering: New Ideas and Emerging Results (ICSE-NIER), pp. 93–96. IEEE (2019)
46. Matthew Sotoudeh, Z.T., Thakur, A.V.: SyReNN: a tool for analyzing deep neural networks. Int. J. Softw. Tools Technol .Transfer. **25**, 145–165 (2023). https://doi.org/10.1007/s10009-023-00695-1
47. Mitra, S., et al.: Formal verification techniques for vision-based autonomous systems–a survey. In: Jansen, N., et al. (eds.) Principles of Verification: Cycling the Probabilistic Landscape: Essays Dedicated to Joost-Pieter Katoen on the Occasion of His 60th Birthday, Part III, pp. 89–108. Springer, Cham (2024). https://doi.org/10.1007/978-3-031-75778-5_5
48. Muhammad, K., Ullah, A., Lloret, J., Del Ser, J., de Albuquerque, V.: Deep learning for safe autonomous driving: current challenges and future directions. IEEE Trans. Intell. Transp. Syst. **22**(7), 4316–4336 (2020)
49. (ONNX), O.N.N.E. https://github.com/onnx/
50. Otter, D.W., Medina, J.R., Kalita, J.K.: A survey of the usages of deep learning for natural language processing. IEEE Trans. Neural Netw. Learn. Syst. **32**(2), 604–624 (2020)
51. Păsăreanu, C., Converse, H., Filieri, A., Gopinath, D.: On the probabilistic analysis of neural networks. In: Proceedings of the IEEE/ACM 15th International Symposium on Software Engineering for Adaptive and Self-Managing Systems, pp. 5–8 (2020)
52. Păsăreanu, C.S., et al.: Closed-loop analysis of vision-based autonomous systems: a case study. In: Enea, C., Lal, A. (eds) Computer Aided Verification. CAV 2023. Lecture Notes in Computer Science, vol. 13964, pp. 289–303. Springer, Cham (2023). https://doi.org/10.1007/978-3-031-37706-8_15
53. Pautov, M., Tursynbek, N., Munkhoeva, M., Muravev, N., Petiushko, A., Oseledets, I.: Cc-cert: a probabilistic approach to certify general robustness of neural networks. In: Proceedings of the AAAI Conference on Artificial Intelligence, vol. 36, pp. 7975–7983 (2022)
54. Prabhakar, P., Rahimi Afzal, Z.: Abstraction based output range analysis for neural networks. Adv. Neural Inf. Process. Syst. **32**, 1–11 (2019)
55. Pramanik, A., Choi, S.W., Li, Y., Nguyen, L.V., Kim, K., Tran, H.D.: Perception-based runtime monitoring and verification for human-robot construction systems. In: 2024 22nd ACM-IEEE International Symposium on Formal Methods and Models for System Design (MEMOCODE), pp. 124–134. IEEE (2024)
56. Santa Cruz, U., Shoukry, Y.: NNLander-VeriF: a neural network formal verification framework for vision-based autonomous aircraft landing. In: Deshmukh, J.V., Havelund, K., Perez, I. (eds.) NASA Formal Methods. NFM 2022. LNCS, vol. 13260, pp. 213–230. Springer, Cham (2022). https://doi.org/10.1007/978-3-031-06773-0_11

57. Schilling, C., Forets, M., Guadalupe, S.: Verification of neural-network control systems by integrating Taylor models and zonotopes. In: Proceedings of the AAAI Conference on Artificial Intelligence, vol. 36, pp. 8169–8177 (2022)

58. Shih, A., Darwiche, A., Choi, A.: Verifying binarized neural networks by Angluin-style learning. In: SAT, pp. 354–370 (2019). https://doi.org/10.1007/978-3-030-24258-9_25

59. Sidrane, C., Maleki, A., Irfan, A., Kochenderfer, M.J.: Overt: an algorithm for safety verification of neural network control policies for nonlinear systems. J. Mach. Learn. Res. **23**(117), 1–45 (2022)

60. Simonyan, K., Zisserman, A.: Very deep convolutional networks for large-scale image recognition. arXiv preprint arXiv:1409.1556 (2014)

61. Singh, G., Gehr, T., Püschel, M., Vechev, M.: An abstract domain for certifying neural networks. Proc. ACM Program. Lang. **3**(POPL), 41 (2019)

62. Singh, G., Gehr, T., Püschel, M., Vechev, M.: An abstract domain for certifying neural networks. Proc. ACM Program. Lang. **3**(POPL), 1–30 (2019). https://doi.org/10.1145/3290354

63. Soori, M., Arezoo, B., Dastres, R.: Artificial intelligence, machine learning and deep learning in advanced robotics, a review. Cogn. Robot. **3**, 54–70 (2023)

64. Sun, X., Khedr, H., Shoukry, Y.: Formal verification of neural network controlled autonomous systems. In: Proceedings of the 22nd ACM International Conference on Hybrid Systems: Computation and Control, pp. 147–156 (2019)

65. Szegedy, C., et al.: Intriguing properties of neural networks. arXiv preprint arXiv:1312.6199 (2013)

66. Tran, H.-D., Bak, S., Xiang, W., Johnson, T.T.: Verification of deep convolutional neural networks using ImageStars. In: Lahiri, S.K., Wang, C. (eds.) CAV 2020. LNCS, vol. 12224, pp. 18–42. Springer, Cham (2020). https://doi.org/10.1007/978-3-030-53288-8_2

67. Tran, H.D., Cai, F., Diego, M.L., Musau, P., Johnson, T.T., Koutsoukos, X.: Safety verification of cyber-physical systems with reinforcement learning control. ACM Trans. Embed. Comput. Syst. (TECS) **18**(5s), 1–22 (2019)

68. Tran, H.D., Cei, F., Lopez, D.M., Johnson, T.T., Koutsoukos, X.: Safety verification of cyber-physical systems with reinforcement learning control. In: ACM SIGBED International Conference on Embedded Software (EMSOFT 2019). ACM, October 2019

69. Tran, H.D., Choi, S.W., Yang, X., Yamaguchi, T., Hoxha, B., Prokhorov, D.: Verification of recurrent neural networks with star reachability. In: Proceedings of the 26th ACM International Conference on Hybrid Systems: Computation and Control, pp. 1–13 (2023)

70. Tran, H.D., Choi, S., Li, Y., Okamoto, H., Hoxha, B., Fainekos, G.: Probstar temporal logic for verifying complex behaviors of learning-enabled systems. In: Proceedings of the 28th ACM International Conference on Hybrid Systems: Computation and Control (2025)

71. Tran, H.D., Choi, S., Okamoto, H., Hoxha, B., Fainekos, G., Prokhorov, D.: Quantitative verification for neural networks using probstars. In: Proceedings of the 26th ACM International Conference on Hybrid Systems: Computation and Control, pp. 1–12 (2023)

72. Tran, H.D., Choi, S., Yamaguchi, T., Hoxha, B., Prokhorov, D.: Verification of recurrent neural networks using star reachability. In: The 26th ACM International Conference on Hybrid Systems: Computation and Control (HSCC), May 2023

73. Tran, H.-D., et al.: Star-based reachability analysis of deep neural networks. In: ter Beek, M.H., McIver, A., Oliveira, J.N. (eds.) FM 2019. LNCS, vol. 11800, pp. 670–686. Springer, Cham (2019). https://doi.org/10.1007/978-3-030-30942-8_39

74. Tran, H.-D., et al.: Robustness verification of semantic segmentation neural networks using relaxed reachability. In: Silva, A., Leino, K. (eds.) CAV 2021. LNCS, vol. 12759, pp. 263–286. Springer, Cham (2021). https://doi.org/10.1007/978-3-030-81685-8_12

75. Tran, H.D., Xiang, W., Johnson, T.T.: Verification approaches for learning-enabled autonomous cyber-physical systems. IEEE Design Test **39**, 24–34 (2020)

76. Tran, H.D., et al.: NNV: The neural network verification tool for deep neural networks and learning-enabled cyber-physical systems. In: 32nd International Conference on Computer-Aided Verification (CAV), July 2020

77. Tran, H.-D., et al.: NNV: the neural network verification tool for deep neural networks and learning-enabled cyber-physical systems. In: Lahiri, S.K., Wang, C. (eds.) CAV 2020. LNCS, vol. 12224, pp. 3–17. Springer, Cham (2020). https://doi.org/10.1007/978-3-030-53288-8_1

78. Tran, K.A., Kondrashova, O., Bradley, A., Williams, E.D., Pearson, J.V., Waddell, N.: Deep learning in cancer diagnosis, prognosis and treatment selection. Genome Med. **13**, 1–17 (2021)

79. Ugare, S., Banerjee, D., Misailovic, S., Singh, G.: Incremental verification of neural networks. Proc. ACM Program. Lang. **7**(PLDI), 1920–1945 (2023)

80. Usman, M., Gopinath, D., Sun, Y., Noller, Y., Păsăreanu, C.S.: NNREPAIR: constraint-based repair of neural network classifiers. In: Silva, A., Leino, K. (eds.) CAV 2021. LNCS, vol. 12759, pp. 3–25. Springer, Cham (2021). https://doi.org/10.1007/978-3-030-81685-8_1

81. Wang, S., Pei, K., Whitehouse, J., Yang, J., Jana, S.: Formal security analysis of neural networks using symbolic intervals. arXiv preprint arXiv:1804.10829 (2018)

82. Wang, S., et al.: Beta-crown: efficient bound propagation with per-neuron split constraints for neural network robustness verification. In: Proceedings of the 35th International Conference on Neural Information Processing Systems. NIPS 2021, Curran Associates Inc., Red Hook, NY, USA (2024)

83. Webb, S., Rainforth, T., Teh, Y.W., Kumar, M.P.: A statistical approach to assessing neural network robustness. arXiv preprint arXiv:1811.07209 (2018)

84. Weng, L., et al.: Proven: Verifying robustness of neural networks with a probabilistic approach. In: International Conference on Machine Learning, pp. 6727–6736. PMLR (2019)

85. Wu, H., et al.: Marabou 2.0: a versatile formal analyzer of neural networks. In: Gurfinkel, A., Ganesh, V. (eds.) Computer Aided Verification. CAV 2024. LNCS, vol. 14682, pp. 249–264. Springer, Cham (2024). https://doi.org/10.1007/978-3-031-65630-9_13

86. Xu, K., et al.: Automatic perturbation analysis for scalable certified robustness and beyond. Adv. Neural. Inf. Process. Syst. **33**, 1129–1141 (2020)

87. Xu, K., et al.: Fast and complete: enabling complete neural network verification with rapid and massively parallel incomplete verifiers (2021). https://arxiv.org/abs/2011.13824

88. Yang, X., Yamaguchi, T., Tran, H.D., Hoxha, B., Johnson, T.T., Prokhorov, D.: Neural network repair with reachability analysis. In: Bogomolov, S., Parker, D. (eds.) Formal Modeling and Analysis of Timed Systems. FORMATS 2022. LNCS, vol. 13465, pp. 221–236. Springer, Cham (2022). https://doi.org/10.1007/978-3-031-15839-1_13

89. Yang, X., Yamaguchi, T., Tran, H.D., Hoxha, B., Johnson, T.T., Prokhorov, D.: Reachability analysis of convolutional neural networks. arXiv preprint arXiv:2106.12074 (2021)
90. Yang, X., Ye, Y., Li, X., Lau, R.Y., Zhang, X., Huang, X.: Hyperspectral image classification with deep learning models. IEEE Trans. Geosci. Remote Sens. **56**(9), 5408–5423 (2018)
91. Zhang, C., Ruan, W., Xu, P.: Reachability analysis of neural network control systems. In: Proceedings of the AAAI Conference on Artificial Intelligence, vol. 37, pp. 15287–15295 (2023)
92. Zhang, H., Weng, T.W., Chen, P.Y., Hsieh, C.J., Daniel, L.: Efficient neural network robustness certification with general activation functions. In: Advances in Neural Information Processing Systems, pp. 4944–4953 (2018)
93. Zhang, Y., Zhao, Z., Chen, G., Song, F., Chen, T.: BDD4BNN: a BDD-based quantitative analysis framework for binarized neural networks. In: Silva, A., Leino, K. (eds.) CAV 2021. LNCS, vol. 12759, pp. 175–200. Springer, Cham (2021). https://doi.org/10.1007/978-3-030-81685-8_8

ModelVerification.jl: A Comprehensive Toolbox for Formally Verifying Deep Neural Networks

Tianhao Wei[1]([✉]), Hanjiang Hu[1], Luca Marzari[1,2], Kai S. Yun[1], Peizhi Niu[1], Xusheng Luo[1], and Changliu Liu[1]

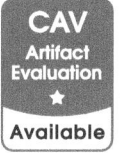

[1] Carnegie Mellon University, Pittsburgh, USA
{twei2,hanjianh,xushengl,cliu6}@andrew.cmu.edu,
luca.marzari@univr.it
[2] University of Verona, Verona, Italy

Abstract. Deep Neural Networks (DNN) are crucial in approximating nonlinear functions across diverse applications, ranging from image classification to control. Verifying specific input-output properties can be a highly challenging task due to the lack of a single, self-contained framework that allows a complete range of various model architecture and input-output properties. To this end, we present `ModelVerification.jl` (`MV.jl`) (https://github.com/intelligent-control-lab/ModelVerification. jl), the first comprehensive, cutting-edge toolbox that contains a suite of state-of-the-art methods for verifying different types of DNNs and input-output specifications. This versatile toolbox is designed to empower developers and machine learning practitioners with robust tools for verifying and ensuring the trustworthiness of their DNN models.

Keywords: Deep Neural Network Verification · Adversarial Robustness

1 Introduction

The use of Deep Neural Networks (DNNs) is becoming increasingly prominent in several applications, including image classification [13,16,24,25], autonomous navigation [6,34,40], robotics [1,18,35,46], and control [27,44,45,47]. The main characteristic of these functions is their ability to approximate complex nonlinear functions often employed in solving these tasks. Nonetheless, while these functions are very efficient, their opaque nature can result in unpredictable and potentially unsafe behavior when small changes in the input, often imperceptible to the human, are performed. Broadly speaking, these functions are subject to so-called "adversarial inputs" [39] that can make them behave unsafely both for the system itself and especially for those around them. Hence, given the applications of DNNs in safety-critical contexts where human life is potentially at risk,

---

H. Hu, L. Marzari, K. S. Yun, and P. Niu—These authors contributed equally to the paper.

© The Author(s) 2025
R. Piskac and Z. Rakamarić (Eds.): CAV 2025, LNCS 15932, pp. 395–408, 2025.
https://doi.org/10.1007/978-3-031-98679-6_18

the need to obtain formal guarantees about the safety of these systems arises and is of paramount importance.

To address this issue, the research field of Formal Verification (FV) of DNNs [26], has emerged as a valuable solution to provide formal assurances on the safety aspect of these functions before the actual deployment in real scenarios. The main goal of FV is to prove (or falsify) a desired input-output relationship (safety property) for a given DNN. More specifically, many methods have been developed to formally verify collision avoidance tasks with standard Feed Forward Neural Networks (FFNNs) or robustness in image classification with Convolutional Neural Networks (CNNs) using reachability analysis [9,14,28,38,42,48], optimization techniques [2,21,22,41], or combining the two approaches [4,19,43,52,53]. Recently, there have also been techniques to find not only an individual violation point in the property's input domain but also to enumerate entire regions that may lead to unsafe behaviors to repair the network in those specific areas [32,33,50].

Despite the considerable advancements made by FV over the years, given the NP-complete nature of the problem [21], there are still several remaining issues, such as scalability, that limit the application of these systems in very large and complex real-world scenarios. Moreover, another limitation of applying FV in realistic scenarios is that existing toolboxes tailored themselves to different assumptions of tasks or properties. Hence, the complexity of the verification landscape in literature implies that users may need to switch between toolboxes or solvers when they intend to employ diverse verification approaches. This necessity poses a significant challenge, as such transitions are often neither convenient nor user-friendly. As a result, using an in-depth and comprehensive pre-deployment formal verification process is hard to achieve, and often, the only guarantees of safety rely on pure empirical evaluations.

To this end, in this work, we present `ModelVerification.jl` (Fig. 1), the first comprehensive cutting-edge toolbox that contains a suite of state-of-the-art methods for verifying different types of DNNs and safety specifications.

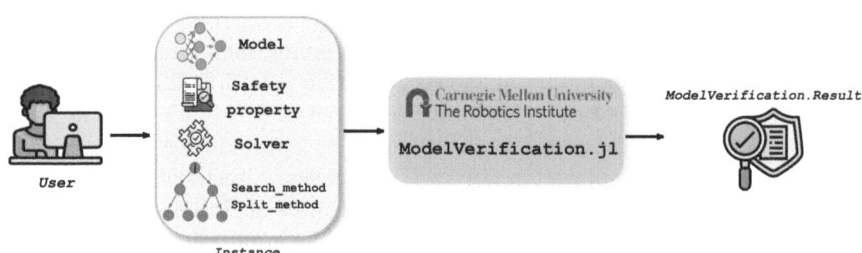

Fig. 1. The user specifies the network, the safety property to check, and the solver. `ModelVerification.jl` provides an assertion of whether the safety property holds.

Our toolbox targets two distinct user categories within the formal verification domain. The first target audience comprises individuals who are relatively new or considered "outsiders" to the FV world. For this latter, our toolbox is designed to be *user-friendly*, accompanied by complete and comprehensive documentation of all the methods developed. Hence, we provide an accessible and educational resource for those looking to learn the intricacies of the field. Concurrently, the second audience consists of researchers already well-versed in FV practices. Our toolbox offers valuable resources to even the sophisticated requirements of experienced practitioners. More specifically, our toolbox is written in Julia [3] language, ideal for specifying algorithms in human-readable form, and with the key *"multiple dispatch"* feature, that enhances the development of an elegant and highly modularized design for `ModelVerification.jl` . From this design, expert users can access the combination of great performing solvers on par with state-of-the-art ones (i.e., we focus not only on user-friendliness but also on toolbox efficiency) and even the possibility of implementing novel strategies of different natures (e.g., combining optimization and reachability) all in a single comprehensive toolbox.

Yet another FV toolbox? The Formal Verification of DNNs is increasingly becoming essential for providing provable guarantees of deep learning models. We refer the interested reader to the following article for a complete taxonomy of the various state-of-the-art methods [26]. In addition to these works mentioned in [26], it is important to mention recent methods such as Verinet [19], MN-BaB [11], α-β-CROWN [43,49,53], which provide the ability to test more complex properties, such as semantic perturbation, in addition to the classic methods based on regression and classification tasks. However, although α-β-Crown, for instance, was the top performer in the last three years of the NN verification competition [5], it lacks support for novel types of DNNs such as Neural Ordinary Differential Equations (NeuralODEs) [31]. To this end, a recent toolbox, NNV 2.0 [29], has arisen to overcome this limitation. Still, the latter presents a lack of support for different deep learning models such as Residual Neural Networks (ResNets) [17], confirming the non-existence of a single, self-contained framework that allows a complete range of verification types. We then have a range of toolboxes such as Juliareach [37], Sherlock [9], jax_verify [8], ReachNN [10], and RINO [15] that mainly focus on specific verification of DNNs (e.g., for Control Systems); and as also pointed out in [29], either they present lack of support for different types of DNNs or are no longer maintained. In contrast, our toolbox covers major state-of-the-art verifiers, including α,β-CROWN [43,49,53], Image-Star [42], DeepZ, Zonotope [14], and different layer types as mentioned before, enabling the user to pick the most appropriate solver for the given problem. Hence, `ModelVerification.jl` is the first self-contained toolbox that supports different verification and safety specification types designed to empower developers and machine learning practitioners with robust tools for verifying and ensuring the trustworthiness of their DNN models.

2   Toolbox Features

To overcome the limitations presented in the previous section, we now discuss the main features and the improvement of `ModelVerification.jl` over the state-of-the-art in four macro categories:

1) *Comprehensiveness*. As previously discussed, a notable constraint of using pre-deployment FV arises from the lack of a unified framework for verifying a broad spectrum of safety models and properties. Notably, existing solvers employ distinct representations for property verification, or they exclusively address particular categories of DNNs, thereby complicating the transition between tools. Consider a scenario where we have a collection of models encompassing both ResNets [17] and NeuralODEs [31] alongside a set of safety properties to be verified. If, for instance, we opt to use the state-of-the-art α-β-CROWN method [43,49,53], it exclusively supports the verification of the former type of networks. Meanwhile, for the latter, an alternative solver such as NNV 2.0 [29] becomes necessary. A critical constraint lies in the fact that these distinct solvers may be implemented following different design architecture strategies or even in different programming languages, as exemplified in this case, where the first solver is coded in Python while the second one is in Matlab. Consequently, accomplishing the verification process, in this case, entails the user's proficiency in both languages and a comprehensive understanding of how safety properties are encoded within the respective toolboxes.

To address such an issue, our primary objective is to provide the community with a tool of maximal comprehensiveness. We report in Table 1 the main features supported by `ModelVerification.jl`.

Table 1. Features supported by `ModelVerification.jl`.

Feature	ModelVerification.jl support
Neural Network	FFNN, CNN, ResNet, and NeuralODE
Activation functions	ReLU, Sigmoid, Tanh
Layers type	FC, Linear, ReLU, MaxPool, AvgPool, Conv, Identity, BatchNorm, Skip, Parallel
Geometries Representation	Hyperrectangle, Polytope, Zonotope, Star, ImageStar, ImageZono, Image Convex Hull, Taylor Model Reachable Set
Verification	Safety, Robustness, Adversarial attack, VNNLIB, Enumeration of (un)safe regions
Reachable set visualization	Layer-by-layer, Exact and Over-approximation visualization

Hence, the main purpose of our toolbox is to provide the possibility to verify all different types of neural networks, starting from the classical FFNNs and CNNs up to the more complicated ResNets and NeuralODEs. Also of primary importance is the support of general squashing activation functions, such as

Tanh and Sigmoid, in addition to the standard ReLU. Moreover, we decide to write ModelVerification.jl in Julia for the following reasons:

- Julia is a language specifically designed for scientific computation, which combines the efficiency of C and the flexibility of Python.
- We have an ample range of libraries available for operations with various complex geometric figures (e.g., *LazySets* [12]). While this gives us prominent performance, it also allows us to encode a wide range of safety properties with consistent geometric representations, resulting in a unified framework as desired.
- Julia's *"multiple dispatch"* feature allows us to adopt a uniform abstract pipeline such that different solvers can share the same function interface. The pipeline is both efficient and easy to follow.

Addressing the comprehensiveness, our toolbox provides the ability to perform several types of verification (Fig. 2), not only safety and robustness, using reachability analysis (Fig. 2a-b), but also the possibility to perform adversarial attack (Fig. 2c) –by exploiting one of the main methods, such as Fast Gradient Sign Method (FGSM), Projected Gradient Descent (PGD) attack, and Auto-PGD. Moreover, our toolbox includes recent exact and approximation methods [32,33,50] even to enumerate the set of (un)safe regions of a given safety property (Fig. 2d). Finally, ModelVerification.jl provides the user with visual representations of the intermediate results of the verification process (i.e., the reachable sets) as depicted in Fig. 3. We also introduce a new type of input set, ImageConvexHull, which contains all possible interpolations of the given seed images. ImageConvexHull is particularly useful for semantic perturbations such as occlusion, rain, fog, and shadow.

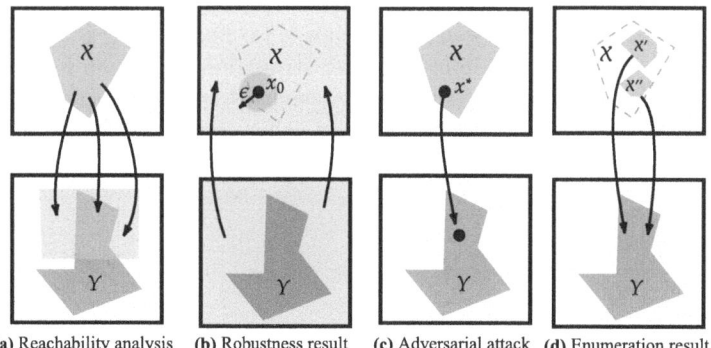

(a) Reachability analysis   (b) Robustness result   (c) Adversarial attack   (d) Enumeration result

Fig. 2. Different types of verification supported in ModelVerification.jl . $\mathcal{X}$ represents the safety property's domain, while $\mathcal{Y}$ the undesired reachable set.

All of these features enable ModelVerification.jl to verify different types of networks and properties in a single framework. We report in Table. 2 the improvements of our toolbox with respect to α-β-CROWN [43,49,53], NNV 2.0 [29], and MN-BaB [11] methods, considered state-of-the-art for formal verification of neural networks.

Table 2. Comparison between `ModelVerification.jl` and existing state-of-the-art toolboxes.

Features	Toolbox - Solver			
	α-β-CROWN	NNV 2.0	MN-BaB	MV.jl
Standard Layers	✓	✓	✓	✓
General Comp. Graph	✓	✓	✓	✓
General non-linearities	✓	✓	✓	✓
GPU support	✓		✓	✓
Reachable set vis.		✓		✓
Input sets	L_p-ball, VNNLIB format	L_∞-ball, Zonotope, Star, Polyhedron, VNNLIB format	L_∞-ball, Zonotope, VNNLIB format	L_p-ball, Polytope, Zonotope, Star, ImageConvexHull, VNNLIB format
Solvers	α-β-CROWN, IBP, CROWN, MIP	Zonotope, Star, NeuralODE	IBP, Zonotope, MN-BaB	α-β-CROWN, IBP, CROWN, Zonotope, Star, MN-BaB, NeuralODE

2) *User-friendliness.* Another major aspect of our toolbox is the ease of use. Our toolbox only requires several lines of code to formulate a verification problem in most cases. We provide comprehensive documentation, facilitating the use of the toolbox through detailed explanations and tutorials and, for Python users, a compiled library of this package such that they can directly call the package from Python itself.

To provide the reader with an intuition of the user-friendliness of our toolbox, let us consider a verification task that considers verifying a ResNet-based NeuralODE. Due to the modularized design chosen for `ModelVerification.jl` and the possibility of combining different solver strategies, we obtain a toolbox that encapsulates a vast range of verification scenarios, avoiding any model architecture modification potentially required in other solvers to meet their specific design.

```
using ModelVerification as MV
model = MV.get_resnet_model("path_to_model")
input_set  = Hyperrectangle(low=[0.9, -0.1], high=[1.1, 0.1])
output_safe_set = Hyperrectangle(low = [2.2, 2.2], high = [2.8, 3.2])
search_method = BFS(max_iter=10, batch_size=1)
split_method = Bisect(1)
prop_method = ODETaylor(t_span=1.0)
verify(search_method, split_method, prop_method, ODEProblem(model, input_set, output_safe_set))
```

More specifically, in `ModelVerification.jl` with a few simple lines of code, reported in the listing above, we can load the desired model and perform the required type of verification, regardless of the dataset we want to use. In particular, our toolbox provides a set of model converters commonly used in the literature, such as ONNX, TensorFlow (Keras), and PyTorch, to name a few, to Flux models, a Julia library for machine learning that contains an intuitive way to define models, just like mathematical notation. In addition, Flux allows differentiable programming of cutting-edge models such as neuralODEs, typically not supported by state-of-the-art (e.g., α-β-CROWN) methods, as previously discussed. As we can notice in the code above, the high-level language exploited in Julia allows for an easy understanding of what is being performed in the verification phase. Moreover, to increase even further the level of clarity, ModelVerification.jl provides the possibility to obtain a set of intra-layer representations of reachable sets obtained during the verification process, as shown in Fig. 3. This visualization shows how the perturbations "diffuse" during the reachability analysis, and how does it affects the final prediction, providing a human conceivable robustness.

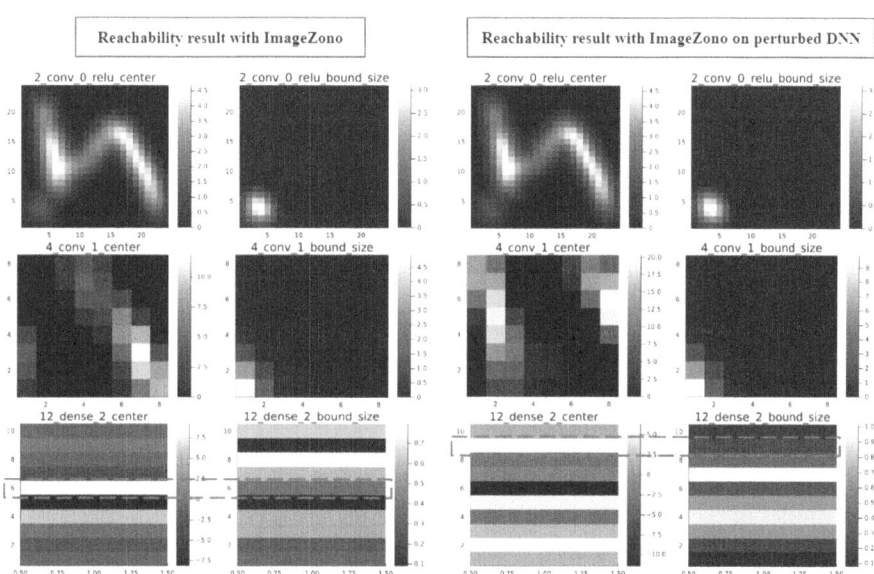

Fig. 3. Explanatory example of visualization of the reachable set layer-by-layer using ModelVerification.jl for a specific robustness verification instance of MNIST dataset. In this example, a single image representing the "five" handwritten digit and a local perturbation in the bottom left corner of the figure is considered. On the left part of the image, we report layers 2, 4, and 12's reachable sets computed using Image-Zono, where each reachable set is visualized using its center and the bound size using a heatmap. On the right, the reachable sets computed using ImageZono for a perturbed DNN are visualized. A convolutional layer and the last dense layers of the DNN are perturbed to visualize their effect on the final prediction. In the last row, we highlighted the predicted class in red. Crucially, we can notice a large scale in correspondence to the lighter row, meaning that the noise is larger.

3) *Extensibility*. Our toolbox follows a highly modularized design, making it easy to understand and customize. Specifically, based on the *"multiple dispatch"*

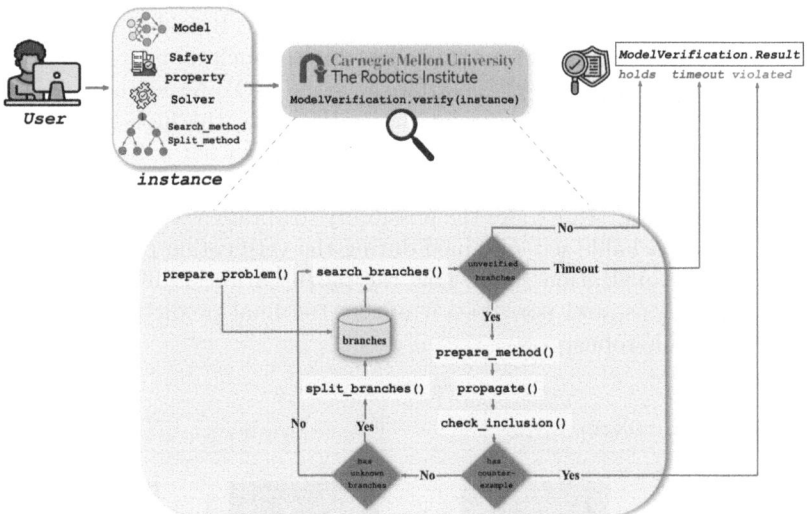

Fig. 4. Computational flow of `ModelVerification.jl` . The user provides the verification problem, including the model, the input set, and the desired output property. Our toolbox follows a branch and bound scheme to divide and conquer the problem. A result will be returned to verify or falsify the property if not timed out.

feature previously mentioned, we developed straightforward and easy-to-follow implementations. We abstract out a general pipeline and modularize `MV.jl` following the standard Branch-and-Bound (BaB) [26] paradigm. In detail, all the verification algorithms implemented in our toolbox divide the hard-to-verify problem into easier problems and proceed to verify the single easier subparts. This results in the possibility of choosing and combining different existing solvers provided in the toolbox to solve each part of the verification process optimally.

In the literature, it is worth noting that some solvers work best exploiting GPU computation, while others heavily rely on the CPU. Crucially, our toolbox supports both GPU and CPU-based methods. This dual support, in combination with an elegant, highly modularized, and well-documented BaB design, enables a key feature of our toolbox with respect to other state-of-the-art methods, as such, the possibility to combine different solvers for any verification purpose. We report in Fig. 4 a high-level overview of the computational flow of `ModelVerification.jl`. As discussed, each base submethod that composes the *verify* function is highly customizable based on the user's necessity. Based on `MV.jl`, neural control barrier functions [20] and neural Hamilton-Jacobi Reachability value functions [51] can be verified.

4) *Efficiency*. Besides prioritizing user-friendliness, the last main feature of `ModelVerification.jl` is concerned with efficiency. Our toolbox provides significant improvements over the first Julia toolbox ever for FV of DNNs called NeuralVerification.jl (NV.jl) [26]. In detail, NV.jl is written in Julia to provide the community with pedagogical and immediate-to-understand implementations, similar to our goal. However, given the pedagogical nature adopted, performance is suboptimal. In contrast, based on the architectural design choices for our toolbox, we are able to achieve user-friendly implementations and, at the same time, efficient results –in terms of verification time and scalability– comparable to, or in certain cases, surpassing those achieved by state-of-the-art solvers, as shown in Sect. 3. Recently, [30] efficiently verifies semantic perturbations on images using zonotope-based reachability analysis, while [7] verifies robust model predictive control leveraging the efficient CROWN [53] implementation in `ModelVerification.jl`.

3   Evaluation

This section demonstrates how versatile `ModelVerification.jl` is in encoding various input-output specifications for various tasks, as well as testing the performance of our toolbox in standard benchmarks from the VNN competition [5] to showcase the efficiency.

3.1   Empirical Evaluation on VNN Benchmarks

The first part of our evaluation concerns the robustness of trained ResNets, in particular, ResNet2b and ResNet4b. This verification is a valuable benchmark of scalability, particularly difficult to verify due to the large number of parameters contained in these architectures. In detail, ResNet2b comprises two residual blocks composed of five convolutional layers plus two linear layers, while ResNet4b has four residual blocks with nine convolutional layers and two linear layers. For this evaluation, we use images from the CIFAR-10 dataset [23] (composed by image size 32×32) with different occlusion perturbations. The occlusion adopted is a 6×6 black block and is randomly placed on the original image. We report in Fig. 5 a set of explanatory images of the type of robustness tested. In this study, a total of 100 images were subjected to verification using *ImageZono* as the solver, and the outcomes are presented in Table 3. All instances yielded

Fig. 5. Examples of the original and the occluded images used for the ResNet verification process.

deterministic results. Notably, the ResNet4b model, characterized by a greater number of layers and enhanced robustness, exhibited a higher number of *holds* instances and thus a longer verification time compared to ResNet2b.

Table 3. Verifying ResNet with occlusion perturbation.

	Holds instance	Violated instance	Unknown instance	#Parameters	Time
ResNet2b	54	46	0	112K	93.51 s
ResNet4b	72	28	0	123K	1086.40 s

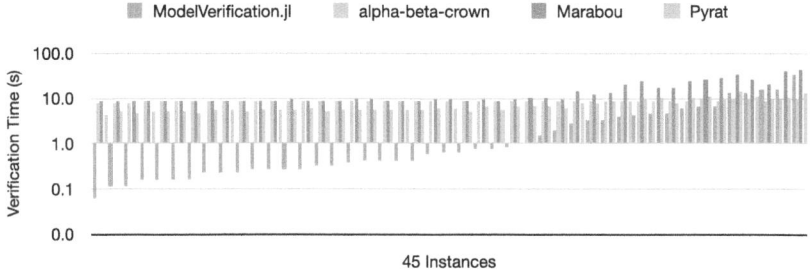

Fig. 6. Verification time of 45 instances in ACAS Xu ϕ_1. `ModelVerification.jl` is the fastest for most of the instances. The average verification time is `ModelVerification.jl`: 3.34 s, α-β-`CROWN`: 8.37 s, `Marabou`: 13.60 s, and `PyRat`: 9.12 s.

We then evaluate `ModelVerification.jl` on a subset of benchmarks from VNN-COMP'23 [36], ACAS Xu property ϕ_1 for 45 different networks that have 13K parameters. We compare with the toolboxes that won the first three places: α-β-`CROWN`, `Marabou`, and `PyRat`. We run our toolbox on an AWS m5 instance following the same VNN-COMP setup [36] as other toolboxes. The results of other toolboxes are directly from the competition. Detailed setting can be found in our toolbox repository. As shown in Fig. 6, our toolbox is faster than other toolboxes for most instances of this property, showcasing its efficiency.

4 Discussion

We introduced `ModelVerification.jl`, a comprehensive toolbox for verifying deep learning models. Our tool is the first cutting-edge toolbox containing a suite of state-of-the-art methods for verifying DNNs, including the verification of feedforward, convolutional, ResNet [17], and NeuralODEs. We believe the easy-to-follow implementation, combined with detailed documentation, provides a valuable and unique resource for using formal verification, even for people new to the subject. Moreover, the wide range of geometries that can be employed to describe both safety properties and different types of verification problems allows even the most experienced users to be able to take full advantage of this tool. For the future development of this toolbox, we want to further optimize the performance of the implemented solvers, including making the code more GPU-friendly, optimizing the general structure to reduce redundant computation, supporting more branching algorithms and solvers, and optimizing memory cost as well as performing a more comprehensive comparison with other state-of-the-art toolboxes.

Acknowledgements. This work is in part supported by Boeing and in part supported by mobility grants for non-EU destinations of the University of Verona's Doctoral School. Tianhao leads the design, implementation and evaluation of the toolbox. Hanjiang, Peizhi, and Xusheng contribute to the toolbox implementation and evaluation. Luca and Tianhao lead the paper writing. Kai and Luca lead the documentation and tutorial.

References

1. Amir, G., Corsi, D., Yerushalmi, R., Marzari, L., Harel, D., Farinelli, A., Katz, G.: Verifying learning-based robotic navigation systems. In: 29th International Conference, TACAS 2023, pp. 607–627. Springer, Heidelberg (2023). https://doi.org/10.1007/978-3-031-30823-9_31

2. Bastani, O., Ioannou, Y., Lampropoulos, L., Vytiniotis, D., Nori, A., Criminisi, A.: Measuring neural net robustness with constraints. Adv. Neural Inf. Process. Syst. **29** (2016)

3. Bezanson, J., Edelman, A., Karpinski, S., Shah, V.B.: Julia: a fresh approach to numerical computing. SIAM Rev. **59**(1), 65–98 (2017)

4. Botoeva, E., Kouvaros, P., Kronqvist, J., Lomuscio, A., Misener, R.: Efficient verification of relu-based neural networks via dependency analysis. In: Proceedings of the AAAI Conference on Artificial Intelligence, vol. 34, pp. 3291–3299 (2020)

5. Brix, C., Müller, M.N., Bak, S., Johnson, T.T., Liu, C.: First three years of the international verification of neural networks competition (vnn-comp). Int. J. Softw. Tools Technol. Transf., 1–11 (2023)

6. Chen, C., Seff, A., Kornhauser, A., Xiao, J.: Deepdriving: learning affordance for direct perception in autonomous driving. In: Proceedings of the IEEE International Conference on Computer Vision, pp. 2722–2730 (2015)

7. Cheng, H., Hu, H., Liu, C.: Robust tracking control with neural network dynamic models under input perturbations. arXiv preprint arXiv:2410.10387 (2024)

8. Dathathri, S., et al.: Enabling certification of verification-agnostic networks via memory-efficient semidefinite programming. Adv. Neural. Inf. Process. Syst. **33**, 5318–5331 (2020)

9. Dutta, S., Jha, S., Sankaranarayanan, S., Tiwari, A.: Output range analysis for deep feedforward neural networks. In: Dutle, A., Muñoz, C., Narkawicz, A. (eds.) NFM 2018. LNCS, vol. 10811, pp. 121–138. Springer, Cham (2018). https://doi.org/10.1007/978-3-319-77935-5_9

10. Fan, J., Huang, C., Chen, X., Li, W., Zhu, Q.: ReachNN*: a tool for reachability analysis of neural-network controlled systems. In: Hung, D.V., Sokolsky, O. (eds.) ATVA 2020. LNCS, vol. 12302, pp. 537–542. Springer, Cham (2020). https://doi.org/10.1007/978-3-030-59152-6_30

11. Ferrari, C., Muller, M.N., Jovanovic, N., Vechev, M.: Complete verification via multi-neuron relaxation guided branch-and-bound. arXiv preprint arXiv:2205.00263 (2022)

12. Forets, M., Schilling, C.: Lazysets. jl: scalable symbolic-numeric set computations. arXiv preprint arXiv:2110.01711 (2021)

13. Gatys, L.A., Ecker, A.S., Bethge, M.: Image style transfer using convolutional neural networks. In: Proceedings of the IEEE Conference on Computer Vision and Pattern Recognition, pp. 2414–2423 (2016)

14. Gehr, T., Mirman, M., Drachsler-Cohen, D., Tsankov, P., Chaudhuri, S., Vechev, M.: Ai2: safety and robustness certification of neural networks with abstract interpretation. In: 2018 IEEE Symposium on Security and Privacy (SP), pp. 3–18. IEEE (2018)

15. Goubault, E., Putot, S.: Rino: robust inner and outer approximated reachability of neural networks controlled systems. In: International Conference on Computer Aided Verification, pp. 511–523. Springer, Heidelberg (2022). https://doi.org/10.1007/978-3-031-13185-1_25

16. Han, Y., Yang, S., Wang, W., Liu, J.: From design draft to real attire: unaligned fashion image translation. In: Proceedings of the 28th ACM International Conference on Multimedia, pp. 1533–1541 (2020)

17. He, K., Zhang, X., Ren, S., Sun, J.: Deep residual learning for image recognition. In: Proceedings of the IEEE Conference on Computer Vision and Pattern Recognition, pp. 770–778 (2016)

18. He, S., Zhao, W., Hu, C., Zhu, Y., Liu, C.: A hierarchical long short term safety framework for efficient robot manipulation under uncertainty. Rob. Comput.-Integrat. Manuf. **82**, 102522 (2023)

19. Henriksen, P., Lomuscio, A.: Efficient neural network verification via adaptive refinement and adversarial search. In: ECAI 2020, pp. 2513–2520. IOS Press (2020)

20. Hu, H., Yang, Y., Wei, T., Liu, C.: Verification of neural control barrier functions with symbolic derivative bounds propagation. In: 8th Annual Conference on Robot Learning (2024). https://openreview.net/forum?id=jnubz7wB2w

21. Katz, G., Barrett, C., Dill, D.L., Julian, K., Kochenderfer, M.J.: Reluplex: an efficient SMT solver for verifying deep neural networks. In: Majumdar, R., Kunčak, V. (eds.) CAV 2017. LNCS, vol. 10426, pp. 97–117. Springer, Cham (2017). https://doi.org/10.1007/978-3-319-63387-9_5

22. Katz, G., et al.: The marabou framework for verification and analysis of deep neural networks. In: International Conference on Computer Aided Verification (2019)

23. Krizhevsky, A., Hinton, G., et al.: Learning multiple layers of features from tiny images (2009)

24. Krizhevsky, A., Sutskever, I., Hinton, G.E.: Imagenet classification with deep convolutional neural networks. Adv. Neural Inf. Process. Syst. **25** (2012)

25. Li, G., Xie, Y., Wei, T., Wang, K., Lin, L.: Flow guided recurrent neural encoder for video salient object detection. In: Proceedings of the IEEE Conference on Computer Vision and Pattern Recognition, pp. 3243–3252 (2018)

26. Liu, C., Arnon, T., Lazarus, C., Strong, C., Barrett, C., Kochenderfer, M.J., et al.: Algorithms for verifying deep neural networks. Found. Trends® Optim. **4**(3-4), 244–404 (2021)

27. Liu, S., Liu, C., Dolan, J.: Safe control under input limits with neural control barrier functions. In: Conference on Robot Learning, pp. 1970–1980. PMLR (2023)

28. Lomuscio, A., Maganti, L.: An approach to reachability analysis for feed-forward relu neural networks. arXiv preprint arXiv:1706.07351 (2017)

29. Lopez, D.M., Choi, S.W., Tran, H.D., Johnson, T.T.: Nnv 2.0: the neural network verification tool. In: International Conference on Computer Aided Verification, pp. 397–412. Springer, Heidelberg (2023). https://doi.org/10.1007/978-3-031-37703-7_19

30. Luo, X., et al.: Certifying robustness of learning-based keypoint detection and pose estimation methods. arXiv preprint arXiv:2408.00117 (2024)

31. Manzanas Lopez, D., Musau, P., Hamilton, N.P., Johnson, T.T.: Reachability analysis of a general class of neural ordinary differential equations. In: International Conference on Formal Modeling and Analysis of Timed Systems, pp. 258–277. Springer, Heidelberg (2022). https://doi.org/10.1007/978-3-031-15839-1_15

32. Marzari, L., Corsi, D., Cicalese, F., Farinelli, A.: The #dnn-verification problem: counting unsafe inputs for deep neural networks. In: International Joint Conference on Artificial Intelligence (IJCAI), pp. 217–224 (2023)

33. Marzari, L., Corsi, D., Marchesini, E., Alessandro, F., Cicalese, F.: Enumerating safe regions in deep neural networks with provable probabilistic guarantees. In: Proceedings of the AAAI Conference on Artificial Intelligence (2024)

34. Marzari, L., Corsi, D., Marchesini, E., Farinelli, A.: Curriculum learning for safe mapless navigation. In: Proceedings of the 37th ACM/SIGAPP Symposium on Applied Computing, pp. 766–769 (2022)

35. Marzari, L., Pore, A., Dall'Alba, D., Aragon-Camarasa, G., Farinelli, A., Fiorini, P.: Towards hierarchical task decomposition using deep reinforcement learning for pick and place subtasks. In: 2021 20th International Conference on Advanced Robotics (ICAR), pp. 640–645. IEEE (2021)

36. Müller, M.N., Brix, C., Bak, S., Liu, C., Johnson, T.T.: The third international verification of neural networks competition (vnn-comp 2022): summary and results. arXiv preprint arXiv:2212.10376 (2022)

37. Schilling, C., Forets, M., Guadalupe, S.: Verification of neural-network control systems by integrating taylor models and zonotopes. In: Proceedings of the AAAI Conference on Artificial Intelligence, vol. 36, pp. 8169–8177 (2022)

38. Singh, G., Ganvir, R., Püschel, M., Vechev, M.: Beyond the single neuron convex barrier for neural network certification. Adv. Neural Inf. Process. Syst. **32** (2019)

39. Szegedy, C., et al.: Intriguing properties of neural networks. arXiv preprint arXiv:1312.6199 (2013)

40. Tai, L., Paolo, G., Liu, M.: Virtual-to-real drl: continuous control of mobile robots for mapless navigation. In: IROS (2017)

41. Tjeng, V., Xiao, K.Y., Tedrake, R.: Evaluating robustness of neural networks with mixed integer programming. In: International Conference on Learning Representations (2018)

42. Tran, H.-D., Bak, S., Xiang, W., Johnson, T.T.: Verification of deep convolutional neural networks using imagestars. In: Lahiri, S.K., Wang, C. (eds.) CAV 2020. LNCS, vol. 12224, pp. 18–42. Springer, Cham (2020). https://doi.org/10.1007/978-3-030-53288-8_2

43. Wang, S., et al.: Beta-CROWN: efficient bound propagation with per-neuron split constraints for complete and incomplete neural network verification. Adv. Neural Inf. Process. Syst. **34** (2021)

44. Wei, T., Liu, C.: Safe control algorithms using energy functions: a uni ed framework, benchmark, and new directions. In: 2019 IEEE 58th Conference on Decision and Control (CDC), pp. 238–243. IEEE (2019)
45. Wei, T., Liu, C.: Safe control with neural network dynamic models. In: Learning for Dynamics and Control Conference, pp. 739–750. PMLR (2022)
46. Wei, T., Ma, L., Chen, R., Zhao, W., Liu, C.: Meta-control: automatic model-based control synthesis for heterogeneous robot skills. In: 8th Annual Conference on Robot Learning (2024). https://openreview.net/forum?id=cvVEkS5yij
47. Xiang, W., Johnson, T.T.: Reachability analysis and safety verification for neural network control systems. arXiv preprint arXiv:1805.09944 (2018)
48. Xiang, W., Tran, H.D., Johnson, T.T.: Reachable set computation and safety verification for neural networks with relu activations. arXiv preprint arXiv:1712.08163 (2017)
49. Xu, K., et al.: Fast and complete: enabling complete neural network verification with rapid and massively parallel incomplete verifiers. In: International Conference on Learning Representations (2021). https://openreview.net/forum?id=nVZtXBI6LNn
50. Yang, X., Yamaguchi, T., Tran, H.D., Hoxha, B., Johnson, T.T., Prokhorov, D.: Neural network repair with reachability analysis. In: International Conference on Formal Modeling and Analysis of Timed Systems, pp. 221–236. Springer, Heidelberg (2022). https://doi.org/10.1007/978-3-031-15839-1_13
51. Yang, Y., Hu, H., Wei, T., Li, S.E., Liu, C.: Scalable synthesis of formally verified neural value function for hamilton-jacobi reachability analysis. arXiv preprint arXiv:2407.20532 (2024)
52. Zhang, H., et al.: General cutting planes for bound-propagation-based neural network verification. Adv. Neural Inf. Process. Syst. (2022)
53. Zhang, H., Weng, T.W., Chen, P.Y., Hsieh, C.J., Daniel, L.: Efficient neural network robustness certification with general activation functions. Adv. Neural Inf. Process. Syst. **31**, 4939–4948 (2018). https://arxiv.org/pdf/1811.00866.pdf

NeuralSAT: A High-Performance Verification Tool for Deep Neural Networks

Hai Duong[1]([✉]) [iD], ThanhVu Nguyen[1] [iD], and Matthew B. Dwyer[2] [iD]

[1] George Mason University, Fairfax, USA
{hduong22,tvn}@gmu.edu
[2] University of Virginia, Virginia, USA
matthewbdwyer@virginia.edu

Abstract. Deep Neural Networks (DNNs) are increasingly deployed in critical applications, where ensuring their safety and robustness is paramount. We present NeuralSAT$_{CAV25}$, a high-performance DNN verification tool that uses the DPLL(T) framework and supports a wide-range of network architectures and activation functions. Since its debut in VNN-COMP'23, in which it achieved the New Participant Award and ranked 4th overall, NeuralSAT$_{CAV25}$ has advanced significantly, achieving second place in VNN-COMP'24. This paper presents and evaluates the latest development of NeuralSAT$_{CAV25}$, focusing on the versatility, ease of use, and competitive performance of the tool. NeuralSAT$_{CAV25}$ is available at: https://github.com/dynaroars/neuralsat.

Keywords: DNN Verification · Satisfiability Solving · VNN-COMP

1 Introduction

Deep Neural Networks (DNNs) have emerged as an effective approach for tackling challenging real-world problems. However, just like traditional software, DNNs can have "bugs", e.g., producing unexpected results on inputs that are different from those in training data, and be attacked, e.g., small perturbations to the inputs by a malicious adversary or even sensor imperfections can result in misclassification [25,37,39,40]. These issues naturally raise the question of how DNNs should be tested, validated, and ultimately *verified* to meet the requirements of relevant robustness or safety standards [18].

To address this question, researchers have developed a wide variety of algorithmic techniques and supporting tools to verify DNNs (§5). As a result, DNN verification has become a vibrant research area, and the community has created the annual DNN verification competition (VNN-COMP) to compare different approaches, showcase the latest advances, and help shape future directions of the field [5]. The first VNN-COMP was established in 2020, and the latest iteration of the competition, VNN-COMP'24, was held with CAV in 2024.

© The Author(s) 2025
R. Piskac and Z. Rakamarić (Eds.): CAV 2025, LNCS 15932, pp. 409–423, 2025.
https://doi.org/10.1007/978-3-031-98679-6_19

Unlike research papers, which often focus on theoretical contributions and has a smaller evaluation scale, VNN-COMP evaluates tools based on their practical performance on a wide range of benchmarks and properties and thus attracts the state-of-the-art in the field including: $\alpha\beta$-CROWN [32], Marabou [33] (successor of Reluplex [19]), nnenum [3], and MN-BaB [15] (successor of ERAN [14]). Among these tools, $\alpha\beta$-CROWN has been the most successful, winning the competitions four consecutive times from VNN-COMP'21 to VNN-COMP'24.

In 2023, we introduced the NeuralSAT$_{\text{VNNCOMP23}}$[1] verification tool in VNN-COMP'23 [6], where it ranked 4th overall and received the New Participation award (and also won the "TLL Verify Bench" benchmark category). We introduced several major improvements such as parallel DPLL(T) and neuron stabilization optimization [13] to define NeuralSAT$_{\text{FSE24}}$, that demonstrated competitive performance with $\alpha\beta$-CROWN on fully-connected networks. We extended NeuralSAT$_{\text{FSE24}}$ to support much larger set of network layer and activation function types with NeuralSAT$_{\text{VNNCOMP24}}$, which participated in VNN-COMP'24, where it ranked 2nd overall behind $\alpha\beta$-CROWN.

In this paper, we describe the latest version NeuralSAT$_{\text{CAV25}}$, which includes further extensions to optimize verification for more complex DNNs; the paper also reports on the extensions in NeuralSAT$_{\text{VNNCOMP24}}$ that have not been previously reported. We focus on features and engineering optimizations in NeuralSAT$_{\text{CAV25}}$ that are essential for creating a high-performance tool. We evaluate NeuralSAT$_{\text{CAV25}}$ in comparison to both NeuralSAT$_{\text{VNNCOMP24}}$ and the latest versions $\alpha\beta$-CROWN, and we illustrate how NeuralSAT$_{\text{CAV25}}$ facilitates ease of use by avoiding the complexities parameter tuning necessary in other verifiers.

Users of NeuralSAT$_{\text{CAV25}}$. We designed the NeuralSAT tool for (i) researchers who want to experiment with DNN verification techniques, and (ii) practitioners who want to verify their networks. For the first type of users, the DPLL(T) framework, which is carefully designed to be modular and extensible, serves as a foundation for incorporating additional algorithmic techniques from the broader SMT and DNN reasoning literature. For the second type of users, NeuralSAT works out of the box and supports various types of network architecture with minimal configuration and tuning. Our goal is to create a high-performance yet easy-to-use DNN verification tool that enables practitioners to employ state-of-the-art DNN reasoning techniques.

2 Background and Overview

2.1 The DNN Verification Problem

Deep Neural Network (DNN). A *deep neural network* consists of an input layer, multiple hidden layers, and an output layer. Each layer contains neurons connected to neurons in previous layers via predefined weights obtained through

---

[1] We use subscripts to distinguish previous versions of NeuralSAT$_{\text{CAV25}}$ from the version discussed in this paper. We use NeuralSAT without a subscript when we refer to the general NeuralSAT line of work.

training with data. A fully-connected (FC) layer is a layer where each neuron is connected to every neuron in the previous layer.

The output of a DNN is computed by iteratively calculating the values of neurons in each layer. Neurons in the input layer receive the input data. Neurons in the hidden layers compute their values through an *affine transformation* followed by an *activation function*, like the popular Rectified Linear Unit (*ReLU*) activation. For ReLU activation, the value of a hidden neuron y is given by $ReLU(w_1v_1 + \ldots + w_nv_n + b)$, where b is the bias parameter for y, $w_i, \ldots, w_n$ are the weights of y, $v_1, \ldots, v_n$ are the neuron values from the preceding layer, $w_1v_1 + \cdots + w_nv_n + b$ represents the affine transformation, and $ReLU(x) = \max(x, 0)$ defines the ReLU activation. A ReLU-activated neuron is *active*, if its input value is greater than zero, or *inactive*, otherwise.

DNN Verification. Given a DNN N and a property ϕ, the *DNN verification problem* asks if ϕ is a valid property of N. Typically, ϕ is a formula of the form $\phi_{in} \Rightarrow \phi_{out}$, where ϕ_{in} is a property over the inputs of N and ϕ_{out} is a property over the outputs of N.

Modern techniques often treat the DNN verification as a *satisfiability* problem [12,13,15,32,33]. More specifically, given a formula α representing the ReLU-based DNN N and the formulae $\phi_{in} \Rightarrow \phi_{out}$ representing the property to be proved, a DNN verifier checks the satisfiability of the formula

$$\alpha \wedge \phi_{in} \wedge \overline{\phi_{out}}. \tag{1}$$

The verifier returns unsat if Eq. 1 is unsatisfiable, indicating that ϕ is a valid property of N, and sat otherwise, indicating the ϕ is not a valid property of N.

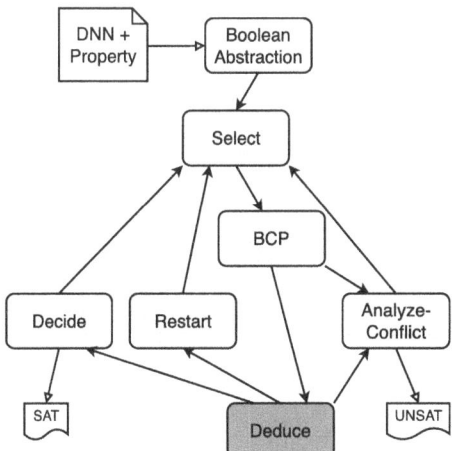

Fig. 1. NeuralSAT overview.

2.2   Overview of `NeuralSAT`

Figure 1 gives an overview of the `NeuralSAT` line of work, which is modeled after the DPLL(T) framework in SMT solving [7,20]. `NeuralSAT` consists of standard DPLL components (non-shaded) and a theory or T-solver (shaded) dedicated for DNN reasoning.

2.3   DPLL Search

`NeuralSAT` treats DNN verification as a search for an activation pattern, represented as an assignment σ which maps truth values to the variables representing the activation status of neurons (`BooleanAbstraction`). In the beginning σ is empty, and `NeuralSAT` uses decision heuristics to select unassigned variables (`Select`) and assigns truth values[2] to them (`Decide`). Briefly, decision heuristics in `NeuralSAT` work by selecting "important" neurons (or inputs) to split. `NeuralSAT` has various decision heuristics to select and will use them interchangeably depending on its optimizations. Currently, it implements greedy, FSB (Filter Smart Branching) [9], and several heuristics based on neuron interval values. Particularly, `NeuralSAT` will change decision heuristics when a reset (discussed later) happens to create different selection orders to avoid the same orders as previous runs.

After each assignment, `NeuralSAT` infers additional assignments caused by the current assignment through Boolean constraint propagation(BCP). Next, it invokes the T-solver (`Deduce`) to check the feasibility of the current assignment in σ. If it is feasible, `NeuralSAT` continues to search for new assignments. Otherwise, `NeuralSAT` detects a conflict, and it learns clauses to remember and backtracks to a previous assignment (`Analyze-Conflict`).

This process repeats until `NeuralSAT` can no longer backtrack, at which point it returns `unsat`, indicating the DNN has the property. Otherwise, it finds a complete assignment for all Boolean variables (i.e., a satisfying activation pattern), and returns `sat`. The user can query for a counterexample input in the case of `sat`.

If the `NeuralSAT` search falls into a local optima, it will *restart* the search by clearing all assignments that have been made. `NeuralSAT` retains learned conflict clauses learned, to avoid reaching the same state in the subsequent search. `NeuralSAT` decides to restart when it reaches (i) a given number of verified branches, (ii) a given number of unverified branches, or (iii) exceeds a timeout. These indicate that NeuralSAT is likely stuck and needs restart.

2.4   `NeuralSAT`-specific Components

`NeuralSAT` follows the standard DPLL algorithm, but includes several components specific for DNN reasoning [13].

---

[2] As described later, `NeuralSAT` uses a parallel DPLL and thus will explore both branches of the decision.

T-Solver. To check that current assignments in σ is feasible with the formula in Eq. 1, the T-solver uses LP solving and polytope abstraction [17,36] to compute neuron bounds from the given precondition and σ, and checks the bounds are feasible with respect to the specified post-condition. Using LP solving and abstraction is standard in modern DNN verification tools [3,13,15,32]. In practice, NeuralSAT employs several polytopes abstraction domains to support a wide range of network types and sizes.

In addition to standard LP solving and abstraction, the T-solver implements *neuron stabilization* [13] by creating and solving custom MILP constraints to determine if a neuron is stable (i.e., it is always active or inactive). If a neuron is stable, the T-solver does not need to guess its activation status, and thus reduces the search space.

Parallel DPLL. NeuralSAT leverages multiprocessing to parallelize its DPLL search. When assigning values to variables, NeuralSAT considers both options (active or inactive) for each variable, and then splits the search space into two disjoint subspaces and processes them in parallel. When a conflict is detected in one subspace, NeuralSAT prunes that subspace and continues the search in the remaining subspaces. This parallelism not only speeds up the process but also facilitates information exchange such as learned clauses among search subspaces.

3   Implemented Features and Optimizations

Table 1. NeuralSAT's features.

Feature	Supported
Network Type	Acyclic computation graphs, e.g., Feed-forward, Residual
Layer Type	FC, CNN, MaxPool, BatchNorm, Softmax
Activation Function	ReLU, Sigmoid, Tanh, Sign, Exp
Abstract Domain	Polytope, Interval
Search Algorithm	Parallel DPLL(T)
Hardware	Multi-core CPU, GPU
Optimization	Adv. Attacks, Input splitting, Large Output Opt., MILP solving
Property	Robustness, Safety
Input	Pytorch, ONNX, VNN-LIB
Output	(sat, unsat, timeout), counter-examples

From our experience evaluating tools and participating in competitions, we found that the novelty described in research papers often does not translate to competitive performance or practical usability. Instead, the implementation details, such as being versatile, easy to use, and employing "engineering" optimizations to improve performance matter perhaps just as much. Table 1 shows features of NeuralSAT, many of which are often overlooked in research papers (e.g., absent in [13]) but are critical for building a long-term and high-performance tool.

Versatility. The work in [13] focused on ReLU-based and fully-connected networks. NeuralSAT has since been extended to support a wide range of network architectures and activation functions. Currently, NeuralSAT works with fully connected (FC), convolutional (CNN), residual (ResNet), batch normalization (BatchNorm) networks, etc. We also support mixtures of different types, e.g., VAEs which are large residual CNN-based networks.

In addition to ReLU, NeuralSAT supports other major activation functions including sigmoid, tanh, and power. Briefly, for these non-ReLU activation functions, we split a neuron at the center of its interval. Unlike ReLU where it becomes linear after splitting, non-ReLU does not, so NeuralSAT splits a single neuron multiple times, if needed, until the problem is verified or timed out.

Note that these are also supported by other DNN verification tools such as $\alpha\beta$-CROWN though the LiRPA library [36]. However, it is straight-forward to extend NeuralSAT to support new layer or activation functions, by modifying the abstractions used in the T-solver to compute the approximation bounds of activation functions over different network layers.

Standard Input and Output Formats. NeuralSAT supports for inputs networks in the standard ONNX format [2] and properties in VNNLIB format [28]. The output of NeuralSAT is reported as unsat (property proved), sat (property disproved), or unknown and timeout (property cannot be proved). NeuralSAT also generates counterexamples for sat results in text format supported by VNN-COMPs.

Fully Automatic, but Configurable. An important decision in designing NeuralSAT is to make it fully automatic and so that for end-users it *"just works"*, perhaps even at the cost of some runtime. Users can simply apply NeuralSAT to check their networks and desired properties without any parameter configuration. For example, NeuralSAT runs on all VNN-COMP benchmarks with *zero* tuning. In contrast, top tools, such as $\alpha\beta$-CROWN, require significant tuning to perform effectively (more details in §4).

However, NeuralSAT has many settings that can be configured by the users, such as the number of threads, number of restarts, timeout, etc. These options are useful for experts who want to explore different settings and optimize the performance of NeuralSAT for their specific problems.

Engineering Optimizations. Despite the focus on theoretical contributions in research, engineering matters! NeuralSAT employs various engineering optimizations to improve performance. First, like most high performing DNN verifiers, NeuralSAT uses adversarial attack algorithms, e.g., derivative-free sampling-based [38] and gradient-based [22] methods, to quickly find counterexamples indicating property violation. Second, NeuralSAT preprocesses and applies heuristics that automatically select appropriate abstractions and algorithms based on input network structures and properties. For example, NeuralSAT focuses on splitting the input ranges for networks with low input dimension and splitting neurons for networks with many inputs (which are the majority of real-world and VNN-COMP DNNs).

In this latest version, $\texttt{NeuralSAT}_{CAV25}$ has two new optimizations. First, for networks with large outputs (e.g., networks in "Cifar100" benchmark with 100 outputs that often cause timeout due to heavy memory usage), $\texttt{NeuralSAT}_{CAV25}$ processes multiple output constraints at once and adjusts abstraction to compute approximations that are less precise, but consume significantly less memory. Second, for networks with small ReLU-based FC layers, $\texttt{NeuralSAT}_{CAV25}$ attempts to solve the problem using MILP solving directly before using the more expensive DPLL(T) search. §4 shows the improvements of these optimizations.

Commodity Hardware. NeuralSAT heavily leverages the power of modern hardware, including multi-core CPUs and GPUs. The parallel search in NeuralSAT uses multi-threading, allowing multiple search subspaces to be processed in parallel. A large part of the theory solver in NeuralSAT is implemented to run on GPUs, which significantly speeds up the computation of neuron bounds. While leveraging hardware is common in DNN verification, the implementation is highly specific to the tool and requires careful engineering to achieve high performance. In VNN-COMP'24[3], NeuralSAT was one of the fastest tools, often outperforming other top competitors.

Well-Tested. NeuralSAT has been rigorously tested on a wide-range of benchmarks, including those in VNN-COMPs and many more. In fact, the benchmarks in VNN-COMP are often easy for NeuralSAT, and we actively seek out more challenging benchmarks to test the tool's capabilities, through our own benchmark generation research [34,35] and collaborations with other researchers and industry partners.

Active Development. NeuralSAT is actively maintained with frequent updates. If the tool does not support a specific problem or benchmark, users are encouraged to open an issue on the project's GitHub page[4], and the team will strive to provide assistance (though in practice people often send emails instead of open Github issues). While the development version of NeuralSAT is quite usable, we aim to release stable versions approximately every 6 months.

Extensibility. As mentioned, NeuralSAT has many optimizations, and their addition was facilitated by the use of DPLL(T). The DPLL(T) framework in NeuralSAT is modular and extensible, consisting of a small core search algorithm and allows users to: add new decision or restart heuristics for DPLL, add new adversarial attacks in preprocessing, or extend the T-solver with additional

---

[3] VNN-COMP'24 no longer measures verification runtime and instead uses timeout.

[4] https://github.com/dynaroars/neuralsat.

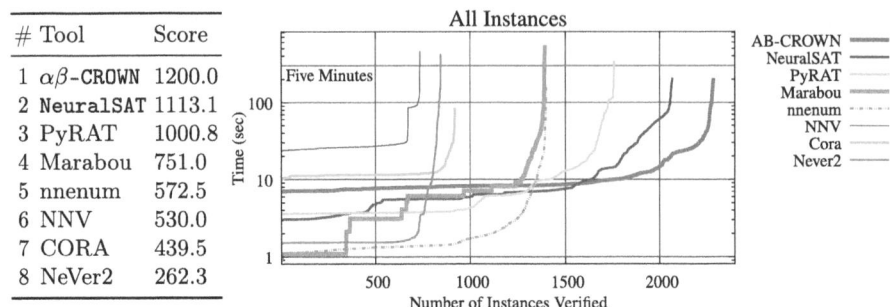

# Tool	Score
1 $\alpha\beta$-CROWN	1200.0
2 NeuralSAT	1113.1
3 PyRAT	1000.8
4 Marabou	751.0
5 nnenum	572.5
6 NNV	530.0
7 CORA	439.5
8 NeVer2	262.3

Fig. 2. VNN-COMP'24 results (of NeuralSAT$_{\text{VNNCOMP24}}$) [5].

abstraction or optimizations for DNN analysis. For example, the neuron stabilization optimization described in §2.2 is an independent function with fewer than 100 SLOCs and integrated via a hook method call into the core DPLL search. Similarly, heuristics are implemented as independent functions and can be easily replaced or extended (e.g., in current implementation decisions and restarts are less than 50 SLOC). NeuralSAT also uses the Gurobi LP solver as a black box and thus can switch to different solvers, e.g., Xpress [16], dReal [11].

Building from Scratch. Originally we considered building NeuralSAT on top of well-known SAT or SMT solvers, such as MiniSat [26] or Z3 [8]. However, we found that these solvers are not well-suited for DNN verification: their architectures and optimizations that are not tailored for DNN reasoning. In our experience, existing SAT/SMT solvers do not do well with logical constraints or formulae representing DNN verification tasks and do not scale to anything beyond the tiniest networks.

To address these limitations, we built NeuralSAT from the ground up as a SAT solver, beginning with a standard DPLL algorithm (§2.3) and extending it with a custom T-solver and specialized optimizations for DNN verification tasks (§2.4). By designing our own solver, we can explore and experiment with new heuristics and optimizations, and quickly add new features, without being constrained by the limitations of existing solvers.

4   Evaluation

4.1   VNN-COMP'24 Results

Figure 2 summarizes the results of VNN-COMP'24 [5]. The table in the Fig. corresponds to Table 35 in Apdx. B of [5] and presents the overall scores and rankings of the tools. The cactus plot corresponds Fig. 28 in Apdx. B of [5] and shows tool performance on all benchmark instances. In summary, NeuralSAT$_{\text{VNNCOMP24}}$ ranks 2nd overall, behind $\alpha\beta$-CROWN and ahead of PyRAT.

4.2   New Results

We present the results of the latest version of $\text{NeuralSAT}_{\text{CAV25}}$. We also compare it with $\text{NeuralSAT}_{\text{VNNCOMP24}}$ and the latest version of $\alpha\beta$-CROWN[5]. As mentioned in §3, the main updates are better handling of networks with large outputs and using MILP solving. We also compare $\text{NeuralSAT}_{\text{CAV25}}$ with $\alpha\beta$-CROWN's default configuration, $\alpha\beta$-CROWN$_{\text{default}}$, to show that $\text{NeuralSAT}_{\text{CAV25}}$ is competitive without any parameter tuning.

Setup. We reuse benchmarks and scripts for tool installation, execution, and scoring from VNN-COMP'24 [5]. In total there are 340 networks (ranging from 0.2K to 68M parameters) and 2058 properties. For, $\alpha\beta$-CROWN$_{\text{default}}$, we run the script provided for $\alpha\beta$-CROWN without a specific configuration (YAML) file and therefore uses its default settings. Details on the benchmarks and scoring system are available in [5] and Github repo[6].

Our experiments were run on a Linux machine with an AMD Threadripper 64-core 4.2 GHz CPU, 128 GB RAM, and an NVIDIA GeForce RTX 4090 GPU with 24 GB VRAM. Because VNN-COMP'24 used Amazon AWS instances which are different than our machine, we experimented with timeouts and settled on 500 s per instance which allowed the verifiers to achieve similar scoring performance as in VNN-COMP'24. All considered tools leverage multiprocessing and GPU processing.

Results. Table 2 shows the results. We report the Rank (#) and % is the percentage of solved problems over all problem instances of the corresponding benchmark. The last two columns break down the number of problems each verifier was able to verify and falsify. For example, for ACAS Xu, all tools other than $\alpha\beta$-CROWN$_{\text{default}}$ were able to verify all 186 problems (139 + 47), and $\alpha\beta$-CROWN$_{\text{default}}$ was only able to solve 113 problems (78 + 35), which is 60.8% of the total problems.

Overall, $\alpha\beta$-CROWN ranks 1st, followed closely by $\text{NeuralSAT}_{\text{CAV25}}$ in 2nd, $\text{NeuralSAT}_{\text{VNNCOMP24}}$ in 3rd, and $\alpha\beta$-CROWN$_{\text{default}}$ last. For $\text{NeuralSAT}_{\text{CAV25}}$ and $\alpha\beta$-CROWN, the results are very close, with $\text{NeuralSAT}_{\text{CAV25}}$ verifying two fewer problems than $\alpha\beta$-CROWN (1296 vs. 1298) and falsifying one fewer problem (981 vs. 982). $\text{NeuralSAT}_{\text{CAV25}}$, with two new optimizations mentioned in §3, has similar performance on most benchmarks and outperforms $\text{NeuralSAT}_{\text{VNNCOMP24}}$ on the remaining ones, with the most significant improvements in "Cifar100" and "Tiny ImageNet" (due to large output optimization) and "Safe NLP" (due to MILP solving).

The results show a significant performance disparity between $\alpha\beta$-CROWN$_{\text{default}}$ and $\alpha\beta$-CROWN, with the latter having fine-tuned 10 parameters, on average, to

---

[5] https://github.com/Verified-Intelligence/alpha-beta-CROWN_vnncomp2024/commit/201f7401b3d8dbaddeda179939a8dc1615f8214a.

[6] https://github.com/ChristopherBrix/vnncomp2024_benchmarks.

Table 2. Results over VNN-COMP'24 Benchmarks

Benchmark	#	Tool	%	Verify	Falsify
ACAS Xu	1	$\alpha\beta$-CROWN	100.0%	**139**	**47**
	1	NeuralSAT$_{\mathrm{CAV25}}$	100.0%	**139**	**47**
	1	NeuralSAT$_{\mathrm{VNNCOMP24}}$	100.0%	**139**	**47**
	4	$\alpha\beta$-CROWN$_{\mathrm{default}}$	60.8%	78	35
Cgan	1	$\alpha\beta$-CROWN	100.0%	**8**	**13**
	1	NeuralSAT$_{\mathrm{CAV25}}$	100.0%	**8**	**13**
	1	NeuralSAT$_{\mathrm{VNNCOMP24}}$	100.0%	**8**	**13**
	4	$\alpha\beta$-CROWN$_{\mathrm{default}}$	33.3%	0	7
Cifar100	1	$\alpha\beta$-CROWN	77.5%	**123**	**32**
	2	NeuralSAT$_{\mathrm{CAV25}}$	76.5%	122	31
	3	$\alpha\beta$-CROWN$_{\mathrm{default}}$	71.0%	110	**32**
	4	NeuralSAT$_{\mathrm{VNNCOMP24}}$	64.5%	98	31
Collins Rul CNN	1	$\alpha\beta$-CROWN	100.0%	**30**	**32**
	1	$\alpha\beta$-CROWN$_{\mathrm{default}}$	100.0%	**30**	**32**
	1	NeuralSAT$_{\mathrm{CAV25}}$	100.0%	**30**	**32**
	1	NeuralSAT$_{\mathrm{VNNCOMP24}}$	100.0%	**30**	**32**
Cora	1	$\alpha\beta$-CROWN	43.9%	**24**	**134**
	1	$\alpha\beta$-CROWN$_{\mathrm{default}}$	43.9%	**24**	**134**
	1	NeuralSAT$_{\mathrm{CAV25}}$	43.9%	**24**	**134**
	1	NeuralSAT$_{\mathrm{VNNCOMP24}}$	43.9%	**24**	**134**
Dist Shift	1	$\alpha\beta$-CROWN	100.0%	**64**	**8**
	1	NeuralSAT$_{\mathrm{CAV25}}$	100.0%	**64**	**8**
	3	NeuralSAT$_{\mathrm{VNNCOMP24}}$	98.6%	63	**8**
	4	$\alpha\beta$-CROWN$_{\mathrm{default}}$	94.4%	60	**8**
Linearize NN	1	$\alpha\beta$-CROWN	100.0%	**59**	**1**
	1	NeuralSAT$_{\mathrm{CAV25}}$	100.0%	**59**	**1**
	1	NeuralSAT$_{\mathrm{VNNCOMP24}}$	100.0%	**59**	**1**
	4	$\alpha\beta$-CROWN$_{\mathrm{default}}$	68.3%	40	**1**
Meta Room	1	$\alpha\beta$-CROWN	98.0%	**91**	**7**
	1	NeuralSAT$_{\mathrm{CAV25}}$	98.0%	**91**	**7**
	1	NeuralSAT$_{\mathrm{VNNCOMP24}}$	98.0%	**91**	**7**
	4	$\alpha\beta$-CROWN$_{\mathrm{default}}$	0.0%	0	0
Nn4sys	1	$\alpha\beta$-CROWN	100.0%	**194**	0
	1	NeuralSAT$_{\mathrm{CAV25}}$	100.0%	**194**	0
	1	NeuralSAT$_{\mathrm{VNNCOMP24}}$	100.0%	**194**	0
	4	$\alpha\beta$-CROWN$_{\mathrm{default}}$	4.1%	8	0

(*continued*)

Table 2. (*continued*)

Benchmark	#	Tool	%	Verify	Falsify
Safe NLP	1	$\alpha\beta$-CROWN	98.1%	**411**	**648**
	1	NeuralSAT$_{\text{CAV25}}$	98.1%	**411**	**648**
	3	$\alpha\beta$-CROWN$_{\text{default}}$	96.9%	401	646
	4	NeuralSAT$_{\text{VNNCOMP24}}$	94.3%	378	640
Tiny ImageNet	1	$\alpha\beta$-CROWN	91.5%	**140**	**43**
	2	NeuralSAT$_{\text{CAV25}}$	91.0%	139	**43**
	3	$\alpha\beta$-CROWN$_{\text{default}}$	89.5%	136	**43**
	4	NeuralSAT$_{\text{VNNCOMP24}}$	72.5%	102	**43**
TLL Verify Bench	1	$\alpha\beta$-CROWN	100.0%	15	17
	1	NeuralSAT$_{\text{CAV25}}$	100.0%	15	17
	1	NeuralSAT$_{\text{VNNCOMP24}}$	100.0%	15	17
	4	$\alpha\beta$-CROWN$_{\text{default}}$	65.6%	5	16
Overall	1	$\alpha\beta$-CROWN	88.8%	**1298**	**982**
	2	NeuralSAT$_{\text{CAV25}}$	88.7%	1296	981
	3	NeuralSAT$_{\text{VNNCOMP24}}$	84.7%	1201	973
	4	$\alpha\beta$-CROWN$_{\text{default}}$	71.9%	892	954

optimize its performance for different benchmarks[7]. In contrast, NeuralSAT$_{\text{CAV25}}$ made no parameter adjustment for any benchmarks, highlighting its ease of use and potential for better performance in unseen benchmarks.

5 Related Work

The literature on DNN verification is rich and rapidly evolving (cf. [21,31]). Here we focus on tools competing in VNN-COMP'24 [5] because they are typically the state of the art and combine multiple effective DNN verification techniques.

Several tools, including NeuralSAT, belong to the BaB approach, which refines bounds computed for subproblems and then splits, or branches, them into subproblems that are solved separately. Marabou [33] (the successor of the popular Reluplex work [19]) encodes verification as constraint problems and uses parallelized split-and-conquer techniques for efficiency. nnenum [3] uses hidden BaB with star sets and several types of zonotope abstractions and focuses strictly on ReLU networks. The mentioned $\alpha\beta$-CROWN [32] combines GPU-accelerated linear bound propagation with advanced BaB techniques, such as cutting planes and neuron splitting, to scale to large networks. While both NeuralSAT and

---

[7] https://github.com/Verified-Intelligence/alpha-beta-CROWN_vnncomp2024/ blob/master/complete_verifier/exp_configs/vnncomp24/ partially consists of VNN-COMP'24 runscripts of $\alpha\beta$-CROWN, which use different configurations (in yaml) on different benchmarks.

$\alpha\beta$-CROWN use BaB and GPU acceleration, they differ widely in everything else, e.g., heuristics and optimizations, with the main distinctions being NeuralSAT prioritize splitting unstable neurons and have strategies borrowed from SAT solving such as restart when it reaches local optima [13].

Other tools use reachability analysis, which overapproximates reachable states to verify properties. CORA [1] employs zonotopes for non-convex enclosures for open-loop and closed-loop verification in control systems. NeVer2 [10] focuses on ReLU-based feedforward networks by using an abstraction-refinement algorithm with symbolic bounds propagation. PyRAT [24] uses abstract interpretation with many domains including intervals, zonotopes, and polyhedra to compute sound overapproximations of reachable states to verify safe and robustness properties. NNV [30] focuses on verifying network-based control systems by integrating the star-set domain [29] with iteratively refinement for precise reachability analysis.

NeuralSAT achieves BaB through its DPLL(T) framework, which provides a strong algorithmic foundation and the flexibility to explore new heuristics and optimizations. NeuralSAT also delivers competitive performance out-of-the-box–an advantage over tools that require significant parameter tuning for good performance.

6   Conclusion and Future Work

NeuralSAT has quickly evolved into a leading performer in DNN verification, achieving similar performance to established competitors like $\alpha\beta$-CROWN. By adopting modular and extensible designs, parallel DPLL(T) search, and advanced optimizations, NeuralSAT performs competitively across a diverse set of benchmarks, demonstrating its robustness and scalability. Its out-of-the-box usability, combined with its potential for further optimization and customization, make it an attractive choice for both researchers and practitioners.

Maintaining competitiveness in the world of rapid advancements requires continuous innovation in both algorithmic research and engineering advancements. We are exploring both algorithmic research, such as compositional reasoning [23,27], which decomposes large verification to more manageable subproblems, and decision heuristics from DPLL, such as VMTF (Variable Move-to-Front) [4], which prioritize variables involved in learned conflict clauses to improve search efficiency, and engineering improvements, such as enhancing parallelization and supporting multi-GPU hardware acceleration.

Acknowledgments. This material is based in part upon work supported by the National Science Foundation under grant numbers 2019239, 2129824, 2200621, 2217071, 2238133, 2319131, 2422036, and by an Amazon Research Award.

Disclosure of Interests. The authors have no competing interests to declare that are relevant to the content of this article.

References

1. Althoff, M.: An introduction to Cora 2015. In: Proceedings of the Workshop on Applied Verification for Continuous and Hybrid Systems, pp. 120–151 (2015). https://doi.org/10.29007/zbkv

2. Bai, J., Lu, F., Zhang, K.: ONNX Open neural network exchange. https://onnx.ai

3. Bak, S.: nnenum: verification of ReLU neural networks with optimized abstraction refinement. In: Dutle, A., Moscato, M.M., Titolo, L., Muñoz, C.A., Perez, I. (eds.) NFM 2021. LNCS, vol. 12673, pp. 19–36. Springer, Cham (2021). https://doi.org/10.1007/978-3-030-76384-8_2

4. Biere, A., Fröhlich, A.: Evaluating CDCL variable scoring schemes. In: Heule, M., Weaver, S. (eds.) SAT 2015. LNCS, vol. 9340, pp. 405–422. Springer, Cham (2015). https://doi.org/10.1007/978-3-319-24318-4_29

5. Brix, C., Bak, S., Johnson, T.T., Wu, H.: The Fifth International Verification of Neural Networks Competition (VNN-COMP 2024): Summary and Results. arXiv preprint arXiv:2412.19985 (2024). https://doi.org/10.48550/arXiv.2412.19985

6. Brix, C., Bak, S., Liu, C., Johnson, T.T.: The Fourth International Verification of Neural Networks Competition (VNN-COMP 2023): Summary and Results (2023). https://doi.org/10.48550/arXiv.2312.16760

7. Davis, M., Logemann, G., Loveland, D.: A machine program for theorem-proving. Commun. ACM **5**(7), 394–397 (1962). https://doi.org/10.1145/368273.368557

8. de Moura, L., Bjørner, N.: Z3: an efficient SMT solver. In: Ramakrishnan, C.R., Rchof, J. (eds.) TACAS 2008. LNCS, vol. 4963, pp. 337–340. Springer, Heidelberg (2008). https://doi.org/10.1007/978-3-540-78800-3_24

9. De Palma, A., et al.: Improved branch and bound for neural network verification via Lagrangian decomposition. arXiv preprint arXiv:2104.06718 (2021). https://doi.org/10.48550/arXiv.2104.06718

10. Demarchi, S., Guidotti, D., Pulina, L., Tacchella, A.: Never2: learning and verification of neural networks. Soft. Comput. **28**(19), 11647–11665 (2024). https://doi.org/10.1007/s00500-024-09907-5

11. dreal: An SMT Solver for Nonlinear Theories of Reals (2024). https://dreal.github.io/

12. Duong, H., Nguyen, T., Dwyer, M.: A DPLL(T) Framework for Verifying Deep Neural Networks. arXiv preprint arXiv:2307.10266 (2024). https://doi.org/10.48550/arXiv.2307.10266

13. Duong, H., Xu, D., Nguyen, T., Dwyer, M.B.: Harnessing neuron stability to improve DNN verification. Proc. ACM Softw. Eng. **1**(FSE), 859–881 (2024). https://doi.org/10.1145/3643765

14. ETH-SRI: ETH Robustness Analyzer for Deep Neural Networks (2021). https://github.com/eth-sri/eran

15. Ferrari, C., Mueller, M.N., Jovanović, N., Vechev, M.: Complete Verification via Multi-Neuron Relaxation Guided Branch-and-Bound. In: International Conference on Learning Representations (2022). https://doi.org/10.48550/arXiv.2205.00263

16. FICO: Xpress Optimization (2024). https://www.fico.com/en/products/fico-xpress-optimization

17. Gurobi Optimization, LLC: Gurobi Optimizer Reference Manual (2022). https://www.gurobi.com

18. Huang, X., et al.: A survey of safety and trustworthiness of deep neural networks: verification, testing, adversarial attack and defence, and interpretability. Comput. Sci. Rev. **37**, 100270 (2020). https://doi.org/10.1016/j.cosrev.2020.100270

19. Katz, G., Barrett, C., Dill, D.L., Julian, K., Kochenderfer, M.J.: Reluplex: an efficient SMT solver for verifying deep neural networks. In: Majumdar, R., Kunčak, V. (eds.) CAV 2017. LNCS, vol. 10426, pp. 97–117. Springer, Cham (2017). https://doi.org/10.1007/978-3-319-63387-9_5

20. Kroening, D., Strichman, O.: Decision procedures. Springer, Heidelberg (2008). https://doi.org/10.5555/1391237

21. Liu, C., Arnon, T., Lazarus, C., Strong, C., Barrett, C., Kochenderfer, M.J., et al.: Algorithms for verifying deep neural networks. Found. Trends® Optim. **4**(3-4), 244–404 (2021). https://doi.org/10.1561/2400000035

22. Madry, A., Makelov, A., Schmidt, L., Tsipras, D., Vladu, A.: Towards deep learning models resistant to adversarial attacks. arXiv preprint arXiv:1706.06083 (2017). https://hdl.handle.net/1721.1/137496

23. Misra, J., Chandy, K.M.: Proofs of networks of processes. IEEE Trans. Softw. Eng. **4**, 417–426 (1981). https://doi.org/10.1109/TSE.1981.230844

24. PyRAT: A tool to analyze the robustness and safety of neural networks (2024). https://pyrat-analyzer.com/

25. Ren, K., Zheng, T., Qin, Z., Liu, X.: Adversarial attacks and defenses in deep learning. Engineering **6**(3), 346–360 (2020). https://doi.org/10.1016/j.eng.2019.12.012

26. Sorensson, N., Een, N.: Minisat v1. 13-a sat solver with conflict-clause minimization. SAT **2005**(53), 1–2 (2005). https://api.semanticscholar.org/CorpusID:63165862

27. Stark, E.W.: A proof technique for rely/guarantee properties. In: Maheshwari, S.N. (ed.) FSTTCS 1985. LNCS, vol. 206, pp. 369–391. Springer, Heidelberg (1985). https://doi.org/10.1007/3-540-16042-6_21

28. Tacchella, A., Pulina, L., Guidotti, D., Demarchi, S.: The international benchmarks standard for the Verification of Neural Networks (2023). https://www.vnnlib.org/

29. Tran, H.-D., et al.: Star-based reachability analysis of deep neural networks. In: ter Beek, M.H., McIver, A., Oliveira, J.N. (eds.) FM 2019. LNCS, vol. 11800, pp. 670–686. Springer, Cham (2019). https://doi.org/10.1007/978-3-030-30942-8_39

30. Tran, H.-D., et al.: NNV: the neural network verification tool for deep neural networks and learning-enabled cyber-physical systems. In: Lahiri, S.K., Wang, C. (eds.) CAV 2020. LNCS, vol. 12224, pp. 3–17. Springer, Cham (2020). https://doi.org/10.1007/978-3-030-53288-8_1

31. Urban, C., Miné, A.: A review of formal methods applied to machine learning. arXiv preprint arXiv:2104.02466 (2021). https://doi.org/10.48550/arXiv.2104.02466

32. Wang, S., et al.: Beta-CROWN: efficient bound propagation with per-neuron split constraints for complete and incomplete neural network robustness verification. Adv. Neural Inf. Process. Syst. **34**, 29909–29921 (2021). https://doi.org/10.48550/arXiv.2103.06624

33. Wu, H., Isac, O., et al.: Marabou 2.0: a versatile formal analyzer of neural networks. In: Gurfinkel, A., Ganesh, V. (eds.) International Conference on Computer Aided Verification, pp. 249–264. Springer, Cham (2024). https://doi.org/10.48550/arXiv.2401.14461

34. Xu, D., Mozumder, N.J., Duong, H., Dwyer, M.: Training for verification: increasing neuron stability to scale DNN verification. In: Finkbeiner, B., Kovács, L. (eds.) Tools and Algorithms for the Construction and Analysis of Systems. TACAS 2024. LNCS, vol. 14572, pp. 24–44. Springer, Cham (2024). https://doi.org/10.1007/978-3-031-57256-2_2

35. Xu, D., Shriver, D., Dwyer, M.B., Elbaum, S.: Systematic generation of diverse benchmarks for DNN verification. In: Lahiri, S.K., Wang, C. (eds.) CAV 2020. LNCS, vol. 12224, pp. 97–121. Springer, Cham (2020). https://doi.org/10.1007/978-3-030-53288-8_5

36. Xu, K., et al.: Automatic perturbation analysis for scalable certified robustness and beyond. Adv. Neural Inf. Process. Syst. **33**, 1129–1141 (2020). https://doi.org/10.5555/3495724.3495820

37. Yang, Z., Shi, J., He, J., Lo, D.: Natural attack for pre-trained models of code. In: Proceedings of the 44th International Conference on Software Engineering, pp. 1482–1493 (2022). https://doi.org/10.1145/3510003.3510146

38. Yu, Y., Qian, H., Hu, Y.Q.: Derivative-free optimization via classification. In: Thirtieth AAAI Conference on Artificial Intelligence (2016). https://doi.org/10.5555/3016100.3016218

39. Zhang, T., Gao, C., Ma, L., Lyu, M., Kim, M.: An empirical study of common challenges in developing deep learning applications. In: 2019 IEEE 30th International Symposium on Software Reliability Engineering (ISSRE), pp. 104–115. IEEE (2019). https://doi.org/10.1109/ISSRE.2019.00020

40. Zügner, D., Akbarnejad, A., Günnemann, S.: Adversarial attacks on neural networks for graph data. In: Proceedings of the 24th ACM SIGKDD International Conference on Knowledge Discovery & Data Mining, vol. 2019-August, pp. 2847–2856. ACM, New York, NY, USA, July 2018. https://doi.org/10.1145/3219819.3220078

Author Index

© The Editor(s) (if applicable) and The Author(s) 2025
R. Piskac and Z. Rakamarić (Eds.): CAV 2025, LNCS 15932, pp. 425–426, 2025.
https://doi.org/10.1007/978-3-031-98679-6

The manufacturer's authorised representative in the EU is Springer
Nature Customer Service Centre GmbH, Europaplatz 3, 69115 Heidelberg,
Germany. If you have any concerns regarding our products, please
contact ProductSafety@springernature.com

Printed and bound by CPI Group (UK) Ltd, Croydon, CR0 4YY
29/04/2026
02099511-0007